The Pioneers of Judicial Behavior

THE *Pioneers* OF
Judicial Behavior

Edited by Nancy Maveety

THE UNIVERSITY OF MICHIGAN PRESS
Ann Arbor

2006   2005   4   3   2

A CIP catalog record for this book is available from the British Library.

Library of Congress Cataloging-in-Publication Data

The pioneers of judicial behavior / edited by Nancy Maveety.
p.   cm.
Includes index.
ISBN 0-472-09822-5 (cloth : alk. paper) —
ISBN 0-472-06822-9 (paper : alk. paper)
1. Judicial process—United States.   I. Maveety, Nancy.

KF8775 .P56   2003
347.73'1—dc21   2002009736

A pioneer should have imagination,
should be able to enjoy the idea of things
more than the things themselves.
—Willa Cather, *O Pioneers!*

It's the vague people who are the pioneers.
—Richard Rorty

Contents

Preface and Acknowledgments

This volume began as a result of a paper I prepared for a panel at the annual meeting of the Southern Political Science Association that commemorated the work of my dissertation supervisor, Woody Howard. But the volume would not have taken shape without discussions I had with Saul Brenner about the reaction to and subsequent empirical testing of Howard's claims about the phenomenon of judicial fluidity in judicial decision making. It is from these discussions, and from Saul's careful and critical reading of my conference paper on Howard's contributions to the study of judicial behavior, that the idea for *Pioneers* grew.

Perhaps it is odd, in this postmodern age of skepticism about scientific progress, cumulative knowledge, and narratives of "discovery," to be speaking of "pioneers" of anything. Perhaps the metaphor is outdated; perhaps it evokes some hegemonic notion of mastery or a naively romantic mythology. Yet the loaded resonance of the term *pioneer* poses the essential question of this volume: In what sense(s) are there pioneers of judicial behavior? Are students of law and courts better or worse for the trails they blazed? Or are we still lost in an untamed wilderness of judicial decision making that can be plausibly navigated in many ways? In 1969, in their book by the same name, Joel Grossman and Joseph Tanenhaus could conjure an image of "the frontiers of judicial research." Can we still?

While there is only one Northwest Passage, in 2001—at the time I write this—there is more than one theory of or approach to understanding judicial behavior. If this is the legacy of the pioneering scholars, it is not an uncomplicated one. For contemporary scholars to accept and even to profit by this kind of eclectic frontier exploration is a challenge best met by fully understanding how the judicial field arrived at such a state and whether we have done the most we could have with our cartographers' maps.

In drafting the party of latter-day explorers who are the contributors to this volume and in soliciting advice on the pioneers of judicial behavior, I am indebted to two chapter authors, Larry Baum and Lee Epstein. Their early enthusiasm for and willingness to sign onto the project were invaluable, in terms of both their vital intellectual feed-

back on my contributions to the volume and their willingness to be utilized as "recruitment devices" in assembling the list of contributors.
(Hopefully, we are not the assembled Donner Party of public law.)
Editing a multiauthor volume is a challenging task, but one that I have
thoroughly enjoyed (especially now that the task is complete) because
of all that I have gained, intellectually and personally, from the contributors. To all of them individually go my sincerest thanks for partic-
ipating and for their faith in their humble editor. (Or perhaps, I should
say instead,"Remember, never take no cutoffs and hurry along as fast as
you can . . .")

While we as coauthors were convinced of the value of this project, its
ultimate existence is the result of the encouragement and support of
our editor at the University of Michigan Press, Jeremy Shine. It has
been my great pleasure to work with him, and for all of his gracious
assistance and general good humor at various stages of the project, I am
deeply grateful. I would also thank the two reviewers Jeremy enlisted to
read and critique the *Pioneers* manuscript; I must express my particular
appreciation to D.H. for a reader's report that made me laugh out loud
at its biting wit—when it wasn't making me cry from its withering, but
witheringly valid, insights. The volume is a better book, and a more
coherent one, because of the efforts of both reviewers.

Finally, all of us who work as scholars in the field of law and courts
are, in the last analysis, indebted to our predecessors.[1] Beverly Blair
Cook once said, in the course of remarks for a roundtable in her honor,
"I am standing on the shoulders of giants."[2] Much of our research as
scholars—as well as the debates that exist within and guide the research
parameters of the judicial field—are certainly the products of the work
of the pioneering scholars of judicial behavior; it is hardly hagiographic
to recognize this. Nevertheless, this volume pays homage to its judicial
pioneers "by mounting a salient critique of some of their weaknesses
based on an appreciation of their strengths."[3] Accordingly, some of our
chapters are duly critical of research directions taken by our scholar-
predecessors and duly critical of the developmental consequences of
certain of their research directions. Giants (in the earth) some may be
(to some); misguided wanderers some may be (to others). We have
tried in this volume to profile them "warts and all," as Harold Spaeth
enthused about the idea of a chapter on himself.

In profiling the scholarship of the pioneers of judicial behavior and
how it has contributed to the current theoretical and methodological
shape of a political science of the courts, we have tried to achieve a balance between critical analysis and explanation of why a particular

scholar might be considered a pioneer. Some of the contributing authors are acquainted with the scholars they profile; others are not. Some of the scholars profiled shared their time and correspondence and offered input into the chapters in the volume. We as coauthors collectively express our thanks for their assistance, and all of us in the judicial field can best acknowledge our scholar-predecessors by recognizing that our intellectual dialogue is enlivened by them and by consideration of theirs as well.

NANCY MAVEETY

NEW ORLEANS, LOUISIANA

OCTOBER 2001

NOTES

1. It is no accident that many of the scholars profiled in this volume have received awards of recognition from their colleagues in the Law and Courts Section of the American Political Science Association. Martin Shapiro received the 2001 Lifetime Achievement Award, which goes to to a senior scholar who has evidenced a distinguished career of scholarly achievement, and J. Woodford Howard Jr. received the 2001 Harcourt College Publisher's Award, for a book or journal article ten years or older that has made a lasting impression on the field of law and courts (awarded for the 1968 article "On the Fluidity of Judicial Choice," *American Political Science Review* 62: 43–56.).

2. Beverly Blair Cook, "Ghosts and Giants in Judicial Politics," *PS: Political Science and Politics* 27 (1994): 78.

3. Alain de Botton, *The Consolations of Philosophy* (New York: Pantheon Books, 2000), 163.

CHAPTER I

The Study of Judicial Behavior and the Discipline of Political Science

Nancy Maveety

> "Let a hundred flowers bloom." End of conversation.
> —Mark Graber, "The Banality of Diversity"

It is ironic that the field that inaugurated the discipline of political science has been beset by an almost perpetual identity crisis.[1] Now part of the lore of the field is Somit and Tanenhaus's 1964 profile of the discipline, which showed that a sample of political scientists ranked contemporary research in public law as among the least significant work being done in political science (55–56).[2] Little appears to have changed since this 1964 survey, if recent anguished discussions of the state of the field and the marginalization of some of its parts, are to be believed.[3]

Public law, as the field was originally known, began as the synthesis of law, history, and philosophy, but a synthesis determined to engage the subject of politics and government empirically. The empiricism of early public law—and thus, early political science—was a descriptive enterprise, emphasizing nineteenth-century physical science's desire to collect, categorize, and comment. Just as the Victorian biologists invested their energies in the categorization of species of flora and fauna, so did the political scientists of the era seek to categorize and describe governmental institutions and constitutional arrangements. Based in *Staatswissenschaft*, the political science taught at German universities in the 1870s, American public law at the turn of the twentieth century embraced "the belief that inquiry akin to that of the natural sciences could ultimately uncover the laws underlying political evolution and development" (Somit and Tanenhaus 1982, 8). Indeed, the work of John Burgess—labeled the father of American political science (Somit and Tanenhaus 1982, 3)[4] and founder of the first school of political science, at Columbia University in 1880—exhibits this faith in the utility of descriptive concepts and objectively perceived facts. Yet despite this use of carefully defined concepts and a comparative, systematic and professionalized analysis of data, Burgess also reveals "an odd combination of the descriptive and the normative" (McClay 1994, xxii) in his seminal work, *The Foundations of Political Science.*[5] His study of the state, "partly an account of the way things actually were, and partly a proclamation of what they ought to become" (McClay 1994, xxii), exhibits the public-spirited, reformist view of the undertaking of political analysis common to scholars of his generation.

It is within the work of this "father" of American political science that we find early evidence of the identity crisis of the public law field. Burgess's interdisciplinary examination of the historical development of specific political and legal traditions

> retained a strong admixture of formalism in both style and content, particularly in its heavy reliance upon the learned examination of a formal documentary and historical record, and the formal and procedural acts that go with it. Such a method had a built-in bias against more vigorous, probing, empirical, skeptical, and pragmatic approaches to the discipline's subject matter. (McClay 1994, xxx)

The realist, antiformalist critique of Burgess's manner of doing political science would soon emerge in the early twentieth century, with the works of Woodrow Wilson, Charles Beard, and Arthur Bentley, and the quest for a behavioral, functionalist and "scientific" approach would soon overtake and define the discipline. But public law, while it partook in this scientific revolution, retained a certain amount of divided loyalty between the methods and worldviews of descriptive (and, to some degree, normative) legal scholarship and empirically rigorous political science.

As political science developed the analytical tools that would fashion the behavioral approach to the study of political phenomena, so too did the perspectives of public law scholars change. By the time of Charles Merriam's 1921 essay, "The Present State of the Study of Politics," scholars of law and courts were already incorporating the epistemological and methodological insights of the legal realists.[6] Leading scholars of public law in the early decades of the twentieth century—Edward Corwin, Robert Cushman, Charles Grove Haines, and Thomas Reed Powell—scorned the mechanistic model of judging embraced by legal formalism, which viewed judges as "value-free technicians who do no more than discover 'the law.'" (Murphy and Tanenhaus 1972, 13) Their early works saw the judicial process as situated in a political context and saw judicial decision making as influenced by overtly political factors. Though many of these scholars engaged in traditional, doctrinal analysis of Supreme Court decisions, they also recognized that those decisions are a mixture of law, politics, and policy and that judges' decisions were influenced by background, training, personality, and value preferences (Murphy and Tanenhaus 1972, 16–17).

Public law's identity crisis, or divided loyalties, persists in the perspective of these early, avowedly realist scholars of courts. For while they saw the judicial institution as an integral part of a political system, and while some—notably, Haines—began to take advantage of the techniques of quantitative analysis of judicial decisions (Haines 1922; Murphy and Tanenhaus 1972, 17), they cautioned that judges' choices (their agency as political actors) are restricted by the legal constraints of precedent and the wording of the Constitution and by the limits of judges' role. Thus, the study of judicial politics could not proceed from the idea of judges as "free" political agents; an understanding of the legal context and its norms remained essential to conceptualize judicial politics and judicial behavior. Moreover, an understanding of the latter would have to proceed from a different methodological basis than the quantitative study of political behavior: public law would continue to concern itself with judicial opinions and with the scholar's informed intuition about and interpretation of legal rules and procedures. Yet there is an irony here. The field of public law, then and now, aspired to both the scientific analysis and the legally informed study of law and courts; in so doing, the field somehow remained peripheral to both political science and legal scholarship.[7] As an excerpt from a recent conference paper illustrates, "Public law is clearly one of the more self-conscious of the subfields in political science, constantly meditating on 'Whither Political Jurisprudence,' . . . congratulating itself on their break from the past and announcing a bold advance into the future . . . only to fall back into doubts as to whether they are taken seriously both in the professions of law and political science" (Helm 1987).

The point of this opening section is not to antagonize the reader with tedious or contentious ancient history but to put into context the field's continuing concern about its research agenda and its concomitant relationship to the discipline—including its ongoing, anguished debate over the suitability of the nomenclature "public law" to label what it studies (Becker 1970b, 145; Vines 1970, 139–40; Baum 1983, 198; Slotnick 1991, 73; Cook 1994a, 83). That the field now generally identifies itself as "law and courts" or "judicial politics" cannot but paper over a fundamental epistemological stumbling block that interferes with the field's integration with the discipline of political science. This epistemological stumbling block is that judges, as political policy-makers, are still part of legal institutions and are constrained by those institutions—by their operative norms and practices. When no less a pioneer of judicial behavior than C. Herman Pritchett cautioned in 1969—during the full flower of the behavioral paradigm of judicial studies—that "judging [is done] in a political context, but it is still judging. . . . Judges make choices, but they are not the 'free' choices of congressmen" (42), then his parallel counsel to "let a hundred flowers bloom" (1968, 219) with respect to research topics and methods in the analysis of law and courts does seem to perpetuate, rather than resolve, the field's collective sense of insecurity. This ecumenical caveat seems to be a conversation stopper, intended only to assuage the guilt of those pursuing the "right" kind of research into law and courts just as it patronizes those who do not. Either that or its plea for genial tolerance further marginalizes the field as a whole from the central concerns and challenges of the political science discipline.

But this would be a cynic's response. To some degree, this volume replicates the ecumenical counsel of Pritchett, and it does so in light of continuing diversification—or, as some would observe less charitably, balkanization (Gibson 1983) or fragmentation (Cook 1994a)—among scholars of the judicial process. But at a time when the judicial politics field is part of a renaissance in the comparative study of courts and constitutionalism and is deeply involved in the application of formal theory to the study of judicial strategy and choice as well as engaged—with legal academics—in a dispassionate reassessment of the legal model of judging, then this counsel has a fresh appeal and a renewed importance. In an era when all positivist, Enlightenment-inspired social science is under attack by the "perspectivism" of postmodernism, a fresh examination of the development, progress, and continued challenges of the study of judicial behavior should proceed without any camp claiming privileged insight into the subject matter. This, at least, is the hope of *The Pioneers of Judicial Behavior*.

This chapter will provide a framework for the reader of the volume and a format with which to appreciate and assess the contributors' individual chapters. My purpose here is twofold: first, I seek to show that the study of judicial behavior has been the vehicle by which the field of "public law" connects to the theoretical and methodological developments in the discipline of political science. Second, I will explain how the study of judicial behavior is currently shaped by three "paradigms"[8] that can be traced to the pioneering research of an early generation of scholars. These scholars were not only pioneers in the development of approaches to the study of judicial behavior but also scholars who saw themselves and were read as integral to the discipline as a whole. Thus, reflection on their work has much to teach us about the project of judicial studies and the state of the discipline.

To aid the reader who is not enmeshed in the internecine struggles of public law scholars, this introduction will trace the intellectual foundations of the three approaches to the study of judicial behavior, approaches that provide the organizational structure for the subsequent chapters of the volume. These are identified as the *attitudinal*, the *strategic*, and the *historical-institutionalist* approaches to the study of judicial behavior. Each is explicated, and its importance to current research in the field is described.

The introductory chapter will also provide a thematic and topical structure that the succeeding chapters on individual pioneers will follow. This structure addresses the following questions: What makes this scholar a pioneer in terms of shaping the development of the study of judicial behavior? How did his/her work help define one of the research approaches to judicial decision making? How have the insights of this scholar's research influenced current work on law and courts, including work outside the field of public law in political science?

Both thematically and organizationally, this chapter seeks to provide a unifying format for the volume as a whole. Additionally, its discussion initiates the book's overarching purpose: to reconnect the field of law and courts to its developmental history and to reengage the field with the concerns of both the discipline of political science and the research agendas of legal scholars. And one final word on this latter front: some readers may find that their "favorite" pioneer—particularly someone who was devoted to analysis of legal systems as a whole or to aspects of the judicial process concerning appointment, recruitment, or the implementation of judicial decisions—has been omitted from our survey of the pioneers of judicial *behavior*. The three contemporary approaches to the study of judicial behavior are necessarily loose categories, but they do not encompass all extant scholarship on courts. This is particularly true of scholarship that does not take as its explanatory focus the decisional behavior of judges. Thus, this volume offers a picture of the foundational work toward three different ways of viewing and explaining judicial behavior as an aspect of policy-making. While this framing risks presenting a crabbed view of the study of judicial decision making, it concentrates attention on scholarship that addresses that aspect of the judicial process that has been most central to the development of the political science of law and courts, the policy-making behavior of judges in a political system. From that body of literature and its coherence and validity as a political science of the judiciary must come any contributions toward interdisciplinary[9] or other broader work on courts.

PUBLIC LAW, JUDICIAL BEHAVIOR, AND POLITICAL SCIENCE

Political science was born as the "science of the state"; most observers would identify its official "birthday" with the founding of the American Political Science Association at Tulane University in 1903. But were an observer to hew to the definition of the discipline provided by its "father," John Burgess, one would encounter a tripartite division heavy with a content that would come to be associated with the judicial politics field. In describing the jurisdiction of the new discipline in 1890, Burgess distinguished political science proper (dealing with political community) from constitutional law (dealing with the regime and the rules of the game) and from public law (dealing with the legislation and policies of particular administrations).[10] Thus, it is fair to say, as Slotnick does, that "within political science, we [the law and courts field] predate most other areas of study, as our work was generally pursued under the label 'public law'" (1991, 67).[11]

That founding father Burgess is now largely a forgotten figure tells us something about the development of the discipline he founded and the concomitant development of the field of public law. The "Teutonic" methodology that Burgess pioneered at Columbia in 1880 and that Herbert Baxter Adams soon installed for the new political science program at Johns Hopkins emphasized comparison: both scholars saw "the historical-comparative approach as the touchstone to the general laws of political behavior and development" (Somit and Tanenhaus 1982, 31). What was initially compared were original documents, charters, and constitutions, but within a decade or two, the comparative approach encompassed political actors, real events, and functioning governments. This move toward a broader empiricism and a greater analytic conceptualization of political forms and phenomena should not disguise the fact that the first American political scientists (1) shared a scientistic[12] point of view and (2) considered legal, institutional "facts" as amenable to analysis from this point of view. Yet both Burgess's and early public law's conceptions of political "science" were soon to be eclipsed, displacing the prominent, foundational role of each.

Over time, the discipline's concerns grew less legalistic—a transformation that could never occur as completely in the domain of "public law" (Slotnick 1991, 71). As political science moved toward greater realism,[13] it moved toward the treatment of the functioning of political institutions as well as their formal structure and toward the investigation of the former through firsthand observation of the phenomenon of concern: political activity. Likewise, political science moved away from the public law content of its roots. Yet the discipline's "original field" only haltingly embraced a Bentleyan-process, protobehavioral approach in the study of its political activity of concern, for that political activity took place within the context of formal, legal institutions, a context that necessitated some descriptive analysis from the older, more historical perspective. Indeed, although public law scholars of the post–World War I generation—such as Corwin, Cushman, Haines, and Powell—all endorsed the tenets of realism, they viewed judicial political actions as constrained by this formal context (Murphy and Tanenhaus 1972, 13–17). Moreover, they viewed the understanding of judicial political actions as constrained by the need to understand the formal, institutional context.

Somewhat unfairly but not surprisingly, then, neither Burgess nor the field of public law is remembered as the progenitor of a "science of politics"—Burgess because he was the target and vanquished foe of a realist methodological revolution and public law because its adoption of realist approaches to studying political activity was tempered by the legalistic subject matter of its study. There is a further explanation for the early twentieth century's demotion of the discipline's founding father and founding field: neither was comfortable with completely abandoning political science's concern for "criticism and education regarding the true ends of the state and how best they may be achieved" (Somit and Tanenhaus 1982, 119, citing Corwin 1929; see also Somit and Tanenhaus 1982, 46–47) As a contemporary commentator has put it, "American political science originated with aspirations to be both truly scientific and a servant of American democratic citizenship"—a belief in "the joint destiny of science and democracy" (Smith 1997, 273, 274).[14] These conflicting desires—to serve American democracy and to be a true "science"—informed Burgess and "public law" and have shaped American political science. But from early on, the discipline's emerging commitment to a value-free political science entailed a jettisoning of things normative or proscriptive as inconsistent with a commitment to unfettered inquiry (Lindblom 1997, 266).[15]

Notwithstanding the empiricist objectives of a neglected giant such as Burgess and the realism of Corwin, the earliest historical-institutionalist pioneer, the work of Charles Grove Haines provided the origins of what was to become behavioralism in public law. His 1922 study of judicial behavior published in the *Illinois Law Review* is distinctive, not only for its nascent attitudinalism but also for its incipient quantitative analysis of judicial decisions. While Haines's realist contemporaries—Corwin, Cushman, and Powell—shared his acknowledgment of the importance of judges' personal values, Haines was unique in employing the new, empirically rigorous methodology for the study of judicial activity. And while a group of quantitatively minded public law scholars met and presented research findings at the Third National Conference on the Science of Politics in 1925 (Murphy and Tanenhaus 1972, 17–18)—a conference engendered by Merriam's APSA Committee on Political Research (Somit and Tanenhaus 1982, 122–25)—Haines's was an inaugural effort to connect the field's subject matter of concern to the developing "science of politics." Haines's work shows that far from being estranged from the new discipline, public law was integral to it and to its methodological developments, even while the field's practitioners struggled with the appropriate definition of the new political "science."

Seen in this developmental context, C. Herman Pritchett's benchmark study of the Roosevelt Court in 1948 was the continuation and a culmination of the long-cherished objective of discovering the political values that underlie judicial decisions. But as Murphy and Tanenhaus comment in their *Study of Public Law* (1972, 18–19), if Pritchett's target was old, his tactics were new. An associate of Merriam's at the University of Chicago, Pritchett was profoundly influenced by Merriam's call for a reconstruction of the methods of political study (Somit and Tanenhaus 1982, 113); in this, Pritchett built on other, more general, influences that were at work within the broader discipline throughout the late 1920s and 1930s. Yet it is equally the case that while pioneering and championing the rigorous study of judicial behavior, Pritchett retained public law's traditional concern for appreciating the judge as a particular kind of political actor whose activity took place within the context of a legal, institutional framework. Pritchett's work, in other words, for all of his laying of the foundation of a new behavioral approach to the study of public law, stressed "the linkage of judicial politics to the concept of law" (Slotnick 1991, 68).

Later judicial behavioralists would lessen this stress as they pursued a truly scientific study of judicial behavior and all that that entailed. But this brief overview of the emergence of the field of public law and judicial politics has demonstrated that public law developed as and subsequently reinvented itself as a field intimately linked with political "science." That some of the field's scholars at times questioned or felt moved to examine the parameters of that science indicates an engagement in, not a disengagement from, the discipline's objectives.

THE PROMISE OF
JUDICIAL BEHAVIORALISM

The behavioral revolution of the 1940s and 1950s was surely the most important watershed in the development of the discipline of political science since Burgess's founding of the Columbia department in 1880. Earlier scholars such as Corwin and Cushman employed an avowedly political analysis of Supreme Court decision making, and other scholars of the period—notably, Alpheus Thomas Mason—pursued a realist approach to constitutional and judicial studies; indeed, the insights of these "old institutionalist" scholars came to inform the contemporary political development approach of historical institutionalism in judicial studies (Clayton 1999, 32). Yet while these doctrinally oriented scholars recognized the same types of political influences on judicial decision making that later behavioral scholars studied (Murphy and Tanenhaus 1972, 15; Clayton 1999, 20), one figure stands out among the early behavioralists in the field of public law, C. Herman Pritchett. Indeed, some would argue that for a decade, there was "little additional construction on the foundation that he built. Those that followed him imitated, rather than added to, his methods" (Murphy and Tanenhaus 1972, 19–20).

The term *behavioral science*—later corrupted to *behavioralism*—was originally coined by a group of quantitatively oriented, "rigorously" inclined social scientists at the University of Chicago. This behavioral political science was "unmistakably a lineal descendant of the antecedent 'science of politics' movement" of the 1920s (Somit and Tanenhaus 1982, 183).[16] The behavioral movement's direction was toward a more scientific practice of political inquiry, with stress laid on the clear-cut formulation of hypotheses and consequent empirical testing of them. Care was to be taken to use concepts that could be firmly attached to the empirical phenomena that they allegedly mapped (Lindblom 1997, 248). This move of political science was toward an avowedly positivist model of science. Though no dogma was ever explicitly espoused or agreed on, the fresh and unbridled (Enlightenment) optimism of behavioralism is captured by some of its tenets: the scientific community's search would be for grand or general theories from which many of the previously discovered "regularities" could be deduced; individuals and their political interactions with other persons were to be a principal focus of research; and research was to be theory guided, rigorous, empirical, and, whenever possible, quantitative as well as value-free, detached, and objective (Easton 1962; Freeman 1991, 27).

Not surprisingly, given political science's history, the behavioral move was engendered by one of the many moments of widespread dissatisfaction with the "state of the discipline." This particular dissatisfaction was inspired by a social science "born" in history, increasingly attempting to distinguish itself from its progenitor by emphasizing theory and method (McDonald 1996, 8), and ultimately developing a causal account of politics "on the model of natural sciences that deny any conscious agency to the phenomena they study" (Smith 1996, 127). Agent-centered ("great man") accounts of political events were part of the personalistic, historical approach that constituted traditional research. Dahl (1961), who calls behavioralism a successful protest movement against traditional political science, provided a brief but detailed effort to account for the specific, situational factors that gave rise to the behavioral movement. Two of the intellectual antecedents he notes are worth mentioning here: Merriam's scientism[17] and Bentley's group, process-oriented analysis, which he applied to the judiciary and which David Truman extended in his judicial chapter in *The Governmental Process* (1951) (Pritchett 1968, 202). Pluralist group theory and the constellation of forces it identified as independent variables—group interests and resources, social background orientations, ideological preferences—thus became a key foundation for the behavioral science of politics, which emphasized explaining particular political events as instances of more general behavioral regularities (Smith 1996, 122, 130).

Pritchett's 1948 *Roosevelt Court: A Study in Judicial Votes and Values, 1937–1947,* aligned judicial politics research with the then current behavioral work in American politics; its focus on decision making resonated with what other political scientists were examining (Slotnick 1991, 74). Pritchett's interest in the social and psychological origins of judicial attitudes and the influence of individual predilections on the judicial decision-making process was thus a facet of a much broader movement in the discipline (Schubert 1963c, 2). With his work, the public law field was christened with a new moniker, judicial process. This renaming suggested not only the growing behavioral mood of the field but also a revised research agenda that focused on the process, not the product, of judicial decision making. As a volume published during the mature, consolidation phase of judicial behavioralism states, "Pritchett . . . foreshadowed and stimulated two new research emphases. One was methodological in character—the utilization of quantitative techniques. The other represented a shift in target from 'what do judges say?' to 'what makes judges behave as they do?'" (Grossman and Tanenhaus 1969, 4).

The behavioralization of judicial studies proceeded from these two new research emphases. One fellow traveler assessed Pritchett's seminal influence on the move from "public law" to "judicial behavior" in the following way:

> First, Pritchett conceptualized the Supreme Court as a small deci-
> sion-making group, whose voting and opinion behavior could
> best be explained in terms of imputed differences in the attitudes
> of individual justices toward the recurrent issues of public policy
> that characterize cases that reach the Court for decision. Second,
> Pritchett based his analysis upon quantitative measurement of a
> large sample of data. (Schubert 1963c, 2)

The attitudinal variable that Pritchett stressed was political liberalism; judicial values, then, reflected broad policy preferences. Nevertheless, judicial values could also incorporate judicial conceptions about proper role.[18] The theoretical premise from which Pritchett's work proceeded was a sociopsychological theory of the formation of attitudes that itself stressed the importance of social background in shaping the attitudes/values expressed in observable behavior and measurable in the same currency. The context for the expression of attitudes was conceptualized as an interest-group-based, pluralist process, which led to two frameworks for examining the political nature of judicial decisions: an intracourt framework, which stressed the importance of a multimember court as a small group, and an extracourt framework, which emphasized the importance of viewing judicial decisions within the context of broader patterns of political conflict (Schubert 1963c, 4–5). The model that Pritchett and subsequent judicial behavioralists formulated to understand political activity at an operational level was a classically behaviorist stimulus-response model, with case facts providing the stimuli and votes—frequently operationalized dichotomously—constituting the response.

That not all public law scholars were entranced by the spell of judicial behavioralism was soon apparent. Of chief concern were the implications of the behavioralists' project and findings for a theory of

democratic government and judicial review.[19] Representative of traditionalists was Wallace Mendelson, who would trenchantly but sourly
observe that behavioral techniques could be legitimately applied to
activist judges, for behavioralism was itself a by-product of libertarian
activism (Mendelson 1963). Intellectually, he objected to the application of behavioral techniques to every member of the modern Supreme
Court and to those judges who "greatly practice" the judge's art, for
these techniques of analysis do not "depict even dimly the subtleties of
the judicial process" (603). To some degree, the humanistic criticism
by Mendelson and others[20] generally resembled the antibehavioralist
reaction, even though the public law traditionalists were not the same
group as the antibehavioralists, who encompassed political theorists,
Straussians, and Left critics of pluralism. The leftists were represented
by the resistance movement, the Caucus for a New Political Science,
organized at the 1967 meeting of the American Political Science Association. These antibehavioralists argued that some things—politics—
cannot be studied scientifically, because to do so distorts what actually
happens; moreover, some things—again, politics—should not be studied scientifically, because in the fallacy of measurement lies the danger
of unethical manipulation (Freeman 1991, 31). The views of the caucus
recall the discipline's unresolved heritage as both a policy "science" and
a progressive enterprise in pursuit of more effective human political
agency by means of a more truly democratic politics (Smith 1997, 275).
Likewise, Mendelson's objections recall the demurrers of the realist
generation of public law scholars to an oversimplification of the judicial
craft. Whether human values are too complex for simplified efforts at
quantification had special resonance for those in the judicial field, given
the heavy normative content of its developmental antecedents.

Mendelson's critique from within the field was one reaction to judicial behavioralism. One might also argue that the behavioral revolution
in judicial studies precipitated the divergence between academic law
and political science in the study of courts, a divergence whose battle
cry was sounded by political scientist Mendelson but given intellectual
expression by law professor Herbert Wechsler. Wechsler, an adherent
to the post–legal realist legal process theory (Kalman 1996, 20, 36–37,
41–42), propounded that the ability and the obligation of law courts to
render "principled decisions," resting on reasons "that in their neutrality and generality" transcend "the immediate result that is achieved" or
the judge who articulates that result, is all that justifies their prestigious
and authoritative role (Wechsler 1959, as quoted in Kalman 1996, 36).
While the "unprincipled" activism of the Warren Court was the real

target of the legal process school (but an activism with whose populist results the legal process scholars agreed), Wechsler's neutral-principles argument and the traditionalist defense of the integrity and objectivity of the judicial office and the rule of law was aimed at any activist—judge or political scientist—who failed to take judicial opinions seriously. As one analyst of the legal scholarship of the 1950s put it,

> "Sophisticated legal scholars" believed they must show that legal and constitutional doctrine underlay judicial opinions. Otherwise, they would be doomed to spend their professional lives presenting the opinions as smoke screens for judges' economic, social, personal, and political preferences. That task could be left to a notable school of historians and *political scientists* who decline to see the legal process as anything more than a chintz cover for the thrust of sheer power and will. (Kalman 1996, 47; emphasis added)

Pritchett himself was sensitive to the limitations of his methodology. In his 1953 study of the Vinson Court, he responded to the potential pitfalls of statistical analyses of judging—charges that included the claims that counting votes as equal in all cases is patently erroneous, that classifying cases in such categories as civil liberties or economic regulation imposes vague and highly subjective criteria on the work of judges, and that classifying cases as involving dichotomous choices oversimplifies the complex of values that may be in conflict. He sought to avoid these pitfalls by combining voting analysis with examination of published opinions and by recognizing that because a final decision could be categorized as for or against a particular value did not mean that the judge saw this value as present or that this was the only value set that was influential (Murphy and Tanenhaus 1972, 126). In other words, he noted the interpretive dimension to quantitative data analysis and sought to avoid a false debate between empiricist and interpretive approaches to political science. Yet his cautious skepticism about the objective nature of and greater analytic precision yielded by any classification of cases was lost on his critics and was, to some degree, deemphasized in the subsequent rush to apply more and more sophisticated quantitative methods to the understanding of judicial behavior. Pritchett's coda, that the judicial process approach had given public law a distinctively *political* orientation and provided it with a vocabulary that makes *discourse* possible with the more methodologically sophisticated sectors of the profession (Pritchett 1968, 219), was already yielding to Glendon Schubert's more partisan pronouncement that a transition had occurred from the study of public law to the study of judicial behavior (1963a, 445).

That Schubert looked back without nostalgia on a public law that "was an exotic bayou, cut off from the mainstream of theoretical and methodological advances in political science" (1963a, 445), tells us much about his behavioral mind-set, but it does not tell us everything about this innovative and influential judicial scholar of the 1960s and 1970s. Schubert's work left a tremendous mark on the study of judicial behavior, most significantly, engendering the current attitudinal model of judging (Segal and Spaeth 1993, 67). But two of his most insightful research directions would not be developed by judicial scholars for more than a decade, to the detriment of the field as a whole.

Schubert took Pritchett's two moves—toward extralegal determinants of judicial decision making and the use of quantification (really, basic summary statistics) to measure these determinants and their effects—and extended them, in terms of depth, sophistication, and precision. One of his contemporary commentators noted that Schubert's 1959 book, *Quantitative Analysis of Judicial Behavior*, "accelerated" the scientific treatment of judicial politics by outlining a method based on a general theory of judicial behavior (Vines 1970, 129–30). Schubert (1959) expanded Pritchett's observation of blocs of justices voting together into a detailed identification of court subgroups, a plotting of their stability over time, and an examination of voting behavior data for evidence of interjudicial influence and leadership. Thus, he refined bloc analysis through measurement by means of indexes of cohesion and adhesion (Schubert 1963c; Vines 1970, 133). Schubert sought, through careful statistical analysis, to find the regularities in the behavior of judges and to identify their structure and origin; his goal was to delineate consistent behavior patterns that are the fundamental structure of judicial institutions (Vines 1970, 135). He adapted a technique from social psychology called scalogram analysis to policy-value judicial research, allowing for the determination of the extent to which judges can be ordered on a (postulated) policy-value continuum (Grossman and Tanenhaus 1969, 11). Schubert's 1965 book, *The Judicial Mind: The Attitudes and Ideologies of Supreme Court Justices, 1946–1963*, became the methodological benchmark for further quantitative research and would later be described as the "turning point" in the use of statistical methods to test hypotheses about courts (Slotnick 1991, 77). Overall, Schubert's work "marked . . . the beginning of the modern era because it represented the first full scale, completely behavioral, methodologically sophisticated effort to develop a theory of judicial decision making in the [Supreme Court]. It also served as a reference point for later inquiries" (Tate 1982, 10).

Two aspects of this "reference point for later inquiries" are worth elaborating, if only because they illustrate that Schubert's research agenda was more diversified than his attitudinal followers or his public law critics give him credit for. One was Schubert's pioneering use of game theory to analyze the strategic dimension of judicial decision making, and the other was his application of the behavioral approach to comparative judicial studies. That neither of these research frontiers were explored contemporaneously with the development of an attitudinal model of judicial behavior suggests that Schubert's work became the central prop of a "normal science" paradigm that was more parched than it might have been.

First, in a 1958 *American Political Science Review* article, his 1959 book, and a subsequent law review piece on certiorari behavior on the Supreme Court (Schubert 1962), Schubert utilized discoveries of rational strategies in strategic game situations to investigate the voting patterns and motivations of swing justices and the "deciding to decide," or certiorari, phase of Supreme Court policy-making. In this, he was part of a general trend in political science to borrow from econometrics to develop formal models depicting politics as comprised of strategically rational, goal-maximizing individual behavior within specific structures of rules. This new enterprise of rational choice theory would aspire to make the discipline a deductive science guided by a unified general theory in extension of neoclassical economics (Freeman 1991, 28–29; Smith 1997, 276; Morton 1999, chap. 2). Although rational economic theory was already making inroads into political science during the 1950s and early 1960s,[21] it differed from classic behavioralism in its agenda for a science of politics. To use a public law illustration, while the psychometric model of judicial decision making—a model Schubert's work largely supported and promoted—postulates a simple and direct relationship between attitudes and voting behaviors (Gibson 1986, 158), game-theoretic modeling eschews successful prediction as the ultimate goal of scientific inquiry and posits a deductive approach to theory (Weisberg 1986, 4). The broad theoretical framework of the economic model of political activity offered to judicial behavior scholarship explicit premises about the bases for judges' decisions, premises that could guide such scholarship to systematically follow their implications for patterns of behavior (Baum 1997, 133–34).[22] Most important of these implications was the role of intervening variables of strategy in the judicial decision-making process. Schubert was not the first, or necessarily the most imaginative, to discuss collegial court behavior as strategic action,[23] but he was foundational in the utilization of game theory for judicial studies.[24] Yet to reiterate, his foundation would not be capitalized on as immediately as were his behavioral/attitudinal innovations.

Second—equally importantly and, alas, almost equally unheeded at the time—Schubert sought from the beginning of his career to extend the utility of his approach to judicial decision making to the comparative context and to cross-cultural comparisons of courts. In this, he was in keeping with the tradition of comparative analysis that had moved such disciplinary founders as Burgess. Schubert's application of bloc analysis to the Michigan Supreme Court and the comparative focus of his volumes on judicial behavior all testify to his desire to develop a general theory of judicial decision making (Schubert 1959, 1963d, 1985; Schubert and Danelski 1969). Again, he was not alone in this desire, as various scholars of the 1960s and early 1970s shared his concern for the comparative study of judicial systems (Schubert and Danelski 1969; Grossman and Tanenhaus 1969; Becker 1970a). Schubert, along with these colleagues, "did not see the judicial behavior field they had created as divided between courts inside and outside the U.S. The empirical approach to studying courts unified their work. They assumed that courts abroad should be a part of the development of judicial behavior. Moreover, they understood that generalizable theory building would have to include cross-cultural studies" (Haynie and Tate 2000, 30). Despite this, Schubert et al.'s clarion call for comparative judicial behavior research atrophied and would not be resuscitated until the late 1980s (Haynie and Tate 2000, 22 ff.), when concern for the political, institutional context of judging was revived by new institutionalist scholars of both strategic and historical persuasions (Epstein and Knight 2000, 644–45).

This litany of accomplishments (one distinguished judicial process scholar was moved to declare, at a recent law and courts roundtable on the topic of this volume presented at the Midwest Political Science Association, that Schubert is "the only pioneer") should not disguise the fact that Schubert was only a part (albeit a very important part) of the behavioralization in judicial studies pursued by a host of other scholars.[25] Nor should Schubert's commitment to behavioral methodology overshadow the fact that he, like others of his generation, saw fit to engage in content analysis of opinions and investigate the role of legal factors, such as stare decisis, on judicial decision making, using "opinion data to complement the insights that we can derive from voting data" (Schubert 1963b, 71). Finally, Schubert's importance to the study of judicial behavior should not detract from the reality that Schubert-style judicial studies were not every judicial scholar's cup of tea. Mendelson's earlier critique of behavioralism was echoed by scholars such as Robert Dixon, who added a new note in a familiar key regarding the increasing abstruseness of the judicial field's quantitative methodology: "How abstract can a profession become," he challenged, "and still serve society?" (1971, 25).

One might also wonder how "isolated" and "unique in its characteristics" (Baum 1983, 197)[26] a field can become and still be of interest to its discipline. This question turns our attention to the intellectual consequences of Schubert's "acceleration" of the scientific objectives of judicial studies. Despite the judicial behavioralists' hopes to reconnect the judicial field to political science generally and to broaden the field's concerns beyond the opinions of the U.S. Supreme Court, their work seemed to have exactly the opposite effect.

FROM ESTRANGEMENT TO A (NEW) INSTITUTIONAL REVIVAL

Crisis would be too strong a word to describe the fallout of the "new" "public law." But by 1970, one of its adherents would already make the following diagnosis:

> As long as the analysis of judicial institutions defined judicial politics as public law, conceptualized and studied by methods endemic to the legal subculture, it developed a vocabulary and a set of methods somewhat marginal to the mainstream of political science. *The turn of judicial studies to a more behavioral orientation brought new problems to light.* Instead of embarking upon macro-analyses of judicial institutions, quantitative studies focused on the Supreme Court, the most visible component of judicial behavioralism, employing sophisticated methodology *but a rather specialized frame of reference.* (Vines 1970, 140; emphasis added)

As the previous survey of Schubert's work suggests, this diagnosis is somewhat extreme. Schubert, as exemplar of the judicial behavioralists, was not a narrow scholar in subject matter or method. However, it is clear that the judicial field behaved more as a consumer of than a contributor to new theory within the discipline of political science. This in itself is not a fatal flaw: the dependency of political science on other disciplines for its innovations is noteworthy, according to a contemporary overview of our origins (Lindblom 1997, 245). But it is true that in its desire to be sophisticated and rigorous and scientific, the study of judicial behavior increasingly buried itself in the examination of that most celebrated and familiar judicial institution, the U.S. Supreme Court, developing, it was claimed, quantitative methods that were not very useful in the study of other federal appellate courts, for example (Vines 1970, 137). To be fair, this "high court bias" was something that Pritchett, Schubert, and other pioneering behavioralists were cognizant of and labored to avoid in their own research agendas.[27] Yet in spite of such warnings, "public law and/or judicial politics dwindled into a marginalized constitutional law–Supreme Court ghetto of little interest to other political scientists"; as public law was reduced to the study of the Supreme Court's constitutional law opinions and votes, it encountered the paradox that it studied only one thing, and the thing is so big as to be unimportant to most political scientists (M. Shapiro 1993, 366).[28]

Making matters worse was the "law avoidance" of contemporary political science—specifically, the fields of American and comparative politics—which contributed to the judicial field's lack of relevance to and status in the discipline (M. Shapiro 1993, 366). These fields, even when engaged in analysis of lawmaking processes and institutions, paid little attention to the content of laws, statutes, and regulations. Their legal ignorance was, unfortunately, something that judicial behavioralism encouraged (though not explicitly or directedly) in its "denigrat[ion of] formal legal and constitutional structures and language as mere appearances behind which real and quantifiable political behavior lurked" (M. Shapiro 1993, 365). Constitutional law—doctrinal analysis—remained an eroded remnant of public law and an undertaking that tied the judicial field to its antediluvian roots: legalistic case analysis and legal structural description. Many judicial behavioralists—aspiring, perhaps, to be like their compatriots in other fields—were ready to jettison such trappings of "fake lawyers" servicing traditional, marginal concerns of political science (Sarat, in Stumpf et al. 1983, quoted in Slotnick 1991, 94). Becker is illustrative (though probably a somewhat extreme version) of such behavioral lambasting of "public law": "For far too long political scientists have played an alien role concerning their interest in the court system. They have played the roles of: lawyer, in attempting case analysis; historian, in sketching judicial biographies and constitutional developments; philosopher, in pondering problems of jurisprudence" (Becker 1970b, 163). Yet, condemning his field with a broad brush, Becker continued, "and statistician, in describing judicial decisions with quantitative exactitude." The judicial decisions to which he referred were those of the U.S. Supreme Court.

Thus, rather than fostering a revivified embrace of the judicial politics field by the discipline of political science, judicial behavioralism seemed to further their estrangement after a fleeting (to continue the trope) rapprochement. Worse yet, "public law" became the arena in which to fight political science's old battles between traditionalists ("constitutional law") and behaviorists ("judicial process").[29] The "return" to normative legal theory in public law political science and an interdisciplinary link to moral philosophy—the interest in constitutional interpretation and constitutional theory that "re-creates" the political theory wing of the field (M. Shapiro 1993, 376)—seemed only to harden the battle lines, further relegating judicial studies to a contentious, strife-ridden, if "exotic bayou" of the disciplinary landscape.[30]

Were this the end of the judicial subfield story, there would be little purpose to this volume beyond nostalgia for what might have been (or, less charitably, beyond continued axe grinding). However, this is not the case: just as behavioralism (ultimately) spurred creative reaction in the discipline of political science, so did judicial behavioralism engender a beneficial diversification in the study of judicial politics. It did so unintentionally and in terms of what might be described as a paradigm struggle. Indeed, Kuhn's (1962) ideas about the structure of scientific revolutions had a delayed but important influence on how political scientists conceptualized their discipline's development:

> When Kuhn's book was read, behavioralists interpreted it their way: 1) scientific revolutions are about paradigm change, 2) a paradigm is an overarching or dominant view of the scope of a discipline and the way it will proceed to conduct inquiry, and 3) the behavioral revolution moved political science from a pre-scientific to a scientific stage in its development. Anti-behavioralists, on the other hand, viewed a single, dominant view of the discipline and its work as closed, stifling, and dysfunctional. (Freeman 1991, 29)

Such quarrels about whether a paradigm shift had occurred in political science and, if so, toward what overarching paradigm began an intensive discussion in the discipline throughout the 1970s and 1980s about whether political science would justify itself as a distinctive professional enterprise by achieving a common scientific paradigm of scientific inquiry, creating a universal explanatory theory, and discovering a scientific method unique to the discipline (Smith 1997, 287, 292). But the Kuhnian analogy suggests that political science is a continuing debate rather than conventional (or idealized) science, that perhaps, "political science as debate might be political science at its best" (Lindblom 1997, 262). This assertion applies to the judicial field and its dialogue over the virtues of judicial behavioralism in the following way.

The research program of judicial behaviorism throughout the 1960s and early 1970s was the pursuit of new empirical analysis based in nonformal theorizing. The theorizing was nonformal because it was based in certain loosely organized ideas about expected empirical relationships in the realm of judicial decision making—ideas coming from observations in previous empirical research (say, Pritchett's) and from general theoretical arguments of behavioralism. The behavioral model as applied to judging—the stimulus (case facts)–intervening attitude–response (judicial vote) model as an abstraction of reality—was nonformal as well because it was "presented as a direct hypothesis or set of hypotheses about the real world and the real things that the researcher [was] interested in explaining" (Morton 1999, 35, 43). Thus, the emphasis in judicial behavior research was on empirically testable theories and generalizing from observable variables (see Epstein and Knight 2000, 637) or on the related quest for better ways to deal with data problems that limit the ability of the empirical research to discover behavioral regularities and "empirical" laws.

This inductive approach left the theoretical basis for such inquiry imprecise or inexplicit, with the empirical search directed somewhat single-mindedly toward continually finding new data or finding new ways to analyze old data (Morton 1999, 20, 16–17). Thus, judicial behavioralists attended to the development of more sophisticated statistical techniques for estimating relationships between various political variables and the key dependent variable, the judicial vote. Likewise, judicial behavioralists concerned themselves with identifying and operationalizing new independent variables on the stimulus side of the judicial behavioral equation.[31] Finally, behavioralism's research program increasingly highlighted the development of judicial data archives for use by investigators in the verification of hypotheses and in the search for empirically supported generalizations[32]—paralleling the objectives of the Michigan school of voting behavior and the creation in 1962 of the Inter-University Consortium for Political and Social Research, a data repository that grew out of Campbell et al.'s survey research for *The American Voter* (1960). All this work was an important and necessary data-generating process and a natural developmental trajectory for empirically based political science. The focus was on knowledge of the empirical world of judicial politics; theory in judicial behavioralism was fused with empirical research and theorizing. In a Kuhnian sense, this focus and its attendant approach constituted the scientific paradigm to which judicial behavioralists—as all behavioralists—were attached.

This focus had two consequences, both somewhat negative from the perspective of behavioralists lauding the discovery of a timeless, dominant paradigm. One was what Becker identified as judicial scholars' consuming interest in describing judicial decisions—particularly those most accessible and considered most important in a policy-making sense, that is, the Supreme Court's—with quantitative exactitude. Thus developed for the judicial field a behavioral variant of the Supreme Court ghetto, increasingly concerned with such specialized empirical questions and quantitative techniques for investigating them that it was of diminishing interest to other political scientists and, frequently, other judicial scholars.[33] Put another way, judicial behavioralists united two epistemological tendencies: one, to view individual actors as the analytic building blocks and to therefore view decisional outcomes as aggregated preferences divorced from either a legal process or a structural/institutional process context (Maltzman, Spriggs, and Wahlbeck 2000, 12); the other, to give in to the traditional public law temptation of personalistic or biographical analysis of judging, albeit quantified (Ranney 1996, 6). Both tendencies narrowed and limited the substantive and theoretical appeal of the judicial field as constituted in the study of judicial behavior.

A second consequence of the focus of judicial behavioralism was the dichotomy it produced in the political science of law and courts, that between the "institutionalist" tendency and the "political behavior" tendency. The differences between these tendencies lay "in the character of their commitment to the discovery of uniformities, in their approach to political institutions, and in the type of data and technique with which they are concerned."[34] Early judicial behavioralism's focus was on testing an empirically derived model of judicial decision making whose assumptions about actors, their goals, and their institutional or structural constraints were not always made explicit.[35] It did not value descriptive institutional study—traditional institutionalism—or carefully attend to the institutional context of judging and moving toward an understanding of how institutional arrangements affect political outcomes.[36] Judicial behavioralism was agnostic to hostile toward study of the process by which law was formed or toward the political and institutional components of lawmaking (Krislov and Krislov 1996, 71). Even pluralist theories of judicial policy-making—that judges enact policies that embody not so much their own personal preferences as the outcomes of interest group political processes (M. Shapiro 1996, 103)—was not what courts' embeddedness in politics meant to the behavioralists.

Dissatisfaction with both these consequences of the judicial behavioral revolution—ghettoization and institutional denial—were testimony to the fact that a paradigm shift had not occurred in the field. Rather, judicial behavioralism—and the criticisms of its attitudinal approach—ultimately produced a "contest" among contested, but not always explicitly specified, theoretical positions. The resulting debate across emergent approaches to the study of judicial behavior has reinvigorated the judicial field without resolving all of its conceptual problems. It is possible that invigoration comes when conceptual problems are not seen as solved; if this is so, it seems clear that the debate over the merits of judicial behavioralism has spawned an alternative research direction for the field of law and courts, albeit one that is loosely structured and still open-ended. This alternative research direction has adopted, as the major part of its agenda, the reconnection of judicial studies to a larger institutional context. It is from this concern for courts as institutions that the three current approaches to the study of judicial behavior come, approaches that include a revivified, more sophisticated, and more self-critical attitudinal model of judging.

JUDICIAL BEHAVIOR IN INSTITUTIONAL CONTEXT(S)

The continued vitality—or, at least, the staying power—of judicial attitudinalism is a product of its predominance among political scientists working in the judicial subfield.[37] Since the late 1960s, it has been both the major approach guiding research into judicial decision making and the major approach to question, supplant, or dethrone in directing and even in justifying further or alternative research. Its predominance, while frequently challenged, nevertheless rested on a secure foundation: its validity as an explanatory model of judicial behavior, where validity meant parsimonious explanation[38] combined with the ability to accurately predict future behavioral outcomes (Spaeth 1995, 297). Simple, neat, and predictively successful—as long as the debate about or contestation over the study of judicial decision making was framed in such terms, the attitudinal model of judging seemed impregnable to critical assault. Various institutionalist critics, however, framed their critiques somewhat more broadly, and their persistence resulted in a certain amount of accommodation by judicial behavioralists, albeit after some initial stonewalling. But it is testimony to the continuing vitality of attitudinal judicial behavioralism that it responded and adapted to its institutionalist critics, just as their attacks (whether directed or more sublimated) on this predominant approach in judicial studies sharpened their particular institutionalist approaches to the study of law and courts.

This diagnosis is aptly illustrated by the fact that a first, critical response to judicial behavioralism developed alongside its intracourt focus on judicial voting behavior. This coterminous yet institutionally grounded judicial research sought to conceptualize courts and their decision making *as part of a larger political context* and *in a larger judicial context*. *Process-based* judicial research, as an institutional approach to the study of law and courts, incorporated two distinct but related research directions, a "political process" line of inquiry and a "legal process" line of inquiry. Political process–based research on judicial decision making harked back to the recognition by Cushman (1925) of the political function performed by the Supreme Court in its constitutional interpretations, of litigation before the Court as a stage in the struggle of contending political forces, and of the broader systemic consequences of major decisions (Grossman and Tanenhaus 1969, 4–5; Murphy and Tanenhaus 1972, 14–15). From this, an approach to judicial process studies developed that addressed the external environment of judicial decisions, attempting to describe judges as participants in and reactive to the political process.[39] Courts, in other words, were part of a political "regime," and their decision making needed to be understood as such. Legal process–based research on judicial decision making, while sharing a concern for the activity of lower federal courts, focused its attention on the legal process itself as one type of a larger category of social behavior. The emphasis, in other words, was increasingly on the *law* aspect of "law and courts." Judges were of course key actors in the legal realm, and legal process–based work investigated judicial roles in the state court context and litigation in the trial court context as avenues for broadening an understanding of judicial decision making (Jacob 1965; Dolbeare 1967; Vines 1969; see Schubert 1963c, 5–6; Grossman and Tanenhaus 1969, 13; Pritchett 1969, 32; Slotnick 1991, 85–86). But paradoxically, one of the contributions of this work on courts in institutional context was the finding that judges are not as central to what happens in lower courts as they are in higher, appellate courts. This finding developed into an orientation: "judicial" scholarship would include the study of law in the hands of a broad range of noncourt legal actors—lawyers, juries, social movements, police, and ordinary people. Legal process–based research moved away from

explaining judicial behavior[40] and ultimately toward the interdisciplinary study of law, culminating in the formation of the Law and Society
Association in 1964 and in—some would claim—the institutionalized
divorce of "law" and "courts" researchers within the field of law and
courts studies.

The "judicial process movement," as Pritchett in 1969 described all
process-based judicial research, paralleled attitudinal judicial behavioralism but was noteworthy for extending judicial politics scholarship's field of inquiry beyond the Supreme Court and its internal workings. In addition, process-based judicial research defended the utility of
comparative judicial studies, using lower federal courts and state legal
systems as the sites for assessing the validity of extant theories of judicial action and as the laboratories for generating new, more generally
applicable theory about the judicial process.[41] Moreover, this research's
emphasis on the external political environment of courts opened the
door for further attention to judicial concern for institutional legitimacy as a crucial element in the explanation of judicial behavior at
home and abroad. This research's emphasis would come to shape indi-
rectly one of the prevailing current approaches to the study of judicial
decision making, the historical-institutionalist approach.

Process-based, institutionally situated judicial research has never
resolved what methodological practice or distinctive analytic approach
should guide further inquiry into the process aspect of judicial decision
making. To an extent, this same failing continues to bedevil historical-
institutionalist judicial scholarship, which builds on its process-based
predecessors' insights. A reason may lie in the fact that scholars interested in broadening the scope of judicial studies to lower courts, trial
courts, and non-U.S. courts have practiced a type of judicial area studies that does not focus on a theory of judicial decision making per se.
Instead, the emphasis has been on ethnographic studies of court systems or of law and legal institutions as part of a generally functionalist[42]
analysis of systemic objectives of dispute resolution, norm enforcement, or regime enhancement. Critics here charge that such work is
idiographic and is oriented less toward drawing generalizations across
different court systems (Gibson 1986, 145) and more toward describing
the cultural meaning of customary behaviors in a legal context (see
Mather 1979, 3, cited in Gibson 1986). Perhaps both practitioners and
critics can agree that with respect to the generation of a general theory
of judging from "comparative" court studies, "unless or until there is a
substantial body of carefully drawn descriptive and inductive research
on which typologies can be drawn and until classifications are made,

the benefits of an analysis of a single setting may be as great, if not greater than, those of comparative studies" (Feeley 1979, xvii; see generally Haynie and Tate 2000). At present, judicial research on non-U.S. and lower court and legal systems retains this descriptive, ethnographic orientation, tabling the question of a "nomothetic" theory of judicial behavior (Gibson 1986, 151) in favor of a cataloging of cross-institutional differences and an identification of the unique factors in local legal cultures. Ironically, of course, it is from such descriptively intensive, single-context studies of the U.S. Supreme Court that judicial behavioralism constituted its generalizable theory of judging as ideology-driven political action. Perhaps the descriptive, "idiographic" agenda of current comparative courts and legal process research awaits such a theoretical culmination.[43]

The debate over the virtues of the attitudinal focus in judicial behavioralism occasioned a second, courts-in-institutional-context research direction in judicial studies. Like the aforementioned political/legal process–based research, this second institutionally grounded research direction was initiated simultaneously with judicial attitudinalism; also like the process-based judicial research, it has not been a homogeneous and unitary research program but a diverse and divergent group of studies concerned with courts in institutional context. Yet unlike the process-based studies, this "new institutionalism" in judicial research quite self-consciously (1) retained the focus on explaining judicial *behavior* and (2) directed attention to the *institutional structure within which judicial decision making occurs.* New institutionalism differed from what Pritchett identified as the "judicial process" movement in its effort to be *systematic* (or at least specific) in accounting for the *institutional factors* affecting judicial choice. Attention to the institutional features of judging sprang from two different methodological camps: neoinstitutionalist formal theory and historical-interpretive institutionalism. These differed in the theoretical bases for their inquiry, as they differed in their definitions of *institutions.* But both attempted to put the politicolegal institutional context back into the judicial behavior equation and, in so doing, laid the groundwork for the two approaches to the study of judicial decision making that currently challenge the attitudinal approach, the strategic and the historical-institutionalist approaches.

For the neoinstitutionalist (or strategic) theorists, inspired by formal or positive political theory, political institutions are conceptualized as structural constraints that, in a collegial decision-making environment, operate to make judicial choices about voting or opinion writing interdependent and a function of actors' strategy for maximizing policy preferences. The effort is to formalize the model of judicial behavior from which testable hypotheses about judging are generated—to derive "a set of precise or abstract assumptions or axioms about the real world presented in symbolic terms that are solved to derive predictions about the real world" (Morton 1999, 61). One way of doing so is for institutional names and norms to be replaced with theoretical constructs with operational meaning at the level of the individual political actor to account for cross-institutional similarities and dissimilarities (Gibson 1986, 152, 155). The choice of abstraction, or what features to abstract of the political reality they represent, has been influenced, in strategic judicial studies, by judicial decision-making research that employed nonformal models or verbal statements about the strategic nature of the empirical judicial world that were given in terms of real observables. Such nonformal research into the interdependent nature of judicial decision making included Walter Murphy's *Elements of Judicial Strategy* (Epstein and Knight 1998, xi–xii; Maltzman, Spriggs, and Wahlbeck 2000, 13) and the work of the social psychology–influenced small-group theorists,[44] all of whom addressed the dynamics of interpersonal persuasion in the multimember court setting. Even Schubert's attitudinally anchored research engendered investigation by him and subsequent scholars into the "strategy" conditioned by certain institutional constraints and conditioning certain judicial voting behavior.[45] But interestingly, the impetus for a positive theory of courts and judicial behavior came originally and most forcefully from two literatures outside of the judicial field proper: spatial voting studies and analyses of legislative coalitions, and legal academics adapting a "separation-of-powers" game structure to understand judicial statutory construction (see generally, Stearns 1997; Smith 1997, 301–2 n.23).[46]

Formal theory, now the disciplinary bête noire that behavioralism once was, has not been enthusiastically embraced as a methodology or a worldview by all law and court scholars—or all political scientists, for that matter. To some, the rational choice scholars are like the behavioralists before them: they tend to assume that policy preferences are fixed and external to political choices (Smith 1996, 123–24) and that human agency is of little intrinsic or explanatory importance (120). Yet unlike the behavioralists, rational choice or strategic scholars stress the understanding of the way in which institutional rules and structures affect the aggregation and expression of preferences and thus empower some actors over others. Indeed, those sympathetic to the approach distinguish behavioralism's view of predetermined human behavior from their own, whereby rational political actors engage in rational calculation of the strategic element in their political "game" and do not simply respond to forces outside of their control (North 1990; Maltzman, Spriggs, and Wahlbeck 2000, 13).

The new institutional "revival" in judicial behavior studies has also included a turn to history that stresses the interpretive character of human knowledge and the constitutive nature of institutions; institutions are defined rather broadly as traditions, contexts, and languages that have at least partially constituted persons and groups as well as their preferences. The emphasis in the research of the historical wing of new institutionalism is (1) political-context sensitive, doctrinal development studies, and (2) analysis of how legal and political institutions changed through history, in ways traceable to different historical conceptions of their purposes, *and how such change influences judicial behavior* (Smith 1996, 134–35, 137). Here, institutions are "not only fairly concrete organizations, such as governmental agencies, but also cognitive structures, such as patterns of rhetorical legitimation characteristic of certain traditions of political discourse" (Smith 1988, 91); institutional settings affect individual judges' capacity to pursue their policy preferences by imposing on them an obligation to act in accordance with particular institutional expectations and responsibilities. In other words, institutions not only structure a judge's ability to act on a set of beliefs—as the strategic neoinstitutionalists claim—but are also a source of distinctive political purposes (Gillman and Clayton 1999, 4–5). This linkage, both conceptual and in terms of research design, among "institutions," policy preferences, and decisional behavior differentiates historical new institutionalists from the political process–based judicial scholars who inform some of the new institutionalists' work. Moreover, historical-institutionalist research turns from the behavioral to the cognitive and affective aspects of *attitudes* and from an instrumental to a constitutive conception of law (Clayton 1999, 28–29). In making this turn, these "new" institutionalists recall the type of work done by "traditional" institutionalists, such as Corwin, Mason, and McCloskey, but the attitudinal thesis of modern judicial behavioralism is the touchstone.

It is true that the historical new institutionalists are spurred in part by old concerns about the discipline's failure to achieve "true science" and by a desire to move beyond the methodological flagellation that political science in general suffers because "the aspiration to be *conventionally scientific* remains strong in the discipline, [and so] discomfort over failure and consequent confusion in the discipline continue"

(Lindblom 1997, 251; emphasis added). But in turning to history to ameliorate feelings of the failure to be scientific, it is not as if historical institutionalists became historians. Unlike historians, who study events to understand them in their peculiar contexts and circumstances, these new institutionalists thought of history as a social scientist would, as a source for generalizations about human behavior that transcend time and place (Wood 2000, 41). In historical sources, this wing of new institutionalism sought for political science an alternative to the self-reproach and consequent disorientation over the failure to practice the scientific method it venerates, which would continue as long as the discipline—or one of its fields—did not "resolve the contradiction between long-standing ideals about method on one hand and feasible productive methods on the other" (Lindblom 1997, 252). The new institutionalist turn to history has far from solved this contradiction—indeed, its critics charge that its failure to be conceptually precise mires it in an inability to generate testable propositions about judicial behavior—for its "productive method" for understanding "the dialectic of meaningful actions and structural determinants" is unclear (Smith 1996, 141, referencing Skocpol 1984 and March and Olsen 1989). Nevertheless, the new institutionalist approach posits an alternative way to discuss institutions and their effect on political action and to move beyond judicial attitudes as an uncomplicated influence on judicial decision making.

New institutionalism in judicial studies offers the promise of reintegrating law and legal academics with the political science of courts as well as—potentially—healing the breach between the institutionalist and political-behavior tendencies in the judicial field. Yet somewhat perversely, the breach that has yet to be healed or really even broached is that between new institutionalists who see institutions as game-theoretic structures that constrain actors' choices and new institutionalists who see institutions as constituting and framing the preferences that actors express in their political roles. In many ways, theirs is the latest cleavage between "scientists" and "interpreters" of politics; the history of the discipline suggests that in such cleavages, the interests of the "scientific" approach eventually predominate. But some new institutionalists'[47] turn to history in judicial studies offers something of potentially great and fairly exclusive value to the field of law and courts: it brings the original, historical focus of early public law back into the mainstream of theoretical and methodological debates over the study of judicial decision making. Whether this is a sign of progress, leading to syncretic judicial research, or of nostalgic backlash that will further mire the field in its own solipsism, it is too soon to tell.

Despite its schizophrenic tendencies, the renewed attention to the institutional context of judicial decision making has had one identifiable, laudable result, engendering a more nuanced, sophisticated behavioral approach: a mature, more engaged, and less exclusionary attitudinal model of judicial behavior. In other words, the criticisms of a spare, ghettoizing, and institutionally agnostic version of the attitudinal approach have yielded a certain amount of syncretism in judicial behavior research. The larger institutional context to which this research would reconnect judicial studies is the *legal* context of judicial decision making that some early judicial behavioralists spurned as epiphenomenal to the ideologically based casting of votes. "Syncretic attitudinalism"—for want of a better label—still aspires to construct a general model of judicial decision making that would animate further research but would be more inclusive and expansive about what such research entails. One candidate for such a model has been expressed as the idea that "judges' decisions are a function of what they prefer to do, tempered by *what they think they ought to do*, but constrained by what they perceive is feasible to do. This . . . integrat[es] attitude theory, including theories linking attitudes to case stimuli, or 'cues,' *role theory*, and theories of institutional, or 'organizational' constraints on decision making" (Gibson 1986, 150; emphasis added). There is clearly some cognizance here of traditional legal scholars' viewpoint that the norms of the legal institutional context shape judicial behavior.

Whether such a unified model explicitly guides a syncretic attitudinalist research agenda, there are signs that contemporary judicial behavior research is at least approaching a more syncretic view of the variables that influence the judicial decision. Contemporary judicial studies are more engaged with multiple approaches to the study of law and courts; they include strategic neoinstitutionalist frameworks informed by the empirical findings of judicial behavioralism (see, for example, Epstein and Knight 1998; Maltzman, Spriggs, and Wahlbeck 2000).[48] Contemporary judicial studies are also less exclusionary in their attitudinal worldview; they are willing to admit that judicial policy preferences might not explain all stages of the judicial decision-making process (Spaeth 1995, 314; Maltzman, Spriggs, and Wahlbeck 2000, 10–11). Similarly, an increasing number of contemporary judicial studies are willing to entertain (and empirically test) the possibility that legal factors like precedent or legal rules are part of the judicial decision

(Wahlbeck 1997; Spriggs and Hansford 1998; Spaeth and Segal 1999; Lindquist and Klein 2001). Perhaps because of this more catholic view of the independent variables in the judging equation, there has been an increasing nexus or cross-pollination between works on law and courts by political scientists and academic lawyers[49]—who are, for all their methodological differences from social scientists, still legal realists. Differences remain, both in terms of the theoretical perspective on judging and the kind of data utilized in analyzing judging, but the gulf between quantitative attitudinal and qualitative legal institutional analysis has narrowed somewhat as both recognize that each is searching to understand patterns in judicial behavior (Baum 1997, 128–31). Generally speaking, theoretically synthetic work on judicial behavior has found endorsement in Baum's reprise of the call to let a hundred flowers bloom with respect to diversity in research (1997, 128). But as with Pritchett's evocation of ecumenicalism thirty years prior, contemporary counsel for a syncretic view of the judicial decision making process risks dismissal by some partisans in the field as the "pious stuff" (Segal and Spaeth 1993, 360).[50]

To conclude, the behavioral movement in judicial studies arose as an effort to link the study of courts to a general methodology for political science. The behavioral theory and quantitative methods of judicial behavioralism flourished for a time but ultimately led to a new kind of estrangement for the judicial field. Still, from this estrangement came a healthy intellectual debate within the field and, most recently, an insistent but as yet unresolved reassessment of the theory and methods for studying judicial decision making—a reassessment that nevertheless *once again links the field to scholarly foment within the discipline between "political behavioralists" and "institutionalists."* One scholar characterized that foment in this way: "Scholars who appear to be fighting over 'causal-scientific' versus 'interpretive' methods are often really opposed over their substantive views of human action. Rather than indulging in methodological ostracism, the challenge is to find ways to explore and debate these more substantive differences more constructively" (Smith 1996, 147). That this scholarly foment is itself still roiling does not diminish the importance of law and courts scholars' involvement in it as political scientists. The study of judicial *behavior*, while sometimes narrow and self-satisfied, sometimes contentious in its claims, has continually kept the field as a whole engaged in the dialogue that is political science generally. And that engagement has at times been furthered by scholars or approaches that challenged and thereby occasioned the revision of the prevailing approach to the study of judicial behavior.[51]

The (re)turn to the institutional context in judicial studies, in its several forms, has challenged the claims, assumptions, and worldview of unadorned attitudinalism. But from where did new institutionalists "revive" an institutional approach to the study of judicial behavior? One source was clearly the work of earlier judicial scholars who never ceded the institutional terrain to judicial behavioralism, the work of the field's foundational scholars, who were consistently writing as part of a theoretical debate about how best to study judicial decision making. Two features of the foregoing developmental saga of the study of judicial behavior are thus significant and merit reiteration. One is that until a paradigm of judicial behavioralism was tirelessly (some would probably say tiresomely) articulated and its class of problems awaiting definition and solution were constituted, no debate over its applicability could ensue. The other is that alternatives to it—other paradigmatic challenges—did not spring from sources external to the scholarship of judicial behavior. Rather, both these developmental features—the articulation of an attitudinal approach and the occasioning of countervailing institutionally oriented approaches—originate in the work of the pioneering scholars of judicial behavior. To return to the debate of these pioneers is to appreciate the complexity in the study of the judicial process and to understand why the current, currently unresolved debate among scholars of law and courts is "public law" "at its best."

THE RELEVANCE OF THE PIONEERS OF JUDICIAL BEHAVIOR: AN OLD DIALOGUE ABOUT THREE CONTEMPORARY APPROACHES

Public law's challenge is to engage in theoretical debate about how to study judging without estranging itself. This has always been public law's challenge, and it has not uniformly risen to meet the test. The common concern of scholars of the judicial process—their interest in explaining the phenomena of judicial behavior—is at times overshadowed by vehement methodological struggles and attendant theoretical battles. The foundational scholars of the judicial field were not immune from such battles, but their dialogue—sometimes nasty, sometimes expansive—was an important aspect of their contributions and a critical element of the development of the law and courts field. What has made certain scholars foundational was their ability, at critical junctures in the field, to articulate and delineate common concerns: overarching research questions, profound implications of those questions, the limits of any one methodology for inquiry (not necessarily their own), even the creative virtue of risk in scholarly inquiry (less competitive academic climes perhaps made risk more likely).

The pioneers of judicial behavior were such scholars. Some are remembered as such; some require a gentle reminder about their status; some took risks that did not pay off or that directed the field down circuitous paths and into what now may seem to be missteps. But lest an examination of the pioneers descend into hortatory affection, we should note this cruel fact: the current shape of the field, with both its problems and its possibilities, is a result of both the advances and the limitations in the work of the pioneering scholars. Seeing both these aspects of their work—its advances and its limits—helps us to understand what work we inherited and what we in the field have done with it. Thus, in attending to the work of these pioneers of judicial behavior, two observations are warranted. First, the modern judicial field was shaped by their research. We cannot understand the current shape of the field and the current nature of its debate among approaches without critically engaging their work. Second, attention to their insights— to some of their "risks," both those that paid off and those that did not—returns contemporary judicial scholarship to the critical moments in its tradition of dialogic synthesis. A tradition of dialogue and synthesis is both appealing and frustrating: there are times when dialogue becomes mired in solving old problems and synthesis results in creating new ones. But without looking at the research of the pioneers and the research that their works spawned, we can neither assess the status of existing research frontiers nor prognosticate on the development of new ones.

Two matters are of immediate moment in this section: what constitutes a "pioneer," and what are the three approaches to the study of judicial behavior that conceptually organize the modern field and order the pioneers themselves? We shall take up each matter in turn.

First, what is a pioneer, and why structure an analysis of the state of the judicial field around such personages? As the previous section suggested, endemic to the study of judicial behavior has been a spirited dialogue among approaches. Dialogue is conducted by individuals, not schools of thought. The volume's task, then, is to identify those scholars who were critical to the methodological and theoretical dialogue that formed and subsequently shaped the field of judicial behavior. Such dialogue was a clear feature of the writings of the pioneering scholars, many of whom were defending themselves from the sallies of the methodological traditionalists of their day. Also, many of the pioneers were exact contemporaries, building on or occasionally challenging each other's work. Even those pioneers who were not contemporaneous were nevertheless engaged in "conversations" with the works and claims of earlier scholars. Finally and most obviously, the writings of certain individuals become the standard around which adherents of an approach rally or become the target of a calibrated response and thus engender further dialogue. The citation of individual researchers' ideas and discoveries is the basis of the cumulative nature of social science. As long as we are attached (by convention, if nothing else) to this element of scientific paradigm building, the work of our predecessors will continue to matter.

Of course, such platitudes beg the real question: to paraphrase recent advertising copy, what becomes a pioneer most? Attributes of eminence are notoriously subjective, but a pioneer of judicial behavior can be described as "an individual whose contribution has been that of systematizing a new field and, in the process, of molding it in the image of his [sic] own thought" (Somit and Tanenhaus 1964, 68). A pioneer might partake of other qualities—having intellectual originality that results in new analytic tools or concepts or functioning as a catalyst and rallying point for new intellectual movements in the field (Somit and Tanenhaus 1964, 67–68). For our purposes, a pioneer is a scholar whose research contributions were theoretically grounded yet distinctively original, essential to the development of the study of judicial behavior, and broad enough in their implications to encourage further experimentation. This is a high enough threshold, but we will add one other element to our definition of a pioneer: *this scholar's work was somehow vital to the intellectual dialogue that shaped the study of judicial decision making and was vital to the constitution of an approach to the study of judicial behavior that shapes that dialogue today.*

Are the pioneers, then, scholars who were never wrong, learned friends partaking in some rarified, gentlemanly debate that was uniformly civil, productive, and progressive? Indeed not: part of the purpose of returning our attention to a group of pioneering scholars is to see them warts and all and to recognize that what at first seemed to be their beauty marks were, in fact, warts. (Just as some warts have turned out to be inspirational, to mix a metaphor.) One way we perceive the strengths and the weaknesses of these scholars and of the field their work shaped is to reexamine/reconstruct the intellectual dialogue in which they were participants. It is clear that the constructiveness of the "public law" dialogue has been marred when adherents of one approach or another have made a claim of absoluteness. That claim often resulted from the temptation to be reductive in one's approach, in the effort to develop the most simple, robust model or rhetorically most convincing theory. (Finger-pointing would be of little use here; were all the judicial behavioralists as guilty of the superficiality that Mendelson gainsaid, then one might cry *j'accuse!*) In examining the work of the pioneering scholars of judicial behavior, one is reminded that such reductive tendencies were not always indulged with the same polemical fervor by the originators of approaches as by the followers of those approaches. It is true that some pioneers more than others explicitly championed the reliance on certain assumptions in formulating a theory of judicial decision making; these scholars, while innovators, could be taken to task by the present for such faults, particularly if their assumptions turned out to be unfounded or naive. Thus, our reassessment of the contributions of the pioneers of judicial behavior is asking a frank question: did this scholar articulate an approach or a distinctive worldview with respect to the study of judging without dictating a closed research agenda? A frank answer allows us to see more clearly (1) what was made of such research agendas and (2) what was made of the work of scholars who did not so clearly proscribe a direction for their research.

Ultimately then, what makes a critical rereading of the scholarship of these pioneers valuable is that from it comes the appreciation that a particular approach does not mandate a single, unifocal research direction. Appreciation of this is the stuff of true dialogue and true syncretic research. If our reassessment of the work of these pioneers shows that many of them were less doctrinaire than their disciples, then, discomforting as this is to realize, it is an important insight into the pitfalls of "normal science" in the law and courts field. Conversely, assessment of the shortsightedness of the pioneering scholarship in judicial studies might also suggest how certain normal science paradigms became entrenched. Contemplating our roots—the bent and misshapen, the thwarted, and the vigorous—may allow current scholars to see the virtue of modesty in making their claims. The pioneers teach by example, both good and bad.

The intellectual foundations of the three current agendas for the study of judicial behavior have their origins in different periods, in the work of different judicial scholars. Our current dialogue brings the work of the pioneering scholars into an implicit conversation with one another and with ourselves. Thus, the scholars identified as pioneers are so identified *because of* their direct association with or connection to one of three approaches to the study of judicial behavior. Other scholars have partaken in the construction of these approaches, but the latter are analytic paradigms because of the theoretical or methodological positions articulated by those identified as pioneers. This brings us to our second definitional duty and larger purpose of *The Pioneers of Judicial Behavior*: an identification of the main approaches that have emerged from the theoretical and methodological debates within the field of public law and judicial behavior studies. Such definition, and elaboration, of the *attitudinal, strategic,* and *historical-institutionalist* approaches to the theory and study of judicial behavior are the goals of this volume as a whole. Therefore, in pursuit of this, each section of the volume will describe each approach and then provide a brief identification of the pioneering scholars grouped under it. We enlist the pioneers in the demarcation of and debate among the three approaches because of (1) their self-conscious identification with attributes of one of them and/or (2) their self-conscious claiming as an ancestor by contemporary practitioners of one of them. Individual chapters within each segment will clarify the reason(s) for a pioneer's association with an approach, assess how this scholar's work significantly influenced its development, and ask whether this construction or interpretation of a pioneer's research is itself a distortion or a limitation—and one that has had importance for the current paradigmatic struggles over the study of judicial behavior.

NOTES

The author wishes to thank Ronald F. King and Lawrence Baum for their valuable comments on an earlier draft of this chapter.

1. Graber (2000, 6) also observes that some flowers should not bloom; he is clearly worried about conversations that at once trivialize and deflect valid concerns about scholarly diversity—and how that diversity is dealt with professionally. He characterizes his essay as opening a "conversation on diversity among people who disagree on what constitutes good public law scholarship and on what constitutes public law scholarship." He then laments the difficulty with such a conversation given the realities of scholarly struggles for professional success and recognition, saying, "still, diversity questions arise that cannot be resolved by proudly declaiming, 'let a hundred flowers bloom'."

I briefly take up the relationship between the diversity in the study of law and courts and the disciplinary structures that shape that study at the close of this chapter. I agree with both Graber and Brandwein (2000) that diversity in the field is not something we can avoid or pretend away: we must deal with it openly. This volume offers one way of doing so through its account of the nature of and reasons for the particular development of three diverse approaches to the study of judicial behavior. This volume argues that these approaches have been conversant with one another, but even when they have not been, it is important to understand why not and to work from there.

Of course, one might also concur with Somit and Tanenhaus, in the 1982 edition of their classic work, *The Development of American Political Science*, that "The Current State of the Discipline" has been "that perennially absorbing topic" (225)—for political scientists, that is. See also Smith 1997, which comments regarding the discipline of political science, "we are now entering one of our periods of transition and heightened uncertainty" (272).

2. Public law's unfavorable ranking was exceeded only by that of political theory.

3. One might note that Martin Shapiro opened his 1993 essay, "Public Law and Judicial Politics," by remarking that the field is one with "a highly problematic status" (365). A recent honorary symposium volume offered the following demoralizing reflection: "alas, all is not well with the subfield intellectually . . . it remains a pale reflection of the dominating political behavior area . . . lacking the visionary intellectual statesmanship that new [sic] fields particularly require" (Krislov and Krislov 1996, 72–73). But see the ray of hope offered for "unification" among judicial specialists in Epstein and Knight 2000, 652–53.

4. Aristotle, of course, can also be saddled with the epithet of the "first" political scientist.

5. This work was Burgess's mature distillation of his most influential treatise, *Political Science and Constitutional Law* (1890).

6. The legal realists included, for example, legal scholars such as Karl Llewellyn and Jerome Frank (see Fisher, Horwitz, and Reed 1993). Probably the most celebrated legal realist aphorism originates with Oliver Wendell Holmes, who observed that "the prophecies of what the courts will do in fact . . . are what I mean by the law" (1897, 461). The legal realist worldview is perhaps typically expressed by one of the early realist scholars of public law, Thomas Reed Powell, in a 1918 article: "This is in a nutshell is my thesis: the logic of constitutional law is the common sense of the Supreme Court of the United States. . . . Judges have preferences for social policies, as you and I" (645, 646, 648). The legal realists and scholars such as Powell lacked a sophisticated analytic method for testing their general theory of judicial decision making, even though Llewellyn would call for legal study with "an ever increasing emphasis on observable behavior (in which any demonstrably probable attitudes and thought patterns should be included)" (1930, 465). Indeed, though the legal realists made law and social science their mantra, spoke of integrating law with political science and its sister social sciences, and looked to the social sciences to define good social policy—for which law was a tool—they never proceeded very far in their attempts. See Kalman 1996, chap. 1, for an interesting discussion of the nexus among law, political science, and the study of the Supreme Court.

7. Even though, at this writing, Law and Courts is the third-largest organized section within the American Political Science Association, with close to nine hundred members, and its membership and e-mail discussion list include numerous legal scholars affiliated with law schools.

8. I use this term somewhat self-consciously but with a tongue-in-cheek attitude as well. There is a sense in which "we are all Kuhnians now" (see Kuhn 1962). As Lindblom (1997) observed about the discipline in the 1940s and 1950s, "for those decades, as perhaps for the present, the term 'political science' was a name given not to a field of conventional scientific inquiry but to a continuing debate" (260). On the use of Kuhn's term *paradigm* in discussing political science or approaches (such as behavioralism) within political science, see Somit and Tanenhaus 1982, 174–75; Freeman 1991, 29; and Smith 1996, 130. For a contemporary evocation of the label *paradigm* to differentiate the worldviews of judicial behavioralists who study only judicial votes and legal scholars who view opinions as the most important outcome of the judicial process, see Maltzman, Spriggs, and Wahlbeck 2000, 150.

9. As Roland Barthes observed in 1972, "in order to do interdisciplinary work, it is not enough to take a 'subject' (a theme) and to arrange two or three sciences around it. Interdisciplinary study consists in creating a new object, which belongs to no one" (Barthes 1989, 72). I take this to mean, as does the author of an essay on academic politics that cites this passage (Garber 2001, 74), that one cannot be "interdisciplinary" until one is "disciplinary," or well disciplined, in at least one traditional field of study. This is because interdisciplinarity is simply the creative end product of what this same author terms "discipline envy," where "envy" is "disciplined"—aspiration to emulate submitted to a regimen of authority and control (60–61).

Concerns about disciplinary "contamination" and "purity" are relevant not only to the intellectual history of political science as a discipline but also to the development of a "theory" of judicial decision making for the public law subfield. Theory is itself the artifact of constituting a field of study; it is the space between the attempt and the idealization of that constituting. But its nature is "why theory always, in a sense, fails; for when it succeeds, it ceases to be theory and becomes fact or *doctrine*" (Garber 2001, 89–90; emphasis added).

10. Somit and Tanenhaus 1982, 24, citing Burgess's *Political Science and Comparative Constitutional Law* (1890).

11. For a less sanguine genealogy, see Schubert 1963a.

12. Somit and Tanenhaus define *scientism* as the belief "that the methodology [of] the natural sciences was appropriate for investigating problems of fundamental concern to political science, and that proper application of this methodology would lead to the development of 'laws' with explanatory and predictive power" (1982, 76).

13. As expressed by Lowell 1909 and Bentley 1908.

14. This public service component of political science even informed no less a proponent of disciplinary scientism than Charles Merriam (see Somit

and Tanenhaus 1982, 110–12). Yet some historians of American political science find in Merriam a symbol of "disciplinary schizophrenia" (Ricci 1984, esp. 57), for Merriam was directly involved in/had preferences about the subject he would scientifically study (see Freeman 1991, 21–22). See also Clayton's chapter in this volume on Edward Corwin's record as a "public scholar."

15. See, as illustrative, Lasswell 1936.

16. Other historiographers of the discipline locate the then most recent use of the term *behavior* in the work of public administration scholar Herbert Simon.

17. Somit and Tanenhaus, who exhibit a penchant for such labels, say that Merriam was the "sire" or "father" or can claim "paternity" for behavioralism (1982, 183–84).

18. As Pritchett himself later spelled out in greater detail (see Murphy and Tanenhaus 1972, 125).

19. As Pritchett himself observed (1968, 198–99).

20. Berns 1963 similarly questioned the relevance of quantitative methods to an understanding of the judicial task.

Mendelson was also embroiled in an epistemological exchange with Harold Spaeth, a defender of what was then termed *jurimetrics*, in the *Journal of Politics* during 1964–66. Mendelson stressed the need to study legal discourse to understand judicial decision making; Spaeth urged the quantitative study of judicial votes, suggesting that reliance on what political actors say about what they have done does not yield scientific evidence about court decisions (see Mendelson 1964, 1966; Spaeth 1965).

21. As exemplified by Downs 1957 and Riker 1962.

22. Rohde and Spaeth (1976) would place Schubert's psychometric attitudinal model of judging within a rational choice framework, positing Supreme Court justices as maximizers of exogeneously determined preferences. However, Rohde and Spaeth would argue that the insulating nature of the Court's institutional features would free the justices to vote their attitudes, to make decisions that approximate as nearly as possible their policy goals (Segal and Spaeth 1993, 68–69; Maltzman, Spriggs, and Wahlbeck 2000, 12).

23. This accolade belongs to Walter Murphy, for his *The Elements of Judicial Strategy* (1964).

24. As Schubert eulogized, "Schubert's (1959) work with game theory constitutes one of the very few attempts that have been made to relate judicial behavior to economic theory, methods, and models of rational choice processes. With the exception, however, of Schubert's (1962) reformulation with up-dated data of one of these game models, no other work along these lines appears to have been forthcoming" (1963c, 6–7). See Segal's chapter in this volume for a discussion of the importance of Schubert's opening of this line of inquiry.

Schubert's interest in the strategic dimension of judicial choice and in the utilization of game-theoretic techniques to clarify that dimension would be furthered in the next decade by David Rohde (see Brenner's chapter in this volume) and in later decades by scholars of the strategic approach to judicial behavior. See also Epstein and Knight's chapter in this volume for a discussion of the importance of Walter Murphy's work in sowing the seeds for the contemporary strategic approach.

25. See the extensive bibliography that accompanies Baum 1997.

26. The full context of the quotation is that the judicial field is "unusually distinctive in that it is both more isolated and closer to unique in its characteristics than are most other fields" of political science (Baum 1983, 197).

27. See, for example, Schubert 1963c, 8. See also Pritchett 1968, 204–5, on the influence of the "upper court myth" on public law research.

28. Some find this comment unnecessarily cryptic or even inaccurate. Perhaps Shapiro is suggesting that in focusing almost exclusively on studies of the U.S. Supreme Court, public law in this period permitted itself to be bracketed as a field devoted to a scholasticism about this "one big thing," a scholasticism that other political scientists penetrated only superficially and thus dismissed as more than they needed to know beyond the readily apparent political dynamics of this "one big thing." There is also the argument that the social-psychological approach of judicial behavioralism was a "scholasticism" that other political scientists, including general Americanists, did not view as relevant to their branches or phenomena of government. Thus, judicial scholars' absorption in the minutia of this approach and its application—this large, unfamiliar, and irrelevant terrain—was beside the point to scholars outside the field. See Epstein and Knight 2000, 640–41. Shapiro's piece was the second survey of the field for the *State of the Discipline II* volume prepared and published by the APSA.

29. This battle lives on, to some degree, in the job ads for the "public law" field in the APSA Personnel Service Newsletter, although the purview of "judicial process" slots has broadened to include formal theory-oriented judicial scholars and expanded into a uneasy symbiotic relationship with practitioners of "law and society" approaches. Today's unholy alliance of public law's many combatants is also disturbed by the field's bifurcated existence within the APSA's annual programming: two distinct sections exist—one for "Law and Courts" and another for "Constitutional Law and Jurisprudence." In September–October 2000, the Law and Courts Discussion List featured a subliminally heated discussion about the relationship between Law and Courts Section/judicial process scholars and judicial researchers whose work is sponsored by the Law and Society Association, an interdisciplinary organization that includes legal sociologists. Reconciliation is notoriously difficult, particularly once a breach has been institutionalized.

30. The battle or "false debate" between empiricist and interpretivist political scientists that Pritchett had sought to avoid was thus joined. While intellectually somewhat of a dead end, this particular debate had practical consequences in terms of professional access to political science journals. Behavioral,

quantitative work—in judicial studies and political science generally—came to predominate in the leading journals and their editors' concerns.

Strangely, public law's submergence in this methodological morass presaged a contemporary battle internal to the discipline over the "bias" in access to the main journal of the profession, the *American Political Science Review*. Complaints against "gatekeeping" by adherents of certain positivist approaches to the study of politics surfaced in a series of letters and e-mail postings ("An Open Letter to the American Political Science Leadership and Members," November 3, 2000), complaints that even gained the derisive attention of the *New York Times* (Eakin 2000).

Disciplinary disputation aside, one could argue that once again, it seems that public law's intellectual battles illustrate the field's engagement—even its "anticipatory" engagement—in the discipline's central methodological and epistemological concerns. This is not to say that the field's particular squabbles precipitated the latter concerns, only that public law is less "exotic" and "cut off" than it might first appear.

31. For example, Tanenhaus's work on cue theory or Ulmer's work on litigant status as influencing the judicial vote. See Carp's and Bradley's chapters in this volume.

32. For example, Harold Spaeth's creation and maintenance of the Supreme Court Judicial Database.

33. That this urge to be as methodologically sophisticated as possible could be off-putting or beside the point, even to other scholars who shared a behavioral mind-set toward judicial studies, is evidenced by Walter Murphy's September 21, 2000, posting to the Law and Courts Discussion List: "One of the reasons that I find much current scholarship on the judicial process rather dull is that few of the contributors, perhaps deafened by their own enthusiastic Eureka's, realize that people like Jack Peltason, Herman Pritchett, and Alpheus Thomas Mason (and Edward Corwin, Robert Cushman, and Charles Grove Haines in an even earlier generation) had long ago said, and in a forgotten language called grammatical English, what has so wonderfully now been 'discovered.'" See also Krislov and Krislov 1996, 71–72, where the authors observe that the single-mindedness of the behavioral approach "has become almost sectarian even within the narrow confines of those who pay attention to judicial studies."

34. The description of this dichotomy resulting from the behavioral revolution is taken from Truman 1968, 559.

35. Allegedly among these inexplicit assumptions was judicial behavioralism's conceptualization of the judicial mind, its rationality, and its resultant amenability to "modeling" according to an attitudinal emphasis. Cook argues that judicial behavioralism was informed by the logic of Aristotle's political inquiry, particularly the influence of "the crisp bivalence of Aristotelianism" (n.d., 5). Behavioralism's empirical models of judicial decision making forced data into bivalent classes (for example, in scalogram analysis) in an effort to

achieve precision; the behavioralist saw "the judge bringing preference and result into conjunction and [was] generally satisfied not to further explore the judicial thought process" (Cook 1994b, 4). Cook would apply a bounded rationality theory and a fuzzy logic model to the study of judicial decision making.

36. An understanding that would become *neo*institutionalism. As representative of such work, see Shepsle 1986, 1989; March and Olsen 1984; and the citations on work coming out of positive political theory in Epstein and Knight 1998, xviii n.1; see also the discussion in this chapter. Of course, to be fair, some behavioral studies—in other words, those that stressed the importance of judicial attitudes in explaining the judicial vote—investigated the role of institutional norms such as the Rule of Four in certiorari review in judicial decisions (see Brenner's and Bradley's chapters in this volume; see also Maltzman, Briggs, and Wahlbeck 2000, 14–15 n.10).

37. A less charitable interpretation of the reason for the predominance of judicial attitudinalism might be what one judicial scholar and member of the Law and Courts discussion listserv identified (albeit in a slightly difference methodological context) as "tribal power." By this term, he was echoing Kuhn, who observed that "to discover how scientific revolutions are effected, we shall . . . have to examine not only the impact of nature and logic, but also the *techniques of persuasive argumentation* effective within the quite special groups that *constitute the community* of scientists" (1962, 93; emphasis added).

38. As Spaeth has put it, "A relatively full account of some phenomenon—such as judicial voting—may contain a larger number of variables [than judicial attitudes]. It is axiomatic, of course, that one may explicate any phenomenon if the number of variables used in the explanation equals the number of times the phenomenon has occurred. Thus, if the reasons given for the Court's decisions in [a] term differ for each of the cases the justices decided, *we have learned nothing systematic* about the justices' voting. All we know is unique—idiosyncratic—to each case" (1995, 297; emphasis added). Spaeth's somewhat derisive tone should not obscure the compelling logic behind his vindication of the "parsimonious" attitudinal model.

39. Works here include Peltason 1955; Dahl 1957; and, from a more historical perspective, McCloskey 1960. See generally Murphy and Tanenhaus 1972, 20; Pritchett 1969, 32.

One article has offered a biographical reason why the political process approach never matured into a fully articulated theory of judicial decision making that would challenge the predominant attitudinal model. Peltason's unfulfilled legacy, for example, was a function of his early "retreat into [university] administration," which left an intellectual void "in charting a sensible domain and pinpointing real-life puzzles for study and realistic ways of approach" (Krislov and Krislov 1996, 73). (Another judicial process scholar, Kenneth Vines, might have provided intellectual statesmanship, given his interest in the development of judicial behavioralism [Vines and Jacob 1963], but he died prematurely.) Yet the political process–based work of scholars such as Dahl and McCloskey arguably was continued in a different vein by the historical-institutionalist approach to judicial behavior (see the discussion in this chapter; see also Gillman's and Adamany and Meinhold's chapters in this volume).

40. For example, Jacob's (1973) work entailed greater emphasis on ethnographic study of the routine of lower courts and less on the overtly political aspects of judicial decision making—that is, judges dealing explicitly with major policy issues (E-mail from Bert Kritzer, September 13, 2000). That Jacob's work more and more gravitated toward a law-and-society orientation and toward a focus on litigant behavior and alternative dispute processing is the reason his otherwise pathbreaking attention to state- and trial-level courts within the judicial field is not considered as pioneering a theoretical approach to judicial *behavior*.

41. The comparative focus of work coming from this process-based research direction would have implications for the contemporary "comparative turn" in judicial studies illustrated by writings such as Jackson and Tate 1992; Brace and Hall 1995; Caldeira and Gibson 1995; Gibson, Caldeira, and Baird 1998 and by the research agenda of the Committee for the Scientific Study of Courts. Of course, it is well to remember that early attitudinalists such as Schubert pursued comparative courts research, albeit from their own behavioralist theoretical position. Moreover, certain current work on non-U.S. courts and judges proceeds from a law-and-society or constitutional ethnography perspective, as is illustrated by the research agenda of the Collective Research Network on Constitutional Ethnography of the Law and Society Association. Not surprisingly perhaps, the "comparative turn" remains hampered by the old, unresolved dichotomy in judicial research between facts/contextual details about specific cases or case studies and a "covering law" or overarching/unified theory of judicial behavior. Of course, to be fair, this latter goal continues to elude U.S. court studies of judicial decision making.

42. Although systems functionalism, coming out of the work of David Easton and Gabriel Almond, was one of the theoretical foundations for the behavioral science of politics (Smith 1996, 130) and was applied with enthusiasm to the study of judicial behavior by Theodore Becker (1970a, 1970b), this research direction fueled the study of political development and modernization and was not carried on in the study of judicial process. Functionalist considerations informed some of the work of M. Shapiro (1980) and certain comparative court analysis (Jacob et al. 1996) but, generally speaking, were not central to the development of theories of judicial decision making.

43. On the importance of theory creation to the constitution of a field of study, see n.9.

44. See Walker's and Maveety and Maltese's chapters in this volume.

45. See Segal's chapter in this volume. The roots of this more explicitly game-theoretic view of judicial choice are seen in the refinements to Schubert's judicial behavioralism by Rohde 1972 and Rohde and Spaeth 1976,

although, in the end, these authors remained convinced that attitudinal variables were determinative.

46. For a genealogy of the current strategic approach to the study of judicial behavior that incorporates these various intellectual influences, see Epstein and Knight's chapter in this volume.

47. This historical turn encompasses the work of the historical institutionalists proper as well as the construction of historical, "analytic narratives" by the strategic neoinstitutionalists (see Bates et al. 1998). Indeed, Epstein and Knight (2000, 643) see in an "*explicit* acknowledgment of the strategic dimension of the historical process" of doctrinal development a way to bridge the gap between strategic institutionalists and historical-interpretive institutionalists.

Conversely, some have claimed that the "new vogue in [historical] institutionalist analysis" is simply a return to "traditional political science" and the old public law of the old institutionalists (M. Shapiro 1989, 89). See also Clayton's chapter in this volume.

48. As both these works observe, the attitudinal model is designed to explain only voting behavior (Epstein and Knight 1998, xii n. b), and the model's applicability to other forms of judicial behavior, such an opinion production, is unclear (Maltzman, Spriggs, and Wahlbeck 2000, 4).

Another attitudinally informed work exploring the utility of a strategic neoinstitutionalist framework is Segal's (1997) examination of extrainstitutional influences on judicial behavior. Though he argues that the political environment does not strongly constrain the justices, his attention to its institutional variables is telling.

49. There is a certain amount of borrowing, or at least cross-reference, between recent works from political scientists and lawyers on the nature of judicial decision making: Tushnet (1999) draws on historical-institutionalist Graber (1993) as well as on the political regime theory of Dahl (1957); Griffin (1996) debates Segal and Spaeth (1993); and Segal and Spaeth (1999) rely on Tushnet's work in critical legal studies (1988) in discussing the judicial use of precedent. Indeed, Segal and Spaeth's findings regarding precedential versus preferential decision making are eerily supportive of the position articulated by Sunstein (1999) with regard to judicial minimalism. For an examination of citation patterns in research by academic lawyers, see F. Shapiro 2000, esp. table 4.

50. Or, less affably, that "fatuous" stuff. As one scholar of the current state of the discipline remarks regarding the polarization of "scientific" from assorted "historical approaches" in political science, "often, various approaches are advancing sharply opposed views of the basic character and driving forces of human action that imply different predictions for behavior in particular circumstances. If they can somehow be shown to be compatible, substantial careful argumentation, not a genial tolerance, is required" (Smith 1996, 142).

The "pious stuff" reference comes from Segal and Spaeth's retort to a "syncretic" overemphasis on the legal or juridical limiting conditions on judicial discretion: "Pious stuff this, fully compatible with modern manifestations of the mythology of judging" (1993, 360).

51. To put a Kuhnian spin on such engagement, one might argue that "a 'take-off' or 'permanent [scientific] revolution' might be envisaged in the case of a community so flexibly organized that the process of paradigmatic reconstruction, or 'scientific revolution,' was constant and continuous" (Pocock 1971, 13–14). Pocock is envisioning multiple linguistic paradigms that might be uncovered in the study of the history of political thought; whether such "permanent revolution" could characterize the community of judicial behavior scholars and their debate over research approaches remains to be seen.

REFERENCES

Adcock, Robert, and David Collier. 2001. "Measurement Validity: A Shared Standard for Qualitative and Quantitative Research." *American Political Science Review* 95:529–46.

Barthes, Roland. 1989. "Research: The Young." In *The Rustle of Language*. Trans. Richard Howard. Berkeley and Los Angeles: University of California Press.

Bates, Robert H., Avner Greif, Margaret Levi, Jean-Larnet Rosenthal, and Barry Weingast. 1998. *Analytic Narratives*. Princeton: Princeton University Press.

Baum, Lawrence. 1983. "Judicial Politics: Still a Distinctive Field." In *Political Science: The State of the Discipline*, ed. Ada W. Finifter, 189–216. Washington, DC: American Political Science Association.

Baum, Lawrence. 1997. *The Puzzle of Judicial Behavior*. Ann Arbor: University of Michigan Press.

Becker, Theodore L. 1970a. *Comparative Judicial Politics: The Political Functionings of Courts*. Chicago: Rand McNally.

Becker, Theodore L. 1970b. "Judicial Theory." In *Approaches to the Study of Political Science*, ed. Michael Haas and Henry S. Kariel, 144–66. Scranton, PA: Chandler Publishing.

Bentley, Arthur F. 1908. *The Process of Government*. Chicago: University of Chicago Press.

Berns, Walter. 1963. "Law and Behavioral Science." *Law and Contemporary Problems* 28:185–212.

Brace, Paul, and Melinda Gann Hall. 1995. "Studying Courts Comparatively: The View from the American States." *Political Research Quarterly* 48:5–29.

Brandwein, Pamela. 2000. "Disciplinary Structures and 'Winning' Arguments in Law and Courts Scholarship." *Law and Courts Newsletter* 10 (summer): 11–19.

Caldeira, Gregory A., and James L. Gibson. 1995. "The Legitimacy of the

European High Court of Justice in the European Union: Models of Institutional Support." *American Political Science Review* 89:356–76.

Campbell, Angus, Phillip Converse, Warren Miller, and Donald Stokes. 1960. *The American Voter.* New York: Wiley.

Clayton, Cornell W. 1999. "The Supreme Court and Political Jurisprudence: New and Old Institutionalisms." In *Supreme Court Decision Making: New Institutionalist Approaches,* ed. Cornell W. Clayton and Howard Gillman, 15–41, Chicago: University of Chicago Press.

Cook, Beverly Blair. 1994a. "Ghosts and Giants in Judicial Politics." *PS: Political Science and Politics* 27:78–84.

Cook, Beverly Blair. 1994b. "Justice Byron White: Fuzzy Rational Actor." Paper presented at the annual meeting of the American Political Science Association, New York.

Cook, Beverly Blair. n.d. "A Rational Fuzzy Set Model of Supreme Court Decision Making." Unpublished manuscript.

Corwin, Edward S. 1929. "The Democratic Dogma and the Future of Political Science." *American Political Science Review* 23:569–92.

Cushman, Robert. 1925. *Leading Constitutional Decisions.* New York: F. S. Crofts.

Dahl, Robert A. 1957. "Decision Making in a Democracy: The Supreme Court as a National Policy Maker." *Journal of Public Law* 6:279–95.

Dahl, Robert A. 1961. "The Behavioral Approach in Political Science: Epitaph for a Monument to a Successful Protest." *American Political Science Review* 55:763–74.

Dixon, Robert G. 1971. "Who Is Listening? Political Science Research in Public Law." *PS: Political Science and Politics* 4:19–26.

Dolbeare, Kenneth M. 1967. *Trial Courts in Urban Politics.* New York: Wiley.

Downs, Anthony. 1957. *An Economic Theory of Democracy.* New York: Harper.

Eakin, Emily. 2000. "Political Scientists Are in a Revolution Instead of Watching." *New York Times,* November 4.

Easton, David. 1962. "The Current Meaning of 'Behavioralism'." In *Achieving Excellence in Public Service: A Symposium,* ed. James C. Charlesworth, 26–48. Philadelphia: American Academy of Political and Social Science.

Epstein, Lee, and Gary King. 2001. "The Rules of Inference." *University of Chicago Law Review* 30:1–93.

Epstein, Lee, and Jack Knight. 1998. *The Choices Justices Make.* Washington, DC: Congressional Quarterly Press.

Epstein, Lee, and Jack Knight. 2000. "Toward a Strategic Revolution in Judicial Politics: A Look Back, a Look Ahead." *Political Research Quarterly* 53:625–61.

Feeley, Malcolm M. 1979. *The Process Is the Punishment: Handling Cases in a Lower Criminal Court.* New York: Russell Sage Foundation.

Fisher, William W., III, Morton J. Horwitz, and Thomas A. Reed, eds. 1993. *American Legal Realism.* New York: Oxford University Press.

Freeman, Donald M. 1991. "The Making of a Discipline." In *Political Science, Looking to the Future: The Theory and Practice of Political Science*, ed. William Crotty, 1:15–44. Evanston, IL: Northwestern University Press.

Garber, Marjorie. 2001. *Academic Instincts*. Princeton: Princeton University Press.

Gibson, James L. 1983. "From Simplicity to Complexity: The Development of Theory in the Study of Judicial Behavior." *Political Behavior* 5:7–49.

Gibson, James L. 1986. "The Social Science of Judicial Politics." In *Political Science: The Science of Politics*, ed. Herbert F. Weisberg, 141–66. New York: Agathon Press.

Gibson, James L., Gregory A. Caldeira, and Vanessa Baird. 1998. "On the Legitimacy of National High Courts." *American Political Science Review* 92:343–58.

Gillman, Howard, and Cornell W. Clayton. 1999. "Beyond Judicial Attitudes: Institutional Approaches to Supreme Court Decision Making." In *Supreme Court Decision Making: New Institutionalist Approaches*, ed. Cornell W. Clayton and Howard Gillman, 1–12. Chicago: University of Chicago Press.

Graber, Mark. 1993. "The Nonmajoritarian Difficulty: Legislative Deference to the Judiciary." *Studies in American Political Development* 7:35–73.

Graber, Mark. 2000. "The Banality of Diversity." *Law and Courts Newsletter* 10 (summer): 5–10.

Griffin, Stephen M. 1996. *American Constitutionalism: From Theory to Politics*. Princeton: Princeton University Press.

Grossman, Joel B., and Joseph Tanenhaus. 1969. "Toward a Renascence of Public Law." In *Frontiers of Judicial Research*, ed. Joel B. Grossman and Joseph Tanenhaus, 3–25. New York: Wiley.

Haines, Charles Grove. 1922. "General Observations on the Effects of Personal, Political, and Economic Influences in the Decisions of Judges." *Illinois Law Review* 17:96–116.

Haynie, Stacia L., and C. Neal Tate. 2000. "Comparative Judicial Politics in the Year 2000 and the Role of Research Collaboration between Indigenous and American Scholars." Paper presented at the annual meeting of the American Political Science Association, Washington, DC.

Helm, Charles. 1987. "The Problem of Judicial Review and Judicial Activism: Disciplinary Boundaries and the 'Rule of Law.'" Paper presented at the annual meeting of the American Political Science Association, Chicago.

Holmes, Oliver Wendell. "The Path of the Law." *Harvard Law Review* 10 (1897): 457–78.

Jackson, Donald W., and C. Neal Tate. 1992. *Comparative Judicial Review and Public Policy*. Westport, CT: Greenwood Press.

Jacob, Herbert. 1965. *Justice in America: Courts, Lawyers, and the Judicial Process*. Boston: Little, Brown.

Jacob, Herbert. 1973. *Urban Justice.* Englewood Cliffs, NJ: Prentice-Hall.

Jacob, Herbert, Erhard Blankenburg, Herbert M. Kritzer, Doris Marie Provine, and Joseph Sanders. 1996. *Courts, Law, and Politics in Comparative Perspective.* New Haven: Yale University Press.

Kalman, Laura. 1996. *The Strange Career of Legal Liberalism.* New Haven: Yale University Press.

Krislov, Samuel, and Daniel Krislov. 1996. "Separating Powers and Compounding Interests." In *Courts and the Political Process: Jack W. Peltason's Contributions to Political Science,* ed. Austin Ranney, 69–98. Berkeley: Institute of Governmental Studies Press, University of California.

Kuhn, Thomas S. 1962. *The Structure of Scientific Revolutions.* Chicago: University of Chicago Press.

Lasswell, Harold D. 1936. *Politics: Who Gets What, When, How.* New York: Whittlesey House, McGraw-Hill.

Lindblom, Charles E. 1997. "Political Science in the 1940s and 1950s." In *American Academic Culture in Transformation,* ed. Thomas Bender and Carl E. Schorske, 243–70. Princeton: Princeton University Press.

Lindquist, Stephanie A., and David Klein. 2001. "Circuit Court Conflicts in the Supreme Court." Paper presented at the annual meeting of the American Political Science Association, San Francisco, CA.

Llewellyn, Karl. 1930. "A Realistic Jurisprudence—The Next Step." *Columbia Law Review* 30: 431–65.

Lowell, A. Lawrence. *APSA 1909 Presidential Address.* Proceedings of the American Political Science Association.

Maltzman, Forrest, James F. Spriggs II, and Paul J. Wahlbeck. 2000. *Crafting Law on the Supreme Court: The Collegial Game.* New York: Cambridge University Press.

March, James G., and Johan P. Olsen. 1984. "The New Institutionalism: Organizational Factors in Political Life." *American Political Science Review* 78:734–49.

March, James G., and Johan P. Olsen. 1989. *Rediscovering Institutions: The Organizational Basis of Politics.* New York: Free Press.

Mather, Lynn M. 1979. *Plea Bargaining or Trial? The Process of Criminal Court Disposition.* Lexington, MA: Lexington Books.

McClay, Wilfred M. 1994. Introduction to *The Foundations of Political Science,* by John W. Burgess, vii–xxxvii. New Brunswick, NJ: Transaction Publishers.

McCloskey, Robert. 1960. *The American Supreme Court.* Chicago: University of Chicago Press.

McDonald, Terrence J. 1996. Introduction to *The Historic Turn in the Human Sciences,* ed. Terrence J. McDonald, 1–14. Ann Arbor: University of Michigan Press.

Mendelson, Wallace. 1963. "The Neo-Behavioral Approach to the Judicial Process: A Critique." *American Political Science Review* 57:593–603.

Mendelson, Wallace. 1964. "The Untroubled World of Jurimetrics." *Journal of Politics* 26:914–22.

Mendelson, Wallace. 1966. "An Open Letter to Professor Spaeth and His Jurimetric Colleagues." *Journal of Politics* 28:429–32.

Merriam, Charles. 1921. "The Present State of the Study of Politics." *American Political Science Review* 15:173–85.

Morton, Rebecca B. 1999. *Methods and Models*. New York: Cambridge University Press.

Murphy, Walter F. 1964. *The Elements of Judicial Strategy*. Chicago: University of Chicago Press.

Murphy, Walter F., and Joseph Tanenhaus. 1972. *The Study of Public Law*. New York: Random House.

North, Douglass C. 1990. *Institutions, Institutional Change, and Economic Performance*. Cambridge: Cambridge University Press.

Peltason, Jack. 1955. *Federal Courts in the Political Process*. New York: Random House.

Pocock, J. G. A. 1971. "Languages and Their Implications: The Transformation of the Study of Political Thought." In *Politics, Language and Time*, ed. J. G. A. Pocock, 3–41. New York: Atheneum Press.

Powell, Thomas Reed. 1918. "The Logic and Rhetoric of Constitutional Law." *Journal of Philosophy, Psychology and Scientific Methods* 15:645–58.

Pritchett, C. Herman. 1948. *The Roosevelt Court: A Study in Judicial Politics and Values, 1937–1947*. New York: Macmillan.

Pritchett, C. Herman. 1953. *Civil Liberties and the Vinson Court*. Chicago: University of Chicago Press.

Pritchett, C. Herman. 1968. "Public Law and Judicial Behavior." In *Political Science: Advance of the Discipline*, ed. Marian D. Irish, 190–219. New York: Prentice-Hall.

Pritchett, C. Herman. 1969. "The Development of Judicial Research." In *Frontiers of Judicial Research*, ed. Joel B. Grossman and Joseph Tanenhaus, 27–42. New York: Wiley.

Ranney, Austin. 1996. "The Political Science of Jack W. Peltason." In *Courts and the Political Process: Jack W. Peltason's Contributions to Political Science*, ed. Austin Ranney, 1–17. Berkeley: Institute of Governmental Studies Press, University of California.

Ricci, David M. 1984. *The Tragedy of Political Science: Politics, Scholarship, and Democracy*. New Haven: Yale University Press.

Riker, William. 1962. *The Theory of Political Coalitions*. New Haven: Yale University Press.

Rohde, David. 1972. "Policy Goals, Strategic Choice, and Majority Opinion Assignment in the U.S. Supreme Court." *Midwest Journal of Political Science* 16:652–82.

Rohde, David, and Harold J. Spaeth. 1976. *Supreme Court Decision Making*. San Francisco: W. H. Freeman.

Schubert, Glendon. 1958. "The Study of Judicial Decision Making as an Aspect of Political Behavior." *American Political Science Review* 52:1007–25.

Schubert, Glendon. 1959. *Quantitative Analysis of Judicial Behavior*. Glencoe, IL: Free Press.

Schubert, Glendon. 1962. "Policy without Law: An Extension of the Certiorari Game." *Stanford Law Review* 14:284–327.

Schubert, Glendon. 1963a. "Behavioral Research in Public Law." *American Political Science Review* 57:433–45.

Schubert, Glendon. 1963b. "Civilian Control and Stare Decisis in the Warren Court." In *Judicial Decision-Making*, ed. Glendon Schubert, 55–77. New York: Free Press.

Schubert, Glendon. 1963c. "Introduction: From Public Law to Judicial Behavior." In *Judicial Decision-Making*, ed. Glendon Schubert, 1–10. New York: Free Press.

Schubert, Glendon. 1963d. *Judicial Decision-Making*. New York: Free Press.

Schubert, Glendon. 1965. *The Judicial Mind: The Attitudes and Ideologies of Supreme Court Justices, 1946–1963*. Evanston, IL: Northwestern University Press.

Schubert, Glendon. 1985. *Political Culture and Judicial Behavior*. Lanham, MD: University Press of America.

Schubert, Glendon, and David Danelski, eds. 1969. *Comparative Judicial Behavior: Cross-Cultural Studies of Political Decision-Making in the East and West*. New York: Oxford University Press.

Segal, Jeffrey A. 1997. "Separation-of-Powers Games in the Positive Theory of Congress and Courts." *American Political Science Review* 91:28–44.

Segal, Jeffrey A., and Harold J. Spaeth. 1993. *The Supreme Court and the Attitudinal Model*. New York: Cambridge University Press.

Shapiro, Fred J. 2000. "Most Cited Legal Books Published since 1978." *Journal of Legal Studies* 29:397–407.

Shapiro, Martin. 1980. *Courts: A Comparative and Political Analysis*. Chicago: University of Chicago Press.

Shapiro, Martin. 1989. "Political Jurisprudence, Public Law, and Post-Consequentialist Ethics: Comment on Professors Barber and Smith." *Studies in American Political Development* 3:88–102.

Shapiro, Martin. 1993. "Public Law and Judicial Politics." In *Political Science: The State of the Discipline II*, ed. Ada W. Finifter, 365–81. Washington, DC: American Political Science Association.

Shepsle, Kenneth A. 1986. "Institutional Equilibrium and Equilibrium Institutions." In *Political Science: The Science of Politics*, ed. Herbert F. Weisberg, 51–81. New York: Agathon Press.

Shepsle, Kenneth A. 1989. "Studying Institutions: Some Lessons from the Rational Choice Approach." *Journal of Theoretical Politics* 1:131–47.

Skocpol, Theda. 1984. "Sociology's Historical Imagination." In *Vision and*

Method in Historical Sociology, ed. Theda Skocpol, 1–21. Cambridge: Cambridge University Press.

Slotnick, Elliot E. 1991. "Judicial Politics." In *Political Science, Looking to the Future: American Institutions*, ed. William Crotty, 4:67–97. Evanston, IL: Northwestern University Press.

Smith, Rogers. 1988. "Political Jurisprudence, the 'New Institutionalism,' and the Future of Public Law." *American Political Science Review* 82:89–108.

Smith, Rogers. 1996. "Science, Non-Science, and Politics." In *The Historic Turn in the Human Sciences*, ed. Terrence J. McDonald, 119–59. Ann Arbor: University of Michigan Press.

Smith, Rogers. 1997. "Still Blowing in the Wind: The American Quest for a Democratic, Scientific Political Science." In *American Academic Culture in Transformation*, ed. Thomas Bender and Carl E. Schorske, 271–305. Princeton: Princeton University Press.

Somit, Albert, and Joseph Tanenhaus. 1964. *American Political Science: A Profile of a Discipline*. New York: Atherton Press.

Somit, Albert, and Joseph Tanenhaus. 1982. *The Development of American Political Science*. New York: Irvington Publishers.

Spaeth, Harold J. 1965. "Jurimetrics and Professor Mendelson: A Troubled Relationship." *Journal of Politics* 27:875–80.

Spaeth, Harold J. 1995. "The Attitudinal Model." In *Contemplating Courts*, ed. Lee Epstein, 296–314. Washington, DC: Congressional Quarterly Press.

Spaeth, Harold J., and Jeffrey A. Segal. 1999. *Majority Rule or Minority Will: Adherence to Precedent on the U.S. Supreme Court*. Cambridge: Cambridge University Press.

Spriggs, James F., II, and Thomas G. Hansford. 1988. "Explaining the Overturning of U.S. Supreme Court Precedent." Paper presented at the annual meeting of the Midwest Political Science Association, Chicago.

Stearns, Maxwell, ed. 1997. *Public Choice and Public Law*. Cincinnati: Anderson Publishers.

Stumpf, Harry P., Martin Shapiro, David J. Danelski, Austin Sarat, and David M. O'Brien. 1983. "Whither Political Jurisprudence: A Symposium." *Western Political Quarterly* 36:533–69.

Sunstein, Cass R. 1999. *One Case at a Time: Judicial Minimalism on the Supreme Court*. Cambridge: Harvard University Press.

Tate, C. Neal. 1982. "The Development of the Methodology of Judicial Behavior Research: A Historical Review and Critique of the Use and Teaching of Methods." Paper presented at the annual meeting of the American Political Science Association, Denver.

Truman, David B. 1968. "The Impact on Political Science of the Revolution in the Behavioral Sciences." In *Readings in the Philosophy of the Social Sciences*, ed. May Brodbeck, 541–60. New York: Macmillan.

Tushnet, Mark. 1999. *Taking the Constitution away from the Courts*. Princeton: Princeton University Press.

Tushnet, Mark. 1988. *Red, White and Blue: A Critical Analysis of Constitutional Law*. Cambridge: Harvard University Press.

Vines, Kenneth N. 1969. "The Judicial Role in the American States: An Exploration." In *Frontiers of Judicial Research*, ed. Joel B. Grossman and Joseph Tanenhaus, 461–85. New York: Wiley.

Vines, Kenneth N. 1970. "Judicial Behavior Research." In *Approaches to the Study of Political Science*, ed. Michael Haas and Henry S. Kariel, 125–43. Scranton, PA: Chandler Publishing.

Vines, Kenneth N., and Herbert Jacob. 1963. *Studies in Judicial Politics*. New Orleans: Tulane University.

Wahlbeck, Paul J. 1997. "The Life of the Law: Judicial Politics and Legal Change." *Journal of Politics* 59:778–802.

Wechsler, Herbert. 1959. "Toward Neutral Principles of Constitutional Law." *Harvard Law Review* 73:1–35.

Weisberg, Herbert F. 1986. "Introduction: The Science of Politics and Political Change." In *Political Science: The Science of Politics*, ed. Herbert F. Weisberg, 3–10. New York: Agathon Press.

Wood, Gordon S. 2000. "Liberalism and Stubbornness." Review of *On Hallowed Ground*, by John Patrick Diggins. *New Republic*, October 30, 38–46.

PART I

The Attitudinal Pioneers

Already familiar from our developmental history of the judicial field is the "first" approach, which inaugurated the study of judicial behavior per se. This is of course the behaviorally inspired *attitudinal* model, which most self-consciously laid claim to being a paradigm. As a theory of judicial behavior and a program for judicial behavior research, it might be succinctly summarized as "Ideology matters." The most salient independent variable explaining the judicial vote was ideological preferences, which were assumed to be fixed (determined by psychological structures or social background characteristics) and exogenous (external to the institutional context or juridical considerations of judges). When considering these latter factors at all, attitudinalists discounted their importance, finding the institutional environment to free Supreme Court justices in particular to vote according to ideology and juridical considerations to function as post hoc rationalizations for ideologically cast votes. The earliest pioneers of the attitudinal approach focused on the measurement of judicial ideology as well as on the predictive validity of ideological preference for understanding the formation of judicial blocs on majoritarian courts. Subsequent scholars investigated the stimulus side of the judicial vote, quantitatively addressing and statistically assessing the effect of case facts and litigant status as cues to which judges responded according to their preexisting attitudes. While it is tempting now to caricature much of the work of the attitudinal pioneers as simplistic, a careful reading of some of it suggests that they were aware of its limitations or lacunae even as they were articulating the behavioral approach. Many of them were concerned in a way that later generations were not with anthologizing the judicial field and thus with pointing to limitations or lacunae or simply to unfinished business. Most exude the ingenuous confidence of scholars embarking on a new research frontier. But clearly, they collectively amassed much empirical evidence that the political preferences of Supreme Court justices could not be dismissed as irrelevant to judicial decision making, as the legalistic models of judging were wont to do. Because of the findings of the attitudinalists, the myth of the robe was henceforth on the defensive.

Confidence of frontiersmen notwithstanding, this section might easily be subtitled "Genesis, Reflection, and Revision" for two reasons. First, it is obvious in an examination of the work of the attitudinal pioneers than many of them—if not most of them—reflected on the implications of their model of judging, both for future research directions in judicial decision-making studies and for the implicit assumptions being made about the nature of judicial behavior and about human political action generally. Second, though this reflective impulse is present in most of the attitudinal pioneers—to a greater or lesser degree—this group of scholars cleaves into two subsets, those focused on and working at the time of the *genesis* of the attitudinal approach and those most concerned with *reflection on* and the *revision of* the attitudinal model *in attitudinal terms*.

The scholar most directly linked to the genesis of the attitudinal approach and most directly assailed by advocates of the myth of the robe was of course the "first" attitudinalist pioneer, C. Herman Pritchett. His work, discussed in the opening chapter, laid the foundation for the behavioral science of judicial politics. Yet, as Lawrence Baum details, there is a good chance that the judicial field would look the same today without Pritchett, although scholarship on judicial behavior would have evolved more slowly. Interestingly, Pritchett's most important legacy for the modern attitudinal model may be his eloquent argument for a conception of judicial behavior that incorporated both legal and policy considerations, even while he is generally remembered as the chief architect of the latter.

Glendon Schubert, the scholar who labored most intensively to apply quantitative methodology to the study of judicial votes as the expression of political preferences, has come to be both celebrated and castigated for developing the attitudinal approach into a research paradigm. As Jeffrey Segal demonstrates, the sophistication of Schubert's methods and the substantive exhaustiveness of his inquiries account for the longevity of the attitudinal model in the study of judicial behavior. Drawing on Schubert's extensive correspondence with other judicial scholars, Segal sketches a profile of a scholar who was constantly refining and expanding his analytical techniques and documents Schubert's dedication to a fully operationalized attitudinal model. In showing how Schubert was consistently pushing the limits of this model, Segal also illustrates how Schubert laid the groundwork for approaches that would come to challenge it. Segal confronts frankly both the criticism that Schubert's attitudinal analysis of judging received at the time of its publication and the challenges the attitudinal model's empirical tests continue to face yet concludes that Schubert's approach to the "judicial mind" stands in the rather exclusive company of few still-vital forty-year-old models of political behavior.

Described by some as a "disciple" of Schubert, S. Sidney Ulmer probably did the most of any attitudinal pioneer to broaden the topical scope of research conducted under the attitudinal paradigm. As Robert Bradley shows, Ulmer was less of a long-ball hitter—a Babe Ruth—than a workmanlike Cal Ripken who demonstrated durability and continuity in producing insights about the judicial process. As such, Ulmer is sometimes dismissed—particularly by contemporary new institutionalists—as a single-minded and somewhat simple-minded clearer of brush on the normal science path of attitudinalism. Bradley takes up this charge, offering what to some may seem a revisionist account of Ulmer's research agenda and overarching theoretical view of courts.

Harold Spaeth, who would surely embrace the label of Schubert's disciple, is—to continue the sporting metaphor—the great oddsmaker of judicial behavior studies, the attitudinalist who most stressed the importance of the predictive validity of behavioral findings. He did the most to place judicial studies on a par, database-wise, with the most empirically intensive and methodologically rigorous parts of American political science. Yet as Sara Benesh asserts, Spaeth's contributions in the area of quantitative data collection and analysis have stymied the expansion of the field into other approaches to the study of judicial behavior. She argues powerfully that Spaeth's work cemented the attitudinal paradigm in a way that has discouraged experimentation and ultimately progress in judicial research. Spaeth is the last of the attitudinal pioneers, then, whose research focused on the genesis (or perhaps more accurately, on the genital maturation) of the attitudinal approach. Yet what have the disciples of this disciple of Schubert made of this work?

Joseph Tanenhaus is the first of the two attitudinal pioneers we would associate most closely with reflection and revision in judicial attitudinalism. He is characterized by Robert Carp as a leader within the field of public law during its critical transition from traditional research to the modern-day use of sophisticated research methodologies grounded in the theoretical orientation of judicial behavioralism. As such, Tanenhaus is the contemporary of early attitudinalists such as Schubert. As a practitioner of attitudinalist scholarship, Tanenhaus attended to both the stimuli of judicial votes and their reception in terms of public support for the decisions of the Supreme Court. But for Carp, Tanenhaus's specific research questions are less significant than the role he played as synthesizer, bridge builder, and educator of the field and the discipline. For his writings as intellectual historian and digester of public law scholarship, Tanenhaus might be assailed—rather snidely—as being a pioneer without being particularly pioneering. Yet Carp makes a strong case for the pertinence of Tanenhaus's efforts to contemporary discussions of the evolution (or stagnation) of the judicial field and to the ongoing dialogue about the relationship between the law and courts field and the discipline of political science.

Finally, the last and most contemporary pioneer of the attitudinal approach, Beverly Blair Cook, has most consistently played the critical role of "reviser" in the behavioral line of research on judicial decision making. Perhaps this is because she herself was an "outsider" to the academic profession, one of the first women to make her mark on a male-dominated field within a male-dominated profession. Eschewing psychobiography, Lee Epstein and Lynn Mather address the importance of Cook's work, which critically examined the pioneering studies of her predecessors. As Epstein and Mather detail, Cook made more of a contribution to the process of accumulating knowledge about judicial politics than to the construction of a general theory of judicial behavior. But her importance in articulating the limits of judicial attitudinalism suggests that the full implication of her work has yet to be felt in the field.

A final comment and a telling fact: the reader will notice that part 1 of this volume is somewhat longer than subsequent sections. There are, quite simply, more attitudinal pioneers in the field of judicial studies, reflecting the predominance of the attitudinal approach as guide and as foil in judicial research. The informal breakdown of the pioneering scholars, too, reflects this double dominance, with the works of Pritchett, Schubert, Ulmer, and Spaeth stressing genesis and guidance and those of Tanenhaus and Cook reflecting, revising, and reminding us that the attitudinal approach has long "foiled" the study of judicial decision making.

CHAPTER 2

C. Herman Pritchett: Innovator with an Ambiguous Legacy

Lawrence Baum

Among all those who have studied judicial behavior, C. Herman Pritchett occupies a special place because he is widely viewed as the one who "blazed the trail" (Schubert 1963c, dedication) for other scholars in the field. Yet his legacy is complex and ambiguous.

Pritchett is remembered for theoretical and methodological innovations that were relatively simple and straightforward in form, innovations that hastened the development of a political science field devoted to the study of judicial behavior. Yet his work also presented more complex formulations of theory and methods. These formulations remain highly relevant to debates in the field, but they have had little impact. An examination of Pritchett's work and his legacy can illuminate both his contributions and the past and present state of the field.

AN OVERVIEW OF
PRITCHETT'S WORK

Pritchett had a long and productive career in the field of judicial politics, publishing for more than forty years. His pioneering work on judicial behavior was concentrated in the first part of that career, from 1941 to 1954. Like most other students of his behavior in his time and a high proportion today, he focused on the Supreme Court.

During that period Pritchett published a series of articles in the *American Political Science Review* (1941, 1945, 1948, 1953) and the *Journal of Politics* (1942, 1946), each analyzing the Supreme Court's behavior in a recent period.[1] The first of those articles, "Division of Opinion among Justices of the U.S. Supreme Court, 1939–1941," was published in the *APSR* in 1941. That article, only nine pages long and written in an undramatic style, opened up a new mode of inquiry into judicial behavior. The articles that followed were similar in their basic approach, though they added new ideas and analytic methods.

In the same period Pritchett wrote two books that consolidated and elaborated on the material in his articles. The first was *The Roosevelt Court*, published in 1948. It was followed by *Civil Liberties and the Vinson Court*, published in 1954. Along with the 1941 article, they constitute Pritchett's most substantial contributions to the understanding of judicial behavior. Of these three works, *Civil Liberties and the Vinson Court*, which is cited least often, presents the most comprehensive conception of judicial behavior.

During the remainder of his career, Pritchett published a diverse body of scholarship. Some of his work dealt with constitutional law, on which he wrote a series of books (1959, 1984a, 1984b) that presented impressive summaries and analyses of the Supreme Court's positions on constitutional issues. *Courts, Judges, and Politics* (1961, 1974, 1979, 1986), which he coedited with Walter Murphy, was an introduction to materials in the judicial process that was widely read over its four editions. These books, of course, dealt in part with judicial behavior.

Pritchett addressed judicial behavior more directly in two other books, *The Political Offender and the Warren Court* (1958) and *Congress versus the Supreme Court, 1957–1960* (1961). The latter book continues to be widely cited, especially by legal scholars. He also wrote two review essays about scholarship on the courts in the late 1960s (1968, 1969b), essays that received considerable attention.

Thus, a discussion focused on Pritchett's early work captures only a portion of his contributions to the study of law and courts. But that focus suits an effort to probe his role as a pioneer in the study of judicial behavior.

We would expect the scholarship of a half century ago to differ from current work, and this is true of Pritchett's judicial behavior scholarship in some respects. In particular, his research was self-contained to a degree that we seldom see in significant research today. Pritchett made almost no explicit use of social science theory as a basis for his conception of judicial behavior. Nor did he link his statistical analyses of the Supreme Court to methodological work in social science or statistics. Rather, he wrote in a matter-of-fact way about how he understood the Court and how he studied it.

One reason for this style was his intended audience. *Civil Liberties and the Vinson Court* was published by the University of Chicago Press. Yet Pritchett said that the book was "written not so much for the specialist as for the interested layman" (viii). Indeed, even his journal articles would have been accessible to nonscholars who were aware of the Supreme Court and its work.

A second reason for Pritchett's style may have been the limited body of relevant scholarship. At the time that he wrote on judicial behavior, there was far less work in theory and methodology for him to use than there would be in the 1960s and beyond. Nor was there any work on judicial behavior that resembled his research. Having relatively little on which to draw, Pritchett may have found it easiest to set out on his own.

Beyond style, the field's evolution over several decades marks Pritchett's scholarship as the work of an earlier era. Theoretical conceptions of judicial behavior and methods for its analysis have advanced enormously since his time, and in some respects Pritchett's work appears quite outdated. But in other respects that work still seems fresh, in part because of the sophistication that he brought to the study of the Supreme Court.

EXPLAINING JUDICIAL BEHAVIOR

Pritchett did not lay out a comprehensive theory of judicial behavior or, more specifically, of Supreme Court decision making. Moreover, his explanation of the justices' behavior evolved between his 1941 *APSR* article and the *Vinson Court* book in 1954. But his writings present a clear perspective on the forces that shape the Court's decisions.

For Pritchett, the justices' positions could be explained primarily by their personal attitudes. This did not mean that other forces were irrelevant. The desire to minimize conflicts with the other branches affected some decisions (1948a, 73; 1961). The Court's workings as a small group affected the justices' behavior in several ways (see, for example, 1954, 229–30, 248–50), and Pritchett recognized that his analyses of the Court were possible only because the Court's collective attitude toward the legitimacy of dissent had changed (1948a, 49–50; 1954, 22). But the justices' attitudes largely determined their choices.

The issue, then, was the relative importance of different kinds of attitudes. Pritchett considered the possible effects of three types of attitudes. The first was attitudes toward the law, specifically justices' belief that their role was to interpret the law accurately. The second was the justices' policy preferences. The third type might be called structural preferences, views about such matters as federalism and the balance between judicial and legislative authority.

For Pritchett and the scholars who followed him, the central issue was the balance between policy preferences and the other two types of attitudes. To what extent did justices simply enact their preferences into law? To what extent did they also act on their readings of the law and views about structural issues? Pritchett's answers to these questions implicitly reflected the influence of legal realism, while he drew more explicitly on an institutionalist conception of judges' behavior.

By the time that Pritchett began writing about judicial behavior, the legal realist movement had become highly influential among academic lawyers (see Fisher, Horwitz, and Reed 1993). At the same time, political scientists who studied the courts widely adopted a realist orientation (for example, Cushman 1925; Swisher 1930; Corwin 1934; see Murphy and Tanenhaus 1972, 13–17). It would have been very surprising if Pritchett had not adopted that orientation.

But realists differed in their views about the relative importance of legal attitudes and policy preferences. All rejected the orthodox theory that judges acted only on their reading of the law, a theory derided by its critics as "mechanical jurisprudence." One version of legal realism pretty much read the law out of judges' decisions, ascribing those decisions almost solely to policy preferences. A more moderate version of realism saw judges as following their preferences within the framework and constraints of legal reasoning.

Pritchett was a moderate realist (1941, 890; 1948a, 14–16). Whatever the origins of this view, he presented it in terms of an institutionalist understanding of the Supreme Court. The similarities between his perspective and that of scholars identified with the new institutionalism decades later is striking. The best example is a two-page passage in the *Vinson Court* book (1954, 186–88), in which Pritchett compared the Supreme Court to Congress in terms of the role of institutions in political decision making.[2] In justifying his moderate realism, Pritchett cited two countervailing elements of the Supreme Court's institutional position.

One was the Court's task within the legal system, which structured the choices of its members. For any justice, according to Pritchett, the Court's

> rules and traditions supply institutional preferences with which his own preferences must compete. . . . What this means, in more concrete terms, is that when a civil liberties case comes to the Supreme Court, the justices are not asked whether they are more or less in favor of civil liberties. They are asked how the Court, consistently with its role as the highest judicial body in a federal system, should dispose of a proceeding, the basic facts in which have been found and the form of which has been given by lower judicial bodies. (1954, 187–88)

The other relevant element of the Court's institutional position was the kinds of cases that it heard. "With its jurisdiction very largely discretionary, the Supreme Court's grist now comprises, for the most part, cases it chooses to hear precisely because they do present difficult questions" (1948a, 30). As a result, the justices' policy preferences come into play.

> For a supreme court, operating in times of crisis, whose grist is almost entirely the hard cases, the difficult problems, the fields where new legislation needs interpretation, the areas of the law where precedents conflict or are nonexistent—on such a court decisions must inevitably reflect the values of the justices who make them. (1948a, 239)

Pritchett emphasized the impact of this second element in freeing the justices from constraints. In comparing the situations of justices and members of Congress, he did not indicate explicitly which were more constrained from voting their convictions. But he did not view the justices as distinctly less free (1953, 322–23; 1954, 186–88). In any event, the justices' freedom was inevitable: "evidence is lacking, despite protestations to the contrary, that any justice has been able to avoid writing his personal preferences into law" (1948a, 67).

Yet Pritchett did not believe that the justices' task of interpreting the law was irrelevant to their decisions because the Court's cases varied in legal difficulty. In some of the Court's unanimous decisions, its unanimity might reflect the irrelevance of the justices' policy preferences. "The fact that all the members of the Court agree in the disposition of the case may mean that the issue involved is one on which the law is so clear and peremptory that any exercise of judicial discretion, guided by an individual set of values, is completely foreclosed" (1948a, 240). Thus, Pritchett gave a prominent place to legal considerations as well as policy preferences in his explanation of the Court's behavior.

Pritchett did not create an explicit category for the type of attitude that I have called structural preferences. In some of his writing, he combined structural preferences with legal considerations, at one point labeling the combined category "institutional preferences" (1953, 323). He was not entirely clear or consistent about the kinds of attitudes that fit under this rubric. He often emphasized respect for precedent, and at various times he cited attitudes concerning the traditions of the law, judicial deference to legislative authority, federalism, and strict versus loose construction of statutes.

Pritchett's most extensive and most systematic analysis of structural preferences related to judicial activism and restraint. In his work on the Vinson Court (1953; 1954, chaps. 10–11) he identified five justices whom he called libertarians: Hugo Black, William O. Douglas, Frank Murphy, Wiley Rutledge, and Felix Frankfurter. As he pointed out, Frankfurter diverged from the other four justices in the more limited support that he gave to civil liberties claims before the Court. Pritchett explained this divergence by distinguishing between activists whose conception of their roles gave free play to their policy preferences (1954, 192) and restraintists (such as Frankfurter) whose view emphasizes "adherence to appropriate judicial standards and proper manipulation of judicial techniques" (1954, 201). This analysis, coupled with his characterization of Oliver Wendell Holmes (1948a, 279), underlines Pritchett's belief that attitudes toward the judicial role could significantly influence the justices' positions.

A reader of Pritchett's work could draw two rather different conclusions about attitudes within and decisions by the Supreme Court. One was that the justices came to their task with various kinds of attitudes and that their choices reflected the mix of those attitudes. Policy preferences were the most powerful, but the others exerted significant influence as well. This, of course, was Pritchett's position. Yet Pritchett's emphasis on the link between policy preferences and votes and the evidence he mustered on systematic voting differences among the justices might lead a reader to a different conclusion: those preferences are the only significant influence on the justices' behavior.

In the next generation of judicial scholars who did quantitative research on Supreme Court behavior, the second view was dominant. Glendon Schubert saw precedent as playing a role at the margins (Schubert 1963a), but his central theme was the strong and direct relationship between policy preferences and votes (Schubert 1963b, 1965, 1974). This was also the consistent position of Harold Spaeth and his collaborators (for example, Rohde and Spaeth 1976; Spaeth 1979).

Why did Pritchett's successors in the quantitative analysis of Supreme Court behavior diverge from his theoretical position? An important part of the answer, I think, is simply a different reading of Supreme Court behavior. In turn, this difference may have reflected the era in which Pritchett's successors did their work. By the late 1950s and 1960s, the continued sharp divisions among the justices along ideological lines underlined the impact of their policy preferences and made it more difficult to believe that they were motivated by the desire to make good law. And judicial restraint had acquired something of a bad odor, largely because of a growing (and justified) skepticism about Justice Frankfurter's motives.

Another part of the answer is methodological. The dimensional approach that Pritchett developed and that his successors refined emphasizes the influence of policy preferences in producing differences among the justices while providing little evidence on the influence of structural preferences or legal considerations. Pritchett did offer one way to probe the impact of these other considerations, quantitative analysis of the relationship between policy preferences and conditions that affected the relevance of structural preferences (1953, 332–33; 1954, 225). Spaeth and his colleagues used the same general approach in a series of studies that, like Pritchett's analysis, focused primarily on Justice Frankfurter.[3] But Pritchett provided no means to analyze the impact of legal considerations on the justices' choices, admittedly a difficult task that has continued to bedevil scholars in the field.

Finally, Pritchett had difficulty in articulating the theoretical relationship between policy preferences and other types of attitudes in Supreme Court decisions. That difficulty underlies the inconsistencies in his position that were discussed earlier. As a result, he provided other scholars with relatively little help in efforts to take into account the full range of judicial attitudes that he described.

There were always scholars who disagreed with the near-exclusive focus on policy preferences that was represented by the work of Schubert and Spaeth. But in the 1950s and 1960s the most visible of these scholars also rejected the premises of quantitative scholarship on the Court (for example, Mendelson 1963, 1964). That rejection helped to harden lines of division among scholars, strengthening the emphasis on justices' policy preferences among scholars who were committed to quantitative analysis.

Things have become more complicated in recent years. Spaeth and Jeffrey Segal maintain an emphasis on policy preferences as bases for choice, arguing for that position with considerable force and eloquence (Segal and Spaeth 1993; Spaeth 1995; Spaeth and Segal 1999). They have been joined by a growing number of scholars who give greater emphasis to strategic considerations in decision making but who share the premise that the justices act almost solely on their policy preferences (for example, Maltzman, Spriggs, and Wahlbeck 2000).

Yet the more complex position that Pritchett took has gained new force. For one thing, a new generation of scholars who do primarily qualitative research resembles its predecessors in questioning the dominance of policy preferences, but scholars in this new generation do so with far greater sophistication than was found in the antibehavioral scholarship of the 1950s and 1960s (for example, Gillman 1993; Kahn 1994; Bussiere 1999).

Further, many of the scholars who take a rational choice perspective find room for legal and role considerations in justices' calculations. In one formulation, the justices do not care about those considerations for their own sake but give weight to them because of the expectations of their audiences (Epstein and Knight 1998). In another, offered by some scholars from other fields and disciplines, accurate interpretation of the law is important to the justices in itself (for example, Shapiro and Levy 1995; Spiller and Tiller 1996).

These scholars differ considerably—sometimes fundamentally—in their viewpoints. But most of them take theoretical perspectives that are linked to the new institutionalism (see Whittington 2000). There would be widespread agreement on the proposition that the decisional calculus of the justices is structured by the Court's characteristics as an institution. For Segal and Spaeth (1993, 69–72), those characteristics liberate the justices from the constraints of the law. But for many other students of the Court, as for Pritchett, its position in the legal system gives weight to considerations other than policy preferences.

These developments have reenergized debates over the attitudes that shape Supreme Court justices' positions. The most prominent result is the new body of research on the impact of precedent on justices' positions (Songer and Lindquist 1996; Brenner and Stier 1996; Spaeth and Segal 1999). One stumbling block for those who see legal or structural attitudes as significant influences on the justices is the lack of substantial progress in developing a framework with which to integrate these attitudes with policy preferences. In this respect, scholars still have not overcome the limitations of Pritchett's theoretical conception.[4]

Pritchett's explanation of Supreme Court behavior had serious shortcomings. That explanation was not grounded in broader social science theory, in part because of the paucity of relevant theory—at least explicitly, the work in that area was largely atheoretical. The generation of scholars that followed Pritchett supplied the theoretical frameworks that had been lacking in his work, most notably Schubert's application of Clyde Coombs's (1964) theory of data and Spaeth's use of attitude theory. In doing so, these scholars linked the analysis of judicial behavior to broader ideas and developments in social science in ways that Pritchett had not. Ironically, these links weakened over time, and much of the scholarship on judicial behavior was largely atheoretical until the revival of explicit theoretical concerns in the 1990s.[5]

Moreover, Pritchett did not give a clear picture of the various considerations that might influence Supreme Court decisions. His writing was ambiguous about the relative importance of and the interactions among the personal attitudes that justices brought to their work. In this respect, Pritchett's effort to take Frankfurter into account may have led Pritchett unnecessarily to complicate his conception of judicial behavior. Nor did Pritchett integrate personal attitudes with other forces, such as the Court's group life. The scholars who followed him also found it difficult to develop integrated theories of judicial behavior, but some made considerable progress toward this goal (for example, Gibson 1983).

Pritchett did advance theory significantly in two respects, though only one caught on. That one, of course, was his presentation of a way to think systematically about the influence of judges' policy preferences on their behavior. That contribution was recognized immediately (Barnett 1949) and helped to spur a new body of scholarship on judicial behavior.

The other was Pritchett's institutionalism. This element of his theoretical work went largely unnoticed, and the recent revival of institutionalism in the study of judicial behavior does not seem to reflect any influence of Pritchett's work (see Clayton and Gillman 1999). Still, his institutional perspective on the Court led to his insights about the interplay of different strands of judicial attitudes, especially legal and policy considerations. His position would not receive universal approval from students of judicial behavior, and he may have overstated the constraints on the justices. Still, he expressed a conception that recent scholars have elaborated and that some have put in more formal terms. In doing so, he was ahead of his time.

STUDYING JUDICIAL BEHAVIOR

By no means was Pritchett the first scholar to analyze judicial behavior with quantitative methods. Among the predecessors of his work in political science were Rodney Mott's (1936) study of influence among state supreme courts and Cortez Ewing's (1938) study of justices' backgrounds (see also Hall 1926). Some scholars in other disciplines also employed quantitative methods to study courts (for example, Frankfurter and Landis 1927; Blackburn 1935). But Pritchett's use of systematic quantitative techniques to analyze the voting behavior of Supreme Court justices was a major step.

The heart of Pritchett's quantitative approach was simple and straightforward. He began by coding the justices' positions into dichotomous categories based on the case outcomes they supported. His primary use of these codings was as a means to measure rates of agreements between pairs of justices. In turn, he used these rates to identify blocs of justices who agreed most often. He also calculated the frequencies with which justices took one or the other side in a set of cases, such as cases in which civil liberties claims were made against state governments. In his 1941 article and in *The Roosevelt Court* (1948a, 257) he scaled the justices from left to right on the basis of the frequency and ideological direction of their dissents.

From the inception of his research, Pritchett recognized two related limitations to the quantitative analyses that he presented. The first was that votes on case outcomes did not provide information on the justices' doctrinal stances. Those stances were the more important component of justices' positions in cases, and they contained more direct evidence of the values that justices were expressing. The second was inherent to the dimensional techniques that he employed: in the absence of external evidence of the justices' preferences, voting alignments in themselves did not establish that the justices were motivated by those preferences.

Both these limitations gave Pritchett reason to pay close attention to the justices' opinions. Indeed, only small portions of the *Roosevelt Court* and *Vinson Court* books were taken up by quantitative analyses. The bulk of both books consisted of close qualitative analysis of the Court's decisions and the justices' opinions in the major areas of the Court's activity. This allocation of space reflected Pritchett's methodological views. While he disagreed with critics who opposed quantitative analysis of judicial decisions, he strongly agreed with the position that "box scores" alone were insufficient to explain those decisions (1954, 189–91).

Qualitative analysis allowed Pritchett to address the first limitation in a straightforward way. Using standard techniques of case reading, he described the Court's collective stance and the justices' individual positions in the various policy areas that the Court addressed. He thereby gained a richer sense of the values expressed by the justices.

The second limitation was not so easily overcome, but Pritchett believed that analysis of opinions could illuminate the justices' preferences. While he did not assume that the content of opinions fully reflected justices' motives and attitudes, he thought that content provided relevant information (1948a, 45, 262). This function surfaced in Pritchett's analysis of Frankfurter. Pritchett did not accept Frankfurter's characterization of his motives at face value (1954, 246) but used that characterization as a starting point in an effort to understand the values that shaped his behavior.

Examining the substance of decisions also allowed Pritchett to determine whether these decisions involved "issues of public policy on which liberals and conservatives might well be expected to differ" (1941, 895). When he found that this was the case, he concluded that "divisions of opinion . . . appear to be for the most part explicable in terms of the opinions of the respective judges on public policy" (898).

His use of the term *appear* is significant: Pritchett knew that close reading of opinions could not circumvent the inherent limitations of dimensional analysis. Thus, he pointed to the need for external evidence of justices' policy preferences. In his *Vinson Court* book (1954, 16), he cited careful biography as a way of linking justices' values with their behavior on the Court (see also 1948a, 239–40). In his 1953 *APSR* article, he suggested that one could probe the bases for Justice Frankfurter's behavior through review of "Frankfurter's record on civil liberties before he became a member of the Supreme Court" (1953, 332 n.42). But Pritchett did not take these steps himself.

Pritchett's quantitative methods were some first, tentative steps toward explanation of Supreme Court behavior through quantitative analysis. Scholars who followed Pritchett in employing dimensional analysis of the justices' votes adopted more sophisticated and more nuanced techniques to map voting patterns and probe the values underlying them (for example, Thurstone and Degan 1951; Schubert 1965; Rohde and Spaeth 1976). Other scholars used causal analysis to explore the antecedents of the justices' values (for example, Ulmer 1973; Tate 1981). David Danelski (1966) and later Segal and Cover (1989) developed the kinds of external measures of preferences whose importance Pritchett had recognized, and the Segal-Cover measure is widely used in Supreme Court research (see Epstein and Mershon 1996).

In a way, however, the most striking trait of the methods used by Pritchett's successors is what they deleted rather than what they added. Among those scholars who analyzed judicial behavior with quantitative techniques, the qualitative analyses of opinions that Pritchett had employed fell into something approaching disuse.

These scholars did not ignore opinions. For one thing, coding cases required reading opinions. Moreover, interpretations of quantitative findings often reflected the same kind of contextual understanding of issues and doctrines that was evident in Pritchett's writing.[6] But the detailed analysis of doctrines that was a hallmark of Pritchett's work generally was absent from the research of Pritchett's successors. As was true of his theory of judicial behavior, the scholars who followed him adopted one part of his methodology and set aside the other.[7]

Here too, there were probably multiple reasons for the divergence between Pritchett and his successors. One reason surely was the growing emphasis on quantitative analysis in political science, especially in the study of American politics. Both in the research process itself and in journal reports of research, quantitative analysis increasingly crowded out qualitative information.

Another likely reason was the influence of judicial realism, especially in its more radical form. For many scholars, case outcomes were what mattered in decisions. In their view, opinions were no more than rationalizations of individual votes and collective outcomes for public consumption. As such, opinions did not illuminate the actual reasons for the justices' positions.[8]

Even if these conditions had not existed, scholars who sought to advance the understanding of judicial behavior might have been drawn to focus on Pritchett's quantitative methods. These methods were clear and relatively easy to follow, and they led to crisp results. In contrast, it was not so clear how to draw insights about judicial behavior from the reading of opinions and how to integrate those insights with findings from analysis of voting patterns, and Pritchett himself did not provide a guide to that process. Moreover, interpretations of opinions undoubtedly seemed highly subjective in comparison with votes.

This does not mean, of course, that qualitative analyses of opinions disappeared from the field. In the 1950s and beyond, some political scientists who studied the Supreme Court continued to undertake such studies. But the field developed something of a bifurcation. On one side of the divide were scholars who devoted themselves entirely or primarily to quantitative analysis of the justices' voting behavior. On the other side were scholars who emphasized qualitative analysis of the justices' opinions. The work of the first group dominated publications on the Court in political science journals, while the second group published primarily in other forums.

As noted earlier, differences in methodology coincided with differences in theoretical position to a considerable degree. Scholars who undertook quantitative analysis typically adopted the position that policy preferences explain nearly everything about the justices' behavior or that justices take other considerations into account only as a means to advance their preferred policies. Scholars who employed qualitative analysis typically argued that considerations related to the law play a substantial role in the decision process.

Of course, there was no logical necessity for this linkage. For example, those legal scholars who espouse radical versions of legal realism generally support their positions with qualitative analysis of decisions (for example, Dalton 1985). But in political science, the linkage became fairly strong. It may be that differences in tastes caused scholars to choose between two divergent paths: what led some to a particular theoretical position also led them to a particular methodological approach.

This does not mean that political scientists who emphasized the linkage between justices' policy preferences and their decisional behavior eschewed qualitative data altogether. Especially in book-length works, they made use of qualitative information about decision processes for illustrative purposes. In *Elements of Judicial Strategy* (1964), Walter Murphy went much further, using information from justices' papers and other sources to probe the kinds of behavior in which a strategic, policy-oriented justice might engage.

That employment of qualitative data continues today. Indeed, the growth of rational choice analysis in the study of judicial behavior has spurred scholars to make greater use of information about decision processes within courts, information that these authors present in both quantitative and qualitative forms (Epstein and Knight 1998; Maltzman, Spriggs, and Wahlbeck 2000).[9] To this extent, use of the two types of data has been integrated.

Yet among political scientists who see the justices as overwhelmingly policy oriented, qualitative analysis of opinions has not been revised as an integral part of research on the Court. Such use of opinions is largely restricted to scholars who argue that attitudes other than policy preferences play central roles in decisions (Gillman 1993; Kahn 1994). To a considerable degree, the reasons that Pritchett's successors did not follow his methodological example remain operative today.

To the extent that the study of judicial behavior remains bifurcated, that bifurcation has long carried with it a degree of intolerance across methodological divides, especially directed by quantitative scholars toward those who do qualitative research. Pritchett noted this kind of intolerance when he offered his famous advice to "let a hundred flowers bloom" (1968, 509). The implication was that scholars who do a particular form of research should at least learn from the findings of scholars who have a different orientation.

Some scholars who carry out quantitative research may be skeptical about what can be learned from qualitative studies. Pritchett pointed to at least part of a response. Not only are the Supreme Court's doctrinal positions more consequential than case outcomes, but the justices' stances on doctrines and the rationales they offer for those stances enrich our understanding of the values that motivate the justices. Though students of judicial behavior can do more than they have done to probe the content of opinions through quantitative analyses,[10] there are limits to such probing; the kinds of close qualitative readings that Pritchett undertook can go further. Thus, to take one example, it probably will be a combination of quantitative and qualitative work that fully illuminates the confusing patterns of Supreme Court votes and doctrines that are currently found in fields such as economic policy (Ducat and Dudley 1987; Hagle and Spaeth 1992).

Moreover, as Herbert Kritzer (1994, 1996) has reminded us, the crispness of quantitative analysis that so many of us find attractive masks a considerable degree of subjectivity. Indeed, interpretation is as inescapable in quantitative analysis as it is in qualitative work. In some respects, it is a different kind of interpretation, and those differences make it all the more attractive to use quantitative and qualitative research on judicial behavior as complements to each other.

Like the theoretical side of his work, Pritchett's methods for the study of judicial behavior had substantial limitations. His quantitative techniques were simplistic by the standards of later work, which offered more sophisticated means to probe the structure of judicial attitudes. Pritchett recognized the limitations of dimensional analysis as a means to explain judicial behavior and pointed to paths for overcoming those limits, but he did not follow those paths himself.

Yet Pritchett's methodological contributions were substantial. His use of systematic quantitative analysis to map attitudes was a major step forward. Moreover, the dimensional approach on which he relied long remained central to the study of judicial behavior. Indeed, the dimensional conception of attitudes that was embedded in his methodology continues to structure scholars' thinking. This conception and the methods associated with it likely would have taken hold even without Pritchett's lead, but he pioneered in their use.

Whatever may be the value of combining quantitative analysis of votes with qualitative analysis of opinions, Pritchett did not demonstrate how to integrate the two systematically. As a result, his approach to the study of Supreme Court behavior did not provide as useful an example for his successors as it could have. In any event, the problem of systematic integration remains unsolved.

PRITCHETT'S LEGACY

Pritchett's scholarly career began with a study of the Tennessee Valley Authority (1943). If he had continued to study administrative behavior rather than turning to judicial behavior, how different would the judicial field be today? As with most counterfactuals, here is no clear answer to that question. But there is a good chance that the field would be largely the same without Pritchett's lead. Almost surely, however, scholarship on judicial behavior would have evolved more slowly. After all, even with Pritchett's example, other scholars did not take substantial research of the same type for many years after his work was first published. But the developments in the Supreme Court and the academic world that helped to produce Pritchett's innovations would have exerted a similar influence on other people in the field.

On both the theoretical and methodological sides, Pritchett took complex approaches that his successors largely abandoned. Among the scholars who analyzed Supreme Court through quantitative methods, his view that justices' positions are a product of multiple sets of attitudes was supplanted by the conception that only policy preferences have a substantial impact on votes. The scholars today who take positions similar to Pritchett's, many of them adopting a similar institutionalist perspective, have done so without apparent influence from his example.

Similarly, Pritchett's combining of quantitative and qualitative analysis of decisions did not provide a persuasive model for other students of judicial behavior. Probably the main reason was that it ran against powerful trends in the discipline, but the absence of a clear guide to this approach also worked against its adoption. The gulf between quantitative and qualitative research that developed after Pritchett's time remains wide today.

In a way, then, it is surprising that Pritchett remains so prominent today and that his prestige has been so high. Undoubtedly, his reputation has been enhanced by the generosity of spirit that characterized both his scholarly work (1968, 1969a, 1969b, 1971) and his personal interactions (see Brigham 1995; Murphy 1995). But the primary reason for his continuing prominence is that he was the first pioneer in what became the leading body of research on judicial behavior. In a sense, he is best understood as a transitional figure who helped usher in a new approach to the study and understanding of the courts. Given the continuing centrality of that approach, it is understandable that Pritchett's work and Pritchett himself remain visible to students of judicial behavior.

NOTES

1. All parenthetical references to years of publication without authors noted are to Pritchett's work.

2. In this passage, Pritchett even cited the strategic considerations involved in congressional voting on amendments that would prohibit discrimination in federally funded programs. That illustration later became a staple of work on congressional strategy (e.g., Enelow 1981).

3. The Spaeth studies (Spaeth 1964; Spaeth and Teger 1982; Spaeth and Altfeld 1986) were more extensive than Pritchett's analysis. Unlike Pritchett, Spaeth's works concluded that Frankfurter's limited support for civil liberties reflected his policy preferences rather than judicial restraint. Their evidence is very convincing (see also Davis 1992). But these analyses were of the Warren Court, and it may be that Frankfurter went through a transitional period—the period analyzed by Pritchett—in which there was a conflict between his policy preferences and his conception of the judicial role.

4. Theoretical formulations in social psychology provide promising bases for the frameworks that students of judicial behavior have not yet developed (e.g., Kunda 1990).

5. This development owes much to the growing use of rational choice theory, both in itself and as a spur to competing perspectives.

6. Indeed, much of the work done by quantitatively oriented scholars would be difficult to carry out without this contextual understanding. One example is the impressive success that Harold Spaeth achieved in predicting the votes of Supreme Court justices (see Spaeth 1979, chap. 6).

7. More precisely, these scholars eschewed qualitative analysis in their research on judicial behavior. Some presented qualitative analyses of doctrine in separate work.

8. This position also provided a theoretical rationale for the choice to code outcomes alone rather than doctrine in quantitative analyses of the justices' behavior.

9. In the work done by scholars outside the judicial behavior field in political science, some formal and quasi-formal analyses examine decisions only in qualitative terms (e.g., Gely and Spiller 1990; Eskridge 1991).

10. One example of work that does take this path is the analyses of doctrinal positions undertaken by Paul Wahlbeck (1997, 1998).

REFERENCES

Barnett, Vincent M., Jr. 1949. "Review: *The Roosevelt Court: A Study in Judicial Politics and Values, 1937–1947.*" *Political Science Quarterly* 64:306–9.

Blackburn, William J. 1935. *The Administration of Criminal Justice in Franklin County, Ohio.* Baltimore: Johns Hopkins University Press.

Brenner, Saul, and Marc Stier. 1996. "Retesting Segal and Spaeth's *Stare Decisis* Model." *American Journal of Political Science* 40:1036–48.

Brigham, John, ed. 1995. "In Memoriam: C. Herman Pritchett." *Law and Courts* 5(2): 16–18.

Bussiere, Elizabeth. 1999. "The Supreme Court and the Development of the Welfare State: Judicial Liberalism and the Problem of Welfare Rights." In *Supreme Court Decision-Making*, ed. Clayton and Gillman, 155–74.

Clayton, Cornell W., and Howard Gillman, eds. 1999. *Supreme Court Decision-Making: New Institutionalist Approaches*. Chicago: University of Chicago Press.

Coombs, Clyde H. 1964. *A Theory of Data*. New York: John Wiley and Sons.

Corwin, Edward S. 1934. *John Marshall and the Constitution: A Chronicle of the Supreme Court*. New Haven: Yale University Press.

Cushman, Robert E. 1925. *Leading Constitutional Decisions*. New York: F. S. Crofts.

Dalton, Clare. 1985. "An Essay in the Deconstruction of Contract Doctrine." *Yale Law Journal* 94:997–1114.

Danelski, David J. 1966. "Values as Variables in Judicial Decision-Making: Notes Toward a Theory." *Vanderbilt Law Review* 19:721–40.

Danelski, David J. 1968. "The Influence of the Chief Justice in the Decisional Process of the Supreme Court." In *The Federal Judicial System: Readings in Process and Behavior*, comp. Sheldon Goldman and Thomas P. Jahnige, 147–60. New York: Holt, Rinehart, and Winston.

Davis, Sue. 1992. "Rehnquist and State Courts: Federalism Revisited." *Western Political Quarterly* 45:773–82.

Ducat, Craig R., and Robert L. Dudley. 1987. "Dimensions Underlying Economic Policy Making in the Early and Later Burger Courts." *Journal of Politics* 49:521–39.

Enelow, James M. 1981. "Saving Amendments, Killer Amendments, and an Expected Utility Theory of Sophisticated Voting." *Journal of Politics* 43:1062–89.

Epstein, Lee, and Jack Knight. 1998. *The Choices Justices Make*. Washington, D.C.: Congressional Quarterly Press.

Epstein, Lee, and Carol Mershon. 1996. "Measuring Political Preferences." *American Journal of Political Science* 40:261–94.

Eskridge, William N., Jr. 1991. "Reneging on History? Playing the Court/Congress/President Civil Rights Game." *California Law Review* 79:613–84.

Ewing, Cortez A. M. 1938. *The Judges of the Supreme Court, 1789–1937: A Study of Their Qualifications*. Minneapolis: University of Minnesota Press.

Fisher, William W., III, Morton J. Horwitz, and Thomas A. Reed, eds., 1993. *American Legal Realism*. New York: Oxford University Press.

Frankfurter, Felix, and James M. Landis. 1927. *The Business of the Supreme Court: A Study in the Federal Judicial System*. New York: Macmillan.

Gely, Rafael, and Pablo T. Spiller. 1990. "A Rational Choice Theory of Supreme Court Statutory Decisions with Applications to the *State Farm* and *Grove City* Cases." *Journal of Law, Economics, and Organization* 6:263–300.

Gibson, James L. 1983. "From Simplicity to Complexity: The Development of Theory in the Study of Judicial Behavior." *Political Behavior* 5:7–49.

Gillman, Howard. 1993. *The Constitution Besieged: The Rise and Demise of Lochner Era Police Powers Jurisprudence*. Durham, N.C.: Duke University Press.

Hagle, Timothy M., and Harold J. Spaeth. 1992. "The Emergence of a New Ideology: The Business Decisions of the Burger Court." *Journal of Politics* 54:120–34.

Haines, Charles Grove. 1922. "General Observations on the Effects of Personal, Political, and Economic Influences in the Decisions of Judges." *Illinois Law Review* 17:96–116.

Hall, Arnold Bennett. 1926. "Round Table on Public Law: Determination of Methods for Ascertaining the Factors That Influence Judicial Decisions in Cases Involving Due Process of Law." *American Political Science Review* 20:127–34.

Hirsch, H. N. 1981. *The Enigma of Felix Frankfurter*. New York: Basic Books.

Kahn, Ronald. 1994. *The Supreme Court and Constitutional Theory, 1953–1993*. Lawrence: University Press of Kansas.

Kritzer, Herbert M. 1994. "Interpretation and Validity Assessment in Qualitative Research: The Case of H. W. Perry's *Deciding to Decide*." *Law and Social Inquiry* 19:687–724.

Kritzer, Herbert M. 1996. "The Data Puzzle: The Nature of Interpretation in Quantitative Research." *American Journal of Political Science* 40:1–32.

Kunda, Ziva. 1990. "The Case for Motivated Reasoning." *Psychological Bulletin* 108:480–98.

Maltzman, Forrest, James F. Spriggs II, and Paul J. Wahlbeck. 2000. *Crafting Law on the Supreme Court: The Collegial Game*. New York: Cambridge University Press.

Mendelson, Wallace. 1963. "The Neo-Behavioral Approach to the Judicial Process: A Critique." *American Political Science Review* 57:593–603.

Mendelson, Wallace. 1964. "The Untroubled World of Jurimetrics." *Journal of Politics* 26:914–22.

Mott, Rodney L. 1936. "Judicial Influence." *American Political Science Review* 30:295–315.

Murphy, Walter F. 1964. *The Elements of Judicial Strategy*. Chicago: University of Chicago Press.

Murphy, Walter F. 1995. "C. Herman Pritchett." *PS: Political Science and Politics* 28:748–50.

Murphy, Walter F., and C. Herman Pritchett, eds. 1961, 1974, 1979, 1986. *Courts, Judges, and Politics: An Introduction to the Judicial Process*. 1st–4th eds. New York: Random House.

Murphy, Walter F., and Joseph Tanenhaus. 1972. *The Study of Public Law*. New York: Random House.

Pritchett, C. Herman. 1941. "Division of Opinion among Justices of the U.S. Supreme Court, 1939–1941." *American Political Science Review* 35:890–98.

Pritchett, C. Herman. 1942. "The Voting Behavior of the Supreme Court, 1941–42." *Journal of Politics* 4:491–506.

Pritchett, C. Herman. 1943. *The Tennessee Valley Authority: A Study in Public Administration.* Chapel Hill: University of North Carolina Press.

Pritchett, C. Herman. 1945. "Dissent on the Supreme Court, 1943–44." *American Political Science Review* 39:42–54.

Pritchett, C. Herman. 1946. "Politics and Values Systems: The Supreme Court, 1945–1946." *Journal of Politics* 8:499–519.

Pritchett, C. Herman. 1948a. *The Roosevelt Court: A Study in Judicial Politics and Values.* New York: Macmillan.

Pritchett, C. Herman. 1948b. "The Roosevelt Court: Values and Votes." *American Political Science Review* 42:53–67.

Pritchett, C. Herman. 1953. "Libertarian Motivations on the Vinson Court." *American Political Science Review* 47:321–36.

Pritchett, C. Herman. 1954. *Civil Liberties and the Vinson Court.* Chicago: University of Chicago Press.

Pritchett, C. Herman. 1958. *The Political Offender and the Warren Court.* Boston: Boston University Press.

Pritchett, C. Herman. 1959. *The American Constitution.* New York: McGraw-Hill.

Pritchett, C. Herman. 1961. *Congress versus the Supreme Court, 1957–1960.* Minneapolis: University of Minnesota Press.

Pritchett, C. Herman. 1968. "Public Law and Judicial Behavior." *Journal of Politics* 30:480–509.

Pritchett, C. Herman. 1969a. "Book Review: *The Supreme Court and Political Freedom; The Supreme Court and Administrative Agencies; The Supreme Court and American Capitalism; Voting Patterns of the United States Supreme Court: Cases in Federalism.*" *Midwest Journal of Political Science* 13:160–63.

Pritchett, C. Herman. 1969b. "The Development of Judicial Research." In *Frontiers of Judicial Research,* ed. Joel B. Grossman and Joseph Tanenhaus. New York: John Wiley and Sons.

Pritchett, C. Herman. 1971. "Book Review: *The Federal Courts as a Political System.*" *American Political Science Review* 65:1183–85.

Pritchett, C. Herman. 1984a. *Constitutional Civil Liberties.* Englewood Cliffs, N.J.: Prentice-Hall.

Pritchett, C. Herman. 1984b. *Constitutional Law of the Federal System.* Englewood Cliffs, N.J.: Prentice-Hall.

Rohde, David W., and Harold J. Spaeth. 1976. *Supreme Court Decision Making.* San Francisco: W. H. Freeman.

Schubert, Glendon. 1963a. "Civilian Control and Stare Decisis in the Warren Court." In *Judicial Decision-Making,* ed. Schubert, 55–77.

Schubert, Glendon. 1963b. "Judicial Attitudes and Voting Behavior: The 1961 Term of the United States Supreme Court." *Law and Contemporary Problems* 28:100–142.

Schubert, Glendon, ed. 1963c. *Judicial Decision-Making.* Glencoe, Ill.: Free Press.

Schubert, Glendon. 1965. *The Judicial Mind: The Attitudes and Ideologies of Supreme Court Justices, 1946–1963.* Evanston, Ill.: Northwestern University Press.

Schubert, Glendon. 1974. *The Judicial Mind Revisited: Psychometric Analysis of Supreme Court Ideology.* New York: Oxford University Press.

Segal, Jeffrey A., and Albert Cover. 1989. "Ideological Values and the Votes of Supreme Court Justices." *American Political Science Review* 83:557–65.

Segal, Jeffrey A., and Harold J. Spaeth. 1993. *The Supreme Court and the Attitudinal Model.* New York: Cambridge University Press.

Shapiro, Sidney A., and Richard E. Levy. 1995. "Judicial Incentives and Indeterminacy in Substantive Review of Administrative Decisions." *Duke Law Journal* 44:1051–80.

Silverstein, Mark. 1984. *Constitutional Faiths: Felix Frankfurter, Hugo Black, and the Process of Judicial Decision Making.* Ithaca: Cornell University Press.

Songer, Donald R., and Stefanie A. Lindquist. 1996. "Not the Whole Story: The Impact of Justices' Values on Supreme Court Decision Making." *American Journal of Political Science* 40:1049–63.

Spaeth, Harold J. 1964. "The Judicial Restraint of Mr. Justice Frankfurter: Myth or Reality?" *Midwest Journal of Political Science* 8:22–38.

Spaeth, Harold J. 1979. *Supreme Court Policy Making: Explanation and Prediction.* San Francisco: W. H. Freeman.

Spaeth, Harold J. 1995. "The Attitudinal Model." In *Contemplating Courts,* ed. Lee Epstein, 296–314. Washington, D.C.: Congressional Quarterly Press.

Spaeth, Harold J., and Michael F. Altfeld. 1986. "Felix Frankfurter, Judicial Activism, and Voting Conflict on the Warren Court." In *Judicial Conflict and Consensus,* ed. Sheldon Goldman and Charles M. Lamb, 87–114. Lexington: University Press of Kentucky.

Spaeth, Harold J., and Jeffrey A. Segal. 1999. *Majority Rule or Minority Will: Adherence to Precedent on the U.S. Supreme Court.* New York: Cambridge University Press.

Spaeth, Harold J., and Stuart H. Teger. 1982. "Activism and Restraint: A Cloak for the Justices' Policy Preferences." In *Supreme Court Activism and Restraint,* ed. Stephen C. Halpern and Charles M. Lamb, 277–301. Lexington, Mass.: Lexington Books.

Spiller, Pablo T., and Emerson H. Tiller. 1996. "Invitations to Override: Congressional Reversals of Supreme Court Decisions." *International Review of Law and Economics* 16:503–21.

Swisher, Carl B. 1930. *Stephen J. Field: Craftsman of the Law.* Washington, D.C.: Brookings Institution.

Tate, C. Neal. 1981. "Personal Attribute Models of the Voting Behavior of U.S. Supreme Court Justices: Liberalism in Civil Liberties and Economic Decisions, 1946–1978." *American Political Science Review* 73:355–67.

Thurstone, Louis L., and J. W. Degan. 1951. "A Factorial Study of the Supreme Court." *Proceedings of the National Academy of Sciences* 37:628–35.

Ulmer, S. Sidney. 1973. "Social Background as an Indicator to the Votes of Supreme Court Justices in Criminal Cases: 1947–1956 Terms." *American Journal of Political Science* 17:622–30.

Wahlbeck, Paul J. 1997. "The Life of the Law: Judicial Politics and Legal Change." *Journal of Politics* 59:778–802.

Wahlbeck, Paul J. 1998. "The Development of a Legal Rule: The Federal Common Law of Public Nuisance." *Law and Society Review* 32:613–37.

Whittington, Keith E. 2000. "Once More unto the Breach: Postbehavioralist Approaches to Judicial Politics." *Law and Social Inquiry* 25:601–34.

CHAPTER 3

Glendon Schubert: The Judicial Mind

Jeffrey A. Segal

Glendon Schubert is the founder of attitudinal model, which arguably remains the dominant model of U.S. Supreme Court decision making. He provided an array of tests for the model that, while supplanted in recent years, were at the cutting edge of judicial behavior for nearly two decades. This alone makes Schubert's contributions enormous. But Schubert also brought game theory to the study of judicial decision making.[1] This chapter will focus on these contributions. My primary sources of information include Schubert's voluminous written works as well as contemporaneous reviews of his work and twelve years of correspondence between Schubert and Harold Spaeth.[2]

Schubert wrote or edited twenty-seven books, published more than 125 articles, founded the field of judicial behavior, and was one of the earliest and most accomplished scholars in a second field, biopolitics. As early as 1963 Theodore Becker referred to "the Schubert school of judicial behavioralism" (1963, 254). He continued, "We prefix Professor Schubert's name because he is its effective founder and most prominent and prolific contributor (255).[3] His disciples included Harold Spaeth and Sidney Ulmer, and his influence continues to be seen to this day.

THE ATTITUDINAL MODEL

BACKGROUND

The attitudinal model has its genesis in the legal realist movement of the 1920s, which itself was a reaction against the traditional legal theories then in vogue. To traditionalists, "courts were portrayed as though they were institutions consisting only of judges; and judges were described exclusively on the basis of the legal parameters defining one aspect of their roles" (Schubert 1964, 1). Against the theory of a static law that judges merely find, the legal realists argued that lawmaking inhered in judging. "I take judge-made law as one of the realities of life" (Cardozo 1964, 14). Indeed, Schubert's 1964 edited volume, *Judicial*

Behavior: A Reader in Theory and Research, opens with works by realists such as Benjamin Cardozo, Jerome Frank, and Charles Grove Haines.

Judicial creation of law did not result because bad jurists sought power for themselves but was the inevitable fallout of an ever-changing society. According to Frank, legal abstractions

> can never be precise, perfect. They must be inexact. If the "environment" were stable, the degree of inexactness could become more negligible and remain relatively fixed. But the economic, political and social problems are ever shifting. (1964, 22)

If judges necessarily create law, how do they come to their decisions? To the legal realists, the answer clearly is not to be found in "legal rules and concepts insofar as they purport to describe what either courts or people are actually doing" (Llewellyn 1931, 1237). Judicial opinions containing such rules merely rationalize decisions but do not cause of them.

Despite the obvious impact of legal realism on attitudinalism, Schubert was greatly critical of the legalist movement, stating that it represented "method without theory" (1964, 9).

> Realism was primarily an academic movement which paralleled the barefoot empiricism characteristic of academic political science at the time. . . . While political science defined its task as the description of "what was going on" in government, or in relationship to it, legal realists undertook the job of describing "what courts actually do." Neither a systematic body of theory to suggest what might be worth observing, nor a set of methodologies which might make possible comparison among whatever observations actually were made, seemed important to either the political scientists or the legal realists in the interbellum period. The consequences, in both instances, was the outpouring (and in substantial degree, the waste) of professional resources in the compilation of aggregates of descriptive data, the cumulative and theoretical value of which was very small. (1964, 11)

Some recognized the need for a scientific, theory-based study of law. Frank, for example, attempted to use the theories of Sigmund Freud and Jean Piaget to explain judicial decisions. Schubert even declared that "the most enduring theoretical influence upon American jurisprudence during this century has come from Freudianism" (1964, 12). Well, no one's perfect. Understandably little has come of this line of work.

Meanwhile, the heretofore misnomered discipline of political science began to test its theories scientifically. This movement, known as behavioralism, argued that

1. Political science can ultimately become a science capable of prediction and explanation. . . .
2. Political science should concern itself primarily, if not exclusively, with phenomena which can actually be observed. . . .
3. Data should be quantified and "findings" based upon quantifiable data. . . .
4. Research should be theory oriented and theory directed. (Somit and Tanenhaus 1967, 177–78)

Behavioralism, according to Schubert, "has little in common with traditional jurisprudence . . . but behavioral concepts of law and uses of methodology do overlap, to some extent, with those of realism." As for traditional works, Schubert wrote, "there is no more justification to expound in detail, in a book on judicial behavior, the views of traditional jurisprudence, than there would be to include a chapter on alchemy in a text on metallurgy, or to include a set of horoscopes in a book of astrophysics" (1964, 9).

Among early behavioral works was a 1948 book by C. Herman Pritchett entitled *The Roosevelt Court*. It systematically examined dissents, concurrences, voting blocs, and ideological configurations from the Court's nonunanimous decisions between 1937 and 1947. Pritchett did not provide a theory of Supreme Court decision making, yet he made the assumptions behind his work quite explicit: "This book, then, undertakes to study the politics and values of the Roosevelt Court through the nonunanimous opinions handed down by the justices" (xi). He also acknowledged that the justices are "motivated by their own preferences" (xii). Its influence was such that Schubert dedicated *Judicial Decision-Making* (1963) "To C. Herman Pritchett, who blazed a trail."

SCHUBERT

Schubert, however, first provided a detailed attitudinal model of Supreme Court decision making. He did so in three major works: *Quantitative Analysis of Judicial Behavior* (1959), *The Judicial Mind* (1965), and *The Judicial Mind Revisited* (1974).

In *Quantitative Analysis*, Schubert applied game theory, bloc analysis, and scalogram analysis to the study of Supreme Court decision making. I will turn to game theory later. But between bloc analysis and scalogram analysis, Schubert concluded that "scalogram analysis . . . offers a much more efficient and less cumbersome method for the analysis of attitudes toward 'issues' than does bloc analysis" (1959, 166). And so concluded most other judicial scholars, with the important exception of Sprague (1968). Thus, I focus on scalogram analysis.

Scalogram analysis, also called cumulative scaling or Guttman scaling, derived from early psychological research on measuring attitudes (Stouffer et al. 1950). Consider, for example, a set of right-to-counsel cases. Cumulative scaling can help us answer two questions: are the justices responding toward these cases based on their attitudes toward the right to counsel, as opposed to some more complicated set of attitudes, possibly one that combined attitudes toward the right to counsel with attitudes toward federalism; and which justices are more liberal or conservative than which other justices? The limitations on the inferences that can be made from cumulative scaling will be discussed following the explanation of the technique.

If the justices are voting strictly on their attitudes toward the right to counsel, then it should be possible to find an ordinal relationship among the justices. An ordinal scale exists if we can rank order each justice in terms of support for right-to-counsel claims. For example, if an ordinal scale exists, we can claim that justice x is more conservative than justice y, and justice y is more conservative than justice z. Further, if this ordinal relationship can be shown to exist, then we can infer that the justices are basing their right-to-counsel decisions on their attitudes toward the right to counsel and not on a more complicated set of values.

The question then becomes, how can we show an ordinal relationship? A simple way would be to count votes. Assume that there are ten right-to-counsel votes. The justice with the most votes upholding the noncounsel convictions might be labeled the most conservative, while the justice voting to strike the most noncounsel convictions might be labeled the most liberal. The simplicity of this approach might seem alluring, but there are problems nevertheless. First, using this procedure, someone will be considered the most procounsel justice, and someone has to be the least procounsel justice. This does not necessarily signify that one is more conservative on the right to counsel than the other. One justice could be very sensitive to federalism questions and will thus invariably vote for the government in state cases regardless of his attitudes toward the right to counsel. Consider for example the following scale in table 1, where cases 1–5 involve state right-to-counsel claims, while cases 6–10 involve federal right-to-counsel claims. A "+"

by convention is a liberal vote (that is, holding the conviction unconstitutional) while a "–" by convention is a conservative vote (that is, holding a conviction valid).

Justice B has more conservative votes, but it is not accurate to say
that she is more conservative on the right to counsel. She is certainly
more conservative on the state cases, but she appears to be more liberal
than justice A on federal cases.

A second problem is that we do not know from this simple counting
which cases are most important. In case 7, A voted conservatively and B
voted liberally. In case 3, B voted conservatively and A voted liberally.
If case 7 were the most important case of the year, while case 3 was
based on a minor technicality, then Justice B might rightfully be considered more liberal. But if case 3 were the most important case and
case 7 involved a minor technicality, then we might want to label justice A more liberal. As demonstrated, merely counting votes does not
allow us to assume ordinality.

Consider instead the following hypothetical pre-*Gideon* cases in
table 2. Case 1 might involve a case where the defendant was a minor in
a capital case. Only two justices, A and B, thought the trial reasonable
and thus cast conservative votes. Case 2 involved a minor in a rape case.
That switched Justice C's vote to conservative. Cases 3 and 4 involved
a minor in a low-level felony, bringing justice D into the conservative
coalition. Case 5 might resemble case 4 except that it involved an
unlearned adult rather than a minor. Case 6 might involve a college-

TABLE 1.   Noncumulative Scale

Case	Justice	
	A	B
1	+	–
2	+	–
3	+	–
4	–	–
5	–	–
6	+	+
7	–	+
8	–	–
9	+	+
10	–	–
	4-6	3-7

educated adult in a minor felony case, while Case 7 might involve an educated adult in a misdemeanor case with the possibility of jail time.

Given that the votes of the justices can be arranged in such a fashion, where once a justice votes conservatively he or she continues to vote conservatively in all less extreme cases, then cumulative scaling theory tells us (1) that the cases might be unidimensional, thus signifying that the justices are basing their votes on their attitudes toward that subject and not on a more complicated set of attitudes, (2) which justices are more liberal or conservative than which other justices, and (3), which cases present the most extreme stimuli.

Of course, it is not likely that any set of cases will perfectly fit the Guttman model. For example, had Justice G voted conservatively in case 3, we could consider such a vote an "error" or nonscale response because the justice had voted liberally in the more extreme cases 1 and 2. If more than 10 percent of the votes in a scale constitute "errors," then by convention, an acceptable cumulative scale is said not to exist.

The existence of a cumulative scale constitutes a necessary but not sufficient condition for the inference of unidimensionality. That is, if an acceptable cumulative scale does not exist, then the cases clearly are not decided on the basis of a single dimension. But the obverse is not true: the existence of an acceptable scale does not necessarily signify the existence of unidimensionality. This point is made most forcefully by Joseph Tanenhaus (1966), who demonstrated that acceptable cumulative scales could be found for all cases during the 1957 term authored by Burton and Clark, all cases from the same term from the Second, Third and Fourth Circuits, and cases decided in May 1957 and 1958.[4] Mendelson's (1963) critique of judicial behavior claims perfect scales for "tenderness toward communism" and a near-perfect scale for "ten-

TABLE 2. A Cumulative Scale

Case	Justice									Total
	A	B	C	D	E	F	G	H	I	
1	−	−	+	+	+	+	+	+	+	7-2
2	−	−	−	+	+	+	+	+	+	6-3
3	−	−	−	−	+	+	+	+	+	5-4
4	−	−	−	−	+	+	+	+	+	5-4
5	−	−	−	−	−	−	+	+	+	3-6
6	−	−	−	−	−	−	−	+	+	2-7
7	−	−	−	−	−	−	−	−	+	1-8
Total	0-7	0-7	1-6	2-5	4-3	4-3	5-2	6-1	7-0	

derness toward murder and manslaughter" (597). Sprague's inability to find acceptable scales over periods of time longer than a single term led him to conclude that while scalogram analysis might be "descriptively useful in the short run," it was "theoretically misleading in the long run" (1968, 50). Moreover, the exclusion of unanimously decided cases, necessary to prevent the artificial inflation of scalogram statistics, artificially inflates the appearance of intracourt divisions that are so crucial to such analyses (Mendelson 1963).

Schubert rather quickly became dissatisfied with the unidimensional restrictions of cumulative scaling. Writing to Spaeth, he declared,

> I have come to doubt very much that a linear continuum (such as Pritchett implicitly postulates, and I myself used in *Q.A.*) can account for the complexity of the patterns of the relationships among the justices. I suspect that the basic task is to discover the locus of points (corresponding to the justices) in an r-dimensional space. In part, my thinking along these lines has been stimulated by Clyde Coombs' theory of data and the procedures for multidimensional unfolding that he and his students have developed over the past decade. . . . One of the difficulties is that, although Coombs presently is writing a book on his theory, the sociometric type of relationship in which I am interested constitutes an advanced part of the theory that he has not yet worked out. (Schubert to Spaeth, December 14, 1960)

Later he wrote,

> A defense of unidimensional models over multidimensional ones for the study of human behavior, based upon any ground other than relative simplicity, must be greeted in the same spirit as one would accord a claim of having squared the circle. (Schubert to Spaeth, August 6, 1964)[5]

Coombs eventually finished *A Theory of Data* (1964), and Schubert, drawing heavily on that research, developed a fully operationalized attitudinal model in *The Judicial Mind* (1965). Schubert assumed that case stimuli and the justices' values could be ideologically scaled. Allow me to illustrate with a modern example. Imagine an affirmative action plan, the legality of which must be determined by the Supreme Court. Assume that a company in a large urban area, in response to previous discriminatory practices, sets a goal of 50 percent minority hires and implements that goal by establishing a hard quota on future hiring. Now imagine a second case, similar to the first in that guilt of discriminatory hiring had been proven but different in that the company simply agrees to include race as one factor among many taken into account in hiring. Both plans are taken to court on the grounds that the hiring plans violate the Civil Rights Act.

According to Schubert's attitudinal model, we can place these cases in ideological space. Since the hard quota is more egalitarian than the soft goal, we place the first case to the left of the second case. This is diagrammed in figure 1, where A represents the first case and B the second. Presumably, any affirmative action case will locate on the line; depending on case characteristics, the case will be to the left of A, between A and B (inclusive), or to the right of B. The more prior justification for the remedy (for example, a finding of purposeful past discrimination) and the less severe the remedy (for example, goals versus quotas), the further to the right the case will fall. The less prior justification and the more severe the remedy, the further to the left it will be. The points on the line where the cases lie are traditionally referred to as j-points.

Next, we place the justices in ideological space. Consider three judges, 1, 2, and 3, who are respectively liberal, moderate, and conservative. They could easily be rank ordered on an ideological scale, with 1 on the left, 2 in the middle, and 3 on the right.

With some additional information, we might be able to go a bit further and say that Judge 1 is liberal enough that he would uphold virtually any affirmative action plan as long as it did not stigmatize particular members of the majority group that is harmed. Thus we could place Judge 1 to the left of case A. Judge 2 might not be quite as egalitarian as justice 1; she would uphold the goals but not the strict quotas. Thus, we could place judge 2 to the right of case A but to the left of case B. Finally, judge 3 might believe that virtually all affirmative action plans are illegal. To this judge, only individuals who have proven that they are the victims of a company's practices are entitled to legal remedy. Thus, we could place judge 3 to the right of case B. The judges are placed in ideological space with the cases in figure 1.

Schubert refers to the positions of the justices as their "ideal points" (i-points), although, as we shall see, the term is a misnomer. According to Schubert, a justice would vote to uphold all convictions that are dominated by (are to the left of) the justice's ideal point and would vote to strike all convictions that dominate (are to the right of) the justice's ideal point. If this is the situation, though, the i-points represent not the ideal points of each justice but the *indifference* point. Justice 1 upholds all convictions to the left of 1, rejects all convictions to the

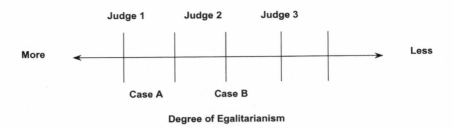

Fig. 1.   Justices and cases in ideological space

right of 1, and is indifferent about whether convictions at 1 are upheld or overturned.

Schubert tested the model not through independent measures of the justices' preferences, case stimuli, or the interaction between them but through a factor analysis of the votes of the justices. He finds that two major scales, political liberalism and economic liberalism, explain the vast majority of the justices' votes.

The Judicial Mind Revisited (1974) was an attempt to replicate *The Judicial Mind* with more sophisticated and reliable techniques. Thus, while Schubert's thinking about the attitudinal model had changed in the preceding decade, he explicitly stuck to the model originally proposed in *The Judicial Mind*. He retested the model using Guttman scaling, principal components factor analysis, oblique factor analysis, and smallest space analysis.

Schubert finds that principal components analysis, oblique factor analysis, and smallest space analysis all essentially lead to the same substantive conclusions but that smallest space analysis works marginally better than the others. Substantively, though Schubert finds evidence of a third and perhaps a fourth dimension at work, he is unable to find any substantive meaning to those dimensions and thus concludes that *The Judicial Mind*'s basic conclusions were correct.

Not surprisingly, these works, though seen as the breakthrough works that they were by many scholars, drew more than their share of contemporary criticism from traditional scholars. Most famously, Mendelson (1963) complained about the use of quantitative methods, the meaninglessness of "law" to judicial behavioralists, the artificial categorization of complex cases, the artificial categorization of complex votes, and the substantive conclusions drawn from such analyses. Theodore Becker, a role theorist, found himself "hard pressed to see how their work even tends toward any theory of *judicial* decision making. Where in their work do they build in the peculiar systemic factors, e.g., the existence of a large body of authoritative precedent; the deeply embedded notion of judicial restraint and *stare decisis*" (1963, 265). The Schubert school is "simply quantitatively *describing*, through very complex tools, that which any informed observer of the Court knows does exist" (261). Albert Rosenthal's attack on *Judicial Mind* and the purported inability of computer-generated statistics to predict Court decisions claims that since the fault is not in the computer,

> the fault must be in the input. We do not have to search far for the flaw. Very early in the book, it is made clear that whoever has indoctrinated the computer has treated the most complex questions of constitutional adjudication, not as delicate problems of weighing competing considerations, but as a test of whether a justice is for or against civil liberties, or of whether he favors the downtrodden or prefers big business; nothing explains a justice's vote except his ideology. (1966, 449)

Of course, Rosenthal's premise is completely wrong, for Schubert's model explained the overwhelming proportion of the Court's decisions. That it does so without resort to factors that traditionalists find essential says more about the relevance of those factors than it does about the deficiencies of the attitudinal model.

UPDATING THE ATTITUDINAL MODEL

The attitudinal model has been updated both theoretically and empirically since Schubert's writings, though not in any way that would appeal to traditional scholars.

Theory

The major theoretical advance to the attitudinal model came in Rohde and Spaeth's *Supreme Court Decision Making* (1976). Whereas Schubert viewed the attitudinal model as a general model of political decision making (1965, 15–21), Rohde and Spaeth provide an explanation for why the justices are able to engage in attitudinal behavior. Influenced by the application of economic notions of rationality to political decisions, they recognize that decisions depend on goals, rules, and situations. While their definitions may have been updated in more recent years, the economics influence is obvious:

Goals. To Rohde and Spaeth, goals simply mean that "actors in political situations are outcome oriented; when they choose among a number of alternatives, they pick the alternative that they perceive will yield them the greatest net benefit in terms of their goals" (1976, 70). To Rohde and Spaeth, as to Schubert, the primary goals of Supreme Court justices in the decision-making process are *policy goals.*

Rules.　　Next, Rohde and Spaeth contend that an actor's choices will depend on the rules of the game, "the various formal and informal rules and norms within the framework of which decisions are made. As such, they specify which types of actions are permissible and which are impermissible, the circumstances and conditions under which choice may be exercised, and the manner of choosing" (1976, 71).

As Segal and Spaeth put it,

> The Supreme Court's rules and structures, along with those of the American political system in general, give the justices, with their lifetime tenure, enormous latitude to reach decisions based on their personal policy preferences. Members of the Supreme Court can further their policy goals because they lack electoral or political accountability, ambition for higher office, and comprise a court of last resort that controls its own caseload. . . . While the absence of these factors may hinder the personal policy-making capabilities of lower court judges or judges in other political systems, their presence enables the justices to engage in rationally sincere behavior. (2002, 92–93)

For example, "if a case on the outcome of a presidential election should reach the Supreme Court . . . the Court's decision might well turn on the personal preferences of the justices" (Segal and Spaeth 1993, 70).

This theoretical updating has itself been controversial, as rational choice scholars find a gaping hole in the independence granted to Supreme Court justices: Congress's ability to overrule the Court on matters of statutory interpretation. The theoretical arguments for judicial deference to Congress are clear: the Court can obtain ultimate outcomes closer to its policy preferences if it sets policy at the spot closest to its ideal point, subject to the constraint that its decision cannot be overruled (Ferejohn and Shipan 1990; Epstein and Knight 1998). Yet these arguments assume that the Court would choose to take a case knowing that it would have to defer to Congress's preferences; that if the Court took such a case, the Court could not opt into constitutional mode; that Congress gets the last move, and so on (Segal 1997). Suffice it to say that these theoretical arguments have not been resolved and ultimately can only be resolved by empirical evidence.

Empirical Tests

Measuring the attitudes and ideology of political elites is a difficult task, as senators, justices, and presidents are unlikely to fill out survey questionnaires provided by scholars, much less fill them out accurately. The solution used by Schubert, and the one commonly used to this day in the congressional literature to measure ideology, is to use votes to measure ideology and then use that ideology measure to explain votes. As Schubert notes in the preface to *The Judicial Mind Revisited*, "the attitudinal differences delineated and denoted obviously are hypothetical rather than empirical constructs, because the data analyzed are based on observations of judicial votes in the decisions of cases—and not even on judicial responses to questionnaire items. . . . We can say no more—and yet no less—than that we cannot reject the theory on the basis of these observations" (1974, xi–xii).

One potential resolution to the circularity problem uses past votes as a measure of the justices' ideology (Epstein and Mershon 1996). While this does in fact resolve the circularity question and provides useful tests for the stability and predictability of judicial attitudes, it nevertheless begs the question of what explains the justices' past votes. If justice A votes liberally in the 1999 term while justice B votes conservatively, their past preferences, as measured by the 1999 term, may well predict their behavior in the 2000 term. But we still lack independent evidence about what caused their behavior in the 1999 term. Thus, past votes may offer an excellent description of the justices' current preferences but cannot qualify as an explanation of the justices' behavior. For finding Supreme Court medians or scaling justices and congressmen, voting behavior may be an excellent measure of preferences. But if our goal is to explain the justices' behavior, we clearly need an independent measure of such preferences.

One such measure uses editorial judgments from leading newspapers about nominees subsequent to their nomination by the president but prior to their confirmation by the Senate. Segal and Cover (1989) found a correlation of .80 between their measure of the justices' attitudes and their decisions in civil liberties cases. More recently, Segal et al. (1995) backdated the Segal and Cover work to cover the Vinson Court and extended the work to cover economic cases. Though their results are not as strong as the original Segal and Cover findings, attitudes still correlate fairly well with justices' votes. Thus, although these works do not demonstrate that attitudes are all that influence Supreme

Court decisions, a claim Schubert explicitly disavowed (1974, xiii), they do demonstrate that attitudes are strong predictors of judicial decisions in the two areas that have made up the bulk of the Court's docket over the past fifty years, civil liberties and economics cases.

Attitudes are only half of the attitudinal model, for the attitudes must interact with case facts. Since Schubert, various scholars have demonstrated the importance of facts/case stimuli in judicial decision making (Segal 1984; Segal and Reedy 1988; McGuire 1990; George and Epstein 1992; Hagle 1992; Ignagni 1994). Of course, case stimuli are also a component of the legal model, so this should be seen as a necessary but clearly not sufficient condition for attitudinal decision making. But the attitudinal model depicted in figure 1, which includes the interaction between case stimuli and attitudes, well explains the justices' search-and-seizure decisions (Segal and Spaeth 2002, chap. 8).

Overall, there are problems with the attitudinal model's empirical tests: Epstein and Mershon (1996) find limits to the preference measures; systematic tests using independent measures of attitudes do not predate the Vinson Court; and areas other than civil liberties and economics have not been well tested (Baum 1997). Nevertheless, even critics of the attitudinal model have conceded its exceptional explanatory ability (Rosenberg 1994; Epstein and Mershon 1996).

Yet while attitudinal influence have by and large been accepted, scholars continue to wonder what else might influence Court decisions. A variety of scholars have presented a series of nonattitudinal factors that might influence the Supreme Court, including public opinion (Mishler and Sheehan 1993), the solicitor general (Scigliano 1971), quality of counsel (McGuire 1993), and legal factors (Kahn 1999). Most prominently, rational choice scholars have argued that the justices do in fact defer to Congress (Spiller and Gely 1992). With the exception of the solicitor general, all of these additional factors remain hotly debated (Segal and Spaeth 2002).

RATIONAL CHOICE

While Schubert is best known as the creator of the attitudinal model, *Quantitative Analysis of Judicial Behavior* (1959) raises questions of concern to game theorists and rational choice scholars.

THE REALLY NEW INSTITUTIONALISM

Twenty-five years before March and Olson (1984) labeled and introduced the "new institutionalism" to political science, Schubert examined the impact of institutional rules on the behavior of judges by comparing the voting patterns of U.S. Supreme Court justices with those of Michigan State Supreme Court justices. His theoretical question of interest was whether life tenure served to limit partisan behavior. Schubert found that while partisan blocs were irrelevant to the U.S. Supreme Court, they were crucial to the Michigan court. "There may, after all, be validity in the assumption that life tenure makes for independence of judges" (Schubert 1959, 142). While Schubert's results may well be time bound, the theoretical question is not, as questions about the influence of institutional design on judicial behavior continue to animate scholars today (Brace and Hall 1990, 1995; Hall 1992; Epstein and Knight 1998).

THE HUGHBERTS GAME

Schubert's explicit examination of game theory in *Quantitative Analysis of Judicial Behavior* began with "The Hughberts Game." According to Schubert's zero-sum game, in any case, the justices in the majority split the policy payoff (set to unity), while dissenting justices receive nothing. Thus, Hughes and Roberts gain utility by being in the smallest possible winning coalition. Because the liberal bloc was smaller than the conservative bloc, Hughberts would always gain more utility by forming a coalition with the Left than it would by forming a coalition with the Right. Schubert's pathbreaking attempt to formalize judicial behavior into the theory of games, though, was not much of a substantive success, as the model sets policy goals to a secondary concern and does not explain dissenting behavior. Indeed, a JSTOR search found only two passing references to "Hughberts" in the past forty years. Far more successful was Schubert's "Certiorari Game."

THE CERTIORARI GAME

In 1972, S. Sidney Ulmer conducted a groundbreaking study whose purpose was to determine whether justices engage in a reversal strategy—that is, whether they vote to hear cases when they disapprove of the lower court's outcome. The results were mixed at best. Indeed, Schubert noted more than a dozen years earlier, "it is manifestly impossible for the Court directly to right all wrongs suffered by litigants in the lower courts" (1959, 254). While there might be some justifications for engaging in an error-correction or reversal strategy, that cannot be the only factor guiding the cert votes of policy-minded justices. First, with several thousand cases confronting the Court annually, justices who voted to review every case with which they disagreed would generate institutional paralysis. Salience will obviously matter. Second, even if the Court could hear all cases with which a justice disagreed, it is not necessarily in that justice's best policy interest to have all such cases reviewed. If the justice will likely lose on the merits, it is preferable that the case not be heard at all. This need to anticipate eventual outcomes led Schubert to examine certiorari from a game-theoretic perspective.

The "Certiorari Game" in *Quantitative Analysis* represents, with the Hughberts game, the first systematic attempt to explain the justices' behavior in game-theoretic terms (Murphy 1964, 3). Schubert examined the strategies of the Court's liberal justices in Federal Employers' Liability Act (FELA) cases. The issue before the Court in such cases was whether the plaintiffs' (railroad workers') evidence was sufficient to permit a jury to decide the question of fact (1959, 215).

From 1942 to 1948, a four-person liberal bloc consisting of Rutledge, Murphy, Black, and Douglas strongly supported the claims of railroad workers against railroads in FELA cases. Given the Court's rule of four, this bloc could control the grant of certiorari but not the decision on the merits. Schubert envisioned four strategies that the justices might use in considering certiorari:

1. Vote for all petitions in FELA cases.
2. Vote for all petitions filed by workers.
3. Vote against all railroad petitions but vote for those worker petitions that had some evidence to support the employees' claim.
4. Vote against all railroad petitions and vote for worker petitions only where the appellate court had overturned a proworker trial court decision.

During this period, the bloc clearly rejected strategy 1, as only one railroad petition out of twenty-five filed was granted cert, but that petition was eventually dismissed as improvidently granted. Nor could the bloc have been playing strategy 2, as 37 percent of worker petitions were denied cert. The Court (and thus, presumes Schubert, the bloc) voted to grant cert in slightly less than half of the workers' petitions that did not meet the criteria of strategy 4. "Presumably, the petitions denied were frivolous and very bad risks" (Schubert 1959, 240). Of those strategy 3 cases that were granted, the workers won eight of eleven cases. Finally, the Court (and again, presumably the bloc) voted to grant cert in thirteen of the fourteen cases in which an appellate court overturned a lower court decision favorable to the employees, winning twelve of the thirteen grants.

The bloc clearly eschewed a simple reversal strategy of voting to hear every antiworker appellate court decision and presumably focused instead only on those where the workers had the best chance of winning, especially those cases where the appellate court reversed a trial court decision favorable to the workers. Unfortunately, Schubert's analysis was limited by the fact that he could only infer the justices' conference votes from the actual granting of cert; he had no data on how they actually voted.

BEYOND SCHUBERT

Schubert's work not only introduced game theory to judicial behavior but also introduced the systematic study of certiorari and certiorari strategies to judicial behavior. While a general discussion of the impact of game theory properly belongs in the Murphy chapter in this volume, I will focus on subsequent works examining the impact of strategic choice in certiorari.

First, Provine (1980, chap. 5), armed with the actual certiorari votes in FELA cases, has contested Schubert's specific conclusions. In subsequent terms, Brennan did not follow Schubert's strategy. The other liberal justices adhered to it between 62 and 100 percent of the time. One can dispute the criterion of success, but Schubert's model provides a reasonably accurate empirical fit.

Second, Schubert's model does not consider the possibility of aggressive grants—voting to hear a case when one liked the lower court outcome to see the case affirmed at the Supreme Court. Such a strategy would be risky, but a justice might be willing to engage in it if she were confident of affirmation.[6] Thus, while sophisticated reversal strategies may be part of the justices' cert process, sophisticated affirmance strategies may be as well.

Third, the empirical literature since Schubert has hotly debated the entire notion of strategic voting on cert. Strong support for strategic certiorari voting can also be found in the early work of Saul Brenner (1979). He assumed that justices will be more likely to behave strategically when there are only four vote to grant cert, because each vote is then essential. He therefore argues that a justice who wants to affirm will not provide the fourth vote unless he or she is quite certain that the Court will in fact affirm. As he predicts, when a four-person certiorari bloc includes justices who want the court to affirm, the affirmance-preferring justices in that bloc will be more likely to prevail than the reversal-preferring justices. He also finds the justices to be less strategic when more than four vote for cert, because in these cases each justice's vote does not affect the decision to hear the case. Voting for cert in such cases neither aids nor hinders the justice's policy designs, making predicted outcomes irrelevant to the decisional outcome. In a later study, Brenner and John Krol (1989) found that justices were more likely to vote for cert if they wanted to reverse, if their side would win on the merits, and if they were liberals on a liberal Court or conservatives on a conservative Court.

Similarly, Caldeira, Wright, and Zorn (1999) find that during the 1982 Court term, justices who were more likely to win on the merits were more likely to vote for cert. These results coincide with the work of Jan Palmer (1982), which found that the justices' votes on cert correlate with their votes on the merits and whether their side wins on the merits.

Not all agree, though. Provine claims that the justices are not motivated by what she called outcome-oriented concerns. Rather, she claims, "a shared conception of the proper role of a judge prevents the justices from exploiting the possibilities for power-oriented [that is, strategic] voting in case selection" (1980, 172). Moreover, Perry claims, "even if one concedes that some cert votes are preliminary votes on the merits, that does not imply that a cert vote involves any strategic or 'sophisticated' voting" (1991, 270). Nevertheless, Perry does not deny the existence of strategic voting, merely its prevalence: "All of the justices act strategically on cert at times, and much of the time none of them acts strategically" (198). Justices on occasion engage in "defensive denials," voting to deny petitions from disfavored lower court decisions to prevent probable affirmance by the Supreme Court, and "aggressive grants," voting to grant petitions from favorable lower court decisions to achieve probable affirmance by the Supreme Court. Blurring the lines in this debate, Brenner, an early proponent of strategic certiorari voting, claims in his work with Krol that when justices who switch their votes between the conference vote on the merits and the final or report vote on the merits are eliminated from consideration, evidence of strategic voting, based on the aggregated votes of all justices, shrinks to statistically significant but substantively meaningless levels. Moreover, Brenner and Krol find no evidence whatsoever for defensive denials. They conclude that their research "buttresses the view that . . . error-correction . . . is extant in certiorari voting but undermines the perception that the prediction strategy is also present" (Krol and Brenner 1990, 342).

One recent study points back in Shubert's direction, but only in general terms of sophisticated strategies. Boucher and Segal (1995) find that the likelihood of winning on the merits is a significant predictor of the justices' cert votes, but only for those justices who wish to affirm. Justices who wish to reverse appear not to consider probable outcomes. These results make a fair amount of sense. A justice wishing to reverse has less to lose than a justice wishing to affirm. Moreover, a justice wishing to reverse can also count on a fairly high prior probability of reversal for any case that is actually granted. But these results are based only on cases in which the Court granted cert.

Among those studies systematically examining prediction strategies, only Caldeira, Wright, and Zorn (1999) includes both grants and denials. While the authors clearly show that the justices take probable outcomes into account, the study does not separate out affirmance- and reversal-minded justices to see if both groups consider probable outcomes. Moreover, Caldeira, Wright, and Zorn calculate each justice's probability of winning on the merits in cases that are denied cert from that justice's probability of winning in cases that are granted cert. This assumes that the two sets of cases are homogenous, when undoubtedly they are not. Thus, while this work, like most of the others before it, points generally in the direction of Schubert's claims, more work remains to be done, with the greatest need being case-specific likelihoods of winning on the merits for both cases that are granted cert and cases that are denied cert.

CONCLUSIONS

There is not room in this chapter to discuss Schubert's contributions to comparative judicial politics (see n.1), oral arguments (Peterson et al. 1992), biopolitics (Schubert 1983),[7] or even academic ideology (Schubert 1967). Indeed, even Schubert's edited volumes have been fantastic successes. Perhaps his best, *Judicial Decision-Making* (1963) includes Ulmer's classic study of the Michigan Supreme Court, Nagel's survey-based study of judicial attitudes, Spaeth's classic B-scale analysis, and Tanenhaus's cue theory article. And little noted by most judicial scholars but well regarded by President Harry S. Truman (1957) is *The Presidency in the Courts* (Schubert 1957).

Despite Schubert's voluminous output, the attitudinal model is his most compelling and influential contribution. The fact that the attitudinal model remains one of the dominant theories of judicial decision making—and perhaps the dominant model of Supreme Court decision making (Epstein et al. 1998)—is truly remarkable. This is best seen by the company of still-vital forty-year-old models: Downs's (1957) theory of party competition, Olson's (1965) theory of interest group development, and Dahl's (1961) pluralist theory of democracy. To paraphrase Richard Nixon, theories come and theories go, but the attitudinal model goes on forever.

1. Either one of these contributions, plus many others, such as his work in comparative judicial research (Schubert 1963, pt. 3; Schubert 1964, chap. 2; Schubert and Danelski 1969), would have been more than enough (*dayenu!*) to warrant inclusion in this volume, but Schubert also played a leading a role in ridding the discipline of one George F. Will, who taught briefly at Michigan State University. "I knew I was in the wrong profession," Will wrote, "when, as a graduate student in political science at Princeton, I opened a scholarly article on 'The Judicial Philosophy of Justice Robert Jackson' and found a mass of equations and graphs" (Will 1983, A23).

2. Spaeth provided access to the letters, and Schubert has generously granted me permission to use them.

3. Schubert dissented from this characterization. "Becker's suggestion of a 'school' is screamingly funny, as I know you are well aware; I don't even belong in such a school myself" (Schubert to Spaeth, November 21, 1963).

4. Of course, this could mean that the justices vote consistently within a single liberal-conservative dimension. The most up-to-date research suggests precisely that (see Clinton 1998). Schubert, though, thought Tanenhaus's problem was that "he fails to distinguish the quite different problems of scaling justices, and scaling cases" (Schubert to Spaeth, April 21, 1961). Schubert's response was to a prepublication version of Tanenhaus's work.

5. But, again, see Clinton 1998 on the continued vitality of unidimensional models.

6. This is probably less true for fact-specific issue areas such as FELA cases.

7. Or, perhaps more interestingly, Schubert 1996 ("The Sexual Choice of Female Primates").

REFERENCES

Baum, Lawrence. 1997. *The Puzzle of Judicial Behavior*. Ann Arbor: University of Michigan Press.

Becker, Theodore L. 1963. "Inquiry into a School of Thought in the Judicial Behavior Movement." *Midwest Journal of Political Science* 7:254–66.

Boucher, Robert, and Jeffrey A. Segal. 1995. "Supreme Court Justices as Strategic Decision Makers: Offensive Grants and Defensive Denials on the Vinson Court." *Journal of Politics* 57:824–37.

Brace, Paul, and Melinda Gann Hall. 1990. "Neo-Institutionalism and Dissent in State Supreme Courts." *Journal of Politics* 52:54–70.

Brace, Paul, and Melinda Gann Hall. 1995. "Studying Courts Comparatively: The View from the American States." *Political Research Quarterly* 48 (March): 5–29.

Brenner, Saul. 1979. "The New Certiorari Game." *Journal of Politics* 41:649–55.

Brenner, Saul, and John F. Krol. 1989. "Strategies in Certiorari Voting on the United States Supreme Court." *Journal of Politics* 51:828–41.

Caldeira, Gregory, John R. Wright, and Christopher J. W. Zorn. 1999. "Strategic Voting and Gatekeeping in the Supreme Court." *Journal of Law, Economics, and Organization* 15 (3): 549–72.

Cardozo, Benjamin. 1964. "The Nature of the Judicial Process." In *Judicial Behavior: A Reader in Theory and Research*, ed. Glendon Schubert. Chicago: Rand McNally.

Clinton, Joshua. 1998. "An Independent Judiciary? Determining the Influence of Congressional and Presidential Preferences on the Supreme Court's Interpretation of Federal Statutes, 1953–1995." Paper presented at the 1998 meeting of the American Political Science Association.

Coombs, Clyde. 1964. *A Theory of Data*. New York: Wiley.

Dahl, Robert. 1961. *Who Governs? Democracy and Power in an American City*. New Haven: Yale University Press.

Downs, Anthony. 1957. *An Economic Theory of Democracy*. New York: Harper and Row.

Epstein, Lee, Valerie Hoekstra, Jeffrey A. Segal, and Harold J. Spaeth. 1998. "Do Sincere Political Preferences Change? A Longitudinal Study of U.S. Supreme Court Justices." *Journal of Politics* 60:801–18.

Epstein, Lee, and Jack Knight. 1998. *Choices Justices Make*. Washington, D.C.: Congressional Quarterly Press.

Epstein, Lee, and Carol Mershon. 1996. "Measuring Political Preferences." *American Journal of Political Science* 40:261–94.

Ferejohn, John, and Charles Shipan. 1990. "Congressional Influence on Bureaucracy." *Journal of Law, Economics, and Organization* 6:1–20.

Frank, Jerome. 1949. *Law and the Modern Mind*. New York: Coward-McCann.

Frank, Jerome. 1964. "Law and the Modern Mind." In *Judicial Behavior: A Reader in Theory and Research*, ed. G. Schubert, 19–27. Chicago: Rand McNally.

George, Tracey E., and Lee Epstein. 1992. "On the Nature of Supreme Court Decision Making." *American Political Science Review* 86:323–37.

Hagle, Timothy M. 1992. "But Do They Have to See It to Know It: The Supreme Court's Obscenity and Pornography Decisions." *Western Political Quarterly* 45:1039–54.

Hall, Melinda Gann. 1992. "Electoral Politics and Strategic Voting in State Supreme Courts." *Journal of Politics* 54:427–46.

Holmes, O. W. 1897. "The Path of the Law." *Harvard Law Review* 10:457–78.

Ignagni, Joseph. 1994. "Explaining and Predicting Supreme Court Decision

Making: The Burger Court's Establishment Clause Decisions." *Journal of Church and State* 36:301–27.

Kahn, Ronald. 1999. "Interpretive Norms and Supreme Court Decision Making: The Rehnquist Court on Privacy and Religion." In *Supreme Court Decision Making: New Institutionalist Approaches*, ed. Cornell W. Clayton and Howard Gillman. Chicago: University of Chicago Press.

Krol, John F., and Saul Brenner. 1990. "Strategies in Certiorari Voting on the United States Supreme Court: A Reevaluation." *Western Political Quarterly* 43:335–42.

Llewellyn, Karl. 1931. "Some Realism about Realism—Responding to Dean Pound." *Harvard Law Review* 44:1222–64.

March, James G., and Johan P. Olsen. 1984. "The New Institutionalism: Organizational Factors in Political Life." *American Political Science Review* 78:734–49.

McGuire, Kevin. 1990. "Obscenity, Libertarian Values, and Decision Making in the Supreme Court." *American Politics Quarterly* 18:47–67.

McGuire, Kevin. 1993. *The Supreme Court Bar: Legal Elites in the Washington Community*. Charlottesville: University Press of Virginia.

Mendelson, Wallace. 1963. "The Neo-Behavioral Approach to the Judicial Process: A Critique." *American Political Science Review* 57:593–603.

Mishler, William, and Reginald S. Sheehan. 1993. "The Supreme Court as a Countermajoritarian Institution? The Impact of Public Opinion on Supreme Court Decisions." *American Political Science Review* 87:87–101.

Murphy, Walter F. 1964. *The Elements of Judicial Strategy*. Chicago: University of Chicago Press.

Olson, Mancur. 1965. "The Logic of Collective Action: Public Goods and the Theory of Groups." Cambridge: Harvard University Press.

Palmer, Jan. 1982. "An Econometric Analysis of the U.S. Supreme Court's Certiorari Decisions." *Public Choice* 39:387–98.

Palmer, Jan. 1990. *The Vinson Court Era: The Supreme Court's Conference Votes: Data and Analysis*. New York: AMS Press.

Perry, H. W. 1991. *Deciding to Decide*. Cambridge: Harvard University Press.

Peterson, Steven, James Schubert, Glendon Schubert, and Stephen Wasby. 1992. Observing Supreme Court Oral Argument: A Biosocial Approach. *Politics and the Life Sciences* 11: 35–51.

Pritchett, C. Herman. 1948. *The Roosevelt Court: A Study in Judicial Politics and Values*. New York: Macmillan.

Provine, Doris M. 1980. *Case Selection in the United States Supreme Court*. Chicago: University of Chicago Press.

Rohde, David, and Harold Spaeth. 1976. *Supreme Court Decision Making*. San Francisco: W. H. Freeman.

Rosenberg, Gerald N. 1991. *The Hollow Hope: Can Courts Bring about Social Change*. Chicago: University of Chicago Press.

Rosenberg, Gerald N. 1994. "Symposium: The Supreme Court and the Attitudinal Model." *Law and Courts* 4:1; 6–8.

Rosenthal, Albert J. 1966. Review of *The Judicial Mind*. *Political Science Quarterly* 81:448–51.

Schubert, Glendon. 1957. *The Presidency in the Courts*. Minneapolis: University of Minnesota Press.

Schubert, Glendon. 1959. *Quantitative Analysis of Judicial Behavior*. Glencoe, IL: Free Press.

Schubert, Glendon, ed. 1963. *Judicial Decision-Making*. New York: Free Press.

Schubert, Glendon, ed. 1964. *Judicial Behavior: A Reader in Theory and Research*. Chicago: Rand McNally.

Schubert, Glendon. 1965. *The Judicial Mind: The Attitudes and Ideologies of Supreme Court Justices, 1946–1963*. Evanston, IL: Northwestern University Press.

Schubert, Glendon. 1967. "Academic Ideology and the Study of Adjudication." *American Political Science Review* 61:106–29.

Schubert, Glendon. 1974. *The Judicial Mind Revisited: A Psychometric Analysis of Supreme Court Ideology*. New York: Oxford University Press.

Schubert, Glendon. 1983. "Aging, Conservatism, and Judicial Behavior." *Micropolitics* 3:135–79.

Schubert, Glendon. 1996. "The Sexual Choice of Female Primates." *Journal of Social and Evolutionary Systems* 19:293–302.

Schubert, Glendon, and David J. Danelski, eds. 1969. *Comparative Judicial Behavior: Cross-Cultural Studies of Political Decision-Making in the East and West*. New York: Oxford University Press.

Scigliano, Robert. 1971. *The Supreme Court and the Presidency*. New York: Free Press.

Segal, Jeffrey A. 1984. "Predicting Supreme Court Decisions Probabilistically: The Search and Seizure Cases, 1962–1981." *American Political Science Review* 78:891–900.

Segal, Jeffrey A. 1997. "Separation-of-Powers Games in the Positive Theory of Congress and Courts." *American Political Science Review* 91:28–44.

Segal, Jeffrey A., and Albert D. Cover. 1989. "Ideological Values and the Votes of U.S. Supreme Court Justices." *American Political Science Review* 83:557–65.

Segal, Jeffrey A., Lee Epstein, Charles M. Cameron, and Harold J. Spaeth. 1995. "Ideological Values and the Votes of U.S. Supreme Court Justices Revisited." *Journal of Politics* 57:812–23.

Segal, Jeffrey A., and Cheryl D. Reedy. 1988. "The Supreme Court and Sex Discrimination: The Role of the Solicitor General." *Western Political Quarterly* 41:553–68.

Segal, Jeffrey A., and Harold J. Spaeth. 1993. *The Supreme Court and the Attitudinal Model*. New York: Cambridge University Press.

Segal, Jeffrey A., and Harold J. Spaeth. 2002. *The Supreme Court and the Attitudinal Model Revisited*. New York: Cambridge University Press.

Somit, Albert, and Joseph Tanenhaus. 1967. *The Development of Political Science*. Boston: Allyn and Bacon.

Spiller, Pablo T., and Rafael Gely. 1992. "Congressional Control or Judicial

Independence: The Determinants of U.S. Supreme Court Labor-Relations Decisions, 1949–1988." *RAND Journal of Economics* 23:463–92.

Sprague, John D. 1968. *Voting Patterns of the United States Supreme Court; Cases in Federalism, 1889–1959*. Indianapolis: Bobbs-Merrill.

Stouffer, Samuel, Louis Guttman, Edward Suchman, Paul Lazersfeld, Shirley Star, and John Clausen. 1950. *Measurement and Prediction*. New York: Wiley, 1950.

Tanenhaus, Joseph. 1966. "The Cumulative Scaling of Judicial Decisions." *Harvard Law Review* 79:1583–94.

Truman, Harry S. 1957. Review of *The Presidency in the Court*. *Midwest Journal of Political Science* 1:92–93.

Ulmer, S. Sidney. 1972. "The Decision to Grant Certiorari as an Indicator to Decision 'On the Merits.'" *Polity* 4:429–47.

Will, George F. 1983. "Marinated in the Math of Baseball." *Washington Post*, April 7, A23.

CHAPTER 4

S. Sidney Ulmer: The Multidimensionality of Judicial Decision Making

Robert C. Bradley

What defines an individual as a *pioneer?* In reflecting on this question, Ulmer in a recent letter suggested that there are basically two ways of determining whether an individual should be so categorized.[1] First, those making the determination could choose a single individual and label her/him the *pioneer.* This determination is often based on identifying the first person either to employ a noteworthy research strategy or to study a previously unexplored but significant concern. The second way would be to select the individual in any given time period who had the greatest impact on a particular field or some substantial subset of that field. Ulmer feels that the second way might be more likely than the first to result in a probative delineation.

For my assessment of Ulmer as a pioneer in the judicial subfield, I will discuss his works in regard to their contributions for shaping our understanding of the decisional processes of the courts in this nation, particularly the Supreme Court. Within that discussion, I will point the attributes and indicators of his efforts at studying the courts that make him truly deserving of the *pioneer* label.

Ulmer demurred in response to my inquiry about the pioneering nature of his research endeavors. Basically, he stated that he would never lay claim to such a title. If others insisted on labeling him a *pioneer*, he would rather defer to their judgment. In that vein, let us proceed to an analysis of his work.

A GENERAL APPRAISAL

When considering Ulmer's published research, one is struck by just how much there is of it. At a roundtable held at the 1989 meeting of the Southern Political Science Association, a group of noted judicial scholars discussed Ulmer's contributions to the judicial subfield. One of the commentators was Tom Walker, a former student of Ulmer's, who first discussed the incredible longevity of Ulmer's academic productivity. Walker pointed out that in 1957 Ulmer started a thirty-year streak of publishing at least one book, book chapter, or article each year. In many of those years, Ulmer had several publications appear in print. For Walker, this provided more than sufficient cause to consider Ulmer not only a Babe Ruth, for the tendency to hit the judicial long ball, but also a Lou Gehrig (or now perhaps Cal Ripken), for longevity in producing valued insights about the courts.[2]

To fully appreciate these comparisons one must note that the number of publishing outlets, particularly in regard to professional journals, is much more numerous now than it was in the decades when Ulmer was most prolific. Much of Ulmer's work appeared in leading political science journals, such as the *American Political Science Review*, *Journal of Politics*, *American Journal of Political Science*, and *Law and Society Review*. Perhaps more as a result of Ulmer's efforts than of those of anyone else, political scientists were kept abreast of judicial research from the late 1950s through the 1980s.

Of course, other audiences, such as undergraduate and graduate students, were also exposed to many of Ulmer's writings by the inclusion of his articles in many edited readers on the courts. These readers were often used as either primary or supplemental texts in judicial-process and behavior courses. Ulmer either wrote original works or had reprinted articles included in readers by Schubert; Goldman and Sarat; Murphy and Pritchett; Goldman and Jahnige; Grossman and Tanenhaus; Nagel; and Glick.[3] This is not an exhaustive list of all the edited volumes focused on judicial process and behavior that featured Ulmer's works, nor does it include readers that focused on other areas of the discipline that included material by him.[4] It is noteworthy that these edited readers were published in the 1960s, 1970s, 1980s, and 1990s and that more than one or two of his articles were reprinted in these different readers. This list also does not include readers edited by Ulmer that included some of his works.[5]

Beyond the value of the amount and longevity of Ulmer's scholarly productivity for the judicial subfield is the breadth and quality of his works. As indicated, one testament to these distinctive attributes is how many of Ulmer's works were and continue to be included in numerous readers on judicial behavior. At the 1989 roundtable, the commentators on Ulmer's contributions to the judicial subfield discussed his works in three areas: certiorari, small-group theory, and microdecisional analysis. Of course, as acknowledged by the commentators, this attempt to put Ulmer's works into three distinct groups was somewhat arbitrary, because his research often overlapped between two or more of the groups.

In assessing Ulmer's contributions to research in the area of certiorari, noted public law scholar Greg Caldeira generally remarked on the impressive quantity of Ulmer's published work, the amount of attention given to his research by other scholars, and the impetus that he provided to other researchers studying the exercise of discretion in granting or denying a writ of certiorari. Caldeira also discussed several significant findings produced by Ulmer's research on certiorari.[6] These would include the impact of litigant status on Supreme Court decisions on certiorari,[7] the predictive value of justices' behavior on cert decisions for decisions on the merits,[8] and the responsiveness of dissenting votes on denials of certiorari to political divisions on the Court.[9]

Ulmer's insights about the multidimensionality of the decisional construct in the area of certiorari are also quite noteworthy. He pointed out that decision making in regard to certiorari extended well beyond just simply granting or denying writs. In deciding the cases to be heard, Ulmer argued that the Court is essentially following three separate yet intertwined agendas: the jurisdictional agenda, composed of litigants' applications for review; the plenary agenda, consisting of the cases accepted for hearing by the Court; and the issue-action agenda, including the issues in the accepted cases addressed by the Court.[10]

Ulmer also contributed significantly to our knowledge of certiorari decision making by extensively studying conflict as a predictive variable. Through his research he clarified considerably the conceptualization of conflict and provided useful guidance for other researchers about how to operationalize the concept. In one study, Ulmer defined a case where conflict was present as where one or more justices dissented and alleged a conflict between the majority decision and a previous Court ruling. Ulmer showed that conflict so defined was significantly associated with the Court's review decisions.[11]

In a later study, Ulmer focused on a much more extensive time period, employed more sophisticated statistical methods, and used a more refined conceptualization of conflict.[12] Basically, he set out to answer three questions: What is the frequency of grants and denials of review in conflict cases? How much weight is given to conflict for granting review? and Does this weight vary across different court periods? To examine these questions, Ulmer defined conflict as the presence of disagreement between federal courts of appeals or between

Supreme Court precedents. He examined the briefs of the petitioning attorneys to determine the presence of conflict. In so doing, Ulmer substantially contributed to the measurement of conflict by noting a difference between cases of genuine and alleged conflict. He pointed out that petitioning attorneys substantially padded their claims of conflict and that the number of cases where genuine conflict existed was substantially smaller than the cases where conflict was claimed. He found that genuine conflict was a statistically significant predictor— stronger than other cues commonly used in prior studies—of the Court's decision to grant review.

Ulmer also contributed to the study of cert behavior by the Court in that he was the first scholar to empirically test the reversal strategy theory as an explanation of cert voting.[13] He tested the underlying presumption of many prior studies on cert voting that justices prefer to hear cases that they want to reverse and found a significant relationship between cert voting and voting on the merits. Ulmer also demonstrated that individual justice certiorari behavior could be modeled similarly to overall Court behavior[14] and that the chief justice and his clerks have a significant impact on certiorari decisions.[15]

Ultimately, as Caldeira pointed out, one of Ulmer's primary contributions is studying certiorari in the theoretical context of access to the Supreme Court. How is access obtained? What impact does getting access to the Court have on its policy decisions? What effect does achieving access to the Court have on the national system of government and on the authoritative allocation of values? These questions greatly concerned Ulmer and continue to be of grave interest to the subfield, partly as a result of his research.[16]

In another area of concern, small-group research on the courts, Ulmer also made many significant contributions, as Tom Walker, an eminent judicial researcher, noted at the 1989 roundtable:

> Although most of his work in this area was completed two decades ago [in the 1960s and early 1970s], it was and continues to be influential. Because, when he did most of that work, the field of judicial behavior was new and standards were formative and the *pioneers* of the field at that time had a great impact.[17]

Ulmer firmly believed that U.S. appellate courts were designed to be collegial and did not become that way by accident. Furthermore, he believed that this collegial nature, particularly for the U.S. Supreme Court, was worthy of scholarly attention to assess its impact on judicial decision making.

Ulmer saw that individuals clearly behaved differently in group settings than on their own. Ulmer's research on these apparent differences
between group and individual settings for judges and justices had three
main thrusts: first, to assess how these differences were empirically
manifested in judicial behavior; second, to determine the implications
of these empirical manifestations for judicial policy-making and, more
broadly, for the legal and political systems; third, and most important,
to enhance the fledgling development of small-group theory with
regard to the courts.

In his monograph *Courts as Small and Not So Small Groups*,[18] Ulmer
discussed a variety of theoretical approaches to the analysis of small-
group behavior as manifested in the courts. Specifically, he examined
whether judges are more likely to make risky decisions (going against
prevailing norms or revealing personal biases) on a collegial court than
on their own. He also examined whether the accuracy of decisions
depended on the number of members of a particular decisional institution, such as a jury or appellate court. Ulmer discussed the formation of
subgroups as well as the flow of communication among them and
examined the influence of a collegial court setting and the exercise of
leadership on judges' choice of role. Much of the discussion in this
monograph was based on Ulmer's previous research.[19]

Throughout this body of research, Ulmer did not contend that
small-group factors either exclusively or primarily determined judicial
behavior on a collegial court. Essentially, Ulmer argued that if other
factors, based in the law, ideology, or psychological motivations, balanced each other out, then small-group determinants could rise to the
forefront in accounting for judicial decision making by an appellate
court.

These small-group determinants appear to resemble structural or
strategic considerations examined by neoinstitutionalists. As James
Gibson notes in his assessment of research on the appellate courts,
Ulmer conducted some of the few investigations of the impact of structural attributes on decision making.[20] For example, Ulmer suggested
that justices in a group setting would occasionally act strategically to
conceal their individual motivations for voting on cases.[21] In another
article, Ulmer argued that justices changed their votes in a case because
of its extreme political implications and out of a desire to protect the
Court as an institution.[22]

The final area in which Ulmer's contributions to the subfield were
discussed at the 1989 roundtable was microdecisional analysis. In discussing this area, Larry Baum, a much-published judicial scholar,

focused extensively on Ulmer's contributions to the development of theory on judicial decision making. As Baum commented, when Ulmer began his judicial scholarship, the idea of a link between Supreme Court justices' deeply held values and their decisional behavior was becoming commonly accepted. Ulmer departed from many of his fellow researchers by not simply documenting the existence of such a link but by wanting to explain why the link existed. Many of Ulmer's attempts to explain this link drew heavily from prevailing theories in the fields of psychology and communications. As Baum stated, Ulmer was distinctive in his desire "to probe the patterns of behavior in theoretical terms, to understand better what underlay them and why it was that there were these consistent seemingly value-based patterns that he had found."[23]

A related contribution that Baum noted is Ulmer's research on change in regard to the link between judicial values and decisional behavior. Ulmer not only pointed out that the direction and intensity of the link could change over time for individual justices and for the Court but also posited and tested theoretical explanations for any observed significant change.[24] Thus, Ulmer challenged prevailing views on the unidimensionality and stability of the link between values and decisions made by a Court or justices.[25]

Ultimately, Ulmer's contributions to microdecisional analysis are even more noteworthy because they are based on quite sophisticated and diverse analytical techniques. Ulmer relied on a wide variety of mathematical models and statistical techniques to conduct his analyses of theoretical propositions about judicial decision making.[26] For example, he used bivariate analysis that relied on the Gamma statistic rather than the more common correlation coefficient, linear and quadratic regression analysis, discriminant function analysis, and factor analysis. Ulmer was the first scholar to extensively discuss and apply discriminant function analysis to the study of judicial behavior.[27] He applied the Poisson statistical function to examine the probability of President Carter's experience of failing to appoint a Supreme Court justice during his term of office.[28] And he developed a quite novel method of assessing whether a change had occurred in a trend of judicial behavior, as reflected in a parabola rather than a linear measure.[29] Of course, it is quite noteworthy that Ulmer researched extensively whether static, linear representations of justices' voting behavior were sufficient to encapsulate trends in justices' behavior over extended time periods. Ultimately, Ulmer demonstrated that curvilinear representations much more adequately displayed the behavior of Supreme Court justices who served for many terms.[30]

To use these various models and techniques, Ulmer frequently had to develop measures and indexes to operationalize particular concepts. He did this either because of the lack of attention paid in prior studies to these concepts or because prior efforts to measure the concepts could be improved on. For example, Ulmer created the interindividual solidarity index to measure leadership on the Court,[31] an index to measure Court turnover,[32] a measure of subject-matter mix for Court decisions,[33] and an index to measure case complexity of Court decisions.[34] He applied the Shapely-Shubik power index, which was developed to study legislative committee behavior, to examine the exercise of power on the Supreme Court.[35] In addition, Ulmer was quite inventive in finding sources of information to utilize these models and techniques, gathering data from justices' votes, docket books, attorneys' briefs, court opinions, and personal papers.

To fully appreciate Ulmer's use of sophisticated models and techniques on a variety of data, one has to remember when he was doing the analysis. In 1960, as a result of his dissatisfaction with the lack of precision in the identification of blocs in prior studies, Ulmer used a modified form of factor analysis to select blocs on the Supreme Court. This analysis was based on the construction of a matrix of correlation coefficients and then the identification of any submatrices using certain criteria. In the same article, Ulmer used some complex indexes based on different statistics to measure leadership and power on the Court.[36] At the time, packaged data sets were not yet readily available, and computers were in their infancy. Powerful personal computers, Internet access to court information sources, and CD-ROMs of court decisions were but the stuff of dreams.

Ulmer's body of research is also notable for the fact that he basically stayed the course in examining court decisional processes. Unlike others, Ulmer concentrated his efforts, after a couple of early forays into other matters, on examining various theoretic explanations of judicial behavior, particularly as evidenced by Supreme Court justices. His research is also quite notable for reflecting the multidimensional and dynamic qualities of judges' and justices' decisions.

In his many analyses of court behavior, Ulmer demonstrated his ability to go outside of the subfield and even the discipline in the search for theoretical constructs to develop explanations. He regularly relied on theories developed in such diverse fields as communication, psychology, economics, mathematics, physics, biology, history, and philosophy. For example, in a 1969 book chapter, Ulmer cited an article from the *Scandinavian Journal of Psychology* to suggest the facial expressions of justices during oral argument as a possible focal point for those interested in studying Court behavior. Ulmer also referenced several articles in eugenics journals to support his use of a specific method of data analysis, extensively discussed findings from communications studies to bolster his theoretical approach, and related the example of the schistosome worm in the Nile Valley to illustrate his point about the interdependence of organic, psychological, and environmental states.[37] In another work, Ulmer discussed at length theories from legal philosophy, psychology, and economics to explain why limits would exist on the amount of change one could expect in judicial behavior.[38] Ulmer strongly believed that the study of decision making, whether by judges or by other political actors, could profit substantially from insights gleaned from researchers in other disciplinary perspectives.

For some, however, Ulmer's use of theoretical concepts drawn from other disciplines to help further explore the motivations of individual judges or justices is not a very fruitful method of studying judicial decision making. To pursue such a course of inquiry reduces the amount of attention available for devotion to its proper area, an examination of the internal and external institutional arrangements. Studying judges as individual decision makers motivated by their preferences without crediting institutional settings gives an incomplete picture of judicial behavior.

The preceding statements can be attributed to adherents of the new institutionalism approach to the study of the courts. Those who subscribe to new institutionalism in their depictions of the history of judicial studies typically portray Ulmer as an attitudinalist.[39] Attitudinalism is argued to be the dominant paradigm for the study of the courts in the political science discipline since the 1950s and 1960s. However, some contend that its dominance is about to end because more scholars are developing an appreciation for the importance of rules, procedures, traditions, and other institutional elements for judicial decision making.[40] Neoinstitutionalism, with its appreciation for the importance of rules and procedures, may soon become the dominant paradigm driving judicial research.

According to new institutionalists, the cornerstones for attitudinalism are that individual judges enjoy unfettered discretion in making decisions and that court policies essentially are the aggregation of individual judicial decisional choices.[41] Based on those premises, attitudinalists argue that preferences or attitudes are the primary, if not sole, determinant of judicial decisions. Thus, once a justice's attitudes are identified and subsequently linked to specific behaviors, other factors need not be studied because they would contribute little, if anything, to explaining those behaviors.[42] And the most common way of identifying justices' attitudes is to examine their votes on the merits in cases.

As one might suspect, new institutionalists use this depiction of attitudinalism as a springboard to launch a series of attacks on that approach to judicial decision making. I believe, however, that the inclusion of Ulmer in the category *attudinalist* as defined by the new institutionalists does not validly encapsulate his works or his conception of the study of the courts. Thus, the new institutionalist criticisms of attitudinalism really miss the mark in regard to Ulmer, but perhaps more importantly, they do a disservice to his contributions to the judicial subfield.

First, Ulmer would not have considered attitudinalism and new institutionalism to be contending approaches to the study of the courts. In fact, Ulmer would not have perceived attitudinalism as supplanting traditionalism or old institutionalism as *the* approach to the analysis of judicial decision-making. As Ulmer wrote,

> The political behavior orientation is not a substitute for other perspectives, but supplements the approaches to knowledge which have been and continue to be the hallmark of more traditional workways. All research into politics and government in the final analysis shares a common goal, i.e. to give meaning to the political phenomena which we experience. This is no less true of the traditional approaches with their focus on events, ideologies, institutions, and structures than of the behavioral orientation which features the analysis of personal and group behavior in a political context.[43]

This was not a onetime sentiment soon forgotten as Ulmer began to amass his considerable scholarly body of research on judicial behavior. In a much later publication, Ulmer echoed these thoughts:

> Research in Court opinions and other sources of information suggests a number of factors that influence decisions on the merits. While no list can be exhaustive, the following would be included on any list of such factors:
>
> 1. Facts and law.
> 2. Stare decisis.

3. The idiosyncratic characteristics of the justices.
4. Law clerks.
5. Small-group factors.
6. The historical, social, and political environment of the Court at the time a decision is made.[44]

Later in the same volume, Ulmer contended, "Students of constitutional law should be consciously aware that justices make decisions on the basis of law—plus other, legally extraneous considerations."[45] While the foci and methodologies of the attitudinalist and new institutionalist approaches may be quite disparate, they share a general goal of understanding political actions and a specific goal of finding more pieces of the "puzzle of judicial behavior" as aptly described in a recent book.[46] A subfield still striving to find answers to fundamental questions about court behavior does not have the luxury of dismissing any approach that might provide substantial insights about judicial decision making.

Nor does a subfield still striving to construct theories of judicial behavior have the luxury of forgetting the efforts of a scholar such as Ulmer, even though the temptation is to heap accolades on a couple of designated giants in the area and focus much attention on the findings of recent studies. By focusing primarily on studies of recent vintage, scholars end up reinventing the wheel by examining the same questions with similar results as research conducted decades earlier but forgotten with the passage of time.

SPECIFIC POINT OF DEPARTURE

To further illustrate that the label *attitudinalist* as employed by new institutionalists does not provide a complete or accurate gauge of Ulmer's record in the judicial subfield, I will discuss briefly his article "Researching the Supreme Court in a Democratic Pluralist System."[47] Given its title, the piece does not appear to fit the narrowly drawn mold of an "attitudinalist" article as configured by new institutionalists. In fact, upon a careful reading of the piece, new institutionalists may well find much with which they agree.

This article argues primarily that research conducted on the U.S. Supreme Court in the confines of the prevailing theory of politics known as democratic pluralism, as most identified in the judicial subfield with Dahl's piece on the Supreme Court as a national policymaker,[48] does not provide an adequate explanation of institutional behavior on the Court. After a brief depiction of democratic pluralism,

Ulmer contends that because it focuses almost exclusively on decisions made at the top of a studied agency, democratic pluralism conveys an incomplete picture of the agency's decisional process. Because so much attention is devoted to decisions on the merits, judicial scholars have not developed a very complete sense of the totality of the Supreme Court's function in the political system. Ulmer contends that scholars must consider and study the multitude of the Court's decisional acts to get a full appreciation of its decision making and ultimately devise explanations for its decisional process.

Ulmer presents a three-dimensional framework for analysis of the Court's exercise of power: (1) whether the power exercised can be seen and is duly noted; (2) whether the exercise of power cannot be seen as a result of institutional secrecy; and (3) whether the exercise of power could be seen except for the limitations of prevailing theory. After briefly explaining and providing examples for the first two dimensions, Ulmer launches into an extensive discussion of the third dimension, thereby pointing out a serious flaw in the prevailing theory (democratic pluralism): it blinds researchers to a number of facets of the Court's exercise of power.

To illustrate the implications of this flaw, Ulmer describes three areas of research that have received little, if any, attention from judicial scholars: summary decisions made by the Court; the selection of cases for plenary consideration; and issue fluidity, which refers to the Court's manipulation of issues presented in petitioners' briefs for plenary review. According to Ulmer (writing in 1979), more research into each of these areas was needed to obtain a fuller appreciation of the Court's conflict-management function in reflecting the social balance of power between competing groups.[49]

Ulmer concludes the article by arguing that to obtain a more complete perspective on the Supreme Court's role in the American political system, we have to lose the blinders imposed by democratic-pluralist theory and look beyond the Court's decisions on the merits. To hold the Court accountable within a democratic framework, we must consider all of its decisions. Also, if meaningful comparisons are to be made between the Court and other decisional institutions, multiple decisional situations in the different institutions must be examined.

This article illustrates quite aptly that Ulmer shares some of the same concerns as the new institutionalists in regard to the study of the Supreme Court. He is interested in developing a better appraisal of the Court's role in the political system. He is concerned about understanding how the Court performs its institutional functions of conflict management and dispute processing in dealing with the demands from various societal groups. How the Court exercises power and how it is held accountable for that exercise of power are also important to Ulmer.

For Ulmer, analysis exclusively based on decisions on the merits cannot provide an adequate explanation of Court behavior. Such analysis yields an extremely limited view of Court decision making. That seems to closely resemble the new institutionalists' primary critique of attitudinalists.

Further, the article displays some of Ulmer's pioneer attributes: his devotion to the development of theory in regard to Supreme Court behavior, his willingness and ability to spark the efforts of others to research various facets of Court decision making, and his ability to concisely summarize the direction and flaws of a research agenda and then suggest specific new approaches for collecting and analyzing information. All are the traits of a pioneer.

CONCLUSION

Because of the number of his publications and the extended time period over which they appeared, Ulmer continues to profoundly impact the judicial subfield. The breadth and quality of those publications—specifically, those dealing with certiorari decisions, small-group theory, and microdecisional analysis—obviously enhance that impact. Ulmer's pioneering theoretical developments and methodological refinements still guide and stimulate others in their research efforts on the courts.[50]

For direct exposure to his insights, writing mastery, and inventiveness, one should read several of Ulmer's writings. One then can appreciate his ability to turn a phrase, make very sophisticated analysis comprehensible, and incorporate ideas and concepts from a wide range of intellectual traditions.

Ultimately, the value of recounting the past efforts of a pioneer such as Ulmer is twofold. First, doing so provides a reminder of the individual's contributions so that others can build on her/his efforts. Second, understanding past efforts makes it possible to heed the pioneer's advice in regard to further inquiry. In this vein, Ulmer would probably state that instead of disparaging the works of those from disparate approaches, the subfield should adopt a much more eclectic perspective. Judicial scholars can fruitfully draw on the research findings produced not only by those of different theoretical orientations in the subfield but also by those elsewhere in the political science discipline and even in other academic disciplines. To paraphrase an old adage, Minds, like parachutes, work best when open."

NOTES

1. Ulmer to author, May 16, 2000.

2. Transcript of remarks at a roundtable in honor of S. Sidney Ulmer, annual meeting of the Southern Political Science Association, Memphis, Tennessee, November 3, 1989, p. 12.

3. Glendon Schubert, ed., *Judicial Decision-Making* (New York: Free Press of Glencoe, 1963); Glendon Schubert, ed., *Judicial Behavior: A Reader in Theory and Research* (Chicago: Rand McNally, 1964); Sheldon Goldman and Austin Sarat, eds., *American Court Systems: Readings in Judicial Process and Behavior* (San Francisco: W. H. Freeman, 1978; 2d ed., New York: Longman, 1989); Walter F. Murphy and C. Herman Pritchett, eds., *Courts, Judges, and Politics: An Introduction to the Judicial Process*, 2d ed. (New York: Random House, 1974); Sheldon Goldman and Thomas P. Jahnige, comps., *The Federal Judicial System: Readings in Process and Behavior* (New York: Holt, Rinehart, and Winston, 1968); Joel B. Grossman and Joseph Tanenhaus, eds., *Frontiers of Judicial Research* (New York: John Wiley, 1969); Stuart S. Nagel, ed., *Modeling the Criminal Justice System* (Beverly Hills, CA: Sage, 1977); Henry R. Glick, ed., *Courts in American Politics: Readings and Introductory Essays* (New York: McGraw-Hill, 1990).

4. See, for example, the serial *Mathematical Applications in Political Science*.

5. Ulmer, ed., *Introductory Readings in Political Behavior* (Chicago: Rand McNally, 1961); Ulmer, ed., *Courts, Law, and Judicial Processes* (New York: Free Press, 1981).

6. Transcript of remarks, 4–5, 7.

7. For example, Ulmer, "Selecting Cases for Supreme Court Review: An Underdog Model," *American Political Science Review* 72 (1978): 902–10.

8. For example, Ulmer, "The Decision to Grant Certiorari as an Indicator to Decision on the Merits," *Journal of Politics* 35 (1973): 286–310.

9. For example, Ulmer and William Nichols, "Changing Patterns of Conflict: Dissent to Denial of Review in the Burger Court," *Journal of Political Science* 7 (1979): 1–23.

10. Ulmer, "Issue Fluidity in the Supreme Court," in *Supreme Court Restraint and Activism*, ed. Charles Lamb and Stephen C. Halpern (New York: D. C. Heath, 1981), 322.

11. Ulmer, "Conflict with Supreme Court Precedent and the Granting of Plenary Review," *Journal of Politics* 45 (1983): 474–78.

12. Ulmer, "The Supreme Court's Certiorari Decisions: 'Conflict' as a Predictive Variable," *American Political Science Review* 78 (1984): 901–11.

13. See Jeffrey A. Segal and Harold J. Spaeth, *The Supreme Court and the Attitudinal Model* (New York: Cambridge University Press, 1993), which references Ulmer's "The Decision to Grant Certiorari as an Indicator to Decision 'On the Merits,'" *Polity* 4 (1972): 429–47.

14. Ulmer, "Modeling the Decisions of Supreme Court Justices: Some Deductive Approaches," in *Modeling the Criminal Justice System*, ed. Nagel.

15. Ulmer, "The Decision to Grant or Deny Certiorari: Further Considerations of Cue Theory," *Law and Society Review* 6 (1972): 637–44.

16. See, for example, Dorothy Marie Provine, "Deciding What to Decide: How the Supreme Court Sets Its Agenda," *Judicature* 64 (1981): 320–33; Gregory A. Caldeira and John Wright, "Organized Interests and Agenda Setting in the U.S. Supreme Court," 82 *American Political Science Review* 82 (1988): 1109–27; H. W. Perry Jr., *Deciding to Decide: Agenda Setting in the United States Supreme Court* (Cambridge: Harvard University Press, 1991).

17. Transcript of remarks, 12.

18. Ulmer, *Courts as Small and Not So Small Groups* (New York: General Learning Press, 1971).

19. For example, Ulmer, "Leadership in the Michigan Supreme Court," in *Judicial Decision-Making*, ed. Schubert; Ulmer, "Toward a Theory of Sub-Group Formation in the United States Supreme Court," *Journal of Politics* 27 (1965): 133–52; Ulmer, "The Use of Power in the Supreme Court: The Opinion Assignments of Earl Warren, 1953–1960," *Journal of Public Law* 19 (1970): 49–67.

20. James Gibson, "Decision Making in Appellate Courts," in *The American Courts: A Critical Assessment*, ed. John B. Gates and Charles A. Johnson (Washington, DC: CQ Press, 1991), 267.

21. Ulmer, "Selecting Cases for Supreme Court Review."

22. Ulmer, "Earl Warren and the Brown Decision," *Journal of Politics* 33 (1971): 689–702.

23. Transcript of remarks, 25, 26.

24. For example, see Ulmer, "Homeostatic Tendencies in the United States Supreme Court," in *Introductory Readings in Political Behavior*, ed. Ulmer; Ulmer, "Parabolic Support of Civil Liberty Claims: The Case of William O. Douglas," *Journal of Politics* 41 (1979): 634–39.

25. See Ulmer, "The Dimensionality of Judicial Voting Behavior," *Midwest Journal of Political Science* 13 (1969): 471–83; Ulmer, "Dimensionality and Change in Judicial Behavior," in *Mathematical Applications in Political Science* 7 (1974): 59–81.

26. See Ulmer, "Mathematical Models for Predicting Judicial Behavior," *Mathematical Applications in Political Science* 3 (1967): 67–95; Ulmer, "The Discriminant Function and a Theoretical Context for Its Use in Estimating the Votes of Judges," in *Frontiers*, ed. Grossman and Tanenhaus.

27. Ulmer, "Mathematical Models," 84; for explanations of this type of analysis, see Ulmer, "Discriminant Function," 352–56; Ulmer, "Supreme Court's Certiorari Decisions," 907–8.

28. Ulmer, "Supreme Court Appointments as a Poisson Distribution," *American Journal of Political Science* 26 (1982): 113–16.

29. Ulmer, "Parabolic Support."

30. Ibid.; Ulmer, "The Longitudinal Behavior of Hugo Lafayette Black: Parabolic Support for Civil Liberties, 1937–1971," *Florida State University Law Review* 1 (1973): 131–53.

31. Ulmer, "The Analysis of Behavior Patterns in the United States Supreme Court," *Journal of Politics* 22 (1960): 629–53.

32. Ulmer, "Exploring the Dissent Patterns of the Chief Justices: John Marshall to Warren Burger," in *Judicial Conflict and Consensus*, ed. Sheldon Goldman and Charles M. Lamb (Lexington: University Press of Kentucky, 1986).

33. Ulmer, "Parabolic Support."

34. Ulmer, "Exploring the Dissent Patterns."

35. Ulmer, "Analysis of Behavior Patterns."

36. Ibid.

37. Ulmer, "Discriminant Function."

38. Ulmer, "Dimensionality and Change."

39. See Forrest Maltzman, James F. Spriggs II, and Paul J. Wahlbeck, "Strategy and Judicial Choice: New Institutionalist Approaches to Supreme Court Decision-Making," in *Supreme Court Decision-Making: New Institutionalist Approaches*, ed. Cornell W. Clayton and Howard Gillman (Chicago: University of Chicago Press, 1999), 45; Cornell Clayton and Howard Gillman, introduction to *The Supreme Court in American Politics: New Institutionalist Perspectives*, ed. Gillman and Clayton (Lawrence: University Press of Kansas, 1999), 1.

40. For example, Cornell W. Clayton, "The Supreme Court and Political Jurisprudence: New and Old Institutionalisms," in *Supreme Court Decision-Making*, ed. Clayton and Gillman, 22–35.

41. Maltzman, Spriggs, and Wahlbeck, "Strategy and Judicial Choice," 44.

42. For support of this assessment, see Lawrence Baum, *The Supreme Court*, 6th ed. (Washington, DC: CQ Press, 1998), 150, which states, "Some scholars argue that the justices' policy preference are essentially a complete explanation of the Court's decisions." He cites Jeffrey A. Segal and Harold J. Spaeth, *The Supreme Court and the Attitudinal Model* (New York: Cambridge University Press, 1993), as reflective of such scholarship.

43. Ulmer, introduction to *Introductory Readings in Political Behavior*, ed. Ulmer, 1.

44. Ulmer, *Supreme Court Policymaking and Constitutional Law* (New York: McGraw-Hill, 1986), 23.

45. Ibid., 30.

46. Lawrence Baum, *The Puzzle of Judicial Behavior* (Ann Arbor: University of Michigan Press, 1997).

47. Ulmer, "Researching the Supreme Court in a Democratic Pluralist System," *Law and Policy Quarterly* 1 (1979): 53–80.

48. Robert A. Dahl, "Decision Making in a Democracy: The Supreme Court as a National Policy Maker," *Journal of Public Law* 6 (1956): 279–95.

49. For examples of such research, see n.16.

50. For example, see Kevin T. McGuire and Barbara Palmer, "Issue Fluidity on the U.S. Supreme Court," *American Political Science Review* 89 (1995): 691–702.

CHAPTER 5

Harold J. Spaeth:
The Supreme Court Computer

Sara C. Benesh

While Glendon Schubert may have been the father of the attitudinal model, it seems safe to assert that Harold J. Spaeth was the dutiful son who, through his hard work, made the business more successful. His is the name most closely affiliated with the attitudinal model of judicial decision making, perhaps because he has been its strongest proponent. No one has been as unequivocal in his devotion to this paradigm of political jurisprudence as Spaeth, and his stalwart demeanor has demanded that scholars of judicial behavior at least contend with its existence. There have been more than 600 citations to the work of Spaeth and two of his coauthors (see table 1)—135 to *The Supreme Court and the Attitudinal Model* alone—and there is scarcely an article written on the behavior of judges that does not in some way deal with the view that they behave ideologically. Even the press is now discussing the party of the appointing president as a relevant consideration in predicting the vote of a given judge, in large part as a result of the prevalence of the attitudinal model in judicial politics.

Through correspondence between Schubert and Spaeth and extensive interviews with Spaeth, we can trace the genesis of the attitudinal movement and thereby better understand what motivated the attitudinal model. The idea that justices' decisions are influenced by their preferred policy positions will be critically examined and its contribution to current scholarship discussed. I also evaluate the other most important contribution of Spaeth to judicial politics: his Supreme Court Judicial Databases. Scarcely a quantitative article produced in the last decade has failed to avail itself of this data source, and the existence of the data has no doubt shaped the way we study the nation's highest court. Has this influence been completely positive, or has the availability of this data stymied research into other fruitful areas?

TABLE 1.   Citations to Spaeth's Work, 1977–2000

Work	Number of Citations
U.S. Supreme Court Databases	59
AJPS 40: Influence of Stare Decisis	19
AJPS 32: Majority Opinion Assignments	13
AJPS 23: Access to the Federal Courts	10
AJPS 15: Analysis and Interp of Dimensionality	12
AJPS 8: Judicial Restraint of Mr. Justice Frankfurter	7
AJPS 6: Judicial Power	15
APQ 16: Ideological Position	3
Annals of the SPSA	4
Behavioral Science: Unidimensionality	11
Contemplating Courts Chapter: The Attitudinal Model	9
Essential Safeguard Chapter: Sandra Day O'Connor	1
Introduction to Supreme Court Decision Making	3
JOP 60: Do Political Preferences Change	2
JOP 57: Ideological Values	19
JOP 55: Ideological Patterns	2
JOP 54: Business Decisions of the Burger Court	5
JOP 27: Jurimetrics and Professor Mendelson	2
JOP 25: Analysis of Judicial Attitudes	15
Journal of Psychology: Effects of Attitudes Toward Situation	5
Judicature 75: Examining an Analogy	5
Judicature 74: Rehnquist Court Disposition	4
Judicature 73: Decisional Trends	10
Judicature 72: Ideology, Strategy and Supreme Court Decisions	6
Judicature 69: If a Supreme Court Vacancy Occurs	6
Judicature 68: Supreme Court Disposition of Federal Court	4
Judicature 68: Burger Court Review of State Court	4
Judicature 67: Distributive Justice	21
Judicial Conflict and Consensus Chapter: Felix Frankfurter	3
Judicial Decision Making Chapter: Warren Court Attitudes	17
Jurimetrics 26: Measuring Power	2
Majority Rule or Minority Will	7
MJPS 5: An Approach to the Study of Attitudinal Differences	5
Multivariate Behavioral Research: Use and Utility	18
Polity 23: Increasing the Size	12
Predicament of Modern Politics	5
Studies in U.S. Supreme Court Behavior	6
Supreme Court Activism and Restraint Chapter	16
Supreme Court and the Attitudinal Model	136
Supreme Court Decision Making	95
Supreme Court Policy Making	30
Warren Court	1
WPQ 44: Voting Fluidity	6
WPQ 42: Defection of the Marginal Justice	7
WPQ 39: Issue Specialization	5
WPQ 38: Influence Relationships	7
WPQ 36: Denial of Access	5
Total Citations	659

Note: This listing taken from the *Social Science Citation Index.* These are citations only to the single-authored work of Spaeth, the coauthored work listing Spaeth as first author, and the two most significant coauthored books, Rohde and Spaeth (1976) and Segal and Spaeth (1973). The listing, therefore, is not complete.

THE ADVENT OF
THE ATTITUDINAL MODEL

One would be hard-pressed to find a public law scholar, a law school professor, or a judicial behavioralist who could not define the attitudinal model. In short, it contends that justices decide cases according to their attitudes in light of the facts of the case. Spaeth is rightly included as a pioneer in this area, as his most influential works have been on Supreme Court decision making; all of his writings contend (or at least conclude) that justices decide cases in accordance with their attitudes. As early as 1965 in *An Introduction to Supreme Court Decision Making*, a tiny volume, Spaeth argued that "Justices are freer than other political actors to base their decisions solely upon personal policy preferences" (63) and provided cumulative scales to prove this contention. With David W. Rohde in 1976, he reaffirmed this position, synthesizing what is now known as the attitudinal model and discussing some strategic accounts of Supreme Court decision making as well. And in 1993, he solidified the case for attitudinal theory in *The Supreme Court and the Attitudinal Model*, written with Jeffrey A. Segal, Spaeth's former student. This work gained even international recognition as a book that Supreme Court scholars should have "constantly by their side" (Hodder-Williams 1994, 522). He continues to argue for the influence of attitudes in Supreme Court decision making, and he and Segal have recently published a revision to his affectionately abbreviated *SCAM*, which he has dubbed *SCAMR—The Supreme Court and the Attitudinal Model Revisited*.

SCAM has received considerable attention and considerable praise. It is said to be "the best work to date on the Attitudinal Model" (Rosenberg 1994, 6), "an invaluable summary of a wide range of empirical work on the Court" (Smith 1994, 8), and a "landmark work" (Gibson 1999, 10). It has also been called "the best of judicial politics scholarship" (Hall 1995, 255) and "a fine and important book" (Caldeira 1994, 486). According to Canon, it is "THE compilation of attitudinal research and THE exposition of the attitudinal model" (1993, 100). The book is enjoyable both for its content and for its style. The language is rife with well-chosen (and large) words and is written in Spaeth's characteristically colorful prose. Hall says that *SCAM* "is exceedingly well written. The witty and sometimes sarcastic comments interspersed throughout the book make it quite enjoyable to read, no small accomplishment for a scientific text" (1995, 255). Of course, the style is not universally appreciated, characterized by Rosenberg as being "marred by numerous disrespectful *ad hominem* attacks" (1994, 7) and criticized by Smith as being "shrill" and "hectoring" in tone (1994, 8).

What is perhaps most remarkable about the attitudinal model, though, is what it is that the legal model is not: the attitudinal model is testable, has been tested, and is empirically verifiable. No one has done with the legal model what Spaeth and company have done with the attitudinal model. Indeed, this is one of Spaeth's major criticisms of the legal model: it is not falsifiable. He has taken great pains to ensure that the attitudinal model has indeed been rigorously tested.

When asked how he came to suspect that attitudes affect Supreme Court decision making, Spaeth cites Schubert's *Quantitative Analysis* (1959) and Spaeth's own reading of the cases. While he had no undergraduate courses in political science, after receiving his doctorate in the field, Spaeth turned his attention to learning quantitative methods of political science and to understanding Supreme Court decision making in the context of these methods. Schubert's book was a major influence on Spaeth, and he maintains that it is the single best, most influential work in public law (2000). That he and Schubert were in touch during the early years of the behavioral revolution and were promoting the idea that judges decide their cases ideologically is probably quite important to the prevalence the attitudinal model now enjoys.

Indeed, there were times when the scholarly community not only resisted the idea of political jurisprudence but also actively fought it. "I took my lumps," says Spaeth, telling stories of conferences during which scholars literally screamed at Schubert's suggestion that judges are political. Spaeth recalls one such meeting in New York in 1960 where the panel was a "lynch mob" (2000). People were appalled that Schubert would denigrate the Court in such a manner. Indeed, the correspondence between the two men in the early 1960s exemplifies the monumental struggle in which they were engaged. Spaeth answered Schubert's lament about the legal profession's reaction to his work:

> I couldn't agree with you more about law professors. Although one expects rather heated argument between those of different ideological and methodological persuasions, the legalists' vehemence goes far beyond rational response. Their overreaction is of classic dimensions. They are, par excellence, the psychopaths of the academic world. Living in a fairyland where they alone have access to and understanding of the oracular pronouncements emanating from the holy of holies, they are mightily afraid of toppling from their pedestals and frustrated at their inability to re-

create the good old slot machine theory days. They comprise, I would say, academe's equivalent of the John Birch Society. Unfortunately, too many members of the Neanderthal claque occupy positions in political science (oops!—pardon me, I mean GOVERNMENT departments). And you seem well on the way to becoming their *bête noir*–in–chief. . . . In connection with the foregoing, I wonder what the reaction of Wallace Mendelson, Helen Shirley Thomas, Harvard Law faculty, and other assorted Frankfurter deifiers is to the recent fracases between God and C. J. Warren. My reaction is that it couldn't have happened to a more deserving bunch. (May 8, 1961)

Spaeth's mention here of the "Frankfurter deifiers" is no doubt a reference to the discovery of ideological behavior in the most self-described "restrained" of the justices. It may be assumed that many took issue with his 1964 article "The Judicial Restraint of Mr. Justice Frankfurter—Myth or Reality?" in which he shows that in cases involving federal regulatory commissions and cases invoking concerns over federalism, Frankfurter was anything but restraintist. In fact, Spaeth finds that "analysis of behavior in the state action and regulatory commission cases regulatory of labor unions and business precludes a judgement that Frankfurter adheres to the canons of judicial restraint. On the evidence, he votes as do the majority of his colleagues—compatibly with their attitudes toward business and labor unions" (37).

Speaking of a 1965 colloquium he gave at Michigan State University, Spaeth tells Schubert, "From the comments and questions from some of the colleagues, a political approach to the Court is still somewhat suspect, but not nearly so much as the questions I got at the APSA panel seemed to indicate. . . . I think we still have a struggle on our hands as far as the legal fraternity's acceptance of the behavioral approach is concerned, to put the matter mildly" (February 1, 1965).

Schubert also described his experiences with the absolute refusal to accept the attitudinal mode of Supreme Court decision making:

Mendelson and I were on a panel together at the Southern Pol. Assn. Meeting in New Orleans earlier this month. He was supposed to comment upon papers by Joe Tanenhaus and by Hans Baade (of the Duke law school) but he spoke only for *less* than two minutes, literally growling that behavioralists didn't know anything, with all of their elaborate techniques, that any intelligent observer in general, and he in particular, hadn't known in advance. Period. He said not another word until, after the formal presentation by the panel, Joe Tanenhaus was responding to the first question from the audience; and Wally stood up suddenly and strode ostentatiously down the center aisle and made his exit. There is no hope that he will be converted; but I think he has signed off. He is through fighting, I believe, and is out of it from here on. (Incidentally 5CA judge John Minor Wisdom sat through the whole session, and remarked (with seeming sincerity, although maybe it was just Southern courtesy) afterwards to me that he had enjoyed the discussion very much. He has a high regard for Ken Vines, who invited him to attend.) (November 30, 1967)

While dispute over the pervasiveness of the attitudinal model continues today, no one now studying the Court could presume to understand its decisions without reference to its attitudinal makeup, and certainly no one would find mention of ideology and judging in the same sentence abhorrent. This is a testament to the work of Schubert and Spaeth. Indeed, while the legal community may still be among the most reticent, one noted legal scholar asserts, "If legal scholars fail to confront the attitudinal model, the resultant legal research will appear increasingly irrelevant" (Cross 1997, 254).

CRITICISM OF THE ATTITUDINAL MODEL

That the debate is not fierce does not mean that it has abated. Many scholars still take issue with the attitudinal model as prescribed by Spaeth, and many different criticisms have been or might be leveled at it. While mechanical jurisprudence has been laid to rest, it is not at all settled that there is *no* room for law in judicial decision making. Indeed, many people argue that these are indeed judges, after all, so their behavior must differ from those of legislators, for example (Pritchett 1969). However, the attitudinal model espoused by Spaeth has most often been, in his eyes, complete and irrefutable. Perhaps largely by design, *SCAM*, probably the strongest presentation of the attitudinal model, presented a "clear target" for those opposed to such an absolute reading of the ways in which judges make their decisions, and many scholars have, as a result, opted to take a shot at it (Caldeira 1994, 486).

The first and probably most frequent criticism with regard to the debate between the attitudinal and the legal models is that Spaeth et al. never really define the legal model in any sort of defensible way. In other words, the legal model presented by Spaeth (1979) and later by Segal and Spaeth (1993) is a straw man. In a review of *Supreme Court Policy Making*, Schmidhauser says, "How refreshing (and realistic) it would be to treat the essential duality of American attitudes toward the Supreme Court and other major federal and state judicial institutions" (1980, 218). Reviewing *SCAM*, Caldeira complains, "They really do not set up any realistic competitor to their model of decision making. I can think of no political scientist who would take plain meaning, intent of the framers, and precedent as good explanations of what the justices do in making decisions. . . . If there is no position other than the attitudinal model and the silly formalism of the legal model, the debate is over" (1994, 485). Canon also worries over the applicability of Spaeth's legal model, arguing that it differs greatly from the one against which Spaeth and Schubert so vehemently fought in the 1960s (1993, 98). Hall agrees, noting that the "legal model that they present is somewhat oversimplified and perhaps does not reflect the full range of considerations that legal theorists would deem important to justices rendering decisions (1995, 254). Rosenberg (1994) argues for a "Legal Model Properly Understood," in which judges have an interpretive philosophy that they follow, and finds support for such a model in *SCAM* itself. "No judge or scholar believes" the legal model espoused by Segal and Spaeth, according to Rosenberg (1994, 7), and, according to Smith (1994), Berger and Bork, cited in *SCAM* as adherents to the legal model presented by Spaeth, only wish the Court would act that way.

Conversely, even noted legal scholars admit to some semblance of the legal model at work in legal scholarship. Cross notes that while strict legal formalism, as he calls it, has gone by the wayside, there remains an interest in some of the claims of the legal model. Strict legal formalism contends that the "path of the law can be identified through reasoned analysis of factors internal to the law[, that] reasoning was central, but reason was superimposed upon common law precedents or statutory texts[, leaving] no room for any judicial individuality, much less any expression of judicial ideology (1997, 255). While he believes that few law professors would admit to being strict formalists, Cross does argue that "a basic formalism pervades legal writing and is difficult to escape" (261). Textual interpretation and precedent remain at the core of judicial decision making, according to adherents to this legal model, making law a constraint on decision making. There may be some political decisions, but they are the exception, not the rule.

Other criticisms concern the "bluntness" of the attitudinal model presented by Spaeth and company. Caldeira says that it is not as simple as "I have policy preference A, so I will enact it." Rather, "the justices maximize their policy preference under the constraints of law, policy, and custom" (1994, 485). While this maximization and the reality of constraints do show up in some of Spaeth's work, it seems that his over-statement of the role of attitudes can be blamed for the reluctance of some to subscribe to his viewpoint. Indeed, that the opinions written by the judges may indeed "merely rationalize decisions" (Segal and Spaeth 1993, 66) does not mean that they do not have legal meaning. The requirement that a judge couch his or her opinion in precedent and legal reasoning may indeed preclude certain outcomes, and that may be a real constraint (Cross 1997). There may also be attitudes about the law that are not examined by attitudinalists. It does appear to be the case that justices differ over the interpretation of certain provisions of the Constitution. (Justice Black in First Amendment cases comes immediately to mind.) Yes, their disagreements can sometimes be char-acterized by liberalism or conservatism, but doesn't it matter that the disagreement is over constitutional interpretation and not merely over the outcome? Perhaps legal attitudes and political attitudes are corre-lated (as with Black and free speech). The attitudinal model does not disentangle those effects (Cross 1997). Perhaps therein lies the effect of the legal model, in variables collinear with the attitudes we so often use as causal factors in decision making. In addition, perhaps legal values trump political values, at least sometimes and for some justices. Cross (1997) offers a nice analogy: attitudinalists wish to show that attitudes matter to judges but would not do so at the cost of valid, reliable, sci-entific research. So too may judges care about political outcomes but would not seek them at the cost of legal integrity.

The maximization of preferences may also be overstated here. Per-haps judges seek to maximize other things, such as leisure, good rela-tions with colleagues, or personal safety (Posner 1995). Justices may also be constrained by things other than the law: jurisdictional rules or the anticipated votes of their colleagues (Knight 1994). And, just maybe, they are concerned with their legitimacy, which would be dam-aged were they to decide cases based wholly on policy preferences. Of course, Spaeth's response to all of this is, "Where's the evidence?" (2000).

Circularity criticisms also are often asserted against the attitudinal model. Critics argue that using past votes to predict future votes is inherently circular. Something caused the Court to vote Z in case X. Later, case Y is decided, and we predict from case X that the justices will again make decision Z. But, what caused the justices to choose decision

Z in case X? The attitudinal model never tells us, or at least we were not so told until its adherents began to search for external measurements of attitudes. Segal and Spaeth attempt to defend themselves against this concern in *SCAM* (1993, 361), but they seem to entirely miss the point. They argue that because they use past cases to predict future cases, no circularity results. While this is not the level of circularity employed in the days of using votes to construct scales and then using those scales to explain decision making, it remains problematic. By saying merely that justices will decide a certain way because that is how they have decided in the past continues to beg the question of why they decided that way. If we assume attitudes, fine, as long as we are clear that attitudes are an assumption. Baum (1994) goes even further, arguing that neither the Segal/Cover scores nor past votes truly tap personal policy preferences; rather, they demonstrate only some behavioral consistency that might be the result of any number of stimuli.

Unanimous cases are not explained or predicted via the attitudinal model either, which is another cause for concern for those who wish to find an explanation for judicial decision making writ large. If we exclude a large proportion of cases from our analysis, claiming that we cannot predict or explain them because of their unanimity, we are certainly missing a large part of the behavior of the Supreme Court. We are then left guessing what happened in those cases. We may posit, for example, that the unanimous decisions are the "easy" ones, but in so doing perhaps we forget *Brown v. Board of Education*. We might argue that these are cases in which there is a clear precedent and therefore a clear outcome, but if that were true, why would the justices take such a case? Perhaps we are led to the conclusion that the justices just do not have attitudes in certain issue or legal areas. This potential explanation has promise, but the possibility of a lack of attitude seems impossible when reading Spaeth's work. This failure to offer some analysis of the Court's unanimous cases surely is a serious one.

In a related matter, Cross (1997) suggests that some cases are easily resolved based entirely on legal principles. This is especially true at levels lower than the U.S. Supreme Court. Focusing on nonunanimous cases or on controversial issue areas, as some of Spaeth's work does, misses these easy cases, thereby underestimating the strength of the legal model. Again though, Spaeth (2000) asks for documentation of such cases.

Sole attention to the Supreme Court has been another concern about Spaeth's work. Many critics argue that judges are able to vote their preferences explicitly because of the Court's unique institutional setup. The argument then turns to the importance of a theory that deals only with one admittedly unique court. While Segal and Spaeth are careful to note that the attitudinal model has not been systematically extended to the lower courts or to the courts of other nations, they suggest that identifying and measuring the attitudes of other judges in light of their institutional constraints should have utility. Still, critics lament the single-minded attention Spaeth has given to this one court, perhaps wishing that he would use his energies elsewhere and more broadly. However, because of the Court's primacy and its extensive role in U.S. society, Spaeth has repeatedly defended his choice of subject. Indeed, he contends (2000) that we are still ignorant about many aspects of the high court.

Not only has Spaeth concentrated on the Supreme Court, but he has also concentrated, in large part, on case outcomes. Because of this concentration, his database uses the case as its unit of analysis. Many critics argue that to fully test the attitudinal model, one must analyze the votes of the individual justices (see, for example, Gibson 1999). Spaeth has recognized this problem and is in the process of converting his database to one wherein justices may be analyzed individually. I discuss this in more detail in the section on Spaeth's premiere quantitative contribution to the field, his databases.

Another question that has been raised about the attitudinal model is whether it is a model or a theory at all or just a means to predict the outcomes of Court cases. In other words, does the attitudinal model add to the explanation of and understanding of decision making? That the justices use their attitudes to decide cases still does not tell us why they might do so. Institutional arguments assuredly can be made for the prevalence of attitudes, and Spaeth makes those arguments. But if justices use their attitudes, what are attitudes, how do we measure them, and why are we surprised that they matter? Might they not matter exactly because justices care about legal reasoning and precedent and the intent of the framers but because they do so differentially? It seems that while empirically, the attitudinal model may arguably have had the greatest impact of any model of judicial behavior, theoretically it is lacking. Indeed, theory is probably Spaeth's weakest area. He has always seen theory building as an inductive exercise and prediction as the ultimate goal. Some observers believe this a dangerous way in which to proceed. Chalmers, for example, argues that "observation statements do not constitute a firm basis on which scientific knowledge can be founded because they are fallible" (1982, 32). He further contends that theories based on induction have "increasingly failed to throw new and interesting light on the nature of science" (36). Perhaps there will be a Court that simply does not fit the attitudinal model. While we might now adhere to the model, there may be a time and an institutional setup that would preclude justices from so deciding. Therefore, as an overarching model of judicial decision making, the attitudinal model, no matter how predictive it is now, may fail. Bueno de Mesquita warns, "Too often we confuse empiricism with theory construction" (1985, 128). Krasner agrees: "Bueno de Mesquita's endorsement of deduction is a more than welcome contribution in a field in which rank empiricism has long held an accepted if not honored place. The behavioral revolution was strongly informed by a new positive, empiricist, and justificationalist epistemology" (1985, 142). Isn't this exactly what the attitudinal model does?

Of course, inductive modes of theory building do have their adherents. Indeed, King, Keohane, and Verba suggest that "theory and data interact" (1994, 46). One might also argue, as Cross does, that the attitudinal model derives from rational choice theory, which seems to make sense. After all, the attitudinal model does indeed argue that judges make their decisions in such a way as to maximize their policy preferences. That the theory may have come from the data, therefore, may be less important than how well the theory does indeed predict and perhaps explain Supreme Court decision making, although many critics argue that the theory only does the former (Smith 1994). Baum argues that while it is common and perhaps acceptable to argue that predicting is the most important criterion of a good theory, he deems such a single goal as unsatisfying: such a solely predictive model does not really explain behavior or provide a "full account" of it (1998, 4). Still, contributions have been made by looking first to the data. Perhaps this is not a completely indefensible way to proceed, especially when Spaeth has provided access to very good data.

THE IMPACT OF
THE ATTITUDINAL MODEL

That the attitudinal model is much debated does not mean that it has not had an impact. As mentioned earlier, it is an unusual article on the courts, especially on the Supreme Court, that does not discuss the possibility of the influence of attitudes on all aspects of decision making. Indeed, citations to Segal and Spaeth (1993), Rohde and Spaeth (1976), and other writings by Spaeth suggest that much work has been influenced by the model of decision making advanced by Spaeth and the attitudinalists. Even work on the lower courts has been influenced by Spaeth. Indeed, the suggestion that perhaps attitudes, tempered by institutional constraints, matter even to lower-court decision making has been confirmed in recent research (see, for example, Songer, Segal, and Cameron 1994). In terms of mere citations, table 1 shows that Spaeth's big attitudinal works are his most cited: *SCAM* was cited 136 times in only seven years; *Supreme Court Decision Making* was cited 95 times; and *Supreme Court Policy Making* was cited 30 times. And looking at mere citations surely underestimates influence, as his work may have motivated many scholars to conduct studies without occasion to actually cite Spaeth.

Of course, many studies have been conducted in attempts to refute the model, thereby lending credence to the view that Spaeth's work has been influential. The true test of the power of an argument is whether other scholars go out of their way to discredit it. Perhaps none has taken the call to refute the attitudinal model more earnestly than Spaeth himself, who, with Brenner and then with Segal, attempted to empirically test the legal model before others did. In *Stare Indecisis* (1995), Spaeth and Brenner argue, "Perhaps it is time to stop asserting that legal variables are obviously important in the Court's decision-making. Perhaps it is time to start testing whether these variables are, in fact, important" (111). The authors attempt to model the decision to formally alter precedent, finding that attitudes rather than legal considerations explain overruling. In an *American Journal of Political Science* workshop and later in the award-winning *Majority Rule or Minority Will* (1999), Spaeth and Segal attempt to apply the vigorous testing they have focused on the attitudinal model to another aspect of the legal model, adherence to precedent. They find, not surprisingly to them, that little evidence supports this aspect of the legal model. However, that they were among the first to try to empirically falsify the claim that precedent matters to Supreme Court justices and constrains their decision making is a testament to the fact that, while many scholars may consider Spaeth an ideologue, blind to any other view of Supreme Court decision making, his major goal is to find the "truth." If doing so means that all of his years spent investigating Supreme Court decision making have been for naught, so be it. He would, I think, be the first to recognize that someone else's model works better than his—provided that could be demonstrated empirically.

Knowledge that judges may be political actors has also leaked into the consciousness of the public and of the press. While such things are admittedly difficult to prove, the current language we use to discuss the act of judging may also result from the prevalence and acceptance of the attitudinal model. From 1970 to 1980, Spaeth wrote an occasional column called the "Supreme Court Computer" in which he predicted the outcome of the cases before the Court. This work drew much attention from the popular media. The *New York Times* praised him, saying, "Jimmy the Greek should look so good" (Stevens 1974). Similarly, the *Christian Science Monitor* proclaimed him "a Supreme Court prophet" (Teare 1973). Stan Isaacs of *Newsday* said that Spaeth was "a peerless prognosticator [and] a significant figure these days" (1974), and Max Lerner proclaimed Spaeth "among the wonders of current constitutional law" (1974). While this sort of prediction may not seem today to be so amazing, it must be remembered that, during this time, people had not fully accepted the role of attitudes in Supreme Court decision making. Surely it was not prognostication or some divinely inspired prophesizing but rather a mere understanding that judges are people and decide cases according to the policy preferences they favor. Had the pundits recognized this phenomenon at the time, Spaeth's prediction record would not have been so notable. But because it was, it may be argued that Spaeth brought this idea to the public, that his column changed the way people viewed the hallowed decisions of the U.S. Supreme Court.

However, even this aspect of Spaeth's career was not without critics. Flango, for example, in his *APSR* review of Rohde and Spaeth, discussed Spaeth's predictions (which appear in the book), especially focusing on his prediction in the Watergate tapes case. Because separation of powers was not a "scalable" category according to Spaeth, he instead used precedent plus the knowledge that the Nixon appointees were conservative on criminal procedure cases to correctly predict the outcome. Flango asks, "How is this procedure at all different from the process law professor Rodell went through to predict the outcome of *Baker v. Carr?*" (1978, 284). Indeed, at the time, many people saw this issue of scaling (which may in many ways now seem ancient although it was state of the art at the time) as suffering from serious flaws. Some critics argued that the scales had no standard error, so it was difficult to determine how close to the real relationship between attitudes and votes a researcher had come (Murphy and Tanenhaus 1972). Another charge against cumulative scaling was that it was circular—scalers used votes to predict votes. That charge evanesced, however, when new cases fit nicely onto scales created using old cases (Spaeth 1965). In any event, Spaeth (2000) argues that cumulative scaling was used largely to explain decisions, not to predict them.

Overall, assertions that the attitudinal model was not influential are difficult to sustain. But perhaps the model's mere prevalence has drawn attention away from other issues worthy of study. Notable among these is the study of Supreme Court opinions and the development of law in certain issue areas. Before the legal realism movement and before the advent of quantitative methods in political science, it seems we knew much more about the jurisprudence of the Supreme Court. Because of this strong attachment to quantitative research and because of the need to justify the inclusion of attitudes in discussions of Supreme Court decision making, the art of tracing jurisprudence and tracing the development of the law has seemingly fallen by the wayside. Perhaps this is an ill result of the primacy of the attitudinal model. Perhaps there is much we do not know about the way in which opinions are crafted, the language the justices use, and the bases on which they rest their decisions because we have become consumed with case outcomes. Pritchett saw this divergence early in his career, and it may be argued that Spaeth deepened this gap between qualitative and quantitative scholarship, perhaps to the detriment of the field.

Perhaps the all-inclusive nature of Spaeth's attitudinal model has also stymied research into the role of legal considerations in judging. True, Spaeth has been the first to attempt to quantitatively test the legal model. However, much more work needs be done. For a long time, perhaps in part because of the split caused by the behavioral revolution, legal scholars and political scientists have ignored one another. Were Spaeth not quite so dismissive of the legal model, perhaps we would have more sophisticated models of decision making that include jurisprudential considerations and explain even more than models that include only attitudes and the facts of the case. "The lack of integration of the attitudinal and legal models," according to Cross, "is most unfortunate" (1997, 309).

THE U.S. SUPREME COURT
JUDICIAL DATABASES

While the attitudinal model is probably seen as Spaeth's greatest substantive contribution to public law, we must not ignore his greatest methodological contribution, the Supreme Court databases and the accompanying empirical study of judicial behavior (Spaeth 1999a, 1999b). Spaeth (2000) explains the databases as born of conceit. He had seen too many quantitative studies that he believed were "garbage in, garbage out." He thus saw the need to standardize data collection of the Court's decisions and to reduce the redundancy inherent in having each scholar collect his or her own data. While he cannot recall exactly when the idea of a multiuser database came to him, Spaeth thinks it was shortly after completing law school at the University of Michigan in December 1981. His received his initial NSF grant for the database in 1983, and preliminary versions of the data were made available in 1987 and 1988. It is first listed at the ICPSR in 1990. The database began, and continues to be updated, on three-by-five cards on which are recorded the justices' votes, the case name and Lawyers' Edition citation, the decision date, the direction of the decision, and the issue involved. He began compiling these cards in the 1950s, using them for his cumulative scaling exercises. He shared this coding scheme with Schubert over the course of their correspondence, and Schubert responded, "I think you have contrived an ingenious way of collecting the data in what I expect will prove to be a very useful form" (April 21, 1961). It appears that Schubert was correct—the databases as later constructed by Spaeth are indeed quite useful. In a special issue of *Judicature*, Epstein calls the databases "the greatest single resource of data on the Court" and "a virtual compendium of 'anything anyone would ever want to know about the Court'—or at least anything that is amenable to quantification" (2000, 225).

The databases contain an impressive array of information. There are currently three separate databases. One covers final voting behavior from the Vinson Court through the most recent term of the Rehnquist Court. The second covers all stages of decision making (cert, merits, and final vote) for the Vinson and Warren Courts. The third adds the Burger conference data to its final vote data. There are a plethora of variables providing an expansive array of information from which to draw. Spaeth puts these variables into several categories: background variables (including jurisdiction, administrative agency action, the source and origin of the case, the reason given for hearing the case, the parties to the case, and the disposition of the case in the court prior to the Supreme Court); chronological variables (including the dates of oral argument, of reargument, if any, and of decision); substantive variables (including legal provision, authority for decision, issue and issue area, and ideological direction of the decision); outcome variables (including the type of decision, the disposition of the case, the winning party, whether there was a formal alteration of precedent, and whether there was a declaration of unconstitutionality); and voting and opinion variables (including the vote in the case and the votes, opinions, and interagreements of the justices) (Spaeth and Segal 2000).

According to Epstein, "there are virtually no social-scientific projects on the Court that fail to draw on [the databases]" (2000, 225).

Indeed, as tables 2 and 3 show, most empirical studies of judicial behavior in the past decade published in the two top political science journals have used the Spaeth data in their analyses. While the overall percentages are less than 50 percent, if one considers only those papers using some sort of data, the number of *APSR* articles relying on the Spaeth databases rises to seven of nine, or 78 percent; for the *AJPS*, the number is fifteen of seventeen, or 88 percent. These numbers undoubtedly could be broken down even further to exclude articles covering the lower courts or those relying on public opinion data. In short, studies of Supreme Court decision making nearly always rely on the Spaeth databases for their empirical work.

Indeed, just by looking at tables 2 and 3, we might discern what we have learned by using the Spaeth databases. First, we have learned much about the conference behavior of the justices through Spaeth's expanded database, which includes conference data from the released papers of the justices. Second, we have learned about the differential success of litigants over time. Third, we have made many advances in understanding coalition formation and interagreement among the justices by having at our disposal four different Courts and the individual votes of those justices. Fourth, work has been done to determine the extent to which public opinion affects the Supreme Court or to which Supreme Court affects public opinion and whether issues heard by the Court each year are salient to the public. And finally, we have learned much about decision making in all respects and across many different types of issues. Since we are only examining papers published in the top two journals, it is worth noting that the breadth of knowledge gained via use of these databases is far wider than that demonstrated here. And much of that work was not done by Spaeth.

An important contribution made by Spaeth's use of his databases is the *Supreme Court Compendium* (Spaeth et al. 2001). This treasure trove of statistics on the Court has been indispensable to judicial scholars. Now in its third edition, the *Compendium* has become a household name among scholars of the Court, and the information ranges widely enough to interest both quantitative and traditional legal scholars. In fact, it has probably brought the database to some of those too intimidated to use it themselves. In reviewing the *Compendium*, Johnson notes "I find little to criticize in this volume. . . . Its extraordinary coverage, the careful documentation of sources and the clear presentation of data represent an outstanding contribution to the field" (1994, 107, 108). This volume is truly another major contribution to the field generated by the Supreme Court database.

TABLE 2. Data Sources for Judicial Research (*American Political Science Review*, 1991–2000)

Article	Citation	Data Source
"Debunking the Myth of Interest Group Invincibility in the Courts"	Epstein and Rowland. 1991. *APSR* 85:205–20.	Self-identified published cases of federal district courts between 1968 and 1980.
"On the Nature of Supreme Court Decision Making"	George and Epstein. 1992. *APSR* 86:323–37.	Self-identified cases from U.S. Reports for 1971–88 terms.
"Ideology, Status, and the Differential Success of Direct Parties before the Supreme Court"	Sheehan, Mishler, and Songer. 1992. *APSR* 86:464–71.	Spaeth Database (Preliminary Version).
"The Supreme Court as a Counter-majoritarian Institution? The Impact of Public Opinion on Supreme Court Decisions"	Mishler and Sheehan. 1993. *APSR* 87:87–101.	Spaeth Database.
"Lawyers, Organized Interests, and the Law of Obscenity: Agenda Setting in the Supreme Court"	McGuire and Caldeira. 1993. *APSR* 87:717–26.	All paid cases on obscenity filed in Supreme Court, 1955–87.
"Antonin Scalia, William Brennan, and the Politics of Expression: A Study of Legal Violence and Repression"	Brisbin. 1993. *APSR* 87:912–27.	No data used.
"Popular Influence on Supreme Court Decisions"	Norpoth, Segal, Mishler, and Sheehan (controversy). 1994. *APSR* 88:711–24.	No data used.
"The Legitimacy of the Court of Justice in the European Union: Models of Institutional Support"	Caldeira and Gibson. 1995. *APSR* 89:356–76.	Eurobarometer.
"Separating Partisanship from Party in Judicial Research: Reapportionment in the U.S. District Courts"	Lloyd. 1995. *APSR* 89:413–20.	Spaeth Database.
"Issue Fluidity on the U.S. Supreme Court"	McGuire and Palmer. 1995. *APSR* 89:691–704.	Data on orally argued cases decided by full opinion during 1988 term.
"Information, Aggregation, Rationality, and the Condorcet Jury Theorem"	Austen–Smith and Banks. 1996. *APSR* 90:34–45.	No data used.
"Strategic Policy Considerations and Voting Fluidity on the Burger Court"	Maltzman and Wahlbeck. 1996. *APSR* 90:581–92.	Spaeth Database.

Title	Citation	Data Source
"The Claim of Issue Creation on the U.S. Supreme Court"	Epstein, Segal, and Johnson. 1996. *APSR* 90:845–52.	Replication.
"Issues, Agendas, and Decision Making on the Supreme Court"	McGuire and Palmer. 1996. *APSR* 90:853–65.	Replication.
"Separation-of-Powers Games in the Positive Theory of Congress and Courts"	Segal. 1997. *APSR*. 91:28–44.	Spaeth Database.
"The Quixotic Search for Consensus on the U.S. Supreme Court: A Cross-Judicial Empirical Analysis of the Rehnquist Court Justices"	Gerber and Park. 1997. *APSR* 91:390–408.	Spaeth Database.
"Convicting the Innocent: The Inferiority of Unanimous Jury Verdicts under Strategic Voting"	Fedderson and Pesendorfer. 1998. *APSR* 92:23–36.	No data used.
"The Public's Conditional Response to Supreme Court Decisions"	Johnson and Martin. 1998. *APSR* 92:299–310.	CBS News/*New York Times* Polls.
"On the Legitimacy of National High Courts"	Gibson, Caldeira, and Baird. 1998. *APSR* 92:343–58.	Eurobarometer and additional surveys.
"Jury Aversion and Voter Registration"	Oliver and Wolfinger. 1999. *APSR* 93:147–52.	American National Election Study.
"The Supreme Court and Local Public Opinion"	Hoekstra. 2000. *APSR* 94:80–100.	Self-conducted survey.
"Strategic Auditing in a Political Hierarchy: An Informational Model of the Supreme Court's Certiorari Decisions"	Cameron, Segal and Songer. 2000. *APSR* 94:101–16.	Segal (1991) search and seizure cases, derived from the Spaeth database.
"In Defense of Unanimous Jury Verdicts: Mistrials, Communication, and Strategic Voting"	Coughlan. 2000. *APSR* 94:375–94.	No data used.
"Jury Verdicts and Preference Diversity"	Gerardi. 2000. *APSR* 94:395–406.	No data used.
"An Experimental Study of Jury Decision Rules"	Guarnaschelli, McKelvey, and Palfrey. 2000. *APSR* 94:407–24.	No data used.

Total using Spaeth Database: 7
Total not using Spaeth: 13
Percentage of Spaeth use: 35%

TABLE 3. Data Sources for Judicial Reserach (*American Journal of Political Science*, 1991–2000)

Article	Citation	Data Source
"Time Binding and Theory Building in Personal Attribute Models of Supreme Court Voting Behavior"	Tate and Hanberg. 1991. *AJPS* 35:460–80.	Spaeth Database (and Schubert's data for 1946–68).
"The Condorcet Jury Theorem, Free Speech, and Correlated Votes"	Ladha. 1992. *AJPS* 36:617–34.	National Election Studies.
"The Etiology of Public Support for the Supreme Court"	Caldeira and Gibson. 1992. *AJPS* 36:635–64.	General Social Survey.
"Integrating Alternative Approaches to the Study of Judicial Voting: Obscenity Cases in the U.S. Courts of Appeals"	Songer and Haire. 1992. *AJPS* 36:963–82.	Votes case by Courts of Appeals judges, 1957–90.
"Lawyers and the U.S. Supreme Court: The Washington Community and Legal Elites"	McGuire. 1993. *AJPS* 37:365–90.	Survey of lawyers participating in Supreme Court litigation.
"Deconstructing the Political Spectacle: Sex, Race, and Subjectivity in Public Desponse to the Clarence Thomas/Anita Hill 'Sexual Harassment' Hearings"	Thomas, McCoy, and McBride. 1993. *AJPS* 37:699–720.	Newspapers, etc.
"Alternative Models of Appeal Mobilization in Judicial Hierarchies"	Atkins. 1993. *AJPS* 37:780–98.	Courts of Appeals judgments, 1983–85.
"Freshman Effects' for Supreme Court Justices"	Hagle. 1993. *AJPS* 37:1142–57.	Spaeth Database.
"The Hierarchy of Justice: Testing a Principal-Agent Model of Supreme Court–Circuit Interactions"	Songer, Segal, and Cameron. 1994. *AJPS* 38:673–96.	Segal (1991) search and seizure (derived from the Spaeth Database) and a sample of Courts of Appeals decisions.
"The Legitimacy of Transnational Legal Institutions: Compliance, Support, and the European Court of Justice"	Gibson and Caldeira. 1995. *AJPS* 39:459–89.	Eurobarometer.

"Specialized Courts, Bureaucratic Agencies, and the Politics of U.S. Trade Policy"	Hansen, Johnson, and Unah. 1995. *AJPS* 39:529–57.	Opinions of the Court of International Trade.
"May It Please the Chief? Opinion Assignments in the Rehnquist Court"	Maltzman and Wahlbeck. 1996. *AJPS* 40:421–43.	Court's docket books, 1987–89 terms.
"The Influence of Stare Decisis on the Votes of United States Supreme Court Justices"	Segal and Spaeth. 1996. *AJPS* 40:971–1003.	Landmark decisions and their progeny.
"Slaying the Dragon: Segal, Spaeth, and the Function of Law in Supreme Court Decision Making"	Brisbin. 1996. *AJPS* 40:1004–17.	No data used.
"The Norm of Stare Decisis"	Knight and Epstein. 1996. *AJPS* 40:1018–35.	Written briefs coded.
"Retesting Segal and Spaeth's Stare Decisis Model"	Brenner and Stier. 1996. *AJPS* 40:1036–48	Landmark decisions and their progeny.
"Not the Whole Story: The Impact of Justices' Values on Supreme Court Decision Making"	Songer and Lindquist. 1996. *AJPS* 40:1049–63.	Landmark decisions and their progeny.
"Norms, Dragons, and Stare Decisis: A Response"	Segal and Spaeth. 1996. *AJPS* 40:1064–82.	No data used.
"The Supreme Court and Federal Administrative Agencies: A Resource-Based Theory and Analysis of Judicial Impact"	Spriggs. 1996. *AJPS* 40:1122–51.	Spaeth Database.
"Policy Convergence in a Federal Judicial System: The Application of Intensified Scrutiny Doctrines by State Supreme Courts"	Kilwein and Brisbin. 1997. *AJPS* 41:122–48.	Spaeth Database.
"Judicial Review and Coordinate Construction of the Constitution"	Meernik and Ignagni. 1997. *AJPS* 41:447–67.	Spaeth Database, Westlaw, Abraham 1986, and Congressional Quarterly Almanac.
"The Public and the Supreme Court: Individual Justice Responsiveness to American Policy Moods"	Flemming and Wood. 1997. *AJPS* 41:468–98.	Spaeth Database.

(*continues*)

TABLE 3. *Continued*

Article	Citation	Data Source
"One Voice among Many: The Supreme Court's Influence on Attentiveness to Issues in the United States, 1947–92"	Flemming, Bohte, and Wood. 1997. *AJPS* 41:1224–50.	Spaeth Database.
"Marshalling the Court: Bargaining and Accommodation on the United States Supreme Court"	Wahlbeck, Spriggs, and Maltzman. 1998. *AJPS* 42:294–315.	Spaeth Database.
"Lobbying for Justice: Organized Interests, Supreme Court Nominations, and the United States Senate"	Caldeira and Wright. 1998. *AJPS* 42:499–523.	Self-conducted surveys of organized interests.
"Acclimation Effects' for Supreme Court Justices: A Cross-Validation, 1888–1940"	Wood, Keith, Lanier, and Ogundele. 1998. *AJPS* 42:690–97.	Spaeth Database and self-collected data.
"Of Time and Consensual Norms in the Supreme Court"	Caldeira and Zorn. 1998. *AJPS* 42:874–902.	Supreme Court Compendium, derived from Spaeth Database.
"From Schubert's The Judicial Mind to Spaeth's U.S. Supreme Court Judicial Data Base: A Crossvalidation"	Djupe and Epstein. 1998. *AJPS* 42:1012–19.	Spaeth Database.
"Inviting Congressional Action: A Study of Supreme Court Motivations in Statutory Interpretation"	Hausegger and Baum. 1999. *AJPS* 43:162–85.	Spaeth Database.
"The Politics of Supreme Court Nominations: A Theory of Institutional Constraints and Choices"	Moraski and Shipan. 1999. *AJPS* 43:1069–95.	Supreme Court nominees between 1949 and 1994.
"Legislative Incentives and Two-Tiered Judicial Review: A Game Theoretic Reading of Carolene Products Footnote Four"	Rogers. 1999. *AJPS* 43:1096–1121.	No data used.
"Measuring Issue Salience" "Ideological Divergence and Public Support for the Supreme Court"	Epstein and Segal. 2000. *AJPS* 44:66–83. Durr, Martin, and Wolbrecht. 2000. *AJPS* 44:768–76.	Spaeth Expanded Database. Spaeth Database.
Total using Spaeth Database: Did not use Spaeth Database: Percentage of Spaeth use:	15 18 45%	

Perhaps this reliance on the Spaeth database is dangerous, however. Perhaps, because such data are available, other fruitful areas are ignored. Perhaps we have become too single-minded in our research, focusing only on quantitative exploration. Perhaps, too, our theorizing has been stunted by the propensity to merely open the database and check to see if potential theories are borne out; if the data do not support these hypotheses, we cast them aside. Undue attention is also paid to the Court as a collective body rather than to the justices' individual behavior. Gibson (1999) bemoans this lack of attention to the individual justice, arguing that if one attempts to test hypotheses about the behavior of judges, one must use the judge rather than the case as the unit of analysis. By their nature, the Spaeth databases have probably promoted scholarly attention to the case as the unit of analysis.

Another problem with the databases is their complexity. Traditional scholars may be intimidated by the length of the codebooks, the decisions necessary to properly use the databases, and the initial lack of value labels, necessitating a constant consultation of the documentation. Indeed, the databases are not foolproof, which some scholars see as a major flaw. If researchers were to open the database and start running models, they would suffer an unfortunate fate, for they will have included non–orally argued cases and per curiams without determining whether doing so is appropriate given the research question at hand. Such researchers will also be counting certain cases two and three times by including multiple dockets, multiple issues, and multiple legal provisions but counting each as a separate case. One of the major hopes for the compilation of these data was that they would allow traditional scholars the opportunity to quantify their work and to make their case studies or judicial biographies more rigorous. Because of the non-user-friendliness of the databases, though, the data are probably being used only by those who are quantitatively sophisticated. And even for them, using the databases can be a challenge.

While Spaeth is not one to cater to the lowest common denominator, he has recognized the need for increased user-friendliness and is taking steps to improve the databases in that respect. He has added value labels so that users might find the definition of a variable and how a variable is coded while exploring the database rather than having to consult the documentation. The documentation itself is being revised and its organization reconsidered. The order in which the variables are found in the database, created for ease in data entry, is being reconsidered in light of user comments. And Spaeth is responsive to questions, tireless in his presentations of the database and instructions for its use, and sympathetic to those who fear data, often doing statistical runs himself to help a fellow scholar. He has also been humble, noting that a database of this size will have errors, ever encouraging users to send "comments, criticisms and corrections."[1] Spaeth has also taken heed of Gibson's complaint about the unit of analysis and has procured an NSF grant to change the unit of analysis of the databases to the individual justice to facilitate analysis at that level and to further encourage judicial biographers and jurisprudes to utilize the database (Benesh and Spaeth 2000).

Regardless of the potential flaws in the databases—flaws one would probably find in any data set not compiled by oneself—the database is well used and has always been very accessible. Spaeth has been quite unselfish, sharing the data early on with impatient scholars and making them publicly available (updated each year) at the Web site of Michigan State University's Program for Law and Judicial Politics (www.ssc.msu.edu/~pls/.pljp). He has made the extensive documentation accompanying the databases readily available and has been quite meticulous in defining and demonstrating the coding used in their construction. Epstein (2000) praises this aspect of the database and the replicability that follows from it. Indeed, Spaeth (2000) has always had as a major goal that other scholars be able to replicate any of the work he has done or, indeed, change any of the coding as they see fit. According to the rates of intercoder reliability, he has succeeded. Of course, when one conducts reliability with people one has trained, one might expect such high levels. Still, this reliability is, as Epstein says, "remarkable" (2000, 225). And the databases' influence has been felt around the discipline. It seems that these databases have stimulated more creative research than they have stymied.

CONCLUSIONS ON THE
WORK OF A TRUE PIONEER

Harold J. Spaeth has influenced many scholars engaged in the study of the Supreme Court in particular and judicial behavior in general. His work has been controversial, but as controversy it has stimulated much research; something a pioneer ought to do. Spaeth has also trained many graduate students—most notably his frequent coauthor, Jeffrey A. Segal—destined to be included in a future volume of this sort. And those not trained by Spaeth have also felt his presence. He attends several conferences every year, typically serving as discussant or chair. And nary a graduate student has not cringed at the realization that Spaeth is in the audience, because of both his physical and his academic presence, or the discovery that he would be their discussant. Spaeth panels are always well attended because they are bound to be entertaining. He has a witty and acerbic way with words, often used expressly for effect, that never lets him go unnoticed. Indeed, it is a pleasure to sit back and enjoy Spaeth's verbal sparring.

In addition to his continued active involvement in professional conferences, Spaeth has maintained an amazingly productive record. When he was awarded the Law and Courts Lifetime Achievement Award in 1997, Lee Epstein referred to Spaeth as the "Energizer bunny," and the allusion is seems accurate. The appendix contains an exhaustive listing of Spaeth's published work. Since receiving the Lifetime Achievement Award, he has published two books (one of which won the 1999 C. Herman Pritchett Award for the best book on Law and Courts), three refereed articles, and numerous conference papers; has received another NSF grant; and is in the process of writing two others at the time of this writing. Before receiving the award, Spaeth averaged 4.5 publications per year (with a book counting as five articles) (Epstein 1997). Subsequently (after his partial "retirement"), the mean has increased to 7.6 publications. His productivity has been truly amazing—more than 175 publications over the course of a forty-year career. Most people take a break when they retire, but fortunately for the field, Spaeth has not. He has several important projects in the works: the transformation of his databases to the justice level of analysis and some analyses stemming from that data source testing legal dissensus; the coding of the Burger Court conference data; a new measure of salience to the Supreme Court justices; and an examination of the little-known practice of relisting in the Court's certiorari process. Other work on the horizon, according to Spaeth, may include an impressionistic presentation of the contents of Powell's papers, an analysis of "join-three" behavior on the Court, and another database project coding the cases denied certiorari by the Court. It seems safe to assume that Spaeth has not run out of ideas. Indeed, he says, "I'm only sorry I'm not starting my career rather than ending it." When asked if he ever will fully retire, Spaeth exclaimed, "I hope not. Gad, what would I do?" (2000).

APPENDIX A: THE WORK OF HAROLD J. SPAETH

BOOKS AND MONOGRAPHS

The Predicament of Modern Politics. Detroit: University of Detroit Press, 1964.
An Introduction to Supreme Court Decision Making. San Francisco: Chandler, 1965.

The Warren Court. San Francisco: Chandler, 1966.

FASCALE: Technical Report no. 29 1968 (with Scott B. Guthery and Stuart Thomas Jr.). East Lansing: Michigan State University Computer Institute for Social Science Research, 1968.

DISFIT: Technical Report no. 72–13 (with Scott B. Guthery). East Lansing: Michigan State University Computer Institute for Social Science Research, 1971.

An Introduction to Supreme Court Decision Making. Rev. and exp. ed. San Francisco: Chandler, 1972.

Classic and Current Decisions of the United States Supreme Court (series of 56 monographs). San Francisco: W. H. Freeman, 1975–79.

Supreme Court Decision Making (with David W. Rohde). San Francisco: W. H. Freeman, 1976.

Supreme Court Policy Making: Explanation and Prediction. San Francisco: W. H. Freeman, 1979.

The Constitution of the United States, 12th ed. (with Edward Conrad Smith). New York: Harper and Row, 1987.

Studies in U.S. Supreme Court Behavior (with Saul Brenner). New York: Garland, 1990.

United States Supreme Court Judicial Database. East Lansing: Michigan State University Program for Law and Judicial Politics, 1990–2000.

The Constitution of the United States (with Edward Conrad Smith). 13th ed. New York: HarperPerennial, 1991.

The Supreme Court and the Attitudinal Model (with Jeffrey A. Segal). New York: Cambridge University Press, 1993.

The Supreme Court Compendium: Data, Decisions, and Development, 3d ed. (with Lee Epstein, Jeffrey A. Segal, and Thomas G. Walker). Washington, D.C.: Congressional Quarterly, 2001.

Stare Indecisis: Alteration of Precedent on the Supreme Court, 1946–1992 (with Saul Brenner). New York: Cambridge University Press, 1995.

Expanded U.S. Supreme Court Judicial Database, 1946–1968 Terms. East Lansing: Michigan State University Program for Law and Judicial Politics, 1995–2000.

Majority Rule or Minority Will: Adherence to Precedent on the U.S. Supreme Court (with Jeffrey A. Segal). New York: Cambridge University Press, 1999.

The Supreme Court and the Attitudinal Model Revisited (with Jeffrey A. Segal). New York: Cambridge University Press, 2002.

BOOK CHAPTERS, CONTRIBUTIONS, AND SYMPOSIA

The Proposed Michigan Constitution: Analyses and Interpretations (contributor). Ann Arbor: Inter-University Faculty Committee on Constitutional Revision, 1963.

"Warren Court Attitudes toward Business." In *Judicial Decision-Making,* ed. Glendon Schubert. New York: Free Press, 1963.

"Race Relations and the Warren Court." *University of Detroit Law Journal* 43 (1965): 255–72.

"The Analysis and Interpretation of Dimensionality: The Case of Civil Liberties Decision Making" (with David J. Peterson). In *American Judicial Behavior*, ed. Saul Brenner. New York: MSS Information Corporation, 1972.

"The Judicial Restraint of Mr. Justice Frankfurter—Myth or Reality?" In *American Judicial Behavior*, ed. Saul Brenner. New York: MSS Information Corporation, 1972.

"The Attitudes and Values of Supreme Court Justices." In *Courts, Law and Judicial Processes*, ed. S. Sidney Ulmer. New York: Free Press, 1981.

"Denying Access in Plenary Cases: The Burger Court" (with Gregory J. Rathjen). In *Courts, Law and Judicial Processes*, ed. S. Sidney Ulmer. New York: Free Press, 1981.

"Activism and Restraint: A Cloak for the Justices' Policy Preferences" (with Stuart H. Teger). In *Supreme Court Activism and Restraint*, ed. S. C. Halpern and C. M. Lamb. Lexington, Mass.: D.C. Heath, 1982.

"Felix Frankfurter, Judicial Activism, and Voting Conflict on the Warren Court" (with Michael F. Altfeld). In *Judicial Conflict and Consensus*, ed. S. Goldman and C. M. Lamb. Lexington: University Press of Kentucky, 1986.

"Jurisdiction." In *Encyclopedia of the American Judicial System*, vol. 2, ed. Robert Janosik. New York: Scribner's, 1987.

"The Dimensions of Civil Liberties Decision Making on the Burger Court." In *Studies in Judicial Behavior: The Vinson, Warren, and Burger Courts*, ed. H. J. Spaeth and S. Brenner. New York: Garland, 1990.

"Sandra Day O'Connor: An Assessment." In *An Essential Safeguard: Essays on the United States Supreme Court and Its Justices*, ed. D. Grier Stephenson. Westport, Conn.: Greenwood, 1991.

"Edwards v. South Carolina," "Graham v. Richardson," "Intermediate Scrutiny," "Judicial Immunity from Civil Damages," "Jurisdictional Consolidation Act," "Juvenile Justice," "Lower Federal Courts," "Plea Bargaining," "Antonin Scalia," and "Strict Scrutiny." In *The Oxford Companion to the Supreme Court of the United States*, ed. Kermit L. Hall. New York: Oxford University Press, 1992.

Symposium on *The Supreme Court and the Attitudinal Model*. *Law and Courts* 4 (1994): 3–12.

"The Attitudinal Model." In *Contemplating Courts*, ed. Lee Epstein. Washington, D.C.: Congressional Quarterly Press, 1995.

"John Marshall." In *The Encyclopedia of Democracy*, ed. Seymour Martin Lipset. Washington, D.C.: Congressional Quarterly, 1995.

"Different Strokes for Different Folks: A Reply to Professor Shapiro's Assessment of the Subfield." *Law and Courts* 6 (1996): 11–13.

"Edwards v. South Carolina" and "Graham v. Richardson." Reprinted in *The Oxford Guide to U.S. Supreme Court Decisions*, ed. Kermit L. Hall. New York: Oxford University Press, 1999.

REFEREED ARTICLES

"Measuring Ideational Identity by Pairing Justices." *American Behavioral Scientist* 3 (1960): 22–23.

"An Approach to the Study of Attitudinal Differences as an Aspect of Judicial Behavior." *American Journal of Political Science* 5 (1961): 165–80.

"Judicial Power as a Variable Motivating Supreme Court Behavior." *American Journal of Political Science* 6 (1962): 54–82.

"An Analysis of Judicial Attitudes in the Labor Relations Decisions of the Warren Court." *Journal of Politics* 25 (1963): 290–311.

"The Judicial Restraint of Mr. Justice Frankfurter—Myth or Reality?" *American Journal of Political Science* 8 (1964): 22–38.

"Jurimetrics and Professor Mendelson: A Troubled Relationship." *Journal of Politics* 27 (1965): 875–80.

"Unidimensionality and Item Invariance in Judicial Scaling." *Behavioral Science* 10 (1965): 290–304.

"FASCALE, a FORTRAN IV Multidimensional Scaling and Factor Analysis Program" (with Scott B. Guthery and Stuart Thomas Jr.). *Behavioral Science* 13 (1968): 426.

"Effects of Attitude toward Situation upon Attitude toward Object" (with Douglas R. Parker). *Journal of Psychology* 73 (1969): 173–82.

"The Use and Utility of the Monotone Criterion in Multidimensional Scaling" (with Scott B. Guthery). *Multivariate Behavioral Research* 4 (1969): 501–15.

"The Analysis and Interpretation of Dimensionality: The Case of Civil Liberties Decision Making" (with David J. Peterson). *American Journal of Political Science* 15 (1971): 415–41.

"The Patentability of Software." *Computerworld* 5 (1971): 1–6.

"DISFIT, a FORTRAN IV Program for Metric Multidimensional Scaling" (with Scott B. Guthery). *Behavioral Science* 17 (1972): 401.

"Is Justice Blind? An Empirical Analysis of a Normative Theorem" (with David B. Meltz, Gregory J. Rathjen, and Michael V. Haselswerdt). *Law and Society Review* 7 (1972): 119–37.

"Is Justice Blind? Comment and Reply." *Law and Society Review* 8 (1973): 155–57.

"Psychometric Modeling." *Computerworld* 8 (1974): 27.

"Access to the Federal Courts: An Analysis of Burger Court Policy Making" (with Gregory J. Rathjen). *American Journal of Political Science* 23 (1979): 360–82.

"Harold J. Spaeth's Rebuttal." *American Bar Foundation Research Journal* (1980): 627–30.

"Kamisar on Confessions: Gentleman and a Scholar." *Res Gestae*, October 24, 1980, 1–5.

"An Outside Educator Views Michigan's Legal Education from the Inside." *Law Quadrangle Notes* 25 (1981): 12–17.

"Computer 9, Supreme Court o." *Barrister* 9 (1982): 8–11, 37.

"Denial of Access and Ideological Preferences: An Analysis of the Voting Behavior of the Burger Court Justices" (with Gregory J. Rathjen). *Western Political Quarterly* 36 (1983): 71–87.

"Distributive Justice: Majority Opinion Assignments in the Burger Court." *Judicature* 67 (1984): 299–304.

"Measuring Influence on the U.S. Supreme Court" (with Michael F. Altfeld). *Jurimetrics Journal* 24 (1984): 236–47.

"A Reply by Spaeth." 1985. *Judicature* 69:366.

"Burger Court Review of State Court Civil Liberties Decisions." *Judicature* 68 (1985): 285–91. (Reprinted in Elliot E. Slotnick, ed. *Judicial Politics: Readings from* Judicature. Chicago: American Judicature Society, 1992.)

"Influence Relationships within the Supreme Court: A Comparison of the Warren and Burger Courts" (with Michael F. Altfeld). *Western Political Quarterly* 38 (1985): 70–83.

"Measuring Power on the Supreme Court: An Alternative to the Power Index" (with Michael F. Altfeld). *Jurimetrics Journal* 26 (1985): 48–75.

"Supreme Court Disposition of Federal Court Decisions." *Judicature* 68 (1985): 245–50.

"Letters: Response by Segal and Spaeth." *Judicature* 69 (1986): 321.

"If a Supreme Court Vacancy Occurs, Will the Senate Confirm a Reagan Nominee?" (with Jeffrey A. Segal). *Judicature* 69 (1986): 186–90.

"Issue Specialization in Majority Opinion Assignment on the Burger Court" (with Saul Brenner). *Western Political Quarterly* 39 (1986): 520–27.

"A Routine to Duplicate Existing dBASE III Records" (with John Valenti). *Social Science Microcomputer Review* 3 (1986): 377–79.

"Ideological Position as a Variable in the Authoring of Dissenting Opinions on the Warren and Burger Courts" (with Saul Brenner). *American Politics Quarterly* 16 (1988): 317–28.

"Majority Opinion Assignments and the Maintenance of the Original Coalition on the Warren Court" (with Saul Brenner). *American Journal of Political Science* 32 (1988): 72–81.

"Consensus in the Unanimous Decisions of the U.S. Supreme Court." *Judicature* 72 (1989): 274–81.

"Decisional Trends on the Warren and Burger Courts: Results from the Supreme Court Data Base Project" (with Jeffrey A. Segal). *Judicature* 73 (1989): 103–7. (Reprinted in Elliot E. Slotnick, ed. *Judicial Politics: Readings from* Judicature. Chicago: American Judicature Society, 1992.)

"The Defection of the Marginal Justice on the Warren Court" (with Saul Brenner and Timothy M. Hagle). *Western Political Quarterly* 42 (1989): 409–25.

"Ideology, Strategy, and Supreme Court Decisions: William Rehnquist as Chief Justice" (with David W. Rohde). *Judicature* 72 (1989): 247–50. (Reprinted as "Rehnquist a Chameleon? It's Just Not So." *Los Angeles Daily Journal*, April 24, 1989.)

"Increasing the Size of Minimum Winning Original Coalitions on the Warren Court" (with Saul Brenner and Timothy M. Hagle). *Polity* 23 (1990): 309–18.

"Rehnquist Court Disposition of Lower Court Decisions: Affirmation Not Reversal" (with Jeffrey A. Segal). *Judicature* 74 (1990): 84–88. (Reprinted in Elliot E. Slotnick, ed. *Judicial Politics*, 2d ed. Chicago: American Judicature Society, 2000.)

"Voting Fluidity and the Attitudinal Model of Supreme Court Decision Making" (with Timothy M. Hagle). *Western Political Quarterly* 44 (1991): 119–28.

"The Business Decisions of the Burger Court: The Emergence of a New Ideology" (with Timothy M Hagle). *Journal of Politics* 54 (1992): 120–34.

"Centralized Research Staff: Is There a Monster in the Judicial Closet?" (with Mary Lou Stow). *Judicature* 75 (1992): 216–21. (Reprinted by the *Michigan Lawyers Weekly* opinion service. Reprinted in Elliot E. Slotnick, ed. *Judicial Politics*, 2d ed. Chicago: American Judicature Society, 2000. For communications from various readers and reply by Stow and Spaeth, see *Judicature* 75 (1992): 289–90.)

"Examining an Analogy: Does the Judicial Monster Eat Chaff?" (with Mary Lou Stow). *Judicature* 75 (1992): 294–337.

"Ideological Patterns in the Justices' Voting in the Burger Court's Business Cases" (with Timothy M. Hagle). *Journal of Politics* 55 (1993): 492–505.

"Ideological Values and the Votes of U.S. Supreme Court Justices Revisited" (with Charles M. Cameron, Lee Epstein, and Jeffrey A. Segal). *Journal of Politics* 57 (1995): 812–23.

"The Influence of *Stare Decisis* on the Votes of U.S. Supreme Court Justices" (with Jeffrey A. Segal). *American Journal of Political Science* 40 (1996): 971–1003.

"Norms, Dragons, and *Stare Decisis*" (with Jeffrey A. Segal). *American Journal of Political Science* 40 (1996): 1064–82.

"Do Political Preferences Change? A Longitudinal Study of U.S. Supreme Court Justices" (with Lee Epstein, Valerie Hoekstra, and Jeffrey A. Segal). *Journal of Politics* 60 (1998): 801–18.

"Equity in Supreme Court Opinion Assignment" (with Sara C. Benesh and Reginald S. Sheehan). *Jurimetrics* 39 (1999): 377–89.

"The U.S. Supreme Court Judicial Data Base: Providing New Insights into the Court" (with Jeffrey A. Segal). *Judicature* 83 (2000): 228–35.

"The Norm of Consensus on the U.S. Supreme Court" (with Lee Epstein and Jeffrey A. Segal). *American Journal of Political Science* 45 (2001): 362–77.

OTHER PUBLICATIONS

Wrote an occasional syndicated newspaper column, "The Supreme Court Computer," 1970–80.

Wrote a column for *Law and Courts,* the newsletter of the Law and Courts Section of the American Political Science Association, 1994–96.

RESEARCH GRANTS

Relm Foundation, 1962–63.
All-University Research Grant, Michigan State University, 1963–94.
National Institutes of Mental Health, 1968–71.
Computer Institute for Social Science Research, Michigan State University, 1971–74.
National Science Foundation, 1984–86, 1986–88, 1988–89, 1992–94, 1994–97, 1997–2000, 2000–2002.

NOTES

This title is taken from the syndicated newspaper column Spaeth wrote from 1970 to 1980. The author wishes to thank Corina Schulz and Don Pashak for their research assistance and Harold Spaeth for the interview and the correspondence with Schubert used herein and for the education and mentorship he provided me.

    1. This can be found at the end of the introduction to the documentation of Spaeth 1999a, iii.

REFERENCES

Baum, Lawrence. 1994. "*The Supreme Court and the Attitudinal Model:* The Critics." *Law and Courts* 4 (spring): 3–5.

Baum, Lawrence. 1998. "What We Don't Know about Judicial Behavior, and Other Musings." *Law and Courts* 8 (spring): 3–4.

Benesh, Sara C., and Harold J. Spaeth. 2000–2002. "Collaborative Research—Individual-Level Analysis of Supreme Court Justices: A Modification to the United States Supreme Court Judicial Databases." National Science Foundation, SBR-9911054.

Bueno de Mesquita, Bruce. 1985. "Toward a Scientific Understanding of International Conflict: A Personal View." *International Studies Quarterly* 29:121–36.

Caldeira, Gregory A. 1994. Review of *The Supreme Court and the Attitudinal Model. American Political Science Review* 88:485–86.

Canon, Bradley C. 1993. Review of *The Supreme Court and the Attitudinal Model. Law and Politics Book Review* 3:98–100.

Chalmers, A. F. 1982. *What Is This Thing Called Science?* Indianapolis: Hackett Publishing.

Cross, Frank B. 1997. "Political Science and the New Legal Realism: A Case of Unfortunate Interdisciplinary Ignorance." *Northwestern University Law Review* 92:251–320.

Epstein, Lee. 1997. "In Honor of Harold J. Spaeth." Remarks at the American Political Science Association annual meeting, roundtable on Harold J. Spaeth, Lifetime Achievement Award Winner, August 28.

Epstein, Lee. 2000. "Social Science, the Courts, and the Law." *Judicature* 83:224–27.

Flango, Victor Eugene. 1978. Review of *Supreme Court Decision Making. American Political Science Review* 72:283–84.

Gibson, James L. 1999. "Selecting Units for Analysis: A Cautionary Note about Methods of Analyzing Cases and Judges." *Law and Courts* 9 (winter): 10–14.

Hall, Melinda Gann. 1995. Review of *The Supreme Court and the Attitudinal Model. Journal of Politics* 57:254–55.

Hodder-Williams, Richard. 1994. Review of *The Supreme Court and the Attitudinal Model. Political Studies* 42:521–22.

Isaacs, Stan. 1974. *Newsday.* July 9.

Johnson, Charles A. 1994. Review of *The Supreme Court Compendium. Law and Politics Book Review* 4:106–9.

King, Gary, Robert O. Keohane, and Sidney Verba. 1994. *Designing Social Inquiry: Scientific Inference in Qualitative Research.* Princeton: Princeton University Press.

Knight, Jack. 1994. "*The Supreme Court and the Attitudinal Model:* The Critics." *Law and Courts* 4 (spring): 5–6.

Krasner, Stephen D. 1985. "Toward Understanding in International Relations." *International Studies Quarterly* 29:137–44.

Lerner, Max. 1974. "Man Predicts High Court Decisions with Accuracy." August 5.

Murphy, Walter F., and Joseph Tanenhaus. 1972. *The Study of Public Law.* New York: Random House.

Posner, Richard A. 1995. *Overcoming Law.* Cambridge: Harvard University Press.

Pritchett, C. Herman. 1969. "The Development of Judicial Research." In *Frontiers of Judicial Research,* ed. Joel B. Grossman and Joseph Tanenhaus. New York: Wiley.

Rosenberg, Gerald N. 1994. "*The Supreme Court and the Attitudinal Model:* The Critics." *Law and Courts* 4 (spring): 6–8.

Schmidhauser, John R. 1980. Review of *Supreme Court Policy Making: Explanation and Prediction. American Political Science Review* 74:217–18.

Schubert, Glendon. 1959. *Quantitative Analysis of Judicial Behavior.* Glencoe, Ill.: Free Press.

Smith, Rogers M. 1994. "*The Supreme Court and the Attitudinal Model:* The Critics." *Law and Courts* 4 (spring): 8–9.

Songer, Donald R., Jeffrey A. Segal, and Charles M. Cameron. 1994. "The Hierarchy of Justice: Testing a Principal-Agent Model of Supreme Court–Circuit Court Interactions." *American Journal of Political Science* 38:673–96.

Spaeth, Harold J. 1999a. *Expanded U.S. Supreme Court Judicial Database.* East Lansing, Mich.: Program for Law and Judicial Politics.

Spaeth, Harold J. 1999b. *United States Supreme Court Judicial Database.* East Lansing, Mich.: Program for Law and Judicial Politics.

Spaeth, Harold J. 2000. Interview by author. Michigan State University, East Lansing, August 14.

Spaeth, Harold J., and Jeffrey A. Segal. 2000. "The U.S. Supreme Court Judicial Database: Providing New Insights into the Court." *Judicature* 83:228–35.

Stevens, William K. 1974. "The Professor's Computer Foretells Court's Rulings." *New York Times*, July 28.

Teare, Jacqueline. 1973. "Professor and his Trusty Computer Have Supreme Court 'Figured.'" *Christian Science Monitor*, June 23, p. 9.

CHAPTER 6

Joseph Tanenhaus:
The "Learned Discipline" of Public Law

Robert A. Carp

The period of scholarly production for Joseph Tanenhaus was abbreviated as a result of his untimely death in 1980 at the age of fifty-six, but his high-quality scholarly writings had a substantial impact on the subfield of public law and indeed on the entire political science discipline. Tanenhaus will be remembered for two separate types of contributions as a public law scholar: (1) his role in the genesis of what would come to be known as the attitudinal model of judicial behavior and (2) his reflections on that model. The first of his contributions was work addressing narrow but important issues of interest to judicial scholars—decisional patterns on the Supreme Court, public attitudes and opinions about the Supreme Court, comparative judicial politics, and new methodological approaches. But the second of his contributions—and, to me, the more important—involved the subfield of public law. Tanenhaus had a tremendous interest in the history, evolution, and theoretical boundaries of the "learned discipline" of political science as a whole and, more specifically, in those of the public law subfield. He began his major research efforts in the 1950s and 1960s, when, in his words, "it seemed to many observers that public law had drifted out of the mainstream of American political science" (Murphy and Tanenhaus 1972, 3). Because of his efforts to introduce more rigorous research methods into the study of judicial phenomenon and, equally important, because of his coauthorship of *The Study of Public Law* (Murphy and Tanenhaus 1972), Tanenhaus significantly helped to resurrect public law within the discipline of political science and to define and secure the boundaries of the subfield. In so doing, he situated the emergent attitudinal approach at the center of the "new" judicial subfield of political science.

TANENHAUS'S CONTRIBUTIONS
TO THE PUBLIC LAW LITERATURE

A brief biographical sketch provides a background for discussion of Tanenhaus the public law scholar. His entire academic training took place at Cornell University, where he received his Ph.D. in 1953. His academic career culminated with his position as professor and chair of the political science department at SUNY, Stony Brook. His most significant professional efforts included membership on the board of editors of the *Midwest Journal of Political Science*, participation in the Law and Society Program of the Northwestern University School of Law, and service as council chair of the Inter-University Consortium for Political Research. During the period of his professional activity, he was the author of numerous articles in both political science and law journals as well as a frequent coauthor and coeditor of important collections on judicial studies and on the discipline of political science. As a scholar, he produced what was cutting-edge research on courts for its time, both substantively and methodologically.

SUPREME COURT DECISION MAKING

Tanenhaus contributed as a coauthor to many studies of Supreme Court justices' behavior, but two such endeavors have had the most longevity and impact on subsequent judicial research. The first of these, and probably the most often cited, was The Supreme Court's Certiorari Jurisdiction: Cue Theory" (Tanenhaus et al. 1963). This piece invented cue theory, and much subsequent research on the phenomenon has been based on this work. It deals with the simple but important question of how Supreme Court justices establish their agenda—that is, how they reduce several thousand requests per year for a hearing on the merits to the hundred or so cases that they agree to consider at length. The authors examine the Court's official primary reasons for granting writs of certiorari as found in what was then called rule 19. The Court said that it would seriously consider granting certiorari if (1) a Court of Appeals decides a point of local law in conflict with local decisions; (2) a Court of Appeals departs from or sanctions departure from the usual course of judicial proceedings; (3) a lower-court ruling conflicts with a Supreme Court ruling; (4) a conflict exists between circuits; or (5) an important question has been decided on which the Supreme Court has not yet ruled.

But are the Court's official reasons an accurate portrayal of what the

Court does? Evidently not, according to the Tanenhaus analysis. In fewer than half of all cases where certiorari was granted are the Court's official reasons of any utility in explaining its behavior. What then might the *real* reasons be? Tanenhaus and his colleagues developed a hypothesis that is both commonsensical and highly intuitive: the justices have neither the time nor the desire to wade through tens of thousands of pages presented to them each year in the form of petitions for writs of certiorari. Rather, the justices must have developed some type of shorthand method for quickly perusing the mountains of paperwork; they must have developed some types of cues that they can readily detect from merely skimming the reams of written material. What might such cues be? The researchers hypothesized that these variables might include such factors as who the parties to the suit were, whether dissension existed on a lower court of appeal, whether a civil liberties subject was involved, and whether an important economic matter was at stake. All hypotheses were tested to determine which ones explained the most variance.

Tanenhaus and his colleagues determined that three of their cues were highly significant predictors of whether the high court would grant certiorari: if the federal government was a party to the suit, if there was dissension on the lower appeals court, and if the case contained a civil liberties issue. If the first of these cues was present, the predicted percentage of granting certiorari was 45; if the second was present, it was 18; and if the third existed, it was 32. If all three were present, the predicted percentage of certioraris reached 80 percent. The authors felt justified in concluding that the cue theory of certiorari is valid (Tanenhaus et al. 1963).

Despite the original contribution of the cue theory article, subsequent research has highlighted its limitations—among them, that its conclusions may have been somewhat time bound. For example, some studies have suggested that a fourth cue has considerable explanatory power—the ideological direction of the lower-court decision. (Songer 1979; Ulmer 1978). In comparing selected periods of the Warren Court (1967 and 1968 terms) and Burger Court (1976 and 1977 terms) on certiorari voting, the analysts reached several conclusions. First, during the liberal Warren Court era, the justices were more likely to review economic cases that had been decided in a conservative manner by the lower court (Armstrong and Johnson 1982), especially when the U.S. government was seeking Court review. Second, and conversely, the more conservative Burger Court tended to review liberal lower-court decisions. Third, the Burger Court was more ready to scrutinize a lower court's civil libertarian position than a lower-court decision limiting civil liberties. In sum, then, the Tanenhaus article was an important first step in the development of cue theory, but its conclusions were somewhat tentative and temporally limited. Cue theory needed and benefited from subsequent research that fleshed out its subtleties and implications, but credit for its original specification still belongs to Tanenhaus and his coauthors.

A second study of Supreme Court decision making with which Tanenhaus is associated is his journal article, "Supreme Court Attitudes toward Federal Administrative Agencies" (1963). This workmanlike piece examines the voting patterns of individual justices in either rejecting or upholding the decisions of ten federal administrative agencies during the 1947–56 terms. Among other things, Tanenhaus found statistically significant evidence for the following hypotheses: (1) members of the Court agree with one another in federal agency cases to a statistically significant degree; (2) the Court and its individual members are more likely to favor federal agencies than to oppose them; (3) the individual justices' voting patterns displayed no statistically significant inconsistencies during the ten-year period; and (4) if agency is held constant, policy and value preferences of statistical significance are revealed in the justices' voting behavior in cases involving organized labor and in lawsuits involving restrictions on competition. While the results of this study may not today sound terribly novel or breathtaking, its significance must be appreciated within the appropriate historical context: the article is part of a first generation of studies that attempted to examine Supreme Court decision making from a rigorous theoretical perspective, using quantifiable data subjected to tests of statistical significance. As such, it is a minor milestone in the shift from qualitative analysis of Supreme Court decisions to modern-day empirical studies; in this, it is analogous to Tanenhaus's work with Walter Murphy on public awareness of and support for the Supreme Court.[1]

COMPARATIVE SCHOLARSHIP

In some ways, it is difficult to single out Tanenhaus's works that make important contributions to the comparative courts literature because virtually all of his major writings take a comparative approach. For example, one of his foremost interests was the question of judicial review, a phenomenon that the United States may have contributed to the political world, but a practice by no means limited to America in the mid–twentieth century. Tanenhaus contended that when considered functionally, "judicial review . . . is one method for resolving disputes over constitutional boundaries. . . . In any political system, no matter how developed or Westernized, the boundaries separating constitutionally permissible behavior from what which is constitutionally proscribed are imprecise enough to cause occasional controversy." He conceded that constitutional courts need not be the institution to resolve such boundary disputes. Rather, in most countries, such a task is performed by institutions such as political parties, religious associations, legislatures, military establishments, or political executives. "But," he noted, "in . . . a few countries . . . judicial bodies [do] actually play . . . a part in settling constitutional boundary disputes" (Tanenhaus 1966b, 1).

Tanenhaus went on to develop a rough model for the ordinal ranking of countries depending on the degree to which they have judicial review. Full judicial review, he argued, meant that "the body exercising judicial review need not be an integral part of the ordinary system of law courts, as is the case in the United States, Canada, Australia, Japan, Norway, Ireland, and India. Therefore, countries which make use of special constitutional tribunals (Austria, Italy, and West Germany) are not *ipso facto* excluded from the roster of those having judicial review. . . . The second assumption is that a judicial body's refusal to enforce or to otherwise legitimize official conduct constitutes judicial review only when the ground for doing so is that the country's constitution has been violated." Finally, "the range of behavior reviewed must cover national (rather than merely regional or local) legislative and executive action" (Tanenhaus 1966b, 1–2).

Tanenhaus's most ambitious project in the comparative area was a reader he prepared with Walter Murphy in 1977, *Comparative Constitutional Law: Cases and Commentary*. Murphy and Tanenhaus argued in the preface that "this book is an effort to look at judicial policy making through actual cases and from a comparative perspective. That perspective, we believe, offers far grater understanding both of certain political problems and of judicial involvement in formulating public policy than does the traditional, ethnocentric approach to judge-made constitutional law as a peculiarly American phenomenon" (1977, ix). The text is divided into three segments: (1) a discussion of the constitutional courts in the political systems of the United States, Germany, Japan, Canada, Australia, and Ireland; (2) specific examples of the activities of these countries' constitutional courts; and (3) an appendix containing key comparative constitutional documents, for example, the Canadian Bill of Rights.

In sum, the work of Tanenhaus and his colleagues in the study of comparative judicial politics was pathbreaking public law research in its day. Sadly, however, the field failed to build on these important early works. It is an irony that after a lapse of almost two decades, the then-chair of the APSA Law and Courts Section, Professor Lee Epstein, strongly chastised her colleagues for ignoring foreign court systems. She concluded her lament with the admonition that "it's time to think about the steps we can take to fill the enormous void that has been created from years, even decades, of neglect of courts abroad" (1999, 3). Tanenhaus, of course, would have nodded in vigorous agreement.

EDUCATING PUBLIC LAW SCHOLARS ABOUT SOCIAL SCIENCE RESEARCH METHODS

A final category of articles authored or coauthored by Tanenhaus was inspired by his strong desire that traditional public law scholars should acquire the research skills and methodologies that were permeating political science as a whole during the 1950s. In addition to insisting that all students entering graduate programs in political science should receive rigorous instruction in statistics, computer use, research design, multivariate analysis, and philosophy of political inquiry, Tanenhaus wrote a number of articles explaining and justifying the use of social science methods for studying the courts. Some of these articles were written for his fellow public law scholars, such as his chapter, "The Application of Social Science Methods to the Study of the Judicial Process," which appeared in Glendon Schubert's essential judicial reader of the 1960s (Tanenhaus 1964)

Tanenhaus also attended to the nexus between social science and law as disciplines. He wrote an essay that documented the use of social science studies in the outcome of important civil rights cases (Tanenhaus 1958), and he subsequently coauthored an article that demonstrated how social science methods could be used in studying the sentencing behavior of judges (Somit, Tanenhaus, and Wilke 1960). This study sought to show lawyers, judges, and law students that there was a verifiable way to answer such questions as whether there is considerable variation in sentencing behavior among judges handling essentially similar cases. Furthermore, however a judge's sentencing patterns might differ from those of his or her colleagues, will the judge's behavior in a given type of case remain generally consistent over any appreciable period of time? In 1966 he used the prestigious *Harvard Law Review* to discuss a technique he had come to value highly, "The Cumulative Scaling of Judicial Decisions" (Tanenhaus 1966a). In this article, he painstakingly described for his legal audience what scaling was and what its underlying assumptions were. He argued that such a technique could provide useful information that could not be obtained as vividly through any other methodology.

In sum, Tanenhaus was strongly committed to the modernization of the public law subfield through introducing its practitioners to the new methodologies and theories that were then having a major impact on the social sciences in general. The full measure of this commitment is seen even more dramatically in an examination of his intellectual leadership role within the discipline of political science and in its public law subfield.

TANENHAUS THE POLITICAL SCIENTIST AND THE DEFINER OF THE PUBLIC LAW SUBFIELD

Tanenhaus was first and foremost a political scientist; only secondarily did he tell his students that he had a special interest in the courts. Colleagues and students recall that his fascination with the discipline itself was more than just the usual interest of a practitioner in his profession. Rather, it was the fascination of a lifelong baseball fan for the ups and down of his or her favorite players and teams. Just as the sports fan might know who played for what team, in what position, and when, Tanenhaus possessed an encyclopedic knowledge of where his colleagues were teaching, how long they had been at their institutions, and what and where they had published. His memory was photographic when it came to the history of the disciplines' journals and the topics they featured. He delighted in talking about which theories were on the rise and which were on the wane and had an equal fascination for which subfields within political science were expanding and at the cutting edge of the discipline and which were receding from that perimeter.

THE POLITICAL SCIENTIST

Tanenhaus's fascination with the internal dynamics of political science manifested itself in a concrete way in the early 1960s when he and Albert Somit began work on an exhaustive survey of the discipline's contours and its practitioners' attitudes and values (Somit and Tanenhaus 1964). After a rigorous series of pretests and after obtaining the advice of several dozen colleagues, the two researchers sent questionnaires to several hundred members of the American Political Science Association. The 431 scholars who responded represented the seven major subfields of the discipline of that era: (1) international relations, (2) American government and politics, (3) comparative government,

(4) political theory, (5) public administration, (6) general politics and political processes, and (7) public law.

This was an opportune time to assess the internal state of the profession because the full impact of the behavioral revolution was first making itself felt. Traditional methods of scholarly inquiry and traditional subjects of research were being challenged by those whose vocabulary included "new" phrases and concepts such as, computer analysis of quantitative data, tests of statistical significance, factor analysis, scaling, and operational definitions. Somit and Tanenhaus found that the profession was in something in a state of turmoil as a result of this behavioral assault. Their data revealed a community of scholars with a distribution of behavioralism scores that is more or less rectangular, or platykurtic. This strongly suggests that there is a continuum of attitudes toward behavioralism with sizable support along most of the continuum. At no point is there an especially heavy concentration of respondents, and only at the outer range of scores does support drop off fairly sharply (Somit and Tanenhaus 1964, 24).

In no subfield was the question of what to make of the behavioral revolution more troubling than in public law. The vast majority of the instructors in this realm described themselves as "con law men"—that is, persons who taught constitutional law primarily from traditional casebooks, often written by lawyers. Such persons may well have read C. Herman Pritchett's highly suggestive *The Roosevelt Court* (1948), which imaginatively employed basic quantitative techniques to analyze systematically the votes of justices in nonunanimous cases between 1937 and 1947. These instructors may have also read Pritchett's sequel, *Civil Liberties and the Vinson Court* (1954). But most public law scholars regarded such behavior thrusts as mere curiosities, and as Murphy and Tanenhaus later noted, "Pritchett's quantitative approach did not immediately begin a new school. . . . [A]lthough many scholars recognized the merit of Pritchett's work, many others, including an occasional Supreme Court justice, deplored his use of statistics, comparing it to 'box scores' in baseball reports" (Murphy and Tanenhaus 1972, 19).

The initial refusal of scholars in the public law field to embrace the behavioral approach had its effect in the discipline, as Somit and Tanenhaus documented and bemoaned in *American Political Science*. The book noted that in a 1953 directory, 18.1 percent of political scientists identified themselves with public law, a number that dropped to 16.4 percent in 1961 and to only 9.1 percent in 1963, the lowest percentage of the seven subfields (Somit and Tanenhaus 1964, 52, 54). Equally disturbing to public law scholars were the numbers showing how other members of the discipline ranked the significance of current scholarship in the various subfields. Comparative government led the field with a score of 3.78, while public law was next to last, with a humiliating score of .394 (56).

The declining number of public law scholars and the tendency of the profession to regard their "traditional, nonbehavioral" scholarship as more and more peripheral to mainline research profoundly affected Tanenhaus. He became convinced that the only way that public law could resurrect itself and regain mainstream status within the profession was to embrace the main tenets and methodological approaches offered by the behavioral movement. More specifically, he believed that mature constitutional law scholars needed to go back to school—as Tanenhaus had done—to study statistics, computer science, and philosophies of political inquiry that lent themselves to empirical verification. Graduate students in public law must be required to take formal courses in these realms as a routine part of their education and should attend summer courses at the University of Michigan that provided more sophisticated training in these subjects. He also felt the strong need to prepare a textbook about the subfield of public law, a book that would teach both students and existing scholars the tools of behavioral trade and what they could offer for public law. The book must also expand the subfield to take in substantive areas of analysis and research other than merely analyzing Supreme Court decisions. Such a book, according to Tanenhaus, could serve as a sort of touchstone for public law scholars and could help to restore the respect of the other members of the profession, who were rapidly relegating public law scholarship into the backwaters of the discipline. Such a work did appear in 1972 when Tanenhaus and Walter Murphy published *The Study of Public Law*, whose contents and significance I will address shortly.

Tanenhaus's fascination with the big picture—that is, with the entire state of political science—was further manifested when a sequel to *American Political Science* appeared in print, *The Development of Political Science from Burgess to Behavioralism* (Somit and Tanenhaus 1967). Somit and Tanenhaus again provided a book that was a first of its kind: an intellectual history and assessment of the entire discipline of political science. This text became required reading for all political science instructors and graduate students, and the fact that the authors were identified with the public law subfield did no harm to its beleaguered status.

In addition to providing a very readable and interesting intellectual history of the discipline, *The Development of Political Science* is perhaps most often cited for its classic outline of what its authors called the "behavioral creed." While Somit and Tanenhaus are quick to point out that the propositions in their creed have been readily borrowed from other scholars, they still deserve credit for distilling them in such a way as to make them particularly relevant to political science scholarship. Moreover, their creed's propositions eventually became applied to scholars in public law when Tanenhaus and Murphy turned their focus to invigorating that subfield with *The Study of Public Law*.

In discussing these key principles of the behavioral creed, Somit and Tanenhaus offer the caveat that "not even the most committed behavioralist necessarily holds all of these views" and that "few . . . would be willing to carry every one of [them] to its logical extreme" (1967, 177).

1. Political science has the potential to become a true science that is capable of explanation and prediction. Such a science might resemble biology more than chemistry or physics, but it is science nonetheless. With this goal in mind, political scientists should address themselves to seeking patterns and regularities in political behavior, and they should think of phenomena in terms of independent and dependent variables. Descriptive studies, while sometimes instructive, should be kept to a minimum, and political scientists should support rigorous, analytic approaches to the development of political theory.

2. The primary focus of political research should be on phenomena that can be observed and measured, such as what a political actor has said or done. Such an actor might be either an individual or a political aggregate. This approach should be preferred over the more traditional institutional approach because of the impossibility of studying such behavior without examining the words and actions of those who carry out political functions.

3. The best data can be put into quantifiable form. Only data in this form can truly lend themselves to a precise statement about political relationships and regularities.

4. Theory must be the guiding light behind all types of political inquiry. In principle, one should begin with a broad, general theory derived from the literature and from there formulate more specific hypotheses about what one expects to derive from the subsequent data analysis. At the same time, the words and the concepts in the theories need to be operationally defined—that is, defined in such a clear, rigorous way that the research could be duplicated by other scholars. Theory could be low level, middle level, or general, but the ultimate goal should be the development of overarching generalizations that explain and interrelate political phenomena in the same way that current proponents of superstring theory hope to do in their integration of the theories of relativity and quantum mechanics.

5. Political science should place a higher value on doing pure research than on seeking to address and resolve contemporary social and political problems. Writing about political reform produces scant important scientific knowledge and is basically an unproductive diversion of time and resources.

6. Because science lacks the capacity to determine the truth or falsity of values (such as equality, free will, good government, and so on), political science should not concern itself with such issues. Political researchers should not be concerned with the great issues of the day except where behavior related to these issues can be empirically examined for a valid scientific purpose.

7. Political science should readily borrow theories, techniques, and approaches from sister disciplines, especially those in other social sciences (such as psychology and economics) and perhaps from the harder sciences (such as biology, botany, and zoology).

8. Political scientists should place much more emphasis on its research methodologies. Anyone earning a Ph.D. should be thoroughly schooled in the use of mathematical models, survey research, multivariate analysis, and game theory. Furthermore, both aspiring graduate students and seasoned scholars should make every effort to be aware of and to put aside as much as possible their value preferences in carrying out their research projects. (Somit and Tanenhaus 1967, 177–79)

Tanenhaus believed (albeit with varied intensity) in all eight tenets of this behavioral creed; he worked ardently to manifest them in his own singular research projects and, more importantly, in his attempts to revitalize and redefine the besieged subfield of public law as he grappled with it in the 1960s.

THE DEFINER OF THE PUBLIC LAW SUBFIELD

Despite his many important studies of judicial behavior, Tanenhaus's main contribution to the subfield stems from his attempts to revitalize the quality, direction, and scope of judicial research. Prior to the publication of *Frontiers of Judicial Research* in 1969 and, more importantly, of *The Study of Public Law* in 1972, public law scholars were declining in number relative to other political science subfields, and other areas of the discipline generally had little esteem for public law work. By the mid-1970s, however, the subfield seemed to have found its way again: more scholars were entering that realm to do teaching and research, and such individuals were publishing in the mainstream journals, the real indication that their work was being taken seriously. Dozens of fine scholars were responsible for this turnabout, but I believe that Tanenhaus was perhaps first among equals when it comes to deserving credit for this regeneration of the public law subfield.

There are several reasons why Tanenhaus was uniquely suited to be a key figure in the renaissance of public law in the 1970s and beyond. First, with his previous research on the history of political science as a discipline (*The Development of Political Science*) and his analysis of the state of the field (*American Political Science*), he possessed the special and unique insights necessary to write a book that defined the intellectual tools and contours of public law (*The Study of Public Law*). His prior disciplinary analyses had given him a keen understanding of what made a field of research productive and respected and what conditions were signs of pathology. Second, the prestige accorded him for his writings about the profession in general made him a highly respected figure throughout the general political science profession. That he was a public law man did nothing to hurt the image of public law within the discipline, and among public law scholars his stature secured him an audience willing to listen when he called for reform and redirection of research efforts.

There were other reasons for Tanenhaus's pivotal position when public law underwent its renaissance. One was that he possessed the theoretical and methodological knowledge essential to an understanding and appreciation of the behavioral movement within the public law subfield. Not only could he call for methodological and theoretical innovations, but he could conduct studies using the tools and insights of the behavioral movement. Furthermore, he was prepared to explain in simple English how his fellow public law scholars and graduate students could employ the latest research techniques. (A good example is chapter 7 of *The Study of Public Law*, "Statistical Methods in the Study of Public Law.") At times, he would even enter the lion's den to explain to lawyers and law students how to scale Supreme Court decisions and why the knowledge produced from doing so was insightful (see, for example, Tanenhaus 1966a).

Finally, Tanenhaus's training, orientation, and experiences with the public law realm gave him a very suitable vantage point from which to call for an inclusive, all-encompassing subfield that did not readily read anyone out of the discipline. This point needs to be emphasized because in the 1960s it became common for many neophyte behavioralists in public law to turn to the works of traditional scholars and say, "That's just not political science," an observation never well taken by older scholars who had long labored in those traditional vineyards. Despite his commitment to the tenets of behavioralism, Tanenhaus was an eclectic scholar with a courteous, patient disposition who much preferred evolution rather than revolution in the subfield. He was trained in a highly traditional manner and consequently enjoyed and appreciated the more traditional forms of scholarship. When it came to methodological and statistical skills, Tanenhaus used to refer to himself as self-taught, and indeed, many contemporary scholars in the discipline had quantitative skills that outshown those of Tanenhaus (including Glendon Schubert and S. Sidney Ulmer). He valued reading Supreme Court decisions; he respected and saw value in judicial biographies and historical analysis as well as in quantitative analysis of data. Because of his attitude toward traditional scholarship, his calls for methodological and theoretical reforms did not fall on totally deaf and unsympathetic traditionalist ears. Just as a centrist justice on the Supreme Court has greater potential to put together a winning coalition, so too was Tanenhaus more likely to expand and unify public law scholars by his inclusive way of defining and refining the subfield. To employ a judicial process trope, his seminal work, *The Study of Public Law*, showed that he was both a good task and social leader.[2]

Prior to the publication of *The Study of Public Law*, Tanenhaus and Murphy organized the Shambaugh Conference on Judicial Research, held at the University of Iowa in the fall of 1967. In addition to Pritchett's opening address, thirteen papers were presented over three days, and the sessions were led by panels of scholars from two dozen colleges, universities, and law schools in the United States, Canada, and Japan. The papers produced at this conference were an indication that the subfield of public law was finding its way back into the political science mainstream. In the introductory chapter of the resulting publication, *Frontiers of Judicial Research*, Tanenhaus and his coeditor, Joel Grossman, took the pulse of the public law subfield and assessed its status within the larger realm of political science. Their commentary begins with this positive observation about the judicial field's self-revision: "Public law is in a state of flux. A field which had for a time drifted close to the outer margins of political science is now fast returning to the fold. As with most other fields in the discipline, recent changes in the scope and methods of judicial research have been sweeping in character and breathtaking in pace" (Grossman and Tanenhaus 1969, 3).

Tanenhaus and Grossman then paid homage to those who had pursued high-level scholarship in the judicial realm in the 1930s and 1940s, including Pritchett, Edward S. Corwin, Robert E. Cushman, Charles Grove Haines, Thomas Reed Powell, Robert K. Carr, Charles Fairman, and Charles Brent Fisher, men whose works Tanenhaus had read and much respected. He saw the behavioral revolution as building on the insights and theories of these more traditional scholars, not as expelling their works from the discipline with the parting taunt so characteristics of the 1960s, "What you did was not political science." In this sense, *Frontiers* both explains and accounts for the genesis of the behavioral or attitudinal approach to the study of judicial decision making and offers a "big tent" message in reflecting on the state of the subfield.

After praising the quantitative studies that had begun to flower in the 1960s, Tanenhaus lent his encouragement to two new trends, both of which were reflected in *Frontiers of Judicial Research:* research on state and lower courts at home and research on constitutional courts in other countries. After arguing that the Supreme Court had been overstudied, he bemoaned the fact that the subfield had focused so little on courts in other countries:

> Perhaps the most striking thing about pre-1963 materials is that virtually none of them dealt with any system other than the United States. Nor, we hasten to add, had nonbehavioralists during the period under discussion done much of anything to show the political relevance of courts, judges, and law outside of the United States. Is there any wonder, then that in the spring of 1963 political scientists in comparative government, general politics, or international relations saw relatively little significance to what public law people were doing? During the years between the two world wars, when the ranks of those engaged in public law research were far thinner than in the contemporary period, we published substantially more of direct concern to our brethren in these other fields than we did from 1948–1962.

Inadequacy of scope can also account for the low ranking of public law by our colleagues in American politics and public administration. Why this is so should be readily apparent. The lion's share of behavioral judicial research from 1948–1962 focused on the United States Supreme Court, and much of that share involved policy values as the principal determinant of judicial decision making—as did most of the reported research on other American courts and judges. All this has now begun to change. (Grossman and Tanenhaus 1969, 24–25)

These are prophetic words with respect to revising the research agenda of judicial behavioralism. In 1999, Lee Epstein, then chair of the Law and Courts Section of the APSA, wrote,

> Over the past decade, observers of the judicial process have drawn attention to the increasingly marginal role played by the U.S. Supreme Court in American society. . . . To support this claim, they point to the Court's declining plenary docket . . . , its inclination to reject especially salient cases . . . , its use of various gate-keeping devices to dispose of controversial cases it has accepted . . . , and its inability to generate social change.
>
> What makes this claim especially intriguing is that it comes at the very same time scholars are taking note of the increasingly important role played by courts in European democracies. As Schwartz (1992) puts it, "Before World War II, few European states had constitutional courts, and virtually none exercised any significant judicial review over legislation. After 1945 all that changed. [They] created tribunals with power to annul legislative enactments inconsistent with constitutional requirements. Many of these courts have become significant—even powerful—actors." Henckaerts and Van der Jeught (1998) agree, asserting that courts in Europe "have played an active role in ensuring the supremacy of constitutional principles."
>
> If these comments are to be believed, then we must confront an essential irony: We judicial specialists continue to focus on the U.S. Supreme Court, despite its (potentially) decreasing importance, and continue (with limited exceptions) to ignore courts abroad, despite their increasing prominence. (1)

If the renaissance that Tanenhaus and others began in the late 1960s had continued, perhaps Epstein's recent lament on the narrow state of the discipline would have been unnecessary.

Paths not taken notwithstanding, the 1972 publication of *The Study of Public Law* was the culmination of Tanenhaus's decade-long effort to redefine, refine, and revitalize the subfield of public law. With his knowledge of the workings and internal dynamics of a learned discipline, with his mastery of both traditional and quantitatively sophisticated research skills, and with his strong desire to bring the public law subfield back to its former cutting-edge status, Tanenhaus was an ideal candidate (along with Murphy) to write this defining piece on the history, research status, and future of public law. The book was a key opportunity for Tanenhaus, appearing as it did during a critical period in the development of the public law subfield. To cite a judicial analogy, just as Chief Justice Marshall had the unparalleled opportunity to write on a blank slate when he penned the key early decisions on the commerce clause and on the taxing and spending powers, so too was Tanenhaus as coauthor of *The Study of Public Law* well positioned to operationalize and define the subfield. The text profoundly affected how public law scholars and graduate students viewed their call to arms and significantly influenced how the rest of political science viewed and evaluated its colleagues in what ten years previously had been an intellectual backwater.

Because of the importance of *The Study of Public Law* to reflection on and revision of the emergent attitudinal approach, a detailed synopsis of—and reflection on—its contents is in order. Chapter 1 begins with a lucid history of the subfield within the broader context of political science. This section was typical Tanenhaus, because he insisted that all of his graduate students have a feel for the larger historical setting in which they worked. When he and Murphy reviewed the works of more traditional scholars such as Pritchett and legal realist school commentators such as Haines, the authors did not ridicule their predecessors for their nontheoretical, nonquantitative approach. Rather, Murphy and Tanenhaus praised the keenness of their forefathers' analysis and revealed that they generated many hypotheses that contemporary behavioralists could readily test. Perhaps the best proof of Tanenhaus's convictions in this regard is found in the book's dedication: "To Robert E. Cushman, 1889–1969, and C. Herman Pritchett," followed by a telling quotation from Ezra Pound: "It was you that broke the new wood, / Now is a time for carving." In addition to an insightful and inclusive review of the contributions of more traditional scholarship, Tanenhaus displayed his continuing belief that public law should have a heavy comparative bent. A discussion of judicial review in the United States is interspersed with references to its functional equivalent in Australia, Japan, Ireland, and other countries.

The comparative theme continues to echo in chapter 2, which addresses "The Political Consequences of Judicial Decisions." The chapter not only discusses key American "political" cases, such as *Brown v. Board of Education* and *Miranda v. Arizona*, but offers comparisons with similar judicial bombshells in countries such as Canada, Ireland, West Germany, Japan, Australia, and India. Tanenhaus also used this chapter to call for research away from the overexamined U.S. Supreme Court. He extolled the usefulness of studies of lower courts' responses to Supreme Court decisions as well as the impact of its politically key decisions.

The third chapter focuses on "Access and Influence"—that is, how easily the government and average citizens have access to judicial review and the degree to which judicial decisions may be affected by the other branches of government. Again using a comparative approach, Murphy and Tanenhaus outline the degree to which obtaining judicial review is easier in some countries than others. The authors also discuss how other political actors, such as the executive and legislative branches, can "correct" or thwart judicial decisions with which these actors disagree. It is clear from this discussion that the authors viewed courts as highly political institutions in continuous interaction with the entire political system. This approach contrasted with prior practice, in which public law scholars focused narrowly on judicial decision making—a phenomenon critically noted by Tanenhaus and his colleagues in 1963.

Chapter 4 reviews the literature on "Judicial Recruitment, Training, and Tenure," offering appropriate comparisons with a score of other nations. The authors not only stress that recruitment is important for its symbolic value but also argue that values and attitudes acquired during the training and recruitment processes have important manifestations in the way jurists subsequently decide cases. The chapter also outlines several models being developed that attempted to relate social background and hereditary factors, as tempered by professional training, to judges' subsequent values and role perceptions, which were then tied empirically to judges' voting patterns.

The fifth chapter explores the ways that public law scholars may legitimately explain and predict individual judges' votes. The authors' eclectic and inclusive philosophy is nowhere more evident than in this chapter, because they accord legitimacy not only to the more behavioral methods for analyzing judicial behavior but also to such traditional methods as opinion analysis (and its more modern counterpart, content analysis, à la the works of Werner Grunbaum) and judicial biography (employing a justice's private papers, as for example, in Mason 1956). Most of the chapter is devoted to a subject for which

Tanenhaus had much enthusiasm, scaling and the utility of scalogram analysis, the leading edge of attitudinally based research. Perhaps indicative of the state of the discipline at that time, the authors explain what scaling is, what its assumptions are, and what it seeks to demonstrate. Murphy and Tanenhaus also defend the technique against a barrage of contemporary criticisms (some of which are still legitimate): "the adequacy of the conventional tests for unidimensionality and scalability, methods for positioning the columns and rows of the scalogram matrix, the designation of cutting points when several seem equally appropriate, the handling of missing data, and the frequent impossibility of developing a unique solution for a given set of data" (1972, 138). Despite all these problems, scaling techniques were still useful because "they do allow analysis to proceed on the basis that litigation may provide judges with several different stimuli rather than merely one" (140).

In chapter 6, "The Group Phase of Decision Making," the authors begin by giving due credit to scholars who had sought to explain appellate court decision making in terms of judges' personal interaction. Scholars such as Murphy and David Danelski who used justices' private judicial papers and judicial biography are cited for traditional but rigorous scholarship in explaining fluidity (changes in justices' votes from the initial, tentative vote at conference to the tallying of the final vote). Murphy and Tanenhaus then explain the new method for empirically measuring judges' influence and interagreement, bloc analysis. After providing several examples of bloc analysis, including its use on foreign courts, the authors outline both the advantages and limitations of this statistical method.

Chapter 7 is the most technical and sophisticated of the book, focusing on the general use of statistical methods in public law research. This discussion includes the use of tests of statistical significance, measurements of association (for example, the Phi coefficient), partial and multiple correlations, residuals, and factor analysis. It is an interesting commentary on the state of the discipline that the authors not only provide arguments for the use of these techniques but even explain how they are performed—most current graduate students would learn about such techniques in introductory methodology courses, but three decades ago, the vast majority of public law scholars were largely untutored in such subjects. Murphy and Tanenhaus deserve credit not only for encouraging public law scholars to learn these new methodologies but also for making the acquisition of them "respectable." The authors were, in effect, saying, "We have learned much from traditional scholarship, but now it is time to move on." Also, by giving traditional scholarship its due respect and by not reading such scholars out of the discipline, as many new converts to behavioralism were wont to do, Murphy and Tanenhaus facilitated public law's move toward expanding its array of research tools and its reorientation around a new, empirically grounded theory of judicial decision making.

The final chapter speculates about the future of public law as a subfield within political science. As is frequently the case with such attempts, there is a fair amount of overlap between predictions about what will happen and beliefs about what should occur. First, Murphy and Tanenhaus predict (hope) that research will turn away from the overstudied U.S. Supreme Court and toward "the operations of trial and intermediate appellate court judges as important political actors in their own right." These lower court judges "help shape policy. They may do so less dramatically but in the aggregate, probably no less effectively—and certainly much more frequently—than do Supreme Court justices" (1972, 216). In this regard, the authors' prediction or prescription seems to have been borne out, given the extensive amount of research done on lower federal courts and on state courts during the past three decades.

The authors also call for and predict more comparative research in public law. They contend that "accurate, detailed, and widespread dissemination of knowledge about the work of constitutional courts will undoubtedly generate more and more truly comparative research" (1972, 216). In retrospect, this call seems to have fallen on somewhat deaf ears, given the dearth of plentiful, good-quality comparative research in recent decades (see Epstein 1999). Murphy and Tanenhaus also predict that "future public law scholarship will [see] increased reliance on quantitative analysis. . . . In the longer run, scholars interested in courts and judges will probably develop more advanced analytical operations as they work closely with statisticians and mathematicians" (216–17). This prediction surely has been borne out, describing the lion's share of public law research published in major journals in recent decades.

The authors also predict that another "feature of future public law scholarship [will be] judicial biographies," both the traditional kind and those relying heavily on psychological analysis (1972, 217). On this matter, their crystal ball seems to have been a bit cloudy. While some fine biographies have been produced since the 1970s (for example, Novick 1989; Smith 1993), the past thirty years have hardly been noted for their plethora of top-grade judicial biographies. Finally, Murphy and Tanenhaus predict that public law will focus more on the development of theory building "grounded in hard empirical research" (220). Great progress has surely occurred in this endeavor in the past third of a century, but few in public law would say that the subfield has a general explanatory theory within its reach. A great deal of thinking and research still need to be done, as the subfield's best minds have recently attested (see, for example, Baum 1997). Yet *The Study of Public Law* stands out as the subfield's first self-conscious, concerted effort to reflect—and to reflect critically—on the theory of judicial decision making that was guiding the area's progress.

CONCLUSION: PUBLIC LAW, THE "LEARNED DISCIPLINE"

The productive period of Tanenhaus's scholarship was comparatively short, lasting from the early 1960s, when his first major writings began to appear in print, until his death in 1980. But during the two decades of his primary scholarly activity, he strongly affected his subfield and discipline. First, it is appropriate to applaud his book chapters and journal articles, frequently coauthored, that focused on narrow but significant topics of interest to judicial behavior scholars of his day. These include his studies of voting behavior of Supreme Court justices (especially the oft-cited article on cue theory); his important work on public opinion support levels for the high court; his groundbreaking theoretical work on comparative judicial studies; and, finally, his writings that tried to educate and persuade public law scholars to dip their toes in the pool of modern research methods.

But I believe that the greatest accolades for Tanenhaus must go to his roles (1) as a historian and definer of political science as a learned discipline and (2) as a leader within the subfield of public law in its critical transition from traditional research to sophisticated, modern research methodologies. His authorship of several books and articles that traced the historical development of political science gave him great prestige within the discipline; moreover, the stature and insights gleaned from those larger works empowered him to do for the subfield of public law what he helped to do for political science as a whole. Public law, like the social science of which it was a part (if not the founding part), was indeed a learned discipline, a cumulative synthesis. Because of Tanenhaus's proficiency and knowledge of traditional research skills and subjects and because of his self-taught methodological abilities, he was in a singular position to lead public law's transition from its traditional posture to one that appreciated empirically based theories, rigorous research methods, and a comparative approach to the study of courts. While his leadership on these points was not equally heeded, his desire to (re)integrate public law within political science and to integrate into public law the emergent attitudinal approach to the study of judging make him a unique but understated pioneer: unique because almost alone among the judicial behavioralists of his day, he sincerely cared about the coherence of the public law subfield; understated because in stressing synthesis and inclusion, he risked creating the impression that he was not pathbreaking. But this impression would be false, for the path that Tanenhaus laid (to indulge in some pioneering language and to playfully borrow a Schubertian public law metaphor) was akin to a bridge connecting an "exotic bayou" with terra firma.[3] His quiet temperament, firm belief that this connection could be made, and ability to talk with both the traditional and behavioral camps strengthened Tanenhaus's capacity to serve as a bridge from old to modern during a tempestuous period in the history of the public law subfield.

NOTES

1. Tanenhaus and Murphy published several important articles between the mid-1960s and 1981 pertaining to public opinion and the U.S. Supreme Court. Such research was funded by the National Science Foundation, and significantly (in terms of public law's linkage with other fields in political science), several other prominent survey research scholars collaborated (e.g., Warren E. Miller, Arthur C. Wolfe, and Arthur H. Miller). The first of these published studies focused on the 1964 presidential campaign of Senator Barry Goldwater, who strongly attacked the Warren Court's liberal decisions as part of his quest for the Oval Office. This study represented the first national survey to ask respondents questions "about their awareness of recent Court decisions" (Murphy and Tanenhaus 1968, 39), meaning that the researchers had no prior data with which to compare their findings. The study's conclusions were intriguing but not definitive. The authors were able "to demonstrate a rather sizable correlation between attitudes toward the Court and support for Goldwater, but [they could] not prove that the campaign was responsible for this correlation." Still, the study did find that the effect of Goldwater's anti-Court campaign "was substantial" (47).

One year later, using this same data set, Tanenhaus and Murphy took a broader look at public opinion and the U.S. Supreme Court: they addressed the important theoretical question of which conditions must exist for a constitutional court to exercise the important function of "boundary maintenance" with maximum effectiveness. The researchers begin by postulating three conditions for this: "The first condition is that the constitutional court be visible. Major decisions cannot have a direct—though they may have an indirect— legitimating impact if they are not perceived. . . . The second condition is a recognition that it is a proper judicial function to interpret and apply the fundamental principles underlying the polity—acceptance, that is, of judges, as guardians of the chastity of the constitution. . . . The third condition is that the court be regarded as carrying out its responsibilities in an impartial and competent manner" (Murphy and Tanenhaus 1969b, 275). This study sought to determine the extent to which these prerequisites for the Supreme Court's legitimation of regime change existed in the United States at that time. The authors addressed the topic by analyzing both "specific" and "diffuse support" for the regime, terms that were then part of the prominent systems analysis theory popularized in political science by David Easton (1965). Murphy and Tanenhaus's data showed "that 27.0 percent of the respondents . . . are aware of the Supreme Court's role and can be classified on the diffuse support scale. Of these classifiable people, about half grant the Court positive diffuse support, three in ten deny it, and two in ten are evasive. In terms of the total sample, and hence presumably the entire adult population of the United States, about one person in eight meets all three of the criteria we established [in the 1968 article]. But this 12.8 percent, it cannot be too strenuously stressed, constitutes a considerable share of the politically attentive public" (Murphy and Tanenhaus 1969b, 295). A 1975 follow-up study reinterviewed some 919 individuals who had been part of the 1969 study, finding that "the level of diffuse support, although moderately and significantly lower in 1975 than in 1966, still remained slightly favorable. In contrast, the level of specific support had increased, but, nonetheless, continued to be strongly unfavorable." Employing a statistical model that controlled for stability enabled Tanenhaus and Murphy to test several hypotheses about the causes of change in diffuse support between 1966 and 1975; hypotheses attributing change to ideological variables found strong confirmation (Tanenhaus and Murphy 1981, 38–39).

While these studies of public opinion and the Supreme Court do not focus on explaining judicial behavior, their high degree of methodological competency and concern with issues at the cutting edge of judicial process research make them significant enough to note as part of Tanenhaus's contributions to public law research.

2. The language concerning social and task leadership comes from the work of David Danelski, discussed by Thomas Walker in this volume.

3. In a 1963 article, Glendon Schubert famously labeled traditional public law scholarship "an exotic bayou, cut off from the mainstream of theoretical and methodological advances in political science" (1963, 445). Proceeding along these metaphorical lines presumably renders judicial behavioralism terra firma. No evaluative ranking is intended by this terminology here, though Schubert surely intended it in his phrasing.

REFERENCES

Armstrong, Virginia C., and Charles A. Johnson. 1982. "Certiorari Decisions by the Warren and Burger Courts: Is Cue Theory Time Bound?" *Polity* 15:141–50.

Baum, Lawrence. 1997. *The Puzzle of Judicial Behavior*. Ann Arbor: University of Michigan Press.

Danelski, David J. 1979. "The Influence of the Chief Justice in the Decisional Process." In *Courts, Judges, and Politics*, 3d ed., ed. Walter F. Murphy and C. Herman Pritchett. New York: Random House.

Easton, David. 1965. *A Systems Analysis of Political Life*. New York: John Wiley and Sons.

Epstein, Lee. 1999. "The Comparative Advantage." *Law and Courts* 9 (3): 1–5.

Grossman, Joel B., and Joseph Tanenhaus, eds. 1969. *Frontiers of Judicial Research*. New York: John Wiley and Sons.

Henckaerts, Jean-Marie, and Stefaan Van der Jeught. 1998. "Human Rights Protection Under the New Constitution of Central Europe." *Loyola International and Comparative Law Journal* 20:475–506.

Mason, Alpheus Thomas. 1956. *Harlan Fiske Stone: Pillar of the Law*. New York: Viking Press.

Murphy, Walter F. 1964. *The Elements of Judicial Strategy*. Chicago: University of Chicago Press.

Murphy, Walter F., and Joseph Tanenhaus. 1968. "Public Opinion and the Supreme Court: The Goldwater Campaign." *Public Opinion Quarterly* 32:31–50.

Murphy, Walter F., and Joseph Tanenhaus. 1969a. "Constitutional Courts and Political Representation." In *Modern American Democracy*, ed. Michael N. Danielson and Walter F. Murphy. New York: Holt, Rinehart, and Winston.

Murphy, Walter F., and Joseph Tanenhaus. 1969b. "Public Opinion and the United States Supreme Court: A Preliminary Mapping of Some Prerequisites for Court Legitimation of Regime Changes." In *Frontiers of Judicial Research*, ed. Joel B. Grossman and Joseph Tanenhaus. New York: John Wiley and Sons.

Murphy, Walter F., and Joseph Tanenhaus. 1972. *The Study of Public Law*. New York: Random House.

Murphy, Walter F., and Joseph Tanenhaus. 1977. *Comparative Constitutional Law: Cases and Commentaries*. New York: St. Martin's Press.

Novick, Sheldon M. 1989. *Honorable Justice: The Life of Oliver Wendell Holmes*. Boston: Little, Brown.

Pritchett, C. Herman. 1948. *The Roosevelt Court: A Study in Judicial Politics and Values*. New York: Macmillan.

Pritchett, C. Herman. 1954. *Civil Liberties and the Vinson Court*. Chicago: University of Chicago Press.

Schubert, Glendon. 1963. "Behavioral Research in Public Law." *American Political Science Review* 57:433–45.

Schwartz, Herman. 1992. "The New Eastern European Constitutional Courts." *Michigan Journal of International Law* 13:741–85.

Smith, Christopher E. 1993. *Justice Antonin Scalia and the Supreme Court's Conservative Movement.* Westport, Conn.: Praeger.

Somit, Albert, and Joseph Tanenhaus. 1964. *American Political Science: A Profile of a Discipline.* New York: Atherton Press.

Somit, Albert, and Joseph Tanenhaus. 1967. *The Development of Political Science: From Burgess to Behavioralism.* Boston: Allyn and Bacon.

Somit, Albert, Joseph Tanenhaus, and Walter Wilke. 1960. "Aspects of Judicial Sentencing Behavior." *University of Pittsburgh Law Review* 21:613–21.

Somit, Albert, Joseph Tanenhaus, and Walter Wilke. 1964. "Aspects of Judicial Sentencing Behavior." In *Judicial Behavior: A Reader in Theory and Research*, ed. Glendon Schubert. Chicago: Rand McNally.

Songer, Donald R. 1979. "Concern for Policy Outputs as a Cue for Supreme Court Decisions on Certiorari," *Journal of Politics* 41:1185–94.

Tanenhaus, Joseph. 1958. "Social Science in Civil Rights Litigation." In *Aspects of Liberty*, ed. Milton Konvitz and Clinton Rossiter. Ithaca: Cornell University Press.

Tanenhaus, Joseph. 1963. "Supreme Court Attitudes toward Federal Administrative Agencies." *Journal of Politics* 22:502–24.

Tanenhaus, Joseph. 1964. "The Application of Social Science Methods to the Study of the Judicial Process." In *Judicial Behavior: A Reader in Theory and Research*, ed. Glendon Schubert. Chicago: Rand McNally.

Tanenhaus, Joseph. 1966a. "The Cumulative Scaling of Judicial Decisions." *Harvard Law Review* 79:1583–94.

Tanenhaus, Joseph. 1966b. "Judicial Review." Unpublished manuscript.

Tanenhaus, Joseph. 1968. "Judicial Review." *International Encyclopedia of the Social Sciences* 8:303–6.

Tanenhaus, Joseph., and Walter F. Murphy. 1981. "Patterns of Public Support for the Supreme Court: A Panel Study." *Journal of Politics* 43:25–39.

Tanenhaus, Joseph, Marvin Schick, Matthew Muraskin, and Daniel Rosen. 1963. "The Supreme Court's Certiorari Jurisdiction." In *Judicial Decision-Making*, ed. Glendon Schubert. New York: Free Press.

Ulmer, S. Sidney. 1978. "Selecting Cases for Supreme Court Review: An Underdog Model." *American Political Science Review* 72:902–10.

CHAPTER 7

Beverly Blair Cook: The Value of Eclecticism

Lee Epstein and Lynn Mather

At a roundtable held in her honor, Beverly Blair Cook remarked that a "scientist who receives a prize has a conventional modest disclaimer— 'I am standing on the shoulders of giants.' My response to being honored by this panel is to point to two lines of predecessors on whose scholarship I have tried to build. One is a line of male giants; the other a line of female ghosts."[1] She went on to describe the contributions of three of those "ghosts," Sophonisba Breckinridge, Alice Paul, and Charlotte Williams.

To be sure, Cook is right: several women have contributed mightily to the study of law and courts yet largely been ignored or, at best, underappreciated. At the same time, however, Cook's comments are characteristically modest. For the extensive and significant scholarship of Beverly Blair Cook—not of Breckinridge, Paul, or Williams—paved the way for women in the field of law and courts. No account of the emergence of judicial behavior within the discipline of political science would be complete without a reckoning of her contributions.

COOK'S CAREER DEVELOPMENT: A THUMBNAIL SKETCH

Cook's progression in the professional world of political science was, like many women of her generation, something short of linear. After receiving a B.A. (with high honors) from Wellesley College in 1948 and a M.A. from University of Wisconsin at Madison in 1949, she served as an instructor of political science at Iowa State University in 1949–50. She then exchanged teaching for family responsibilities, marrying and staying home and rearing four children.

In 1960, she resumed her graduate work at Claremont University and Graduate School, receiving her Ph.D. from Claremont in 1962. Cook then took an assistant professorship at California State University at Fullerton, where she gained tenure in 1966. In that same year, she met Neil Cotter, another political scientist, at a NSF summer seminar at Virginia Polytechnic Institute; they married five weeks later.

In 1967, Cook, Cotter, and their combined brood of eight moved to the University of Wisconsin at Milwaukee. At first, it seemed that Cook and her husband would be unable to work together in the department of political science. The university told her that its nepotism rule barred married couples from obtaining tenure in the same department, so Cook transferred to the School of Social Welfare for a year, "while [she] helped the university discover that the rule was unwritten and in any case contradicted federal law" (Cook 1994b, 80). With that matter resolved, she moved back to the political science department, where she would produce some of her most important work and where she would remain until her retirement in 1989.

To term Cook retired, though, is something of a misnomer. From her home in Atascadero, California, she continues to write at an astonishing pace. Her essays in the 1990s have offered a measure of significant U.S. Supreme Court decisions (1993), commented on the Court's agenda (1994a), considered opinion assignment on the Burger Court (1995), analyzed the decision of Justice Blackmun (1996), and presented biographies of important women judges (Cook 1998). In her latest work, to be published in *Judicature*, she applied "fuzzy logic" to the Supreme Court's legal language (Cook forthcoming). Her service to the profession also continues. Over the past decade or so, Cook served on Project '87, the joint American Historical Association–American Political Science Association (APSA) Committee on the Bicentennial of the Constitution. More recently, she was elected to the executive committee of the APSA's Law and Courts section.

TOWARD THE STUDY OF JUDICIAL BEHAVIOR: SOME CONTEXTUAL NOTES

At the time Cook was studying for her Ph.D., an intellectual struggle of sorts was ensuing in the field of "public law," as it was then called in political science. The traditional approach to law and courts centered on judicial opinions and appellate court doctrine. Scholars such as Edward Corwin and Robert Cushman drew on history, political theory, and constitutional law to scrutinize and parse Supreme Court opinions. Others, however, including Jack Peltason and Victor Rosenblum, rejected the centrality of legal doctrine, emphasizing instead the process by which law emerges from and reflects political forces. Martin M. Shapiro summarized the essence of this new "political jurisprudence" as "a vision of courts as political agencies and judges as political actors" (1964b, 297).

Viewing judges as political actors led judicial scholars to apply the latest techniques and theories of political science to the study of courts and judicial decision making. The behavioral revolution in political science during this period thus provided a further challenge to traditional legal approaches by introducing scientific ways of studying judicial behavior and legal phenomena. C. Herman Pritchett pioneered the study of judicial behavior beginning in the 1940s with a firm rejection of traditionalists' exclusive focus on legal doctrine. Pritchett's classic *American Political Science Review* article (1941) examined justices' voting patterns in an attempt to understand systematically their divisions of opinion. He subsequently published several influential studies of the Roosevelt and Vinson Courts (for example, Pritchett 1948, 1954).

This intellectual engagement was perhaps in its most heated stage during the 1960s, when Cook was beginning her scholarship in the field. Important journals published acrimonious debates between proponents of traditional legal perspectives, political approaches, and scientific approaches (Shapiro 1964b; Kort 1964; Mendelson 1964a, 1964b, 1966; Spaeth 1965). Articles such as Schubert's (1967) delineated the key players and their views of the field of judicial behavior. And seminal books, such as Walter F. Murphy's *Elements of Judicial Strategy* (1964), Glendon A. Schubert's *The Judicial Mind* (1965), and Martin M. Shapiro's *Law and Politics in the Supreme Court* (1965a) were published.

Thomas G. Walker (1994) documents how firmly research on judicial politics established itself in the discipline. Walker found that in 1964, for the first time, judicial process articles outnumbered constitutional law pieces in three influential political science journals, and this trend continues today.[2] He also noted that theoretical innovation exploded, with attitude theory, systems theory, social background theory, role theory, fact pattern analysis, game theory, incrementalism, and others used in attempts to explain courts and judicial behavior.

COOK'S MAJOR
SCHOLARLY CONTRIBUTIONS

Although Cook was not initially part of this heyday, she became a major player during the 1970s. Part of the explanation for her ascendancy lies in the enormous breadth of her research program. We see hints of this in her first book, *The Judicial Process in California* (1967), in which she set out themes that she would revisit in subsequent projects. In this work she demonstrated that the judicial process was an essential part of the political process, that political party of judges was directly related to judicial selection, that judges' identity (background, age, race, gender, and class) mattered, that trial court and appellate court judges were important judicial actors, and that a complete understanding of courts necessitated consideration of participants other than judges—lawyers, interest groups, police, and litigants.

Cook also became known for the many different methodological approaches she used in her scholarship. She has always allowed the nature of the problem to dictate the methodology employed. Included in her research on judges are comparative analyses of individuals and of courts across different locations and different time periods. She has drawn on case studies, legal doctrine, personal interviews, judicial biographies and memoirs, broad surveys, historical data, and quantitative statistical data. Cook also has done what too few of us do in our research: she has reexamined primary data collected by others to generate new ideas for analyzing issues.

In short, Cook's earliest research shows the importance of asking interesting questions, thinking theoretically, invoking a wide range of sources, and rigorously and sensitively analyzing data. These traits continued to characterize her later work, but her horizons grew substantially. Over the past three decades, she has skillfully explored questions involving criminal sentencing, judicial administration, and decision making, among many others. Some of these studies rest on careful description and empirical analysis, others explore policy issues and questions of reform, and still others are highly theoretical. She also has demonstrated the usefulness of borrowing from other scholarly literatures—psychology, anthropology, social history, criminal justice, and even biology—to improve our understanding of courts and judges.

So great is its diversity that Cook's work cannot be characterized in a single phrase. Still, we have little hesitation suggesting that her most important contributions came in the areas of socialization, political and legal culture, and women on the bench.[3]

SOCIALIZATION

Some of Cook's earliest research focused on socialization to explain judicial decisions. Defining socialization as "individual learning of the behavioral patterns and the values of institutional roles" (1971b, 253), Cook was among the first to recognize socialization's importance for understanding what judges do. Initial pieces considered ways in which court systems attempt to socialize new judges. For example, in an article published in the *Washington University Law Quarterly* (1971b), she took up two questions relating to the introductory seminars established by the federal government to train new judges in effective case management and processing techniques: Why were they established, and what impact did they have? By invoking a wide range of data sources, Cook demonstrated that socialization through these seminars failed to have the desired effect of making courts more efficient.[4]

Cook's articles on judicial socialization not only were theoretically and methodologically innovative but were also, in at least one regard, substantively distinct from much of the research being produced by her male counterparts. While most of Cook's peers, including many of those profiled in this volume, tended to focus on U.S. Supreme Court justices, she set her sights on the life experiences of state and federal trial judges.[5] In so doing, she played a role in rewriting the agenda for a generation of researchers to come. They heeded her warning that our understanding of the judicial process would be incomplete unless we incorporated other judicial bodies into our work. Empirical studies of trial courts flourished during the late 1970s and 1980s (see, for example, Eisenstein and Jacob 1977; Mather 1979; Feeley 1979; Boyum and Mather 1983). But most of this research centered on criminal courts; much more remains to be done to understand civil courts and to develop broader theories of trial courts.

Cook also had mixed success in convincing her political science colleagues to undertake further investigations explicitly aimed at uncovering the effect of socialization on judicial behavior. To be sure, within a few years of publication of her article in the *Washington University Law Quarterly*, a scattering of work appeared, most notably Alpert, Atkins, and Ziller (1979) and Carp and Wheeler (1972), as well as some related studies, including Milton Heumann's (1978) research on how judges learn about plea bargaining and John Paul Ryan et al.'s (1980) survey and analysis of the work of state trial judges.[6] But this research rarely appeared in political science journals. Indeed, an electronic search of articles published in political science journals since 1980 yielded only one mention of "judicial socialization" or "the socialization of judges," and that mention was in passing.[7]

Conversely, the topic of judicial socialization receives regular coverage in sociolegal journals and law reviews. That it intrigues scholars in other disciplines and in the nation's law schools is not too difficult to explain, for it is the same reason that Cook finds it attractive: socialization offers an explanation of judicial decisions that, while not ignoring the role of politics, incorporates legal norms and social context. For example, in her study of the sentencing decisions made by black and white trial court judges, Cassia Spohn, a professor of criminal justice (though a political scientist by training) argues that judicial socialization "produces a subculture of justice and encourages judges to adhere to prevailing norms, practices, and precedents" (1990, 1212). This may explain why sentencing decisions reached by judges of different races may be less dissimilar than some expect. Likewise, in her work on how judges decide divorce cases, professor of law Marsha Garrison argues that "judicial discretion at divorce is not as unlimited as statutory law alone would suggest." That is so, at least in part, because of judicial socialization, which helps to "establish a perimeter beyond which judicial decisions are unlikely to stray" (1996, 413; for similar sentiments, see, for example, Schneider 1991; Bierman 1995). Moreover, numerous articles in the law reviews consider the degree to which judicial socialization affects not only decisions but also other aspects of judicial behavior, such as the just, ethical, neutral, and expeditious processing of cases (see, for example, Goldberg 1985; Gavison 1988; Geyh 1993).

Most of this research examines judges' on-the-job socialization, but Cook's work also explores the effects of prebench experiences on decisions. For example, in her 1973 *Cincinnati Law Review* article, she seeks to explain the sentencing behavior of federal district judges in draft cases. This piece shows both her interest in judicial attitudes (for example, how, in sentencing draft resisters, judges might have been shaped by prior military service or age) and her concern with the structure of the political environment of judges (for example, how judges might have been affected by American Legion group pressure, by the extent of draft offense caseload, or by political party dominance in the district).

Seen in this way, while Cook's work on socialization exemplifies the attitudinal approach to an extent, it also reflects the concerns of historical institutionalism. And, in fact, we see strains of Cook's ideas about the importance of socialization in contemporary research that invokes this approach. In comparing the institutionalist perspective to the attitudinal model, Whittington explicitly makes this point:

> Patterns of legal training, personnel selection, and judicial socialization all serve to shape how the Court approaches an individual case. By taking judicial preferences as given, the attitudinalists place in the background much of what formed the status quo more generally. The systematic intellectual and material processes that restrict the range of possible judicial outcomes are ignored. The attitudinalist model tells us a great deal about how a given justice is likely to vote in a case that raises particular issues,

but it tells us little about how such cases arose, how those issues had been framed, and why the justices approach their task in these ways. (2000, 621–22)

Given the insights historical institutionalists provide into key background variables that produce judicial attitudes (along with the insights of 1970s law professors and political scientists who focused on socialization), we have little hesitation in advising contemporary scholars who stress the relationship between institutional norms and judicial behavior to return to some of the original socialization studies, including Cook's, and to heed the theoretical, substantive, and methodological lessons these works offer.

POLITICAL AND LEGAL CULTURE

Cook's research on the impact of political and legal culture on judicial behavior reflects a second major theme in her work and represents a contribution for which she is widely cited. Her efforts to explain judging in trial courts led her to identify local culture as a necessary but not a sufficient explanation for judicial behavior (1983). In her study (1979b) showing the high correlation between criminal sentencing by state and federal judges in the same locality (despite their different legal frameworks), and in her piece (1983) comparing federal sentencing across regions of one state, Cook joined others scholars such as Thomas Church (1982) and James Eisenstein, Roy B. Flemming, and Peter F. Nardulli (1988) in demonstrating the importance of local legal culture. Exactly what the concept of local legal culture represents nevertheless remains a contested issue. Kritzer and Zemans (1993), for example, see culture simply as a residual of unexplained variation among courts, although most other scholars see substantive and useful content in the concept.

Equally controversial are Cook's most important contributions to the study of political culture, those that investigate whether courts consider or mirror the public's views when rendering judgments. This seemingly simple question has generated immense scholarly interest and debate. Despite decades of research, analysts have resolved neither the question of why federal judges, who do not require electoral support to retain their jobs, would consider public opinion in their decisions nor the question of whether they in fact do so.

It is beyond debate that Cook's work (1973, 1977, 1979a) provides the starting point for virtually all important analytic discussions of public opinion and trial courts. As Gregory A. Caldeira noted in his review of the field, "Some dispute the findings and interpretations, but Beverly Cook has done important research on this topic and, without doubt, has drawn scholarly interest" (1991, 317).

Cook's 1977 article in the *American Journal of Political Science* well illustrates Caldeira's point. In it, she invokes a "representational" model to explain the sentences issued by federal district court judges in cases involving draft offenders. Her primary argument is that for a variety of reasons, we might expect to find a relationship between public opinion and judicial decisions, even for judges who do not face reelection. First, socializing experiences teach judges that public opinion is a legitimate consideration in their sentencing. Second, the recruitment process virtually guarantees that nominees will share the attitudes and values of the local community in which they will serve. Or, to put it another way, the selection system for federal judges embeds them in the political culture of their districts. Finally, the fact that judges watch television and read newspapers means that they will have some knowledge of the prevailing public mood. Cook's argument for her approach foreshadows that of today's judicial scholars, who are again seeking to compare judicial politics with legislative and administrative politics: "New models for research on judicial decisions should include concepts which also fit legislative and administrative processes, so that comparisons of political authorities in the three branches can be empirically rather than ideologically based" (1977, 593).

In the remainder of the article, Cook tests her representational approach as well as rival explanations—the legal, bureaucratic, and sociopsychological models—against data carefully assembled from public opinion surveys and from court sentencing records.[8] She applies a path model analysis to examine the relationship between the variables over time. The results indicate that public opinion correlates highly with judicial sentences.

Cook's work is not without its critics. Herbert Kritzer, for example, questions whether judges were responding to public opinion or to their "own doubts about the war, or their opinions concerning the degree of governmental commitment to the war" (1979, 198). Nonetheless, Cook's findings have withstood the test of time and are widely cited in accounts of public opinion and the courts (for example, Marshall 1989; Caldeira 1991). Her results also have been vindicated in several, though not all, subsequent studies. Work by James Kuklinski and John E. Stanga (1979) indicates that state judges, even those who rarely face electoral competition, bend to public sentiment. With regard to federal appellate jurists, Marshall finds that at the very least, U.S. Supreme

Court rulings do not deviate significantly from the views of the citizenry:

> Most modern-day Court decisions reflect public opinion. When a clear-cut poll majority or plurality exists, over three-fifths of the Court's decisions reflect the polls. By all arguable evidence, the modern Supreme Court appears to reflect public opinion about as accurately as other policy makers. (1989, 97)

Mishler and Sheehan go even further, suggesting that changes in the public's ideological mood have a causal effect on macrolevel output: the justices "are broadly aware of fundamental trends in the ideological tenor of public opinion, and . . . at least some justices, consciously or not, may adjust their decisions at the margins to accommodate such fundamental trends" (1993, 89). Conversely, Norpoth and Segal (1994) assert that public opinion has virtually no influence on Supreme Court voting behavior. Instead, they find that Court appointments made by President Nixon in the early 1970s caused a sizable ideological shift in the direction of Court decisions. Thus, the illusion that the Court was echoing public opinion was created by the entry of conservative justices rather than by sitting justices modifying their preferences to conform to the changing views of the public.

The three most recent efforts to relate court decisions to public opinion, Stimson, MacKuen, and Erikson (1995); Mishler and Sheehan (1996); and Flemming and Wood (1997), which also concern the U.S. Supreme Court, fall somewhere between Mishler and Sheehan and Norpoth and Segal, leading to the obvious conclusion that this debate is far from over. These works do, however, shore up the enduring nature of the question Cook raised and perhaps underscore the need to move away from the U.S. Supreme Court to consider, as Cook did, federal trial court judges. Owing to the greater variation in these judges' political environments, a renewed focus on their behavior would enable us to maximize leverage on the general question of the relationship between public opinion and judicial behavior.

And, yet, for all the focus on the substantive question Cook raised, her research strategy sometimes goes neglected in treatments of public opinion. When she was writing in the 1970s, judicial specialists avoided competitive model testing—that is, they would select a particular theoretical approach to decision making and test its predictions, and only its predictions, against data. Today, many researchers claim that this tack was probably unwise since judicial decisions can best be explained by invoking models that integrate many different kinds of theories (see, for example, George and Epstein 1992; Hall and Brace 1992). We might go so far as to say that today, at least in the area of public opinion, it would indeed be a rare piece that did not take into account alternative explanations. But, as noted earlier, Cook first had this important intuition and adopted it in her work. Seen in this way, she truly was a pioneer of the judicial process, a researcher two decades ahead of her time.[9]

WOMEN JUDGES

Under what circumstances are women selected to serve as jurists? Do female jurists bring a different voice to the bench? In recent years, these questions have captured the imagination of a slew of political scientists—as well they should. With two women now on the U.S. Supreme Court and with their numbers growing on the lower federal courts and state supreme courts, it seems only natural that this question move to the fore of social scientific research on the judicial process. But even before Sandra Day O'Connor took her seat on the Court, Cook had undertaken what would become an extensive and fruitful research program on women jurists. It is no exaggeration to write that virtually all contemporary writings on the selection of female judges and their impact owe their origin to her studies.

Judicial Selection

Cook's research on judicial selection began in 1977, when she traversed the country interviewing women judges and collecting other relevant information.[10] In the late 1970s, she amassed an enormous database on all female state, local, and federal judges in the United States and used it in a series of articles to explore how and when women were selected for the bench (1981a, 1982, 1984a). She advanced and tested ideas about a state's political culture, court size and organizational structure, political party influence, and method of judicial selection as well as the place of women in the legal profession and in state offices (Cook 1984a, 1984b, 1986). Among her more important findings is that women will become more than mere tokens in the courts only if there are increases in three key factors: (1) the number of judgeships, (2) the number of eligible women, and (3) the number of "gatekeepers" (those who select judicial candidates) who will give serious consideration to women.

Another of her important contributions was brought to light by Sheldon Goldman, one of the nation's leading authorities on judicial selection. In his review of Cook's work, Goldman made particular note of her article on Florence Allen (1981a), the first woman federal judge and a candidate for at least ten of twelve vacancies on the Supreme Court that occurred during the Roosevelt and Truman administrations (Mather 1994, 76). But, of course, Allen never received an appointment, even though, as Cook demonstrated, Allen's background (except for her sex) was comparable to others who had served on the Court.

Why did Allen fail and O'Connor succeed? Cook takes up this question in yet another intriguing study (1982). The most significant of the several answers she derives is that Roosevelt did not perceive that Allen would help his political fortunes. Public opinion polls showed that in 1938 only 37 percent of Americans favored the appointment of a women to the Court (1982, 318), and groups representing women's interests were not seen as central to passage of FDR's programs. As Cook demonstrates, the political environment had turned significantly by the late 1970s, enabling Reagan to do what Roosevelt found politically untenable: elevate a woman to the Court.

Still, Cook's work on Allen does more than answer an important research question. It also shows the importance of archival research. While many scholars toiling in the field rely exclusively on published reports or records, Cook draws extensively on judicial papers available in the Library of Congress, various presidential libraries, and the National Archives, among other repositories. The value of such data is evident in Cook's publications on Allen and on several other female judges (see, for example, Cook 1993). This information enables scholars to capture nuances of political phenomena that may be lost in the sometimes sterile world of statistics and that may have some bearing on the hypotheses under investigation.

Impact of Women on the Bench

Cook's archive-based research on judicial selection continues, as does her work on the equally important question of whether women bring a distinct voice to the bench, a question that has bearing on many areas of study, including constitutional interpretation, feminist jurisprudence, and judicial behavior. In fact, scholars now working in all these fields have attempted to address the topic, but Cook set the agenda for this entire line of inquiry. She was among the first to propose that female judges would be more likely than their male counterparts to advance prowoman positions in cases centering directly on the status of women (1981a), and she was one of the first to suggest that women would adopt positions that would conform to those of their male colleagues in other kinds of disputes (1978).

O'Connor's 1982 appointment to the bench provided Supreme

Court scholars with the opportunity to assess these predictions. Suzanna Sherry's (1986) examination of O'Connor's opinions revealed a more communitarian and contextual perspective than opinions authored by Rehnquist; the study also asserts that O'Connor's votes for civil rights claimants lend support for the hypothesized "feminine voice in constitutional adjudication." Later and more systematic investigations of O'Connor's votes qualified these conclusions somewhat. While Sue Davis also found greater support from O'Connor than from her male colleagues in claims of discrimination, Davis concluded that the data "do little to support the assertion that O'Connor's decision making is distinct by virtue of her gender" (1993, 139); rather, O'Connor may simply be more liberal than Rehnquist on issues of civil rights (see Brown, Parmet, and O'Connell 1999 for a similar conclusion).

With O'Connor as an n of one, it was obviously difficult for scholars to go much further in assessing U.S. Supreme Court behavior. Accordingly, a long line of judicial specialists have sought to assess predictions of gender-based decision making by looking at lower federal court judges (Walker and Barrow 1985; Davis, Haire, and Songer 1993; Aliotta 1995; Segal 1997; Crowe 1998) and at state-level judges (Kritzer and Uhlman 1977; Gruhl, Spohn, and Welch 1981; Allen and Wall 1993; Molette-Ogden 1998). In an early study of the voting behavior of President Jimmy Carter's appointees to the U.S. district courts, for example, Walker and Barrow (1985) observed significant differences between male and female judges in several legal areas but not in some of the arenas that Cook anticipated, such as gender discrimination and affirmative action.

In contrast come studies of gender and decision making based on votes in the U.S. courts of appeals that find differences in these substantive areas and, in so doing, bolster Cook's suggestions about importance of gender for judicial decisions in certain legal areas. Davis, Haire and Songer, for example, examined federal appellate vote patterns and found that in two of three areas (employment discrimination and search and seizure; the third was obscenity), there is "some support for the thesis that women judges bring a different perspective to the bench" (1993, 132). Similarly, Crowe (1998) found female judges on the courts of appeals significantly more likely than their male colleagues to vote for plaintiffs in sex discrimination cases.

Intriguingly, one of the most recent efforts along these lines, Segal's (1997) analysis of President Clinton's appointees to the federal district courts, falls somewhere between these earlier studies. She found that women appointees supported minorities in seventeen of the thirty-four cases she analyzed; for men, the figure was eight of twenty-eight. Yet Segal detected no discernible differences between male and female judges in cases involving women's issues.

Results at the state level are equally mixed. While studies by Kritzer and Uhlman (1977) and Gruhl, Spohn, and Welch (1981) reveal no significant differences between male and female judges, work by Allen and Wall (1987, 1993) is more promising for Cook's thesis. Allen and Wall argue that "the data indicate that the preponderance of women justices . . . behave as Outsiders when deciding appeals which focus on women's issues" and those involving criminal rights (1987, 239).

Clearly, then, just as in the area of public opinion, far more research is necessary before we can reach conclusions about the veracity of Cook's predictions. Yet again as in public opinion, without her pioneering effort, the literature would be far less developed than it is.

PROFESSIONAL AND
POLITICAL ACTIVITIES

Cook's contributions to political science do not end with her research: over the past thirty years, she has been honored as a distinguished leader in the profession. Her long list of professional activities includes stints as vice president of the APSA (1986–87) and of the Midwest Political Science Association (1982–84) and as chair of the APSA's section on Law and Courts (1981). She has also served on the editorial board of the *Western Political Quarterly* and on the program committees of the APSA (1982), the Midwest Political Science Association (1972), and the Western Political Science Association (1981). Finally, Cook made a major contribution to the field in her capacity as a member of the board of overseers of the National Science Foundation's project on the U.S. Supreme Court. That board guided the collection of a staggering amount of data on the Court, with the final product (Spaeth 1999; updated annually) now in wide use. So impressive are her scholarly and professional contributions that in 2000 the APSA's Law and Courts section bestowed on her its highest honor, the Lifetime Achievement Award.

Among all these accomplishments, though, it is probably fair to say that Cook is proudest of her role in the founding of the National Association of Women Judges (NAWJ).[11] Her association with the NAWJ began in 1977–78, when she was interviewing women state court judges. As she traveled around the country, she "discovered that the women had no knowledge of women judges in other states and cities." Based on the work she had been conducting on early women lawyers,

Cook "recognized the similarity of the women judges' situation to that of women lawyers one hundred years earlier and thought that it was time for them to form an organization."

Cook brought the idea to two of the judges she had interviewed. One of them, Joan Klein, followed up and organized a "constitutional convention" of women judges. Cook gave the keynote address at that meeting, suggesting that female judges should create their own sister-hood, just as the first women lawyers did.

As the association began to take shape, Cook continued her involve-ment. In fact, through the NAWJ she played a major role in bringing the organizational strength of women to the attention of the (pre-O'Connor) Supreme Court.[12] As Cook tells the story,

> [I arranged] to have women judges attending the 1980 NAWJ convention in Washington, D.C., march together into the Supreme Court building for the special tour to impress the jus-tices with [their] number. . . . I developed this strategy because of the report that Truman consulted with Chief Justice Vinson about the possibility of appointing Florence Allen; Vinson con-sulted with the brethren, and they expressed their discomfort at the idea of a woman in their private conferences.

Heeding this historical lesson, Cook thought it strategically sensible to confront Chief Justice Burger with the fact that a large number of women would soon be eligible for service on the Court. "If they entered the building en masse," as Cook put it, "then all the justices as well as the other (overwhelmingly male) personnel in the building would also understand that the day would soon come when a women would join their conferences."

Cook's message was delivered and apparently received. Chief Justice Burger was amazed "when he walked into the huge assembly room and saw the standing-room-only crowd," composed exclusively of women. Just one month later, the justices dropped, from courtroom courtesy and the official reports, the term *Mr.* and exactly a year later, O'Con-nor ascended to the bench.

Reflecting on her involvement with the women judges' visit to the Court and the NAWJ more generally, Cook acknowledged that it was "unusual" for social scientists and lawyers to engage in this sort of cooperation. Perhaps that would be true for most of us, but that is cer-tainly not the case for Beverly Blair Cook, whom we have come to know as an intellectual leader and role model for a generation of schol-ars—men and women—of the judicial process.

CONCLUDING THOUGHT:
THE VALUE OF ECLECTICISM

In more than one way, Cook is a different kind of pioneer. As the preceding section suggests, her professional activities highlighted her interest in gender as a factor in judging and her concerns about gender as an element of professional development and advancement in both law and political science. Through such activities and through her academic presence in the judicial field, she has been an important role model in a way her fellow (but male) pioneers were not.

Moreover, Cook is a different kind of attitudinal pioneer. As previous sections have detailed, much of Cook's research pushed the scholarly boundaries of the attitudinal model by seeking to understand the relationships among institutional norms, judicial policy preferences, and judicial behavior. Cook pushed these boundaries methodologically, allowing the nature of the research question to determine the research method utilized. She also intellectually pushed the boundaries of attitudinalism, incorporating into an explanation of judging the same legal norm and social context factors stressed by the alternative, historical-institutionalist approach to the study of judicial behavior. Though Cook never explicitly made this claim, her work constitutes some of the earliest practical revision of the attitudinal approach by an attitudinal scholar. In exploring the value of eclecticism in judicial research, Cook provided a new pathway from judicial attitudes to the institutional settings that frame the expression of those attitudes.

NOTES

We adopt some of the material in this chapter from our previous writings on Cook (see Epstein 1996; Mather 1994).

1. The roundtable was held at the 1992 meeting of the American Political Science Association. Cook's remarks are available in Cook 1994a.

2. Walker 1994 examined all articles published by the *APSR*, the *American Journal of Political Science*, and the *Journal of Politics*.

3. It also bears noting that Cook was one of the first to conduct systematic research on black judges. For an early example, see Cook 1971a.

4. As we will describe, Cook's interest in judicial socialization remains unabated, though her later work focuses more heavily on the effect on judicial decisions of life experiences rather than of experiences occurring on the bench. Lawrence Baum made this point when he described Cook's research on Sandra Day O'Connor, which he deemed a "sensitive treatment of [her] life experiences and how those experiences affected her values on the bench" (quoted in Mather 1994, 77).

5. When Cook accepted her APSA award in 2000, she explained that choices about her research sites and methods were often dictated by family circumstances. Trial courts or appellate circuits were more accessible than the Supreme Court.

6. Based on a survey of all trial judges on courts of general jurisdiction throughout the country, the data in Ryan et al. 1980 provide a wealth of information on trial judges that scholars today could profitably use and replicate.

7. We searched the political science journals in J-STOR.

8. In a January 9, 2001, E-mail to us, Cook commented on her difficulty in obtaining usable sentencing data for this study. The Administrative Office of the Courts had only just begun to collect individual case data, and federal judges were quite distrustful of the AOC. Cook explained that the office "agreed to send me the data on the sentences without identification of the sentencing judge but made the mistake of including the judge code in the printout. Then I spent several months breaking the code and cross-checking my [biographical] IDs with reported cases and court clerks in order to associate a judge with each sentencing choice."

9. Baum makes this point, though in a somewhat different way: "although multivariate models are now common in the field, Cook was among those who first showed how this kind of analysis could be done and how much we could learn from it" (quoted in Mather 1994, 77).

10. A Florence E. Eagleton grant (from the Center for the American Woman and Politics, Eagleton Institute) supported this research. In addition to the Eagleton grant, Cook has received support from the National Endowment for the Humanities, the Ford Foundation, and the Social Science Research Council.

11. Cook relayed the information that follows to Elaine Martin (Cook to Martin, May 31, 1993) and was kind enough to supply us with a copy of the letter.

12. Cook relayed the information in this paragraph to Epstein (Cook to Epstein, January 23, 1994).

REFERENCES

Aliotta, Jilda M. 1995. "Justice O'Connor and the Equal Protection Clause: A Feminine Voice?" *Judicature* 78:232–35.

Allen, David W., and Diane E. Wall. 1987. "The Behavior of Women State Supreme Court Justices: Are they Tokens or Outsiders?" *Justice System Journal* 12:232–45.

Allen, David W., and Diane E. Wall. 1993. "Role Orientations and Women State Supreme Court Justices." *Judicature* 77:156–65.

Alpert, Lenore, Burton M. Atkins, and Robert C. Ziller. 1979. "Becoming a Judge: The Transition from Advocate to Arbiter." *Judicature* 62:325–35.

Bierman, Luke. 1995. "The Dynamics of State Constitutional Decision-Making: Judicial Behavior at the New York Court of Appeals." *Temple Law Review* 68:1403–56.

Boyum, Keith O., and Lynn Mather, eds. 1983. *Empirical Theories about Courts.* New York: Longman.

Brown, Judith Olans, Wendy E. Parmet, and Mary E. O'Connell. 1999. "The Rugged Feminism of Sandra Day O'Connor." *Indiana Law Journal* 32:1219–93.

Caldeira, Gregory A. 1991. "Courts and Public Opinion." In *The American Courts: A Critical Perspective*, ed. John B. Gates and Charles A. Johnson. Washington, D.C.: Congressional Quarterly Press.

Carp, Robert A., and Russell Wheeler. 1972. "Sink or Swim: The Socialization of a Federal District Judge." *Journal of Public Law* 21:359–93.

Church, Thomas. 1982. "Examining Local Legal Culture: Practitioner Attitudes in Four Criminal Courts" Washington, D.C.: National Institute of Justice.

Cook, Beverly Blair. 1967. *The Judicial Process in California.* Belmont, Calif.: Dickenson.

Cook, Beverly Blair. 1971a. "Black Representation in the Third Branch." *Black Law Journal* 1:260–81.

Cook, Beverly Blair. 1971b. "The Socialization of New Federal Judges: Impact on District Court Business." *Washington University Law Quarterly* 1971: 253–79.

Cook, Beverly Blair. 1973. "Sentencing Behavior of Federal Judges: Draft Cases—1972." *University of Cincinnati Law Review* 42:597–633.

Cook, Beverly Blair. 1977. "Public Opinion and Federal Judicial Policy." *American Journal of Political Science* 21:567–600.

Cook, Beverly Blair. 1978. "Women Judges: The End of Tokenism." In *Women in the Courts*, ed. Winifred L. Hepperle and Laura Crites. Williamsburg, Va.: National Center for State Courts.

Cook, Beverly Blair. 1979a. "Judicial Policy: Change over Time." *American Journal of Political Science* 23:208–14.

Cook, Beverly Blair. 1979b. "Sentencing Problems and Internal Court Reform." In *The Study of Criminal Courts*, ed. Peter Nardulli. Cambridge, Mass.: Ballinger.

Cook, Beverly Blair. 1981a. "The First Woman Candidate for the Supreme Court." *Supreme Court Historical Society Yearbook* 1981:19–35.

Cook, Beverly Blair. 1981b. "The Impact of Women Judges upon Women's Legal Rights: A Prediction from Attitudes and Simulated Behavior." In *Women, Power, and Political Systems*, ed. Margherita Rendel. New York: St. Martin's.

Cook, Beverly Blair. 1982. "Women as Supreme Court Candidates: From Florence Allen to Sandra Day O'Connor." *Judicature* 65:314–26.

Cook, Beverly Blair. 1983. "Sentencing the Unpatriotic: Federal Trial Judges in Wisconsin during Four Wars." In *The Quest for Social Justice*, ed. Ralph Aderman. Madison: University of Wisconsin Press.

Cook, Beverly Blair. 1984a. "Women Judges: A Preface to Their History." *Golden Gate Law Review* 14:573–610.

Cook, Beverly Blair. 1984b. "Women on the State Bench: Correlates of Access." In *Political Women: Current Roles in State and Local Government*, ed. Janet Flammang. Beverly Hills, Calif.: Sage.

Cook, Beverly Blair. 1987. "Women Judges in the Opportunity Structure." In *Women, the Courts, and Equality*, ed. Laura L. Crites and Winifred L. Hepperle. Newbury Park, Calif.: Sage.

Cook, Beverly Blair. 1993. "Measuring the Significance of U.S. Supreme Court Decisions." *Journal of Politics* 55:1127–39.

Cook, Beverly Blair. 1994a. "A Critique of the Supreme Court's 1982 Agenda: Alternatives to the NYU Model." *Justice System Journal* 17:135–51.

Cook, Beverly Blair. 1994b. "Ghosts and Giants in Judicial Politics." *P.S.: Political Science and Politics* 27:78–84.

Cook, Beverly Blair. 1995. "Justice Brennan and the Institutionalization of Dissent Assignment." *Judicature* 79:17–23.

Cook, Beverly Blair. 1996. "Justice Blackmun and the Attitudinal Model." Presented at the annual meeting of the American Political Science Association, San Francisco, September.

Cook, Beverly Blair. 1998. "Annette Abbott Adams," "Florence E. Allen," "Georgia P. Bullock," and "Marion J. Harron." In *American National Biography*. New York: Oxford University Press.

Cook, Beverly Blair. Forthcoming. "The Fuzzy Logic of the Supreme Court's Legal Language." *Judicature*.

Crowe, Nancy. 1998. "Diversity on the Federal Bench: The Effect of Judges' Sex and Race on Judicial Decision Making." Paper presented at the annual meeting of the Law and Society Association, Aspen, Colo.

Davis, Sue. 1993. "The Voice of Sandra Day O'Connor." *Judicature* 77:134–39.

Davis, Sue, Susan Haire, and Donald R. Songer. 1993. "Voting Behavior and Gender on the U.S. Courts of Appeals." *Judicature* 77:129–33.

Eisenstein, James, Roy B. Flemming, and Peter F. Nardulli. 1988. *The Contours of Justice: Communities and Their Courts*. Boston: Little, Brown.

Eisenstein, James, and Herbert Jacob. 1977. *Felony Justice: An Organizational Approach to Criminal Courts*. Boston: Little, Brown.

Epstein, Lee. 1996. "Beverly Blair Cook." In *Women in Law*, ed. Rebecca Mae Sakolar and Mary L. Volcansek. Westport, Conn.: Greenwood.

Feeley, Malcolm. 1979. *The Process Is the Punishment*. New York: Russell Sage.

Flemming, Roy B., and B. Dan Wood. 1997. "The Public and the Supreme Court: Individual Justice Responsiveness to American Policy Moods." *American Journal of Political Science* 41:468–98.

Garrison, Marsha. 1996. "How Do Judges Decide Divorce Cases? An Empirical Analysis of Discretionary Decision Making." *North Carolina Law Review* 74:401–552.

Gavison, Ruth. 1988. "The Implications of Jurisprudential Theories for Judicial Election, Selection, and Accountability." *Southern California Law Review* 61:1617–62.

George, Tracey E., and Lee Epstein. 1992. "On the Nature of Supreme Court Decision Making." *American Political Science Review* 86:323–37.

Geyh, Charles Gardner. 1993. "Informal Methods of Judicial Discipline." *University of Pennsylvania Law Review* 142:243–331.

Goldberg, Susan L. 1985. "Judicial Socialization: An Empirical Study." *Journal of Contemporary Law* 11:423–51.

Gruhl, John, Cassia Spohn, and Susan Welch. 1981. "Women as Policymakers: The Case of Trial Judges." *American Journal of Political Science* 25:308–22.

Hall, Melinda Gann, and Paul Brace. 1992. "Toward an Integrated Model of Judicial Voting Behavior." *American Politics Quarterly* 20:147–68.

Heumann, Milton. 1978. *Plea Bargaining: The Experiences of Prosecutors, Judges, and Defense Attorneys.* Chicago: University of Chicago Press.

Kort, Fred. 1964. "Comment on 'The Troubled World of Jurimetrics.'" *Journal of Politics* 26:923–26.

Kritzer, Herbert M. 1979. "Federal Judges and Their Political Environments: The Influence of Public Opinion." *American Journal of Political Science* 23:194–207.

Kritzer, Herbert M., and Thomas M. Uhlman. 1977. "Sisterhood in the Courtroom: Sex of Judge and Defendant in Criminal Case Disposition." *Social Science Journal* 14:77–88.

Kritzer, Herbert M., and Frances Kahn Zemans. 1993. "Local Legal Culture and the Control of Litigation." *Law and Society Review* 27:535–57.

Kuklinski, James H., and John E. Stanga. 1979. "Political Participation and Government Responsiveness: The Behavior of California Superior Courts." *American Political Science Review* 73:1090–99.

Marshall, Thomas. 1989. *Public Opinion and the Supreme Court.* Boston: Unwin Hyman.

Mather, Lynn. 1979. *Plea Bargaining or Trial? The Process of Criminal Case Disposition.* Lexington, Mass.: Lexington Books.

Mather, Lynn. 1994. "Introducing a Feminist Pioneer: Beverly Blair Cook." *P.S.: Political Science and Politics* 27:76–78.

Mendelson, Wallace. 1964a. "Response." *Journal of Politics* 26:927–28.

Mendelson, Wallace. 1964b. "The Untroubled World of Jurimetrics." *Journal of Politics* 26:915–22.

Mendelson, Wallace. 1966. "An Open Letter to Professor Spaeth and His Jurimetrical Colleagues." *Journal of Politics* 28:429–32.

Mishler, William, and Reginald Sheehan. 1993. "The Supreme Court as a Countermajoritarian Institution? The Impact of Public Opinion on Supreme Court Decisions." *American Political Science Review* 87:716–24.

Mishler, William, and Reginald Sheehan. 1996. "Public Opinion, the Attitudinal Model, and Supreme Court Decision Making: A Micro-Analytic Perspective." *Journal of Politics* 56:169–200.

Molette-Ogden, Carla E. 1998. "Female Jurists: The Impact of Their Increased Presence on the Minnesota Supreme Court." Ph.D. diss., Washington University, St. Louis.

Murphy, Walter F. 1964. *The Elements of Judicial Strategy.* Chicago: University of Chicago Press.

Norpoth, Helmut, and Jeffrey A. Segal. 1994. "Popular Influence on Supreme Court Decisions." *American Political Science Review* 88:711–16.

Pritchett, C. Herman. 1941. "Divisions of Opinion among Justices of the U.S. Supreme Court." *American Political Science Review* 35:890–98.

Pritchett, C. Herman. 1948. *The Roosevelt Court: A Study in Judicial Politics and Values.* New York: Macmillan.

Pritchett, C. Herman. 1954. *Civil Liberties and the Vinson Court.* Chicago: University of Chicago Press.

Rowland, C. K., Robert A. Carp, and Ronald A. Stidham. 1984. "Judges' Policy Choices and the Value Basis of Judicial Appointments: A Comparison of Support for Criminal Defendants among Nixon, Johnson, and Kennedy Appointees to the Federal District Courts." *Journal of Politics* 46:886–902.

Ryan, John Paul, et al. 1980. *American Trial Judges.* New York: Free Press.

Schneider, Carl E. 1991. "Discretion, Rules, and Law: Child Custody and the UMDA's Best-Interest Standard." *Michigan Law Review* 89:2215–98.

Schubert, Glendon. 1965. *The Judicial Mind: The Attitudes and Ideologies of Supreme Court Justices, 1946–1963.* Evanston, Ill.: Northwestern University Press.

Schubert, Glendon. 1967. "Academic Ideology and the Study of Adjudication." *American Political Science Review* 61:106–29.

Segal, Jennifer A. 1997. "The Decision Making of Clinton's Nontraditional Judicial Appointees." *Judicature* 80:279.

Shapiro, Martin M. 1964a. *Law and Politics in the Supreme Court: New Approaches to Political Jurisprudence.* New York: Free Press.

Shapiro, Martin M. 1964b. "Political Jurisprudence." *Kentucky Law Journal* 52:294–345.

Sherry, Suzanna. 1986. "The Gender of Judges." *Law and Inequality* 4:159–69.

Spaeth, Harold J. 1965. "Jurimetrics and Professor Mendelson: A Troubled Relationship." *Journal of Politics* 27:875–80.

Spaeth, Harold J. 1999. *United States Supreme Court Judicial Database.* Ann Arbor: Inter-University Consortium for Political and Social Research, study 6557.

Spohn, Cassia. 1990. "The Sentencing Decisions of Black and White Judges: Expected and Unexpected Similarities." *Law and Society Review* 24:1197–1216.

Stimson, James A., Michael B. MacKuen, and Robert S. Erikson. 1995. "Dynamic Representation." *American Political Science Review* 89:543–65.

Walker, Thomas G. 1994. "The Development of the Field." Paper presented at the Columbus Conference on the State of the Field of Judicial Politics, Columbus, Ohio.

Walker, Thomas G., and Deborah J. Barrow. 1985. "The Diversification of the Federal Bench: Policy and Process Ramifications." *Journal of Politics* 47:596–617.

Whittington, Keith E. 2000. "Once More unto the Breach: Post-Behavioralist Approaches to Judicial Politics." *Law and Social Inquiry* 25:601–34.

PART 2

The Strategic Pioneers

Coming out of the theoretical limitations of the attitudinal approach—indeed, making its appearance even as the attitudinal model was maturing, methodologically—is the second, strategic approach to the study of judicial behavior. As a theory of judicial behavior and a program for judicial behavior research that resisted some of the more reductionist tendencies of judicial attitudinalism, it might be succinctly summarized as "group dynamics matter." It is important to recognize that the pioneers of the strategic paradigm were not generally game theorists, nor were they informed by positive political theory. Most were grounded in the social-psychological theory that spawned behavioralism's emphasis on attitudes and their origins in social background. But to this focus on individual judicial ideology, the pioneers of the strategic approach to the study of judicial behavior added the importance of small-group, leadership, and interdependent decision-making factors in the explanation of judicial choice. Rather than dismissing the importance of socially determined political attitudes, these scholars pointed to their interaction with collegial choice, institutional rule, and role orientation variables in affecting judicial decisions, including opinion coalition formation. From these somewhat unsystematic observations, strategic neoinstitutionalists saw the opportunity to develop formal models of the strategic situations and institutional constraints within with judges seek to express their policy preferences.

Appropriately, Lee Epstein and Jack Knight take on the task of profiling the foundational pioneer of the strategic approach to judicial behavior, Walter Murphy. Their coauthorship is appropriate, for Murphy, like Cook, whom Epstein profiled with Lynn Mather in chapter 7, addressed the limits of an ideological model of judging as well as the limitations of an approach that focused on judicial decision making as a discrete, individual act of preference expression. Murphy's incorporation, however implicitly, of the notion of strategic rationality as the key to understanding judicial behavior has provided an important starting point for the development of a new analytic paradigm. Epstein and Knight's coauthorship is also doubly appropriate because their recent work on the strategic approach to judicial decision making has most evoked and most self-consciously expressed indebtedness to Murphy's insights. But they also raise another issue: Why did Murphy's insightful 1964 work on judicial strategy fail to find a receptive audience at the time it appeared, and why has it now gained a following among political scientists and legal academics?

If Murphy laid the general theoretical groundwork for the strategic paradigm, J. Woodford Howard Jr. provided it with one of the key questions with which it would challenge the attitudinal approach: What explains the fluidity of judicial choice, if attitudes are so fixed and determinative? Nancy Maveety and John Maltese show that Howard's claim that judges change their minds as a result of intervening, collegial factors served as a catalyst for both attitudinal research responses, challenging the empirical validity of his claim, and for strategic research that sought to systematically identify and account for the small-group variables Howard proposed. That Howard's 1968 study of decisional fluidity relied primarily on qualitative methods in making its contribution to understanding of judicial behavior is also significant, for it precipitated a larger discussion about how factors allegedly influencing judicial decisions should be measured and how claims regarding judicial action should be tested.

Another scholar who stressed the importance of interpersonal influence in collegial court decision making, David Danelski was also part of a critical dialogue regarding the problems that plagued new attitudinal model of judicial behavior. Thomas Walker highlights Danelski's early work, developing typologies of leadership strategies, as providing his most lasting insight into the judicial process. Danelski's somewhat unsystematic observations about judicial strategic interaction were grounded in a social-psychological theory of interpersonal relations in small groups, but the absence of a general framework for the explanation of behavior ultimately made social psychology less attractive than rational economic theory as a means to integrate theory and empirical findings. While subsequent judicial scholars would not follow Danelski's social-psychology path, they would wrestle with their own explanations for the undeniably strategic phenomena he identified.

Unlike the other pioneering scholars of a strategic approach to judicial behavior, David Rohde was a rational choice scholar who for a time turned his attention to decision making on the Supreme Court. His theoretical and methodological foundation gave him a fairly unsentimental perspective on the judicial institution and a capacity to formalize its institutional dynamics almost acontextually. In his chapter on

Rohde, Saul Brenner applies his unsentimental perspective to Rohde's proto-game-theoretic analysis of the Court as a cooperative decision-making setting, finding that Rohde's rich theoretical models were consistently not supported by empirical evidence. Yet this discrepancy generated a substantial amount of research attempting to bridge the gap between strategic models of judging and behavioral evidence about judging, more generally raising the question of what a "scientific theory" of judicial behavior is.

Like the judicial attitudinalists, the current practitioners of the strategic approach argue strenuously for the scientific study of judicial decision making. This emphasis on the necessity of a "science of judging" is less pronounced among the strategic pioneers, with the possible exception of Rohde. Perhaps such rhetoric is less overt in the works of Murphy, Howard, and Danelski because their call for attention to the institutionally framed group dynamics of judicial decision making came within the context of an already extant scientific paradigm, that of attitudinal judicial behavioralism. The group-based orientation toward understanding judicial choice was seldom framed by the strategic pioneers as "scientific": it fell to their successors in the judicial field to posit that institutional constraints and institutional goals could be (or had to be) part of a systematic theory of interdependent judicial decision making.

CHAPTER 8

Walter F. Murphy: The Interactive Nature of Judicial Decision Making

Lee Epstein and Jack Knight

Since his days in the Marine Corps, Walter F. Murphy has conceptualized the world in strategic terms. Just as no military commander can
expect to win a battle without taking into account the position and
likely actions of his opponents, no jurist can expect to establish policy
that members of society will respect unless he or she is attentive to the
preferences and likely actions of those members. Or so Murphy has
argued in now-classic works on the complex strategic situations confronting U.S. Supreme Court justices in their dealings with their colleagues (e.g., Murphy 1964) or with relevant members of the policy-
making community (e.g., Murphy 1962b).

In this chapter we detail the major role Murphy's scholarship has
played in initiating the strategic revolution that is now under way in the
field of law and courts (see Cameron 1994; Epstein and Knight 2000).
But to focus exclusively on those studies would be to miss Murphy's
contributions to so many other areas of inquiry. Accordingly, we
devote the first section to an overview of his research, with emphasis on
its recent direction. Next, we turn to his work on strategic interactions
between the Court and other political organizations and among the
justices. We begin with a description of the central studies and then
move to the question—puzzle, really—of why several decades elapsed
before scholars begin to heed the lessons in those works. We end with
a detailed discussion of their impact on contemporary thinking about
law, courts, and judges.

AN OVERVIEW OF
MURPHY'S SCHOLARSHIP

From the time she conceptualized this volume through the day she
selected her authors, Nancy Maveety located Walter F. Murphy in this
section on strategic pioneers. We agree with Maveety's choice: if there
is a strategic pioneer—and we believe there is—it is Murphy. But,

frankly, as even Maveety would concede, she could have placed a chapter on Walter F. Murphy in almost any section. His contributions to the study of law and courts are that great and that varied.

Table 1 makes this crystal clear, depicting Murphy's work over time and across four substantive areas: judicial behavior, law and society, comparative law and courts, and constitutional interpretation.[1]

In perusing the table, at least two interesting patterns emerge. First, the great bulk of Murphy's work on judicial behavior came in the 1960s; indeed, with the exception of new editions of *Courts, Judges, and Politics* (Murphy and Pritchett 1961, 1974, 1979, 1986; Murphy, Pritchett, and Epstein 2001), he has moved away from this line of research, writing almost as much on the Pope—whether fiction or not (see, e.g., Murphy 1979, 1982, 1987a)—as he has on matters of legal process and politics. That Murphy is included in a volume on the pioneers of judicial behavior is thus a testament to the staying power of his early research.

Second, his interest in constitutional interpretation and jurisprudence, while present over the entire course of his career, has grown even stronger with time. Notice the four bottom cells in the table, representing Murphy's research during the 1990s: the two in the judicial behavior and law and society columns are empty; those reflecting his work on constitutionalism, here and abroad, are loaded with intriguing studies, published in a wide range of outlets.

That Murphy now spends the bulk of his time working on jurisprudence and doctrine is not particularly surprising to him or to his many students and colleagues. Quite the opposite: for Murphy, this stage of his career represents a return to his first love, political theory. In fact, he went to graduate school at the University of Chicago to study with Leo Strauss, perhaps the most prominent political theorist in the United States at the time, rather than with C. Herman Pritchett, the most prominent judicial specialist of his day. Or as Murphy puts it, "Pritchett was *a* reason I went to Chicago; Strauss was *the* reason."[2] Murphy took more courses with Strauss than with any other professor, including Pritchett, and would have wound up writing his dissertation with Strauss had he not been "the type who told you what to do, how to do it, and what you would find." Finding himself unable to work with the great theorist, Murphy turned to Pritchett, who moved Murphy in the direction of empirically grounded work on judicial politics.

Murphy may have found Strauss's approach to his dissertation students distasteful, but Murphy never lost his taste for political theory. He simply combined his interest in it and in judicial politics to make a

TABLE 1. Walter F. Murphy's Contributions to the Study of Law and Courts

Judicial Behavior/ Process	Law and Society	Comparative Constitutionalism	American Constitutional Interpretation/ Jurisprudence
The 1950s			
Murphy 1959a	Murphy 1959c		Murphy 1958, 1959b)
The 1960s			
Murphy 1961, 1962a, 1962b, 1962c, 1964, 1965b, 1966; Murphy and Pritchett 1961	Birkby and Murphy 1964; Murphy and Tanenhaus 1968; Murphy and Tanenhaus 1969b	Murphy and Tanenhaus 1969a	Murphy 1965a
The 1970s			
Murphy and Pritchett 1974; Murphy and Pritchett 1979; Murphy and Tanenhaus 1972	Murphy 1974; Murphy, Tanenhaus and Kastner 1973	Murphy and Tanenhaus 1977	Murphy 1978
The 1980s			
Murphy and Pritchett 1986	Tanenhaus and Murphy 1981	Murphy 1980	Lockard and Murphy 1980; Lockard and Murphy 1987; Murphy 1986; Murphy, Fleming, and Barber 1986
The 1990s			
	Murphy and Tanenhaus 1990	Murphy 1991, 1993a, 1993b, 1995b, 1998	Lockard and Murphy 1992; Murphy 1987b, 1990, 1992, 1995a; Murphy, Fleming, and Barber 1995

Note: Because Murphy maintains only an abbreviated vitae, we cannot be certain that this table lists all of his published research relating to law and courts. But searches of various electronic databases indicate that, at the very least, the table covers his major works.

"natural" move to jurisprudence. This is clear in his recent work, which is consciously theoretical, yet his concern with the doctrine is never far from the surface even in his earliest studies of judicial behavior. While many scholars writing in the 1960s—including Glendon Schubert and S. Sidney Ulmer—aimed their cannons at explaining justices' votes, Murphy pointed his at understanding the law as articulated by the Court. This is a critical distinction, we believe, between Murphy and the attitudinal pioneers represented in this volume, and one to which we return shortly.

MURPHY AND THE
STRATEGIC ACCOUNT

Without doubt, we could devote this chapter in its entirety to Murphy's doctrinal and jurisprudential analyses. But, given the purpose of this volume—to illuminate contributions made by prominent scholars to the study of judicial behavior—we focus instead on Murphy's role in moving the strategic account of judicial decisions from an intriguing idea to a rapidly expanding and influential form of analysis. We divide our discussion into three parts. The first two describe the initial rise and demise of the strategic account within the law and courts field. That rise began in the 1950s and reached its zenith with publication of Murphy's *Elements of Judicial Strategy* (1964). Given the central role Murphy's contributions played during this period, the discussion necessarily incorporates a description of them. After detailing the demise of the strategic account, which occurred in the early 1970s and persisted through the early 1990s, we consider solutions to the puzzle of why this demise occurred.

Before moving to these topics, we want to be clear about what we (e.g., Epstein and Knight 1998) and Murphy (e.g., 1964) mean by the "strategic account." On this account (1) social actors make choices to achieve certain goals, (2) social actors act strategically in the sense that their choices depend on their expectations about the choices of other actors, and (3) these choices are structured by the institutional setting in which they are made (see, generally, Elster 1986). Defined in this way, the account belongs to a class of nonparametric rational choice explanations as it assumes that goal-directed actors operate in strategic or interdependent decision-making context.

It does not assume that the actors—including judges—pursue one particular goal. Under the strategic account, researchers must specify a priori the actors' goals; researchers may select any motivation(s) that they believe particular actors hold. We emphasize this point because it is the source of a great deal of confusion in the judicial literature, with some scholars suggesting that on the strategic account the only goal actors pursue entails policy.

We understand the source of this confusion: virtually every existing strategic account of judicial decisions posits that justices pursue policy—that is, their goal is to see public policy (the ultimate state of public policy) reflect their preferences. This includes Murphy's work (e.g., 1964) as well as most of ours (e.g.., Epstein and Knight 1998). But again, this need not be the case; under the strategic account, researchers could posit any number of other goals, be they jurisprudential or institutional.

Because this point becomes important in the concluding section of this chapter, where we discuss Murphy's impact on contemporary scholarship, and because so much confusion exists over it, we drive it home even further with the simple example shown in figure 1, which depicts a hypothetical set of preferences regarding a particular policy—for example, a civil rights statute.[3] The horizontal lines represent a (civil rights) policy space ordered from left (most liberal) to right (most conservative); the vertical lines show the preferences (the most preferred positions) of the actors relevant in this example: the median member of the current Congress (M) and of the key current committees and other gatekeepers (C) in Congress that make the decision about whether to propose civil rights legislation.[4] We also identify the current committees' indifference point ($C(M)$) "where the Supreme Court can set policy which the committee likes no more and no less than the opposite policy that could be chosen by the full chamber" (Eskridge 1991a, 381). To put it another way, because the indifference point and the median member of current Congress are equidistant from the committees, the committees like the indifference point as much as they like the most preferred position of Congress: they are indifferent between the two. Finally, we locate the status quo (X), which represents the intent of the legislature that enacted the law.

Suppose the Court has a case before it that requires interpretation of a civil rights law: Where would it place policy? Under the strategic account, the answer depends on the goals of the justices. If they are motivated to see the outcome reflect as closely as possible their policy preferences, they will interpret the law in the $C(M)$-C interval, with the exact placement contingent on the location of their ideal point. Placing policy there will deter a congressional attempt to overturn. Now, suppose instead that the justices' goal is to interpret the law in line with the intent of the enacting legislature (that is, to follow a jurisprudence of

Fig. 1.   Hypothetical set of preferences regarding civil rights policy. (*Note:* X is the status quo (intent of enacting Congress); $C(M)$ represents the current committees' indifference point (between their most preferred position and that desired by M); M denotes the most preferred position of the median member of Congress; C is the most preferred position of the key current committees (and other gatekeepers) in Congress that make the decision about whether to propose legislation to their respective houses. Adapted from Ferejohn and Weingast 1992a.)

original intent) but also to avoid an override attempt by the current Congress. If the justices were so motivated (and assuming that the president and pivotal veto player in Congress are to the right of X), the Court will place policy at $C(M)$.

THE RISE OF THE STRATEGIC ACCOUNT

The sort of model we use in figure 1 to demonstrate the flexibility (and importance) of goals within the strategic account has been invoked over the past decade or so by a group of (mainly) business school and legal academics who tout positive political theory (PPT) as an appropriate framework for the study of judicial decisions.[5] Though a survey of positive political theorists makes clear that "considerable" disagreement exists over the meaning of the term PPT, the theorists tend to coalesce around the following definition: "PPT consists of non-normative, rational-choice theories of political institutions" (Farber and Frickey 1992, 461). For us, the key point is that positive political theorists typically adopt the assumptions of the strategic account, as Walter F. Murphy originally set it out.

Yet, based on at least the early PPT writings, one would think that the injection of strategic analysis into the study of judicial politics began with them; in fact, they say that the field owes its origins to a 1989 dissertation written by Brian Marks, a student of economics at Washington University (see, e.g., Ferejohn and Weingast 1992a, 574).[6] This is not so. As we suggested previously, nearly thirty years before Marks produced his "locus classicus" (Cameron 1994), political scientists—including Murphy and several other of the founders of the modern-day study of courts and law—implicitly or explicitly invoked strategic approaches to studying judicial decision making.

Indeed, though Marks may be the starting point for modern-day

positive political theorists, Glendon Schubert, more typically associated with social-psychological theories of judicial decision making (see,
e.g., Schubert 1965; Segal and Spaeth 1993, 67–69), was one of the first
political scientists to apply rational choice theory to political problems.
In his 1958 review of the field of law and courts, Schubert included a
section he called "game analysis." He wrote that the "judicial process is
tailor-made for investigation by the theory of games. Whatever may be
their obligations as officers of courts, attorneys frequently play the role
of competing gamesmen, and the model of the two-person, zero-sum
game certainly can be applied to many trials . . . and to the behavior of
Supreme Court justices" (1022). Schubert provided several examples,
including one that applied game theory[7] to the voting behavior of two
Supreme Court justices—Roberts and Hughes—during a crucial historical period, the New Deal (the "Hughberts" game). In so doing, he
showed that the justices were strategic decision makers; only by recognizing their interdependency, Schubert argued, could they maximize
their preferences.

Schubert's application may have been crude, but it was important in
two regards. First, it demonstrated that approaches based on assumptions of rationality—specifically, game theory—could be applied to
important political problems.[8] Although scholars working in most
fields of political science (but not necessarily law and courts) now take
this for granted, it was not so clear in 1958. Game theory was relatively
new in the social sciences, and it was usually applied to social science
problems by economists in pursuit of explanations of economic phenomena. Second, Schubert's work generated interest in other legal
applications of the rational choice paradigm—or, at the very least, it
encouraged scholars working in the field to think about the interdependent nature of judicial decision making. One of the most influential
exemplars—if not the most influential—was Murphy's 1962 *Congress
and the Court*.[9]

Prior to his work on Congress, Murphy of course had read Pritchett's research on the justices of the Roosevelt Court era (1941, 1948).
These works, especially *The Roosevelt Court*, were seminal in many
regards, not the least of which was that they moved legal realism from
the sole province of law school professors to the realm of political scientists, who had previously been reluctant adherents. Like Holmes,
Brandeis, and later adapters of sociological jurisprudence, Pritchett
argued that justices are simply motivated by their own preferences,
with rules based on precedent nothing more than smoke screens
behind which to hide values and attitudes. Or, to put it in modern-day

language, he was perhaps the first political scientist to view justices as "single-minded seekers of legal policy" (George and Epstein 1992, 325).

This intuition about the goals of justices provided the basis for Murphy's work (1962b) on Congress-Court interactions, but in that work he pushed the analysis one step further.[10] Working with interview data, Court cases, information collected from manuscript collections, congressional hearings, and the like, Murphy shows that if justices are single-minded seekers of policy, they necessarily care about the law, broadly defined. And if justices care about the ultimate state of the law, then they may be willing to modulate their views to avoid an extreme reaction from Congress and the president.[11] Murphy, in other words, tells a tale of shrewd justices who anticipate the reactions of the other institutions and take those reactions into account in making decisions. The justices he depicts would rather hand down a ruling that comes close to but may not exactly reflect their preferences than see Congress completely reverse the decision in the long run.

Murphy's work on Congress and the Court thus clearly if implicitly adopted the strategic assumption of Schubert's "Hughberts" game and, at the same time, underscored the importance of the policy goals brought to light in *The Roosevelt Court*. Still, Murphy's *The Elements of Judicial Strategy* (1964), which came on the heels of the Congress-Court book, most fully embraced the notion of interdependent interaction and explicitly found its grounding in strategic accounts of politics.

The core arguments of *Elements of Judicial Strategy* are the same ones that Murphy and Schubert advanced earlier: (1) Supreme Court justices are policy oriented; (2) they act strategically to further their goals; and (3) their interactions are structured by institutions. The new contribution came in the blending of Schubert's earlier focus on internal decision making with Murphy's stress on the external constraints placed on the Court by Congress and the president. Under Murphy's framework, strategic interaction exists not only between the Court and the other branches of government but also among the justices. As Murphy later described *Elements*, "It took as its point of departure the individual Supreme Court justice and tried to show how, given his power as one of nine judges and operating within a web of institutional and ideological restraints, he could maximize his influence on public policy" (Murphy and Tanenhaus 1972, 24). *Elements* supported this account in much the same way as did *Congress and the Court*, by culling (in this case, from various justices' private papers) stylized stories that in one way or another reinforced the central thesis.

That Murphy arrived at these views is not terribly surprising. By 1964, the rational choice paradigm was beginning to take hold in the political science literature with publication of Downs's classic work on political parties, *An Economic Theory of Democracy* (1957), and Riker's *The Theory of Political Coalitions* (1962). Murphy surely was heavily influenced by some of this thinking. In the preface to *Elements*, he wrote, "Almost as jarring to some readers as quotations from private papers will be my use of terms which are familiar to economic reasoning and the theory of games but which are alien in the public law literature" (1964, x). In 2000, Murphy reiterated *An Economic Theory of Democracy*'s central role in helping him to "crystallize [his] ideas." Indeed, in 1960, when he first started working in justices' papers, he did not "know what [he] was doing." He had read some of Schubert's strategic work, but because of its emphasis on voting, it was less interesting to him than were various biographies, especially Mason's *Harlan Fiske Stone* (1956). In those works, Murphy could see strategic behavior's importance for the doctrine articulated by the Court rather than simply for its votes. Murphy thought that this was a critical distinction because both he and Pritchett believed that there were limits to the vote studies of the sort Schubert and others were then undertaking.

Still, not until a year later, in 1961, when he was reading Downs's work on a train, did the *Elements* framework pop into Murphy's head. He now knew to what use he would put the judicial papers he had been reading.

THE DEMISE OF THE STRATEGIC ACCOUNT

While Murphy was working on *Elements*, reactions from the scholarly community were not favorable.[12] Alpheus Mason thought that Murphy's emphasis on behind-the-scenes maneuvering on the Court was "going to stir up snakes." Schubert was dismayed that Murphy was not setting up hypotheses and systematically mining information from the justices' papers to test these theories and was concerned about Murphy's emphasis on process and doctrine rather than on votes.

But once *Elements* appeared, scholars found aspects of the work attractive—or at least attractive enough to continue in its path. Particularly noteworthy was Howard's examination of "fluidity" (1968), which attempted to provide more systematic support for one of Murphy's key observations: judges "work" changes in their votes and "permit their opinions to be conduits for the ideas of others" through "internal bargaining" (44). Howard's methodology resembled Murphy's in its reliance on a small number of important cases, but Howard cast his argument in general terms: "it may come as some surprise to political scientists how commonplace, rather than aberrational, judicial flux actually is." He further claimed that "hardly any major decision [is] free from significant alteration of vote and language before announcement to the public" (44).

Howard's article was not the last of the post-*Elements* pieces. Into the next decade, analysts applied theories grounded in assumptions of rationality (especially game theory) to study opinion coalition formation and jury selection (see, e.g., Rohde 1972). In fact, by the 1970s, there had been enough work invoking game-theoretic analysis in particular that Saul Brenner wrote a bibliographic essay devoted exclusively to the subject (1979).

Perusal of the works on Brenner's list, however, reveals that most were not explicit applications of game theory or were conducted in the late 1960s. We do not have to search too long to explain this trend away from approaches that assume rationality: scholars eschewed strategic analysis in favor of four "determinants" of judicial behavior drawn from the social-psychological paradigm:

1. *The social background/personal attribute* hypothesis, which asserts that a range of political, socioeconomic, family, and professional background characteristics accounts for judicial behavior or at least helps to explain the formation of particular attitudes (see, e.g., Nagel 1961; Schmidhauser 1962; Tate 1981; Tate and Handberg 1991; Ulmer 1970, 1973; Vines 1964).

2. *The policy-oriented values (attitudinal)* hypothesis, which claims that political attitudes toward issues raised in cases explain judicial votes (see, e.g., Goldman 1966, 1973; Pritchett 1948; Rohde and Spaeth 1976; Schubert 1960, 1965; Spaeth and Parker 1969). Schubert's version of this theory came from the psychometric research of Coombs and Kao (1960) and Guilford (1961).

3. *The role* hypothesis, which suggests that judges' normative beliefs about what they are expected to do either act as a constraint on judicial attitudes or directly affect judicial behavior (see, e.g., Becker 1966; Carp and Wheeler 1972; Cook 1971; Gibson 1978; Glick and Vines 1969; Grossman 1968; Howard 1977; James 1968; Jaros and Mendelson 1967; Ungs and Baas 1972; Vines 1969; Wold 1974). Judicial specialists adopted this theory from the work of Campbell (1963) and Rokeach (1968) (see Gibson 1978).

4. *The small-group* hypothesis, asserting that the "need to interact in a face-to-face context" affects the behavior of judges on collegial courts (Grossman and Tanenhaus 1969, 15; see also Atkins 1973; Danelski 1960; Snyder 1958; Ulmer 1971; Walker 1973). This hypothesis draws heavily on the work of experimental social psychologists studying conformity, deviance, and leadership in small groups (see Goldman and Sarat 1978, 491; Ulmer 1971).

To be sure, these approaches differ from one another at the margins. But because they draw from the same paradigm (social-psychological), they are complementary in their core beliefs about the way people make decisions. As Grossman and Tanenhaus put it, "these hypothesized determinants can be traced back to the simple action stimulus-response model. . . . This S-R model, of which there are now several variants, conceptualized the votes of judges as responses to stimuli provided by cases presented to them for decision" (1969, 10–11; see also Gibson 1978, 917).

Conceptualized in this way, the social-psychological paradigm is quite distinct from the economic approach offered by Murphy: while Murphy's justices are preference maximizers who make decisions to further their goals with regard to the preferences and likely actions of other relevant actors and to the institutional context, the stimulus-response justices are policy seekers who further their goals with reference to their own normative and policy-based preferences (see generally Barry 1978). Even small-group approaches, which seem to have more in common with strategic analysis than the other approaches do, lack clear-cut notions of interdependent interaction. At a minimum, most scholars invoking this approach in their empirical work rely less on rational choice logic and more on variants of the social-psychological paradigm. For example, they note that judges occasionally conform to the behavior of their colleagues but do not necessarily do so to further their goals; rather, the motivation seems to be the desire to retain friendly relations with colleagues (for a summary of this literature, see Goldman and Jahnige 1976).

In pointing out these differences, we do not mean to imply that strategic and social-psychological accounts of judicial decisions have nothing in common. Both certainly acknowledge the importance of goals, and small-group theory is obviously concerned with group context. But the fact that social-psychological approaches do not acknowledge a strategic component to decision making is a point of distinction between the two approaches and one that we cannot stress enough, for it can lead to very different predictions about judicial behavior.

Return to figure 1, which depicts a hypothetical set of preferences regarding civil rights policy. Suppose justice A was confronted with the task of interpreting a law that fell in this policy space; further suppose that her most preferred position is X, the status quo. Theoretically speaking, if justice A is motivated in the way assumed by, for example, those personal attribute models that suggest a direct connection between background factors and voting, the prediction is simple enough: she would always choose X regardless of the positions of her colleagues or, more relevant here, of congressional actors. Even though she realizes that if she selects X, the current Congress will attempt to override her policy placement, it does not matter to her because she makes decisions that are accord with her background characteristics, which do not change after she has ascended to the bench. The strategic account, conversely and as noted earlier, supposes that justice A would choose $C(M)$, the point closest on the line to her most preferred position that Congress would not overturn.

EXPLAINING THE DEMISE

If there is any doubt that predictions from variants of the social-psychological model dominated thinking about law and courts by the 1980s, figure 2 should dispel it. The data on the number of judicial articles published between 1970 and 1989 in the *American Political Science Review* that invoked the social-psychological paradigm and others are clear: within a decade of the publication of *Elements of Judicial Strategy*, work adopting variants of that paradigm was pervasive, accounting for sixteen of the twenty-seven articles published in the discipline's flagship journal. During this period, only two essays attentive to any variant of choice approaches appeared, and one of them (Smith 1988) was a critical assessment.

In all of this, the question remains why scholars so fully embraced the social-psychological paradigm and so fully spurned the sort of strategic analysis Murphy conducted in *Elements*. Two answers come to mind. Schwartz contends that the primary answer lies in the notion of equilibrium predictions: Murphy "only identifies strategies that *might* be pursued under some circumstances. Often such a pronouncement is immediately followed by a disclaimer that the contrary strategy might be more appropriate in other circumstances. The problem is that he derives no tight predictions about exactly when we should expect to see certain behaviors as opposed to others" (Schwartz 1997).

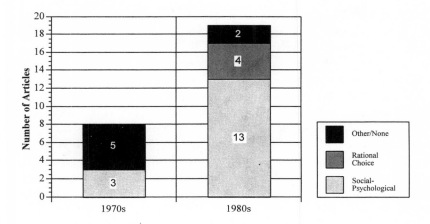

Fig. 2.   Major theories invoked in articles published in the *American Political Science Review*, 1970–89. (Data from Epstein and Knight 2000, 633.)

There is certainly some merit to this view. In direct contrast to other early advocates of rational choice theory, such as Downs (1957) and Riker (1962), Murphy did not write down any models and derive equilibria that others could go out and test, as a multitude of scholars did with the predictions contained *An Economic Theory of Democracy* and *The Theory of Political Coalitions.* Even more to the point, Murphy's "predictions" were a good deal more ambiguous (as Schubert initially complained to Murphy) than those offered by early adherents of social-psychological approaches. Compare, for example, a Murphy hypothesis with one offered by Schubert:

Murphy: "When a new Justice comes to the Court, an older colleague *might* try to charm his junior brother." (1964, 49)

Schubert: "In accordance with modern psychometric theory, which generalizes the basic stimulus-response point relationship, Supreme Court cases are treated as raw psychological data. . . . Each case before the Court for decision is conceptualized as being represented by a stimulus (*j*) point. . . . The combination of the attitudes of each justice toward these same issues also may be represented by an ideal (*i*) point. . . . Obviously how the case will be decided will depend upon whether a majority or minority of the *i*-points dominate the *j*-point. If a majority of *i*-points dominate, then the value or values raised in the case will be upheld or supported by the decision 'of the court'; and if, to the contrary, the j-point dominates a majority of i-points, then the value or values raised will be rejected." (1960, 91)

Yet scholars gleaned predictions from Murphy's work and attempted to test them. This was certainly true of work on vote fluidity (see Brenner 1989; Howard 1968) and is true of the current crop of strategic work, much of which explicitly identifies *Elements* as its starting point (see, e.g., Epstein and Knight 1998; Maltzman, Spriggs, and Wahlbeck 2000). In other words, Murphy may not have laid out predictions as boldly as did the other rational choice theorists or those who advocated variants of the social-psychological model, but his work contained sufficient intuitions of judicial behavior that other scholars could in turn write down models, solve them, develop behavioral predictions, and assess those predictions against data.

If it was not the lack of precise expectations that led scholars to dismiss the strategic account, why, then, did they do so? We believe the explanation lies in the nature of those tests and in the results they generated—an explanation, we and Murphy think, that is a more faithful representation of the tenor of the times. During the 1960s, as Murphy made clear to us, the great battles in the field of judicial politics were not between proponents of the rational choice and social-psychological models but between traditionalists and behavioralists; between those who believed that social scientists should develop realistic and generalizable explanations of social behavior and those who did not; and, increasingly, between those who believed scholars could quantify behavior and those who did not share such beliefs (Walker 1994). To be a scientist in the world of judicial politics by the 1970s was to value data and to believe in the power of statistics. It is thus hardly surprising that scholars working in the social-psychological tradition triumphed over their strategically minded counterparts. Beginning with Pritchett's *The Roosevelt Court* (1948) and culminating with Segal and Spaeth's *The Supreme Court and the Attitudinal Model* (1993), such scholars have claimed to gather a tremendous amount of systematic support for their theory. Unlike Murphy, they typically refrained from detailed analyses of particular litigation (the modus operandi of the traditionalists) and instead focused on large samples of Court cases, claiming to predict their dispositions with a good deal of success.

Furthermore, in addition to asserting that the key premises of variants of the social-psychological model held up against systematic, data-intensive investigations, scholars also argued that Murphy's strategic view did not withstand similar scrutiny. A critical work here is Brenner (1989), which reassessed Howard's contention that voting fluidity was rampant on the Court. Brenner compared votes cast in conference with those in the published records for "major" and "nonmajor" decisions. Although he found minimal change in case disposition (about 15 percent), his results for vote shifts were rather dramatic: in 48 percent of the major cases and in 59 percent of the nonmajor cases, at least one justice changed his vote. Still, Brenner concluded that Howard (and, by implication, Murphy) was largely incorrect, that considerable stability exists in voting. And Brenner's interpretation became the prevailing wisdom among judicial specialists (Goldman and Sarat 1989, 466). With Brenner's rendition of his study, the massive amounts of data analysts have gathered to support the social-psychological model, and the significance that political scientists in this field attached to large-scale statistical studies, it is easy to understand why decision-making theories grounded in assumptions of rationality virtually failed to make any substantial showing in political science journals during the 1970s and 1980s.

THE (RE)EMERGENCE OF THE RATIONAL CHOICE PARADIGM

We would be loathe to write that the tide has fully turned, for surely that is not the case. Just a few years ago, scholars were still claiming that "the attitudinal model is a, if not *the*, predominant view of Supreme Court decision making" (Segal et al. 1995, 812). But just as surely a change is in the wind, with Murphy's more strategically oriented approach beginning to take hold. The signs are everywhere. At the outset, we noted the existence of a growing and influential group of law and business school professors who advocate use of the strategic account as Murphy set it out. And the approach is now reemerging in political science journals and conference papers (see Epstein and Knight 2000).

We do not, of course, mean to imply that these studies are a monolith: they are not. Rather, they typically focus on one of the two sets of strategic relations Murphy identified in *Congress and the Court* and *Elements of Judicial Strategy*, those between the Court and relevant political actors (especially Congress and the president) (e.g., Eskridge 1991a, 1991b, 1994) and those among the justices (e.g., Maltzman, Spriggs, and Wahlbeck 2000). Not only does the recent spate of studies parallel Murphy's work in this regard, but his fingerprints are all over these works as well. In reviewing these studies we make this point with force.

We also consider several voids and how a return to Murphy's work can help to fill them.

In *Congress and the Court*, as we already have mentioned, Murphy sought to demonstrate that Supreme Court justices must keep their eyes on Congress to come as close as possible to attaining their policy goals. A large and growing body of research examining the constraints that the U.S. separation-of-powers system imposes on the political branches' ability to establish efficacious policy has embraced this insight.

These separation-of-powers studies come in many variants. Early ones formalized Murphy's ideas—consciously or otherwise[13]—using simple spatial models (of the sort depicted in figure 1) to develop implications about how justices might interpret statutes given their interest in maximizing policy preferences. These works then assess those implications through qualitative or doctrinal analyses. Among the most influential of these are studies by William N. Eskridge Jr., a professor at Yale Law School (1991a, 1991b, 1994). In considering the course of civil rights policy in the United States, Eskridge identified many U.S. Supreme Court decisions that would be difficult to explain if the justices voted solely on the basis of their policy preferences (e.g., instances of the relatively conservative Burger Court reaching liberal results).

Hence, the question emerged: If not straight preferences, then what? Eskridge's intuition was the same as Murphy's: the separation-of-powers system induces strategic decision making by Supreme Court justices. In other words, if the justices' goal is to establish national policy that is as close as possible to their ideal points, they must take into account the preferences of other relevant actors (here, Congress and the president) and the actions these others are likely to take. Justices who do not make such calculations risk congressional overrides and thus risk seeing their least preferred policy become law.

Eskridge formalized this intuition in his Court/Congress/president game (the SoP game), which unfolds on a one-dimensional policy space over which the relevant actors have single-peaked utility functions (see n.4). All these actors, Eskridge assumes, have perfect and complete information about the preferences of the other actors and about the sequence of play. As figure 3 depicts, the Court begins the game by interpreting federal laws. In the second stage, legislative gatekeepers (congressional committees and/or leaders) can introduce legislation to

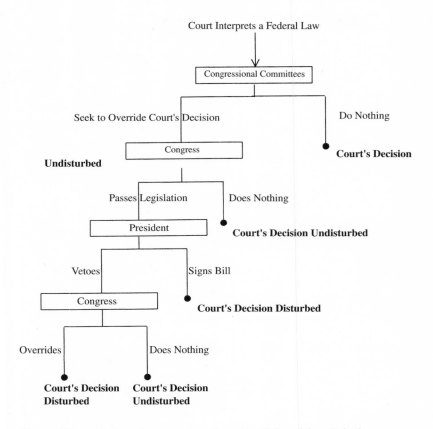

Fig. 3.   The separation-of-powers system in action. (Adapted from Eskridge 1991a, 1991b.)

override the Court's decision; if they do so, Congress must act by adopting the committees' recommendation, enacting a different version of it, or rejecting it. If Congress takes action, then the president has the option of vetoing the law. In this depiction, the last move rests with Congress, which must decide whether to override the president's veto.

By invoking simple spatial models, Eskridge notes the existence of two different regimes with regard to the Court (illustrated in figure 4), one in which the Court is not constrained by one or more political actors and one in which it is. Based on the ideal points depicted in figure 4a, the equilibrium result is $x = J$. In other words, the Court is

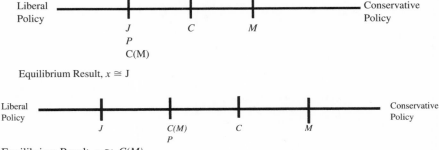

Fig. 4. Hypothetical distribution of preferences. (*Note: J* is the justices' preferred position based on the attitudes of the median member of the Court; *M* and *P* denote, respectively, the most preferred positions of the median member of Congress and the president; *C* is the preferred position of the key committees in Congress that make the decision about whether to propose legislation to their respective houses; and *C(M)* represents the commitees' indifference point (between their preferred position and that desired by *M*). (Adapted from Eskridge 1991b.)

free to read its sincere preferences into law. Figure 4b yields a very different expectation. Because the Court's preferences are now to the left of $C(M)$, it would vote in a sophisticated fashion to avoid a congressional override; the equilibrium result is $x = C(M)$.

Eskridge explores these regimes in much the same way as did Murphy, providing a largely qualitative examination of particular Court cases. Eskridge also reached many of the same conclusions—for example, in interpreting legislation, we learn that the intent of the enacting Congress is far less important to policy-preference-maximizing justices than are the preferences and likely actions of the current Congress.

Eskridge is a legal academic. Beginning in about 1996, political scientists moved into the picture. Some followed in Murphy's and Eskridge's footsteps, conducting largely qualitative analyses of the constraints on the Court imposed by the separation-of-powers system (see, e.g., Epstein and Walker 1995; Knight and Epstein 1996). Others assessed their predictions with large-scale data sets (see, e.g., Martin 1998; Segal 1997). These studies and others undertaken by those identifying themselves as positive political theorists have reached mixed results, though, on balance, the findings support the Murphy-Eskridge perspective. Exemplary is work by Spiller (e.g., Bergara, Richman, and Spiller 1999; Spiller and Gely 1992), which concludes that it is difficult to make sense of Court decisions without taking into account the preferences of the other political organizations. Conversely, Segal writes that "evidence of strategic behavior at other stages of the Court's decisions suggests that the justices can act in a sophisticated fashion *when they need* to do so. But the institutional protections granted the Court mean that with respect to Congress and the presidency, they almost never need to do so" (1997, 42–43).

Despite these mixed conclusions, the studies resemble one another in an important respect: virtually all the existing separation-of-powers literature asserts that the constraint is far more—or, at the extreme, exclusively—operative in cases calling for the Court to interpret statutes than in cases asking the Court to assess statutes' constitutionality.[14] The rationale behind this claim is straightforward: Congress has the power to overturn the Court's interpretations of laws, but, at least according to the U.S. Supreme Court (most recently in *Dickerson v. United States* [2000]), the legislature cannot overturn the Court's constitutional decisions (at least not by simple majorities; Congress must propose constitutional amendments). Given the infrequency with which Congress takes this action—and the frequency with which it disturbs the Court's statutory interpretation decisions[15]—many scholars have argued that the justices need not be too attentive (or, again at the extreme, at all attentive) to the preferences and likely actions of other government actors in constitutional disputes.

Is there thus any reason to suppose that the strategic account, as Murphy developed it, applies to cases involving constitutional questions? *Congress and the Court* suggests several such reasons, with a significant one being the weapons other actors can use to punish justices for their decisions in constitutional cases. Congress may not easily overturn these rulings, but, as Murphy notes, it can hold judicial salaries constant, impeach justices, and pass legislation to remove the Court's ability to hear certain kinds of cases. Although the legislature rarely deploys these weapons, their existence may serve to constrain policy-oriented justices from acting on their preferences.

Murphy provides examples of this phenomenon in action, but the most well known are perhaps the Court's decisions in *Watkins v. United States* (1957) and *Barenblatt v. United States* (1959). In these cases, the justices considered similar constitutional questions pertaining to the rights of witnesses to refuse to answer questions put to them by congressional committees investigating subversive activities in the United States. In *Watkins*, they ruled for the witness, but in *Barenblatt* they ruled against him. Figure 5, which provides an approximation of the

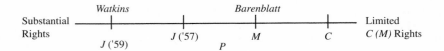

Fig. 5. Approximate distribution of preferences about the rights of witnesses in subversive activities cases, 1957–59. (*Note:* The policy, rights of witnesses, pertains to the right of witnesses to refuse to answer questions put to them by congressional committees investigating subversive activities in the United States. J ('57) is the most preferred position of the Court in 1957; J ('59) is the most preferred position of the Court in 1959; M, C, and P are the most preferred positions, respectively, of the median member of Congress, the relevant congressional committees, and the president; $C(M)$ denotes the indifference point of congressional committees.) (Adapted from Epstein and Knight 1998, 153.)

ideal points of the key players, depicts Murphy's explanation for the seeming shift. At the time the cases were decided, Murphy tells us, the Court was to the left of (more liberal than) Congress, the president, and key congressional committees. Given this configuration, the Court's decision in *Watkins*, which put the policy at its ideal point, provided the committees with incentive to take action to override its decision or to harm the Court in other ways. That is because the committees preferred any point on the line between $C(M)$ and M/P to J; Congress and the president would have been amenable to override proposals because these actors also preferred M/P to J. And, in fact, in response to *Watkins* and other liberal decisions, members of Congress offered up numerous Court-curbing laws, including some that would have removed the Court's jurisdiction to hear cases involving subversive activities. Therefore, in *Barenblatt*, the Court had every reason to misrepresent its true policy preferences to protect its legitimacy and reach a result to the right of the congressional median (M)—precisely the course of action that the Court took.

This is but one example; we could develop scores of others from Murphy's work. But the larger point should not be missed: Murphy's perspective is worth a hard look. We urge scholars to bring the same tools to bear on cases involving constitutional interpretation as on those requiring the Court to engage in statutory interpretation. Perhaps the effect of the separation-of-powers system is less, but we, like Murphy, do not believe it is nonexistent.

STRATEGIC INTERACTIONS
AMONG THE JUSTICES

Since the early 1990s, scholars have produced a substantial amount of work that explicitly identifies *Elements of Judicial Strategy* as its starting point—work that considers strategic interactions among the justices. To the extent that it seeks to develop a conceptualization of judicial decisions, some of this new wave of research is actually quite close to Murphy's seminal book. Along these lines, we would point to our work, *The Choices Justices Make* (Epstein and Knight 1998), which attempts to follow the example set by *Elements:* we develop a picture of justices as strategic seekers of legal policy and explore how such justices make choices. Other research has stressed the importance of formal analysis, with the central idea as follows: if scholars want to explain a particular line of decisions or a substantive body of law as the equilibrium outcome of the interdependent choices of the judges and other actors, they must demonstrate why the choices are in equilibrium, and a formal model is an essential feature of such a demonstration (Caldeira 1999; Kornhauser 1992a, 1992b; Schwartz 1992). A third set of scholars has translated the strategic intuition into variables, which are explored in statistical models. We think here of Maltzman and his colleagues, Spriggs and Wahlbeck, who have investigated a wide range of strategic behavior, from the selection of a majority opinion writer to the decision to join a particular opinion coalition (see Maltzman, Spriggs, and Wahlbeck 2000; Maltzman and Wahlbeck 1996a, 1996b; Wahlbeck, Spriggs, and Maltzman 1998).

However varied the contemporary research, it, like the separation-of-powers studies, shares a common feature: as mentioned earlier, virtually all of this work assumes that justices pursue policy goals. We certainly understand why this is the case: a vast amount of empirical support exists for the importance of this motivation. Moreover, *Elements*, the starting point for so much of this research, treated this goal as paramount. Nonetheless, Murphy's work counsels that, while this may be the primary objective, it is not necessarily the only one. Another arena that *Elements* brings to light is institutional legitimacy, or the judicial motivation to ensure that the Court remains a credible force in American politics, in the eyes of both the public and public officials. Such a concern may manifest itself in a number of ways, such as selecting cases for review that have the potential to influence political, social, or economic policy—or avoiding such cases under particular political circumstances.

And Murphy's more recent return to questions of jurisprudence reminds us of the role that doctrine and principle can play in judicial decision making. As our earlier analysis suggests, the oft-cited conflict between jurisprudential and strategic approaches to the courts is vastly overstated. If justices are motivated by doctrine and principle (rather than policy) and are concerned with effectively instantiating those doctrines and principles into the content of law, they will adapt their decisions both to the goals of other relevant actors and to the institutional context in which they make their choices. In so doing, justices act strategically and thus are a proper subject for the approach Murphy has advocated throughout his career.

But, again, the general point should not be missed: scholars invoking the strategic account perhaps ought devote more attention to considering other judicial motivations (see, generally, Baum 1997). That they can do so, as we noted earlier, is one of the nice features of the account; it is, simply put, flexible enough to accommodate a wide range of goals. That they should do so is a direct lesson from Murphy's important and prescient body of work.

NOTES

We are grateful to the National Science Foundation for supporting our work on strategic decision making (SBR-9320284, SBR-9614130).We adapt several passages in this chapter from some of that work (e.g., Epstein and Knight 1998, 2000).

1. The categories in table 1 are not and need not be mutually exclusive, as many of Murphy's studies themselves demonstrate (e.g., Murphy 1965a, 1995a; Murphy, Pritchett, and Epstein 2001). Nonetheless, for purposes of discussion and analysis, we placed each work—based on its predominant theme—into a single cell.

2. Unless otherwise indicated, all unattributed quotes from Walter F. Murphy are from an interview we conducted with him on February 19, 2000, in St. Louis, Missouri.

3. We adapt the discussion in this and the next paragraph from Ferejohn and Weingast 1992a.

4. In denoting these most preferred points, we assume that the actors prefer an outcome that is nearer to that point than one that is further away. Or, to put it more technically, "beginning at [an actor's] ideal point, utility always declines monotonically in any direction. This . . . is known as single-peakedness of preferences" (Krehbiel 1988, 259, 263). We also assume that the actors possess complete and perfect information about the preferences of all other actors and that the sequence of policy-making unfolds as follows: the Court interprets a law; the relevant congressional committees propose (or do not pro-

pose) legislation to override the Court's interpretation; Congress (if the committees propose legislation) enacts (or does not enact) an override bill; the
president (if Congress acts) signs (or does not sign) the override bill; and Congress (if the president vetoes) overrides (or does not override) the veto. These
are relatively common assumptions in the legal literature (see, e.g., Eskridge
1991a, 1991b; see also fig. 3).

5. This group includes Eskridge (1991a, 1991b, 1994) of the Yale Law
School; Farber (Farber and Frickey 1991, 1992) of the University of Minnesota
School of Law; Kornhauser (1992a, 1992b, 1995) of New York University Law
School; Rodriguez (1994) of the University of San Diego Law School; Spiller
(Gely and Spiller 1990; Spiller and Gely 1992) of the Haas School of Business
(Berkeley); Spitzer (Cohen and Spitzer 1994) of the University of Southern
California Law Center; and Cross and Tiller (1998), both of the Graduate
School of Business at the University of Texas. These law and business profes-
sors are joined by a few political scientists, most of whom developed their rep-
utations as students of Congress (e.g., Ferejohn and Weingast [1992a, 1992b]
and Cameron [Cameron 1994; Cameron Segal, and Songer 2000]). See, generally, Shapiro 1995.

6. More specifically, they claim that Marks (1989) gave rise to a major part
of the PPT research program, the separation-of-powers games more fully
developed in Eskridge 1991a, 1991b, 1994; Ferejohn and Weingast 1992a,
1992b; Epstein and Walker 1995, to name just a few. For a discussion of this
line of inquiry and Murphy's role in it, see the subsequent section on "Strategic Interactions between the Court and External Political Actors."

7. Game theory provides a potent set of tools for examining social situations involving strategic behavior—that is, situations in which the social outcome depends on the product of the interdependent choices of at least two
actors.

8. Other articles published around the same time also pointed to the
promise of game theory in political science (see, e.g., Shapley and Shubik
1954).

9. Another was Pritchett 1961, which was published the year before Murphy's work. That both student and mentor were working on similar books at
about the same time is something of a coincidence, though certainly reflective
of the times, a period during which Congress was considering various Court-
curbing measures. Pritchett's work grew out of a series of Minnesota lectures
he delivered on the subject; Murphy's interest was piqued after he attended
some congressional hearings and conducted interviews with several senators,
including Lyndon Johnson.

10. To put it in contemporary terms, Murphy uses the intuitions of the
attitudinal model (discussed in the next section) to study the relationship
between Congress and the Court, but he extended those premises and demonstrated that the resulting behavior may differ from what attitudinalists postu-
late.

11. Reactions can vary from overturning decisions through legislation to holding judicial salaries constant to impeaching judges. Murphy's general point is that the lack of an electoral connection does not negate strategic behavior on the part of nonelected actors.

12. The information in this paragraph comes from our interview with Murphy (see n.2).

13. As we implied earlier, some of the initial studies, produced mainly by legal academics and business school professors—the positive political theorists—did not acknowledge their debt to Murphy primarily because they did not know of his research. That has changed, with virtually all PPT now regularly citing his books and articles.

14. Exceptions, to lesser and greater extents, are Epstein and Knight 1998; Fisher 2001; Martin 1998; Meernik and Ignagni 1997; Murphy 1964; Rosenberg 1992.

15. Between 1967 and 1990, Congress overrode some 120 Court decisions (see Eskridge 1991a).

REFERENCES

Atkins, Burton M. 1973. "Judicial Behavior and Tendencies toward Conformity in a Three Member Small Group: A Case Study of Dissent Behavior on the United States Court of Appeals." *Social Science Quarterly* 54:41–53.

Barry, Brian. 1978. *Sociologists, Economists, and Democracy*. Chicago: University of Chicago Press.

Baum, Lawrence. 1997. *The Puzzle of Judicial Behavior*. Ann Arbor: University of Michigan Press.

Becker, Theodore R. 1966. "A Survey Study of Hawaiian Judges: The Effect of Decisions on Judicial Role Variations." *American Political Science Review* 60:677–80.

Bergara, Mario, Barak Richman, and Pablo T. Spiller. 1999. "Judicial Politics and the Econometrics of Preferences." Typescript, University of California-Berkeley.

Birkby, Robert H., and Walter F. Murphy. 1964. "Interest Group Conflict in the Judicial Arena: Group Access to the Courts." *Texas Law Review* 42:1018–48.

Brams, Steven J., and Morton D. Davis. 1976. "A Game-Theory Approach to Jury Selection." *Trial* 13:47–49.

Brenner, Saul. 1979. "Game Theory and Supreme Court Decision Making: A Bibliographic Overview." *Law Library Journal* 72:470–75.

Brenner, Saul. 1989. "Fluidity on the United States Supreme Court: A Reexamination." In *American Court Systems*, ed. S. Goldman and A. Sarat. New York: Longman.

Caldeira, Gregory A. 1999. "Sophisticated Voting and Gate-Keeping in the Supreme Court." *Journal of Law, Economics, and Organization* 15:549–72.

Cameron, Charles M. 1994. "Decision-Making and Positive Political Theory (or, Using Game Theory to Study Judicial Politics)." Paper presented at the annual meeting of the Conference Group on the Scientific Study of Judicial Politics, Columbus, Ohio.

Cameron, Charles M., Jeffrey A. Segal, and Donald R. Songer. 2000. "Strategic Auditing in a Political Hierarchy: An Informational Model of the Supreme Court's Certiorari Decisions." *American Political Science Review* 94:101–16.

Campbell, Donald T. 1963. "Social Attitudes and Other Acquired Behavioral Dispositions." In *Psychology: A Study of Science*, ed. S. Koch. New York: McGraw-Hill.

Carp, Robert A., and Russell Wheeler. 1972. "Sink or Swim: The Socialization of a Federal District Judge." *Journal of Public Law* 21:359–93.

Cohen, Linda R., and Matthew L. Spitzer. 1994. "Solving the *Chevron* Puzzle." *Law and Contemporary Problems* 57:65–110.

Cook, Beverly Blair. 1971. "The Socialization of New Federal Judges: Impact on District Court Business." *Washington University Law Quarterly* 1971: 253–79.

Coombs, Clyde M., and Richard C. Kao. 1960. "On a Connection between Factor Analysis and Multidimensional Unfolding." *Psychometrika* 25:210–31.

Cross, Frank B., and Emerson H. Tiller. 1998. "Judicial Partisanship and Obedience to Legal Doctrine: Whistleblowing on the Federal Courts of Appeals." *Yale Law Journal* 107:2155–76.

Danelski, David J. 1960. "The Influence of the Chief Justice in the Decisional Process of the Supreme Court." Paper presented at the annual meeting of the American Political Science Association, New York.

Downs, Anthony. 1957. *An Economic Theory of Democracy*. New York: Harper and Row.

Elster, Jon. 1986. *Rational Choice*. New York: New York University Press.

Epstein, Lee, and Jack Knight. 1998. *The Choices Justices Make*. Washington, D.C.: CQ Press.

Epstein, Lee, and Jack Knight. 2000. "Toward a Strategic Revolution in Judicial Politics: A Look Back, a Look Ahead." *Political Research Quarterly* 53:625–61.

Epstein, Lee, and Thomas G. Walker. 1995. "The Role of the Court in American Society: Playing the Reconstruction Game." In *Contemplating Courts*, ed. L. Epstein. Washington, D.C.: CQ Press.

Eskridge, William N., Jr. 1991a. "Overriding Supreme Court Statutory Interpretation Decisions." *Yale Law Journal* 101:331–417.

Eskridge, William N., Jr. 1991b. "Reneging on History?: Playing the Court/Congress/President Civil Rights Game." *California Law Review* 79:613–84.

Eskridge, William N., Jr. 1994. *Dynamic Statutory Interpretation*. Cambridge: Harvard University Press.

Farber, Daniel A., and Philip P. Frickey. 1991. *Law and Public Choice.* Chicago: University of Chicago Press.

Farber, Daniel A., and Philip P. Frickey. 1992. "Foreword: Positive Political Theory in the Nineties." *Georgetown Law Journal* 80:457–76.

Ferejohn, John, and Barry Weingast. 1992a. "Limitation of Statutes: Strategic Statutory Interpretation." *Georgetown Law Review* 80:565–82.

Ferejohn, John, and Barry Weingast. 1992b. "A Positive Theory of Statutory Interpretation." *International Review of Law and Economics* 12:263–79.

Fisher, Louis. 2001. "Congressional Checks on the Judiciary." In *Congress Confronts the Court: The Struggle for Legitimacy and Authority in Lawmaking,* ed. C. C. Campbell and J. F. Stack. Lanham, Md.: Rowman and Littlefield.

Gely, Rafael, and Pablo T. Spiller. 1990. "A Rational Choice Theory of Supreme Court Decision Making with Applications to the *State Farm* and *Grove City* Cases." *Journal of Law, Economics, and Organization* 6:263–300.

George, Tracey E., and Lee Epstein. 1992. "On the Nature of Supreme Court Decision Making." *American Political Science Review* 86:323–37.

Gibson, James L. 1978. "Judges' Role Orientations, Attitudes, and Decisions: An Interactive Model." *American Political Science Review* 72:911–24.

Glick, Henry, and Kenneth N. Vines. 1969. "Law-Making in the State Judiciary: A Comparative Study of the Judicial Role in Four States." *Polity* 2:142–59.

Goldman, Sheldon. 1966. "Voting Behavior on the United States Courts of Appeals, 1961–1964." *American Political Science Review* 60:374–83.

Goldman, Sheldon. 1973. "Conflict on the U.S. Courts of Appeals, 1965–1971: A Quantitative Analysis." *University of Cincinnati Law Review* 42:635–58.

Goldman, Sheldon, and Thomas R. Jahnige. 1976. *The Federal Courts as Political System.* 2d ed. New York: Harper and Row.

Goldman, Sheldon, and Austin Sarat, eds. 1978. *American Court Systems: Readings in Judicial Process and Behavior.* San Francisco: W. H. Freeman.

Goldman, Sheldon, and Austin Sarat, eds. 1989. *American Court Systems: Readings in Judicial Process and Behavior.* 2d ed. New York: Longman.

Grossman, Joel B. 1968. "Dissenting Bloc on the Warren Court: A Study in Judicial Role Behavior." *Journal of Politics* 30:1068–90.

Grossman, Joel B., and Joseph Tanenhaus, eds. 1969. *Frontiers of Judicial Research.* New York: Wiley.

Guilford, J. P. 1961. "Factorial Angles to Psychology." *Psychological Review* 68:1–20.

Howard, J. Woodford, Jr. 1968. "On the Fluidity of Judicial Choice." *American Political Science Review* 62:43–56.

Howard, J. Woodford, Jr. 1977. "Role Perceptions and Behavior in Three U.S. Courts of Appeals." *Journal of Politics* 39:916–38.

James, Dorothy. 1968. "Role Theory and the Supreme Court." *Journal of Politics* 30:160–86.

Jaros, Dean, and Robert Mendelson. 1967. "The Judicial Role and Sentencing Behavior." *Midwest Journal of Political Science* 11:471–88.

Knight, Jack, and Lee Epstein. 1996. "On the Struggle for Judicial Supremacy." *Law and Society Review* 30:87–130.

Kornhauser, Lewis A. 1992a. "Modeling Collegial Courts. I: Path Dependence." *International Review of Law and Economics* 12:169–85.

Kornhauser, Lewis A. 1992b. "Modeling Collegial Courts. II. Legal Doctrine." *Journal of Law, Economics, and Organization* 8:441–70.

Kornhauser, Lewis A. 1995. "Adjudication by a Resource-Constrained Team: Hierarchy and Precedent in a Judicial System." *Southern California Law Review* 68:1605–29.

Krehbiel, Keith. 1988. "Spatial Models of Legislative Choice." *Legislative Studies Quarterly* 13:259–319.

Lockard, Duane, and Walter F. Murphy. 1980. *Basic Cases in Constitutional Law.* 1st ed. New York: Macmillan

Lockard, Duane, and Walter F. Murphy. 1987. *Basic Cases in Constitutional Law.* 2d ed. Washington, D.C.: CQ Press.

Lockard, Duane, and Walter F. Murphy. 1992. *Basic Cases in Constitutional Law.* 3d ed. Washington, D.C.: CQ Press.

Maltzman, Forrest, James F. Spriggs II, and Paul J. Wahlbeck. 2000. *Crafting Law on the Supreme Court.* Cambridge: Cambridge University Press.

Maltzman, Forrest, and Paul J. Wahlbeck. 1996a. "May It Please the Chief? Opinion Assignments in the Rehnquist Court." *American Journal of Political Science* 40:421–43.

Maltzman, Forrest, and Paul J. Wahlbeck. 1996b. "Strategic Policy Considerations and Voting Fluidity on the Burger Court." *American Political Science Review* 90:581–92.

Marks, Brian. 1989. "A Model of Judicial Influence on Congressional Policy-Making: *Grove City v. Bell.*" Ph.D. diss., Washington University, St. Louis.

Martin, Andrew D. 1998. "Public Policy, the Supreme Court, and the Separation of Powers." Paper presented at the annual meeting of the American Political Science Association, Boston.

Mason, Alpheus T. 1956. *Harlan Fiske Stone: Pillar of the Law.* New York: Viking.

Meernik, James, and Joseph Ignagni. 1997. "Judicial Review and Coordinate Construction of the Constitution." *American Journal of Political Science* 41:447–67.

Murphy, Walter F. 1958. "Civil Liberties and the Japanese American Cases: A Study in the Uses of Stare Decisis." *Western Political Quarterly* 11:3–13.

Murphy, Walter F. 1959a. "Lower Court Checks on Supreme Court Power." *American Political Science Review* 53:1017–31.

Murphy, Walter F. 1959b. "Mr. Justice Jackson, Free Speech, and the Judicial Function." *Vanderbilt Law Review* 12:1019–45.

Murphy, Walter F. 1959c. "The South Counterattacks: The Anti-NAACP Laws." *Western Political Quarterly* 12:371–90.

Murphy, Walter F. 1961. "In His Own Image: Mr. Chief Justice Taft and Supreme Court Appointments." *Supreme Court Review* 1961:159–93.

Murphy, Walter F. 1962a. "Chief Justice Taft and the Lower Court Bureaucracy." *Journal of Politics* 24:453–76.

Murphy, Walter F. 1962b. *Congress and the Court: A Case Study in the American Political Process.* Chicago: University of Chicago Press.

Murphy, Walter F. 1962c. "Marshalling the Court: Leadership, Bargaining, and the Judicial Process." *University of Chicago Law Review* 29:640–72.

Murphy, Walter F. 1964. *The Elements of Judicial Strategy.* Chicago: University of Chicago Press.

Murphy, Walter F. 1965a. "Deeds under a Doctrine: Civil Liberties in the 1963 Term." *American Political Science Review* 59:64–79.

Murphy, Walter F. 1965b. *Wiretapping on Trial.* New York: Random House.

Murphy, Walter F. 1966. "Courts as Small Groups." *Harvard Law Review* 79:1552–72.

Murphy, Walter F. 1974. "Explaining Diffuse Support for the United States Supreme Court: An Assessment of Four Models." *Notre Dame Lawyer* 49:1037–44.

Murphy, Walter F. 1978. "The Art of Constitutional Interpretation: A Preliminary Showing." In *Essays on the Constitution of the United States*, ed. M. J. Harmon. Port Washington, N.Y.: Kennikat Press.

Murphy, Walter F. 1979. *The Vicar of Christ.* New York: Macmillan.

Murphy, Walter F. 1980. "An Ordering of Constitutional Values." *Southern California Law Review* 53:703–60.

Murphy, Walter F. 1982. "What If Peter Had Been Pope during World War II?" In *What If?* ed. N. W. Polsby. Lexington, Mass.: Lexington Books.

Murphy, Walter F. 1986. "Who Shall Interpret the Constitution?" *Review of Politics* 48:401–23.

Murphy, Walter F. 1987a. "Inching toward the New Jerusalem: How an Imperfect Pope Might Do a Little Good in an Imperfect World." In *If I Were Pope*, ed. C. Lund. Chicago: Thomas More Press.

Murphy, Walter F. 1987b. "*Slaughter-House, Civil Rights,* and Limits on Constitutional Change." *American Journal of Jurisprudence* 32:1–22.

Murphy, Walter F. 1990. "The Right to Privacy and Legitimate Constitutional Change." In *The Constitutional Bases of Social and Political Change in the United States*, ed. S. Slonim. New York: Praeger.

Murphy, Walter F. 1991. "Civil Law, Common Law, and Constitutional Democracy." *Louisiana Law Review* 52:91–136.

Murphy, Walter F. 1992. "Staggering toward the New Jurisprudence of Constitutional Theory." *American Journal of Jurisprudence* 37:337–57.

Murphy, Walter F. 1993a. "Constitutions, Constitutionalism, and Democracy." In *Constitutionalism and Democracy: Transitions in the Contemporary World*, ed. D. Greenberg. New York: Oxford University Press.

Murphy, Walter F. 1993b. "Excluding Political Parties: Problems for Democratic and Constitutional Theory." In *Germany and Its Basic Law*, ed. P. Kirchhof and D. P. Kommers. Baden-Baden: Noms Verlagsgesellschaft.

Murphy, Walter F. 1995a. "Merlin's Memory: The Past and Future Imperfect of the Once and Future Polity." In *Responding to Imperfection: The Theory and Practice of Constitutional Amendment*, ed. S. Levinson. Princeton: Princeton University Press.

Murphy, Walter F. 1995b. "What Is It Interpreters Interpret? A Response to Professor Delperee." In *Constitutional Justice under Old Constitutions*, ed. E. Smith. The Hague: Kluwer Law International.

Murphy, Walter F. 1998. "May Constitutional Democracies 'Outlaw' a Political Party?" In *Politicians and Party Politics*, ed. J. C. Greer. Baltimore: Johns Hopkins University Press.

Murphy, Walter F., James E. Fleming, and Sotirios A. Barber. 1995. *American Constitutional Interpretation*. 2d ed. Westbury, N.Y.: Foundation Press.

Murphy, Walter F., James E. Fleming, and William F. Harris II. 1986. *American Constitutional Interpretation*. Mineola, N.Y.: Foundation Press.

Murphy, Walter F., and C. Herman Pritchett. 1961. *Courts, Judges, and Politics*. 1st ed. New York: Random House.

Murphy, Walter F., and C. Herman Pritchett. 1974. *Courts, Judges, and Politics*. 2d ed. New York: Random House.

Murphy, Walter F., and C. Herman Pritchett. 1979. *Courts, Judges, and Politics*. 3d ed. New York: Random House.

Murphy, Walter F., and C. Herman Pritchett. 1986. *Courts, Judges, and Politics*. 4th ed. New York: Random House.

Murphy, Walter F., C. Herman Pritchett, and Lee Epstein. 2002. *Courts, Judges, and Politics*. 5th ed. Boston: McGraw-Hill.

Murphy, Walter F., and Joseph Tanenhaus. 1968. "Public Opinion and the Supreme Court: The Goldwater Campaign." *Public Opinion Quarterly* 32:31–50.

Murphy, Walter F., and Joseph Tanenhaus. 1969a. "Constitutional Courts and Political Representation." In *Modern American Democracy*, ed. M. Danielson and W. F. Murphy. New York: Holt, Rinehart, and Winston.

Murphy, Walter F., and Joseph Tanenhaus. 1969b. "Public Opinion and the U.S. Supreme Court." In *Frontiers of Judicial Research*, ed. J. B. Grossman and J. Tanenhaus. New York: Wiley.

Murphy, Walter F., and Joseph Tanenhaus. 1972. *The Study of Public Law*. 1st ed. New York: Random House.

Murphy, Walter F., and Joseph Tanenhaus. 1977. *Comparative Constitutional Law: Cases and Commentaries*. New York: St. Martin's Press.

Murphy, Walter F., and Joseph Tanenhaus. 1990. "Publicity, Public Opinion and the Court." *Northwestern University Law Review* 84:983–1036.

Murphy, Walter, Joseph Tanenhaus, and Daniel L. Kastner. 1973. *Public Evaluations of Constitutional Courts: Alternative Explanations*. Beverly Hills, Calif.: Sage.

Nagel, Stuart S. 1961. "Political Party Affiliations and Judges' Decisions." *American Political Science Review* 55:843–50.

Pritchett, C. Herman. 1941. "Divisions of Opinion among Justices of the U.S. Supreme Court." *American Political Science Review* 35:890–98.

Pritchett, C. Herman. 1948. *The Roosevelt Court*. New York: Macmillan.

Pritchett, C. Herman. 1961. *Congress versus the Supreme Court, 1957–1960*. Minneapolis: University of Minnesota Press.

Riker, William H. 1962. *The Theory of Political Coalitions*. New Haven: Yale University Press.

Rodriguez, Daniel B. 1994. "The Positive Political Dimensions of Regulatory Reform." *Washington University Law Quarterly* 72:1–150.

Rohde, David W. 1972. "Policy Goals and Opinion Coalitions in the Supreme Court." *Midwest Journal of Political Science* 16:208–24.

Rohde, David W., and Harold J. Spaeth. 1976. *Supreme Court Decision Making*. San Francisco: W. H. Freeman.

Rokeach, Milton. 1968. *Beliefs, Attitudes, and Values: A Theory of Organization and Change*. San Francisco: Jossey-Bass.

Rosenberg, Gerald N. 1992. "Judicial Independence and the Reality of Political Power." *Review of Politics* 54:369–98.

Schmidhauser, John R. 1962. "*Stare Decisis*, Dissent, and the Backgrounds of the Justices of the Supreme Court of the United States." *University of Toronto Law Review* 14:194–212.

Schubert, Glendon. 1958. "The Study of Judicial Decision-Making as an Aspect of Political Behavior." *American Political Science Review* 52:1007–25.

Schubert, Glendon. 1960. *Constitutional Politics: The Political Behavior of Supreme Court Justices and the Constitutional Policies That They Make*. New York: Holt, Rinehart, and Winston.

Schubert, Glendon. 1965. *The Judicial Mind: The Attitudes and Ideologies of Supreme Court Justices, 1946–1963*. Evanston, Ill.: Northwestern University Press.

Schwartz, Edward P. 1992. "Policy, Precedent, and Power: A Positive Theory of Supreme Court Decision Making." *Journal of Law, Economics, and Organization* 8:219–52.

Schwartz, Edward P. 1997. "The New Elements of Judicial Strategy." Paper presented at the annual meeting of the Midwest Political Science Association, Chicago.

Segal, Jeffrey A. 1997. "Separation-of-Powers Games in the Positive Theory of Law and Courts." *American Political Science Review* 91:28–44.

Segal, Jeffrey A., Lee Epstein, Charles M. Cameron, and Harold J. Spaeth. 1995. "Ideological Values and the Votes of U.S. Supreme Court Justices Revisited." *Journal of Politics* 57:812–23.

Segal, Jeffrey A, and Harold J. Spaeth. 1993. *The Supreme Court and the Attitudinal Model*. New York: Cambridge University Press.

Shapiro, Martin. 1995. "From the Section Chair." *Law and Courts* 5:1–3.

Shapley, L. S., and Martin Shubik. 1954. "A Method for Evaluating the Distribution of Power in a Committee System." *American Political Science Review* 48:791–92.

Smith, Rogers M. 1988. "Political Jurisprudence, The 'New Institutionalism,' and the Future of Public Law." *American Political Science Review* 82:89–108.

Snyder, Eliose. 1958. "The Supreme Court as a Small Group." *Social Forces* 36:232–38.

Spaeth, Harold J., and Douglas R. Parker. 1969. "Effects of Attitude toward Situation upon Attitude toward Object." *Journal of Psychology* 73:173–82.

Spiller, Pablo T., and Rafael Gely. 1992. "Congressional Control or Judicial Independence: The Determinants of U.S. Supreme Court Labor-Relation Decisions." *RAND Journal of Economics* 23:463–92.

Tanenhaus, Joseph, and Walter F. Murphy. 1981. "Patterns of Public Support for the Supreme Court: A Panel Study." *Journal of Politics* 43:24–39.

Tate, C. Neal. 1981. "Personal Attribute Models of Voting Behavior of U.S. Supreme Court Justices." *American Political Science Review* 75:355–67.

Tate, C. Neal, and Roger Handberg. 1991. "Time Binding and Theory Building in Personal Attribute Models of Supreme Court Voting Behavior, 1916–88." *American Journal of Political Science* 35:460–80.

Ulmer, S. Sidney. 1970. "The Use of Power in the Supreme Court: The Opinion Assignments of Earl Warren, 1953–1960." *Journal of Public Law* 19:49–67.

Ulmer, S. Sidney. 1971. *Courts as Small and Not So Small Groups.* Morristown, N.J.: General Learning Press.

Ulmer, S. Sidney. 1973. "Social Background as an Indicator to the Votes of Supreme Court Justices in Criminal Cases." *American Journal of Political Science* 17:622–30.

Ungs, Thomas, and Larry R. Baas. 1972. "Judicial Role Perception: A Q-Technique Study of Ohio Judges." *Law and Society Review* 6:343–66.

Vines, Kenneth N. 1964. "Federal District Court Judges and Race Relations Cases in the South." *Journal of Politics* 26:338–57.

Vines, Kenneth N. 1969. "The Judicial Role in the American States: An Exploration." In *Frontiers of Judicial Research*, ed. J. B. Grossman and J. Tanenhaus. New York: Wiley.

Wahlbeck, Paul J., James F. Spriggs II, and Forrest Maltzman. 1998. "Marshalling the Court: Bargaining and Accommodation on the Supreme Court." *American Journal of Political Science* 42:294–315.

Walker, Thomas G. 1973. "Behavioral Tendencies in the Three-Judge District Court." *American Journal of Political Science* 17:407–13.

Walker, Thomas G. 1994. "The Development of the Field." Paper presented at the Columbus Conference on the State of the Field of Judicial Politics, Columbus, Ohio.

Wold, Jon T. 1974. "Political Orientation, Social Backgrounds, and Role Perceptions of State Supreme Court Judges." *Western Political Quarterly* 27:239–48.

CHAPTER 9

J. Woodford Howard Jr.: Fluidity, Strategy, and Analytical Synthesis in Judicial Studies

Nancy Maveety and John Anthony Maltese

At first glance, J. Woodford Howard Jr., the Princeton-trained student of Alpheus T. Mason (another pioneer discussed in this volume), may look more like a traditional public law scholar than a prototypical pioneer of judicial behavior. But looks can be deceiving. Though often associated with judicial biography (Howard 1968a)—the classic genre of the traditional approach—his work is multifaceted. It reflects an ecumenical approach that is wary of oversimplification and of doctrinaire views. It is, like his life and teaching, balanced. Howard forever exhorted his students (two of whom are the authors of this chapter) to use a variety of approaches to illuminate judicial behavior. Though critical of many of these approaches, his favorite catchphrase was, "Don't throw the baby out with the bathwater!"

As important as Howard's work in judicial biography has been, his two most influential pieces may well be his 1968 article for the *American Political Science Review*, "On the Fluidity of Judicial Choice" (which was a direct outgrowth of research for his biography of Associate Justice Frank Murphy), and his 1981 book, *Courts of Appeals in the Federal Judicial System*. Either one would serve as ample evidence of his standing as a pioneer of judicial behavior.

Although we will be concentrating largely on the contributions of "Fluidity," we must make a few preliminary observations about *Courts of Appeals*. Notwithstanding important articles by others (e.g., Goldman 1966; Richardson and Vines 1970), Howard's book was the first comprehensive analysis of the courts of appeals. Although limited by time and funding to the Second, Fifth, and District of Columbia Circuits, Howard examined the courts of appeals as a system, used them as a springboard for an inquiry into the concept of judicial role theory, and created a database of nearly five thousand cases that he coded, analyzed, and traced as they flowed through the circuits. In an age when computer technology was cumbersome (don't drop the cards!), this data collection effort was particularly impressive. *Courts of Appeals* was one of the first major judicial studies to buck the prevailing (and still dominant) upper-court bias in the study of public law. This work laid the foundation for several empirical studies of lower courts, including a multiuser database on courts of appeals decisions funded by the National Science Foundation (Songer 1997). Howard's analysis of the flow of litigation also led scholars to examine more closely those factors that affect the circuit court's agenda (Davis and Songer 1989; Harrington and Ward 1995) and to test the influence of hierarchical considerations on appeals court decision making (Songer, Segal, and Cameron 1994). *Courts of Appeals* was also unique in that it provided scholars with substantial insights on the perspectives of those sitting on the appeals courts. By blending a quantitative analysis of judicial voting and workload data with interviews with judges, Howard explored and tested the varying dimensions that underlie the concept of role orientation. His findings encouraged scholars to test further the relationships between institutional practices and judicial decision making. Systematic studies of judicial behavior on the courts of appeals (e.g., Songer, Sheehan, and Haire 2000), as well as more general studies of lower courts, clearly owe much to the Howard's legacy.

Despite this use of quantitative data to sketch a picture of judicial behavior on the courts of appeals, Howard appealed to his readers to remember that "each statistic represents human beings" (1968a, xxv) and lamented that concentration on "the abstractions of litigation flow and judicial roles leech the flesh and blood from litigants and judges in action" (1968a, xxiv). Seeking to look beyond the abstractions, Howard embraced the view that the question was not whether judges make law, but when, where, and how much (pace Cardozo). The *why* behind the when and where and how much could only be revealed by including the individual and the context as part of the equation.[1] That helps to explain his fascination with judicial role, not only in *Courts of Appeals* but also in his 1977 *Journal of Politics* article on role perception as well as in his desire to view decision making on the courts of appeals in the context of the system within which the judges operated. Most importantly, the *why* is the root of his suspicion of oversimplified attitudinal models, which he challenged most directly in his article on fluidity of judicial choice.

Written during the ascendance of quantitative judicial behaviorism, "Fluidity" served as a bold challenge to the public law subfield. By 1968, when the article was published, many judicial scholars had embraced the attitudinal approach as an explanation for decision making by U.S. Supreme Court justices. Yet the subfield remained bitterly divided between what Howard referred to as "quantifiers" and "qualifiers" (Tanenhaus, quoted by Howard 1968b, 43). Howard now says that "Fluidity" should be understood in the context of that fight. His goal, he says, was "to find a middle ground and to refine theory by deflating excessively rigid and ideological constructs from both sides" of the debate (2000).

In that effort to find a common ground, Howard stressed that most qualifiers and quantifiers agree that "judging is a value-laden rather than a value-free art" (1968b, 43). The core debate is not about whether attitudes matter but about how one infers those attitudes and what one can actually predict by knowing those attitudes. Quantifiers infer attitude from aggregate votes, qualifiers from reading opinions. Thus, Howard seemed to be saying that both quantifiers and qualifiers are realists but that "extremes of advocacy" over methodological differences obscure that fact (1968b, 43). In "Fluidity," he attempted to bridge the divide between the quantifiers and qualifiers by "contributing to the analytical synthesis which must come if the discipline is to make a concerted advance in understanding judicial behavior" (1968b, 43).

Howard admits that he had particular concerns about "the oversimplified, single-factor, attitudinal model," although his criticisms were meant to refine rather than debunk the attitudinal model (2000). According to the attitudinal model, a judge's ideology and the presence of ideological blocs on the Court accounted for judicial votes. Once justices' ideological positions were identified and scaled, their votes could be easily quantified. Judicial attitudes served as the predictor of judicial votes, with aggregate data analysis of the patterns that emerged used to validate these claims.

Howard found this to be too simplistic. He argued that both the quantifiers and the qualifiers gave "insufficient attention to the intervening variables operating in a collegial court [that] mediate significantly between individual [judicial] attitude and behavior" (1968b, 44). He cited the "fluidity of judicial choice"—the fact that judges change their minds about how to vote on specific cases—as the evidence for this mediation and suggested different types of fluctuating choices that could only be explained by these intervening small-group or institutional variables. According to Howard, the intervening variables that he posited were a by-product of his larger goal: to deflate single-factor analysis and lay the groundwork for a more complex model of judicial decision making. The variables were simply "a way of ordering the complexity" (Howard 2000).

As seminal works often do, Howard's article speaks as freshly today to the public law subfield as it did when it was first published. Unfortunately, this is partly because the subfield remains methodologically divided among attitudinalists, legal traditionalists, and the most recent entrants to the dispute, strategic theorists who utilize the insights of a rational choice approach. However, what has changed since Howard first wrote is an increasing awareness among many proponents of these different approaches of the synthetic relationship between the explanatory variables they emphasize. Evidence of this contemporary sensitivity to synthesis in explaining judicial behavior can be found in several recent writings. Baum's *The Puzzle of Judicial Behavior* (1997) offers an overview of extant work in judicial politics and sees a common interest among judicial scholars in examining certain questions. In arguing for an ecumenical approach to the examination of the goals that motivate judicial actors, Baum highlights Howard's work as one of the four best qualitative studies of judicial behavior. In addition, Clayton and Gillman's *Supreme Court Decision Making* (1999) suggests that scholars be pluralistic in the search for variables—including institutional characteristics within which judges are embedded—that influence the position a justice takes. Maltzman, Spriggs, and Wahlbeck's work is indicative of this trend: for them, "the principal task of judicial scholars is to provide theories for and empirical evidence of the circumstances under which various factors affect justices' decisions" (1999, 58; see also Maltzman, Spriggs, and Wahlbeck 2000). Finally, recent issues of the *American Political Science Review* and the *Journal of Politics* have included articles on judicial consensus that combine attention to institutional and to ideological variables in the analysis (Gerber and Park 1997) and on the effect of judicial politics variables on the development of legal rules (Wahlbeck 1997).

Despite these encouraging signs, judicial scholars are all too often limited to a particular methodological and theoretical paradigm, which encourages them to dismiss or devalue work outside of it. As an important early challenge to the attitudinal model of judicial decision making, Howard's piece demanded attention (and possibly rebuttal) from more behaviorally oriented judicial scholars. Thus, a second, more positive reason for the continued relevance of Howard's piece is the reaction it engendered across the methodological camps of the subfield—for example, the many quantitative studies of fluidity in voting that it generated (Brenner 1995). Moreover, by fostering the use of the justices' docket books and other private papers by both traditional and behavioral judicial scholars, Howard's piece helped keep qualitative research alive as a legitimate means for understanding judicial decision making.

More recently, Howard's insights have been embraced by contemporary scholars interested in the strategic considerations that inform judicial choice, offering a potential bridge between small-group theory and neoinstitutional models of judicial behavior. In emphasizing the importance of group dynamics and institutional role constraints on judicial decision making, "On the Fluidity of Judicial Choice" addresses many of the same concerns as the contemporary strategic model of judicial action. This model and, more generally, the new institutionalism in the analysis of judicial politics stress the interactive and interdependent nature of judicial decision making and aspire to heal the continuing breach between attitudinalists and legalists (Gillman 1996–97; Epstein and Knight 1998; Maltzman, Spriggs, and Wahlbeck 2000). Howard seemed to speak for these scholars in 1968 when he said that "the intervening variables of strategy and style, in my judgment, are so critical in judicial decision making that they cannot be excluded from any stimulus-response model without distorting results and reducing the reliability of the most carefully constructed attitudinal inferences" (1968b, 52).

We contend that Howard's concept of fluidity, at times questioned by judicial behaviorists as overemphasized, at least regarding the frequency of fluidity in voting, and possibly inconsistent with the ideological model of judging, has reemerged as a prominent aspect of current neoinstitutional work on judicial politics and promises to be a core principle of the (re)new(ed) strategic understandings of judicial action. To illustrate this, we will first briefly summarize the major claims of Howard's 1968 article. We will then comment on the initial interpretation and critique of fluidity by some of his attitudinal colleagues. Finally, we will discuss the recent growth in work on strategic variables affecting judicial choice, noting the ways in which Howard's identification and understanding of fluidity may inform current theories of group dynamics in judicial behavior.

I

Reprinted in several well-known and widely circulated readers on judicial process, "On the Fluidity of Judicial Choice" is a classic in the field. Its deceptively simple thesis is that Supreme Court justices exhibit fluidity of choice in that they change their votes, alter the language of their opinions, and permit their opinions to be conduits for the ideas of others. Noting that Walter Murphy had observed judicial flux in the face of internal bargaining in his classic book, *The Elements of Judicial Strategy* (1964), Howard used the recently opened papers of Justice Frank Murphy to further document fluidity. Based on conference notes, docket books, and unpublished opinion drafts from these papers, Howard suggested that judicial flux is commonplace rather than aberrational (1968b, 44). He argued that fluidity of choice is "so extensive in empirical reality" (44) that it compromised the ability to infer individual attitudes from opinions or aggregate votes, because these opinions and votes were products of group behavior. The existence of fluidity called attention to the group interaction on collegial courts that "intervenes between attitude and action and *qualifies both*" (43; emphasis added). In other words, because votes and opinions frequently change in response to intracourt influences, votes and opinions are not necessarily reliable indicators of attitude, ideology, or jurisprudential philosophy.

This assertion—particularly as to votes, which was tantamount to heresy for advocates of the ideological model of judging—required two elements of proof: evidence of the (extensive) phenomena of fluidity, and identification of a behavioral gap between ideology and choice, a gap to be filled by reference to intervening group variables that inflate or deflate the effect of ideology on choice. Howard offered a typology of flux, a classification of fluid choices according to the type of intervening variable at work. He thus identified and illustrated three types of fluidity: that attributable to the "freshman effect" (unstable attitudes resulting from the assimilation of new members to the Court); that responding to the "strategic variables of massing the Court and of institutional loyalties" (concerns for maximizing the Court's collective force and safeguarding its power and legitimacy); and that resulting from changing factual perceptions of a particular judge (1968b, 45–47). By Howard's admission, the third type of fluidity was the most difficult to prove and the most complicated to explain. But the existence of these phenomena of flux allowed him to conclude that votes and opinions— or the lack thereof—are crude measures of attitude, for "the ideological commitment manifest in both may be lower and the basis of choice far more pragmatic than either imply on their face" (49).

In addressing the gap between ideology and choice, Howard argued that there are many cases in which personal ideologies have been moderated or exaggerated by group interaction (1968b, 49–50). He saw the vote switching of Black and Douglas, for example, as testimony to the naïveté of "attitudinal automatism." Although the state of theory at the time (perhaps currently as well) did not permit him to generalize about which kind of mediation would result from group interaction on the bench, he speculated that the systematic application of role theory to the appellate process would yield a more richly developed theory of judicial process and generate testable hypotheses about judicial decision making. Howard's contributions to role theory analysis are well known (Howard 1977, 1981), and the importance of judicial role orientation as an intervening variable in ideological models of judging remains pertinent today. Again, one need only peruse a public law article in a recent issue of the *APSR* and notice the authors' concluding comments: "our supposition [is] that *role conceptions* are the principal reason why individuals become more nonconsensual in voting and opinion-writing on the Supreme Court than they were on a lower appellate court" (Gerber and Park 1997, 406).

By drawing attention to the many group factors (including institutional norms such as role) that mediated between judges' ideological predispositions and their final votes, Howard challenged attitudinal quantifiers to "face squarely the probability and effect of fluid judicial choices on their modal categories and attitudinal inferences" (1968b, 55). Moreover, his identification of the phenomenon of fluidity was a caution to qualitative classifiers, many of whom used opinions and their substantive interpretation in the same uncomplicated way as the quantifiers used votes. His goal was not to discredit or dismantle the ideological approach but to force it to confront the situational and complex nature of judicial decision making in its models. In so doing, he was somewhat ahead of his subfield, as demonstrated by some attitudinalists' skeptical reactions to his fluidity thesis.

II

In discussing the concept of fluidity, Howard stressed that judicial decision making, while very much motivated by individual belief systems, was subject to important group dynamics. As a result, the main artifacts of the decision-making process—opinions and votes—are group outcomes, from which individual attitudes must be inferred. Biographical and archival data show that judges change their minds (and their votes), and unless we are to presume that judges are quixotic and that their attitudes are unstable, some nonideological variables must account for this flux.[2] Howard identified small-group factors as those that influence both fluidity and individual expressions of preference generally. In sum, the existence of fluidity of judicial choice pointed to a somewhat diminished causal role for personal ideology in judicial decision making.

One initial reaction from Howard's judicial behavior colleagues was interrogative: how frequent, pervasive, and, thus, significant is judicial fluidity? If it is infrequent—if, in fact, judicial votes on the merits of cases are fairly stable throughout the decision process—then the intervening small-group variables would not seem to significantly mitigate ideology's effects on voting. Ideological models of judicial voting behavior would thus be restored to their position of preeminence as explanatory models.

One attitudinalist who wrote a series of articles examining—or, in his words "reconsidering"—fluidity was Saul Brenner (1980, 1982). Brenner was concerned not only with the frequency of fluidity but also with its types and impact in specific cases. In a piece that was a synthesis of some of his earlier works and had wide exposure in a popular reader of judicial process studies, Brenner conducted a quantitative investigation comparing the original and final votes on the merits of cases during the Vinson Court. Utilizing the private papers and docket books of various Vinson justices as his data source, he concluded that "the finding that in 86% of the votes the justices voted the same way at both stages supports the contention that the final vote scale is a good index of attitudes" (1989, 483). He did allow, however, that the great amount of consensus voting between the original and final votes on the merits suggested that consensus norms might be an equally powerful explanatory factor. Consensus norms—like role, small-group, and institutional factors—clearly could be the kind of intervening variables that Howard identified as affecting the judicial vote.

The concept of fluidity received a more recent and more directly attitudinalist reevaluation in a 1991 article by Timothy Hagle and Harold Spaeth. Hagle and Spaeth asked whether the attitudinal model itself can explain fluidity in judicial voting; in other words, they did not presume that voting fluidity and an ideological explanation of judicial behavior are incompatible. Drawing on previous work on the ideological variables associated with the breakup of minimum winning coalitions on the Court (e.g., Brenner and Spaeth 1988: Brenner, Hagle, and Spaeth 1989), Hagle and Spaeth argued that ideological closeness between the vote-shifting justice and the ideologically marginal justice in dissent explained the voting fluidity of the former (1991, 122). As the authors freely admitted, the scope of their inquiry was narrow: it looked only at vote shifts from majority to minority coalitions and did not address opinion fluidity, simply that of votes. Nevertheless, their study indicated that fluidity, as they define it, is consistent with the attitudinal model and, moreover, that Howard's small-group variables (as

Hagle and Spaeth operationalize them) do not seem to influence the proportion of fluidity voting (1991, 123–25).

In a theoretical reassessment of fluidity voting, Brenner and Robert Dorff (1992) focus on conformity of a justice from the minority at the original vote on the merits to the majority at the final vote, the most frequent type of fluidity voting as measured by stability of pairs of votes (i.e., the original and the final vote on the merits). The authors concede that it makes sense to conclude that small-group variables function in an interactive way with attitudinal variables, for "small group variables usually will influence the final vote of the minority-majority justice *even if* we expect him to shift to the majority based on what we know about his attitudes" (200; emphasis added). Though Brenner and Dorff do not test hypotheses about specific small-group or institutional variables, and though they emphasize that Howard overestimated the amount of fluidity voting that occurs, their piece suggests that Supreme Court decision making is more complex than the attitudinal model proposes.

This selection of attitudinalist reactions to Howard's fluidity argument suggests several things. First, though earlier studies questioned the frequency of the phenomenon, by the early 1990s fluidity was part of the attitudinal model's discourse as it became increasingly sensitive to some of its own limits in inferring attitudes from votes (see Segal and Cover 1989; Segal, Epstein, and Cameron 1995). Second, the attitudinal scholars seemed much more taken with the concept of fluidity than with the group factors Howard evoked to explain its incidence. Indeed, in a recent study of issue fluidity on the Supreme Court, the authors commented that because of Howard's work, "we *know* how the justices change *as a function of the issues in the case*, not how the issues in a case change as a function of the justices" (McGuire and Palmer 1995, 692; emphasis added). As the italicized passage indicates, the study assumes that an ideological model of judicial response to issue stimuli adequately explains voting fluidity. Thus, the phenomenon of fluidity did not provide the impetus to build bridges across methodological and theoretical divides within judicial process studies. Conversely, Howard's linking of fluidity with small-group-theory explanations of court behavior arguably helped spawn a number of studies that examined the group dynamics surrounding judicial decision making, including patterns of interjudicial influence, leadership, and opinion coalition formation (Ulmer 1971; Rohde 1972; Danelski 1978; Altfeld and Spaeth 1984).

Among the variables that this body of work examined were the strategic variables of institutional loyalty and uniting the Court—in

Howard's words, the justices' concerns for "maximiz[ing] their collective force and safeguard[ing] the power and legitimacy of the Court among its reference groups" (1968b, 46). Although the effect of personal ideology on judicial decision making was not discounted, and even though some small-group approaches lacked clear-cut notions of interdependent, goal-oriented interaction, the public law literature was beginning to reconsider institutional or collegial court factors.

III

One way to assess the influence of an article on subsequent works is to use a citation index, documenting the number of references to the article in question. The advantage of this method is precision and quantifiability of results; the disadvantage is the insensitivity of the measure (citation) to the phenomenon of interest (influence). Sometimes, the latter is indirect (mediated by other, later works that draw on the original article) or diffuse (part of a cumulative, theoretical response to certain recurring questions). Howard's fluidity article has had, we think, direct as well as indirect and diffuse influence on the contemporary strategic approach to the study of courts.

Generally speaking, the small-group approach to the study of judicial behavior finds contemporary expression in the current new institutionalist and strategic approaches to court politics. We make this assertion even though the small-group approach highlights the influence of nonpolicy variables (such as role orientation or concern for institutional legitimacy) on judicial choice and proceeds from a social-psychological model of behavior, while certain strategic approaches focus on policy variables' influence on judicial choice and proceed from an economic model of behavior (see n.2). The overlap lies, we think, in the recognition that rationalities of action or deliberate bargaining and strategizing are activities constituted by an evolving set of normative institutional perspectives (Gillman 1999, 74–75; Epstein and Knight 2000, 31, 43) and by the interdependent judicial interactions that help to construct those perspectives. Indeed, Howard's intervening variables accounting for fluidity have much in common with the broad range of factors or "missions" identified by the new institutionalism in judicial studies as salient to judicial decision making. Although institutionalist approaches differ about how to define institutions, rules and norms, and the role or worldview of institutional officeholders (Smith 1988; Gillman 1996–97, 7, 9–10; Epstein and Knight 1997, 6–7; Gillman 1999), it is clear that all institutionalists are interested in moving beyond personalistic variables such as ideological preference to explain judicial action. Echoing Howard's emphasis on the importance of strategy and style variables in judicial decision making, Rogers Smith notes that a broad conceptualization of institutional factors would shed light on both "the causal determinants of the vote [and] on the patterns of discourse used to rationalize the vote" (1988, 104). Howard Gillman sketches the relationship between strategic institutionalists (those influenced by rational choice theory) and interpretive institutionalists (those utilizing sociological or historical methods to address institutional development) in this way: interpretive institutionalists would identify the range of judicial motivations and concerns relevant to judicial choice, and strategic institutionalists would investigate which of these motivations can be productively translated into rational choice models of judicial decision making as interdependent choice (1997, 12–13). With respect to the debate about how to conceptualize a neoinstitutionalist study of courts, the influence of Howard's work has been indirect, mediated by a body of literature on courts as small groups that identifies explanatory variables that are contextual or situational to courts as institutions.

One feature of the strategic institutionalist approach stands out as directly parallel with Howard's work: a concern, if not a fascination, with the collegial nature of decision making on multimember courts. To this awareness of the group context in which judges act, proponents of the strategic model add that judges are "goal-directed, single-minded seekers of policy" (Epstein 1995, 5) as well as rational bargainers in a situation in which many institutional norms frame, delimit, and shape individual expressions of policy. In other words, while judges may have an ideal point in terms of policy preference, they are willing to shift its expression (i.e., their vote) under group pressures and institutional constraints to maximize the likelihood of a collective outcome that is closest to their preferred position.

The foundations of the strategic approach to judicial process studies are often summarized as oppositional to the prevailing attitudinal model. According to Lee Epstein and Jack Knight, two exponents of rational choice institutionalism, "justices may be primarily seekers of legal policy, but they are not unsophisticated actors who make decisions based merely on their ideological attitudes. Instead, judges are strategic actors who realize that their ability to achieve their goals depends on a consideration of the preferences of other actors, of the choices they expect others to make, and of the institutional context in which they act" (1997, 4). In sum, and in a sentence that reaffirms Howard's position in 1968, with a slight change of vocabulary, Epstein and Knight propose that judicial choice can best be explained as strategic behavior rather than merely as the response to ideological values.

Epstein and Knight's indebtedness to Howard's insights is clear in their work on strategic interaction on the Supreme Court. Indeed, they directly reference Howard (as well as Walter Murphy, whose work was a foundation for Howard's inquiry) in providing a definition of strategic action on the bench: the phenomenon whereby judges "work changes in their votes . . . through internal bargaining" to further their own policy objectives, under the limitations imposed by legal and political institutions (Epstein and Knight 1995, 8). Howard's conceptualization of fluidity, they state, should be interpreted as part of an early effort to develop objective indicators of strategic activity; in fact, they use fluidity as one of several such indicators in their research on strategic behavior on the Supreme Court (1995, 15, 19–20; Epstein and Knight 2000, 629–30). Epstein and Knight further observe that for both the rational choice approach and the Murphy-Howard strategic view of courts, there is a linkage of the judicial vote with policy choice, unlike the attitudinal model's emphasis on predicting the dichotomous vote choice of reverse or affirm and subsequent lack of attention to the factors that shape courts' policy outputs (1995, 10, 13) A book-length study by the same authors, presenting a strategic account of judicial decisions, confirms the direct influence of Howard's work on fluidity on the contemporary paradigm of rational choice institutionalism in public law (see Epstein and Knight 1998).

Another recent piece that shows the direct influence of Howard's conceptualization of fluidity is Maltzman and Wahlbeck's 1996 article, "Strategic Policy Considerations and Voting Fluidity on the Burger Court." Maltzman and Wahlbeck define the strategic model, with which they identify, as "portray[ing] justices as responding to the positions articulated by other justices" (583). Arguing for "a more nuanced role for the influence of policy preferences on justices' votes" (582), they focus on the context of the decision-making process. They explicitly agree with Howard that intracourt factors affect fluidity, addressing both the dynamics of the coalition-building process and institutional considerations to develop a multivariate model of the causes of judicial fluidity. By providing empirical evidence to support a conclusion that fluidity is a function of strategic policy calculations, Maltzman and Wahlbeck confirm Howard's assessment of the public law subfield: judicial behavior requires a richer understanding than the attitudinal model affords (1968b, 591). It is worth noting, however, that some fluidity cannot be explained in terms of the rational choice models that have been advanced. For example, not all fluidity is "strategic" in reactive, policy goal–oriented terms: justices, as Howard pointed out, might shift their votes from conference to the final decision because of "additional thought and homework" (1968b, 47).

This emphasis on judges as legal policymakers is an important part of historical-interpretive models of strategic judicial behavior. As Gillman suggests, the Court is an institution in which the justices are not engaged in policy-making per se, as both the attitudinalist and many rational choice scholars claim, but rather in deciding "actual disputes based on their understanding of the law" (1999, 10). This view is compatible with Howard's statement that "the evidence of the 1940's lends greater credence to the lawyer's ideal of the judicial process as a system of reasoning" (1968b, 55). Thus, it is possible that Howard's piece fostered the use of historical, interpretive new institutionalism to study the Court in the 1990s. Indeed, some scholars who champion this approach have extensively mined the justices' private papers in attempting to explain decision making in a single case or in a group of cases in an area of the law (Maveety 1996; Bussiere 1999).

Other strategic rationality/game-theoretic approaches to judicial studies suggest a more diffuse influence for Howard's insights regarding the "intervening variables operating in a collegial court setting [that] mediate between individual attitude and behavior" (Howard 1968b, 44). Although there is a literature within judicial process studies that applies game-theoretic models of behavior to judicial action (see Brenner 1979) while tracing some of its inspiration to the "Murphy-Howard strategic view," much of the current work by positive political theorists and legal scholars investigating separation-of-powers games owes less to small-group theory or judicial process studies generally than to spatial models of voting from legislative studies (see, e.g., Cameron 1993). One suspects that the highly formalized nature of such model building—the almost acontextual definition of strategic action as sophisticated voting—results in theoretical scholarship that discards many of the situational and the institutional variables relevant to judging that Howard stressed (but compare the neoinstitutional model presented by Cameron, Segal, and Songer 1993). Nevertheless, it is evident that the positive political theory of group dynamics on the bench presumes the existence of a type of judicial fluidity in its separation-of-powers-game models of court behavior, whereby judges' votes are changeable depending on the degree to which the preferences of other actors (including judicial colleagues) facilitate judges' expressions of their true preferences through voting (Ferejohn and Weingast 1992;

Schwartz 1992; Cohen and Spitzer 1993; see also Boucher and Segal 1995). Many positive political theorists are interested in exploring how the decision-making rules or institutional norms of multimember bodies provide opportunities for strategic representation and maximization of actors' preferences (Spiller 1992; Kornhauser and Sager 1993; Schwartz, 1993).

Because of the lack of sustained empirical verification or even institutionally based explanation for many of positive political theorists' assertions, their accounts of the strategic environment in which judges act have been challenged by some judicial process scholars. New institutionalists who defend interpretive understandings of the historical context in which judges act posit that positive political theorists "need to be mindful to develop a conception of 'institution' that is capable of capturing the various motivations that institutional actors might possess and the various influences on their behavior exerted by institutional forces" (Gillman 1999, 77). The attitudinalists' general response to the current strategic model is itself revealing with respect to the long-term influence of Howard's understanding of the nonideological variables that affect judicial choice. One attitudinal scholar observes that "the extent to which any vote or decision by any justice is influenced by the actions or perspective actions of her colleagues is an empirical question . . . justices do not inevitably behave 'strategically'" (Brenner 1997, 3). For Brenner and those like him, it is possible to conceive of strategic behavior that is neither sophisticated nor involves bargaining and is in fact a sincere expression of preferences "because [the judge] has concluded that by expressing his views he is more likely to achieve a specific instrumental and policy-oriented goal" (Brenner 1997, 4). In other words, it is possible for behavior to be strategic and sincere. Arguably, this is exactly what Howard postulated when he stated that ideology may be inflated or deflated as a result of group interaction, that various factors—including conversion, evangelism, and a milieu of advocacy—may result in ideological inflation (1968b, 49–50) or sincere expression of preference, to use the contemporary vocabulary.

One attitudinalist who attempts to test the validity of the strategic institutionalist model and particularly the separation-of-powers game as applied to courts is Jeffrey Segal. Segal's 1997 study examines Supreme Court voting records in statutory civil rights cases, comparing the behavioral record with the expectations predicted by the attitudinal (sincere voting) and separation-of-powers game (sophisticated voting) models of judicial action. He concludes that judges vote according to the expectations of the attitudinal model, with rational sincerity with regard to congressional preferences. Yet some of Segal's concluding comments suggest that attitudinalists consider legal and institutional variables relevant to an ideological model of judicial choice. He notes the possibility that sophisticated actions vis-à-vis Congress may show up in majority opinions even if such actions are not apparent in judicial voting patterns, though the linkage between votes and policy positions makes this unlikely in any systematic fashion (42 n.42). In addition, he admits that there is evidence of strategic behavior at the prefinal vote on the merits stages of the Court's decisions (see Boucher and Segal 1995), suggesting that "the justices can act in a sophisticated fashion *when they need to* do so. But the institutional protections granted to the Court mean that with respect to Congress and the presidency, they almost never need to do so" (42–43). Like Brenner, Segal is unwilling to concede too much to the strategic model of judicial action and its nonideological explanatory variables, but both authors seem willing to incorporate institutional/small-group/strategic factors into attitudinal theorizing.[3]

By relocating the study of judicial behavior in an institutional and group context, contemporary attitudinal scholarship avoids the ideological reductionism and oversimplification that Howard decried in 1968. Research paradigms in judicial process studies, which were once considered independent of each other, now seem to operate (and define themselves) in a much more interdependent fashion. Examination of the merits of the current new institutional approach to the study of courts—by attitudinalists, academic lawyers, game theorists, and various practitioners of institutionalism—clearly has revived an important methodological and theoretical debate about the nature and objectives of the public law subfield (Baum 1997). Perhaps such colloquy will finally realize Howard's hope of "helping to sharpen the theoretical tools that will enable us collectively to cut through the judicial process' fierce complexity" (1968b, 56). In drawing attention to the fluidity of judicial choice and the variables responsible for it, Howard's work has been both a substantive foundation for subsequent research questions and a catalyst for the ongoing dialogue about research design.

NOTES

Nancy Maveety delivered an earlier version of this paper for "Biography, Fluidity, and Constitutional Interpretation: The Contributions of J. Woodford Howard Jr. to the Study of Judicial Politics," at the annual meeting of the Southern Political Science Association, Norfolk, Virginia, November 5–8,

1997. She wishes to thank Lee Epstein and Saul Brenner for their invaluable and insightful comments on this earlier version.

1. Howard's position here has continued relevance to and special pertinence for contemporary comparative judicial studies, as is evidenced by Vanberg's recent comments regarding the necessary blending of rational choice modeling with case study work: "data limitations imposed by the rules of procedure of European courts as well as the centrality of expectations in strategic analysis—provide reason to think that there is a place for qualitative [interview-based] evidence in contemplating statistical work as we evaluate theories of judicial behavior" (1999, 5).

2. Even if judges are considered "policy maximizers," as some proponents of strategic rationality models of judging would assert, judges' vote switches are a response to the group decision-making context because changes in vote that represent "the best that they can do" are reactive to their colleagues' policy preferences, role orientations, institutional concerns, and interpretive commitments. Such nonideological factors are relevant whether one conceptualizes small-group variables as the product of a social-psychological or an economic rationality model of judicial decision making. If the strategic model is truly "agnostic" about the content of justices' goals, then a multiplicity of political purposes presumably influences justices' strategic calculations. See Gillman and Clayton 1999, 9; Maltzman, Spriggs, and Wahlbeck, 1999, 60; Epstein and Knight 2000, 631 n.16.

3. Brenner's position on this is to say that attitudes are very important in explaining the final vote on the merits. In other settings, however, he allows that attitudes are usually important, but so are other variables. He is willing to posit a rational choice model of judging where appropriate but believes it is not appropriate when the goal is obvious and easy to achieve. Complex models, he warns, are invariably unrealistic. The authors owe this clarification to exchanges with Brenner.

REFERENCES

Altfeld, Michael F., and Harold J. Spaeth. 1984. "Measuring Influence on the U.S. Supreme Court." *Jurimetrics Journal* 24:236–47.

Baum, Lawrence. 1997. *The Puzzle of Judicial Behavior*. Ann Arbor: University of Michigan Press.

Boucher, Robert J., and Jeffrey A. Segal. 1995. "Supreme Court Justices as Strategic Decision Makers: Aggressive Grants and Defensive Denials on the Vinson Court." *Journal of Politics* 57 (August): 824–37.

Brenner, Saul. 1979. "Game Theory and Supreme Court Decision Making: A Bibliographic Overview." *Law Library Journal* 72:470–75.

Brenner, Saul. 1980. "Fluidity on the United States Supreme Court: A Reexamination." *American Journal of Political Science* 24 (August): 526–35.

Brenner, Saul. 1982. "Fluidity on the Supreme Court, 1956–1967." *American Journal of Political Science* 26 (May): 388–90.

Brenner, Saul. 1989. "Fluidity of the Supreme Court: A Reconsideration." In *American Court Systems: Readings in Judicial Process and Behavior*, 2d ed., ed. S. Goldman and A. Sarat, 479–85. New York: Longman.

Brenner, Saul. 1995. "Fluidity in Voting on the U.S. Supreme Court: A Bibliographic Overview of the Studies." *Law Library Journal* 87 (spring): 380–86.

Brenner, Saul. 1997. "Comment: A Useful Definition of Strategic Behavior to Study the Supreme Court." *Law and Courts Newsletter* 7 (summer): 3–4.

Brenner, Saul, and Robert Dorff. 1992. "The Attitudinal Model and Fluidity Voting on the United States Supreme Court." *Journal of Theoretical Politics* 4 (2): 195–205.

Brenner, Saul, Timothy M. Hagle, and Harold J. Spaeth. 1989. "The Defection of the Marginal Justice on the Warren Court." *Western Political Quarterly* 42 (September): 409–25.

Brenner, Saul, and Harold J. Spaeth. 1988. "Majority Opinion Assignment and the Maintenance of the Original Coalition on the Warren Court." *American Journal of Political Science* 32 (February): 72–81.

Bussiere, Elizabeth. 1999. "The Supreme Court and the Development of the Welfare State: Judicial Liberalism and the Problem of Welfare Rights." In *Supreme Court Decision Making*, ed. Clayton and Gillman, 155–74.

Cameron, Charles M. 1993. "New Avenues for Modeling Judicial Politics." Paper presented at the Conference on the Political Economy of Courts, Rochester, N.Y., October 15–16.

Cameron, Charles M., Jeffrey A. Segal, and Donald R. Songer. 1993. "Law Creation and Signaling in the Judicial Hierarchy." Paper presented at the annual meeting of the Midwest Political Science Association, Chicago, March 9.

Clayton, Cornell, and Howard Gillman, eds. 1999. *Supreme Court Decision Making.* Chicago: University of Chicago Press.

Cohen, Linda R., and Matthew L. Spitzer. 1993. "Judicial Deference to Agency Action: A Rational Choice Theory and an Empirical Test." Paper presented at the Conference on the Political Economy of Courts, Rochester, N.Y., October 15–16.

Danelski, David J. 1978. "The Influence of the Chief Justice in the Decisional Process of the Supreme Court." In *American Court Systems: Readings in Judicial Process and Behavior*, ed. S. Goldman and A. Sarat, 506–19. San Francisco: Freeman.

Davis, Sue, and Donald Songer. 1989. "The Changing Role of the U.S. Court of Appeals: The Flow of Litigation Revisited." *Justice System Journal*, 13:323–30.

Epstein, Lee. 1995. "Studying Law and Courts." In *Contemplating Courts*, ed. L. Epstein, 1–13. Washington, D.C.: Congressional Quarterly Press.

Epstein, Lee, and Jack Knight. 1995. "Documenting Strategic Interaction on the U.S. Supreme Court." Paper presented at the annual meeting of the American Political Science Association, Chicago, August 31–September 3.

Epstein, Lee, and Jack Knight. 1997. "The New Institutionalism, Part II." *Law and Courts Newsletter* 7 (spring): 4–9.

Epstein, Lee, and Jack Knight. 1998. *The Choices Justices Make.* Washington, D.C.: Congressional Quarterly Press.

Epstein, Lee, and Jack Knight. 2000. "Toward a Strategic Revolution in Judicial Politics: A Look Back, a Look Ahead." *Political Research Quarterly* 53:625–61.

Ferejohn, John A., and Barry R. Weingast. 1992. "A Positive Theory of Statutory Interpretation." *International Review of Law and Economics* 12:263–79.

Gerber, Scott, and Keeok Park. 1997. "The Quixotic Search for Consensus on the U.S. Supreme Court: A Cross-Judicial Empirical Analysis of the Rehnquist Court Justices." *American Political Science Review* 91 (June): 390–408.

Gillman, Howard. 1996–97. "The New Institutionalism, Part I." *Law and Courts Newsletter* 7 (winter): 6–11.

Gillman, Howard. 1997. "Placing Judicial Motives in Context: A Response to Lee Epstein and Jack Knight." *Law and Courts Newsletter* 7:10–13.

Gillman, Howard. 1999. "The Court as an Idea, Not a Building (or a Game): Interpretive Institutionalism and the Analysis of Supreme Court Decision Making." In *Supreme Court Decision Making,* ed. Clayton and Gillman, 65–87.

Gillman, Howard, and Cornell Clayton. 1999. "Beyond Judicial Attitudes: Institutional Approaches to Supreme Court Decision Making." In *Supreme Court Decision Making,* ed. Clayton and Gillman, 1–12.

Goldman, Sheldon. 1966. "Voting Behavior in the United States Courts of Appeals, 1961–1964." *American Political Science Review* 60:374–83.

Hagle, Timothy, and Harold J. Spaeth. 1991. "Voting Fluidity and the Attitudinal Model of Supreme Court Decision Making." *Western Political Quarterly* 44 (March): 119–28.

Harrington, Christine, and Daniel Ward. 1995. "Patterns of Appellate Litigation, 1945–1990." In *Contemplating Courts,* ed. Lee Epstein. Washington, D.C.: Congressional Quarterly Press.

Howard, J. Woodford, Jr. 1968a. *Mr. Justice Murphy: A Political Biography.* Princeton: Princeton University Press.

Howard, J. Woodford, Jr. 1968b. "On the Fluidity of Judicial Choice." *American Political Science Review* 62 (March): 43–56.

Howard, J. Woodford, Jr. 1977. "Role Perceptions and Behavior in Three U.S. Courts of Appeals." *Journal of Politics* 39:916–38.

Howard, J. Woodford, Jr. 1981. *Courts of Appeals in the Federal Judicial System: A Study of the Second, Fifth, and District of Columbia Circuits.* Princeton: Princeton University Press.

Howard, J. Woodford, Jr. 2000. Interview by authors.

Kornhauser, Lewis A., and Lawrence G. Sager. 1993. "The One and the

Many: Adjudication in Collegial Courts." *California Law Review* 81 (January): 1–59.

Maltzman, Forrest, James F. Spriggs II, and Paul J. Wahlbeck. 1999. "Strategy and Judicial Choice: New Institutionalist Approaches to Supreme Court Decision Making." In *Supreme Court Decision Making*, ed. Clayton and Gillman, 43–63.

Maltzman, Forrest, James F. Spriggs II, and Paul J. Wahlbeck. 2000. *Crafting Law on the Supreme Court: The Collegial Game*. New York: Cambridge University Press.

Maltzman, Forrest, and Paul J. Wahlbeck. 1996. "Strategic Policy Considerations and Voting Fluidity on the Burger Court." *American Political Science Review* 90 (September): 581–92.

Maveety, Nancy. 1996. *Justice Sandra Day O'Connor: Strategist on the Supreme Court*. Lanham, Md.: Rowman and Littlefield.

McGuire, Kevin T., and Barbara Palmer. 1995. "Issue Fluidity on the Supreme Court." *American Political Science Review* 89 (September): 691–702.

Murphy, Walter. 1964. *The Elements of Judicial Strategy*. Chicago: University of Chicago Press.

Richardson, Richard J., and Kenneth N. Vines. 1970. *The Politics of Federal Courts*. Boston: Little, Brown.

Rohde, David. 1972. "Policy Goals and Opinion Coalitions in the Supreme Court." *Midwest Journal of Political Science* 16:208–24.

Rowland, C. K., and Robert Carp. 1996. *Politics and Judgment in the Federal District Courts* Lawrence: University Press of Kansas.

Schwartz, Edward P. 1992. "Policy, Precedent, and Power: A Positive Theory of Supreme Court Decision-Making." *Journal of Law, Economics, and Organization* 8:219–52.

Schwartz, Edward P. 1993. "Information, Agendas, and the Rule of Four: Nonmajoritarian Certiorari Rules for the Supreme Court." Paper presented at the annual meeting of the Public Choice Society, New Orleans, March.

Segal, Jeffrey A. 1997. "Separation of Powers Games in the Positive Theory of Congress and Courts." *American Political Science Review* 91 (March): 28–44.

Segal, Jeffrey A., and Albert D. Cover. 1989. "Ideological Values and the Votes of U.S. Supreme Court Justices." *American Political Science Review* 83 (June): 557–65.

Segal, Jeffrey A., Lee Epstein, and Charles M. Cameron. 1995. "Ideological Values and the Votes of U.S. Supreme Court Justices Revisited." *Journal of Politics* 57 (August): 812–23.

Smith, Rogers M. 1988. "Political Jurisprudence, the 'New Institutionalism,' and the Future of Public Law." *American Political Science Review* 82 (March): 89–107.

Songer, Donald R. 1997. *The United States Courts of Appeals Database*. Ann Arbor, Mich.: Inter-University Consortium for Political Research.

Songer, Donald R., Jeffrey A. Segal, and Charles M. Cameron. 1994. "The

Hierarchy of Justice: Testing a Principal-Agent Model of Supreme Court–Circuit Court Interactions." *American Journal of Political Science* 38:673–96.

Songer, Donald R., Reginald S. Sheehan, and Susan B. Haire. 2000. *Continuity and Change on the United States Courts of Appeals.* Ann Arbor: University of Michigan Press.

Spiller, Pablo. 1992. "Rationality, Decision Rules, and Collegial Courts." *International Review of Law and Economics* 12 (2): 186–90.

Ulmer, S. Sidney. 1971. *Courts as Small and Not So Small Groups.* New York: General Learning Press.

Vanberg, Georg. 1999. "Strategic Behavior and Empirical Testing." Paper presented at the annual meeting of the Conference on the Scientific Study of Judicial Politics, Texas A&M University, October 21–23.

Wahlbeck, Paul J. 1997. "The Life of the Law: Judicial Politics and Legal Change." *Journal of Politics* 59 (August): 778–802.

CHAPTER 10

David J. Danelski: Social Psychology and Group Choice

Thomas G. Walker

The pioneers of any successful intellectual endeavor invariably are individuals of great independence of thought. Breaking away from the past requires a scholar to bring a fresh perspective to an academic field, often fueled by the theories and methods of other disciplines. It demands the ability to develop new questions and to frame old questions differently, to identify analytical weaknesses that others overlook, and to suggest new methods to solve old problems. It takes a good bit of intellectual courage to withstand inevitable criticism from the established community and a great deal of scholarly confidence to persevere when mainstream publication outlets are inhospitable to new ideas.

David J. Danelski shares these traits with the other members of judicial behavior's pioneering generation. Beginning in 1960 and continuing to the present, Danelski developed innovative approaches to the study of judicial politics that appeared in scores of books, articles, and professional papers. His research employed perspectives from different theoretical perspectives and often provided a bridge between them.

THE MAKING OF A JUDICIAL BEHAVIORALIST

David Danelski's first calling was not to the academy but to the legal profession. Born to a Wisconsin couple in 1930 and the eldest of seven children, Danelski developed a love of learning early in his childhood. At the age of nineteen he began the study of law at DePaul University, before he had finished his undergraduate studies at St. Norbert College. On receiving his law degree, Danelski joined the U.S. Navy. While stationed in Seattle, he specialized in criminal law, first as a military prosecutor and then as a defense attorney. When his service obligation was completed, Danelski decided to remain in Washington, initiating a private law practice in Mt. Vernon, a small city in the northwestern part of the state.

Danelski's career path began to change in 1955, when he received a call from the dean of the local junior college, desperately seeking a temporary instructor to substitute for a longtime professor who was ill. Danelski agreed to step in, although he had little academic training for the classes in economics and psychology that he was required to teach. Shortly thereafter, the college asked him to remain on staff. His teaching assignments expanded to other disciplines. He even taught a course on "English for Practical Nurses" and directed a college play (Stokes 1981). In preparing for his varied classroom assignments, Danelski read widely in several disciplines. In the course of his preparation, he came across C. Herman Pritchett's *The Roosevelt Court* (1948). Danelski found Pritchett's application of both the law and theories of human behavior to the study of judicial politics enormously appealing. As a consequence, Danelski decided to leave his law practice to study under Pritchett at the University of Chicago.

Under Pritchett's guidance, Danelski read widely in psychology, sociology, political science, and law. He began forming a theoretical approach to judicial behavior that had a psychosociological base. This approach theoretically grounded his dissertation research on the role of the chief justice of the United States. After spending three years at Chicago, Danelski accepted a position at the University of Illinois in 1959, combining full-time teaching with continued work on his dissertation.

In 1960, while still an instructor at Illinois, Danelski presented a paper at the American Political Science Association that had a major impact on his career. "The Influence of the Chief Justice in the Decisional Process of the Supreme Court" (1960b) was based on his dissertation research. Danelski explained the power of the chief justice from a theoretical perspective grounded in the work of small-group psychology. His views of the way the Supreme Court operated were quite unlike the more traditional historical and legal approaches that dominated the field as the discipline entered the 1960s.

In contrast to today's practice, professional meetings at that time scheduled relatively few paper presentations, with each attracting rather large audiences. The reaction to Danelski's paper was immediate and hostile. Those in attendance found unacceptable his deviation from more accepted approaches. It was impossible, many argued, to generalize about the justices of the Supreme Court from social psychology, a discipline that built its theories largely on artificial experiments with undergraduate students as subjects.

The rejection of his paper and the stinging criticism it received took

Danelski by surprise. As the session ended, however, two individuals offered their support. The first was Samuel Krislov, who told Danelski that the widespread negative reaction was really a positive sign that he was engaged in important and pathbreaking work. The second was Walter Murphy, who had overlapped with Danelski for a year at Chicago. Murphy approached Danelski with the news that he and Herman Pritchett wanted to publish the paper in *Courts, Judges, and Politics*, a new anthology on which they were working. In spite of this support, the dejected Danelski immediately checked out of the Statler-Hilton Hotel, leaving the convention early to visit a friend in New York.

Danelski, of course, was not alone in being the target of harsh criticism. Other judicial behavior pioneers experienced similar hostility at professional meetings and in printed reactions to their early writings. Whatever disappointment Danelski may have suffered at that APSA meeting quickly passed, however, and he never considered abandoning the approach he found so satisfying. He completed the dissertation in March 1961 and began an illustrious career as a scholar, holding distinguished appointments at the University of Washington, Yale University, Cornell University, and Stanford University as well as a deanship at Occidental College.

Although Danelski left the private practice of law when he moved to Chicago, he never completely gave up his legal work. In 1960, while still an instructor at Illinois, Danelski defended a biology professor who was fired for arguing in the school newspaper that premarital intercourse should be condoned. During the mid-1960s he represented civil rights groups such as the Student Nonviolent Coordinating Committee and the Freedom Democratic Party in Mississippi. During his years on the faculty of the University of Washington, Danelski served as counsel for the American Civil Liberties Union. In 1978 he left his position at Cornell to resume the full-time practice of law in Seattle, but the next year he was lured back into academe with a professorship at Stanford. Danelski took emeritus status at Stanford in 1993 at the relatively young age of sixty-three. He did so to focus his full professional attention on research.

CONTRIBUTIONS TO STRATEGIC APPROACHES TO JUDICIAL BEHAVIOR

As is the case with several of the judicial behavior pioneers, Danelski's work is difficult to force into a single theoretical category. Once the boundaries imposed by the more traditional approaches to judicial politics were set aside, the new generation of judicial scholars borrowed from the full gamut of the social sciences to identify theories that would unlock some of the mysteries of judicial behavior. Today we tend to divide those various approaches into two general categories: those that rely on sociopyschological theories, and those that use rational actor models derived from the economics literature (Epstein and Knight 2000).

Sociopsychological theories include approaches that emphasize the influence on judges' behavior of personal attributes, political/legal attitudes, and role orientations. These schools of thought are often said to share a common stimulus-response mechanism. That is, judges behave the way they do because their social backgrounds, role orientations, and ideologies predispose them to do so. Influenced by their personal characteristics, they respond almost automatically to the stimuli presented by specific cases.

Rational actor models, conversely, posit that judges act strategically to attain their goals. The essential elements of this approach, as Epstein and Knight describe it, are "(1) social actors make choices in order to achieve certain goals, (2) social actors act strategically in the sense that their choices depend on their expectations about the choices of other actors, and (3) these choices are structured by the institutional setting in which they are made" (2000, 626).

Danelski's work is clearly more informed by sociopsychological theories than by economic models. Yet the concerns of his early research and the questions he confronted clearly provide a bridge between the two approaches. Danelski has not formally embraced the rational choice approach, nor has he incorporated formal theory into his analyses as contemporary game theorists do, yet his informed intuitions clearly lead him to view judges as strategic actors working within legal institutions. His work influenced much of the early rational choice research on judges, and the questions he posed have been central to later work conducted by strategic behavior theorists. Unlike many of the sociopsychological scholars, Danelski clearly understood that judges had individual goals, that those goals could not be attained by ignoring other actors, and that institutional factors had a strong impact on whether judges reached their goals.

THE STUDY OF INTRA–SUPREME COURT INFLUENCE

Any analysis of Danelski's impact on the field must start with his dissertation research (1961). Although never published as a single volume or appearing as a series of articles, Danelski's dissertation had a significant influence in the developing field of judicial behavior. His research focused on judicial leadership, especially emphasizing influence patterns within the Supreme Court.

At the heart of his research is the recognition that the Court is a collegial body that makes decisions based on majority rule. As a consequence, individual justices cannot achieve their institutional or policy goals by acting alone. Instead, a justice depends on the preferences and actions of other members of the Court. To be successful, then, justices must be able to influence other justices. Any member of the Court may exercise leadership, but the chief justice is in the best position to do so.

Danelski argues that influence is not sought for influence's sake. Instead, he claims that the chief justice exercises leadership with four goals firmly in mind. The first two are policy oriented: the attainment of "a majority vote for the chief justice's position" and "written opinions satisfactory to him." The second two are institutional goals: "social cohesion in the Court" and "unanimous opinions" (1960b, 3).

Danelski's analysis of the way in which the chief justice leads the Court is based on the work of social and group psychologists. Relying heavily on the research of Bales (1950, 1953, 1958), Slater (1955), and Berkowitz (1953) for both theoretical principles and methodological strategies, Danelski posits two varieties of leadership on collegial bodies such as the U.S. Supreme Court, task leadership and social leadership. The task leader is the member of the Court who keeps the justices focused on the business at hand. The task leader usually makes more suggestions, orients the discussion more effectively, and frames questions more clearly than do other members of the Court. Task leaders tend to offer their opinions readily and defend them successfully. Task leadership, however, is not without its negative implications. Because the task leader continuously drives the group to complete its work, conflict, tension, and antagonism often occur. As a consequence, social leadership must emerge to relieve tension, reinforce solidarity, and tend to the members' emotional needs. The Court functions most effectively, according to Danelski, when both forms of leadership are present.

Danelski discusses how the Court's institutional arrangements provide the chief justice with the most advantageous position from which to exercise these forms of leadership. Doing so effectively means that the Court's actions will tend to meet the chief's goals. During the case selection stage, the chief justice exercises considerable control over the process by initially making recommendations on which certiorari petitions should be dismissed and which should be fully discussed. As the presiding officer during oral argument, the chief justice can extend the time allotted for an attorney's presentation. In the decision-making conference, the chief justice speaks first, framing the issues for the discussion and offering initial suggestions for how the case should be decided. Danelski describes the conference as the "matrix of leadership in the Court," the stage at which the chief justice can "persuade his colleagues that his views of the case and his doctrinal ideas ought to prevail" (Steamer 1986, xi). After an initial vote is taken, the chief justice, when voting with the majority, appoints the justice who will draft the Court's opinion. In exercising this power, the chief justice has considerable influence over the shape of the final decision and the size of the majority. Finally, during the opinion writing and circulation process, the chief justice may actively engage in bargaining and negotiation to influence the final outcome.

Danelski examines how three chief justices, William Howard Taft, Charles Evans Hughes, and Harlan Fiske Stone, exercised the leadership potential inherent in the office. Presenting evidence gathered from the justices' private papers, official court records, newspaper accounts, biographies, and other sources, Danelski carefully evaluates how the three chiefs used their power to influence Court outcomes.

Danelski portrays Taft as a modestly effective leader. Taft was ill-suited to exercise substantial task leadership. He admitted, for example, that he had little influence over the certiorari process and often found himself in the minority on case selection issues. Instead, he generally deferred to allow the more intellectually able Willis Van Devanter to lead the Court in efficiently completing its tasks. Taft was content to exercise social leadership. In doing so, he gained the respect of his colleagues, played a crucial role in the maintenance of the Court as an institution, yet still retained some influence of over the Court's policy-making process by forging a fruitful alliance with Van Devanter.

Because Hughes occupied both task and social leadership positions on the Court, Danelski classifies Hughes as a very influential chief justice. Armed with a photographic memory, a strong intellect, and a genial personality, Hughes maintained good relations with his colleagues and steered the Court in a direction he preferred. Hughes understood well the importance of norms and procedural rules. Hughes, for example, developed the "special list" procedure in which the chief justice would identify those petitions for certiorari that he believed did not merit discussion. Making such initial recommendations gave the chief justice an advantage in influencing the Court's determination of its docket.

Stone was a much less effective leader than his immediate predecessor. Having chafed under Hughes's more rigid and formal leadership, Stone provided little direction for the justices in conference. Unlike Hughes, Stone did not start discussions of pending cases with clear, suggested solutions, nor did he maintain full control of the deliberations. In many ways Stone continued to play the role of an associate justice rather than that of a leader of a decision-making group. This resulted in a general lack of task leadership, a void partially filled by Hugo Black. The heated debates that characterized conferences during Stone's tenure frequently led to tense relations and ruffled feathers. The situation called for effective social leadership. Although Stone was liked and respected by his colleagues, he failed to use his position to soothe tempers and promote cohesiveness, preferring instead to be a full combatant in the battles that marked his administration. As a result, dissents and separate opinions reached historic levels (Walker, Epstein, and Dixon 1988; Caldeira and Zorn 1998).

While Danelski did not take the conventional route of publishing his work as a book or series of articles, his research was widely disseminated. Danelski presented two important papers from his dissertation project at professional meetings. The first was an analysis of the chief justices' use of the opinion assignment power as a method of influence (1960a), and the second was his paper on the role of the chief justice that received so much criticism at the 1960 meeting of the American Political Science Association (1960b). The judicial influence paper was initially printed in abridged form in the first edition of Murphy and Pritchett's *Courts, Judges, and Politics* (1961), and the essay has continued to appear in subsequent editions of this reader (for the latest edition, see Murphy, Pritchett, and Epstein 2001). Other judicial process anthologies also reprinted Danelski's paper (Goldman and Jahnige 1968; Goldman and Sarat 1978; Grossman and Wells 1988). Unlike many pioneering works in judicial behavior, Danelski's paper on the leadership of the chief justice also was reprinted in books targeting a broader American politics and political behavior audience (Barber 1964; Wolfinger 1966; Wildavsky and Polsby 1968; Kessel, Cole, and Seddig 1970; Keynes and Adamany 1971). Danelski's work may well have enjoyed greater circulation as a repeatedly reprinted convention paper than it would have as an independent publication. Given the exposure the paper received, Danelski found little reason to pursue other publishing outlets for his dissertation-based work.

Although Danelski based his intra-Court influence work on sociopsychological theories, his research clearly helped lay the foundation for the more explicitly strategic studies that were to follow. This influence was clearly felt by those whose work followed his. In the preface to *Elements of Judicial Strategy* (1964), a work frequently cited as one the earliest efforts to inject notions of strategic behavior into the study of the judicial process, Walter Murphy thanks Danelski for his contributions to the manuscript. In "Marshalling the Court," arguably the most important portion of this classic volume, Murphy cites the importance of Danelski's work on the chief justice's influence. More than three decades later, in the preface to their more contemporary and more systematic application of rational choice theory to the work of the Court, Lee Epstein and Jack Knight (1998) also thank Danelski and allow that his influence can be seen throughout their volume.

These acknowledgments are clearly justified. Although we cannot see in Danelski's writing a systematic, rigorous explication of principles flowing from rational choice models, the elements of a strategic theory of judicial behavior are clearly present. In addition, his research on intra-Court influence (1960b) was contemporaneous with Schubert's early work, which for the first time explicitly used game-theory models to understand voting on the Supreme Court (Schubert 1958, 1962, 1964).

Danelski's (1960a, 1960b) examination of the chief justice's exercise of the opinion assignment power provides a good example of his recognition of a strategic component in the behavior of Supreme Court justices. First, Danelski specifies the policy and institutional goals of the chief justice. The ultimate goal, of course, is a unanimous opinion consistent with the chief's views, but concerns over fairness and workload distribution also play a role. Second, Danelski spells out what is at stake in the opinion writing process, examining such factors as public acceptance of the ruling, the breadth of the precedent set, and the size of the majority. Third, Danelski develops explicit opinion assignment rules that the chief justice should follow to achieve his goals. These rules are clearly strategic in nature, requiring the chief to take into account the other justices' preferences. Finally, Danelski examines data from the justices' private papers to determine the extent to which Taft, Hughes, and Stone assigned opinions consistent with these strategic prescriptions.

Danelski's work set the stage for future examinations of opinion assignment power. Such studies have held the attention of judicial behavior scholars over the past several decades. Ulmer's research (1970), for example, extended Danelski's analysis by examining Earl Warren's exercise of the opinion assignment power. Similarly, Slotnick

(1978, 1979) published a series of articles evaluating opinion assignment patterns from Taft through Burger. Brenner (1982) and subsequently Maltzman and Wahlbeck (1996) explicitly applied strategic analysis to the opinion assignment power. These studies, and others of a similar vein, cite Danelski's work as the initial attempt to understand the use of opinion assignments as a means of judicial influence. In fact, subsequent studies employing increasingly sophisticated statistical and theoretical tools have continued to confront the same questions and evaluate the same hypotheses that Danelski laid down during the early period of pioneering studies of judicial behavior.

Danelski's treatment of persuasion and bargaining provides an additional illustration of research that laid groundwork for future strategic analyses of judicial behavior. Danelski examines how a chief justice can affect the outcome of cases by actively attempting to persuade other members of the Court. These efforts may seek to bring the Court to a position favored by the chief or may be part of the chief justice's strategy to achieve unanimity in the Court's decision. In addition, the chief justice may use his informal authority to determine when a case outcome is announced, thereby truncating or extending the period during which bargaining and negotiation take place. Danelski documents well, for example, the successful efforts of Chief Justice Stone to change his colleagues' views. Among the other illustrations, Danelski cites *Edwards v. California* (1941), in which Stone persuaded Justice Byrnes to change his conference vote, resulting in an opinion based on the commerce clause rather than the privileges and immunities clause. Danelski provides additional data documenting the numerous times Stone influenced the content of opinions by suggesting additions and deletions.

Danelski's work on bargaining and persuasion encouraged additional studies using similar data sources but with a theoretical focus derived more directly from rational choice principles. We have already noted Murphy's *Elements of Judicial Strategy* (1964) as the classic work on strategic approaches to judicial negotiation and persuasion. In more recent years, scholars such as Epstein and Knight (1998) and Maltzman, Spriggs, and Wahlbeck (2000) have used more refined theoretical and methodological tools to probe judicial bargaining from a strategic perspective. Similarly, scholars examining judicial leadership from more conventional perspectives both in the United States (Ducat and Flango 1976; Steamer 1986) and abroad (Paterson 1982) have relied significantly on Danelski's early findings. In each case, scholars interested in bargaining and negotiation can trace a significant root of their research lineage to the research questions addressed in Danelski's early work.

THE STUDY OF JUDICIAL SELECTION

The publication of Danelski's *A Supreme Court Justice Is Appointed* (1964) followed closely on the heels of his examination of intra-Court influence. Once again, Danelski's work is the product of meticulous analyses of archival materials guided by social science theory. What started out as a small but interesting project on the 1922 appointment of Pierce Butler grew quickly in complexity and breadth as Danelski dug deeper into the story. The final result was a major work of history and social science.

Danelski starts with a straightforward question: What accounts for a Republican president's appointment of a self-taught corporate lawyer with no significant political experience, a man born to Irish immigrant parents who was both a Democrat and a Roman Catholic? To sort out the possible explanations for this event, Danelski carefully reconstructs the key events, beginning with William Rufus Day's resignation from the Court and culminating in Butler's taking the oath of office.

The book has three major sections. The first describes well Butler's background and personality as well as the key executive branch personnel involved in filling the vacancy. The second section is a careful piecing together of all the relevant interactions that led to Butler's appointment. And the third section develops a theoretical explanation for the appointment.

As in his work on intra-Court influence, Danelski approaches the problem with a theoretical eye steeped in the sociopsychological literature. Yet once again, Danelski's intuitions decidedly reveal a method of interpretation closely related to contemporary strategic analysis. First, Danelski examines all of the relevant actors and establishes their motivations. Second, he realizes that the nomination of a Supreme Court justice requires the assent of multiple players. No single actor can determine the outcome. Third, institutional norms (such as the geographic and religious representation expectations) help structure the process. And finally, to achieve their preferences, the participants must act in a strategic fashion, understanding the other players' goals and anticipating their moves. Two key chapters dealing with the nomination and action by the Senate Judiciary Committee begin with explicit statements that strategy is a crucial element in the successful appointment of a Supreme Court justice.

More than any previous work on judicial selection, Danelski's book gives a full account of the active players in the process. Of course, this description includes the expected participants such as President Warren Harding, Attorney General Harry Daugherty, and various key legislators. But Danelski also goes far beyond the institutions constitutionally required to participate in the formal presidential nomination/ Senate confirmation process. A major contribution is Danelski's examination of the roles played by members of the Supreme Court, especially Chief Justice Taft and Justice Van Devanter. Danelski also goes behind the scenes to highlight the campaigns launched to secure the nomination for Butler and for competing candidates, especially Second Circuit Judge Martin Manton of New York. The prominent role of interest groups, such as the Roman Catholic hierarchy; business leaders in the mining, finance, and rail industries; academicians; and progressive political groups, is carefully documented. The entire process is very much a series of political moves and countermoves, with the participants taking into account the preferences of a variety of other players.

In the final three chapters of the book Danelski outlines his theoretical explanations for the events that led to Butler's appointment, basing much of the explanation on a theory of transactions. By this term, Danelski refers to "the phenomena of man perceiving, describing, and otherwise acting in process with his environment . . . in fields of connected activity" (1964, 146). This approach acknowledges, as do those who take a strategic view of judicial politics, that outcomes depend on interactions among various players within institutional environments that are shaped by norms and expectations.

Once again, Danelski's scholarship can be viewed as a bridge between the sociopsychological approach and the rational choice strategic position. While Danelski's work clearly recognizes that the politics of judicial selection involves a series of strategic interactions, he does not subscribe to the simple notion that political behavior can be adequately understood in terms of strategic moves taken within institutional environments to obtain preferred outcomes. The sociopsychological side of his training informs Danelski that the process is far more complex. For example, Danelski emphasizes the importance of perceptions. Not all players in the judicial selection game have perfect information or equal degrees of information about the process as it unfolds. Perhaps even more importantly, the players have different perceptions of the facts at their disposal. These differences make unreasonable any assumptions about the players operating with the same store of knowledge. Similarly, Danelski underscores the role of personality. Not all players in the judicial selection process have the same capabilities. Personality factors make some players more effective at carrying out the roles necessary for a successful outcome. In the politics of the Butler appointment, Chief Justice Taft's assertive and gregarious personality allowed him to have a much more influential hand in the process than did President Harding's more passive, nonconfrontational personality. Danelski clearly holds that strategic approaches are incomplete without taking into account the psychological dimensions of human behavior.

Studies of Supreme Court appointments have become fairly common. They range from broad historical accounts (Abraham 1999) to studies of one or more appointments placed in the context of contemporary social science theory (for example, Cameron, Cover, and Segal 1990; Overby et al. 1992; Ruckman 1993). Many of these studies were provoked by the controversial appointments of Clement Haynsworth, G. Harrold Carswell, Robert Bork, and Clarence Thomas and naturally include questions about political motivations and the role of interest groups.

Danelski's research on the Butler appointment predated all of these (see also Danelski 1965). Danelski wrote at a time when Supreme Court appointments, with few notable exceptions, were not highly publicized, political events and before it was widely understood that ideological, economic, and religious interest groups played a significant role in the process. He documented for the first time the complex web of interactions that take place even in a generally noncontroversial appointment. He made us understand that Supreme Court appointments do not just happen but are the product of vigorous campaigns and countercampaigns, often taking place outside the public's view. He demonstrated that political actors supporting a candidate for the Court have clear motivations for doing so, often based on policy preferences and predictions about the future justice's voting behavior (Brownell 1965–66; Smith 1966).

CONTRIBUTIONS TO THE METHOD OF STUDYING JUDICIAL POLITICS

Although Danelski is best known for his substantive contributions to our knowledge of judicial behavior, his insights into methodological issues are also worthy of attention. He shared with other judicial behavior pioneers concerns about data, measurement, and inference. Yet Danelski was always slightly outside the mainstream of the judicial behavior movement on methodological matters. He often relied on approaches that were not widely accepted by those students of judicial behavior who broke most abruptly from traditional scholarship on law and courts, and he sometimes addressed weaknesses in the field's leading methodological practices.

This section highlights three areas of Danelski's work: his application of social science theory to archival data, his attempt to develop measures of attitudes independent of judicial votes, and his use of comparative approaches to the study of courts. In each instance he was one of first scholars delve into these subjects. And in each case the judicial behavior movement initially moved away from the directions in which his work pointed, only to realize much later the error of doing so.

THE APPLICATION OF SOCIAL SCIENCE THEORY TO QUALITATIVE DATA

A hallmark of the judicial behavior movement is often characterized as its radical methodological break from more traditional approaches to the study of law and courts. Specifically, the dominant scholars of the early period rejected legal, historical studies in favor of statistically driven quantitative analysis. Glendon Schubert, S. Sidney Ulmer, Harold Spaeth, and others led the way by employing cumulative scaling, factor analysis, correlation and regression, simultaneous equations, bloc analysis, and other statistical methods not previously applied to judicial phenomena. Using such tools to analyze quantifiable data, most commonly voting behavior data, became the standard in the judicial behavior field.

Other judicial scholars, however, did not join the rush to use the most sophisticated statistical methods available. Instead, these pioneers examined judges from the perspective of social science theory but through qualitative methods. Danelski, along with others such as Walter Murphy and J. Woodford Howard Jr., clearly fall into this category. They can be credited for expanding the variety of sources that can be used to uncover the secrets of how judges behave as well as for systematizing the use of qualitative analysis.

Danelski's work is based heavily on the examination of vast amounts of primary and secondary documents. Most importantly, Danelski mined collections of the justices' private papers to reconstruct interactions among the members of the Court. Danelski supplemented these collections with published materials, letters, and biographical accounts by the justices and other actors.

While historians and biographers had previously used private judicial papers as sources of factual information, Danelski culled and interpreted data from these sources guided by social science theory. Scholars who use such archival materials owe much to Danelski's original efforts. Murphy (1966) has credited Danelski with being the first scholar to merge the use of the theoretical concepts of small-group psychology with evidence gathered from judicial papers to obtain a better understanding of what occurs inside the Supreme Court. Theodore Becker (1964), a critic of much of the work done by the pioneering generation of judicial behaviorists, agreed that Danelski's work with private papers was fresh, innovative, and of heuristic importance that cannot be underestimated. The primary advantage of Danelski's approach is its ability to allow the scholar to reconstruct interactions that occur within the Court, interactions that are not directly observable. According to Becker, this procedure is much superior to the approach used by quantitative scholars who attempt to infer unobserved activity from voting data or opinion support patterns. Although Danelski's work was a clear break from the past, traditional scholars valued his approach as well. Noted legal historian G. Edward White, for example, described a volume by Danelski and Tulchin (1973) as "the finest single piece" on Charles Evans Hughes (1988, 531).

As the judicial behavior movement moved into the mid-1960s, the qualitative approaches as practiced by Danelski and others were quickly overshadowed by the statistical methods of more quantitatively oriented scholars. Qualitative methods were perceived as excessively impressionistic and lacking the rigor required for the confirmation of scientific hypotheses. In more recent years, however, the use of private papers as a primary data source for the examination of judicial behavior has undergone a considerable renaissance (see, for example, Epstein and Knight 1998; Maltzman, Spriggs, and Wahlbeck 2000). In part, this resurgence has resulted from collections of private papers, such as those of Justices Brennan, Marshall, and Powell, that have recently become available, presenting researchers with new materials for examination. In addition, scholars have developed a renewed appreciation of the advantages provided by such primary materials, reaffirming the positions taken by Danelski, Murphy, Howard, and others at the beginning of the judicial behavior movement.

ALTERNATIVE METHODS OF MEASURING JUDICIAL ATTITUDES

From the early 1960s until the more contemporary period, the field of judicial behavior has been dominated by the attitudinal model. Schubert, building on the work of Pritchett and the legal realists, was the first scholar to present a fully developed attitude theory of judicial behavior (see, for example, Schubert 1965). In more recent years, this theory has been advocated prominently by Harold Spaeth and Jeffrey Segal (see, for example, Segal and Spaeth 1993). This school of thought, based on theories developed in psychology, posits that justices' behavior is determined by their personal policy preferences or ideologies. It is a simple stimulus-response model. Each judge has an ideological position, called an ideal point, that determines his or her response to specific cases. For example, a Supreme Court justice has a relatively fixed position regarding how extreme protest activity may become before it ceases to be protected by the First Amendment and is vulnerable to government regulation. Explaining and predicting the votes of judges requires nothing more than determining the position of the case stimuli relative to the judge's ideal point.

While studies based on the attitudinal model have been very successful at predicting the votes of Supreme Court justices, they are vulnerable to criticisms of logical circularity. Such attacks focus on the problem of measuring judicial attitudes. For years, attitudes were measured by examining previous judicial votes. Thus, a justice who had a conservative voting record was classified as having conservative attitudes. Applying that conservative classification to subsequent votes would invariably lead to the conclusion that a judge with conservative attitudes will vote for conservative case outcomes. But this circular line of reasoning really proved nothing more than that the decision records of judges are relatively consistent over time. There was no measure of attitudes independent of the behavior in question.

Very early in the development of the attitudinal model, a small group of scholars realized the logical problem presented by the attitudinal research and sought to find an improved way to test attitudinal theories (see, for example, Nagel 1963). Prominent among these scholars was Danelski. In an important article published in the *Vanderbilt Law Review*, Danelski (1966) offered a method of measuring judicial attitudes independent of the justices' votes. Using value analysis techniques developed by Ralph K. White (1944) and Charles E. Osgood (1959), Danelski examined public addresses made by Pierce Butler and Louis Brandeis prior to their Supreme Court appointments, identifying themes that might identify the values each justice embraced. Danelski gave special attention to the positions Butler and Brandeis expressed on matters related to a laissez-faire philosophy. He found, not surprisingly, that their public statements indicated that Butler supported laissez-faire but that Brandeis opposed it. Danelski then used statistical techniques such as cumulative scaling and factor analysis to examine the positions taken by members of the Court on economic regulation cases in the 1935–36 terms. The results showed that Butler and Brandeis sharply differed in the way they voted and did so in a direction that Danelski's content analysis of their public speeches would have predicted. Danelski's article is important because it demonstrates the attitude-behavior link by using a measure of attitudes independent of the justices' votes.

While Danelski's method worked relatively well for the analysis of two members of the Court, the obstacles to extending such analysis to large numbers of justices were too great to become a standard way of measuring judicial attitudes. As indicated by the reprinting of Danelski's article in important volumes on the judicial process (Goldman and Jahnige 1968; Goldman and Sarat 1978; Ulmer 1981), attitudinal theorists were cognizant of the problem Danelski addressed. Studies of judicial ideology, however, continued to use judicial votes as the primary method of determining a judge's ideology well into the 1980s, seemingly accepting the circularity difficulties as an unavoidable weakness. Only after Jeffrey Segal and Albert Cover (1989) published a measure of attitudes based on the estimations provided by major editorial writers did judicial scholars have a workable and reliable index of judicial attitudes based on measures independent of the vote.

Danelski's work on judicial values of course contributed to more than just the methodological debate over the best ways to measure attitudes. First, he demonstrated that justices perceive case stimuli in different ways, that judicial values are complex and multidimensional, and that scholars must determine the interaction between values and case stimuli to predict decisional outcomes. Second, his research did much to explicate the roll of values in intra-Court conflict and its resolution (Danelski 1967, 1986). And finally, in a 1970 piece that Gibson (1983, 28) described as "pathbreaking," Danelski extended his work on values to analyze the ideology of Harold H. Burton under two institutional settings, the Senate and the Court.

COMPARATIVE JUDICIAL BEHAVIOR

In the latter part of the 1960s, Danelski directed his attention to courts in other nations. In so doing, he became one of the few members of the pioneering generation of judicial behavioralists to engage in comparative research. Danelski's primary attention was focused on courts and judges in Japan, a nation with a developing judiciary in the aftermath of World War II. Because of postwar Allied influence, the Japanese judiciary has significant similarities to the U.S. system. Yet marked differences between the two nations provide an opportunity for fruitful comparative analysis. Danelski's research on Japan was based on fieldwork conducted over several years and was enhanced by a close association with Takeo Hayakawa, a social scientist interested in applying the theories and methods of the young judicial behavior movement to the courts in Japan (see, for example, Hayakawa 1964). Danelski's designation as a senior Fulbright-Hays scholar in 1968–69 recognized the importance of his comparative judicial behavior research.

Danelski's first examination of the Japanese judicial process was "The Supreme Court of Japan: An Exploratory Analysis," written in 1966 and subsequently published in an edited volume on comparative judicial behavior (Danelski 1969b). This piece explores the importance of status and prestige on the Japanese high court, the role of hierarchy in the appointment process, and the decisional patterns of the individual justices. Also published in 1969 was Danelski's "The People and the Court in Japan," which examines the relationship between the Supreme Court and the Japanese citizen, focusing especially on the slowly evolving prestige of the Japanese court following World War II. Included in this research is an examination of the "People's Review," a process whereby Japanese voters are periodically called on to approve or disapprove the continued tenure of the justices. In addition, Danelski has examined the political impact of the Japanese Supreme Court (1974) and the rise of judicial review in Japan (1990). Throughout all of his work on the Japanese judiciary, Danelski draws comparisons to the U.S. case. This body of work also highlights some of Danelski's most extensive use of statistical methods, including factor analysis and small-space analysis.

Perhaps Danelski's most important contribution to the comparative study of courts was his volume on comparative judicial behavior coedited with Glendon Schubert (Schubert and Danelski 1969). The book offers to students of the judicial process a collection of the some of best comparative judicial behavior studies of that era. Unfortunately, the sustained wave of comparative judicial behavior research that Danelski and Schubert hoped to ignite did not immediately come to pass. With few exceptions, the most visible work on judicial behavior remained fully fixed on the U.S. case. The field's failure to focus on comparative research resulted from many factors, including limited research support and the obstacles imposed by language differences. In addition, the initial work in comparative judicial research too often applied theories developed specifically for the U.S. context, leading to somewhat disappointing results. However, the field experienced a major rebirth in comparative studies in the late 1990s, with scholars appreciating once again the intellectual advantages of the comparative approach that attracted scholars such as Danelski and Schubert many years before.

CONCLUSION

A striking feature of Danelski's career is his large number of research firsts. He was the first to examine intra-Court leadership and influence patterns, the first to analyze systematically opinion assignment processes, the first to map the complex interactions that result in appointments to the Supreme Court. He was among the initial scholars to organize and interpret qualitative data through social science theories, to confront questions of ideology measurement, and to cast the research spotlight on courts of other nations. These accomplishments required Danelski not only to break away from the work of traditional legal scholars but also occasionally to refuse to march in lockstep with mainstream judicial behavioralists.

Danelski's work often provided a bridge between competing schools of thought and frequently opened the door to research questions that younger generations of judicial politics scholars could pursue armed with their new theoretical insights and methodological skills. Scholarly pioneers are measured not only by their successful break from the past but also by the significance of the work that builds on theirs. Measured by these standards, the judicial behavior field owes David Danelski a great deal.

REFERENCES

Abraham, Henry J. 1999. *Justices, Presidents, and Senators: A History of the U.S. Supreme Court Appointments from Washington to Clinton.* Lanham, Md.: Rowman and Littlefield.

Bales, Robert F. 1950. *Interaction Process Analysis: A Method for the Study of Small Groups.* Cambridge, Mass.: Addison-Wesley Press.

Bales, Robert F. 1953. "The Equilibrium Problem in Small Groups." In *Working Papers in the Theory of Action,* ed. Talcott Parsons, Robert F. Bales, and Edward A. Shills. Glencoe, Ill.: Free Press.

Bales, Robert F. 1958. "Task and Social Roles in Problem-Solving Groups." In *Readings in Social Psychology,* ed. Eleanor E. Maccoby, Theodore M. Newcomb, and Eugene L. Hartley. New York: Holt.

Barber, James David, ed. 1964. *Political Leadership in American Government.* Boston: Little, Brown.

Becker, Theodore L. 1964. *Political Behavioralism and Modern Jurisprudence: A Working Theory and Study in Judicial Decision-Making.* Chicago: Rand McNally.

Berkowitz, Leonard. 1953. "Sharing Leadership in Small, Decision-Making Groups." *Journal of Abnormal and Social Psychology* 48 (April): 231–38.

Brenner, Saul. 1982. "Strategic Choice and Opinion Assignment on the U.S. Supreme Court: A Reexamination." *Western Political Quarterly* 35 (June): 204–11.

Brownell, Herbert. 1965–66. Review of *A Supreme Court Justice Is Appointed*, by David J. Danelski. *Harvard Law Review* 79 (November): 220–22.

Caldeira, Gregory A., and Christopher J. W. Zorn. 1998. "Of Time and Consensual Norms in the Supreme Court." *American Journal of Political Science* 42 (July): 874–902.

Cameron, Charles M., Albert D. Cover, and Jeffrey A. Segal. 1990. "Senate Voting on Supreme Court Nominees: A Neoinstitutional Model." *American Political Science Review* 84 (June): 525–34.

Danelski, David J. 1960a. "The Assignment of the Court's Opinion by the Chief Justice." Paper presented at the annual meeting of the Midwest Conference of Political Scientists, Bloomington, Ind.

Danelski, David J. 1960b. "The Influence of the Chief Justice in the Decisional Process of the Supreme Court." Paper presented at the annual meeting of the American Political Science Association, New York.

Danelski, David J. 1961. "The Chief Justice and the Supreme Court." Ph.D. diss., University of Chicago.

Danelski, David J. 1964. *A Supreme Court Justice Is Appointed.* New York: Random House.

Danelski, David J. 1965. "A Supreme Court Justice Steps Down." *Yale Review* 54 (March): 411–25.

Danelski, David J. 1966. "Values as Variables in Judicial Decision-Making: Notes toward a Theory." *Vanderbilt Law Review* 19 (June): 721–40.

Danelski, David J. 1967. "Conflict and Its Resolution in the Supreme Court." *Journal of Conflict Resolution* 11 (March): 71–86.

Danelski, David J. 1969a. "The People and the Court in Japan." In *Frontiers of Judicial Research*, ed. Joel B. Grossman and Joseph Tanenhaus. New York: John Wiley.

Danelski, David J. 1969b. "The Supreme Court of Japan: An Exploratory Analysis." In *Comparative Judicial Behavior: Cross-Cultural Studies of Political Decision-Making in the East and West*, ed. Glendon Schubert and David J. Danelski. New York: Oxford University Press.

Danelski, David J. 1970. "Legislative and Judicial Decision-Making: The Case of Harold H. Burton." In *Political Decision-Making*, ed. S. Sidney Ulmer. New York: Van Nostrand Reinhold.

Danelski, David J. 1974. "The Political Impact of the Japanese Supreme Court." *Notre Dame Lawyer* 59 (June): 955–80.

Danelski, David J. 1986. "Causes and Consequences of Conflict and Its Resolution in the Supreme Court." In *Judicial Conflict and Consensus*, ed. Sheldon Goldman and Charles M. Lamb. Lexington: University Press of Kentucky.

Danelski, David J. 1990. "The Origins of Judicial Review in the United States and Japan." *Policy Studies Journal* 19 (fall): 151–60.

Danelski, David J., and Joseph Tulchin. 1973. *The Autobiographical Notes of Charles Evans Hughes.* Cambridge: Harvard University Press.

Ducat, Craig R., and Victor E. Flango. 1976. *Leadership in State Supreme Courts: Roles of the Chief Justice.* Beverly Hills, Calif.: Sage.

Epstein, Lee, and Jack Knight. 1998. *The Choices Justices Make.* Washington, D.C.: CQ Press.

Epstein, Lee, and Jack Knight. 2000. "Field Essay: Toward a Strategic Revolution in Judicial Politics: A Look Back, a Look Ahead." *Political Research Quarterly* 53 (September): 625–61.

Gibson, James L. 1983. "From Simplicity to Complexity: The Development of Theory in the Study of Judicial Behavior." *Political Behavior* 5:7–49.

Goldman, Sheldon, and Thomas P. Jahnige, comps. 1968. *The Federal Judicial System: Readings in Process and Behavior.* New York: Holt, Rinehart, and Winston.

Goldman, Sheldon, and Austin Sarat, eds. 1978. *American Court Systems: Readings in Judicial Process and Behavior.* San Francisco: Freeman.

Grossman, Joel B., and Richard S. Wells, eds. 1988. *Constitutional Law and Judicial Policy Making.* 3d ed. White Plains, N.Y.: Longman.

Hayakawa, Takeo. 1964. "Civil Liberties in the Japanese Supreme Court." In *Judicial Behavior*, ed. Glendon Schubert. Chicago: Rand McNally.

Kessel, John H., George F. Cole, and Robert G. Seddig, eds. 1970. *Micro-Politics.* New York: Holt, Rinehart, and Winston.

Keynes, Edward, and David W. Adamany, eds. 1971. *The Borzoi Reader in American Politics.* New York: Knopf.

Maltzman, Forrest, James F. Spriggs II, and Paul J. Wahlbeck. 2000. *Crafting Law on the Supreme Court: The Collegial Game.* New York: Cambridge University Press.

Maltzman, Forrest, and Paul J. Wahlbeck. 1996. "May It Please the Chief? Opinion Assignments in the Rehnquist Court." *American Journal of Political Science* 40 (May): 421–43.

Murphy, Walter F. 1964. *The Elements of Judicial Strategy.* Chicago: University of Chicago Press.

Murphy, Walter F. 1966. "Courts as Small Groups." *Harvard Law Review* 79 (June): 1565–72.

Murphy, Walter F., and C. Herman Pritchett, eds. 1961. *Courts, Judges, and Politics: An Introduction to the Judicial Process.* New York: Random House.

Murphy, Walter F., C. Herman Pritchett, and Lee Epstein, eds. 2001. *Courts, Judges, and Politics.* 5th ed. New York: McGraw-Hill.

Nagel, Stuart S. 1963. "Off the Bench Judicial Attitudes." In *Judicial Decision-Making*, ed. Glendon Schubert. New York: Free Press of Glencoe.

Osgood, Charles E. 1959. "The Representational Model and Relevant Research Methods." In *Trends in Content Analysis*, ed. Ithiel de Sola Pool. Urbana: University of Illinois Press.

Overby, L. Marvin, Beth M. Henschen, Michael H. Walsh, and Julie Strauss. 1992. "Courting Constituents? An Analysis of the Senate Confirmation Vote on Justice Clarence Thomas." *American Political Science Review* 86 (December): 997–1003.

Paterson, Alan. 1982. *The Law Lords.* Toronto: University of Toronto Press.

Pritchett, C. Herman. 1948. *The Roosevelt Court: A Study in Judicial Politics and Values, 1937–1947.* New York: Macmillan.

Ruckman, P. S., Jr. 1993. "The Supreme Court, Critical Nominations, and the Senate Confirmation Process." *Journal of Politics* 55 (August): 793–805.

Schubert, Glendon A. 1958. "The Study of Judicial Decision-Making as an Aspect of Political Behavior." *American Political Science Review* 52 (December): 1007–25.

Schubert, Glendon. 1962. "Policy without Law: An Extension of the Certiorari Game." *Stanford Law Review* 14 (March): 284–327.

Schubert, Glendon. 1964. "The Power of Organized Minorities in a Small Group." *Administrative Science Quarterly* 9:133–53.

Schubert, Glendon. 1965. *The Judicial Mind: The Attitudes and Ideologies of Supreme Court Justices, 1946–1963.* Evanston, Ill.: Northwestern University Press.

Schubert, Glendon, and David J. Danelski, eds. 1969. *Comparative Judicial Behavior: Cross-Cultural Studies of Political Decision-Making in the East and West.* New York: Oxford University Press.

Segal, Jeffrey A., and Albert D. Cover. 1989. "Ideological Values and the Votes of U.S. Supreme Court Justices." *American Political Science Review* 83 (June): 557–65.

Segal, Jeffrey A., and Harold J. Spaeth. 1993. *The Supreme Court and the Attitudinal Model.* New York: Cambridge University Press.

Slater, Philip E. 1955. "Role Differentiation in Small Groups." *American Sociological Review* 20 (June): 300–310.

Slotnick, Elliot E. 1978. "The Chief Justice and Self-Assignment of Majority Opinions: A Research Note." *Western Political Quarterly* 31 (June): 219–25.

Slotnick, Elliot E. 1979. "Who Speaks for the Court? Majority Opinion Assignment from Taft to Burger." *American Journal of Political Science* 23 (February): 60–77.

Smith, Paul S. 1966. Review of *A Supreme Court Justice Is Appointed*, by David J. Danelski. *American Historical Review* 71 (January): 728–29.

Steamer, Robert J. 1986. *Chief Justice: Leadership and the Supreme Court.* Columbia: University of South Carolina Press.

Stokes, Donald. 1981. "Danelski Straddles Three Professions." *Stanford University Campus Reports*, February 25.

Ulmer, S. Sidney. 1970. "The Use of Power in the Supreme Court: The Opinion Assignments of Earl Warren, 1953–1970." *Journal of Public Law* 19:49–67.

Ulmer, S. Sidney, ed. 1981. *Courts, Law, and Judicial Processes.* New York: Free Press.

Walker, Thomas G., Lee Epstein, and William J. Dixon. 1988. "On the Mysterious Demise of Consensual Norms in the United States Supreme Court." *Journal of Politics* 50 (May): 361–89.

White, G. Edward. 1988. *The American Judicial Tradition.* New York: Oxford University Press.

White, Ralph K. 1944. "Value Analysis: A Quantitative Method for Describing Qualitative Data." *Journal of Social Psychology* 19 (May): 351–58.

Wildavsky, Aaron, and Nelson Polsby, eds. 1968. *American Governmental Institutions.* Chicago: Rand McNally.

Wolfinger, Raymond E., ed. 1966. *Readings in American Political Behavior.* Englewood Cliffs, N.J.: Prentice-Hall.

CHAPTER 11

David Rohde: Rational Choice Theorist

Saul Brenner

David Rohde was one of the first scholars to test a formal rational choice model regarding decision making on the U.S. Supreme Court (1972a, c). I will critique this model as well as his other judicial research. But prior to doing so, I will place his research in its historical context.

Epstein and Knight (1995) view the history of the uses of rational choice theory to study decision making on the U.S. Supreme Court in terms of three eras. The first era lasted from 1958 until the early 1970s. This period, which coincided with the flowering of the behavioral study of decision making on the Court, is associated with a number of innovative rational choice studies. One can easily mention Glendon Schubert's game-theory research (1958), Walter Murphy's masterful *Elements of Judicial Strategy* (1964), Woody Howard's pioneering fluidity piece (1968), Sidney Ulmer's study of the error correction strategy (1972), and David Rohde's formal studies regarding minimum winning coalitions on the Court (1972a, 1972c) and majority opinion assignment (1972b). According to Brenner, this early research "appeared to be rich and imaginative and in the eyes of some Supreme Court scholars showed the importance of rational choice theory for studying decision making on the Court" (1998, 364).

Epstein and Knight (1995), however, classify the second era of rational choice scholarship as a period of decline. This period lasted from the early 1970s until 1988. Epstein and Knight attribute this decline to the triumph of the attitudinal model, which is based on the assumption that the justices' vote at the final vote on the merits is a product of sincere voting in accord with their attitudes. As a consequence, there is no room for strategic variables to operate, at least at this vote.

Rational choice Supreme Court research also declined in the second period because the behavioral scholars of the time were unimpressed with the research from the pioneering period. A number of scholars showed Schubert's game-theory research to be flawed (see Brenner

1979a). Almost no scholar faulted Murphy's *Elements of Judicial Strategy* (1964), but this is not surprising because Murphy offered examples of strategic behavior and did not maintain that his examples represented the usual patterns on the Court. Brenner (1980, 1982) showed that Howard (1968) probably overestimated the amount of fluidity in voting between the conference vote on the merits and final vote. In any event, the presence of fluidity between these two votes hardly suggests that either vote is strategic. Baum (1979) was originally unimpressed with Ulmer's error correction study (1972), but all behavioral scholars, including Baum (1997, 79), now accept Ulmer's conclusion that there is a relationship between the vote to grant cert and the vote to reverse at the final vote. Ulmer's conclusion, however, is unexciting because voting to grant cert to reverse a lower court decision one dislikes does not constitute a clear example of strategic voting (see Baum 1997, 112). Finally, numerous scholars criticized Rohde's research, as this chapter will show.

In short, both because of the success of the attitudinal model and because of the criticism directed against most of the rational choice studies from the pioneering era, rational choice theory was not perceived in the middle period as a promising theoretical approach. It is not surprising, therefore, that when this kind of research was again aggressively pursued, it was pursued by law professors, economists, and business professors, many of whom believed that they had pioneered this approach. These scholars created a third era, which has lasted from 1988 to the present. A number of judicial scholars in political science turned to this orientation as well, particularly after the publication of Segal and Spaeth's *The Supreme Court and the Attitudinal Model* (1993). In reaction to this book, these scholars sought an alternative to the attitudinal model. Some championed rational choice institutionalism (see, e.g., Epstein and Knight 1998; Maltzman, Spriggs, and Wahlbeck 2000), while others posited formal deductive models (see, e.g., Hammond, Bonneau, and Sheehan 1999). Scholars in both traditions noted and explored Rohde's pioneering research. Maltzman, Spriggs, and Wahlbeck (2000), for example, devoted a chapter in their impressive book to coalition formation on the Court and another to the assignment of the majority opinion. Rohde's research was presented and confronted in both chapters. Indeed, as I will argue in the body of this chapter, Rohde's main contribution is that he raised a number of important questions that became the agenda for judicial scholars in the second and third eras.

DAVID ROHDE

Rohde received a Ph.D. in political science from the University of Rochester in 1971. He spent almost all of his academic career at Michigan State University, where he is presently a University Distinguished Professor. Most of Rohde's academic research concerns Congress and elections. On April 15, 2000, he was selected as fellow of the Council of the American Academy of Arts and Sciences.

Rohde was the first school trained formal rational choice scholar to investigate decision making on the Supreme Court. His judicial research consists mainly of an examination of the size of opinion coalitions on the Court (Rohde 1972a, 1972c, 1977; Rohde and Spaeth 1976, 193–210) and an investigation into the variables associated with majority opinion assignment on the Court (Rohde 1972b; Rohde and Spaeth 1976, 172–92).

THE SIZE OF OPINION
COALITIONS ON THE COURT

Rohde's first study (1972c) was based on the theoretical ideas of William Riker, who introduced the "size principle" to the study of politics:

> In n-person games, where side payments are permitted, where players are rational, and where they have perfect information, only minimum winning coalitions occur. (1962, 32)

In Rohde's second study (1972a), however, he turned to the theoretical ideas of Robert Axelrod (1970), who argued that under certain conditions the actors will form ideologically connected minimum winning (MW) coalitions and that these coalitions will minimize the conflicts of interest among the members of the coalition.

Walter Murphy argued that an opinion writer on the Court will seek a MW vote for his opinion, but even after such a vote is obtained, he may bargain for additional votes:

> The marginal value of another vote is never zero, though the asking price may exceed its real value and may have to be rejected. In the judicial process a 5–4 decision emphasizes the strength of the losing side and may encourage resistance and evasion. The greater the majority, the greater the appearance of certainty and the more likely a decision will be accepted and followed in similar cases. (1964, 65–66)

It is uncertain, however, whether Murphy was referring to the size of an opinion coalition (i.e., the winning coalition formed by the writer of the opinion of the Court and the justices who joined his opinion) or to the size of the decision coalition (i.e., the winning coalition formed by the justices who voted for the winning outcome, whether they joined the opinion of the Court or not). S. Sidney Ulmer (1965) examined Supreme Court voting during the 1946 through 1961 terms and concluded that subgroup formation was not based on Riker's size principle. In response to Ulmer's article, Rohde (1972c) argued that Ulmer had inspected *decision* coalitions but that only *opinion* coalitions can be expected to be MW.

Rohde (1972a), like Murphy, viewed opinion coalition formation on the Court as a bargain between the majority opinion writer and the other justices wherein the majority opinion writer modifies her ideal opinion in exchange for the other justices' votes. The majority opinion writer will desire an opinion that mirrors her policy position, but she would be willing to alter her ideal opinion to obtain four additional votes for it, so that her opinion will be an authoritative opinion of the Court instead of a mere plurality opinion. Unlike Murphy, however, Rohde argued that the majority opinion writer would be unwilling to change the opinion after an MW vote is obtained and the other justices will not join unless changes are made. As a consequence, opinion coalitions on the Court will tend to be MW. Indeed, based on Axelrod (1970), opinion coalitions will tend to be both MW and ideologically connected. I will evaluate Rohde's model based on the less demanding requirement that the winning coalition will be MW whether it is ideologically connected.

This model, however, pertains only to nonthreat cases. In threat cases, when the Court "chooses to persist in the policy direction that produced the threat," "some of the justices will . . . acquiesce silently in spite of their disagreement" with the Court's opinion "to present a united front against the threat" (Rohde and Spaeth 1976, 197). As a consequence, Rohde argued, the opinion coalitions will tend to be larger than MW. Rohde tested the model by inspecting the opinion coalitions in the nonthreat civil liberties cases on the Warren Court. He discovered (1972a) that 40 percent of cases were five-person coalitions, and 63 percent were either five- or six-person coalitions. He also found that in threat cases, the opinion coalitions tended to be eight- or nine-person or five- or six-person in about equal proportions. Rohde argued that six-person opinion coalitions ought to be treated as MW because the opinion writer, "uncertain about the behavior of other members" and concerned about securing a majority vote for the opinion, might make "his policy broader than . . . necessary and thus [gain] the assent of more than the minimum number of justices" (1972a, 218). This contention regarding six-person opinion coalitions is a convenient argument, and not everyone is willing to accept it. Rohde was impressed with his results and claimed that they supported his nonthreat theoretical model.

But a number of scholars disputed this claim (Giles 1977; Brenner 1979b, 1998; Brenner and Arrington 1980; Epstein and Mershon 1993; Hammond, Bonneau, and Sheehan 1999). Regarding Rohde's nonthreat results, Giles (1977) compared the size of the opinion coalitions with the size of the decision coalitions and discovered that the opinion coalitions were much more likely to be equivalent in size with the decision coalitions than to be MW. Rohde (1977) replied that Giles's finding can be explained on the basis of the judicial norm against the writing of unnecessary concurring opinions.

Brenner (1979b) noted that the 40 percent and the 63 percent obtained by Rohde for the nonthreat cases were below the random amounts of 49.2 percent and 82 percent. But there are good argument why Rohde's results for the nonthreat cases should not be compared with the random amounts (see Hoyer, Mayer, and Bernd 1977; Rohde 1977).

In addition, Brenner (1979b) showed that in the 1946–55 era, 50 of the Court's 130 MW (five or six) conference coalitions (i.e., the decision coalition formed by the conference vote on the merits) were larger at the opinion vote. In other words, even when a tentative MW coalition was in place, with specific justices having voted for the outcome favored by the opinion writer and with the other justices either voting for the opposite outcome (the usual situation) or not voting, additional votes were obtained for the majority opinion 38 percent of the time. This result undermines the claim that opinion coalitions in nonthreat cases are MW.

Perhaps we do not need a fancy measure to conclude that Rohde's MW hypothesis was not supported. The fact that only 40 percent of the opinion coalitions were MW and the presence of a large number of unanimous coalitions may suggest this conclusion. Epstein and Mershon (1993) so argue, and there is merit in their argument.

Brenner (1998) noted that Rohde's nonthreat results are particularly unimpressive because he was inspecting three conditions that make MW coalitions more likely: (1) he was treating nonthreat cases, when

the justices had no incentive to form a united front against some outside threat; (2) he was focusing on civil liberties cases—that is, cases
that are often of sufficient importance that the justices are more likely
to write or join a concurring or a dissenting opinion when they disagree
with some part of the Court's opinion; and (3) he was examining a
period of time (the Warren Court) when consensus norms were weak.

Not only were a number of scholars unimpressed with Rohde's nonthreat results, but some of them also were unimpressed with his threat
results. Brenner and Arrington (1980), for example, showed that the differences in the size of the opinion coalitions on the Warren Court are
not associated with a comparison of the threat cases with the nonthreat
cases (as defined by Rohde) but rather with a comparison of the racial discrimination cases and all other civil liberties cases. It appears that the justices will form a united front against a threat only when it is severe.

Why was neither Rohde's threat hypothesis nor his nonthreat
hypothesis supported? Regarding the threat results, Ulmer (1977)
questioned whether outside groups that may threaten the Court would
be particularly interested in how many justices supported the Court's
opinion. Perhaps they are more likely to be interested in whether the
president and Congress defend or oppose the Court's decision.

But why were Rohde's more important nonthreat results not supported? I can suggest two possible reasons: first, Rohde assumed that
the majority opinion writer is interested only in an opinion that mirrors
his policy preferences and one that obtains a MW vote. Yet one can
easily list a number of other goals that a majority opinion writer in a
nonthreat case might be pursuing:

1. an opinion that pleases the justices who voted with him at the
   conference vote on the merits;
2. an opinion that picks up the maximum number of votes;
3. an opinion that increases the probability that the outcome that
   won at the conference vote on the merits will also win at the
   final vote;
4. an opinion that reduces tension between the majority and the
   minority on the Court (McLauchlan 1972);
5. an opinion that is "emphatic and unambiguous" (Palmer 1990,
   132);
6. an opinion that is "acceptable to the general public" (Palmer
   1990, 132);
7. an opinion that is acceptable to future Courts, to the lower
   court judges, and to the president and Congress;

8. an opinion that appeals to legal scholars (Palmer 1990, 132); and

9. an opinion that can be "completed quickly or at least before the end of the term" (Palmer 1990, 132).

I suspect that goals 1 and 8 are particularly important to most majority opinion writers. Yet none of these nine goals are associated with a MW opinion coalition. Baum emphasized goals 2 and 7 and argued that

it is not clear that strategy-minded judges would seek a minimum winning coalition. For instance, judges concerned with the reactions of other institutions or with long-term developments in their own court might prefer large majorities for majority opinions. (1997, 105)

Second, we can also view coalition formation from the perspective of the individual justice who decides whether to join the opinion coalition. Why, in a nonthreat case, might such a justice join that coalition even after a MW vote is obtained?

I can suggest various attitudinal, strategic, and small-group reasons for this behavior.

1. He agrees with the opinion because it coincides with his own views without accommodation (attitudinal).
2. She agrees with the opinion because her views have been accommodated (Murphy 1964, 64–65) (strategic).
3. He believes that the writing of a concurring or a dissenting opinion will raise the salience of the majority opinion (strategic).
4. She wishes to please the opinion writer with the expectation that the opinion writer will join her opinions in future cases (strategic).
5. He believes that Court opinions are strengthened with outside audiences and with future Courts when they are supported by a maximum number of votes (strategic).
6. She wants to be on the winning side (small-group).
7. He does not wish to take the time and effort necessary to write a persuasive concurring or dissenting opinion (small-group).
8. She does not care a great deal whether the Court's opinion is written one way or the other because the case is not particularly salient to her (small-group).
9. All the other justices have already joined the majority opinion,

and the remaining justice feels uncomfortable as the sole hold-out (small-group).

Epstein and Mershon (1993) argue that justices who do not agree with all aspects of the Court's opinion are likely to join if they are ideologically close to it and they are loyal to the Court as an institution.

Hammond, Bonneau, and Sheehan (1999) also posited a formal model. They assumed that the justices are rational actors who want the Court to adopt policies that are as close as possible as the justices' ideal points. The authors argued that as a consequence of attempting to achieve this goal, the majority opinion coalitions that are likely to form will not necessarily be MW. Rather, the size of these coalitions will depend on (1) the relative locations of the justices' ideal points, (2) the relationship between the state of the law and the justices' ideal points, and (3) the identity of the justice who is writing the majority opinion (35). These three scholars also argued that the MW coalitions that do occur are not necessarily the result of the bargaining over the content of the majority opinion. Rather, such coalitions are more likely to be the result of these three variables (15, 38).

All this speculation is interesting, but what does the empirical evidence suggest regarding the conditions under which an individual justice is likely to join the majority opinion? Maltzman, Spriggs, and Wahlbeck (2000, chap. 5) discovered that on the Burger Court, a justice was more likely to join an early draft of the majority opinion when

1. the justice was ideologically close to the majority opinion writer;
2. the justice was ideologically close to the majority opinion coalition that had already formed;
3. the justice was ideologically closer to the majority opinion author than to the closest dissenting opinion author;
4. the justice voted with the majority coalition at the conference vote;
5. there were few amicus briefs on the merits in the case (in other words, the case was politically less salient);
6. there was already a majority vote for the Court's opinion;
7. the majority opinion writer had joined that justice's majority opinions in the past;
8. the end of the Court's term was approaching; and
9. certain internal activities that signaled a willingness to join the majority opinion were present (four hypotheses).

It is reasonable to believe that virtually all of these variables will influence whether a given justice will join the majority opinion. Yet none of them necessarily suggests a MW opinion coalition.

In addition, Brenner, Hagle, and Spaeth (1990) compared MW conference coalitions and opinion coalitions on the Warren Court and discovered four variables associated with a larger than MW opinion coalition: nonsalience, the dissenter at conference vote ideologically closer to conference coalition, the breakup of the conference coalition (i.e., shift by the Court from reverse to affirm, or the converse), and the conference coalition voting to reverse.

Ulmer contended that one of the problems with Rohde's opinion coalition model is "the presence of multiple games and multiple intergame relationships—all of which seem to require more detailed attention than Rohde has given" (1977, 252). Ulmer also argued that the contribution to knowledge made by this model and other formal Supreme Court models that he explored was "not overwhelming" (259). Nevertheless, he welcomed these models "for the stimulation [they offer] to new thought and for the pressure [they apply] to thinking through our theories more systematically than is customary in judicial studies" (259). I strongly concur with this statement. Among the questions suggested by Rohde's imaginative opinion coalition study are

1. What goals are majority opinion writers pursuing when they write the majority opinion?
2. How often and under what conditions will the majority opinion writers succeed in achieving these goals?
3. How often and under what conditions
   (a) will the majority opinion accommodate the views of the other justices?
   (b) will the other justices join the majority opinion?
   (c) will the opinion coalition be MW, less than MW, or unanimous?
   (d) will opinion coalition be smaller, larger, or the same size as the conference coalition?
   (e) will the opinion support a different outcome than that supported by the Court at the conference vote on the merits?
4. Is there a relationship between the size of the opinion coalition on the Court and the acceptance of the decision by external groups, by the lower courts, and by future Supreme Courts?

Numerous studies since 1972 have attempted to answer many of these questions. In short, Rohde set the research agenda for a host of interesting questions.

THE ASSIGNMENT OF THE
MAJORITY OPINION

Most Supreme Court scholars believe that the assignment of a justice to write the majority opinion is important because the majority opinion writer has substantial control over its content. (For a rare dissent from this view, see Hammond, Bonneau, and Sheehan 1999.) As Ulmer stated,

> Each judge being unique, each opinion reflects, to some extent, the particular attributes of the writer—his conception of the law, his previous positions, his facility with language and concepts and so on. Who writes may affect a court decision's acceptability, its value as precedent or future guide, and the support of other judges. (1970, 51–52)

Who writes the majority opinion may also influence how many justices will vote for it and perhaps whether the outcome that won at the conference vote on the merits will also win at the final vote.

Thus, a number of judicial scholars investigated majority opinion assignment on the Court (for a list up to 1991, see Brenner 1991). Rohde was one of the earliest scholars to do so. Rohde assumed (1972b) that opinion assigners would want majority opinions reflecting their policy preferences. The ideal way to achieve this goal is for assigners themselves to write all majority opinions. But Court norms and work-load demands do not allow opinion assigners to behave in this way. Thus, they are likely to do the second-best thing, assigning majority opinions to the ideologically closest justices.

In MW cases, Rohde argued, the opinion assigner might be concerned about the possible future behavior of the pivotal justice (i.e., the justice in the conference coalition who was ideologically most distant from the opinion assigner and who presumably joined the opinion coalition last). If this justice is a marginal justice (i.e., ideologically closest to the dissenters), he might defect to the other side and, if none of dissenters at the conference vote switch to the other side, cause the breakup of the conference coalition. If the pivotal justice is the extreme justice in the conference coalition (e.g., the most liberal in a liberal coalition), she might fail to join the main opinion and, as a consequence, cause the main opinion to become a plurality opinion. Rohde assumed that assigning the majority opinion to the pivotal justice would forestall these two kinds of defections. As a consequence, in the MW cases the pivotal justices are likely to be favored in opinion assignment. Rohde tested these two hypotheses by examining the Warren Court's civil liberties cases and concluded that both theories were supported.

Rathjen (1974), however, inspected economic cases between 1959 and 1969 and discovered that the opinion assigner and the justice or justices ideologically closest to him were not favored in opinion assignment. Rohde (Rohde and Spaeth 1976) accepted this finding and concluded that only in the more salient civil liberties cases is his first hypothesis supported, while in the less salient economic cases the opinion assigner will use his assignment power to equalize the number of opinions assigned to each justice.

Hammond, Bonneau, and Sheehan argue that it is not always rational for opinion assigners to assign the opinion to the ideologically closest justice. At times, opinion assigners would benefit from selecting justices who are farther away ideologically (1999, 13).

Rohde's finding regarding the pivotal justice was partially confirmed by Brenner and Spaeth (1988), who inspected MW (5-4, 4-3) coalitions at the conference vote on the merits on the Warren Court and discovered that the marginal justice, whether pivotal or not, was assigned to write 46.3 percent of the majority opinions, more than double the random expectation of 20.2 percent. But Brenner and Spaeth also found no relationship between the assignment of the majority opinion to the marginal justice in MW cases and his defection to the other side. In other words, this justice defected or failed to defect at approximately the same rate whether he was chosen to write the majority opinion.

But neither Brenner and Spaeth (1988) nor any one else was able to present any reason that could be empirically tested for why the marginal justice was favored in opinion assignment. I suspect that this behavior, like most behaviors, is based on multiple goals, none of which are central. If this is true, then this topic is probably not a good candidate for a formal rational choice model simply because it is difficult to test formal models when multiple goals are being pursued. When opinion assigners select pivotal justices to write majority opinions in MW cases, the assigners are choosing the justices in the conference coalition furthest away ideologically and, therefore, least likely to draft opinions that reflect the assigners' policy preferences.

In short, Rohde contributed to the study of judicial behavior by presenting data that showed that the justice or justices ideologically closest to the opinion writer and the pivotal justice were favored in opinion assignment. Although the first finding has been modified by subsequent research, the second (regarding the pivotal justice) has held up

over time. But neither Rohde not anyone else has shown why this justice or the marginal justice is favored.

Whatever the merits of both studies, it cannot be denied that Rohde
presented two rich theoretical models, both of which generated a substantial amount of subsequent research. On this basis alone, Rohde was
one of the pioneers in the study of judicial behavior and in the study of
it from a strategic perspective.

NOTE

I thank Larry Baum for his critique of an earlier version of this chapter.

REFERENCES

Axelrod, Robert. 1970. *Conflict of Interest: A Theory of Divergent Goals with
Applications to Politics.* Chicago: Markham.

Baum, Lawrence. 1979. "Judicial Demand—Screening and Decisions on the
Merits: A Second Look." *American Politics Quarterly* 7:109–19.

Baum, Lawrence. 1997. *The Puzzle of Judicial Behavior.* Ann Arbor: University
of Michigan Press.

Brenner, Saul. 1979a. "Game Theory and Supreme Court Decision Making: A
Bibliographic Overview." *Law Library Journal* 72:470–75.

Brenner, Saul. 1979b. "Minimum Winning Coalitions on the U.S. Supreme
Court: A Comparison of the Original Vote on the Merits with the Opinion
Vote." *American Politics Quarterly* 7:384–92.

Brenner, Saul. 1980. "Fluidity on the Supreme Court: A Reexamination."
American Journal of Political Science 24:516–35.

Brenner, Saul. 1982. "Fluidity on the Supreme Court, 1956–1967." *American
Journal of Political Science* 26:388–90.

Brenner, Saul. 1991. "Majority Opinion Assignment on the U.S. Supreme
Court: A Bibliographic Overview of the Social Science Studies." *Law Library
Journal* 83:763–69.

Brenner, Saul. 1998. "Rational Choice and Supreme Court Decision Making:
A Review Essay." *Southeastern Political Review* 26:366–76.

Brenner, Saul, and Theodore S. Arrington. 1980. "Some Effects of Ideology
and Threat upon the Size of Opinion Coalitions on the United States
Supreme Court." *Journal of Political Science* 8:49–58.

Brenner, Saul, Timothy Hagle, and Harold J. Spaeth. 1990. "Increasing the
Size of the Minimum Winning Coalition on the Warren Court." *Polity*
23:309–18.

Brenner, Saul, and Harold J. Spaeth. 1988. "Majority Opinion Assignments
and the Maintenance of the Original Coalition on the Warren Court."
American Journal of Political Science 32:72–81.

Epstein, Lee, and Jack Knight. 1998. "Documenting Strategic Interaction on the U.S. Supreme Court." Paper presented at the annual meeting of the American Political Science Association, Chicago.

Epstein, Lee, and Jack Knight. 1997. *The Choices Justices Make*. Washington, D.C.: Congressional Quarterly Press.

Epstein, Lee, and Carol Mershon. 1993. "The Formation of Opinion Coalitions on the U.S. Supreme Court." Paper presented at the annual meeting of the Midwest Political Science Association, Chicago.

Giles, Micheal W. 1977. "Equivalent versus Minimum Winning Opinion Coalition Size: A Test of Two Hypotheses." *Journal of Politics* 21:405–8.

Hammond, Thomas H., Chris W. Bonneau, and Reginald S. Sheehan. 1999. "Toward a Rational Choice Spatial Model of Supreme Court Decision-Making." Paper presented at the annual meeting of the American Political Science Association, Atlanta.

Howard, J. Woodford, Jr. 1968. "On the Fluidity of Judicial Choice." *American Political Science Review* 62:43–56.

Hoyer, R. W., Lawrence S. Mayer, and Joseph L. Bernd. 1977. "Some Problems in Validation of Mathematical and Stochastic Models of Political Phenomena: The Case of the Supreme Court." *Journal of Politics* 21:381–403.

Maltzman, Forrest, James F. Spriggs II, and Paul J. Wahlbeck. 2000. *Crafting Law on the Supreme Court: The Collegial Game*. New York: Cambridge University Press.

McLauchlan, William P. 1972. "Research Note: Ideology and Conflict in Supreme Court Opinion Assignment, 1946–1962." *Western Political Quarterly* 25:16–27.

Murphy, Walter. 1964. *The Elements of Judicial Strategy*. Chicago: University of Chicago Press.

Palmer, Jan. 1990. *The Vinson Court Era: The Supreme Court's Conference Votes*. New York: AMS Press.

Rathjen, Gregory J. 1974. "Policy Goals, Strategic Choice, and Majority Opinion Assignments in the U.S. Supreme Court: A Replication." *Midwest Journal of Political Science* 18:713–24.

Riker, William H. 1962. *The Theory of Political Coalitions*. New Haven: Yale University Press.

Rohde, David W. 1972a. "Policy Goals and Opinion Coalitions in the Supreme Court." *Midwest Journal of Political Science* 16:208–24.

Rohde, David W. 1972b. "Policy Goals, Strategic Choice, and Majority Opinion Assignments in the U.S. Supreme Court." *American Journal of Political Science* 16:652–82.

Rohde, David W. 1972c. "A Theory of the Formation of Opinion Coalitions in the U.S. Supreme Court." In *Probability Models of Collective Decision Making*, ed. Richard G. Niemi and Herbert F. Weisberg, 165–78. Columbus, Ohio: Charles E. Merrill.

Rohde, David W. 1977. "Some Clarification Regarding a Theory of Supreme Court Coalition Formation." *American Journal of Political Science* 21:409–13.

Rohde, David W., and Harold J. Spaeth. 1976. *Supreme Court Decision Making.* San Francisco: W. H. Freeman.

Rohde, David W., and Harold J. Spaeth. 1989. "Ideology, Strategy, and Supreme Court Decisions: William Rehnquist as Chief Justice." *Judicature* 72:247–50.

Schubert, Glendon. 1958. "The Study of Judicial Decision Making as an Aspect of Political Science." *American Political Science Review* 52:1007–25.

Segal, Jeffrey A., and Harold J. Spaeth. 1993. *The Supreme Court and the Attitudinal Model.* New York: Cambridge University Press.

Ulmer, S. Sidney. 1965. "Toward a Theory of Sub-Group Formation in the United States Supreme Court." *Journal of Politics* 27:133–52.

Ulmer, S. Sidney. 1970. "The Use of Power in the Supreme Court: The Opinion Assignment of Earl Warren, 1953–1970." *Journal of Public Law* 19:49–67.

Ulmer S. Sidney. 1972, "The Decision to Grant Certiorari as an Indicator to Decision 'On the Merits.'" *Polity* 4:429–47.

Ulmer, S. Sidney. 1977. "Modeling the Decisions of the U.S. Supreme Court Justices: Some Deductive Approaches." In *Modeling the Criminal Justice System*, ed. Stuart S. Nagel, 247–62. Beverly Hills, Calif.: Sage Publications.

PART 3

The Historical-Institutionalist Pioneers

Discomfort about the "science" of judicial politics and a recent "historic turn" in the human sciences (McDonald 1996)[1] gave momentum to the third currently viable approach to the study of judicial decision making—even though this approach is the one with the most established roots in the historical development of the field of public law. This *historical-institutionalist* approach to the study of judicial behavior is least integrated with work out of the other two approaches. Here, behavior is situated and contextual, but in a different sense than the rational choice strategic approach imputes. As a theory of judicial behavior and a program for judicial behavior research, the historical-institutionalist approach is difficult to succinctly summarize, but a possible definition might be that institutionally constituted norms, powers and preferences matter because they inform behavior, but they also reconstitute the institutional context in which actors act. Inspired by both "old" institutionalists and judicial process scholars who examined judicial decisions as part of a political regime, the historical-institutionalist approach reconceptualizes the study of judicial behavior as an unabashedly interpretive project. Informed by the ways in which past actions and institutions constitute the powers and preferences of agents in contemporary politics, this approach seeks to discern patterns of historical evolution and political development that demonstrate that conscious, jurisprudential decisions of judicial actors matter, that they can reshape structural contexts and thus shape future decisions.

The historical-institutionalist pioneers are the most eclectic and diverse of the three groups of scholars who have influenced the current shape of the judicial field. Not only are they eclectic and diverse in approach, but they are also the most chronologically diversified group of pioneering scholars to be discussed. Indeed, the earliest historical-institutionalist pioneer, Edward Corwin, anticipated the rise and perhaps the decline of judicial behavioralism. As Cornell Clayton argues, Corwin's defense of a historically grounded, normative political science of courts offers both a foundation for the interpretive strand of new institutionalism and an interdisciplinary contextualization of the behavioralist impetus in judicial studies. Corwin presents for Clayton an important jumping-off point for assessing the continuities and the discontinuities of "institutional" scholarship on judicial behavior; Corwin, too, remains an essential bridge between the work of political scientists and academic lawyers on the nature and purpose of judicial decision making in a democratic system. Corwin's concern for—and mixed success in achieving—the normative and prescriptive aspect of public law studies is keenly felt in the title of Clayton's chapter, "Public Scholar."

A second "old" institutionalist—but like Corwin, a realist for his day—Alpheus Thomas Mason also predates the behavioral revolution in public law, just as his work straddles constitutional law and judicial behavior analysis. While some observers now consider his pioneering work in judicial biography an aspect of his traditionalism, his explorations of the historical and institutional contexts in which his biographical subjects operated stressed the links between those justices' decision making and those political contexts. Sue Davis examines the ways in which Mason's work reflects many of the underlying assumptions and shaped many of the methods of new institutionalism. In so doing, she asks us to consider the relationship between judicial biography and the descriptive focus of the study of judicial behavior that ensued from it, as well as the uneasy relationship between atheoretical, narrative studies of judging and the generation of more systematic, theoretically animated approaches to behavioral phenomena.

Just as attitudinal pioneers such as Tanenhaus and strategic pioneers such as Howard and Danelski presided over and commented on the transition between traditional doctrinal analysis of judicial politics and the emergent school of judicial behavioralism, Robert McCloskey addressed this transition in his work linking Supreme Court politics to the agenda of the larger political system. Just as Pritchett reminded behavioral scholars of the mix of legal and policy considerations in judicial action, McCloskey assumed that judges are both empowered and restricted by their "courtly" attributes. Howard Gillman links McCloskey with the research agenda of historical institutionalism in his adoption of macro or regime approaches to the study of courts. While more recent literature has modified and refined McCloskey's research design, his work, like Corwin's, remains vital for contemporary readers concerned with the problem of judicial institutional legitimacy, just as it remains significant as a connector between political science and legal scholarship on the role of the Supreme Court in the American political system.

The discussion of Robert Dahl demonstrates the marked eclecticism of the list of historical institutionalist pioneers, for Dahl is not ordinarily celebrated or even noted as a judicial scholar. Yet this major twentieth-century political scientist and architect of pluralist theory left his mark on the judicial field by writing one journal article that spawned an entire literature on judicial process. David Adamany and Stephen Meinhold take up the challenge of proving Dahl's pioneer status, even while they examine the critical stance taken by much of the research responding to Dahl's thesis that the Supreme Court is a national policymaker more often than it is truly countermajoritarian. In raising the issues of the Court's legitimacy and its relationship to majority party coalitions, Dahl invited work that empirically tested his claims but did so in a framework that retained a sensitivity to the institutional, political context of judicial behavior.

The most recent of the historical institutionalist pioneers and the last scholar appraised in the volume took his work in directions consonant with new institutionalism, particularly in his focus on the institutional functions of judicial norms. Martin Shapiro, like many of the attitudinalist pioneers who were his contemporaries, recognized early on that "political jurisprudence" was not limited to the U.S. judicial (or Supreme Court) context and that any general theory of judicial decision making based in an operative context demanded comparative court analysis. Herbert Kritzer singles out Shapiro among the pioneers of judicial behavior for stressing a broad institutional perspective in adjudging judging. Similarly, Kritzer notes that the breadth and inventiveness of Shapiro's work hamper its easy categorization and may have limited direct reliance on it in generating a theory of judicial behavior. That Shapiro is the only one of the pioneers of judicial behavior—historical-institutionalist or otherwise—whose work substantially informed the non-court-centered research agenda of law and society scholarship is telling, too: Shapiro's efforts to analyze the legal and political contexts that shape judicial decision making eventually took him—and took a subset of the law and courts field—further into those contexts and further away from Schubert's concern for the "judicial mind."

The opening chapter alluded to the implications of this drift away from the *judicial* in judicial studies. The historical-institutionalist approach to judicial decision making offers one avenue for reclaiming drifters by enlarging the conception and exploration of the institutional context of judging. Yet that enlargement entails a risk: just as the research of many of the historical-institutionalist pioneers was so broad in scope and method as to risk being labeled *history* or *sociology*, so too is some work by contemporary practitioners of historical-institutionalist court studies dismissed by other judicial scholars as insufficiently a political science of courts. Interdisciplinarity and contextualization of phenomena, then as now, are perilous because they challenge existing boundaries, categories, and bounded and categorical ways of thinking. Yet such bounded and categorical ways of thinking define and constitute academic disciplines and what they study (often *by* what they study) and give meaning to findings and evaluative standards for assessing claims to meaning. There is a certain mushiness and flabby holism to unmethodical interdisciplinary methods and the unbridled putting of things in context. As a recent essay on the relationship between shared standards for the validity of measurements and contextual specificity in social science research comments, "if pushed to an extreme, the 'claim to context dependency' threatens to 'make impossible the collective pursuit of empirical knowledge'" (Adcock and Collier 2001, 534).

Still, we would do well to remember that "what is taken to contaminate different disciplines varies as the prestige (and intellectual accomplishments) of other disciplines change" (Garber 2001, x). To mix several metaphors, the work of the historical-institutionalist pioneers is particularly useful for current judicial scholars since those pioneers served on the front lines during a prior period of disciplinary and intradisciplinary "contamination" as well as a prior period of fractious debate over validity of measurement. Rather than relive their battles, current scholars might profit from a study of their tactics, successful and less so, lest the law and courts field become an "invitation to nostalgia, a longing for a lost unitary knowledge or a lost unitary self" enraptured only by "the narcissism of small differences" (Garber 2001, 89, 54).

NOTE

1. The references cited in this section are listed in the references to chapter 1.

CHAPTER 12

Edward S. Corwin as Public Scholar

Cornell W. Clayton

That the primary task of political science is today one of popular education, and that therefore it must still retain its character as a "normative," a "telic," science, is then, my thesis. Why, indeed, should there be another natural science anyway? The general obtuseness of the laboratory sciences to social values is boasted by their would-be imitators, and is as notorious as it is infantile. With modern physics and chemistry brandishing sticks of dynamite with the insouciance of a four year old, what could be more preposterous than to induct political science into the same nursery of urchins?

—Edward S. Corwin, "The Democratic Dogma and Political Science"

INTRODUCTION:
CORWIN AS PIONEER

Few, if any, modern political scientists have so influenced American constitutional law and the way political science understands it as Edward S. Corwin. At Princeton University from 1905 until 1946, Corwin became the premier teacher and educator. He succeeded to Woodrow Wilson's former position as McCormick Professor of Jurisprudence and served as the first chair of Princeton's politics department. His students included men of political power (John D. Rockefeller III, Allen Dulles, Adlai Stevenson, Syngman Rhee) as well as eminent scholars (Raymond Leslie Bueil, Alpheus T. Mason, and Clinton Rossiter, to name only a few).[1] Under Corwin's direction, Princeton's politics department became the disciplinary center for study of what the U.S. Constitution means. He paved the way for his successors at Princeton, Mason and Walter Murphy (two other pioneers in this volume), and the eventual establishment of the "Princeton school" of constitutional studies that is today associated with such names as Murphy, Sanford Levinson, James Fleming, and Sotirios Barber.

As an academic, Corwin achieved the highest honor in his discipline, serving as the president of the American Political Science Association in 1931. He published more than 20 books, 150 scholarly articles, and nearly 250 book reviews and letters. Many of his works are classics that remain staple readings in political science departments and law schools around the country. His ideas remain as vital today as when first penned. Indeed, a quick review on Lexis-Nexis reveals that Corwin's work was cited in law reviews more than 487 times between 1990 and 2000 alone—a remarkable record considering that his last scholarly work was authored more than forty years ago.

More important to Corwin than academic honors, however, was his public standing as the preeminent constitutional authority of his day. Corwin was a *public scholar*, a force in the real world of politics. As a political commentator and an adviser to two presidents, he was involved in remaking the same constitutional structures he spent his life studying. He is one of the few nonlawyers (and perhaps the only political scientist) in the modern era to be considered seriously for a seat on the U.S. Supreme Court. Although that appointment never came, his ideas "changed the minds of men in the seats of power in Washington as in the seats of learning around the country, . . . and American constitutional law—not just the law taught by professors, but the law debated by senators and proclaimed by judges—has never been quite the same since he first took his incisive pen in hand" (Rossiter 1955, xi). Indeed, Corwin's scholarship has been cited more frequently in Supreme Court opinions than probably all other modern political scientists combined,[2] more than twenty-seven times and in some of the most important cases this century.[3]

If Corwin differs from other pioneers in this volume, it is in his view of the role and purpose of political science. Trained as a historian, Corwin grappled with what it meant to be a political scientist when the discipline was still in its infancy. For him, political science was a *part of*, and not *a-part from*, the world of democratic politics that it aspires to understand. In this sense, political science must always be a normative or, in Corwin's words, a "telic" science. The goal of the political scientist was to "educate" the public to better understand what a commitment to democratic ideals required. For those interested in public law—and it was public law, not judicial behavior, in Corwin's day—the term meant giving guidance to judges and other policymakers about what law in a democracy ought to be. "If judges make law," Corwin argued, "so do commentators" (1923, 74).

Corwin's view of the purposes of political science had both theoretical and methodological implications. He anticipated both the rise (and decline?) of behavioralism and other efforts to emulate the natural sciences. In a 1929 article in the *American Political Science Review*, Corwin argued against transforming political science into a positivist, "laboratory science," a transformation that he believed would leave the discipline "sterile" and marginalized. This critique of the nascent developments in the discipline also remains as vital today as when first penned. Corwin's warning against excessive "scientific" zeal and the flight from questions of normative relevance has in recent years been echoed in the pages of the *New York Times* (Eakin 2000), the *New Republic* (Cohn 1999), and, in more scholarly tones, in the pages of the *American Political Science Review* (Smith 1988). Corwin's astonishingly "postbehavioral" conception of the goals of political science, far more than disagreements over methodological approach, remains, I argue, the core difference between historical-institutionalist scholars of judicial behavior, from whatever generation, and those public law scholars within the attitudinal or strategic choice traditions.

Unlike some authors in this volume, I have no personal experience with the pioneer about whom I write. I was not a student of Corwin, nor was I trained at Princeton. I have not written a biography of Corwin, as did Kenneth Crews (1985, 1986), nor exegeses of his work, as have Richard Loss (1976, 1981–88), Clinton Rossiter (1955), or Gerald Garvey (1962). In short, I am not a Corwin expert. To those who wish to know more about Corwin's life and ideas, I can recommend these other excellent sources.

I do, however, admire Corwin as a political scientist—his method, his understanding of the discipline, and his conception of public law scholarship. Ironically, like many political scientists of my generation, I was trained when the behavioralist approach was at its peak in the United States. The work of Corwin and other early institutionalists, such as Robert Cushman, Charles Grove Haines, and Thomas Reed Powell, received little attention and was generally considered unscientific and obsolete. It was not until I went abroad for graduate studies that I was introduced to the work of this earlier generation of American public law scholars. In a sense, then, my respect for their work is much like that of a third-generation immigrant: their second-generation parents eschew the old country, embarrassed by its old ways, but the third generation, secure in its native identity, returns to rediscover all that is good about the old country and its traditions.

Still, it takes nothing from the brilliance of Corwin's work to note that its strength—his insistence that normative concerns should guide empirical inquiry—is also its most serious weakness. If his career illustrates what is desirable and excellent about a historical-institutionalist approach to studying law and courts, it may also alert us to some of its limitations.

The remainder of this essay sketches Corwin's career and major scholarly contributions. It then discusses the main outlines of his constitutional theory and his views about the role of the Court in the U.S. constitutional system. Finally, it turns to Corwin's understanding of political science as a historically grounded, normative enterprise and how approach this informed his views on judicial behavior. Corwin's understanding of judicial behavior, together with the force and longevity of his own work, provides an important foundation for the revival of a "new" historical institutionalism in the public law field, and the chapter concludes with some comments about this relationship.

THE CAREER AND SCHOLARSHIP OF EDWARD S. CORWIN

Edward S. Corwin was born near Plymouth, Michigan, in 1878. His early interest in history and politics came together in 1896, when he was a student at the University of Michigan, which had an exceptionally strong program in constitutional studies, led by Thomas Cooley and distinguished historian Andrew McLaughlin. In researching a paper for McLaughlin, Corwin was struck by the Supreme Court's decision in the 1857 *Dred Scott* case. The Court had not previously construed the due process clause as a substantive limitation on congressional power, and neither Corwin nor McLaughlin could understand where this interpretation of the clause originated (Crews 1985, 4–5). Thus began Corwin's lifelong fascination with the Court's due process jurisprudence and its connection to "higher law" values.

After graduating in 1900, Corwin taught high school for two years and then returned to Michigan in 1902 to pursue graduate studies under McLaughlin. In 1904 Corwin accepted a fellowship at the University of Pennsylvania, where he received his Ph.D. in history in 1905 under the direction of eminent historian John Bach McMaster. On McMaster's recommendation, Corwin traveled to Princeton in June 1905 to interview with its new president, Woodrow Wilson. Wilson was instigating a new "preceptor" program that envisioned faculty serving not only as lecturers but also as mentors and friends to students. Corwin was hired and quickly became one of Princeton's most respected preceptors and teachers. In 1911 he was made a full professor.

While at Princeton, Corwin developed a lasting if mercurial friendship with Wilson. Although they often disagreed over college governance matters, Corwin won Wilson's respect as a scholar. In 1908, he asked Corwin to coauthor the revised edition of his American history book, *Division and Reunion* (Wilson and Corwin 1921). Wilson eventually left Princeton, was elected governor of New Jersey, and then ran for the presidency. As a Progressive, Corwin had written in early support of the Sixteenth Amendment and a fair income tax (1912a). But he was also a Republican and had clashed publicly with Wilson over his criticism of Theodore Roosevelt, whom Corwin greatly admired. Nevertheless, out of loyalty to his friend and colleague, Corwin threw his support to Wilson in the 1912 presidential election. Once Wilson assumed office, Corwin's personal connection to the president elevated the professor's public status and lent prestige and credibility to his academic writing.

Corwin's scholarship during this period began to focus on the three great constitutional issues of the day: (1) the scope of federal power; (2) the role of the Court and the doctrine of judicial review; and (3) presidential authority. In 1913 Corwin published *National Supremacy: Treaty Power versus State Power*, in which he argued that the federal treaty power was not restricted by the reserved powers of the states and could thus be used to effect social legislation otherwise beyond the national government's delegated authority. He sent a copy of the book to Wilson, who responded unenthusiastically in a letter: "I do not feel by any means as confident as you do as to the power of the Federal Government in the matter of overriding the powers of the states" (quoted in Crews 1985, 12). This and other disagreements over Wilson's domestic policy led to Corwin's disenchantment, and by 1916 he was publicly criticizing Wilson and writing in support of his Republican opponent, Charles Evans Hughes (Corwin 1916).

Despite Corwin's defection, Wilson was reelected and the United States soon entered the war against Germany. There was a brief rapprochement between the men, and Corwin worked for the administration in the wartime Committee on Public Information, editing a compendium on the war entitled *War Cyclopedia* (Paxson, Corwin, and Harding 1918). In 1917, he published his first book on the presidency, *The President's Control of Foreign Relations*, tracing the historical development of presidential authority to conduct foreign affairs and advocating its further expansion. In other articles, however, Corwin began to recognize the war's effect in shifting legislative powers over other areas. Evincing a concern to which he would return in later life, he expressed apprehension about the radical changes in governmental authority and the expansion of presidential power brought about by World War I (1917b).

Following the war, Corwin once again found himself at odds with Wilson. Corwin sided with his friend Henry Cabot Lodge, the president's chief congressional critic, in the dispute over the League of Nations. Although Corwin supported the idea of a world body, he argued that without restrictions on U.S. obligations in international disputes—restrictions favored by Lodge and opposed by Wilson—the agreement would violate American sovereignty (Corwin 1919a). His opposition was devastating to the agreement, not only because of his growing reputation as a constitutional scholar but also because of his close ties to Wilson.[4] Despite these political disagreements, Corwin's relationship to Wilson endured. In 1918 Corwin succeeded to Wilson's former position as McCormick Professor of Jurisprudence, and in 1921 Corwin authored another edition of Wilson's *Division and Reunion*.

At around the same time, Corwin entered his most prolific period of scholarship. His reputation as a public scholar was cemented by regular letters to national newspapers and contributions to widely read liberal periodicals such as the *New Republic*, the *Nation*, and the *Weekly Review*. With the *Lochner* era in full swing, Corwin delved headlong into the origins of the Court's controversial jurisprudence. In 1914 he published one of his most definitive articles, "The Basic Doctrine of American Constitutional Law" and gathered together a series of other previously published articles into a book entitled *The Doctrine of Judicial Review*. In these works, Corwin rejects the formalist's insistence that law is autonomous from politics, arguing that the constitutional justification for judicial review was rooted in the natural rights ideology of the framers.

In 1919 Corwin published *John Marshall and the Constitution*, examining Marshall's impact on the Court and his influence over early constitutional understandings. Corwin argued that Marshall's nationalism was not original but reflective of the framers' own views. The book not only marked Corwin as a leading expert on the great chief justice but pioneered judicial biography as a genre of political science separate from history. In later years, Corwin's student, Alpheus T. Mason, expanded this method and turned judicial biography it into a virtual subfield of public law.[5]

During the next decade, Corwin published three more books and some forty articles, including many of his most important contributions to constitutional theory.[6] In "The Worship of the Constitution" (1920) and "Constitution v. Constitutional Theory" (1925), he debunks popular veneration for the Constitution and the framers intent, or what he termed the framers' "political science." Such "blind reverence," he argued, had been thoroughly repudiated by the historical reality of the Civil War and the political acceptance of Lincoln's vision of a nation greater than the Constitution. The framers' theories, he concluded, could no longer serve as the foundation for constitutional law in the twentieth century. He elaborated on this theme and proposed an alternative way of understanding the basis of constitutional authority in perhaps his most celebrated essay, "The 'Higher Law' Background of American Constitutional Law" (1928).

With Progressives out of power during this period, Corwin also began to focus more attention on the discipline of political science. In 1924 politics emerged from history and economics as an independent department at Princeton; Corwin became the first chair of the new department, holding that position until 1936. Although he taught a variety of courses at Princeton, his favorite—the course he pioneered—was Constitutional Interpretation. In 1920 Corwin authored his most widely read book, *The Constitution and What It Means Today*, now in its fourteenth edition (Corwin 1978). A shorter version of that book, originally authored by Corwin and Jack Peltason in 1949, *Understanding the Constitution*, is now in its fifteenth edition (Corwin, Peltason, and Davis 2000). They remain probably the longest continuously used textbooks on the U.S. Constitution. By teaching constitutional law as a body of legal doctrines contingent on broader social, economic, and historical forces, Corwin wedded constitutional study to the social sciences and virtually created the classroom model for the infant field of public law (Mason 1981, 146).

In 1931, Corwin was honored with the presidency of the American Political Science Association. His presidential address, "Social Planning under the Constitution," displayed his trademark wit and his overriding concern that political science remain relevant to the world of politics. Criticizing both big business and President Hoover's efforts to cope with the Great Depression, Corwin sarcastically called the president's program the "with the help of God" plan (1932, 2). Political science, Corwin argued, must be prepared to play an important role in assisting government policymakers in dealing with economic crisis. Corwin argued that the government ought to expand its role in economic planning, and he criticized the Court's *Lochner*-era decisions as creating a false barrier to the regulatory state. The Constitution of 1789 was itself "an instance of social planning," he argued. By contrast, the *Lochner* Court's constitutional law dates to an altogether unappreciated extent from this side of the year 1890, and so is fully a century younger than the Constitution itself; and especially is this true of those doctrines and principles concerning which the social planner needs feel special concern. These are not, in the main, the outgrowth of earlier precedents; more often they are the repudiation of them. They derive from a point of view which became dominant with the Court about 1890. (1932, 4)

His speech, delivered in December 1931, foreshadowed the constitutional upheavals of the next decade. The following year, the Great Depression condemned Hoover's presidency and swept Franklin D. Roosevelt into office. Corwin understood, as few others could, the challenge that Roosevelt's New Deal posed to the idea of constitutional governance in the United States. It was, he said in 1933, a test of "the capacity of the Constitution to absorb a revolution" ("NRA Constitutional" 1933, 3). He immediately began writing in support of the New Deal and criticized Supreme Court resistance to the doctrinal changes it required. In *The Twilight of the Supreme Court* (1934), he predicted that the New Deal would mark the emergence of legislative authority and the eclipse of judicial authority as the primary source of constitutional interpretation. When the Court remained recalcitrant, he wrote *The Commerce Power versus States Rights* (1936), criticizing the Court's narrow interpretations of Congress' interstate commerce powers and its misunderstanding of constitutional federalism. After the Court's retreat in 1937, Corwin returned to assess the Court's diminished constitutional role in *Court over Constitution* (1938). The declining role of the Court as constitutional interpreter was acceptable, he argued, only with caution and only with strong presidential leadership to make Congress more responsive to the democratic impulse and the needs of the people. Finally, at the close of the decade, he wrote *The President: Office and Powers* (1940), in which he examined the historical growth of presidential power and the office's capacity to provide the leadership necessary for the new constitutional system. This book, which remains a classic of presidential studies, established the "institutional model" of the presidency, isolating and analyzing each of the president's functions and powers.

During the 1930s, several strands of Corwin's work came together. Roosevelt's strong leadership led to popular legislation that altered relationships between federal and state governments, between Congress and the president, and between government regulatory power and individual property rights. The Court's doctrines of the previous forty years had to change, and a new constitutional theory had to replace that of the framers and of the *Lochner* Court. Corwin had positioned himself perfectly to become the New Deal's chief constitutional theorist.

In 1935 Corwin went to work for Roosevelt's administration as a legal adviser to the Public Works Administration. In 1936 he became special assistant and consultant to Attorney General Homer S. Cummings, advising on constitutional law and helping to litigate important cases such as *Carter v. Carter Coal Co.* (1936). When the Court struck down both the National Industrial Recovery Act and the Bituminous Coal Conservation Act in 1936, Corwin wrote profusely for newspapers and magazines and took to the radio and lecture circuit to attack the Court's decisions. The attorney general forwarded Corwin's articles to the president, and Corwin soon was mentioned as a leading candidate for the Court. He joked with students about the possibility, but after Roosevelt's landslide reelection in 1936, Corwin had good reason to believe that such an honor was in fact imminent.[7]

Instead, Corwin's career reached a watershed in 1937. Corwin's commitment to public scholarship, to the political scientist as normative critic and advocate, came back to haunt him. Corwin had previously argued that the Court should remedy the constitutional impasse by simply correcting its New Deal rulings in subsequent decisions. He brushed aside proposals for constitutional amendment, and, although he backed a mandatory judicial retirement age, he argued against changing the size of the Supreme Court to effect its decisional outcomes (1937a). So, when Roosevelt sent the Court-packing bill to Congress in February 1937 and Corwin came to its defense, its not surprising that the politically flexible Corwin became the subject of criticism.

Corwin was the principal academic spokesman for the president's plan during Senate hearings in March 1937.[8] In fact, Corwin was one of the few prominent scholars to support the proposal. The plan was roundly condemned by Harold W. Dodds, president of Princeton, and Andrew McLaughlin, Corwin's old mentor. It was also rejected by a prestigious committee formed at the Brookings Institution that included Dean Acheson, Thurmond Arnold, Charles Clark, Robert Cushman, Charles Grove Haines, and Corwin (Special Committee 1937). Despite his position as chair of the committee, Corwin was unable to persuade the other members to support the president's plan.

At the hearings, Nebraska Democrat Edward R. Burke bluntly asked Corwin about his earlier views and his changed position on expanding the size of the Court. Corwin's response was, "I live and learn." But his testimony failed to persuade the Senate, and his public inability to explain the reversal of his own views on Court-packing proved deeply embarrassing. Corwin was widely criticized for abandoning scholarly objectivity and becoming a partisan advocate. Some even called into question his commitment to academic freedom and to Princeton's honor code.[9] Because a Court nomination would require another Senate hearing, Corwin's hopes for becoming a justice were dashed. He continued to be mentioned as a possible nominee, but the White House never called.

Corwin's disappointment over the Court appointment seriously colored his views after 1937. His thinking and writing became increasingly more conservative and critical of Roosevelt. Corwin continued to support the New Deal, but in the popular press he began to criticize FDR's leadership and his failure to respect the two-term "constitutional understanding" on presidential incumbency. In 1940, Corwin returned to his Republican roots, writing in support of Willkie's campaign and criticizing Roosevelt's foreign policy and his appointments to the Court (1940a). Corwin later supported Eisenhower and also became a personal friend and supporter of Richard Nixon's (Crews 1985, 45–47).

Corwin's scholarship turned to the constitutional problems wrought by World War II. In *The Constitution and World Organization* (1944), he argued that the Constitution posed few problems for U.S. entry into international organizations and that the United States should assume a global leadership role. In 1953 he cochaired, with Lucius Clay and John W. Davis, the Committee for Defense of the Constitution by Preserving the Treaty Power, a group formed to oppose the Bricker Amendment and efforts to curtail federal authority to enter international agreements or treaties.

Corwin had, however, became increasingly concerned about the "aggrandizement" of presidential power. In three books, *Total War and the Constitution* (1947), *A Constitution of Powers in a Secular State* (1951), and *The Presidency Today* (written with Louis W. Koenig, 1956), Corwin recognized that the Court could no longer be an effective check on government, especially power that had been increasingly accumulating in the presidency. Corwin now looked for political rather than legal limitations on presidential power. Criticizing Congress for abdicating so much of its authority, he advocated a more effective use of its power over the purse to limit future accretion of power in the presidency.

In contrast to the growing prestige given his presidential scholarship, Corwin's status as the premier Supreme Court scholar waned following the Court-packing controversy. By the 1950s Corwin's ideas were increasingly overshadowed by those of a new generation of academic lawyers—including Alexander Bickel and Herbert Wechsler—trained in the academic legal realism and historical method that Corwin himself helped establish.

Nevertheless, Corwin continued to write prolifically about the Court and grappled with the consequences of the same constitutional changes he had earlier espoused. In *Constitutional Revolution, Ltd.* (1941), he argued that the 1937 shift in constitutionalism had made political theory explicit rather than latent in constitutional jurisprudence, and he warned that judges might now become increasingly results oriented in their decision making. In "The Dissolving Structure of Our Constitutional Law" (1945) and "The Passing of Dual Federalism" (1950), Corwin examined the New Deal's impact on constitutional structures of power such as separation of powers and federalism. Expressing concern that the American "system had lost resiliency," he worried that "what was once vaunted as a Constitution of rights, both state and private, had been replaced by a Constitution of powers." And he wondered whether the acceptance of "cooperative federalism" had so diminished the power of state governments, that they could be "saved for any useful purpose, and thereby saved as the vital cells that they have been heretofore of democratic sentiment, impulse, and action" (1950, 23).

Corwin also recognized that the abandonment of the doctrines of inherent limitations on government regulatory authority would necessitate a larger role for the Court in protecting basic civil liberties (1940c). He criticized some of the specifics in the Court's emerging civil liberties jurisprudence, especially its free speech decisions (1952) and its establishment clause decisions (1948b). However, in *Liberty against Government* (1948a), Corwin supported the Court's new role in protecting individual rights. Nevertheless he worried that ideas of fundamental rights, untethered from traditional higher law concepts, might lead to populist demands for equalization of conditions and a principle of equality that would wind up producing servitude rather than freedom (1948a).

While Corwin's shift in partisan loyalties after 1937 is undeniable, too much can be made of shifts in his scholarship. Corwin never retreated from the "constitutional revolution" of 1937, a term he coined. He continued to defend the positive state as a proper instrument of the sovereign legislative authority and to argue for a reduced role for judicial power in interpreting the U.S. constitutional tradition.

Although he saw the aggrandized presidency as a threat to the idea of limited government, he thought the appropriate response was political, not legal. And he continued to think that the Court's pre-1937 views of federalism and separation of powers were logical absurdities. Corwin's fundamental concern about the modern dilemma of maintaining effective but limited government remained steady throughout his career. Before 1937, that concern led him to buttress constitutional authority for effective government; after 1937, he recognized the need to find new ways to limit government power.

CORWIN'S CONSTITUTIONAL THEORY

A thorough explication of Corwin's constitutional theory is beyond the scope of this essay.[10] Although he never wrote a single synthesis of his evolving ideas about constitutional theory, after retiring from Princeton in 1946 and while working for the Library of Congress he wrote .and edited the massive *The Constitution Annotated: Analysis and Interpretation* (Corwin 1953). This work comes close to a comprehensive account of his descriptive scholarship on constitutional history and law. Yet Corwin's true contribution consists in the fact that unlike earlier theorists of the U.S. Constitution, such as Kent, Story, and Cooley, he developed a theory entirely independent of the framers' intentions and sought to replace rather than justify existing constitutional law and legal doctrines.[11] In this sense, Corwin was perhaps the first to develop a truly postrealist constitutional theory. By explicitly tying developments in constitutional law to evolutions in social-political thought, he denied the autonomy of law as a separate discipline and made constitutional jurisprudence a branch of normative political philosophy. That his ideas about the Constitution became perfectly conventional within his own life is a mark of his success in replacing the old order.

Corwin's constitutional theory began as a reaction to the Gilded Age constitutionalism of Thomas Cooley and its doctrinal spawn, the laissez-faire, or *Lochner*-era, versions of dual federalism, judicial review, and due process or vested rights. The first of these, Corwin recognized, had created a governmental no-man's-land where business could escape regulation by both the federal and state governments. It withheld broad powers from the federal government by reserving them to the "sovereign" states but at the same time held states incompetent to regulate economic activity that was interstate in nature. Corwin realized that the doctrine of dual federalism gained authority from its historical association with the father of the Constitution, James Madison.

But Corwin also understood that the laissez-faire version of dual federalism—much like earlier versions used to argue for state interposition
and secession—rested on an idea of state sovereignty whose historicity
was vulnerable.

Corwin argued that Madison did not champion state sovereign pre-
rogatives until after the constitutional convention (1912b). Instead,
Madison and the framers had embraced a nationalist version of dual
federalism, the same one elaborated by their federalist disciple, John
Marshall, in *McCulloch v. Maryland* (1819). Thus, Corwin argued, the
Marshall Court, not the *Lochner* Court, was true to the framers' history:
"That vision of national unity which indubitably underlies the Constitution was after all the vision of an aristocracy conscious of a solidarity
of interests transcending state lines" (1919b, 126). At the very least,
Corwin concluded, the Constitution was at the time of its ratification
compatible with both the state-sovereignty and nationalist variants of
federalism, and thus it was up to Marshall to establish the precedent in
McCulloch.

Yet if the Constitution created a nationalist framework of sovereignty, what limits existed on its authority, and who was to enforce
them? Corwin argued that the two great achievements of American
courts, the doctrine of vested rights and the doctrine of judicial review,
were interwoven and needed to be historically unraveled. Both laissez-
faire variants of these doctrines, Corwin believed, rested on a historically contingent view of the Constitution in which the framers
embraced the idea of "common right and reason and natural law" (1911,
306). Corwin disagreed with his contemporary Charles Beard, who had
argued that the framers had clearly intended the institution of judicial
review to better protect their economic privileges against populist legislation. Instead, Corwin argued, "judicial review of acts of Congress is
clearly a result of inference rather than of explicit grant, and while many
drew this inference at the time of the Constitution's framing and adoption, others did not" (1937b, 3). The doctrine's acceptance became
inevitable, however, only because the framers' belief in natural rights
was transferred to the written Constitution. The legal basis for judicial
review was then supplied by a view of the Constitution as embodying a
higher law enforceable by the courts and the legal formalists' distinction
between "making policy" and "interpreting law," the assumption that
judges "alone really *know* the law" (1914b, 572).

Key to the doctrine's survival and later development into the judicial
supremacy variant of the *Lochner*-era Court, however, was its connection to the doctrine of vested rights, or the Lockean idea of natural

property rights as antecedent to government. Corwin called this "The Basic Doctrine of American Constitutional Law" (1914a), and it stood at the heart of the Court's due process jurisprudence. In short, this doctrine held that legislative power was inherently limited and that "quite independently of the written Constitution, [legislative power] is not absolute, but constrained both by its own nature and by the principles of republican government, natural law and social compact." Blackstone had relied on this idea to develop the doctrine of parliamentary sovereignty as the bulwark against royal encroachments on property rights. By contrast, the framers' fear of popular majorities and the threat they posed to vested rights, Corwin suggested, "lies at the very basis of the whole system of judicial review, and indeed of our entire constitutional system." Consequently, judicial review and American constitutional law generally "has for its primary purpose not the convenience of the state but the preservation of individual rights" (1911, 306).

Yet if Corwin understood clearly the ideological foundations of American constitutional law, the problem with which he grappled was how to dislodge constitutional law from those foundations and find new ones while remaining faithful to the idea of constitutionalism. In his most important essays on this subject, "The Worship of the Constitution" (1920), "Constitution v. Constitutional Theory" (1925), "The 'Higher Law' Background of American Constitutional Law" (1928), and "The New Deal in Light of American Political and Constitutional Ideas" (1936), Corwin argues that history had made the framers' ideas untenable as a basis for constitutional law in the twentieth century. Lincoln's attack on the old constitutional order had undermined the sanctity of the framers' intent and had democratized the American political order. Moreover, the legal realism of the late nineteenth and early twentieth centuries had undermined both the legal formalist distinction between law and politics and the belief in the possibility of an objectively knowable "natural justice" or a "brooding omnipresence" that operated above the positive law.

Most importantly, Corwin argued, modern society had transformed the nature of liberty and its consequent relationship to government. Rejecting a purely negative conception of liberty rights, Corwin argued that government was not the enemy of freedom in the modern world. Neither Locke nor the framers could have foreseen the degree to which concentrated private ownership would become "a source of power over other people's lives" and the consequent need for strong government to check the tyranny of private economic power. "From a purely *negative* concept restrictive of legislative power," Corwin explained, "liberty thus becomes a *positive* concept calling for legislative implementation and protection" (1937b, 531). In this sense, then, government economic regulation in the twentieth century was "more fairly represented as an effort to realize the Lockean and early American conception of property rights (and liberty) . . . than as an attempt to overthrow it" (1936b, 93).

With this recognition, Corwin's historicism moved beyond mere description, becoming transformative and normative. One must not only understand the Constitution's values against the historical-intellectual milieu of the framers but also understand that those values embrace different institutional forms in different historical settings. Corwin could now retain faith in the fundamental purposes of the Constitution while abandoning the framers' "political science" with respect to particular institutional structures. This allowed him to completely reconceptualize the relationship at the heart of the Constitution. No longer would government power need to be held constant by judicial reference to vested rights; now, "man and his happiness are the fixed points of reference—all else is relative, and hence subject to alteration, amendment, or rejection, as circumstances may require" (1936b, 84).

The implications of this theory for constitutional law and the role of the Court followed. Since the Constitution's claim to supremacy could no longer be rooted in its content, or the idea that it embodied certain absolute natural rights, it must now be rooted in its source, the sovereign people as lawmakers. The Constitution was now the people's law rather than the law of some higher, transcendental source. It was "adaptive" and "living" and should be interpreted "as a living statute, palpitating with the purpose of the hour, reenacted with every waking breath of the American people, whose primitive right to determine their institutions is its sole claim to validity as a law and as the matrix of law under out system" (1925, 303).

Years before Alexander Bickel proclaimed the countermajoritarian difficulty as the central problem in constitutional theory (1962), Corwin had recognized its source and resolved it. The difficulty—justifying judicial review in a democracy—was rooted in the historical transformation of constitutional authority from higher law concepts to democratic sovereignty. Its solution required a reduced role for the Court and a larger role for the democratic branches as interpreters of the Constitution. Constitutional meaning became fixed, to the extent it ever does, not as a result of judicial application in particular cases but as a result "of a continued harmony of views among the three departments. It rests, in other words, in the last analysis on the voting power of public opinion" (1938, 6–7). Judicial review was not at an end: it "still has its uses, and important ones," to ensure that the Constitution functioned as an "instrument of power . . . for achievement of progress" and that "the Constitution of a progressive society keeps pace with that society" (1936b, 92). But the era of a judicial supremacy under the pretended enforcement of due process had ended.

Finally, Corwin brought symmetry to his historical analysis. The adaptive Constitution was, after all, what the framers had in mind. New Deal constitutionalism, to the extent that it was revolutionary, was only a "response to a revolution which had already occurred in the facts of everyday living—the kind of revolution which Madison had in mind when he wrote in the *Federalist:* A system of government, meant for duration, ought to contemplate these revolutions, and be able to accommodate itself to them" (1936b, 92–93). And the kind that Corwin's great hero, John Marshall, had in mind when he declared in *McCulloch v. Maryland* (1819) that the Constitution is "intended to endure for ages to come, and, consequently, to be adapted to the various crises of human affairs."

Subsequent scholarship has attacked key points in Corwin's historical analysis, especially his view of Madison's federalism and Marshall's constitutional adaptivity (Garvey 1962). Others have offered defenses against Corwin's dismissal of the higher law conception of constitutional authority (Loss 1981–88, vol. 1).[12] Corwin's contemporary, Thomas Reed Powell, articulated what may remain the strongest argument against Corwin's abandonment of original intent as an interpretive guide to the Constitution: those who abandon it "must give us in [its] place some guides to the way of wisdom in making an indefinite series of practical [political] judgements" (1925, 309). Whose politics should thus replace the authority of the framers?[13] Still, Corwin's ideas remain important and powerful. It might easily be argued that little of original significance has been added to American constitutional theorizing in the half century that has followed.

CORWIN ON JUDICIAL BEHAVIOR AND HISTORICAL INSTITUTIONALISM

The social sciences have today become fragmented, and labels such as *historical institutionalism, behavioralism,* and *rational choice* take on more meaning than they should.[14] Corwin certainly did not think in such terms, though it is clear that history served as the medium of his political science. His commentary on contemporary politics offered historical perspective. He understood presidential powers from their historical growth. He reflected on the judiciary's role by revealing its evolution through the years. He developed a constitutional theory that embraced the historically contingent meaning of its values. History, one biographer noted, "was Corwin's means of grasping the present and building for the future . . . he demonstrated that lessons from the past could guide politics of the present" (Crews 1985, 20).

For Corwin, however, understanding history was the method, not the purpose, of the discipline. Modern political science, he argued, was the "belated offspring of eighteenth-century rationalism, and has taken all its ideals from that source. It sprang from the same matrix as the democratic dogma, and it has heretofore fought in the same ranks and for the same causes as its older relative" (1929, 571). The historical method was thus the way he explored the normative questions central to democratic governance.

Corwin's generation of political scientists had embraced the philosophical realism of the early twentieth century, forcing them to adopt less descriptive, idealized understandings of law and the state. No longer could law and the state be viewed as simple reflections of human nature; they were now reconceptualized as a set of historically evolving normative patterns or institutions that were themselves subject to change through reflection and political choice. Analyzing the development of those patterns and making informed judgments about their continued desirability from the democratic standpoint was the purpose of political science.[15]

Like later behavioral scholars, the leading public law scholars of this time—Corwin, Haines, Powell, Cushman, and Beard—were all legal realists. While they relied on methods of doctrinal and historical analysis, their goal was to understand how law and individual judicial decisions were related to the political forces of democracy. Indeed, in their history of the field, Murphy and Tanenhaus point out that these doctrinally oriented or institutional scholars fully understood the same types of political influences on judicial decision making—ideological, strategic, personal—that later behavioral scholars studied (1972, 13–15). No clearer statement of the realist view is found than in the preface to Cushman's classic 1925 textbook, *Leading Constitutional Decisions:* "The Supreme Court does not do its work in a vacuum. Its decisions on important constitutional questions can be understood in their full significance only when viewed against the background of history, politics, economics, and personality surrounding them and out of which they grew" (p. iii). Or as Corwin conceived judicial decision making, "the constitutional document is little more than a taking-off ground; the journey out and back occurs in a far different medium, of selected precedents, speculative views regarding the nature of the Constitution and the purposes designed to be served by it, and unstated judicial preferences" (1937b, 532).

Corwin's specific contribution to our understanding of judicial behavior must thus be understood as a reflection of his realistic conception of law. But it must also be understood against the view of politics adopted by other contemporary realists and by the behavioralists who followed. Corwin's realism did not lead him to accept a reductionist account of politics—the view that politics is simply the process of who gets what. He rejected much of the popular criticism of the *Lochner*-era Court, which portrayed the justices as simply reading their own economic preferences into the Constitution, a charge echoing Holmes's famous dissent in *Lochner v. New York* (198 U.S. 45, 1905) that "The 14th Amendment does not enact Mr. Herbert Spencer's Social Statics." This idea that judges used law to mask the imposition of their own policy preferences had received important academic support in the work of Beard, whose *The Supreme Court and the Constitution* (1912) and *An Economic Interpretation of the Constitution of the United States* (1913) portrayed both the framers and subsequent judges as consciously using judicial review as a device to secure economic privileges for the propertied class.

Corwin attacked Beard's history and his view of judicial motivation (1914c). Rather than individual-level interests or preferences, Corwin emphasized that judicial decisions were structured by politics at a deeper level. Unlike Beard and the Court's popular critics, Corwin's analysis did not focus on what the Court did as a matter of policy (or on whose interests were advanced) but on what its members believed about the law. Corwin argued that Spencerian ideas of social Darwinism were so pervasive at the turn of the century that they shaped judicial attitudes about the law at the cognitive level. They had been propounded and accepted by society as a set of natural physical laws, on the same footing as gravity or the evolution of species. So it was quite natural that judges would accept these ideas as axiomatic without conscious thought, believing it a happy coincidence that an objective reading of the law reflected those same values. As Corwin notes in one of his more sardonic passages, the naturalness of social Darwinism "came inevitably to impress the naif, simple-minded men who made up the Court of that day, while by an equal inevitability, they proceeded to spin from it a new constitutional law" (1934, 49).

Corwin believed that judicial bias was rarely the consequence of duplicity or insincerity on the part of judges; rather, it was the product of historically changing ideological structures, or institutions, that framed judicial thought and constituted the nature of individual judicial preferences. Other political scientists of Corwin's generation shared this understanding of judicial decision making. Haines, for example, wrote in 1922, "A complex thing like a judicial decision involves factors, personal and legal, which carry us to the very roots of human nature and human conduct. Political prejudice, the influences of narrow and limited legal training with antiquated legal principles and traditions, or class bias having little or no relation to wealth or property interest, are more likely to affect the decision of judges than so-called 'economic interests'" (1922, 49). But no one developed this approach to understanding judicial behavior as prolifically and profoundly as Corwin. His emphasis on the historical-ideological context of judicial decision making and constitutional development, rather than mere internal logic of legal doctrine or the willful imposition of individual judicial preferences, thus represents Corwin's most significant contribution to judicial behavior scholarship.

Guided by his conception of political science's democratic purpose and his belief that political behavior was rational and normatively driven, Corwin was troubled by the behavioralists' effort to emulate the natural sciences. In his most important statement on this subject, "The Democratic Dogma and the Future of Political Science" (1929), he argues that efforts to develop a "laboratory" or "predictive science" of political behavior required a certainty about human motivation that human reason and freedom simply did not permit. Moreover, the methods of such a science required processes of experimentation that simply were not possible in the political world; one simply could not isolate or control for the influence of single factors or variables. Politics would always be too messy, too interconnected, too historically situated and organic in its operation to be vulnerable to positive or formal modeling.

He was especially skeptical of the ability of quantitative methodology to shed light on important political questions. In his presidential address to the APSA, for example, he quipped that if "political science begins talking algebra, it will make no great practical difference whether the people who understand it do so or not" (1932, 3). Even earlier, in his 1923 report to the National Conference on the Science of Politics, Corwin rejected the use of quantitative methods in public law: in contrast to other fields, quantitative methods could tell us little about judicial motivation. Instead, he argued, an "adaptation of the historical method" was the best hope for moving the field "from a purely subjective to a relatively objective basis" (1924, 148).

This is not the place to discuss the merits of the behavioral approach to the study of politics or the validity of attitudinal and rational choice models within the law and courts field.[16] It is worth noting, however, that those who question these approaches do so for reasons echoing Corwin's original concerns, especially his view that positive methodology leads to a reductionist conception of politics and an inability to analyze questions of political motivation (Smith 1988, 1992; Burgess 1993; McCann 1996; Clayton 1999; Gillman 1999). Many new institutionalists have thus returned to the historical method to examine political influences over law and judicial behavior. For example, Howard Gillman (1993) has used the historical-institutionalist approach to challenge prevailing views about judicial decision making during the *Lochner* era. Ronald Kahn (1994) has used this approach to describe the actions of the Burger Court. Mark Graber (1995) has used historical institutionalism to examine the historical development of the doctrine of judicial review and its relationship to democracy. Susan Burgess (1992) and Keith Whittington (1999a) have used it to explore the role of the elected branches in the construction of constitutional meaning. And I have used this approach to make normative arguments about the Supreme Court's administrative jurisprudence (1994) and to explain decision making by the Rehnquist Court (1999).

There are important differences between the new and old historical institutionalisms that merit more attention than can be given to them here. One important distinction is the willingness on the part of new institutionalists to accept a more porous and dynamic conception of institutions and to deemphasize the formal structures of state power and authority as the focus of analysis. While earlier institutional scholars tended to focus on formal structures such as judicial doctrines or constitutional provisions, new institutionalists may be more inclined to emphasize the role of informal norms, myths, and background patterns of social meaning, such as religion, class, race, and gender (see, e.g., Smith 1995; Gillman 1999). I have argued elsewhere that the abandonment of formal or tangible institutions as the subjects of study, especially the move away from linkages to the state, may make it difficult for the new institutionalists to aspire to rigorous normative and empirical analysis (Clayton 1999). Conversely, focusing on the culturally embedded values that attach to informal institutions may place new institutionalists in a better position to understand how institutions have contingent meanings based on the relative power relationships and cultural traditions of different social groups and classes.

Regardless of how institutions are conceptualized, what unifies the new and old institutionalisms is a belief that political science ought to care deeply about the real political world of which it is part and that it must therefore "remain a 'normative,' a 'telic,' science." Corwin reminds us that there is nothing in this purpose that "inhibits one's using scientific, statistical, or any other device of intellectual precision" (1929, 591). The key is for political scientists to intelligently "choose their tools and techniques for the task at hand rather than *vice versa*" (1930, 3). That requires realizing that the "destiny of political science is to do more expertly and more precisely what it has always done; its task is criticism and education regarding the true ends of the state and how best they may be achieved. So far as it contributes to this end, the more of scientific method the better" (1929, 592).

Corwin's commitment to the normative purposes of political science made him the quintessential "public scholar." Ironically, it also damaged his credibility as a scholar at a crucial time in his career. The quest for "scientific" objectivity and the separation of *is* and *ought* questions not only became the impetus for the behavioral revolution that followed Corwin but was also the basis for criticism of Corwin's scholarship and may have put an end to his ambition to a seat on the nation's highest court. In short, what made Corwin's academic work relevant to the real political world also cast a shadow over its authority as an impartial guide. This central problem of how social scientists can retain scientific status for themselves and their subjects while acting as arbiters of social goals and values is a conundrum with which Corwin struggled. It also continues to confront those who have resurrected the historical-institutionalist approach. However, postmodernist critiques of behavioral and other positivist approaches to the social sciences have significantly weakened their claim to objectivity as well, and they consequently find themselves moved to the same side of this question. Why then should political scientists be driven by a normative conception of the discipline? Corwin's response, though not fully resolving the problems, remains perhaps the best answer:

Why should the political scientist spend his time measuring stereotypes planted in the public mind by other people when he could be planting some of his own? The issue, indeed, is not whether the political scientist can have his cake and eat it too, but whether he shall trade his cake for a mass of pottage. And why should society be barred from having a few arbiters of social values who know what scholarly method is, as well as so many of the other sort? (1929, 591–92)

NOTES

1. In Corwin's day, Princeton was an all-male institution.

2. A 1959 study of the use of legal periodicals in Supreme Court opinions named Corwin as the only political scientist among the ten most cited authors (see Newland 1959).

3. The twenty-seven cases in which Corwin's work is cited in an opinion were obtained from a search of Supreme Court opinions on Lexis-Nexis. The cases include: *Yarborough v. Yarborough* (1933), *Adamson v. California* (1947), *Youngstown Sheet & Tube Co. v.* Sawyer (1952), *Abington School District v. Schempp* (1963), *Miranda v. Arizona* (1966), *Nixon v. Fitzgerald* (1982), *New York v. United States* (1992), and, most recently, *Washington v. Glucksberg* (1997).

4. See "Wilson's Friend Flays League at Hoboken Forum," *Hudson Observer*, October 7, 1919.

5. For a discussion of judicial biography in political science and Mason's contributions, see Davis's chapter in this volume.

6. Corwin's books during this period included *The Constitution and What It Means Today* (1920), *The President's Removal Power under the Constitution* (1927), and *The Democratic Dogma and the Future of Political Science and Other Essays* (1930).

7. See, for example, Louis Lyons, "The World's Wise Men," *Boston Globe*, June 19, 1936, 20; and "Savant Indorses F.D.R. Court Plan," *Atlanta Constitution*, February 8, 1937, 1. For a general discussion of the possible appointment, see Crews 1985, 26–31.

8. This account of Corwin's role in the Court-packing controversy and the Senate hearing is drawn from Crews 1985, 28–32.

9. See "Corwin vs. Consistency," *Daily Princetonian*, March 20, 1937, 2; and "Academic Freedom in Discussing the Supreme Court," *Princeton Alumni Weekly*, April 2, 1937, 550.

10. The most thorough treatment of Corwin's constitutional theory is Garvey 1962. See also Loss's (1981–88) introductory essays.

11. For more on the differences between Corwin and earlier constitutional theorists, see Mason and Garvey 1964, ix–xii; Loss 1981–88, 2:19–21.

12. For a contemporary argument along these lines, see Dworkin 1996.

13. For a political scientist's thoughtful alternative to the "default position" defense of original intent, see Whittington 1999b.

14. For thoughtful discussion of this point, see Graber 1999, 2000.

15. See Ethington and McDonagh 1995. I have argued elsewhere that real-

ism differentially affected how political science and the legal academy came to think about law (see Clayton 1999).

16. But see Clayton and Gillman 1999; Gillman and Clayton 1999.

REFERENCES

Beard, Charles. 1912. *The Supreme Court and the Constitution.* New York: Macmillan.

Beard, Charles. 1913. *An Economic Interpretation of the Constitution of the United States.* New York: Macmillan.

Bickel, Alexander. 1962. *The Least Dangerous Branch: The Supreme Court at the Bar of Politics.* Indianapolis: Bobbs-Merrill.

Brigham, John. 1996. *The Constitution of Interests: Beyond the Politics of Rights.* New York: New York University Press.

Burgess, Susan. 1992. *Contest for Constitutional Authority: The Abortion and War Powers Debates.* Lawrence: University Press of Kansas.

Burgess, Susan. 1993. "Beyond Instrumental Politics: The New Institutionalism, Legal Rhetoric, and Judicial Supremacy." *Polity* 25:445–59.

Clayton, Cornell. 1992. *The Politics of Justice: The Attorney General and the Making of Legal Policy.* New York: M. E. Sharpe.

Clayton, Cornell. 1994. "Separate Branches—Separate Politics: Judicial Enforcement of Congressional Intent. *Political Science Quarterly* 109:843–72.

Clayton, Cornell. 1999. "The Supreme Court and Political Jurisprudence: New and Old Institutionalism." In *Supreme Court Decision-Making: New Institutional Approaches,* ed. Clayton and Gillman.

Clayton, Cornell W., and Howard Gillman, eds. 1999. *Supreme Court Decision-Making: New Institutional Approaches.* Chicago: University of Chicago Press.

Cohn, Jonathan. 1999. "When Did Political Science Forget about Politics? Irrational Exuberance." *New Republic,* October 25, 25–31.

Corwin, Edward S. 1911. "The Establishment of Judicial Review." *Michigan Law Review* 9:283–316.

Corwin, Edward S. 1912a. "Income Tax Ratification." *New York Evening Post,* January 25, 8.

Corwin, Edward S. 1912b. "National Power and State Interposition, 1781–1861." *Michigan Law Review* 10:535–51.

Corwin, Edward S. 1913. *National Supremacy: Treaty Power versus State Power.* New York: Holt.

Corwin, Edward S. 1914a. "The Basic Doctrine of American Constitutional Law." *Michigan Law Review* 12:247–76.

Corwin, Edward S. 1914b. *The Doctrine of Judicial Review: Its Legal and Historical Basis and Other Essays.* Princeton: Princeton University Press.

Corwin, Edward S. 1914c. Review of *An Economic Interpretation of the Constitu-*

tion of the United States, by Charles Beard." *History Teacher's Magazine* 5 (February): 65–66.

Corwin, Edward S. 1916. "A 'Firm' Foreign Policy." *New York Evening Post*, October 26, 8.

Corwin, Edward S. 1917a. *The President's Control of Foreign Relations*. Princeton: Princeton University Press.

Corwin, Edward S. 1917b. "War, the Constitution Molder." *New Republic*, June 9, 153–55.

Corwin, Edward S. 1919a. "An Examination of the Covenant." *Review*, June 7, 77–80.

Corwin, Edward S. 1919b. *John Marshall and the Constitution: A Chronicle of the Supreme Court*. New Haven: Yale University Press.

Corwin, Edward S. 1920a. *The Constitution and What It Means Today*. Princeton: Princeton University Press.

Corwin, Edward S. 1920b. "The Worship of the Constitution." *Constitutional Review* 4:3–11.

Corwin, Edward S. 1923. Review of *The Law of the American Constitution*, by Charles K. Burdick. *Michigan Law Review* 22:84–86.

Corwin, Edward S. 1924. "Round Table VI. Public Law." *American Political Science Review* 18:148–54.

Corwin, Edward S. 1925. "Constitution v. Constitutional Theory: The Question for the States v. the Nation." *American Political Science Review* 19:290–304.

Corwin, Edward S. 1927. *The President's Removal Power under the Constitution*. New York: National Municipal League.

Corwin, Edward S. 1928. "The 'Higher Law' Background of American Constitutional Law." *Harvard Law Review* 42:149–85, 365–409.

Corwin, Edward S. 1929. "The Democratic Dogma and the Future of Political Science." *American Political Science Review* 23:569–92.

Corwin, Edward S. 1930. *The Democratic Dogma and the Future of Political Science and Other Essays*. Yenching Political Science Series. Shanghai: Kelly and Walsh, Ltd.

Corwin, Edward S. 1932. "Social Planning under the Constitution—A Study in Perspectives." *American Political Science Review* 26:1–27.

Corwin, Edward S. 1934. *The Twilight of the Supreme Court*. New Haven: Yale University Press.

Corwin, Edward S. 1936a. *The Commerce Power versus States Rights: "Back to the Constitution."* Princeton: Princeton University Press.

Corwin, Edward S. 1936b. "The New Deal in Light of American Political and Constitutional Ideas." Reprinted in Loss, ed., *Corwin on the Constitution*, vol. 3.

Corwin, Edward S. 1937a. "Congress, Supreme Court Could Solve Constitutional 'New Deal' Issues." *Progressive*, January 16, 7–9.

Corwin, Edward S. 1937b. "Standpoint in Constitutional Law." *Boston University Law Review* 17:513–32.

Corwin, Edward S. 1938. *Court over Constitution: A Study of Judicial Review as an Instrument of Popular Government.* Princeton: Princeton University Press.

Corwin, Edward S. 1940a. "E. S. Corwin Comes out in Support of Willkie Because of Third Term and Foreign Relations." *Daily Princetonian*, October 26, 1–4.

Corwin, Edward S. 1940b. *The President: Office and Powers.* New York: New York University Press.

Corwin, Edward S. 1940c. "Statesmanship on the Supreme Court." *American Scholar* 9:159–63.

Corwin, Edward S. 1941. *Constitutional Revolution, Ltd.* Claremont, Calif.: Claremont Colleges.

Corwin, Edward S. 1944. *The Constitution and World Organization.* Princeton: Princeton University Press.

Corwin, Edward S. 1945. "The Dissolving Structure of Our Constitutional Law." *Washington Law Review* 20:185–98.

Corwin, Edward S. 1947. *Total War and the Constitution.* New York: Alfred A. Knopf.

Corwin, Edward S. 1948a. *Liberty against Government: The Rise, Flowering, and Decline of a Famous Juridical Concept.* Baton Rouge: Louisiana State University Press.

Corwin, Edward S. 1948b. "The Supreme Court as National School Board." *Thought* 23:665–83.

Corwin, Edward S. 1950. "The Passing of Dual Federalism." *Virginia Law Review* 36:1–24.

Corwin, Edward S. 1951. *A Constitution of Powers in a Secular State.* Charlottesville, Va.: Michie.

Corwin, Edward S. 1952. "Bowing out 'Clear and Present Danger.'" *Notre Dame Law Review* 27:325–59.

Corwin, Edward S. 1953. *The Constitution of the U.S. Annotated: Analysis and Interpretation.* U.S. Congress, Senate, 82nd Cong., 2nd sess., 1953. 5. Doc. 170.

Corwin, Edward S. 1978. *Edward S. Corwin's The Constitution and What It Means Today.* 14th ed. Rev. Harold W. Chase and Craig R. Ducat. Princeton: Princeton University Press.

Corwin, Edward S., and Jack W. Peltason. 1949. *Understanding the Constitution.* New York: Sloane.

Corwin, Edward S., Jack W. Peltason, and Sue Davis. 2000. *Corwin and Peltason's Understanding the Constitution.* Fort Worth, Tex.: Harcourt College.

Corwin, Edward S., and Louis W. Koenig. 1956. *The Presidency Today.* New York: New York University Press.

Crews, Kenneth D. 1985. *Edward S. Corwin and the American Constitution.* Westport, Conn.: Greenwood Press.

Crews, Kenneth D., ed. 1986. *Corwin's Constitution: Essays and Insights of Edwin S. Corwin.* New York: Greenwood Press.

Dworkin, Ronald. 1996. *Freedom's Law: The Moral Reading of the American Constitution.* Cambridge: Harvard University Press.

Eakin, Emily. 2000. "Political Scientists Are in a Revolution Instead of Watching." *New York Times,* November 4, 1–4.

Ethington, Philip, and Eileen McDonagh. 1995. "The Common Space of Social Science Inquiry." *Polity* 28:85–90.

Garvey, Gerald. 1962. "Corwin on the Constitution: The Content and Context of Modern American Constitutional Theory." Ph.D. diss., Princeton University.

Gillman, Howard. 1993. *The Constitution Besieged: The Rise and Demise of Lochner Era Police Powers Jurisprudence.* Durham: Duke University Press.

Gillman, Howard. 1999. "The Court as an Idea, Not a Building (or a Game): Interpretive Institutionalism and the Analysis of Supreme Court Decision-Making," in Clayton and Gillman, eds., *Supreme Court Decision-Making: New Institutional Approaches.*

Gillman, Howard, and Cornell W. Clayton. 1999. *The Supreme Court in American Politics: New Institutionalist Interpretations.* Lawrence: University Press of Kansas.

Graber, Mark. 1995. "The Nonmajoritarian Difficulty: Legislative Deference to the Judiciary." *Studies in American Political Development* 7:35–73.

Graber, Mark. 1999. "Historical Institutionalism as/and Scholarship." *Law and Courts Newsletter* 9:14–15.

Graber, Mark. 2000. "The Banality of Diversity." *Law and Courts Newsletter* 10:4–10.

Haines, Charles Grove. 1922. "General Observations on the Effects of Personal, Political, and Economic Influences in the Decisions of Judges." Reprinted in *Judicial Behavior: A Reader in Theory and Research,* ed. Glendon Schubert. Chicago: Rand McNally.

Kahn, Ronald. 1994. *The Supreme Court and Constitutional Theory.* Lawrence: University Press of Kansas.

Loss, Richard, ed. 1976. *Presidental Power and the Constitution: Essays by Edward Corwin.* Ithaca: Cornell University Press.

Loss, Richard, ed. 1981–88. *Corwin on the Constitution.* 3 vols. Ithaca: Cornell University Press.

Mason, Alpheus T. 1981. "Corwin, Edward Samuel." In *Dictionary of American Biography.* John A. Garraty, ed. (supp. 7, pp. 146–47). New York: Charles Scribner's Sons.

Mason, Alpheus T., and Gerald Garvey, eds. 1964. *American Constitutional History: Essays by Edward S. Corwin.* New York: Harper and Row.

McCann, Michael. 1996. "Causal versus Constitutive Explanations (or, On the Difficulty of Being So Positive . . .)." *Law and Social Inquiry* 21:457–82.

Murphy, Walter, and Joseph Tanenhaus. 1972. *The Study of Public Law.* New York: Random House.

Newland, Chester A. 1959. "Legal Periodicals and the United States Supreme Court." *Midwest Journal of Political Science* 3:58–74.

"NRA Constitutional, Prof. Corwin Says." 1933. *New York Times*, November 7, 3.

Paxson, Frederic L., Edward S. Corwin, and Samuel B. Harding, eds. 1918. *War Cyclopedia: A Handbook for Ready Reference on the Great War.* Washington, D.C.: U.S. Government Printing Office.

Powell, Thomas Reed. 1925. "Comment on Mr. Corwin's Paper." *American Political Science Review* 19:306–15.

Rossiter, Clinton. 1955. "Prefatory Note," in *The "Higher Law" Background of American Constitutional Law*, by Edward S. Corwin. Ithaca: Cornell University Press.

Smith, Rogers. 1988. "Political Jurisprudence, the 'New Historical,' and the Future of Public Law." *American Political Science Review* 82:89–108.

Smith, Rogers. 1992. "If Politics Matters: Implications for a 'New Institutionalism.'" *Studies in American Political Development* 6:1–36.

Smith, Rogers. 1995. "Ideas, Institutions and Strategic Choices." *Polity* 28:135–40.

Special Committee on the Constitution. 1937. *Memorandum of the Special Committee on the Constitution: Special Committee Memorandum Number One.* Washington, D.C.: National Policy Committee.

Whittington, Keith E.. 1999a. *Constitutional Construction: Divided Powers and Constitutional Meaning.* Cambridge: Harvard University Press.

Whittington, Keith E. 1999b. *Constitutional Interpretation.* Lawrence: University Press of Kansas.

Wilson, Woodrow, and Edward S. Corwin. 1921. *Division and Reunion: With Additional Chapters Bringing the Narrative down to the End of 1918.* New York: Longmans Green.

CHAPTER 13

Alpheus Thomas Mason:
Piercing the Judicial Veil

Sue Davis

I first encountered Alpheus Thomas Mason's work when I was an undergraduate in the early 1970s. *American Constitutional Law* (Mason and Beaney 1954) was the textbook in my first constitutional law course.[1] Then, as a graduate student at the University of California, Santa Barbara a few years later, I read *Free Government in the Making* (1949) in Gordon Baker's course in American political thought.[2] A number of years passed before I realized that those two books represented only a small portion of Mason's work. He published twenty-two books in addition to a vast number of articles. He is best known, however, for his pioneering studies in judicial biography. Indeed, in the 1960s Mason was often considered to be the preeminent judicial biographer in the country. His award-winning *Brandeis: A Free Man's Life* (1946) and *Harlan Fiske Stone: Pillar of the Law* (1956) not only offered a myriad of detail about the early lives and developing ideas of those justices but explored the inner dynamics of the Court, revealing the extent to which it operated as a political institution. In 1964 he extended his examination of the Court as a political institution with his study of the office of the chief justice in *William Howard Taft: Chief Justice.*

Mason's biographies moved far beyond traditional doctrinal analysis to examine in rich detail the historical, political, and institutional contexts in which his justices operated and explored the links between those contexts and judicial decision making. As Clyde Spillenger wrote, Mason revealed the Supreme Court "as a human and political institution" (1993, 723). He not only explored the relationships among the justices but also the connections between the Court and the other institutions of the federal government. In keeping with this book's theme, this chapter focuses primarily on the ways that Mason's work reflected an institutionalist perspective and how it provided a foundation on which the new historical-institutionalist scholars have built. His approach was thoroughly historical, building as it did on the work of his mentor and predecessor, Edward S. Corwin. Moreover, Mason's judicial biographies and studies of the Supreme Court invariably linked judicial decision making to American political ideas. Indeed, as Walter F. Murphy observed, "Alph looked on each decision of the Supreme Court as, if not a morality play, at least as a clash of political theories. His constant intellectual goal was to seek out the bases for 'free government' and the roles that ideas and actors played in moving the United States closer to that concept" (2000).

After graduating from Dickinson College in 1920, Mason entered graduate school at Princeton University and earned his Ph.D. in politics in 1923. He taught at Trinity College (now Duke University) in Durham, North Carolina, for two years and then returned to Princeton as an assistant professor in the department of politics. Just as he had during Mason's days as a graduate student, Corwin continued to play a major role in the development of the younger man's scholarship and teaching.[3] Indeed, Corwin's influence continued even after his retirement in 1946, when Mason became McCormick Professor of Jurisprudence at Princeton, a position he occupied until he retired in 1968. He died in 1989.

In 1965 John P. Frank referred to Mason as "the country's foremost judicial biographer" and noted that he was the only major biographer in American history to have written about three justices (369). Jack W. Peltason speculated that Mason might "be known in history as the man who made judicial biography worthwhile" (1964, 227). After Mason's death, Murphy noted that if Mason "did not invent the field of judicial biography, he perfected it" (1990, 72).

The full-scale, scholarly judicial biography began in 1916 with Albert J. Beveridge's publication of the first volume of *The Life of John Marshall*. Nevertheless, as Peltason noted, the increasing interest in judicial biography during the 1940s coincided with the rise of legal realism (1964, 215). Indeed, judicial biographies would become increasingly popular once scholars began to recognize that judges did not simply discover the law in precedent and statutes but that extralegal factors also had an important impact on justices' decision making. If the political, social, and economic environment influences Supreme Court decisions, and if the justices' values and intra-Court interaction affect votes and opinions, analysts of the judiciary need all the information they can get about the lives of the justices—information that is invariably found in the best judicial biographies.

JUSTICE BRANDEIS:
INSTITUTIONAL CONTEXT

Two major themes lie at the center of the new historical institutional-ism, an approach that rose to prominence in the subfield of law and courts during the last fifteen years of the twentieth century (see, for example, March and Olsen 1984). First, institutional arrangements and social processes are profoundly important in understanding polit-ical phenomena. Indeed, it is essential to recognize institutions as independent forces in the judicial decision-making process. For the new institutionalists, the relationship between political actors and institutional structures is interactive—political actors both shape and are shaped by those structures. Second, the new historical institution-alism denies that the behavior of political actors can be explained solely with reference to instrumentalist rational self-interest. The new institutionalists argue that politics invariably "involves processes of normative persuasion and deliberation through which political actors come to transform their senses of their interests and their very identi-ties" (Smith 1992, 5). In other words, institutions shape the interests and values of political actors, and those interests and values also influence institutions.

Alpheus Thomas Mason's judicial biographies stand out as precur-sors to new historical-institutionalist scholarship. Mason's historical approach developed under Corwin's influence and remained a con-stant. Mason consistently assigned a preeminent role to the historical and social contexts in which a justice's ideas and values evolved. He also undertook thorough examinations of justices' impact on the Supreme Court as well as of the institution's effect had in shaping its members' preferences. Moreover, he consistently refused to explain the behavior of justices in simple terms of rational self-interest. Indeed, Mason's jus-tices were individuals whose interests and values were shaped by a com-plex combination of historical, institutional, and social factors.

Mason's first full-scale biography, *Brandeis: A Free Man's Life*, offered an in-depth treatment of the justice's life and work, but it was not Mason's first study of the justice. He published two earlier volumes, *Brandeis: Lawyer and Judge in the Modern State* (1933) and *The Brandeis Way: A Case Study in the Workings of Democracy* (1938). Mason's institu-tionalist perspective was discernible even in these early works, which also reflected the growing influence of legal realism. For example, he declared, "Constitutional theory usually reflects the training, and also the economic and social background of the judge himself. The judge does not and cannot live in a vacuum. He is, and ought to be, influenced by the life about him" (1933, 2). Moreover, Mason criticized the Court for invalidating economic and social legislation and for continuing to adhere to an outmoded formalistic method of decision making. He called on justices to study social and economic data so that the Court might keep pace with changing conditions. In examining Brandeis's life and work, Mason emphasized the justice's commitment to social justice and his belief that the law must be flexible enough to keep abreast of changing social and economic conditions. Institutions, as Mason explained Brandeis's beliefs, must keep in touch with the "outer world" (1933, 25). Regarding the famous Brandeis Brief, Mason inferred that once the Supreme Court adopted the method of considering social and economic facts in support of challenged legislation, it would continue to do so: "And one thinks the Court assumed at least an implied obligation to insist upon this new method of dealing with similar cases—certainly before setting legislation aside" (1933, 109).

In *The Brandeis Way*, Mason examined the Massachusetts Savings Bank Life Insurance, which Brandeis founded, as an example of his social and political philosophy. What stands out most about Mason's analysis is Brandeis's commitment to the proposition that political ideas and institutions must adapt to the realities of twentieth-century industrial society. Thus, the facts of social and economic life made it necessary for the role of government to expand to protect individual liberties and democracy. Indeed, the meaning of liberty and democracy were invariably connected to changing economic facts and institutions. The same was true for the law, as Mason explained. Brandeis conceived of the law as "never an abstract thing, divorced and set apart, but an integral factor at work in our mental climate and social life. Legal and constitutional questions are not found isolated as if in compartments, but are rooted throughout our entire social and economic being" (1938, 25).[4]

Brandeis gave Mason access to his nonjudicial papers and documents, memoranda, diaries, notebooks, and personal correspondence. Those materials; interviews with Brandeis's family, friends, and professional associates; and a vital understanding of the early years of the twentieth century made it possible for Mason to place his study of Brandeis squarely in historical and institutional context. In *Brandeis: A Free Man's Life* (1946), Mason most clearly linked Brandeis's numerous activities on behalf of reform—including unionization, worker management, and the setting of maximum hours and minimum wages—to early-twentieth-century economic and social conditions. Mason explains Brandeis's 1908 introduction of the Brandeis Brief in *Muller v.*

Oregon (in defense of an Oregon statute limiting women's working hours) as an application of his ideas about the need for regulation of industry amid industrial America's rapidly changing conditions.

The Brandeis Brief was to have a major impact on the law, as the Court began to accept the introduction of extralegal facts and as Brandeis, after his ascension to the Court in 1916, continued to use the method of bringing in facts from outside a particular case. For example, in his dissent from the decision to invalidate the Washington statute prohibiting private employment agencies from charging fees for finding jobs for workers, Brandeis pointed to the "chronic problem of unemployment—perhaps the gravest and most difficult problem of modern industry. . . . Students of the larger problem of unemployment appear to agree that establishment of an adequate system of employment offices or labor exchanges is an indispensable first step toward its solution" (*Adams v. Tanner*, 244 U.S. 590 [1917], quoted in Mason 1946, 517).

Mason also emphasized that Brandeis's early dissents represented an innovation in judicial method—the dissenting opinion as an educational tool "to explore and illumine not only the law but also the relations which law governs, bringing to bear relevant law reports, secular literature, information from pertinent sources in a persuasive demonstration of what the law ought to be in terms of social justice" (1946, 518). Brandeis's method was particularly apparent in labor cases, where he consistently applied his earlier conviction that workers must have the right to organize and insisted on the principle of the presumption of constitutionality. In Mason's estimation, Brandeis's dissents had an important impact on the Court not only because his views on major constitutional issues eventually prevailed but also because they brought a new approach to collegial decision making. In addition, in his dissenting opinions in the cases after World War I involving freedom of expression, Brandeis was quick to point out the inconsistency in protecting property and contract rights but not civil liberties. In 1920, when the majority upheld a Minnesota statue that prohibited the teaching of pacifism, he dissented, noting his

> difficulty in believing that the liberty guaranteed by the Constitution, which has been held to protect against state denial the right of an employer to discriminate against a workman because he is a member of a trade union, the right of a businessman to conduct a private employment agency . . . although the legislature deems it inimical to the public welfare, does not include liberty to teach, either in the privacy of the home or publicly, the doctrine of

pacifism. . . . I cannot believe that the liberty guaranteed by the Fourteenth Amendment includes only liberty to acquire and to enjoy property. (*Gilbert v. Minnesota*, 254 U.S. 325 [1920], quoted in Mason 1946, 564)

It is noteworthy that analyzing Brandeis, Mason implicitly rejected the notion that the behavior of political actors can be explained with reference to calculated, rational self-interest. Brandeis was a wealthy corporate lawyer by 1895, yet he became convinced that he had a public responsibility, an obligation to work for the public interest and to limit the power and wealth of big business and industry.

Mason devoted only one quarter of *Brandeis: A Free Man's Life* to the justice's work on the Court. This limited treatment of Brandeis's twenty-three years on the Court resulted from Mason's inability to secure access to the justice's judicial papers. Justice Brandeis gave control of his Court papers to Felix Frankfurter, who refused to allow Mason access. According to Clyde Spillenger, Frankfurter had not approved of Mason's earlier work on Brandeis and believed that "no mere professor of politics could properly elucidate the work of the Supreme Court" (Spillenger 1993, 725). Thus, when Mason wrote to Frankfurter in 1940 asking about letters and documents that might be relevant to the Brandeis biography, Frankfurter passed the inquiry back to Brandeis and noted that "my experience with Mason and the quality of his work would not lead me to select him for such a delicate and creative and art-demanding enterprise" as a biography of Brandeis (quoted in Spillenger 1993, 725). Brandeis then advised Frankfurter not to disclose Court-related information that the justice had related during their long years of correspondence. Even though Brandeis's request did not apply specifically to the judicial working papers that he had given to Frankfurter, he later told Mason later that he felt justified in denying the author access to the papers because a tacit "mutual understanding" led him to believe that these were Brandeis's wishes. Years later, when Mason had begun his study of the office of the chief justice, he again asked Frankfurter to allow him access to Brandeis's judicial papers. Frankfurter, who had by that time given unrestricted access to the papers to Paul Freund and Alexander Bickel, continued to deny access to Mason, noting that Brandeis had "very rigorously enjoined me not to make available to you, in connection with your biography, anything he wrote to me regarding Court matters. His reasons for this restriction apply even more rigorously of course to access to his working papers" (quoted in Spillenger 1993, 726).

HARLAN FISKE STONE: THE
EVOLUTION OF A JUSTICE AND
INTRA-COURT DYNAMICS

In contrast to the limited access he had to Brandeis's papers, Mason had full access to the papers of Harlan Fiske Stone, which the chief justice's family loaned to him. Thus, with *Harlan Fiske Stone: Pillar of the Law*, Mason became the first judicial biographer to utilize a twentieth-century justice's Court papers: as Mason put it, with those papers, he managed to get inside the conference. Thus, Mason's biography of Stone became the first study of the Supreme Court to explore the inner workings of the institution. Just as with Brandeis, Mason made an effort to explore every facet of Stone's life and to put it into historical context. He visited the places of Stone's youth; met with former professional associates, family, and friends; and in general immersed himself in the chief justice's life.

Mason's work reflected an understanding of the requirements of studying judicial decision making that would later become more self-conscious and systematic in the hands of the new institutionalists. The new historical institutionalism acknowledges that all political behavior must be explained with some reference to individual values, attitudes, and personalities (Gillman and Clayton 1999). The new institutionalists nevertheless recognize the importance of looking beyond the policy preferences of individual justices to the contexts in which they operate. Institutional arrangements and cultural contexts, these scholars emphasize, are central factors in a political actor's choices. Moreover, justices may well develop a sense of obligation to act in certain ways that are consistent with the expectations and responsibilities of the Court. In short, institutional norms and contexts have a major impact on a justice's attitudes and goals. In turn, as justices develop goals and behave accordingly, the justices have their own impact on the Court.

Although Mason's biography of Stone came close to winning a Pulitzer Prize,[5] it was severely criticized by some academic reviewers, particularly law professors who felt that the biographer had lost his objectivity, that he did not present an objective portrait of Stone but "the man as he saw himself. Indeed probably few biographers have so completely and successfully identified themselves with their subjects as Mason has with Stone" (Kurland 1957, 1321). Some commentators, moreover, found inaccuracies in Mason's treatment of the case law and considered his revelations about intra-Court relationships to be inappropriate and unproductive, even vulgar (see, for example, Dunham

1957). More important for present purposes, however, *Harlan Fiske Stone: Pillar of the Law*, like other institutionalist political science work at the time, reflected a broad concern with institutions and contexts as important sources of a justice's decision making. Although Mason did not engage in a systematic analysis of institutional influences, he described in great detail early-twentieth-century social, economic, and political conditions and thus provided a rich historical context for his study of Stone's work on the Court. Moreover, Mason paid great attention to the development of Stone's legal and political ideas and methods from the beginning of his career as a law professor, through his time as dean of Columbia Law School and attorney general, to the end of his tenure as chief justice. Mason conjectured connections between Stone's pre-Court experiences and his decision making on the Court. For example, during World War I, Stone, then dean of Columbia Law School, was a member of a board of inquiry that handled the cases of conscientious objectors. Later, amid the patriotic and intolerant frenzy that followed the war, he helped to settle a case of a faculty member who had been forced to resign because he had expressed opposition to forcing conscientious objectors to fight. In 1920 Stone served on a committee of protest against Attorney General A. Mitchell Palmer's "Red Raids." Stone expressed his conviction that the

> only methods which hold out promise for the triumph of democratic institutions over the assaults now directed against them are firm but impartial adherence to the law by those in authority, and ceaseless and untiring efforts to educate and enlighten these men and especially the class to whom they make their appeal, together with the fullest discussion and most searching analysis of the doctrines which they preach. (quoted in Mason 1956, 114)

Mason suggested that Stone's support for the preferred-freedoms doctrine, the basis of which he articulated in the *Carolene Products* footnote, and his lone dissent in the first flag-salute case could be traced to those earlier experiences (*United States v. Carolene Products Co.*, 304 U.S. 144 [1938]; *Minersville School District v. Gobitis*, 310 U.S. 586 [1940]).

Mason also noted that in 1915 Stone disagreed with Brandeis's contention that if the law, lawyers, and judges were to keep pace with changing conditions, legal thinkers needed to study "economics and sociology and politics which embody the facts and present problems of today" (quoted in Mason 1956, 118). Stone argued instead that ideas of social and political justice must not be substituted for valid principles of judicial decisions. But by 1923 his views had shifted so that he could express some support for sociological jurisprudence, the goal of which, as he wrote, was to "establish in our legal thinking that trinity of juridical theory—logic, history, and the 'method of sociology'—as the source of all true legal doctrine" (quoted in Mason 1956, 120). Although Stone agreed that the law needed to adapt, he favored some scientific and systematic development that would be free from the problems of both codification and sociological jurisprudence. Mason summarized the changes in Stone's view as follows.

> Thus the period of Stone's deanship was a time of intellectual turmoil, of increasing awareness that, without considerable modification, the common law system of justice could not survive. The system was imperiled from without as well as from within. The problem, as he conceived of it, was to find ways of enabling the law to cope with the impact of industrialism without doing violence to the genius of the common law, or to his own intellectual and political inheritance.
>
> In 1912 he derided social justice as "absolutely without value" as a "test for the correctness of judicial decisions." Three years later he denounced its proponents as calamity howlers, attempting "to formulate law on the basis of the legislator's view of what is sound public policy based upon his observations of social conditions." In 1923 he recognized that sociological jurisprudence need not be tied inextricably to the political aspirations of captious "do-gooders." Sociological jurisprudence had a contribution to make—in checking the actual operation of legal rules, in measuring their effectiveness in controlling human behavior, in ascertaining the facts of "social utility." "But," he insisted, "we must have other resources if we are to make of the common law the great and abiding system which it may become." (Mason 1956, 123–24)

Stone became an associate justice in 1925, a time that Mason describes as dominated by exploitative large-scale business with leaders preaching the "gospel of goods." Stone joined an activist conservative Court headed by Chief Justice William Howard Taft, a Court that, in Mason's assessment, construed as sacrosanct liberty of contract and the rights of large-scale business against government regulation. That context stands out prominently in Mason's exploration of Stone's judicial career. Moreover, in his study of Stone, Mason described some of the most important developments in the Court's history, including its hostility to economic regulation, the constitutional crisis engendered by

President Franklin Roosevelt's response to that hostility, and the Court's adoption of a new role as guardian of individual rights.

Stone's position on the constitutionality of economic regulation was unknown when he joined the Court, but in 1927 he wrote a dissenting opinion for himself, Oliver Wendell Holmes, and Brandeis objecting to the majority's decision invalidating a New York law that restricted the markup on theater tickets to fifty cents more than the price printed on the ticket. While the majority condemned the law as an exercise in price fixing, Stone argued that the regulation was within the state's power in a situation where "a combination of circumstance seriously curtails the regulative forces of competition, so that buyers and sellers are placed at a disadvantage in the bargaining struggle that a legislature might reasonably anticipate serious consequences to the community as a whole" (*Ribnik v. McBride*, 277 U.S. 350 [1928], quoted in Mason 1956, 239). Stone soon allied himself with Holmes and Brandeis against the conservative majority's determination to use the due process clause of the Fourteenth Amendment to invalidate state regulations. In 1928 Stone delivered an address to the American Bar Association, castigating the majority for resorting to what he referred to as stultifying formulas to protect property from government regulation.

According to Mason, Stone's relationships with Holmes and Brandeis had a major impact on Stone's understanding of the law: "In Holmes and Brandeis the newcomer found an approach to the law and a breadth of view upon which he could build his own" (1956, 254). The Three Musketeers thus supported each other in the struggle against the old formalistic jurisprudence. As a result, the initially warm relationship between Stone and Chief Justice Taft cooled considerably. Stone wrote few majority opinions and dissented more frequently. He expressed his reluctance to dissent and said that he would

> often acquiesce in opinions with which I do not fully agree so you may know how strongly I have really felt in order to participate in so many dissents as I have recently. But where a prevailing view rests upon what appear to me to be false economic notions, or upon reasoning and analogies which will not bear analysis, I think great service is done with respect to the future development of the law, in pointing out the fallacies on which the prevailing view appears to rest even though the particular ruling made should never be overruled. (quoted in Mason 1956, 260)

Taft retired in 1930, and in the midst of rumors that Stone would be Herbert Hoover's choice for chief justice, the president nominated

Charles Evans Hughes to the position. Like its predecessor, the Hughes Court was polarized over the constitutional status of economic regulations and the relationship between the federal government and the states. Furthermore, as Mason made clear, it was necessary to view the dynamics of the Court in conjunction with Great Depression economic conditions, Hoover's inability to deal with the crisis, and Franklin Delano Roosevelt's election.

The majority subsequently struck down legislation that was central to the New Deal, prompting a constitutional crisis. After Roosevelt was reelected in 1936 with 98 percent of the electoral vote, he introduced the Court-packing plan, which would have added a new position on the Court for every justice who had reached the age of seventy and did not retire. Roosevelt's plan would have allowed him to nominate six new justices, who would be crucial in forming a majority to uphold New Deal programs. Mason explains the continuing evolution of Stone's legal and political views against this background. In late 1935, for example, the justice noted that new ideas had come to him "in light of recent history." He wrote, "Judges ought to be more prayerful. I am going to develop the habit. . . . When we attempt to be God, or even to do the job of the legislature, the reduction of what we do to its lowest terms is very revealing and in the long run, I hope, is going to be very useful" (quoted in Mason 1956, 399).

Stone's opinions began to reflect increasing fervor, perhaps, Mason noted, because "none of his colleagues foresaw more clearly the disaster that might follow in the wake of judicial decisions warped to satisfy the purblind demands of practical politics" (1956, 402). When a six-person majority invalidated the tax provision of the Agricultural Adjustment Act in early 1936, Stone wrote a dissent that was strong enough to prompt Justice Owen Roberts, the author of the majority opinion, to complain to the chief justice. Although Hughes did not raise the issue with Stone, the chief suggested that Roberts discuss it with Brandeis, who probably prompted Stone finally to soften the tone of his dissent (Mason 1956, 408).[6]

According to Mason, commentators relied on Stone's dissent to denounce the majority for usurping the powers of Congress and substituting their own views for those of elected officials. Indeed, Stone's dissent and Roberts's majority opinion framed the debate in the law journals and in the popular literature. As a result, Stone was viewed as a liberal and an enthusiastic supporter of the New Deal. The justice's view, however, was more closely linked to his conception of a judge's proper role: "My duty as a judge is simple and explicit. It is to see that the Constitution functions. It is not for the judge to approve or disapprove social policy in his decisions" (quoted in Mason 1956, 417).

Stone opposed Roosevelt's proposal to pack the Court on the grounds that it would interfere with the function of the judiciary: "Granting all the faults that are attributed to the Court, it still embodies in its traditions and habits of work, and in the performance of its functions essential to our form of government, values which are inestimable" (quoted in Mason 1956, 445). Still, Stone conceded that some change in the Court was necessary. Despite his efforts to avoid involvement, Stone was drawn into the controversy. Roosevelt invoked the justice's dissenting opinions when in announcing the Court-packing plan, and the president's opponents tried to get Stone to publicly denounce the scheme. Although he did not speak out on the matter, his somewhat ambivalent position meant that both sides claimed his support. Mason's description of Stone's important role in the constitutional crisis brought sharply into focus an image of the Court as an institution operating in conjunction with the broader political system.

Mason also emphasizes Stone's role in the Court's adoption of a new role as protector of individual rights with his famous footnote 4 in *United States v. Carolene Products* in 1938. The second and third paragraphs of the footnote, Mason notes, were drafted by Stone's law clerk, Louis Lusky, and Stone adopted them with only minor changes. The footnote manifested Stone's increasing concern for civil liberties and his conviction that the Court had a responsibility to protect them. Indeed, the day after the decision was announced, he wrote to a colleague of his deep concern "about the increasing racial and religious intolerance which seems to bedevil the world, and which I greatly fear may be augmented in this country" (quoted in Mason 1956, 515).

Access to Stone's Court papers meant that Mason was able to examine the interaction between Stone and his colleagues concerning the drafting of opinions. Thus, readers are offered a view of the way that Stone—when he was in the majority—worked to get a final opinion that was most consistent with own views. Similarly, when Stone was in dissent, he negotiated with the other dissenters and the members of the majority so that the opinions would be as strong as possible. Indeed, what stands out most in Mason's exploration of Stone's tenure on the Court is the way the author delved into the justices' negotiations between the first draft and final version of an opinion.

In 1941 Roosevelt nominated Stone to replace Hughes as chief justice. When Stone assumed the center chair, Mason observed, the Court's procedures became noticeably more relaxed. Stone labored to get "his team of wild horses to pull together," but the task became increasingly difficult, particularly in light of the fact that the new Roosevelt Court no longer divided along clear economic lines (Mason 1956, 578–81). During Stone's tenure, disagreement among the justices increased, concurring opinions proliferated, and by the end of his second term, nearly half of the decisions contained a dissent. Moreover, the justices ceased to confine their disputes to the conference and increasingly expressed disagreement in their opinions. Mason attributed such developments primarily to the complex nature of the issues, noting that the differences were "but a normal, healthy part of decision-making in a free society" (quoted in Mason 1956, 605). In addition, Mason pointed out that because Stone was convinced that disagreements should be worked out rather than glossed over, he allowed more discussion of the issues than had either Taft or Hughes. Overall, however, Mason observed a lack of "convincing evidence that the Chief Justice proved especially adept in smoothing troubled waters" (1956, 612).

The impact of Stone's tenure as chief justice has been the focus of several studies of the Court's decision-making process, all of which have built on Mason's work. David J. Danelski (1978) asserted that Stone's style of presiding over conferences and assigning opinions was lacking in the qualities of either social or task leadership. Thomas Walker, Lee Epstein, and William Dixon (1988) concluded that Stone's style of leadership was a major factor in the demise of the institutional norm of consensus. David M. O'Brien (1999) challenged that conclusion, pointing to a variety of institutional factors that contributed to the erosion of the norm of consensus. The way Mason connected Stone's leadership to a variety of factors—including the interaction among the justices and the Court's relationship to the other branches of the federal government—further reveals Mason's work to be squarely in the institutionalist tradition.

WILLIAM HOWARD TAFT:
THE CHIEF JUSTICE IN
INSTITUTIONAL PERSPECTIVE

Mason published his study of Chief Justice William Howard Taft just four years before retiring from Princeton. Mason conceived the work as the first installment of a comprehensive analysis of the office of the chief justice of the United States, but he did not complete that project. It is possible that he found his historical approach and the discontinuities of the office of the chief justice to be incompatible.[7]

Like Mason's studies of Brandeis and Stone, *William Howard Taft: Chief Justice* placed its subject firmly in historical context and emphasized the connections between the Court and the development of American political ideas. Taft began his career in the last quarter of the nineteenth century. Profoundly influenced by the ideas of social Darwinist William Graham Sumner, Taft was strongly opposed to populist and progressive reform. He was instead dedicated to reforming the judicial system to make it more efficient and thus more powerful. Indeed, he advocated discretionary review for the Supreme Court almost twenty years before the Judiciary Act of 1925. The conservative Taft, according to Mason, saw an important link between judicial reform and the continued protection of property rights against popular reform: "By putting its own house in order, the legal profession might counteract the disruptive influence of wild-eyed reformers" (Mason 1964b, 54).

Taft argued that the judiciary should not be merely an auxiliary check but should constitute the primary check on majorities. He continued his campaign to reorganize the judiciary after he left the presidency and became a law professor at Yale. As chief justice, he faced considerable opposition from some members of Congress, particularly in the early 1920s, when there was a great deal of criticism of the Court. Indeed, in 1924 the Progressive Party's platform included a constitutional amendment giving Congress the authority to reenact a statute that the Court had invalidated (Mason 1964b, 92). Taft was faced with the task of winning approval of his reform proposals from the Senate Judiciary Committee, which contained some of the Court's harshest critics. He characterized those senators as "the wretched personnel of the Judiciary Committee," the individuals "'least fitted for the Judiciary Committee' who had sought places on it because they could not enhance their 'reputation as lawyers in any other way'" (quoted in Mason 1964b, 95).

The picture that Mason painted of Taft's efforts on behalf of judicial reform represents the institutionalist approach at its best insofar as it underlines the extent to which the legislature imposes constraints on the power of the chief justice and the judiciary in general. Taft's proposal to give the chief justice authority to assign district judges to any of the U.S. circuits failed; his plan for a judicial conference, headed by the chief justice, that would recommend legislation and revision of the rules of procedure also met with serious opposition. To members of both the House and Senate Judiciary Committees, Taft seemed to be trying to usurp the power of Congress to establish courts. To many it seemed that Taft was trying to transform the federal judiciary into a Prussian military organization or a judicial system similar to that of Britain, with its lord chancellor. Nevertheless, in 1922 Congress approved legislation that established the chief justice as head of the federal judiciary and created the judicial conference with the power to suggest legislation.

The important task of giving the Court control over its own docket remained. Taft assigned two justices, Willis Van Devanter and James McReynolds, to help the Senate Judiciary Committee draft such a bill. The chief justice also assisted, and Justice George Sutherland helped by presenting the proposal to the committee. Thus, justices rather than members of Congress drafted the bill. With passage of the Judiciary Act of 1925, the only portion of Taft's reform agenda that remained unfulfilled was the unification of the Federal Rules of Procedure, with the Supreme Court in charge of formulating the rules. The chief justice lobbied doggedly for that reform, but because it was invariably viewed by members of Congress as a measure that would further aggrandize the power of the judiciary, it failed. Taft used the same lobbying tactics to secure congressional support for the construction of a building for the Supreme Court.

The summary of Chief Justice Taft's important contribution to the administration of the Supreme Court reveals the extent to which interinstitutional dynamics permeate Mason's analysis.

> Taft's lobbying has no precedent in Supreme Court annals. Few of his predecessors were either prepared for or capable of plunging into the shifting congressional tides. . . . Years of public service had educated Taft in the ways of party politics. After leaving the White House, he canvassed the nation in quest of support for judicial reform. By the time he ascended to the bench, thousands of influential Americans knew that he favored far-reaching correctives. Bringing to the Court a definite program, he launched it within days after his appointment. He drafted legislation, exerted vast influence on individual legislators, pressed his program at congressional hearings, enlisted the support of the American Bar Association members and newspaper editors. By utilizing in various combinations these instruments of power, he got much of what he wanted. (Mason 1956, 137)

Just as in *Harlan Fiske Stone: Pillar of the Law*, Mason's analysis of Taft's work on the Court included a detailed discussion of the manner in which the chief justice managed intra-Court dynamics. Unlike

Stone, Taft made every effort to "mass the Court." He tried to persuade by example, frowned on dissents, exploited personal courtesy and charm, maximized the assignment and reassignment powers, and relied on the expertise of his associates (1956, 198). Although Mason's study of Taft has been characterized as an "informative but bland account . . . a workmanlike job at best" (Spillenger 1993, 732), it clearly provided that basis on which subsequent studies of studies of the institutional workings of the Court would build.

THE SUPREME COURT AND AMERICAN POLITICAL THOUGHT: MASON'S INSTITUTIONALIST APPROACH

The preceding discussion of Mason's judicial biographies emphasized the extent to which he used a thoroughgoing institutionalist perspective. Institutionalism also dominates Mason's two books on the Supreme Court, *The Supreme Court: From Taft to Warren* (1958) and *The Supreme Court: Palladium of Freedom* (1962).[8] His treatment of the doctrine of liberty of contract serves as a telling illustration. The influence of legal realism is readily apparent—Mason severely criticized the justices for grafting their theories and political agendas onto the Constitution and emphasized the extent to which the old notion that judges merely discover the law was an inaccurate description of the process of decision making. It is important that Mason also linked the Court's activism during the *Lochner* era to the structure of the Constitution and the resulting tension between popular sovereignty and judicial review. Moreover, he emphasized the link between the doctrine of liberty of contract and the social Darwinism of Herbert Spencer. In Mason's assessment, although the doctrine of liberty of contract was inconsistent with the Constitution, it was nevertheless grounded in some of the basic ideas in American constitutionalism that could be traced back to the founding.

More recently, scholars who have adopted the new historical-institutionalist perspective have reinterpreted the jurisprudence of the *Lochner* era. Howard Gillman (1993), like Mason, links judicial doctrine to the ideology structured into the Constitution by the framers and traces changes in that doctrine to industrialization and the rise of the modern state. But Gillman challenges the traditional view that early-twentieth-century judicial decisions striking down economic regulations represented an abuse of judicial power. Analyzing the Court's decisions in light of the constitutional ideology that was averse to class politics, Gillman argues that the judiciary was acting in a way that was consistent with an established constitutional tradition by maintaining a distinction between valid economic regulations that legitimately promoted a genuine public purpose and invalid class legislation that was designed to advance the special or partial interests of particular groups or classes.

Overall, the theme that runs most prominently through Mason's studies of the Supreme Court is the shifting perception of the Court's role in the U.S. political system. That the Court makes policy and has a responsibility for protecting rights and balancing the distribution of powers among the various institutions of government was a given for Mason. As *The Supreme Court: Palladium of Freedom* concluded

> The Court is the palladium of free government. Its decisions, based on reason and authority, have a moral force far exceeding that of the purse or sword. . . . The Court's firm command over the hearts and minds of men is not unrelated to the contemplative pause and the sober second thought its restraining power entails. The Justices inform by both precept and example. They make vocal and audible the ideals and values that might otherwise be silenced. Far from discouraging civic responsibility, judicial decisions and Supreme Court opinions are among the greatest educational forces in America. In passing judgment on living issues, in resolving complexities which are at any given moment puzzling and dividing us, it teaches the demanding lesson of free government. (178)

CONCLUSION

Alpheus Thomas Mason, a pioneer in judicial biography, never neglected the institutional context of his subjects. The design of the Constitution, the ideas that predominated in the late eighteenth century, and the nation's major nineteenth-century transformation as a result of industrialization invariably played a prominent role in his studies. Moreover, his work emphasized the interplay among the Supreme Court, the presidency, and Congress as well as the relationships among the nine justices and the constraints the dynamics of those relationships imposed on judicial decision making. Finally, Mason's judicial biographies explored not only the impact that each of his justices had on the Supreme Court but also the institutional constraints under which his subjects worked. More recently, new historical-institutionalist scholars have built on the foundation that Mason established. In so doing, they have developed new interpretations and have sought to clarify links between institutional factors and judicial decision making.

NOTES

I am most grateful to Walter F. Murphy for his valuable advice and for providing a copy of Mason's autobiography. I am entirely responsible for errors or misinterpretations.

1. Subsequent editions were coauthored first by William M. Beaney and then by D. Grier Stephenson.

2. This work is a collection of readings with introductory essays. (Subsequent editions were published, with the 4th ed. [1985] coedited by Gordon E. Baker.) Mason and Leach 1959 contains the essays without the readings.

3. Under the system of precepts, the courses are managed by a senior faculty member, with junior faculty acting as precepts, running seminars within the course in which students meet in small groups to discuss assigned reading material. Murphy reports that Corwin allowed Mason to teach constitutional interpretation only once in twenty years—when Corwin was in China (2000).

4. Mason (1941) also published a study of Brandeis's role in the Pinchot-Ballinger affair, which involved an attempt by President Taft to cover up a scheme developed by his secretary of the interior to sell government-owned lands in Alaska to private commercial interests. There were congressional hearings to investigate the matter, and Brandeis represented *Collier's Weekly*, a journal threatened with a libel suit for publishing a report about governmental improprieties.

5. Joseph P. Kennedy is reputed to have engaged in some maneuvering on behalf of John F. Kennedy's *Profiles in Courage*, which ultimately won the Pulitzer that year.

6. The case was *United States v. Butler*, 297 U.S. 1 (1936).

7. Walter F. Murphy (2000) also pointed out that Mason's lifelong commitment to teaching could have contributed to his failure to complete the study of the office of the chief justice. He taught his courses with a historical approach and connected them to his research. The chief justiceship, however, was not conducive to the development of such a course.

8. Later published as *The Supreme Court: From Taft to Burger* (1979).

REFERENCES

Beveridge, Albert J. 1916–19. *The Life of John Marshall.* 4 vols. Boston: Houghton Mifflin.

Clayton, Cornell W., and Howard Gillman, eds. 1999. *Supreme Court Decision-Making: New Institutionalist Approaches.* Chicago: University of Chicago Press.

Danelski, David J. 1978. "The Influence of the Chief Justice in the Decisional Process of the Supreme Court." In *American Court Systems: Readings in Judicial Process and Behavior*, ed. Sheldon Goldman and Austin Sarat. San Francisco: W. H. Freeman.

Dietze, Gottfried. 1964. *Essays on the American Constitution: A Commemorative Volume in Honor of Alpheus T. Mason*. Englewood Cliffs, NJ: Prentice-Hall.

Dunham, Allison. 1957. Review of *Harlan Fiske Stone: Pillar of the Law*, by Alpheus T. Mason. *University of Chicago Law Review* 24:794–97.

Frank, John P. 1965. Review of *William Howard Taft, Chief Justice (1964–65)* by Alpheus Thomas Mason. *Michigan Law Review* 64:363–70.

Gillman, Howard. 1993. *The Constitution Besieged: The Rise and Demise of Lochner Era Police Powers Jurisprudence*. Durham, NC: Duke University Press.

Gillman, Howard, and Cornell W. Clayton. 1999. "Beyond Judicial Attitudes: Institutional Approaches to Supreme Court Decision-Making." In *Supreme Court Decision-Making: New Institutionalist Approaches*, ed. Cornell W. Clayton and Howard Gillman, 1–12. Chicago: University of Chicago Press.

Kurland, Philip B. 1957. Review of *Harlan Fiske Stone: Pillar of the Law*, by Alpheus T. Mason. *Harvard Law Review* 70:1318–25.

March, James G., and Johan P. Olsen. 1984. "The New Institutionalism: Organizational Factors in Political Life." *American Political Science Review* 78:734–49.

Mason, Alpheus Thomas. 1932. "Brandeis: Student of Social and Economic Science." *University of Pennsylvania Law Review* 80:799–841.

Mason, Alpheus Thomas. 1933. *Brandeis: Lawyer and Judge in the Modern State*. Princeton: Princeton University Press. Later published as *Brandeis and the Modern State* (Washington, DC: National Home Library Foundation, 1936).

Mason, Alpheus Thomas. 1938. *The Brandeis Way: A Case Study in the Workings of Democracy*. Princeton: Princeton University Press.

Mason, Alpheus Thomas. 1941. *Bureaucracy Convicts Itself*. New York: Viking Press.

Mason, Alpheus Thomas. 1946. *Brandeis: A Free Man's Life*. New York: Viking Press.

Mason, Alpheus Thomas. 1949. *Free Government in the Making: Readings in American Political Thought*. New York: Oxford University Press.

Mason, Alpheus Thomas. 1956. *Harlan Fiske Stone: Pillar of the Law*. New York: Viking Press.

Mason, Alpheus Thomas. 1958. *The Supreme Court from Taft to Warren*. Baton Rouge: Louisiana State University Press.

Mason, Alpheus Thomas. 1962. *The Supreme Court: Palladium of Freedom*. Ann Arbor: University of Michigan Press.

Mason, Alpheus Thomas. 1964a. *The States Rights Debate: Antifederalism and the Constitution*. Englewood Cliffs, NJ: Prentice-Hall.

Mason, Alpheus Thomas. 1964b. *William Howard Taft: Chief Justice.* New York: Simon and Schuster.

Mason, Alpheus Thomas. 1987. "In Pursuit of Happiness: A Teacher's Story." Unpublished manuscript.

Mason, Alpheus Thomas. 1979. *The Supreme Court from Taft to Burger.* 3d ed. Baton Rouge: Louisiana State University Press. (Originally published as *The Supreme Court from Taft to Warren* [1958].)

Mason, Alpheus Thomas, and William M. Beaney. 1954. *American Constitutional Law: Introductory Essays and Selected Cases.* Englewood Cliffs, NJ: Prentice-Hall.

Mason, Alpheus Thomas, and Richard H. Leach. 1959. *In Quest of Freedom: American Political Thought and Practice.* Englewood Cliffs, NJ: Prentice-Hall.

Murphy, Walter F. 1990. "Alpheus Thomas Mason." *PS: Political Science and Politics* 23:71–73.

Murphy, Walter F. 2000. Letter to author, July 17.

O'Brien, David M. 1999. "Institutional Norms and Supreme Court Opinions: On Reconsidering the Rise of Individual Opinions." In *Supreme Court Decision-Making: New Institutionalist Approaches,* ed. Cornell W. Clayton and Howard Gillman, 91–113. Chicago: University of Chicago Press.

Peltason, J. W. 1964. "Supreme Court Biography and the Study of Public Law." In *Essays on the American Constitution: A Commemorative Volume in Honor of Alpheus T. Mason,* ed. Gottfried Dietze, 215–27. Englewood Cliffs, NJ: Prentice-Hall.

Smith, Rogers M. 1988. "Political Jurisprudence, the 'New Institutionalism,' and the Future of Public Law." *American Political Science Review* 82:89–108.

Smith, Rogers M. 1992. "If Politics Matters: Implications for a 'New Institutionalism.'" *Studies in American Political Development* 6:1–36.

Spillenger, Clyde. 1993. "Lifting the Veil: The Judicial Biographies of Alpheus T. Mason." *Reviews in American History* 21:723–34.

Walker, Thomas G., Lee Epstein, and William J. Dixon. 1988. "On the Mysterious Demise of Consensual Norms in the United States Supreme Court." *Journal of Politics* 50:362–89.

CHAPTER 14

Robert G. McCloskey, Historical Institutionalism, and the Arts of Judicial Governance

Howard Gillman

[Throughout American history], certain dominant judicial interests take form, certain dominant values emerge, and the Court can be observed struggling to formulate a judicial role that will reinforce those interests and values within the subtle limit of judicial capability.
—Robert G. McCloskey, *The American Supreme Court*

Pioneer may not be the right word to describe Robert Green McCloskey. From his position in Harvard's government department in the 1950s and 1960s, he paid very little attention to putative social science innovations in the study of law and courts. His former students cannot recall him ever talking about judicial behaviorism; the reductionist psychology and politics of Schubert-style analysis could not be reconciled with McCloskey's more nuanced (but also less testable) view of the elements that shape the Court's decisions. Unlike some contemporary advocates of rational choice, McCloskey did not view Walter Murphy's *The Elements of Judicial Strategy* (1964) as an important methodological breakthrough. McCloskey liked the book a lot—in fact, he wrote a laudatory letter strongly recommending Murphy's promotion at Princeton—but mostly because of Murphy's sophisticated reading of the Court's recent history and his useful summary of the sorts of political considerations that justices routinely take into account. McCloskey put that book in the same category as another book published a few years earlier, Richard Neustadt's *Presidential Power* (1960), a thoughtful (historically grounded) summary of a similar set of issues relating to the exercise of power in a different branch of government. This was high praise, but not because either of these works pioneered advances in the social sciences. They just made the field smarter about the nature of institutional politics.

In the mid-1950s, when McCloskey turned his attention from intellectual history to Supreme Court politics, he considered himself to be working out of a tradition that had been started by Edward Corwin, Thomas Reed Powell, Charles Warren, Charles Grove Haines, and Alpheus Mason and that was being extended by contemporaries such as C. Herman Pritchett, Jack Peltason, Walter Murphy, and (soon enough) McCloskey's student, Martin Shapiro, among others. They differed somewhat in their approaches, but they all shared a belief that scholars had to view the Court as part of the larger structure of American politics. Corwin, Powell, Warren, and Haines had pioneered historical-political analyses of Supreme Court decision making (see Murphy and Tanenhaus 1972). McCloskey appreciated how Mason had made everyone aware of bargaining and strategic decision making on the Supreme Court (see esp. Mason 1956, 360–65, 399–402; 1958); McCloskey also thought that Pritchett (1948, 1954) had usefully pointed out emergent voting blocs on the modern Court. McCloskey drew on this work, but he was not the sort to think that it could be improved through the development of more formal or sophisticated methods. What was needed, if anything, was additional work that proffered some smart theoretical syntheses of the historical record. McCloskey did this better than almost anyone. But more than that, as he thought about the emergent Warren Court in real time, he also offered innovative perspectives on the Court's role in the political system, the Court's relationship to American politics more broadly, and the nature of the Court's institutional capabilities. In the process, McCloskey helped transform the disparate elements of "traditional" public law scholarship into the serious practice of historical-institutional analysis.

In ignoring some of the methodological developments that the field of public law would later embrace to a fault, McCloskey reflected the common sense of his department. The government department at Harvard was, as Martin Shapiro recalls, as close to a history department as any political science department in the United States. Students would learn about Dahl, Truman, Arrow, Riker, March, and Simon, but the faculty was more interested in politics than political science as such, which meant immersion in theory and history—diplomatic, institutional, legal, intellectual, and otherwise. It also meant that there were no obvious boundaries between empirical and normative scholarship. Value-free politics was oxymoronic; after all, what was the point of writing about something like the Supreme Court unless one wanted to say something about its role in the political system?

In this department, McCloskey was originally an intellectual historian interested in how particular "areas of American life" related to the currents of American political development (McCloskey 1951, vi). In 1951 he wrote *American Conservatism in the Age of Enterprise, 1865–1910*, a well-regarded analysis of conservative thought that blended a historian's sensitivity to context with a passion for democratic values.[1] Even after turning his attention to other matters, McCloskey, not his friend and colleague, Louis Hartz, taught the department's seminars in American political thought. McCloskey never strayed too far from these roots. In his classic political history, *The American Supreme Court* (2000), he wrote that because "the members of the Supreme Court are children of their times," a "chronicle of Court doctrine tends to be, in a general way, an intellectual history of America" (122).[2]

But McCloskey's work amounted to much more than an intellectual history of Supreme Court doctrine, and in the following sections I will draw attention to those lines of argument and analysis that make up his brand of historical institutionalism. They include the following claims: (1) institutions should be understood in terms of the distinctive "roles" they play within a larger structure of governance and authority; (2) these roles are normative (and must be engaged as such) but also reflect constellations of power and interest within changing historical contexts; (3) the Supreme Court's institutional characteristics shape the distinctive way in which justices attempt to exercise power and maintain their authority and legitimacy; and (4) the Court's capacity to exercise power depends on its ability to generate sufficient support for its role from powerful interests and constituencies.

Given this understanding of the nature of institutions, it is no wonder that McCloskey would also insist on a more holistic and interpretive approach to institutional behavior. He knew that

> there were those who would confine all evaluation to the historical-technical category [of legal accuracy] and would pronounce it illegitimate even to consider the issues of power or ethics. There are others so dedicated to a value-oriented assessment that they regard legalistic strictures as mere pettifoggery, and probably still others who would prefer to think of the Court purely in terms of its power to govern. It might be sufficient comment on such viewpoints to say that, whatever our preferences, these three different judgment criteria persist in turning up in the debates over judicial behavior; we cannot tame the subject to our own liking, however pleasant this might be. (1972, 293)

Given the nature of the institution, he considered it inevitable and important that scholars debate the role of law in the Court's decisions, but he also consistently pointed out that the justices of every historical era made claims about the special role of courts in the political system, and he believed that understanding these claims was essential both to a complete empirical account of the Supreme Court and to a normative assessment of the institution's practices. By offering his own normative and empirical assessments of the Supreme Court in American politics, McCloskey helped push public law scholarship toward what one of his students referred to as "political jurisprudence" (Shapiro 1964, 1984).

THE SUPREME COURT'S ROLE IN THE POLITICAL SYSTEM

Public law scholarship in the 1970s and 1980s treated the Supreme Court as having one fairly abstract role in the political system—to act as a "policymaker." This characterization allowed researchers to treat the Court as the institutional equivalent of any other policy-making branch of government. In turn, this assumption led to a focus on how judges' personal characteristics influenced their policy-making choices. Little attention was paid to the ways in which the Court's institutional characteristics or the larger system-wide expectations about the proper functions of courts influenced the kind of policy-making the justices chose to engage in or avoid. Theoretically, the dominant approaches to the study of Supreme Court politics—focusing on the "personal policy preferences" of the decision makers (the justices)—could have just as easily applied to the actions of local school boards.

By contrast, when McCloskey first began writing about the Court in 1956, he believed that the point of departure for any understanding of this institution was the particular role that it played in the political system. He began his 1956 article "The Supreme Court Finds a Role" by distinguishing those ("the innocent") who "subscribed, more or less whole-heartedly, to the amiable myths of our native jurisprudence" that "courts are the mere instruments of the law, and can will nothing" from those ("the initiated") who believe that law is merely what the judges say and that the Supreme Court is a "participant in the formation of public policy" (McCloskey 1972, 129).[3] He agreed that "the innocent" view was "beyond any reasonable hope of mending," but he still felt it was necessary to warn the initiated that "no sophisticated observer imagines that the Court is simply a free-wheeling superlegislature" (130). Like all institutions, the Court's behavior reflected its caretakers' beliefs about the proper place of their institution in the political system—in other words, institutions act as if they have a distinctive role to play in a larger system of shared powers and responsibilities. As McCloskey put it in *The American Supreme Court*, the Court's actions "can be broadly understood as an endless search for a position in American government that is appropriate" to particular historical circumstances (2000, 15).

Underlying this search was a shared consensus among the justices about the basic "constitutional powers and duties" of their institution. There has been a long-standing understanding among most national power holders that "the judiciary will help in charting the path of governmental policy," and from that has developed "a rough division of labor" that assumes "that the legislature can focus largely on the task of 'interest representation,' while passing on to the courts a substantial share of the responsibility for considering the long-term constitutional questions that continually arise" (2000, 10–11). While McCloskey was aware that the legislature often spoke for constitutional traditions and that the judiciary often represented interests, he thought that this distinction was a useful starting point for understanding the particular way in which the Court established and reestablished its place among the institutions of national government. Put another way, to understand the Supreme Court, it was best to start with Article III of the Constitution, which laid out the Court's basic institutional responsibilities (deciding cases and controversies) and preoccupations (clarifying the meaning of federal law, including the Constitution). The Court's role, therefore, is to make policy with respect to a specific set of issues—most notably relating to the limits on the powers of various institutions in the political system—but not necessarily all issues (for example, setting the prime rate). This role was broad enough to involve the Court in most important public policy debates but was also distinct enough to allow observers to pay attention to the ways in which the Court differed from the Congress or the presidency.

SUPREME COURT DECISION MAKING AND PATTERNS OF POLITICAL INTEREST

Within these broad boundaries, McCloskey understood that the Court "is an agency in the American governing process, an agency with a mind and a will and influence of its own" (2000, xv). He also believed it important to emphasize the ways in which the justices' minds were typically aligned with certain dominant values and interests. Toward this end, McCloskey identified three great periods of constitutional development: 1789 to the close of the Civil War, when the justices focused primarily on the "value of preserving the American Union"; 1865 to 1937, when concerns about Union were replaced with concerns about the role of government in regulating capitalism; and 1937 to the mid-1950s, when debates about economic regulation were replaced by new questions about civil rights and liberties in the age of Jim Crow and totalitarianism (2000, 15–16, 67–69, 121–23). Similarly, when McCloskey first took interest in the emergent Warren Court in 1956, he suggested that the Court's post-1937 jurisprudence could be organized into three distinct phases: the phase of "judicial New Dealism," when the justices seemed mostly to be "concerned to protect the values that had been enshrined by more recent political history"; a second phase when the Court reacted in "uncertain and inchoate" ways to the challenge of totalitarianism; and a "phase of maturity," arrived at during the just completed 1955 term, when the Court attempted to reconcile a commitment to national security with a commitment to civil rights and liberties (1972, 133–36). In general, "the interests and values, and hence the role, of the Court have shifted fundamentally and often in the presence of shifting national conditions. . . . It is hard to find a single historical instance when the Court has stood firm for very long against a really clear wave of public demand" (2000, 230).

McCloskey was not alone in urging readers to link Supreme Court politics to certain dominant interests in particular historical periods. This had been a hallmark of the historical work of Corwin, Warren, Haines, and Mason. Moreover, a year after McCloskey started writing about the Warren Court, Robert Dahl published his now-famous article "Decision-Making in a Democracy: The Supreme Court as a National Policy-Maker" (1957), in which he argued that the Supreme Court almost always aligned itself with the prevailing coalitions of the national government. Dahl's version of the argument was more quantitative than McCloskey's and more clear about how the mechanism of judicial appointments made it likely that the Supreme Court would be broadly interested in upholding acts of Congress. But Dahl paid a price for his methodology, since his discussion of the Supreme Court as a policymaker paid no attention to the substance of the Court's policies or to its role as a national supervisor of state behavior.[4] While not narrowly "reproducible" in the same way as Dahl's study, McCloskey's more interpretive and historical orientation had some compensations, such as abilities to trace the Court's attitude toward state lawmaking, to move beyond decision-making patterns to provide an explanation for the substance of judicial policy-making, and to spell out the circumstances under which the Court would be inclined to impose limits on national power rather than just "legitimate" it by upholding legislation.

McCloskey was always careful to situate the Court's policy preferences within the dominant policy debates of a particular political context. The ahistorical language of *liberal* and *conservative* was not adequate for understanding the concerns of Federalist justices at the beginning of the republic or the various ways in which Jacksonian justices reconciled their views of federalism, commercial development, and slavery. McCloskey knew that the Court typically lined up with dominant opinion, but he also knew that there was no need to assume that the Court would not turn its power against the national government, particularly at times when dominant power holders were themselves divided on the appropriateness of national legislation, as with the expansions of national regulatory authority in the 1890s and early 1900s, the battle over the New Deal in the mid-1930s, Truman's seizure of the steel plants, or even the campaign against so-called subversives in the 1950s.

Much of McCloskey's best work on the Warren Court consisted of a careful tracing of how judicial opinion reflected the ways in which political leaders were reacting to changing circumstances: the consensus after 1937 around the "New Deal mentality" of innovative national economic regulation and support for labor; the reaction against labor and "subversives" in the 1940s; the 1950s efforts to promote a vision of more "humane democracy" through increasing judicial supervision of civil rights and domestic security programs. His efforts to trace the cautious rise of the Warren Court's more "activist" approach to civil liberties continued in his 1957 article, "Useful Toil or the Paths of Glory?" in which he continued explore whether the Court might be making "a transition between the extreme forbearance of the Vinson Court and a future period of full-scale judicial activism" (1972, 160). The inclination of at least some justices toward a more aggressive role "is stimulated by certain contemporary factors," including "the encouragement of what may loosely be called the liberal community"; at the same time, "whether the Court is preparing to move ahead to dubious battle or settle for the lesser glory and risk may be a difficult question precisely because it is now in process of determination" (1972, 188–89, 161). Within a year, after Congress reacted to the Court's modest efforts to impose some statutory or procedural limits on the domestic subversion program, McCloskey commented that the context had changed in such a way as to encourage the Court to pull back from the implications of some of its broader pronouncements (1958b).

One of the principal benefits of adopting this approach was that, unlike judicial behavioralists, McCloskey could say something about the origins of judicial attitudes. Rather than treat the source of the justices' preferences as irrelevant to public law scholarship, McCloskey wanted to make it a centerpiece. This was simply part of the overall process by which the Court could be seen as part of a larger political system, one that often shared the Court's concerns and preoccupations and that sometimes battled with the justices over how best to cope with these contexts.

Moreover, this careful attention to the justices' claims about their proper role in the political system also allowed McCloskey to engage them as normative and not merely empirical-explanatory features of judicial politics. His 1958 collection of *Essays in Constitutional Law* was prompted by his interest in constructing a more modern "theory about the place of the Constitution and the Court in our socio-political order," which he considered to be "one of the most pressing items on the agenda of those who think and care about government in the United States" (1958a, 12, 19). As a passionate advocate of democratic values, he supported much of the Court's work on behalf of "humane democracy," but when Congress tried to fight back, he suggested that

> it is not perhaps too early to sound a soft note of alarm, to urge that the Court's existing role in the American polity is a noble and appropriate one, to hope that the justices will go slow in reasserting their sometime place at the vortex of politics. . . . The Court has served both the judicial tradition and the American republic most usefully when it has kept to a path of duty more consistent with its real expertise—insisting upon a decent regard for regularity and fairness, enforcing the plain command of the Constitution when it was really plain, but respecting the judgment of the other branches always, and most especially in those matters of high political decision that are the peculiar responsibility of the legislative and executive authorities. (1972, 190–91)[5]

THE ARTS OF
JUDICIAL GOVERNANCE

McCloskey's efforts to show the relationship between the Court's role and various historical contexts were, in many respects, extensions of the sort of intellectual history to which he was accustomed. What made him an institutional analyst rather than merely a doctrinal historian was his sensitivity to the political challenges facing the justices as they attempted to secure their place in the political system. McCloskey helped us better understand how "the Court learned to be a political institution and to behave accordingly" (2000, 231).[6]

McCloskey placed particular emphasis on the challenges presented to these policymakers by virtue of their special institutional setting. He insisted that there are "limitations implied by the fact that the Supreme Court is expected to be both a 'court' in the orthodox sense of the word and something very much more as well." It was "perfectly true" for critics to point out that the Supreme Court "is a willing, policy-making, *political* body." But this view "tended to foster an oversimplification of its own":

> "legal realists," impressed by the discovery that the Supreme Court was more than a court, were sometimes prone to treat it as if it were not a court at all, as if its "courthood" were a pure facade for political functions indistinguishable from those performed by the legislature. Such a view bypasses everything that is really interesting about the institution and obscures, as much as the discredited old mythology ever did, its true nature. (2000, 11–12)

McCloskey believed that the need to reconcile policy-making and judicial functions accounts for the constraints on the Court's ability to promote a preferred role in the political system. "The Court's claim on the American mind derives from the myth of an impartial, judicious tribunal whose duty it is to preserve our sense of continuity with the fundamental law. . . . Though the judges do enter this realm of policy-making, they enter with their robes on, and they can never (or at any rate seldom) take them off; they are both empowered and restricted by their 'courtly' attributes." To fail to take this into account would be "to align the judicial power squarely with the legislative power and to erase the differentiation of function that is the Court's basis for being." It would also be to ignore one of the first lessons learned by the justices, "that their tribunal must be a court, as well as seem one, if it is to retain its power. The idea of fundamental law as a force in its own right, distinguishable from today's popular will, can only be maintained by a pattern of Court behavior that emphasizes the separation" (2000, 12–13).

Among other things, McCloskey meant to point out certain obvious aspects of judicial politics that were underappreciated when the focus was merely on courts as generic policymakers. He noted how judges could exercise power only in the context of a properly presented case and even then had only a limited set of tools on which to rely—mostly striking down or upholding others' actions. These modest options could be used impressively, but as the mainstay of the Court's arsenal, they paled in comparison to the weapons at the disposal of Congress and the president. McCloskey also suggested the Court, like all institutions, had to be mindful of the political system's general expectations about what a legitimate exercise of power looks like, and this required the Court to find a role in the political system that was more or less in tune with popular opinion or the preferences of powerful constituencies. This view led him to offer important insights into the early development of judicial power, such as the Jay Court's refusal to offer an official opinion on the legality of the Neutrality Proclamation or to take up administrative responsibilities relating to the settlement of the claims of war veterans. As he put it, "the refusal to perform 'non-judicial' functions reflected a shrewd insight—that the Court's position would ultimately depend on preserving its difference from the other branches of government" (2000, 20).

Like most judicial scholars who lived through the New Deal battles, he was also extremely mindful of how the Supreme Court's potential vulnerability to the other branches' reactions when those institutions felt that the Court was overreaching. In his Supreme Court history, McCloskey carefully situated John Marshall's maneuvering in *Marbury v. Madison* in the context of the Jeffersonians' concerns about (if not outright hostility toward) judicial power (including the Chase impeachment), and he placed great significance on Marshall's decision to uphold the Republican repeal of the Judiciary Act of 1801. Marshall's battles with Spencer Roane and the Virginia Supreme Court in cases such as *Cohens v. Virginia* received similar treatment (see Graber 1995). While McCloskey did not use the specific language of rational choice (see Knight and Epstein 1996), he was assuredly aware of the idea of strategic decision making. Before he began his examination of the Marshall Court's constitutional vision, McCloskey stressed that those judges had "begun to learn the arts of judicial governance: the necessity to avoid, if possible, head-on collisions with the dominant political forces of the moment; the undesirability of claiming too much too soon; the great advantage of taking the long view, especially when others take the short; the usefulness of identifying judicial claims to authority with the claims of the Constitution" (2000, 34).

With these assumptions, McCloskey expressed both support and concern for the Warren Court's developing commitment to civil rights and liberties. He did not think that the Court should buckle under to the pressures of Congress; after all, "if John Marshall's court had recoiled whenever opposition in Congress seemed probable, the cor-

nerstones of American constitutionalism would never had been laid"
(1972, 194). At the same time, "a Court which exalts civil liberties must
take care that it be able to reach and supervise the governmental
devices by which civil liberties may be infringed." He was heartened
that few on the Court followed Justice Clark's practice of almost complete deference to Congress on issues of civil liberties, but by 1958
McCloskey also thought that "the civil liberties position adopted by the
Chief Justice and Justices Black and Douglas smacks strongly of the
judicial absolutism of the pre-1937 era," and he expressed satisfaction
that "a working majority seems firmly planted on a middle ground
between this contingent on the one extreme and Mr. Justice Clark on
the other" (1972, 217–19).

McCloskey was not alone in his preoccupation with these interinstitutional struggles in the late 1950s. These same events also sent Pritchett (1961) and Murphy (1962) to the typewriter to provide an even
more focused account of judicial politics in context. (See also Murphy
1959 on lower court resistance to *Brown*.) In "Deeds without Doctrines" (1962a), McCloskey noted that the Court's restraint in the face
of congressional protests "has helped to temper the critical climate"
(1972, 222).[7] But when in 1962 he became the first political scientist
asked to write the high-profile foreword to the *Harvard Law Review*,
McCloskey (1962c) focused on a new development that concerned
him—the justices' decision to enter the political thicket of reapportionment. He noted that "it is hard to recall a decision in modern history
which has had such an immediate and significant effect on the practice
course of events, or—against excepting the *Segregation Cases*—which
seems to contain such a potential for influencing that course in the
future." For McCloskey, the key question was whether "the subject will
turn out to be judicially manageable," and his major concern about this
move was that it ran the risk of undermining the central "differentiation of function" that distinguished courts from legislatures in the
political system. Assuming that "a prudent court will seek always to
minimize doctrinal developments that cut so close to the very fulcrum
of judicial power," McCloskey noted that the Court now had the
option either of requiring merely that legislatures following certain
procedural requirements for popular consent of districting decisions or
of requiring that the courts "go behind these procedural considerations
and undertake to approve or disapprove the actual distribution of legislative seats," focusing on per capita equality and then evaluating
whether departures based on geography, economics, or other local factors should be considered "reasonable." He believed that this second

approach "carries the judiciary into an uncircumscribed realm of moral and practical choices that is indistinguishable from the legislative realm and in which judicial competence to judge wisely is something less than self-evident" (1972, 266, 277–78, 283–85, 288).[8]

At the same time, given the extraordinary willingness of state courts and legislatures to reexamine their systems of apportionment, McCloskey did admit that it is

> as if the decision catalyzed a new political synthesis that was already straining, so to speak, to come into being. . . . Court decisions have not always generated such a ready—almost over-ready—spirit of compliance. When a decision fails to strike a responsive chord in the public breast, the tendency is at best to abide by its minimum compulsions grudgingly interpreted. The tendency suggested by early reactions to the reapportionment decision seems very different from this, and it may warrant the conjecture that the Court here happened to hit upon what the students of public opinion might call a latent consensus. (1972, 266)[9]

McCloskey had expressed elsewhere that the Supreme Court needed to be mindful of public opinion when it exercised power, and it was possible that, in this context, the latent consensus might provide the Court with enough cover to proceed more aggressively than he would have expected based on the historical record. Still, it would soon be clear that the Warren Court's more confident assertions of judicial power after 1961 had prompted McCloskey to rethink his traditional emphasis on prudence and caution, and within a short time he was in a position to more fully develop an alternative basis for the exercise of judicial power.

JUDICIAL POWER AND CONSTITUENCIES OF SUPPORT

Two years after McCloskey's *Harvard Law Review* essay, Murphy (1964) provided an outstanding summary of the sorts of considerations that McCloskey believed to be central to the art of judicial governance. In a 1965 essay entitled "Principles, Power, and Values," McCloskey called Murphy's *The Elements of Judicial Strategy* "by far the most thorough discussion to date of the Supreme Court and the power question," meaning the elements that determine "whether the Court has the power to do a thing, as distinguished from the question of whether it has the right to do it" (1972, 304–5).[10] McCloskey's writings had previously focused on the circumstances that typically required the Supreme Court to exercise power cautiously. In coming to grips with the mature Warren Court, McCloskey was ready to talk more about the political determinants of judicial activism.

In *The American Supreme Court*, he noted that while "judges have no organized party machine to call on," this does not mean "that the Court has no constituency. . . . No institution in a democratic society could become and remain potent unless it could count on a solid block of public opinion that would rally to its side in a pinch." For the Court, this has traditionally meant two kinds of supporters, those "who are attached to the idea of the rule of law" and "those who happen to be gratified by the course of policy that judges are pursuing at the moment" (2000, 47). In reviewing the Court's political difficulties in the late 1950s, McCloskey noted that *Brown* "had created an atmosphere of sectional hostility and laid the basis for an alliance between the proponents of segregation and the proponents of harsh anti-subversive laws" (1972, 193). But now he also noticed that while "resistance and retaliation from some quarters may tend to restrict the Court's power, . . . support from other quarters may simultaneously augment it." This was another way of saying "that the Court's power is not entirely its own, that its capability depends in part on a preponderance of friends over enemies" (1972, 307–8).

McCloskey reached a more expansive understanding of the nature of judicial power by the time he wrote his final essay, "Reflections on the Warren Court," published in 1965, nine years after he had begun his journey with this institution.[11] Since he had started writing about the Court, the justices had "developed 'judicial activism' to a degree that at least matches the record of the 'Old Court' of the 1920s and 1930s and that certainly exceeds the record of any other Court in our constitutional history." On issues of segregation, censorship, religious observance, criminal law, reapportionment, the investigation of "subversives," the postal power, and even the issuance of passports, the Court exerted unprecedented directives; moreover, unlike earlier Court actions, these were designed not to protect custom against innovation but rather to break down tradition in favor of more innovative practices. "Even Marshall, with all his ambition and daring, might well be daunted by the prospect of governing a self-willed, dynamic nation in as many important ways as the Warren Court has sought to govern America" (1972, 326, 343). McCloskey was willing to acknowledge that some of these changes might have been brought about by changes in the Court's personnel, especially the replacement in 1948 of Murphy and Rutledge with Clark and Minton and the 1961 retirements of Frankfurter and Whittaker and the appointment of Goldberg. But McCloskey also thought more was at work.

For one, McCarthyism had receded into the background, while Eisenhower made it clear that "the clock would not be turned back either on New Deal liberalism or on Roosevelt-Truman international-ism." The anti-Court legislation considered in 1958 did not pass, sug-gesting that the alliance of segregationists and antisubversives would not be particularly dangerous to the Court. The Eisenhower and Kennedy administrations, along with their Congresses, were also fairly inactive on important issues in domestic politics, and it is "possible that the Court can be thought of as filling a vacuum left by the other branches of government" just as it had in the 1920s. Moreover, while the Court lost the traditional support of the business community and commercial lawyers and earned new enemies among white southerners "and advocates of state-enforced piety," it "also acquired some new champions" among "Negroes and Northern liberals of various types." If the 1964 election was any test, it appeared as though the Court had picked just the right allies at the right time: "Anti-judicialism was for the first time being associated with one of the worst popular defeats in electoral history," and President Lyndon Johnson "helped [to] carry into office an extra contingent of liberal congressmen [and] to decimate the array of those most likely to join an anti-Court movement." Finally, after years of carrying the load, the Supreme Court found that the other branches of the national government were finally ready to address the issue of racial discrimination (McCloskey 1972, 351–60).

In light of this holistic assessment of the political system, this advo-cate of judicial caution predicted that, at least in the short term, "the Court can continue to perform its present influential functions in the governmental process without much likelihood of providing a damag-ing reaction." The presidency, the Congress, and public attitudes all seemed to be working in the Court's favor. There was even reason to think that the justices might have helped themselves by bringing a national consensus over its role into being; in a sense, the Court might be building its own constituency of support (McCloskey 1972, 363). The question of whether the Court's exercise of bold power could be sustained ultimately depended as much on the balance of power between the Court's supporters and its opponents as on the wise exer-cise of judicial statecraft.

MCCLOSKEY'S LEGACY

Because McCloskey struggled with history as it was unfolding, many of his judgments inevitably were overtaken by subsequent events. As his former student Sandy Levinson points out in his updated conclusion to *The American Supreme Court,*

> Whatever else can be said about the past forty years of the Supreme Court's behavior, it certainly does not appear to accord with Robert McCloskey's advice that it proceed by careful incremental steps and avoid "a series of leaps and bounds." . . . The Court appeared to learn as its lesson from the past not the merit of cautious, crablike movement but rather that the American public, for all of its grumblings, was quite willing to accept a great deal of political tutelage from it. (McCloskey 2000, 236)

To be fair, McCloskey did come to better understand the circumstances that permitted the bold exercise of judicial power. And, as Levinson quickly adds, McCloskey's basic lesson about the relationship between Court power and the support of powerful constituencies did receive a significant rehabilitation with the publication of Rosenberg's (1991) more systematic analysis of the Court and social change. Just as McCloskey highlighted in 1965 the significance of the other two branches finally joining the Court's efforts on civil rights, so too did Rosenberg make the politics of cooperation central to an understanding of the Court's effectiveness (and lack thereof). McCloskey would not disagree with Rosenberg's basic point that expecting the Court alone to act as a force for social change was a hollow hope, although McCloskey might be willing to give the Court more credit for adopting a role that helped set in motion a chain of events making change more possible. Before deciding, he would want to spend more time reconstructing the history.

There is no question that McCloskey's holism and aversion to trends in social science theory and methodology diminished his influence on political science scholarship for some time. Other pioneers in this volume believed that work such as McCloskey's reflected a stubborn, traditional attachment to personal, subjective narrative at the expense of hardheaded, verifiable, empirical analyses. They worked hard to move the discipline toward methods of inquiry that were more explicitly anchored in uncontestable observations and falsifiable hypotheses. The field undoubtedly benefited from these developments. But it should also be recognized that something was lost when our subject matter was transformed from the art of political analysis to the science of politics. McCloskey knew that beneath the smooth veneer of numbers and models was the contingency of history, the judgment of power holders, and the vital question of what role these institutions should play in the political system. For many of his generation, including Pritchett, Murphy, and Shapiro, who had reached scholarly maturity under the influence of Corwin and Mason, the single-factor emphasis on judicial ideology or the abstract discussion of strategic interaction provided useful precision but too often did so at the expense of what was most important—politics, actual politics, as lived in history. McCloskey never said an unkind word about developments in the field, but he refused to join because he preferred an approach that treated the subject (in the words of Rogers Smith) as "if politics matters" (1992).

Almost twenty years after McCloskey's death, an effort was made to revitalize public law's interest in examining power holders (such as judges) from within particular institutional and historical settings. Smith's (1988) argument for the "new institutionalism" was premised on his belief that something had been missing from our accounts of judicial politics ever since public law became dominated by behavioralism and rational choice. While this work was "valuable," it also tended to "treat the resources, the institutional environment, and especially the very values and interests of political actors as exogenous, as determinants of political-choice situations that shape events while remaining more or less impervious to conscious human direction themselves." Moreover, "when limited inquiries dominate the field of research, too many of the decisive elements in politics are left unexplored," with the result being "a restricted, atemporal view of politics" where "political action, such as judicial decision making, then inevitably seems a tedious, crassly self-interested, and rather ineffectual game among programmed players" (1988, 95–96). The alternative view encouraged by Smith was one in which

> political institutions appear to be "more than simply mirrors of social forces." They are themselves created by past human political decisions that were in some measure discretionary, and to some degree they are alterable by future ones. They also have a kind of life of their own. They influence the self-conception of those who occupy roles defined by them in ways that can give those persons distinctively "institutional" perspectives. Hence

such institutions can play a part in affecting the political behavior that reshapes them in turn—making them appropriate as units of analysis in their own right. (1988, 95)

There is little in this agenda with which McCloskey would have disagreed. Perhaps, then, the time is ripe for a new generation of scholars to consider how his analysis of the art of judicial governance might provoke new and better research agendas—not for the purpose of dominating the field with a new hegemonic framework, but just to keep alive a style of inquiry that explores aspects of judicial politics that are too often missed by our more positivistic colleagues.

In considering this question, we should keep in mind the various ways in which we have already improved on some of McCloskey's efforts. For example, rather than merely discussing the Court in historical context, some scholars have explored the advantages of tying Supreme Court politics to party realignment theory (see Adamany 1973; Funston 1975; Gates 1992; Lasser 1985), which was in its infancy at the time McCloskey started writing about the Court (see Key 1955, 1959).[12] Among other things, this work also provided a framework for understanding how conflicts might develop between the Court and the political system, particularly when the justices act in ways that provoke partisan conflict or resist the new order forged by a realignment (Gates 1999).

Then again, abstracting from history is not the only way to improve on McCloskey's analysis. For example, writing in a more McCloskeyan vein (albeit with much more original research), Mark Graber (1998) provided an impressive historical reconstruction of party politics in the time of Marshall to show how Marshall's decisions over time were much more in tune with dominant sentiment than one might guess if one assumes (with McCloskey) that the chief justice was leading a Federalist Court in an era of Jeffersonian democracy. Similarly, Kevin McMahon has taken his cue from new institutionalist approaches to argue that simple efforts to relate judicial decisions to background characteristics of the political system (such as realignments) "diminishes the importance of institutional action" and the specific calculations made by actual power holders. This leads him to offer an important overview of the Roosevelt administration's policy on race, emphasizing how "FDR's management of intraparty cleavages in conjunction with his pursuit of a new institutional arrangement drove his administration's judicial policy," in turn paving the way for the constitutional order that soon resulted in *Brown v. Board of Education* (2000,

21–22). Cornell Clayton (1999) has also explored how the structure of American politics in the 1980s and 1990s shapes judicial appointments and decision-making on the Rehnquist Court. And maybe most appropriately, Powe (2000) has modeled his sweeping and comprehensive political history, *The Warren Court and American Politics*, explicitly on the example of McCloskey's work.[13]

While McCloskey focused on the Court creating its own role in the political system, scholars have since pointed out that judicial power sometimes flows out of decisions made by the political branches. In his classic discussion of the "nonmajoritarian difficulty" Graber (1993) argues that there are circumstances under which it is in the interest of party leaders or presidents to have courts take the lead in addressing certain contentious issues. He focuses on slavery, antitrust, and abortion, but it would be useful to have the analysis applied to other areas as part of an effort to extend McCloskey's speculations on the determinants of judicial power (see also Gillman 2002). Some of this work is already being done in the context of comparative judicial politics, with special attention to the constituencies that benefit from expanded judicial power (see Hirschl 2000).

Finally, McCloskey's inclination to start with the Court's role in the political system can still provide a useful rubric for researchers who want to examine the distinctiveness of judicial power (Gillman 1999). Some have used this language to reconceptualize important periods in the Court's history; for example, Casto (1995) has suggested that the justices in the 1790s thought of themselves as performing a "national security" role. Others have used this starting point to incorporate into their discussion of Supreme Court politics the influence of law, as understood by the interpreters, rather than as modeled by researchers (Brigham 1978; Bussiere 1997; Cushman 1998; Gillman 1996, 1993; Kahn 1994; O'Neill 1981; Perry 1991; for an overview, see Gillman 2001). Like McCloskey, none of these scholars is starry-eyed about the role of law. All understand that Supreme Court decision making reflects the justices' ideology. But there is also some interest in seeing whether the art of judicial politics sometimes leads the justices to take jurisprudence into account, either out of a sense of professional obligation or as part of the art of judicial governance, wherein they attempt to convey a role that (at least) seems distinct from that of other institutions in the political system.

McCloskey died in 1969. During his last few years he was working on a manuscript on the modern Supreme Court, and he had completed his chapters on the Stone and Vinson Courts. Martin Shapiro commented that they clearly showed "the value of an approach that is fundamentally historical but also acutely sensitive to the situation of the decision-makers at the time they had to make their decision" (McCloskey 1972, viii).[14] Increasing numbers of public law scholars believe that after decades of trying to abstract away from history, the time has come once again to explore the advantages of immersing our subjects in their history. As we continue to move forward, we may find some value in rediscovering some of the pioneers we left behind.

NOTES

1. McCloskey ended the book this way: "clarity is not served by perpetuating a myth which identifies an unregulated economic order with democracy. That notion was the result, as we have seen, of a corrosion of national ideals so pervasive that it apostatized the American political tradition. In one form or another, the confusions thus inaugurated have survived to clog the channels of public policy ever since. Democracy, however, is condemned to no such misalliance. Economic regulation of business enterprise raises grave issues, but no question of the betrayal of democracy is involved. The master concern of democracy in America is not business but humanity; and the problem of social control should be judged with that truth in mind" (1951, 174).

2. This book was originally published in 1960. Citations in this chapter are to the third edition, as revised by McCloskey's former student, Sandy Levinson.

3. Almost all of McCloskey's essays were posthumously collected by Martin Shapiro and republished in McCloskey 1972. (The main exception is McCloskey 1962b.) For the sake of convenience, this chapter will cite page numbers from the book version rather than from the original essays.

4. Subsequent work on Dahl's thesis has called into question some of his findings about the Court's role in the political system. See esp. Adamany 1973; Casper 1976.

5. See also his more famous evaluation of the Court's history, written in 1958 during the Court-Congress battles: "The Court's greatest successes have been achieved when it has operated near the margins rather than in the center of political controversy, when it has nudged and gently tugged the nation, instead of trying to rule it. . . . The Court ruled more in each case when it tried to rule less, and that paradox is one of the clearest morals to be drawn from this history" (2000, 234).

6. McCloskey's work was related to but quite different than the work being done by "process scholars" such as Peltason (1955) and Krislov (1965), who were more influenced by David Truman. McCloskey's focus, like that of Pritchett, Murphy, and Shapiro, was on how Supreme Court politics was linked to regime politics and how the justices oriented themselves to the polit-

ical system. Still, all of these scholars viewed themselves as moving beyond the sort of intellectual history that was a mark of Corwin's generation into something more in line with the kind of political-institutional analysis that was developing in political science. Many of these scholars also believed that the shift toward an individual level of analysis, looking simply at judicial preferences, was also a shift away from a serious political understanding of the Court—useful in many respects, and certainly in tune with exciting work in voting behavior, but not very helpful in giving us a perspective on how the Court fits into a larger system of institutional arrangements. One of these scholars commented to me that it was like trying to understand congressional legislation as if it were the sum of congressional biographies.

7. The main thesis of McCloskey 1962a was that immediately before Frankfurter's retirement, the justices had not been able to develop a coherent role or rationale as it related to their civil rights jurisprudence, and the result was a fragmentation of opinions that made it nearly impossible for the Court to satisfy the demands of the school of "reasoned elaboration"—those law professors who insisted that the judicial power should be rooted in clear principles that are rationally justified and applied (see Wechsler 1961). Three years later, Walter Murphy (1965) wrote what amounted to a rebuttal to that article; however, that essay never refers to McCloskey. One way to reconcile these two discussions is to assume that by 1965, there was much more coherence to Warren Court liberalism than there was in 1961. In any event, there is no reason to think that McCloskey took any offense; as mentioned earlier, around that same time he wrote in strong support of Murphy's promotion at Princeton.

8. This concern led McCloskey that same year to worry about a new incarnation of substantive due process (1962b).

9. In the article version of this essay, McCloskey places at n.14 an elaborate three-page discussion of all state efforts to respond to the decision. In the version printed in McCloskey (1972, 266), Shapiro replaces that extensive analysis with a reference to Dixon 1968 for a discussion of "the general pattern of response."

10. Among the other books that McCloskey placed alongside Murphy's were Lasswell and Kaplan 1950; Neustadt 1960; Peltason 1955, 1961; and Pritchett 1961. He also cited Dahl 1957.

11. In this essay he also finally offered his acknowledgments of the behavioral revolution in the form of some rudimentary statistics on voting patterns. Even here, though, he was careful to defend the virtues of interpretivism: "This trend [toward activist civil liberties decision making] and its accelerating pace are evident enough I believe from the kind of impressionistic, bird's eye view that has just been described. If statistics did not confirm the impressions, one would suspect some flaw in the counter or some ambiguity in the counted. But the fact is that tabulation and comparison do seem to bear out the foregoing account faithfully, and this may comfort those with a taste for quantifiable data and a suspicion of intuitive conclusions" (1972, 338).

12. Many of these scholars appropriately cite Dahl 1957 as their point of departure. While this action is understandable, there is also reason to think that realignment theory's emphasis on periodic historical adjustments in judicial decision making is at least as consistent with McCloskey's view of Supreme Court politics in the sense that, in both cases, the justices are seen as struggling to find an acceptable role in changing circumstances. At the same time, as Smith points out (1988), these approaches to Supreme Court politics also assumed that judicial decision making was little more than abstract policy-making. These analyses tend to treat the Court's distinctive institutional characteristics as essentially irrelevant to the analysis.

13. This is not too surprising, considering that Powe's close colleague at the University of Texas is Sandy Levinson. For other examples of work along these lines, see Burgess 1992; Fisher 1988; Friedman 1993; Gillman and Clayton 1999; Griffin 1996; Klarman 1996; and, to a lesser extent and for a very different purpose, Ackerman 1991.

14. Shapiro added perceptively that McCloskey's writings on the Court were remarkably autobiographical, the work of a scholar whose temperament was judicious but who also believed in "the dignity and autonomy of the individual" (McCloskey 1972, vii). As McCloskey reflected on the Warren Court, he found a way to reconcile his deeply cautious nature with the bold civil rights agenda of this remarkable institution. In the end, his analysis of Supreme Court politics and the nature of judicial decision making was driven by the same concern that led him to write that first book and especially to end it with the claim that the "master concern of democracy in America" was "humanity" and that "the problem of social control should be judged with that truth in mind" (1951, 174).

REFERENCES

Ackerman, Bruce. 1991. *We, the People: Foundations.* Cambridge: Belknap Press of Harvard University Press.

Adamany, David. 1973. "Legitimacy, Realigning Elections, and the Supreme Court." *Wisconsin Law Review* 1973:790–846.

Brigham, John. 1978. *Constitutional Language: An Interpretation of Judicial Decisions.* Westport, CT: Greenwood.

Burgess, Susan R. 1992. *Contest for Constitutional Authority: The Abortion and War Power Debates.* Lawrence: University Press of Kansas.

Bussiere, Elizabeth. 1997. *(Dis)Entitling the Poor: The Warren Court, Welfare Rights, and the American Political Tradition.* University Park: Pennsylvania State University Press.

Casper, Jonathan D. 1976. "The Supreme Court and National Policymaking." *American Political Science Review* 70:50–63.

Casto, William R. 1995. *The Supreme Court in the Early Republic: The Chief Jus-*

ticeships of John Jay and Oliver Ellsworth. Columbia: University of South Carolina Press.

Clayton, Cornell. 1999. "Law, Politics, and the Rehnquist Court: Structural Influences on Supreme Court Decision Making." In *The Supreme Court in American Politics: New Institutionalist Interpretations,* ed. Howard Gillman and Cornell Clayton. Lawrence: University Press of Kansas.

Cushman, Barry. 1998. *Rethinking the New Deal Court: The Structure of a Constitutional Revolution.* New York: Oxford University Press.

Dahl, Robert. 1957. "Decision-Making in a Democracy: The Supreme Court as a National Policy-Maker." *Journal of Public Law* 6:279–95.

Dixon, Robert G., Jr. 1968. *Democratic Representation: Reapportionment in Law and Politics.* New York: Oxford University Press.

Fisher, Louis. 1988. *Constitutional Dialogues: Interpretation as Political Process.* Princeton: Princeton University Press.

Friedman, Barry. 1993. "Dialogue and Judicial Review." *Michigan Law Review* 91:577–682.

Funston, Richard. 1975. "The Supreme Court and Critical Elections." *American Political Science Review* 69:795–811.

Gates, John. 1992. *The Supreme Court and Partisan Realignment: A Macro- and Micro-Level Perspective.* Boulder, CO: Westview.

Gates, John. 1999. "The Supreme Court and Partisan Change: Contravening, Provoking, and Diffusing Partisan Conflict." In *The Supreme Court in American Politics: New Institutionalist Interpretations,* ed. Howard Gillman and Cornell Clayton. Lawrence: University Press of Kansas.

Gillman, Howard. 1993. *The Constitution Besieged: The Rise and Demise of Lochner Era Police Powers Jurisprudence.* Durham: Duke University Press.

Gillman, Howard. 1996. "More on the Origins of the Fuller Court's Jurisprudence: Reexamining the Scope of Federal Power over Commerce and Manufacturing in Nineteenth-Century Constitutional Law." *Political Research Quarterly* 49:415–37.

Gillman, Howard. 1999. "The Court as an Idea, Not a Building (or a Game): Interpretive Institutionalism and the Analysis of Supreme Court Decision-Making." In *Supreme Court Decision-Making: New Institutionalist Approaches,* ed. Cornell W. Clayton and Howard Gillman. Lawrence: University Press of Kansas.

Gillman, Howard. 2002. "How Political Parties Use the Courts to Advance Their Agendas: Federal Courts in the United States, 1875–1891." *American Political Science Review* 96 (August): 511–24.

Gillman, Howard. 2001. "What's Law Got to Do with It? Judicial Behavioralists Test the 'Legal Model' of Judicial Decision Making." *Law and Social Inquiry* 26:465–504.

Gillman, Howard, and Cornell Clayton, eds. 1999. *The Supreme Court in American Politics: New Institutionalist Interpretations.* Lawrence: University Press of Kansas.

Graber, Mark. 1993. "The Non-Majoritarian Difficulty: Legislative Deference to the Judiciary." *Studies in American Political Development* 7:35–73.

Graber, Mark. 1995. "The Passive-Aggressive Virtues: *Cohens v. Virginia* and the Problematic Establishment of Judicial Power." *Constitutional Commentary* 12:67–92.

Graber, Mark. 1998. "Federalist or Friends of Adams: The Marshall Court and Party Politics." *Studies in American Political Development* 12:229–66.

Griffin, Stephen M. 1996. *American Constitutionalism: From Theory to Politics.* Princeton: Princeton University Press.

Hirschl, Ran. 2000. "The Political Origins of Judicial Empowerment through Constitutionalization: Lessons from Four Constitutional Revolutions." *Law and Social Inquiry* 25:91–148.

Kahn, Ronald. 1994. *The Supreme Court and Constitutional Theory.* Lawrence: University Press of Kansas.

Key, V. O. 1955. "A Theory of Critical Elections." *Journal of Politics* 17:3–18.

Key, V. O. 1959. "Secular Realignment and the Party System." *Journal of Politics* 21:198–210.

Klarman, Michael J. 1996. "Rethinking the Civil Rights and Civil Liberties Revolutions." *Virginia Law Review* 82:1–67.

Knight, Jack, and Lee Epstein. 1996. "On the Struggle for Judicial Supremacy." *Law and Society Review* 30:87–120.

Krislov, Samuel. 1965. *The Supreme Court in the Political Process.* New York: Macmillan.

Lasser, William. 1985. "The Supreme Court in Periods of Critical Realignment." *Journal of Politics* 47:1124–87.

Lasswell, Harold D., and Abraham Kaplan. 1950. *Power and Society: A Framework for Political Inquiry.* New Haven: Yale University Press.

Mason, Alpheus Thomas. 1956. *Harlan Fiske Stone: Pillar of the Law.* New York: Viking Press.

Mason, Alpheus Thomas. 1958. *The Supreme Court from Taft to Warren.* Baton Rouge: Louisiana State University Press.

McCloskey, Robert G. 1951. *American Conservatism in the Age of Enterprise, 1865–1910.* New York: Harper and Row.

McCloskey, Robert G. 1956. "The Supreme Court Finds a Role." *Virginia Law Review* 42:735–60.

McCloskey, Robert G. 1957. "Useful Toil or the Paths of Glory?" *Virginia Law Review* 43:803–35.

McCloskey, Robert G., ed. 1958a. *Essays in Constitutional Law.* New York: Vintage Books.

McCloskey, Robert G. 1958b. "Tools, Stumbling Blocks, and Stepping Stones." *Virginia Law Review* 44:1029–55.

McCloskey, Robert G. 1960. *The American Supreme Court.* Chicago: University of Chicago Press.

McCloskey, Robert G. 1962a. "Deeds without Doctrines." *American Political Science Review* 56:71–89.

McCloskey, Robert G. 1962b. "Economic Due Process and the Supreme Court: An Exhumation and Reburial." *Supreme Court Review* 1962:34.

McCloskey, Robert G. 1962c. "Foreword: The Reapportionment Cases." *Harvard Law Review* 76:54–74.

McCloskey, Robert G. 1965. "Reflections on the Warren Court." *Virginia Law Review* 51:1229–70.

McCloskey, Robert G. 1972. *The Modern Supreme Court.* Cambridge: Harvard University Press.

McCloskey, Robert G. 2000. *The American Supreme Court.* 3d ed. Rev. Sanford Levinson. Chicago: University of Chicago Press.

McMahon, Kevin J. 2000. "Constitutional Vision and Supreme Court Decisions: Reconsidering Roosevelt on Race." *Studies in American Political Development* 14:20–50.

Murphy, Walter F. 1959. "Lower Court Checks on Supreme Court Power." *American Political Science Review* 53:1017–31.

Murphy, Walter F. 1962. *Congress and the Court: A Case Study in the American Political Process.* Chicago: University of Chicago Press.

Murphy, Walter F. 1964. *The Elements of Judicial Strategy.* Chicago: University of Chicago Press.

Murphy, Walter F. 1965. "Deeds under Doctrine: Civil Liberties in the 1963 Term." *American Political Science Review* 59:64–79.

Murphy, Walter F., and Joseph Tanenhaus. 1972. *The Study of Public Law.* New York: Random House.

Neustadt, Richard. 1960. *Presidential Power: The Politics of Leadership.* New York: Wiley.

O'Neill, Timothy J. 1981. "The Language of Equality in a Democratic Order." *American Political Science Review* 75:626–35.

Peltason, Jack W. 1955. *Federal Courts in the Political Process.* New York: Random House.

Peltason, Jack W. 1961. *Fifty-eight Lonely Men: Southern Federal Judges and School Desegregation.* New York: Harcourt, Brace, and World.

Perry, H. W., Jr. 1991. *Deciding to Decide: Agenda Setting in the United States Supreme Court.* Cambridge: Harvard University Press

Powe, Lucas A., Jr. 2000. *The Warren Court and American Politics.* Cambridge: Harvard University Press.

Pritchett, C. Herman. 1948. *The Roosevelt Court: A Study in Judicial Politics and Values, 1937–1947.* New York: Macmillan.

Pritchett, C. Herman. 1954. *Civil Liberties and the Vinson Court.* Chicago: University of Chicago Press.

Pritchett, C. Herman. 1961. *Congress versus the Supreme Court, 1957–1960.* Minneapolis: University of Minnesota Press.

Rosenberg, Gerald. 1991. *The Hollow Hope: Can Courts Bring about Social Change?* Chicago: University of Chicago Press.

Shapiro, Martin. 1964. *Law and Politics in the Supreme Court: New Approaches to Political Jurisprudence.* New York: Free Press.

Shapiro, Martin. 1978. "The Supreme Court from Warren to Burger." In *The New American Political System*, ed. Anthony King. Washington, D.C.: American Enterprise Institute.

Shapiro, Martin. 1984. "Recent Developments in Political Jurisprudence." *Western Political Quarterly* 36:541–48.

Shapiro, Martin. 1986. "The Supreme Court's 'Return' to Economic Regulation. In *Studies in American Political Development*, ed. Karen Orren and Stephen Skowronek. New Haven: Yale University Press.

Smith, Rogers M. 1988. "Political Jurisprudence, the 'New Institutionalism,' and the Future of Public Law." *American Political Science Review* 82:89–108.

Smith, Rogers M. 1992. "If Politics Matters: Implications for a 'New Institutionalism.'" *Studies in American Political Development* 6:1–36.

Wechsler, Herbert. 1961. *Principles, Politics, and Fundamental Law*. Cambridge: Harvard University Press.

CHAPTER 15

Robert Dahl: Democracy, Judicial Review, and the Study of Law and Courts

David Adamany and Stephen Meinhold

The appearance of a chapter on Robert Dahl in this volume will surprise many who are not public law scholars. While Professor Dahl is certainly among the most influential political scientists of our time, he is rarely thought of as a student of the courts or judicial process. Indeed, Dahl does not meet the usual criteria for the pioneers included in this volume: he has neither written a substantial body of law and courts scholarship nor mentored a cadre of personally trained disciples who have contributed to the law and courts field and are able to examine the influence of his work. Instead, Dahl made his mark with a single article.[1] When he published "Decision Making in a Democracy: The Supreme Court as a National Policy-Maker" in 1957, Dahl instantly made what has proven to be one of the most influential and enduring contributions to the modern study of law and courts. As testament to the article's influence, in 2000 Professor Dahl received the first Harcourt College Publisher's Award, given by the Law and Courts Section of the American Political Science Association for a book or journal article at least ten years old that has made a lasting impression on the field of law and courts. How is it that a single article in a relatively unknown journal propelled its author to the status of judicial pioneer?

"Decision Making in a Democracy: The Supreme Court as a National Policy-Maker" appeared in a 1957 special symposium on the Supreme Court in the *Journal of Public Law*.[2] The symposium, edited by Louis Pollock, included eleven invited manuscripts, of which Professor Dahl's was one of only two written by a political scientist. Dahl's essay was brief, sixteen pages, with few footnotes.[3] In August 2000, we asked Professor Dahl how he had come to write an article on the Supreme Court for a symposium in a relatively obscure law journal. He surprised us by confessing that he had no recollection of who invited him to contribute or why; indeed, he seemed somewhat surprised by our report of the article's extraordinary influence on judicial studies and the frequency with which the essay was and continues to be cited. With the benefit of hindsight, it is more apparent to us why Dahl's article has been so influential. First, Dahl addressed the foundational controversy surrounding judicial review in America, whether it can be squared with a representative democracy. Second, he connected this controversy to several major lines of inquiry that have characterized modern political science.

THE FOUNDATIONAL CONTROVERSY OVER JUDICIAL REVIEW

Dahl entered the debate about the democratic nature of judicial review at a critical juncture. Most of the nation's politicians, commentators, and senior scholars remembered well the epic struggle between the New Deal and the old Court, which defined discussions of the Supreme Court at least until the end of the Warren Court and perhaps to the present day. This conflict between judicial policy-making and popular sovereignty had, moreover, emerged again in the years just before Dahl wrote—in *Brown v. Board of Education* (347 U.S. 483 [1954], 349 U.S. 394 [1955]), in the Court's tentative entry into national controversies about whether domestic communist political activity was constitutionally protected, and in the Court's cases dealing with the scope of the rights of criminal defendants.

In deft strokes, Dahl argued persuasively that when the Supreme Court reviews the constitutionality of federal statutes enacted by elected officials representing a majority of the nation's voters, justices exercise discretion, make policy choices, and therefore engage in the national political process. Dahl thus appeared to reinforce the position both of New Deal Democrats in the 1930s and of southern Democrats and conservative Republicans in the 1950s—namely, that in exercising the power of judicial review, the Supreme Court acts undemocratically. Then, turning this objection to judicial review on its head, Dahl asserted and sought to demonstrate empirically that the Supreme Court's policy-making is largely democratic in nature, rarely obstructing the important policies of national lawmaking majorities and largely ineffectual on the rare occasions when it does so.[4] Moreover, Dahl argued, the normal operation of American politics usually assures that the Court acts in concert with the will of the lawmaking majority and that the Court advances majoritarian policies by endowing them with an aura of legitimacy. Thus, the power of judicial review is structurally undemocratic but functionally democratic.

In reaching this conclusion, Dahl eschewed the contemporary liberal justification for judicial review, that the Supreme Court does, or at least ought to, provide a bulwark for the protection of minority rights in a democracy.[5] He empirically demonstrated that the Court had not performed a minority-rights function through history,[6] and he suggested that the Court should not be expected to do so.[7] Looking at the Court's invalidations of federal law that took the longest time to overrule, Dahl found that the Court often invoked the "Fifth, Thirteenth, Fourteenth, and Fifteenth Amendments to preserve the rights and liberties of a relatively privileged group at the expense of the rights and liberties of a submerged group: chiefly slaveholders at the expense of slaves, white people at the expense of colored people, and property holders at the expense of wage earners and other groups" (1957, 292).[8]

PROFESSOR DAHL, THE SUPREME COURT, AND MODERN POLITICAL SCIENCE

Dahl's influence on studies of the Supreme Court reached well beyond his asserted resolution of the controversy over the democratic nature of judicial review, however. Dahl's essay tapped into several main lines of thinking and methodology that have framed modern political science. Dahl was interested not in judicial reasoning or judicial doctrine—the earlier modes of judicial scholarship used by such political scientists as Wallace Mendelson, David Fellman, and, to some degree, Edward S. Corwin—but in the Supreme Court's policy outcomes. Using simple arithmetic techniques, Dahl counted judicial outcomes: How many federal statutes had the Supreme Court overturned? How many of these Court decisions were overturned within four years of enactment, when their sponsoring lawmaking majority might still be in existence, and how many after longer periods? How many of the decisions had important national policy consequences, and how many only a minor policy impact? In this simple quantification of case outcomes, Dahl's work was closer to the judicial behavioralists of his time—such as Pritchett, Schubert, and Ulmer—who defined the dominant mode of judicial studies through the end of the twentieth century.[9]

However, unlike the behavioralists, Dahl's unit of analysis was the Court as an institution rather than its individual members, the justices. Dahl counted and analyzed the Court's policy decisions, not the votes of individual justices on those decisions. And he did so because he believed that judicial policies were shaped by the Court's interactions with other institutions—the presidency and Congress through the appointments process and the amendment process. In this, Dahl reached back to an older institutional political science and forward to the new institutionalist judicial studies that began in the late 1990s. His fundamental insight—one that links old and new institutionalism—was that Supreme Court politics makes little sense if judges are conceptualized as individual, independent, and thus potentially countermajoritarian decision makers; judging, rather, must be placed within the context of regime politics, or the agendas of ruling coalitions.

Dahl's article tapped other wellsprings of modern political science. His analysis connected judicial studies to the theory of critical elections (and political regimes) framed by V. O. Key Jr. in his seminal 1955 article.[10] Noting "the Jeffersonian alliance, the Jacksonian, the extraordinarily long-lived Republican dominance of the post–Civil War years, and the New Deal alliance," Dahl argued that because of the appointments process, "the Supreme Court is inevitably a part of the dominant national alliance" and therefore "supports the major policies of the alliance" (1957, 293). As a result, the Court's policies are likely to be consistent with majority will as reflected in the dominant political alliance.

Again, however, Dahl was ahead of his time. He provocatively suggested, without further elaboration, that the Court might play a significant independent role in policy-making during "short-lived transitional periods when the old alliance is disintegrating and the new one is struggling to take control of political institutions" (1957, 294)—that is, during periods of electoral realignment. And he saw the possibility that in a few instances "when the [national lawmaking] coalition is unstable with respect to certain key policies . . . the Court can intervene in such cases and may even succeed in establishing policy" (294). Dahl does not specifically discuss the instability that occurs in the majority coalition when new issues arise that divide it, but his analysis suggests that the Supreme Court might play an important policy-making role in such periods and could help shape the coalition's electoral position on these issues.[11] Dahl also does not anticipate an extended period in which there is no dominant majority coalition—a period of dealignment—but his analysis nonetheless suggests that such a period would create conditions in which policy activism by the Supreme Court could effectively occur.[12]

Finally, Dahl's analysis points to important issues in the study of public opinion. Here, uncharacteristically, Dahl's analysis is not entirely clear. He notes that the "Supreme Court . . . possesses some bases of power of its own, the most important of which is the unique legitimacy attributed to its interpretations of the Constitution" (1957, 293). "This legitimacy the court jeopardizes," he says, "if it flagrantly opposes the major policies of the dominant alliance" (293). Elsewhere, however, Dahl describes the Court's relationship to public opinion somewhat differently: "The main task of the Court is to confer legitimacy on the fundamental policies of the successful coalition" (294). These two assertions suggest very different but not necessarily inconsistent relationships between the public and the Court. First, the public esteems the Court as an institution, perhaps because of its role in interpreting the Constitution or because of its stature as a constitutionally established institution, thereby creating an independent basis of power for the Court. Second, the public's reverence for the Constitution leads to the recognition that the Court's most distinctive function is to interpret the Constitution. Presumably because the public believes the Court makes such interpretations independently and according to clear rules, the Court may confer legitimacy on the policies of the elected branches when it declares those policies consistent with the Constitution. Both lines of inquiry—the foundations of institutional authority among the public and the mechanisms by which governmental policy gains public acceptance—have been core concerns of students of American democracy and public opinion since Dahl penned "Decision Making in a Democracy." Dahl connected both lines of inquiry not only to the judiciary but also to the relationships among the judiciary, the other branches, and the dominant political coalition.

PROFESSOR DAHL AND THE CONTINUING CONTROVERSY OVER THE DEMOCRATIC NATURE OF JUDICIAL REVIEW

With the triumph of the behavioral approach in judicial studies, the normative debate about the democratic implications of judicial review waned as a central concern of political science following the publication of Dahl's essay. But judicial review remained a central concern of legal scholarship for several more decades, and the main themes of Dahl's essay appeared and reappeared. Charles Black Jr. (1960) soon sought to rehabilitate the power of judicial review from the liberal perspective. Seizing on the idea that the Court's affirmance of challenged federal statutes legitimated them, Black argued that the principal impact of judicial review was to support democracy by garnering public support for national government policies, especially among the losers of those policy struggles, by declaring them constitutional and thus "legitimate." The occasions when the Court strikes down statutes support its legitimating power by assuring the public that the Court makes discriminating judgments about what is constitutional and what is not. "The power to validate is the power to invalidate," he said. "If the Court were deprived . . . of its real and practical power to set bounds to governmental action, or even of public confidence that the Court regards this as its duty . . . then it must certainly cease to perform its central function of unlocking the energies of government by stamping governmental actions as legitimate. If everybody gets a Buck Rogers badge, a Buck Rogers badge imports no distinction" (53).

At about this same time, Black's Yale colleague, Alexander Bickel, in his renowned *The Least Dangerous Branch*, identified the "countermajoritarian difficulty" as the central challenge to the Supreme Court.[13] Bickel too rejected the minority-rights justification for judicial review. When the Supreme Court acts against the majority will, he argued, it was likely to be wrong on the substance of policy, as judged by history, and this was as likely to be true of decisions that the Court perceived as protecting minority rights as of other decisions.[14] Bickel then turned Black and Dahl's legitimacy-conferring argument on its head: the Court should not affirm decisions of the lawmaking branches when those policies are contrary to constitutional values because doing so would legitimate those policies, and it cannot strike down such policies, except when neutrally implementing constitutional values, without engaging in countermajoritarian policy-making. Hence, Bickel argued, the Court should usually invoke its doctrines of abstention and avoidance to abjure entirely policy-making. Bickel regarded the Court's legitimacy-conferring power, which Dahl and Black deemed a democratic function, as potentially strengthening government decisions at odds with constitutional values.

In 1980 John Hart Ely attempted to dissolve the countermajoritarian difficulty by arguing that the Court could strengthen democracy by exercising judicial review to protect those rights essential for the operation of the majoritarian political system. Judicial review on behalf of political expression, association and assembly, ballot access and the right to vote, and similar political processes advances rather than defeats democracy. The protection of groups subject to such community prejudice that their views could not gain a hearing in the majoritarian political process—such as African Americans and gays and lesbians—might also advance democratic values. However, Ely's comprehensive analysis of the Court's recent constitutional decisions demonstrated, as might be expected, that the justices, while sometimes protecting political rights, range far and wide to overturn many other majoritarian policies.

Also in 1980, Jesse Choper argued that the Court should focus on individual and minority rights but should do so without limiting itself to political rights. Choper joined the consensus among legal scholars that the exercise of judicial review was inherently undemocratic. Moreover, based on a searching review of the devices available to the elected branches to reverse the Court, he concluded that these democratic checks either required nondemocratic extraordinary majorities or were largely ineffectual. And echoing another of Dahl's themes, Choper argued that the Supreme Court has limited political capital and therefore has only a limited capacity to invalidate majority policies without endangering its power and its legitimacy with policymakers and the public. In a review of the Court's decisions, he concluded that in the two decades or so after Dahl wrote, the Court's work had been largely the protection of individual and minority rights.

Arguing that the constitutional structure of federalism allows states to protect their own interests and the constitutional separation of powers allows the president and Congress to safeguard their respective prerogatives, Choper said that the Court should eschew judicial review in these areas. Instead, it should expend its limited political capital—a concept akin to Dahl's concern about the Court's fragile institutional legitimacy—to secure the rights of individuals and minorities, because the majoritarian political system provides them few protections elsewhere. Moreover, reviewing the Court's recent record, Choper argued that the justices had been vigorous in protecting minority rights (1980, 79–108). Ely and Choper thus rejected both Dahl's thesis that because the appointment process necessarily makes the Court part of the dominant political coalition, the Court is not likely to align itself with minorities and his empirical analysis that the Court does not in fact do so. A more recent review of the Court's decisions invalidating federal, state, and local actions infringing liberties suggests that Dahl's assessment may have been closer to the mark and that the Court's activism on behalf of minority rights was limited to a period from the 1960s to the 1980s (Baum 1996, 210–16).

The fundamental difference in these approaches is clear: Dahl reached his conclusions through the description and analysis of institutions, political processes, and judicial policies; Bickel, Ely, and Choper went beyond description to prescribe how the Court should exercise its authority. And, as might be predicted, the Court's behavior has not conformed to those prescriptions. In recent decades, the Court has not emphasized avoidance and abstention but has instead been very active in policy-making. The Court also has not limited its policy-making to the protection of democratic political processes. And despite Baum's recent (1996) persuasive analysis, consistent with Choper's argument, that the contemporary Court has emphasized cases involving minority rights, leaving foreign policy to the executive and domestic regulation, budget, and taxation to Congress, the Court has most recently exhibited heightened activism in formulating federalism doctrines. The Court's recent findings that federalism limits congressional power under the commerce clause, protects state governments from regulatory legislation on sovereignty grounds, and expands state immunity from lawsuits under Article III and the Eleventh Amendment suggest neither abstention from policy-making nor a judicial commitment to safeguarding majoritarian political processes or more generally to protecting individual rights.

The democratic nature of judicial review continues to frame much constitutional scholarship by legal scholars, either overtly or implicitly. But since Choper's *Judicial Review and the National Political Process*, the emphasis has largely shifted away from political and structural analysis.[15] Debates over appropriate means of constitutional interpretation, the coherence of judicial policies, the Court's capacity effectively to initiate change, the existence of unenumerated constitutional rights, and the appropriate scope of judicial review have been more prominent. Dahl's essay had little to say directly about these controversies. Prescription about the means by which the justices should construe the Constitution are largely irrelevant to Dahl, because his analysis is rooted in evidence that the Court invalidates few federal statutes and that the Court—as a result of the appointment process and its role as part of the national political coalition—generally develops doctrines consistent with the policy preferences of the lawmaking majority.

Several aspects of Dahl's analysis may be subject to revision in light of changes in American politics, as we subsequently point out. But these revisions have little to do with principled prescriptions about the Court's proper policy-making role in a democratic society. Instead, the potential revisions to Dahl's analysis can largely be explained within his broad framework of the Court's role within the American political process and its relationship to other governmental institutions.

PROFESSOR DAHL AND
HIS CRITICS: THE FIRST
TWENTY YEARS

More than a decade passed before challenges from within political science emerged to the Dahl thesis, and then they came quickly. In 1973, David Adamany challenged the legitimacy-conferring function Dahl attributed to the Supreme Court. Adamany suggested that the preconditions for Dahl's legitimation hypothesis would include higher public regard for the Court than for the elected branches, public belief that the Court engaged in constitutional interpretation, and public knowledge of the Court's decisions affirming federal laws. Relying on a small body of published studies of public opinion about the Supreme Court, Adamany concluded that there was insufficient empirical support for the legitimacy-conferring function. Moreover, he argued that if the Court had such a function, during realigning periods, when the Court, dominated by justices from the old coalition, was likely to obstruct the new lawmaking majority, it would also "delegitimate" policies of the lawmaking coalition. Adamany did not find, however, that in realigning periods the Court engaged in a heightened rate of invalidations of laws enacted by the new lawmaking majority. Instead, employing historical materials, he showed more generalized conflict between the Court and the lawmaking branches, especially the president, during these periods.

Just two years later, Richard Funston (1975), in the *American Political Science Review*, challenged Adamany's analysis of judicial review during realigning periods. Funston found that the annual average number of Supreme Court invalidations of federal law during realigning periods was greater than during stable eras between realignments and concluded that Dahl was correct: during the long periods of stable party government, the presidential appointment power assures that the Court is part of the lawmaking majority, so decisions overturning federal laws occur infrequently. When a new lawmaking majority is emerging, however, justices from the old regime engage in an unusual number of invalidations of federal laws adopted by the new regime.

But Beck (1976) and Canon and Ulmer (1976) quickly noted that by averaging the number of invalidations in realigning periods, Funston (1970) had allowed the large number of invalidations of New Deal policy to unduly inflate the average for all realigning periods. In fact, the Court had not invalidated an extraordinary number of federal laws during most realigning periods. This conclusion appeared at odds with a narrow suggestion that Dahl had advanced earlier—that in short-lived transitional periods when one majority coalition was being replaced by another, the Court might be more assertive in making policy. Ironically, however, Beck and Cannon and Ulmer's findings also suggested support for Dahl's broader thesis: that the Court would rarely be out of line with the nation's lawmaking majorities, because if the justices did not go their own way during realigning periods, they would be unlikely to do so during stable periods of majority-party dominance.

The tempest over the Court's activism in realigning periods had scarcely quieted when the Dahl thesis came under broader and more forceful attack from another direction. Jonathan Casper (1976) argued that the Dahl thesis was time bound and was an artifact of Dahl's narrow definition of judicial review. Including the Warren Court era and taking into account statutory interpretation and judicial review of state and local laws, the Supreme Court, Casper argued, emerges in the modern period as an important independent policymaker, especially in the protection of minority rights. Dahl could not have foreseen the minority rights activism of the Warren Court, of course. And there has as yet been no definitive assessment of whether the Warren Court period ushered in a new, enduring minority-rights function for the Court or was an aberration. But in the past several years, the Court has reentered the fray about the scope of national authority in the federal system.

Whether Casper was correct that the Court plays a larger role in the protection of minority rights than Dahl had envisioned, Casper probably missed the mark in arguing that Dahl had not broadly enough defined judicial policy-making. The lawmaking branches can, by majority vote, revise statutes to overturn the Court's statutory interpretations, thereby meeting Dahl's majority criterion for democratic government. And although tentative in his 1957 essay, Dahl acknowledged elsewhere that the invalidation of local laws might be viewed as an assertion of policy by the national lawmaking majority, carried out by a Supreme Court that, through the appointments process, largely reflects that majority's policy preferences. But the development of the doctrine of incorporation, which gives the same meaning to most provisions of the Bill of Rights and to the due process clause of the Fourteenth Amendment, may cause some invalidations of state laws or constitutional provisions to become binding on the federal government as well—a sort of incorporation in reverse. No one has yet reviewed Professor Dahl's thesis about the Court's national policy-making role by examining the impact of the Supreme Court's invalidations of state laws and constitutions on federal law.

CONTEMPORARY CHALLENGES AND THE REVIVAL OF THE DAHL THESIS

The mainsprings of Dahl's analysis were the existence of long-enduring, dominant national political coalitions and the efficacy of the presidential appointment power in binding the Supreme Court to the policy preferences of those lawmaking majorities. Justices who are part of the dominant national political coalition are unlikely to invalidate federal laws, especially those embodying important policies of the contemporary lawmaking majority, thus minimizing both the frequency and the importance of judicial review of federal statutes. Dahl's empirical analysis affirmed both results. The processes conforming the Supreme Court's policies to those of the dominant national political coalition may break down, as Dahl suggested in passing, during transitions from one national lawmaking majority to another—that is, when there is no stable lawmaking majority—and when the national lawmaking coalition lacks consensus on major issues, thus giving the Court some latitude to choose among policy outcomes.

Many commentators believe that for various reasons, the modern period reflects fundamental changes in American politics. The most important of these is electoral dealignment, the advent of an extended period in which there is no dominant political coalition and thus no stable, enduring lawmaking majority.[16] Taylor has argued that earlier analyses of judicial review by electoral eras cannot be extended beyond 1968 because, "although the coalition that assumed power in the election of 1932 no longer dominates either the electoral or policymaking processes, no realignment in the traditional sense has taken place" (1992, 360). Other facts support such a conclusion: since 1968 the nation has elected Republican presidents six times and Democrats three times; the Senate has been in Republican hands a bare majority of the time but is now essentially evenly divided; and the House of Representatives has been in Democratic hands a majority of the time but shifted to a narrow Republican majority that has declined steadily since 1994. In short, neither party has dominated national electoral politics on a sustained basis.

Dahl did not foresee such a turn in American politics. But the absence of an enduring national political coalition creates conditions similar to those that occur when there is a transition from one dominant national political coalition to another or when a national lawmaking coalition is divided with respect to major policies—both conditions that Dahl foresaw. Under these circumstances, he speculated, the Court might engage independently in significant national policy-making. Dahl did not suggest what behavior by the Court might occur under such circumstances, but an increase in judicial invalidations of federal laws would certainly be one manifestation. And, indeed, the rate of invalidations does appear to have significantly increased after 1968, from an average of one case every two years to an average of nearly 1.8 cases each year.[17]

In the 1980s and 1990s, several veins of political science revived and confirmed a number of Professor Dahl's suggestions, though sometimes with different evidence and for different purposes. The Court's role as a democratic institution has gained support from studies showing congruence between the justices' policies and public opinion and from relatively new but still tentative evidence that the Court might influence public acceptance of policy, thus reviving the idea that the Court might perform a legitimacy-conferring function. Heightened judicial activism would appear at odds, however, with Dahl's characterization of the Court as an institution that only rarely challenges the lawmaking branches on important policy issues. And the emergence over three decades of an electoral system without a clearly dominant majority party coalition both casts doubt on Dahl's thesis about how the Supreme Court's policy-making remains within the framework of majority preferences and revives interest in his passing suggestion that the Court find opportunities to be more assertive in policy formulation when no dominant political coalition is in charge in Washington. New studies of the appointment of justices also raise questions about Dahl's central reliance on the appointment process to assure that the Court's policies remain consonant with the will of the lawmaking majority. Indeed, several of these themes interact in ways that both contradict and reinforce Dahl's overall thesis.

Pointing out that "public opinion polls are of relatively recent origin" and that national elections rarely allow an inference about public preferences on specific policies, Professor Dahl argued that "for the greater part of the Court's history . . . there is simply no way of establishing with any high degree of confidence whether a given alternative was or was not supported by a majority or a minority of adults or even of voters" (1957, 283–84). He was therefore clear from the beginning that his measure of the democratic nature of judicial policy-making— the infrequency with which the Court invalidated the work of lawmaking majorities on important policies—was a surrogate.[18] However, by the mid-1980s, public opinion polls of one kind or another had been conducted for almost half a century, and scholars began to closely examine the relationship between the Court's decisions and public opinion.

Early studies employing polls about a limited number of specific Court policies showed mixed public reaction, with the public supporting decisions ordering desegregation and reapportionment but opposing the Court's defendants' rights and affirmative action decisions (Murphy and Tanenhaus 1968; Adamany and Grossman 1983). However, looking more broadly at surveys of public preferences and comparing them to the main lines of the Court's policy directions—including some of its most controversial decisions of the 1960s and 1970s, criticized as judicial activism—Barnum (1985) found congruence between the Court's policies and public opinion, thus putting a majoritarian cast on judicial review. In a more far-ranging analysis, looking at more issues over even longer periods, Marshall (1989) identified 130 Court decisions that could be compared with surveys of public attitudes on issues and found that about 63 percent of those Court decisions were congruent with public opinion.

Recent studies continue to emphasize the congruence between public opinion and Supreme Court policy-making. Examining opinion polls and the justices' policies from 1958 through 1989, Mishler and Sheehan concluded that the data "suggest the existence of a responsive Court whose decisions not only reflect changes in public opinion but also serve to reinforce and legitimize opinion change in an iterative process" (1993, 87, 96). Others, too, found a relationship between the Court's decisions and the public mood on national policy (Stimson, Mackuen, and Erikson 1995). These studies were soon criticized because, while showing congruence between public opinion and Supreme Court policies, they did not demonstrate that this congruence occurred because individual justices followed or were influenced by public sentiment (Norpoth and Segal 1994). The possibility remained strong, therefore, that as public opinion evolved but individual justices with fixed judicial ideologies remained on the bench, the Supreme Court's policies would not remain consistent with majority will.

Responding to this concern, Mishler and Sheehan (1996), following their earlier analysis, examined the relationship between public opinion and the policy preferences of individual justices. Over a forty-year period, they concluded that about half the justices to some degree shifted policy positions in directions similar to changes in public opinion and that about a third of the justices did so to a substantial degree. Their conclusions appear to be confirmed by Flemming and Wood (1997), who examined the voting patterns of twenty-one justices on six issue areas from 1956 to 1989 and found that in five issue areas (but not in civil rights), the justices' votes tended to follow changes in the public's ideological mood.

Contemporary studies examining the relationship between public opinion and Supreme Court policies may prove both too much and too little. Dahl argued that the Court would usually act consonantly with the lawmaking majority, and public opinion studies confirm his hypothesis. But Dahl was concerned about a particular type of decision—those affirming or rejecting policies, especially important policies, of the lawmaking majority in Congress and the presidency. Today's public opinion studies fall short of responding to that concern. They show general congruence between Supreme Court policies of all kinds and public opinion but do not demonstrate that when the Court specifically acts on its own by invalidating the policies of the lawmaking majority, the justices act in congruence with public opinion and can thus claim to act democratically. Whether there is congruence between those Supreme Court policies that invalidate actions of the lawmaking branches—the policies about which Dahl was specifically concerned— and public opinion remains unresolved.

The opinion studies also prove too little. They do not address convincingly the mechanisms for keeping the Court in line with public opinion. Mishler and Sheehan suggest that it happens through "a political socialization process where public opinion alters the Court's ideology by causing one or more incumbent justices to change their individual attitudes. . . . Our analysis, then, does not argue against the attitudinal model of judicial decision making but in favor of a more subtle version in which individual attitudes are treated not as static and immutable but as fluid and dynamic" (1994, 722). This mechanism for judicial change has not yet been confirmed, and it is difficult to think of a study design that would do so. By contrast, Dahl's answer was clear: the appointment of justices, at more or less regular intervals, by presidents who are part of a long-enduring national political coalition would keep the Court in line with the will of lawmaking coalitions.

Contemporary analysis may occur in a changed context, however. As previously pointed out, there has not been a clear nationally dominant electoral coalition or a stable lawmaking majority for at least three decades. Who is appointed to the Court may therefore depend more on short-term shifts in control of the presidency, potentially leaving the

Court in the hands of opposition partisans when control again shifts to the other party. What Dahl perceived as occasional and quickly corrected lags in Court conformance to the lawmaking majority during realigning periods may now be long lags, occurring with regularity.

Dahl observed that "over the whole history of the Court, on the average one new justice has been appointed every twenty-two months," but he noted the "truly exceptional" situation that Franklin Roosevelt faced, failing to make a single Supreme Court appointment during his first term (1957, 285). Since 1968, however, the period between appointments has stretched to twenty-nine months, and the appointments have occurred at different frequencies during Democratic and Republican presidencies. Richard Nixon and Gerald Ford made five appointments during an eight-year period, Ronald Reagan made three appointments during his eight-year term, and George Bush made two more during the ensuing four-year term. By contrast, Jimmy Carter made no appointments in four years, and Bill Clinton made two in eight years. In short, Republicans held the presidency for twenty years and made ten appointments at an average rate of one every twenty-four months; Democrats held the presidency for twelve years and made just two appointments—an average of one every seventy-two months. The likelihood that the Court will be out of step with lawmaking majorities is thus heightened during periods of dealignment, and the potential for conflict between democratic decision making and the Court has increased in ways that Dahl could not have foreseen.

Whether for these reasons or for others, the Court appears to have become more active in overturning the policies of the lawmaking majorities. Taylor (1992) reports that the Court decided ninety-two cases invalidating federal laws in the republic's first 179 years and forty such cases in the ensuing 22 years, more than tripling the rate of invalidations. By another measure, the Court has been about four times as active in striking down federal laws from 1960 through 1996 than it was during the preceding 171 years (Baum 1996).[19] Whether this greater level of activism is caused by the loss of presidential influence over the Court because of dealignment or by some other reason is not clear, but there is at least some question about Dahl's conclusion that the Court would not often engage in policy-making at odds with the lawmaking majority.

There are, finally, new questions about the impact of the president's appointment power in influencing the direction of the Supreme Court. Noting that one of Woodrow Wilson's Supreme Court appointments was "wasted, from a policy point of view, on McReynolds," Dahl (1957,

290) acknowledged that presidents could sometimes name justices at odds with presidential policies or simply miscalculate appointees' likely decisions. For the most part, however, the evidence through history is that justices' policies are generally consonant with the policy views of their appointing presidents. And an examination of the civil rights votes by justices appointed by Presidents Eisenhower, Kennedy, Johnson, Nixon, and Ford found general consistency between justices' votes and presidential policies as reflected in presidential statements. However, about a third of justices compiled an overall civil rights voting record that veered away from the ideology expressed in presidential statements (Heck and Shull 1982).

In the modern period, however, there may be a somewhat greater tendency for justices either to act independently or to significantly shift their views once on the Court. President Eisenhower's reported chagrin at the policies pursued by Earl Warren and William Brennan may be the best-known instance of remorse. But Harry Blackmun's shift to the left and Lewis Powell's unanticipated liberalism on certain issues were certainly at odds with Nixon's stated intention to appoint conservatives to the Court. The extraordinary lack of agreement between George Bush's two appointees—David Souter and Clarence Thomas— rebuts the suggestion that the president's appointees are likely to share his policy views.

Of five recent presidents (Roosevelt, Truman, Eisenhower, Nixon, and Reagan) who appointed either four or five justices, blocs large enough usually to assure control of the Court, only three (Truman, Nixon, and Reagan) found their appointees acting as a cohesive group (Lindquist, Yalof, and Clark 2000). Moreover, bloc cohesion sometimes varied on different issues. Thus, Truman's appointees were cohesive on civil rights but not on economic issues—a surprising result because economic policy was the core of the New Deal–Fair Deal coalition. This analysis does not, of course, consider whether presidents—Kennedy, Johnson, Bush, and Clinton—who each appointed two justices achieved influence on the Court through cohesive voting by their appointees, but it appears that Byron White, appointed by Kennedy, did not hew to a liberal position over time and that Souter and Thomas, appointed by Bush, were in substantial disagreement from the beginning. Some reconsideration is therefore in order of Dahl's argument that the appointment process will serve as a sufficient device for assuring policy conformance between the Court and the lawmaking majority.

A related inquiry is whether the lawmaking branches are more assertive than in the past in attempting to reverse Supreme Court decisions inconsistent with policies of elected officials. Dahl's thesis that the Court's policies will not long be at odds with those of the lawmaking majority may retain its vitality, even if the processes for assuring conformity have evolved. There is no recent study examining the fate of Supreme Court overrulings of federal law, but a study looking more broadly at Supreme Court decisions at odds with the policies of elected officials reveals only a very small number of occasions when Congress passed legislation attempting to reverse the Court (Meernik and Ignagni 1997). Of 569 cases from 1954 through 1990 in which the Court struck down a federal law ($n = 65$), a state law ($n = 497$), or a presidential executive order ($n = 7$), Congress completely acquiesced in 78 percent of the decisions (i.e., neither house brought reversal legislation to the floor for a vote), one house voted to reverse 15 percent of the Court's decisions, and both voted to override 7 percent. This is a very small number of reversals, and it seems likely that very few of these overturned the Court's invalidations of federal law on constitutional grounds because of the limited means available for that purpose. While the question remains open, it does not seem likely that any weakening of the lawmaking majority's influence over the Court through the appointment power has been offset by an expansion of the majority's authority to overrule Court decisions in other ways.

Most of the recent studies of public opinion and the Supreme Court have focused on the democratic or representational nature of the Supreme Court rather than on the legitimacy-conferring function asserted by Dahl. However, the controversy over the Court's ability to confer legitimacy on public policy has continued. Nearly twenty years ago, Baas and Thomas (1984) conducted three controlled experiments with college students to test whether policies were more highly approved by panels of students who were told that the policies stemmed from the Supreme Court and the Constitution than by panels of students who were presented the same policies without attribution to the Court and Constitution. On none of the sixteen controversial policies submitted to students in the three experiments did attribution to the Court increase approval. Skepticism about the legitimacy-conferring function was heightened by Marshall's (1987) examination of eighteen instances from the 1930s to the 1980s in which public opinion polls about policies were available both before and after Supreme Court decisions on the same issues. On nine policies, the Supreme Court's decision was followed by a shift in public opinion away from the Court's policies; on six, opinion shifted in the direction of the

Court's policies; and on three, there was no change in the public's views.[20]

In the 1990s, however, there was new, albeit limited, support for the Court's potential to shape public opinion about policy. The Supreme Court was found to have high visibility and strong support among the public—both general support for it as an institution and more specific support for its role in making policy, including policies unpopular with the public (Gibson, Caldeira, and Baird 1998). Another study of public response to the abortion cases suggests that on issues where there is already majority support cutting across group lines, a decision by the Court may spur movement toward the Court's policy among those who hold dissenting opinions within each group. However, where majorities of relatively well defined groups within the population hold an opinion contrary to the Court's policy—such as Roman Catholics on the abortion issue—the impact of judicial action is likely to be consolidation of opinion within the group, thus contributing to polarization rather than consensus within the population as a whole (Franklin and Kosaki 1989). A later study confirmed that Court decisions about the death penalty caused heightened division within the public as unity increased within population subgroups that differed from one another (Johnson and Martin 1998). This study also found, however, that subsequent decisions on the same subject had little additional effect on public opinion.

Focusing on a single religious freedom case and conducting surveys in the community from which the case arose and separately in the larger geographic region, Hoekstra and Segal (1996) concluded that after the Court handed down its decision, public opinion overall moved in the same direction as the Court's decision in both geographic areas. Consistent with a theory that responses are different among subgroups, especially those opposed to the Court's decision, the authors found that opinion shifted less toward the Court's policy among those ideologically opposed to it, the more highly educated, residents of the immediately affected community, and those whose initial opinions were strongly held. Change toward the Court's opinion was influenced by extensive use of the media for information, by residing in the surrounding region rather than in the directly affected community, and by preexisting favorable evaluations of the Supreme Court. The authors recognize that it is unclear how the dynamic of public support for the Court's opinion in a case affecting a defined region might apply to national policies—that is, those adopted by Congress and the president, Dahl's national lawmaking majority. But Hoekstra and Segal's evidence that local public opinion follows Supreme Court decisions about local issues reopens the door to Dahl's legitimacy-conferring function.

The revival of interest in Court's legitimacy-conferring function faces enormous hurdles, however. Hoekstra (2000) examined opinion change following Supreme Court decisions—two on civil liberties, two on economic issues—in four communities from which those cases arose and in the immediately surrounding regions. Although opinion changed at different rates depending on respondents' previous evaluations of the Court, residence (local community, surrounding region), and initial attitude toward the case, she concluded that the decision caused changes in public evaluations of the Court. This reopens the issue left unclear by Dahl's discussion of public opinion and the Court: whether the institution's legitimacy or its ability to confer legitimacy on the policies of other decision makers is at stake when the Court is active in policy-making. If decisions by the justices cause citizens to reevaluate the Court itself rather than causing opinion to shift toward the Court's policy results, and if opinion is not shifted by Court decisions, then they do not legitimate decisions of the lawmaking majority.

THE DAHL THESIS INTO ITS FIFTH DECADE

Professor Dahl's remarkable essay will continue to provoke analysis and debate and to be extensively cited. The reasons are both simple and complex. His principal concern was the basic structural contradiction between policy-making by elected officials, periodically accountable to the electorate, on the one hand, and policy-making by appointed justices, subject to no periodic review by the voters, on the other. Dahl is uncompromising in his classification of this structural arrangement as contrary to democratic principles. Attempts by the Court's defenders and apologists to convert its power of judicial review into a democratic function will necessarily confront Professor Dahl's careful argument to the contrary.

Yet Dahl argued simultaneously that the Court's power to veto legislation by lawmaking majorities could be functionally reconciled with representative government in the United States. This analysis turned not on the logic of structural arrangements but rather on a complex empirical analysis—some parts systematically undertaken by Professor Dahl, some parts only suggested. His systematic empirical findings—that the Court's decisions overturning federal laws do not support a "democratic" rationale that the Court protects minority rights, that the

Court rarely overturns "important" policies of the lawmaking branches, that these few countermajoritarian decisions are generally overturned in a short time, that stable electoral alliances dominate American politics for extended political eras, and that the presidential appointment power usually keeps the Court in line with the lawmaking majority during these stable coalition periods—will continue to be subject to reanalysis as the conditions of U.S. politics change. The propositions that Dahl advances without empirical analysis are particularly provocative: that the Supreme Court may have greater latitude to make policy during unstable periods when one dominant political coalition is being displaced by another or when a stable coalition is itself divided on some significant issue on which the Court might act; that the Court has legitimacy as an institution among the public; and that because of its association with the Constitution and its normal reticence in policy-making, the Court has the ability to confer legitimacy on the policies of the elected departments by holding those policies constitutional.

The most difficult challenge for analysts of Professor Dahl's empirical assertions—both those he tested and those he suggested—is to calculate the effect of their conclusions on his larger argument that the Court fits comfortably into the nation's system of representative government, not as a matter of logic but rather as a fact confirmed by political behavior. Dahl has created an intricate fabric of empirical analysis and assertion that leads to a larger conclusion about the character of judicial review in a democratic polity. Tugging at this thread or that thread of that fabric gives play to the growth of data, the increasingly rigorous methods, and the substantial body of midlevel theory that has developed in several branches of political science since 1957. But the larger challenge that will compel continuing interest in Dahl's brief essay is whether and how our treatment of the interwoven threads will change the picture of the Supreme Court's role in American democracy that Dahl has woven from them.

Those accepting this challenge include contemporary historical-institutionalists such as Mark Graber, who assess the Supreme Court as "an important site for struggles between various winners of American politics" (1999, 29). For these scholars, who see the Court as part of a political system made up of various political coalitions, judicial review is a political instrument used by some coalitions or by factions within coalitions that may only partly control the elected branches of the national government. Litigation before the Supreme Court may be viewed both as struggles over policy and as struggles between the different constitutional visions of those competing coalitions and of factions within those coalitions (Graber 1999, 40). While this approach emphasizes the role of the Supreme Court as an institution in the political system and is therefore closely linked to the new institutionalist research agenda in judicial studies, it is a perspective on the Court that finds its origin in Dahl's work.

As Dahl asked, "To anyone who holds that at least one role of the Court is as a policy-making institution . . . a serious and much debated question arises, to wit: Who gets what and why? Or in less elegant language: What groups are benefited or handicapped by the Court and how does the allocation by the Court of these rewards and penalties fit into our presumably democratic political institutions?" (1957, 281). Those questions and Dahl's answers to them will continue to provide impetus to judicial scholars reawakened to the importance of the Court's institutional context.

NOTES

1. Dahl has referred to the U.S. Supreme Court and to judicial review in several other works. However, with one small exception—his acknowledgment that judicial review by a national supreme court may be a means to carry out the policies of national majorities against local lawmaking majorities in states, provinces, or other regional governments—these other references essentially confirm and repeat the main themes established in his groundbreaking 1957 essay.

2. The *Journal of Public Law* later became the *Emory Law Journal*.

3. Of its thirty-one footnotes, only eight referred to other authors (including two to the same author), and two of those cited reference works from which Dahl had drawn data. The remaining footnotes simply documented the manner in which Dahl had categorized Supreme Court decisions invalidating acts of Congress or cited constitutional amendments overturning Supreme Court decisions.

4. Dahl examined only Supreme Court decisions striking down federal laws within four years of enactment, a convention designed, he said, to reasonably identify only those cases that overturned the policies of a national lawmaking majority still likely to be in existence. This convention has flaws, as we will subsequently note. However, using that approach, Dahl concluded that of thirty-eight such invalidations, twelve occurred during the New Deal era standoff between the Court and FDR, and only seven of the twelve were on important policy matters. All seven, Dahl argued, were overruled within a few years. Of the remaining twenty-six cases invalidated within four years of enactment, fifteen involved important policy issues. Of these, the Court reversed itself on ten, Congress changed its policies on two others to accept the Court's

decisions, and the ultimate policy outcome was unclear in the remaining three. Overall, then, Dahl argued that twenty-two cases overturned important congressional policies within four years of enactment, and in seventeen of those, the Court overruled itself and in two others the Congress overtly accepted the Court's policy decision. It is this tally of cases on which Dahl based his assertion that the Court rarely overturned important policies of the lawmaking majority and that when it did, its decisions didn't endure. No one has yet repeated this analysis to include the Court's invalidation of federal statues in the period since Dahl wrote, during which the Court has been more active in reviewing federal laws.

5. In our August 2000 discussion with Professor Dahl, he surprisingly indicated that he was rethinking the question of how institutional structures—including judicial review—might create protections for minority and individual rights. While surprising to those of us who have plumbed the reasoning of "Decision-Making in a Democracy," Dahl's renewed attention to this question is entirely consistent with his intellectual conviction that important questions about how to define, develop, and sustain democracy are always open to renewed analysis and deliberation.

6. "Do we have evidence in [cases in which the Court has held legislation unconstitutional within four years after enactment] that the Court has protected fundamental or natural rights and liberties against the dead hand of some past tyranny by the lawmakers? The evidence is not impressive. In the entire history of the Court there is not one case arising under the First Amendment in which the Court has held federal legislation unconstitutional. If we turn from these fundamental liberties of religion, speech, press and assembly, we do find a handful of cases—something less than ten—arising under Amendments Four to Seven in which the Court has declared acts unconstitutional that might properly be regarded as involving rather basic liberties. [Citations omitted.] An inspection of these cases leaves the impression that, in all of them, the lawmakers and the Court were not very far apart; moreover, it is doubtful that the fundamental conditions of liberty in this country have been altered by more than a hair's breadth as a result of these decisions. However, let us give the Court its due; it is little enough" (Dahl 1957, 292).

7. "Even without examining the actual cases, it would appear, on political grounds, somewhat unrealistic to suppose that a Court whose members are recruited in the fashion of Supreme Court justices would long hold to norms of Right or Justice substantially at odds with the rest of the political elite" (Dahl 1957, 291).

8. Citations to cases in Dahl's text have been omitted.

9. The analysis of the voting behavior of individual justices remains a powerful element in judicial studies five decades after Pritchett introduced it as a method for analyzing the political nature of judicial decision making (e.g., Segal and Spaeth 1993).

10. See also Key 1959. Sundquist 1983 offers a comprehensive statement of realignment theory and electoral realignments through history.

11. See Adamany 1980, which suggests how the Court played a role in shaping majority-coalition policies during some, but not all, periods leading up to critical elections.

12. See Taylor 1992, which suggests that since 1968 there has been no dominant political party coalition and discusses the Court's policy-making role during that period.

13. "The reality [is] that when the Supreme Court declares unconstitutional a legislative act or the action of an elected executive, it thwarts the will of the representatives of the actual people of the here and now; it exercises control, not on behalf of the prevailing majority, but against it" (Bickel 1962, 17).

14. Bickel 1970 criticized the decisions of the Warren Court both because the policies underlying them had not been successful and because the people had not ultimately accepted them.

15. An exception may be Bruce Ackerman's trilogy, of which the first two volumes have been published (1991, 1998). Ackerman argues that at critical times in American history, national leaders, supported overwhelmingly by the people, engage in acts of popular sovereignty that lead to transformations of constitutional meaning, thus linking the Supreme Court to national leaders and popular movements as well as giving constitutional interpretation a popular sanction. Ackerman's transformational periods include the founding period, the Civil War and its aftermath, and the New Deal, all of which are included in any set of realigning periods identified by social scientists who study electoral cycles.

16. There is a large literature on dealignment; see, e.g., Inglehart and Hochstein 1972; Norpoth and Rusk 1982; Dalton, Beck, and Flanagan 1984; Niemi and Weisberg 1993.

17. Dahl 1957 (282 n.4) reported 78 cases declaring one or more provisions of federal law unconstitutional from 1789 through 1955. Taylor 1992 (352, 366) counted 91 such cases through 1968 and 132 such cases through 1990. So, in the twenty-two years following the end of the New Deal coalition in 1968, the Court invalidated federal laws in 41 cases, an average of about 1.8 each year, compared to one every two years from the beginning of the republic through 1968.

18. In some respects, Dahl's search for a direct measure of public opinion about judicial policy is surprising, because much of Dahl's other work emphasizes the pluralist rather than majoritarian nature of American democracy—the formulation of policy through the interaction of an array of groups, often with widely differing resources, and the differential advantages in policy-making achieved by groups as a result of their differential influence on and access to the formal structures of government.

19. Baum (1996) reports 135 federal statutes declared unconstitutional from 1789 through 1959 (an annual rate of .42) and 63 from 1960 to 1996 (an annual rate of 1.7).

20. Thus, through the 1980s, there was virtually no scholarly support for the existence of the legitimacy-conferring function.

REFERENCES

Ackerman, Bruce. 1991. *We the People: Foundations.* Cambridge: Harvard University Press.

Ackerman, Bruce. 1998. *We the People: Transformations.* Cambridge: Harvard University Press.

Adamany, David. 1973. "Legitimacy, Realigning Elections, and the Supreme Court." *Wisconsin Law Review* 1973:790–846.

Adamany, David. 1980. "The Supreme Court's Role in Critical Elections." In *Realignment in American Politics,* ed. Bruce Campbell and Richard Trilling. Austin: University of Texas Press.

Adamany, David, and Joel Grossman. 1983. "Support for the Supreme Court as National Policymaker." *Law and Policy Quarterly* 5:405–37.

Baas, Larry, and Dan Thomas. 1984. "The Supreme Court and Policy Legitimation: Experimental Tests." *American Politics Quarterly* 12:335–60.

Barnum, David. 1985. "The Supreme Court and Public Opinion: Judicial Decision Making in the Post–New Deal Period." *Journal of Politics* 47:652–65.

Baum, Lawrence. 1996. *The Supreme Court.* 6th ed. Washington, D.C.: Congressional Quarterly Press.

Beck, Paul Allen. 1976. "Critical Elections and the Supreme Court: Putting the Cart after the Horse." *American Political Science Review* 70:930–32.

Bickel, Alexander. 1962. *The Least Dangerous Branch.* Indianapolis: Bobbs-Merrill.

Bickel, Alexander. 1970. *The Supreme Court and the Idea of Progress.* New York: Harper and Row.

Black, Charles L., Jr. 1960. *The People and the Court.* Englewood Cliffs, N.J.: Prentice-Hall.

Canon, Bradley, and S. Sidney Ulmer. 1976. "The Supreme Court and Critical Elections: A Dissent." *American Political Science Review* 70:1215–18.

Casper, Jonathan. 1976. "The Supreme Court and National Policy Making." *American Political Science Review* 70:50–63.

Choper, Jesse. 1980. *Judicial Review and the National Political Process.* Chicago: University of Chicago Press.

Dahl, Robert. 1957. "Decision Making in a Democracy: The Supreme Court as a National Policy-Maker." *Journal of Public Law* 6:279–95.

Dalton, Russell J., Paul Allen Beck, and Scott C. Flanagan. 1984. "Electoral Change in Advanced Industrial Democracies." In *Electoral Change in Advanced Industrial Democracies: Realignment or Dealignment?* ed. Dalton, Flanagan, and Beck. Princeton: Princeton University Press.

Ely, John Hart. 1980. *Democracy and Distrust.* Cambridge: Harvard University Press.

Flemming, Roy, and B. Dan Wood. 1997. "The Public and the Supreme Court: Individual Justice Responsiveness to American Policy Moods." *American Journal of Political Science* 41:468–98.

Franklin, Charles, and Liane Kosaki. 1989. "Republican Schoolmaster: The U.S. Supreme Court, Public Opinion, and Abortion." *American Political Science Review* 83:751–72.

Funston, Richard. 1975. "The Supreme Court and Critical Elections." *American Political Science Review* 69:795–811.

Gibson, James, Gregory Caldeira, and Vanessa Baird. 1998. "On the Legitimacy of National High Courts." *American Political Science Review* 92:343–58.

Graber, Mark. 1999. "The Problematic Establishment of Judicial Review." In *The Supreme Court in American Politics: New Institutionalist Interpretations*, ed. H. Gillman and C. Clayton. Lawrence: University of Kansas Press.

Heck, Edward, and Steven Shull. 1982. "Policy Preferences of Justices and Presidents: The Case of Civil Rights." *Law and Policy Quarterly* 4:27–38.

Hoekstra, Valerie. 2000. "The Supreme Court and Local Public Opinion." *American Political Science Review* 94:89–100.

Hoekstra, Valerie, and Jeffrey Segal. 1996. "The Shepherding of Local Public Opinion: The Supreme Court and Lamb's Chapel." *Journal of Politics* 58:1079–1102.

Inglehart, Ronald, and Avram Hochstein. 1972. "Alignment and Dealignment of the Electorate in France and the United States." *Comparative Political Studies* 5:343–72.

Johnson, Timothy, and Andrew Martin. 1998. "The Public's Conditional Response to Supreme Court Decisions." *American Political Science Review* 92:299–309.

Key, V. O. 1955. "A Theory of Critical Elections." *Journal of Politics* 17:3–18.

Key, V. O. 1959. "Secular Alignment and the Party System." *Journal of Politics* 21:198–210.

Lindquist, Stephanie, David Yalof, and John Clark. 2000. "The Impact of Presidential Appointments to the U.S. Supreme Court: Cohesive and Divisive Voting within Presidential Blocs." *Political Research Quarterly* 53:801–6.

Marshall, Thomas. 1987. "The Supreme Court as an Opinion Leader." *American Politics Quarterly* 15:147–68.

Marshall, Thomas. 1989. *Public Opinion and the Supreme Court*. Boston: Unwin Hyman.

Meernik, James, and Joseph Ignagni. 1997. "Judicial Review and Coordinate Construction of the Constitution." *American Journal of Political Science* 41:447–67.

Mishler, William, and Reginald Sheehan. 1993. "The Supreme Court as a Countermajoritarian Institution? The Impact of Public Opinion on Supreme Court Decisions." *American Political Science Review* 87:87–101.

Mishler, William, and Reginald Sheehan. 1994. "Popular Influence on Supreme Court Decision-Making: A Response." *American Political Science Review* 88:711–22.

Mishler, William, and Reginald Sheehan. 1996. "Public Opinion, the Attitudinal Model, and Supreme Court Decision Making: A Micro-Analytic Perspective." *Journal of Politics* 58:169–200.

Murphy, Walter, and Joseph Tanenhaus. 1968. "Public Opinion and the United States Supreme Court." *Law and Society Review* 2:357–82.

Niemi, Richard G., and Herbert F. Weisberg. 1993. "Dealignment and Realignment in the Current Period." In *Controversies in Voting Behavior*, 3d ed., ed. R. Niemi and H. Weisberg. Washington, D.C.: CQ Press.

Norpoth, Helmut, and Jerrold G. Rusk. 1982. "Partisan Dealignment in the American Electorate." *American Political Science Review* 76:522–37.

Norpoth, Helmut, and Jeffrey Segal. 1994. "Popular Influence on Supreme Court Decisions." *American Political Science Review* 88:711–16.

Rohde, David, and Harold Spaeth. 1976. *Supreme Court Decision-Making*. San Francisco: Freeman.

Scigliano, Robert. 1971. *The Supreme Court and the Presidency*. New York: Macmillan.

Segal, Jeffrey, and Harold Spaeth 1993. *The Supreme Court and the Attitudinal Model*. New York: Cambridge University Press.

Stimson, James, Michael Mackuen, and Robert Erikson. 1995. "Dynamic Representation." *American Political Science Review* 83:543–65.

Sundquist, James L. 1983. *The Dynamics of the Party System: Alignment and Realignment of the Political Parties in the United States*. Rev. ed. Washington, D.C.: Brookings Institution.

Taylor, John B. 1992. "The Supreme Court and Political Eras: A Perspective on Judicial Power in a Democratic Policy." *Review of Politics* 54:345–68.

CHAPTER 16

Martin Shapiro: Anticipating the New Institutionalism

Herbert M. Kritzer

I can imagine Martin Shapiro relaxing in his study with a glass of excellent California wine and opening Howard Gillman and Cornell Clayton's collection of essays, *The Supreme Court in American Politics: New Institutionalist Interpretations* (1999). Within a few minutes, he would be jumping up and down and shouting, "This is what I said thirty-five years ago!!!" And in fact, probably the best description of Shapiro's work, starting with his 1964 book (and the earlier articles that formed the basis of the book), *Law and Politics in the Supreme Court*, is that it anticipates what we today call new institutionalism.

In anticipating the developments of the 1990s, Shapiro's work serves as a bridge, perhaps the *key* bridge, between traditional institutional analysis of the judicial branch and the work of the new institutionalists. His application of what he labels "political jurisprudence" draws heavily on the traditional institutionalist work of Corwin, Mason, and McCloskey (with whom Shapiro studied at Harvard) while taking that work in directions that have become the new institutionalism. His scholarship constitutes a significant contribution to institutional analysis along at least three different dimensions:

understanding courts and court processes as institutions;
understanding the institution of courts in the larger political system; and
understanding the institutional functions of judicial norms.

Shapiro's work starts with a focus on the American context but moves in a comparative direction starting in the mid-1970s. In the discussion that follows, I consider three interrelated strands of work:

his definition of political jurisprudence and his early application
of that concept to institutional analyses of the Supreme Court
and administrative law;

his efforts to apply political jurisprudence beyond the American
context; and

his theoretical analyses of the judicial norm of stare decisis.

In this necessarily brief essay, I will neglect many areas of Shapiro's
scholarship (e.g., his later work on administrative law and his most
recent work on the European Court of Justice).

THE CONCEPT OF POLITICAL JURISPRUDENCE

The transition from the old to the new institutionalism is central to
Shapiro's concept of political jurisprudence. This term appears in the
subtitle of his first book, *Law and Politics in the Supreme Court*, and as the
title of Shapiro's 1964 essay in the *Kentucky Law Journal*. In Shapiro's
words, the "core of political jurisprudence is a vision of courts as political agencies and judges as political actors" (1964b, 196). The implication is that courts and judges can and should be subjected to the same
type of analysis routinely applied to other institutions of government
and their institutional actors.[1] While his institutionalist predecessors—
Corwin, Mason, and McCloskey—wrote about the Court's institutional features, they typically emphasized what made the Court unique
among the three branches of government rather than what made the
Court one of several distinctly political institutions within the American scheme of governance.

Political jurisprudence, the roots of which Shapiro traces to sociological jurisprudence[2] and legal realism (1964b, 294), encompasses a
range of analyses of the Supreme Court and courts more generally.
These include interest group use of the courts (after David Truman's
The Governmental Process), the Court as policymaker (after Robert
Dahl's "Decision Making in a Democracy: The Supreme Court as a
National Policy-Maker"), judges' decisions as reflecting underlying
attitudes (after Glendon Schubert's early work as well as that of Herman Pritchett), and justices as members of a small group subject to
leadership and group dynamics (after work by Eloise Snyder, Sidney
Ulmer, Walter Murphy, and David Danelski). Political jurisprudence
captures all of these threads in "an attempt to treat the Supreme Court
as one government agency among many—as part of the American
political process, rather than as a unique body of impervious legal technicians above and beyond the political struggle" (1964a, 15).[3]

Today this argument seems trite. Among political scientists, even
the most vehement proponents of "legal" explanations of Supreme

Court decisions accept the major or even central role of justices' preferences. Scholars in the legal academy may argue about whether justices' attitudes *should* be as important as they are, or scholars may argue that *some* justices are driven by attitudes (almost always the justices with whom the scholars disagree), but here, too, virtually no one would argue that the justices are simply legal technicians who apply neutral principles of analysis to arrive at neutral results. However, in the early 1960s, when what Shapiro called political jurisprudence was beginning to displace the more traditional approach associated with "public law" within political science, the movement came under fierce attack. The dominant school of analysis, reflected in the writing of political scientists such as Robert McCloskey and Wallace Mendelson and prominent legal academics such as Alexander Bickel, endorsed a view of "judicial modesty" that sought to show that the actions of courts and judges were grounded in legal principles (Bickel 1962) or at least in neutral principles (see Wechsler 1959). This approach had reasserted itself in the wake of Herman Pritchett's controversial book, *The Roosevelt Court* (1948), which dared to posit the importance of justices' values in decision making—a rather ironic response given the controversy of a decade earlier over the "nine old men" of the Supreme Court. As with the reaction to Pritchett's work, the developments Shapiro labeled political jurisprudence produced a vocal assault from the establishment. Paul Mishkin, in the foreword to the *Harvard Law Review*'s issue devoted to analyses of the Supreme Court's 1964 term, remarked that although political jurisprudence "has core soundness, carried too far it exerts a corrosive effect upon the symbolic ideals and the felt duty of fealty to Court decisions" (68). Even a decade later, prominent legal academics found it necessary to attack political jurisprudence. Archibald Cox delivered a set of lectures on the Supreme Court at Oxford in 1975; in the published version of those lectures, he specifically cites *Law and Politics in the Supreme Court* as representing a "school of political scientists in the United States that likens the Court to purely political agencies" that by "substituting a manipulative for a moral view of the judge's role" ultimately would "raise questions of [the Court's] legitimacy and thus undermine both the Court and the impact of its decisions" (1975, 106, 107–8).[4]

While Shapiro defined political jurisprudence to include attitudinal approaches to the study of justices' voting decisions, his work turned more on thinking about the Supreme Court and courts more generally as agencies of government. In this focus, he adopted an institutional approach. What differentiated his institutional approach from that of his institutional predecessors was his concern with the politics of institutions and institutional relationships. That is, Shapiro's institutionalism was that of political institutions rather than of legal institutions. He was concerned about the strengths and weaknesses of courts as institutions intimately involved in creating, shaping, and/or interpreting policy. He wanted to compare courts to other institutions in this broadly defined policy process. Law, in Shapiro's view, is a tool of policy rather than some lofty ideal of behavior that stands above the political fray.

EXPLICATING POLITICAL JURISPRUDENCE I: *Law and Politics in the Supreme Court*

The core of political jurisprudence is that courts are courts, but courts are also political institutions—hence the linking of *jurisprudence* with *political*. Shapiro sees courts as amenable to the same type of analysis as other political institutions; however, that does not mean that he sees courts as just another political institution. While he rejects efforts to set courts above politics, such as that represented by Herbert Wechsler's "neutral principles" (1959), Shapiro recognizes that courts interact in the political/governmental system in different ways than do legislative and administrative agencies. These differences serve to distinguish the role of courts in the policy process. *Law and Politics in the Supreme Court* develops this argument in detail. The thrust of Shapiro's analysis is that the Supreme Court's role in the policy process varies substantially from area to area. The variations depend on factors such as the need for technical expertise, the level of detail involved in the area, the constitutional or statutory nature of issues, and the nature of the policy implementation process.

Central to Shapiro's analysis is the relationship between the Supreme Court and other actors. He develops an argument that today we would label principal-agent theory. The Supreme Court must be attuned to what those it seeks to influence or direct will in fact do. Simply saying X wins and hence Y must do whatever X has sought to have it do is insufficient; the Court must persuade Y that there is a good reason that the Court is saying that X wins; the result is that the Court must provide "carefully reasoned and consistent opinions" (Shapiro 1964a, 24). The opinions not only persuade the loser of the need to conform to the Court's position but also (1) guide future actors in predicting the likely outcome of future cases and (2) present an image consistent with popular and professional expectations of neutrality (31). In one sense, Shapiro acknowledges attitudinalists' arguments that the Court's opinions are rationalizations, but unlike the attitudinalists, he goes on to identify the other functions of opinions vis-à-vis the policy process. Court decisions are more than naming winners and losers: they are one of the major vehicles through which the Supreme Court provides guidance to its "agents," whether they are lower courts, executive agencies, or the legislative branch of government. While political scientists have used the terminology of principal-agent theory to understand the relationship between the Supreme Court and other governmental actors (Brent 1999; Songer, Segal, and Cameron 1994), the emphasis has been on the Court's decisions more than on its opinions. Shapiro's analysis implies that we need to consider not just the direction of what the Court is doing but also what the Court is saying about why it is reaching the decision it is reaching.

If Shapiro were writing this book today, he might well point to the example of *Oncale v. Sundowner Offshore Services Inc* (523 U.S. 75 [1998]) as an example of the principal-agent theory of Supreme Court opinions in action. In *Oncale* the court unanimously ruled that workers could sue for claims of same-sex sexual harassment. Looking at winners and losers, *Oncale* appears to be a clear win for harassment victims and liberal groups such as the American Civil Liberties Union. However, the opinion, written by Justice Scalia, has turned out to limit more generally claims of sexual harassment. In the opinion, Scalia observes, "Title VII prohibits 'discriminat[ion] . . . because of . . . sex,'" and continues,

> [The plaintiff] must always prove that the conduct at issue was not merely tinged with offensive sexual connotations, but actually constituted discrimina[tion] . . . because of . . . sex. . . .
>
> [Title VII] does not reach genuine but innocuous differences in the ways men and women routinely interact with members of the same sex and of the opposite sex. The prohibition of harassment on the basis of sex requires neither asexuality nor androgyny in the workplace; it forbids only behavior so objectively offensive as to alter the "conditions" of the victim's employment. "Conduct that is not severe or pervasive enough to create an objectively hostile or abusive work environment—an environment that a reasonable person would find hostile or abusive—is beyond Title VII's purview." We have always regarded that requirement as crucial, and as sufficient to ensure that courts and juries do not mistake ordinary socializing in the workplace—such as male-on-male horseplay or intersexual flirtation—for discriminatory "conditions of employment."

We have emphasized, moreover, that the objective severity of harassment should be judged from the perspective of a reasonable person in the plaintiff's position, considering "all the circumstances." In same-sex (as in all) harassment cases, that inquiry requires careful consideration of the social context in which particular behavior occurs and is experienced by its target. A professional football player's working environment is not severely or pervasively abusive, for example, if the coach smacks him on the buttocks as he heads onto the field—even if the same behavior would reasonably be experienced as abusive by the coach's secretary (male or female) back at the office. The real social impact of workplace behavior often depends on a constellation of surrounding circumstances, expectations, and relationships which are not fully captured by a simple recitation of the words used or the physical acts performed. Common sense, and an appropriate sensitivity to social context, will enable courts and juries to distinguish between simple teasing or roughhousing among members of the same sex, and conduct which a reasonable person in the plaintiff's position would find severely hostile or abusive. [Citations omitted.]

The result of the opinion, as distinct from the decision favoring victims of same-sex sexual harassment, has been to disadvantage sexual harassment victims more generally. Trial courts are granting summary judgment and being upheld on appeal on the grounds that the plaintiff failed to prove a gender basis for the alleged discrimination or that even relatively aggressive behavior by male coworkers was "ordinary socializing" (Greenburg 1999). What mattered in this case was the opinion, not the outcome, which is precisely why Shapiro argues that to understand the Court's role in the policy process we must look to what the justices say as much or more than what they do. Other actors in the policy process are constantly attuned to what the justices say (Shapiro 1964a, 39–40).

In one sense, this is because many cases raise multiple issues. In *Oncale*, the Court clearly addressed two related but distinct issues: Does Title VII extend to same-sex sexual harassment? What types of behavior are actionable under Title VII? In other cases, the separate issues may be quite unrelated to one another (e.g., *Craig v. Boren*, 429 U.S. 190 [1976], which had both a major question regarding standing and a major question of equal protection). Shapiro observes that analysts must fall back on relatively traditional approaches of legal analysis of fact patterns and the issues that they raise to identify and separate out the distinct issues (1964a, 36). The multiple issues serve to structure the Court's decision, and this structuring lies more in the hands of the parties than in the Court as policymaker.[5] More generally, the issues presented to the Court constrain the range of policy choices the justices can make (37); unlike other agencies, which can initiate policy change *sua sponte* (to use the legal term), the Court is limited to the cases and by the records that come before it, although the justices can certainly invite issues to be brought.

The bulk of *Law and Politics in the Supreme Court* examines the different kinds of political roles the Supreme Court plays in five different areas of decision making: review of congressional investigations, labor law, federal tax policy, representation (*Baker v. Carr*, 369 U.S. 186 [1962] and its aftermath), and antitrust. In his analysis, Shapiro pays attention to winners and losers but is more interested in understanding how the Court's decisions influenced other actors in the policy and political process. Shapiro looks closely at what the Court says because of his argument that the Court's words ultimately guide the other actors. With an updating of the cases covered, the discussions of the various areas could readily be found in a volume of writing by new institutionalists (Clayton and Gillman 1999; Gillman and Clayton 1999). His analyses are not simply a lawyer's doctrinal discussion; instead, he closely examines the give-and-take among institutional actors seeking to stake out positions and communicate those positions to players. Shapiro sees communication of positions and expectations as central to the policy-making process, and the justices must pay careful attention to what they say in their opinions because of their communication value. The reasoning and reference to prior cases are not simply rationalization; rather, they are an essential road map of the justices' thinking that others in the policy process—lower courts, agencies, Congress—must consider. In a fundamental sense, the opinions are a major element what some have called the "separation of powers" game (see Epstein and Walker 1995; Eskridge 1991a, 1991b; Knight and Epstein 1996; Marks 1989; Segal 1997); a key element of that game is information, and the opinions provide information—albeit not always unambiguous information—to the legislators who must decide how to respond to the Court's decisions, a point made by those who look not just at Court's response to legislators but also at the legislators' response to the Court's decisions (see Eskridge 1991a; Melnick 1995; Pickerill 2000).

Through his case studies, Shapiro demonstrates the strengths and weaknesses of the Court's major institutional advantage: functioning as a generalist in a world of specialized policy subsystems—for example, agencies, subcommittees, and interest groups (see such classics as Heclo 1978; Lowi 1969).[6] One result is that the Court has difficulty dealing with extremely technical, nitty-gritty areas such as the federal tax code (Shapiro 1964a, 154–67). The Court's generalist nature means that it can be most effective as an intervener in the policy/political process when it can make broad pronouncements that establish general principles of action. Without getting into the debate over whether the Court is a "hollow hope" (Rosenberg 1991), decisions such as those in the wake of *Baker v. Carr* led to significant changes in the composition of legislative bodies at the state level.[7] In other areas, the Court is thrust into the policy process by other actors (e.g., by Congress in the area of antitrust) as a means to allow the delegating entity to avoid making difficult decisions; the generalist nature of the Court does not well equip it to deal with the complexities of economic reality raised by significant antitrust issues, as the recent/current Microsoft case demonstrates: What expertise would the Supreme Court bring to the resolution of thorny technical issues that the law seems to assume a court can sort out? Nonetheless, the Court (or at least the courts) must decide these cases and in so doing must make choices that are fundamentally political. While the form of the Court's decision process may differ from that used by administrative and legislative bodies, and while the Court may make reference to legal standards rather than political interests, the Court is making political choices as well as legal choices when it decides cases. In making these choices, the Court itself determines its role vis-à-vis the other institutions of government.

EXPLICATING POLITICAL JURISPRUDENCE II: *The Supreme Court and Administrative Agencies*

Four years after the publication of *Law and Politics in the Supreme Court*, Shapiro published *The Supreme Court and Administrative Agencies* (1968b), which shifted the focus from legal areas where the Supreme Court plays a major lawmaking role to areas where it, along with administrative agencies, plays a "supplementary" lawmaking role. The areas explored in *Law and Politics* generally concerned either constitutional pronouncements (e.g., apportionment, institutional powers, free speech, and so on) or effective congressional delegation to the Court of major lawmaking responsibilities (antitrust, important elements of labor law). As discussed earlier, Shapiro's analyses of these areas emphasized the Court's political role and the importance of the Court's opinions for the larger political process.

In this second book,[8] Shapiro continues to move his application of political jurisprudence beyond the constitutional realm that then dominated political scientists' writings about the Supreme Court. Shapiro describes this as part of an effort to move the research agenda for courts scholars "outward and downward . . . to lower courts and bodies of law other than constitutional" (letter to author, May 15, 2000). This was not surprising, given that Shapiro saw courts' role in the political system in very broad terms. In his first year of teaching at Harvard, he created a course called American Judicial Government, so titled so that it would fall right next to V. O. Key's course on American Party Government.

The Supreme Court and Administrative Agencies examines the Court's political role in its relations with a variety of administrative agencies, with particular focus on the Patent Office and the Federal Power Commission. Shapiro chose these two agencies because they represent "near to the two extremes of judicial review of administrative decision making; one at which the Supreme Court persists in major opposition to agency policy, the other where the Court acquiesces in the agency position, imposing only a very marginal check on its actions" (1968b, 264). In both of these areas, the agencies and the Court function in the context of relatively well specified legislation and hence assume a supplementary lawmaking role within the boundaries set by statute. In contrast to the constitutional arena, in these areas "judicial policy making . . . can rarely move public policy more than a few degrees off the directional line set by the statute" (21).

The core of Shapiro's argument is that the Supreme Court and the administrative agencies function as competing subordinate lawmakers within a particular policy domain. The terms of the competition are set by the statute, and hence the law made by the Court and the agencies tends to lie at the margin rather than the core of setting policy. In some areas (e.g., antitrust and labor), because of the huge gaps left by congressional enactments, the courts may play a more central role (see Shapiro 1968b, 25–26), but even here the courts are engaged in subordinate lawmaking and are subject to being reined in by Congress whenever it so chooses.

The agencies and the courts differ in how they go about their subordinate lawmaking. Shapiro argues that many of the supposed differences are less than would appear to be the case at first glance. For example, stare decisis, supposedly a particular feature of judicial process, can be viewed as a specialized form of incrementalism. (See the subsequent section on stare decisis for a detailed discussion of the topic.) For Shapiro, the biggest difference comes back to that between the generalist and the specialist rather than any uniquely legal style. The judicial setting may also allow for the participation of interests excluded from the administrative setting, the result of which is to make the court venue in a sense more political than the administrative setting. Moreover, the Supreme Court's "actions are less important as discrete pronouncements on legal-doctrinal questions than as episodes in the evolution of public policy" (Shapiro 1968b, 226). This of course assumes that the Supreme Court acts in response to administrative agencies; in reality, very few agency decisions are appealed to the courts, and when cases make it to the Supreme Court, the Court tends to defer to the agencies.[9] There are, of course, exceptions, such as when a new administration attempts to sharply change long-standing administrative decision patterns without congressional action and those affected swamp the courts with appeals, as in the early 1980s in response to the Reagan administration's efforts to reduce the Social Security disability rolls (see Mezey 1988). Both because the courts sometime stand in opposition to administrative action and because of the importance of a policy process that is open to involvement and influence,[10] the courts are important actors even when the role they play is that of subordinate lawmaking.

Administrative law remained a central part of Shapiro's work, reflecting his belief that courts are important politically for the full range of areas they touch. However, Shapiro's efforts to move courts scholarship "outward and downward" was by no means limited to the nonconstitutional decisions of the U.S. Supreme Court. The agenda of political jurisprudence extended to courts outside the United States and to areas of law, customarily labeled private law, long ignored by political scientists. In the next two sections, I discuss these threads of Shapiro's pioneering efforts.

EXTENDING POLITICAL JURISPRUDENCE TO COMPARATIVE STUDIES

Shapiro's 1981 book, *Courts: A Comparative and Political Analysis*, represents his most comprehensive effort to extend political jurisprudence beyond the U.S. context. While interest in comparative judicial studies grew throughout the 1990s (Epp 1998; Holland 1991; Jackson and Tate 1993; Jacob et al. 1996; Kenney, Reisinger, and Reitz 1999; Stone 1992; Tate and Vallinder 1995), *Courts* was published at a time when courts were largely ignored both by U.S. political scientists who defined their field as comparative politics and by non-U.S. political scientists studying their own countries.[11] Outside of the United States, courts were (and largely still are) seen as something apart from politics and hence not an appropriate focus of study by political scientists.[12] In *Courts*, Shapiro seeks to bring the comparative study of courts to a wider view within political science and to do so by developing the argument that the political jurisprudential view—that courts should be thought of as political agencies of government and judges as political actors—extends to courts from diverse countries.

Shapiro's strategy is to take on the idealized view of courts as triadic dispute resolvers whereby two disputants turn to a third party to obtain a resolution based on existing principles of law. According to this view, courts are distinguished by four characteristics: "independence, adversariness, decisions according to preexisting rules, and 'winner-take-all' decisions" (1981, vii). His core argument is that these characteristics, taken together, represent the basis of the "courts are different" or the "courts are not political" perspective. Shapiro does not reject the position that judges *may* exhibit independence, that the judicial process *may* be adversarial, that decisions *may* reflect preexisting rules, or that courts *may* make "winner-take-all" decisions. Rather, he argues that examples contradicting these propositions are not simply rare exceptions but routine or dominant events even in settings where the proposition is taken most seriously. Courts, according to Shapiro's analysis, routinely replace adversarial contests with mediational processes and seek to find compromise solutions rather than declaring one party the winner; neutrality on the part of judges is often more stylized than real, and judges cannot avoid going beyond even the most comprehensive preexisting rules to deal with inevitably unique situations. Most fundamentally, the role of courts and judicial processes is to maintain the legitimacy of the regime, and most elements of the court system serve to advance this function.

The thrust of Shapiro's analysis is straightforward. When one looks closely at the prototype and nature of the deviations from the prototype, it is apparent that the courts function largely in support of the political regime. When it is in the interest of the regime to appear neutral and above fray between the disputants, the courts put this image forward. Conversely, the structure of judicial selection, appellate process, nonadjudicatory dispute resolution, and so forth work to support the interests of the regime in terms of stability and legitimacy. On the subject of appeal, for example. Shapiro observes that

appellate institutions are more fundamentally related to the political purposes of central regimes than to the doing of individual
justice. [With regard to conflict resolution] appeal [is] an important political mechanism for both increasing the level of central
control over administrative subordinates and for ensuring the
authority and legitimacy of rulers. . . . When trial courts or first-
instance judging by administrators is used as a mode of social control, appeal is a mechanism for central coordination of local control. (1981, 52–53)[13]

Shapiro goes on to label appeal a "mode of hierarchical political management" that also provides some assurances of fairness to the disputants (54). But even on the fairness dimension, of most importance is
the role of appeal in counteracting the fundamental instability of the
court's triadic form: as soon as the adjudicator makes a decision, the
triad becomes a two-against-one structure. Appeal provides a mechanism of reassuring the loser of a fair process, thereby maintaining the
political legitimacy of the authority under whose auspices the court
functions. The importance of perceptions of a fair process have been
confirmed in the years since *Courts* by the "procedural justice" work in
law and psychology (see Lind and Tyler 1988; Tyler 1990).

Vital to Shapiro's argument about the political importance of appeal
for the central regime is the near-universal use of some appeals procedure. As a test of this point, Shapiro examines a legal/judicial system
that does not involve an appeals mechanism, *kadi* courts in Islam. The
thrust of Shapiro's analysis is that the absence of appeal mechanisms
reflects the absence of centralized authority. Where there is centralized
secular authority, mechanisms of appeal are superimposed on the
Islamic system. Shapiro looks specifically at the Ottoman Empire and
argues that while there was no institutionalized appellate structure, the
divan (council of the sultan) functioned as an appellate body, hearing
complaints against lower-level officials including *kadis*, although there
was a dominant tendency to support the *kadis*, which in turn would be
consistent with the political argument Shapiro makes about the role of
appeal.

A second central theme of the "legal" view of courts is the role of
independence as a central characteristic of the adjudicator. For
Shapiro, the question concerns independence from whom or from
what. While it is easy to show the tension between independence and
accountability in the jumble of selection systems used in the United
States, other countries have adopted systems that ostensibly insulate

judges from "politics." Shapiro argues that while adjudicators may be independent of the immediate parties to a private dispute, they are not independent of the political regime, even in systems that design selection systems to be outside the day-to-day political arena. In most countries, although the judiciary is separate from the "political" branch of government, the bureaucratic structure of judiciary and the resultant recruitment and promotion systems insure a form of centralized control that reflects the regime's interests (see esp. Abe 1995; Lafon 1991).

Shapiro focuses on England for his analysis of judicial independence. He does not argue that English judicial independence is mythical but rather that there is less independence than at first appears to be the case. Courts in England developed largely as part of the centralization of power: the common law courts enunciated and enforced the law that was common to the king's dominion; the courts of equity served as the vehicle for the king's chancellor, the chief administrative officer of the realm and the "conscience of the king" (Shapiro 1981, 85), to deal with gaps and problems in the common law and its writs. By the mid–nineteenth century, the hierarchical structure of the English court system was more or less in place (although courts have been combined, renamed, abolished, and so forth over the past 150 years, the major structure has remained recognizable), and the subordination of the courts to parliamentary supremacy was firmly established (including Parliament's power to create and abolish courts at will). Until recently (that is, since *Courts* was published), the central regime's interests have been kept largely out of the traditional courts by creating specialized administrative tribunals to deal with issues arising from the implementation of government policy; unlike the United States, appeals from tribunals to the courts were rarely permitted. (For a discussion of the few exceptions, see Karlen 1963, 132–33.)

Shapiro discusses evidence of some involvement of judges in reviewing actions of government officials starting as early as the 1940s and 1950s and culminating in the 1958 Tribunals and Inquiries Act (1981, 118–21), but he suggests that those changes were nothing more than "the judges' refusal finally to be pushed entirely out of the field of judicial review of administrative decisions" (121).[14] Subsequent developments raise questions about Shapiro's skepticism: over the past twenty years, there has been a sharp increase in the frequency of judicial review (see Sunkin 1993), which is handled by a specially designated panel of judges from the Queen's Bench Division of the High Court, which is known as the Divisional Court (Jacob et al. 1996, 151–52). In addition, European law has begun to increase the courts' role relative to Parliament: the Human Rights Act of 1998, which became effective in October 2000, incorporated the European Convention of Human Rights into British law and almost certainly will further shift power to the courts.

Yet this increasing role of courts does not negate Shapiro's argument. The selection of judges of the high courts is largely in the hands of the lord chancellor, who is a member of the ruling government cabinet.[15] While the lord chancellor relies on staff in the Lord Chancellor's Department for much of the work of judicial selection, and while there have been calls to change selection processes and criteria to make the process more open, nothing in the proposals significantly changes the focus on candidates who are safe in the political sense. While occasionally, someone may find his or her way to the bench and subsequently act in a genuinely independent fashion, the strong norm today of promotion up the judicial ladder; High Court judges are selected mostly from those serving in part-time judicial positions such as recorder, and the High Court judges are the primary source of Appeal Court judges, who in turn are the primary pool of candidates for the Judicial Committee of the House of Lords (see Malleson 1997).[16] This means that those who are too independent, at least vis-à-vis the policy of the sitting government, are unlikely to move up the judicial hierarchy. One interesting but as yet unanswered question is whether judges selected by the lord chancellor of one party are more likely to strike down the actions under a government of the other party.

Finally, regarding the limited nature of judicial independence, recent research provides further evidence in support of the view that courts serve first the regime and then the parties. A number of studies of court outcomes have built on Marc Galanter's distinction between "haves" and "have nots": by and large, haves come out ahead in litigation, Galanter argues, because of institutional and resource advantages that accrue to "repeat players" who both learn how to use the system and have a long-term stake in how the system operates (1974). One generally consistent result of the studies of court outcomes, both at the appeals level and the trial level, is that government litigants are more successful than nongovernment litigants. Most researchers have interpreted these patterns as reflecting the government litigant as the consummate repeat player (Farole 1999, 1054–55; Songer, Sheehan, and Haire 1999, 830). However, a more political interpretation is that courts have a built in bias toward or deference to the regime of which they are a part (Farole 1999, 1056). In some ways, this makes sense because government litigants often are actually resource poor rather than resource rich, and many government legal departments in the United States are marked by high turnover as young attorneys move through, gain experience, and go off to find their fortunes. It is interesting that Shapiro has never weighed in with this observation, which his work in *Courts* can be seen as anticipating; then again, no one who has reported the pattern of governmental dominance has connected it to Shapiro's argument about the limitations of judicial independence vis-à-vis the governments for which the judges work.

STARE DECISIS AND POLICY-MAKING IN THE COURTS

As should be clear from the preceding discussion, one of the central themes of Shapiro's work is that the courts are intimately involved in the policy-making process. Of course, this view is not original to Shapiro; rather, Shapiro's institutional approach to understanding the role of courts in policy-making distinguishes his work. Importantly, a central element of his analysis revolves around the uniquely judicial/legal concept of stare decisis, an issue that he discusses in a set of three interrelated articles. Through this stare decisis trilogy, he not only shows the strong links between policy-making in the courts and in the other institutions of government but also ultimately reconstructs a role for stare decisis in areas of policy-making that the courts dominate. This reconstructed role differs sharply from traditional jurisprudential views of stare decisis, which continue to reappear in attacks on the so-called legal model of Supreme Court decision making by proponents of the attitudinal model (see Brenner and Spaeth 1995; Segal and Spaeth 1996; Spaeth and Segal 1999). By focusing largely on private law issues, this work on stare decisis extends analyses based on political jurisprudence in additional areas long neglected by political scientists.

The first of the trilogy articles was "Stability and Change in Judicial Decision-Making: Incrementalism or Stare Decisis?" (1965).[17] This article is part of the "task of political jurisprudence," which is an effort to "describe the functional similarities, difference and interrelationships of courts to other political agencies, and, in light of this description, prescribe what the courts might best contribute to the political system." The article's specific goal is "to describe a method of decisionmaking that is shared by courts and other political agencies" (136).

As the title suggests, the common form of decision making Shapiro seeks to attribute to the courts is incrementalism (as described in the work of James March [see Cyert and March 1963] and Charles Lindblom [1959, Braybrooke and Lindblom 1963] and as exemplified in

Aaron Wildavsky's *Politics of the Budgetary Process* [1964]). Incremental-ism, Shapiro observes, is "a method of decision-making that proceeds by a series of incremental judgments as opposed to a single judgment made on the basis of rational manipulation of all the ideally relevant considerations" (1965, 37). Shapiro's explication of incrementalism is straightforward, focusing on elements such as "margin-dependent choice," "themes" rather than "rules," "serial analysis and evaluation," satisficing, standard operating procedures, feedback loops, and so on.

Shapiro contrasts incrementalism to what he labels the theory of stare decisis: "there are rational and immutable legal principles imbed-ded somewhere in the life of the law and . . . the technique of stare deci-sis facilitates the legal system's discovery of those principles" (1965, 142). Shapiro argues that incrementalism is a much better description of the process of judicial policy-making than is stare decisis, in no small part because of the fundamental flaws of the classical view of stare deci-sis (i.e., judges typically had a variety of alternative lines of precedent from which they might choose, and there is no way of specifying which line of precedent was correct). The core of Shapiro's analysis is that precedent is best conceived not as an immutable line of binding princi-ples but as reflecting a particular style of incrementalism.

As a source of the incrementalist view within common law jurispru-dence, Shapiro turns to the work of Karl Llewellyn (1960). Llewellyn sees U.S. courts at midcentury as engaged in a process of incremental policy change—that is, lines of precedent do not reflect "fluctuations around a locus of principle, but as the record of a series of marginal adjustments designed to meet changing circumstances" (Shapiro 1965, 142). Shapiro's concern here is not so much with who wins and who loses in specific cases but rather with the evolution of legal doctrine that guides the actions of potential future litigants. His position is that while attitudinal explanations might go a long way—even all the way—toward accounting for wins and losses, more institutional explanations of processes and norms are required to account for the policies reflected in judicial doctrines. Judges may seek to move policy in par-ticular directions, but the norms of incrementalism inherent in the institution of the common law limit the amount of movement judges can justify on most occasions; although judges can have clear and immediate impact on the parties in the case at hand, the impact of any one decision on future parties is more limited because of the incremen-talist constraint.

Incrementalism thus allows for more freedom than does the tradi-tional view of stare decisis. At the same time, incrementalism recognizes the "lawyer's and judge's concern for precedent, stability, [and] long-standing practice" (Shapiro 1965, 155). Incrementalism allows— even encourages—lawyers and judges to seek out new paths; at the same time, incrementalism limits the degree of departure for those paths. The result is stability and gradual change coexisting in the law without a mechanical adherence to prior decisions. Judicial choice is real and inevitable; however, judges' freedom to choose among alternatives is incremental in nature, not an unbridled freedom to make radical departures to achieve policy goals.

As indicated by its title, "Decentralized Decision-Making in the Law of Torts" (1968a), the second article in the stare decisis trilogy, looks at the evolution of tort policy through a process of decentralized decision making. In this analysis, Shapiro views stare decisis primarily "in terms of socialization, of essentially tribal experience into which new initiates are integrated through ritual and education" (49). Shapiro chooses tort policy because it is an area traditionally dominated by the courts rather than the legislatures. Moreover, there are more than fifty distinct tort regimes within the United States, but they have a striking resemblance to one another. Shapiro asks what accounts for the fact that we do see a number of radically different tort regimes. Nothing requires that Wisconsin's tort regime closely resemble that of Arizona: although a Wisconsin practitioner might look at Arizona and see significant differences (and vice versa), a *bengoshi* from Japan or an *avocat* from France would see a single system with very minor variations.

Shapiro finds the answer to the puzzle of similarity in the flow of communication among the disparate decision makers combined with "(1) a common culture and historical experience, (2) a common professional discipline, (3) shared channels of communication and incentives to use them, and (4) a piecemeal system of messaging that leads to large volume, constant communication" (1970, 51). The result of all of these factors is the emergence of a "collective opinion" (51). The norms of the system require decision makers to be attentive to decisions of others, and the system of publication of appellate decisions insures that there is a large flow of communication. The receivers of these communications share a common perspective on their significance and see them through very similar perceptual screens. These commonalities result from core law school curriculums that differ little in content; the similar content in turn flows from the almost universal case method of teaching and the dominance of a small number of very similar casebooks for teaching key areas of the law (e.g., torts).[18] Shapiro traces the evolution of doctrine vis-à-vis some important issues in tort (e.g., "attractive nuisance," "charitable immunity") to show how courts in disparate jurisdictions incrementally sought out solutions to new problems created by technological and social developments as well as how these solutions become crystallized through writing of academics and through the Restatement of Torts. In some ways, Shapiro is describing the analogic reasoning process that marks common law legal reasoning (see Levi 1961). What distinguishes Shapiro's analysis is that he sees this as very much at one with policy development in institutions other than the courts. That is, while there may be some unique communication tools and some unique language, the accretion of case law is the quintessential incremental process.

While much of the debate over the role of courts in American society has turned on the movement of public issues from the legislative arena to the judicial arena, Shapiro raises the fascinating question of movement in the other direction. Whereas some issues have traditionally been seen as political and properly the realm of the "political" branches of government (e.g., provision of government services and legislative districting), others have been accepted as properly the realm of the courts (the classic private law issues of tort, contract, property, and inheritance). Just as the failure of the political branches to deal with key issues in their realm has led courts to assert authority, the failure of the courts to deal with key issues in their traditional areas have led the political branches to act (e.g., marital property, punitive damages, joint and several liability). Thus, while the courts are subordinate, supplementary lawmakers in some areas, in others the courts are the primary lawmakers, with the legislative branch playing the supplemental role.

The last leg of the stare decisis trilogy, "Toward a Theory of Stare Decisis" (1972), turns further to communication theory to specify how we might understand the role of case law and hence stare decisis in judicial policy-making/decision making. On one level, the norm of stare decisis is primarily an organizing principle of legal discourse in a common law system. Implicitly, this contrasts to the code law systems of Europe, which rely on treatises explicating code provisions rather than incremental and redundant communication inherent in a system claiming to rely on precedent. This distinction's importance lies in the contrast between redundancy and information that Shapiro emphasizes from communications theory: redundancy is important when information is low.

What is the significance of the fact that judicial decisions and judicial arguments in the form of lawyers' briefs emphasize redundancy while suppressing information? Emphasizing redundancy goes hand in hand with the incremental view Shapiro presented in the earlier articles in the trilogy. If cases were treated as genuinely unique, requiring new perspectives and new approaches, that would constitute pressure for unique solutions to each case. Redundancy emphasizes commonalities and provides choices among existing solutions. To the degree that a case does present a unique combination of issues and that those issues are communicated through reference to a variety of different cases, this communication serves to focus the decision maker on the referenced cases, which in turn shapes the decision ultimately reached to look like those cases rather than as something entirely new.

The lawyer's need to provide redundancy through as much case law support as possible for the lawyer's argument leads to cross-citation among jurisdictions, even when the decisions of a court in one jurisdiction have, even under the strictest rules of precedent, no binding authority on a court in another jurisdiction. Yet the practice of cross-citation further homogenizes the legal policy at issue across jurisdictions. Thus, the norms of stare decisis (i.e., finding support for a proposed decision in prior decisions) communicates from one court to others what the first court has done. Shapiro observes that the "survival of *stare decisis*, particularly in 'common law' areas of law, as the dominant mode of legal discourse" reflects the redundancy of communication it represents, assisting judges in choosing among a wide range of options in a way that results in incremental policy change (1972, 133). "*Stare decisis* does not yield single correct solutions" (133) but remains relevant because of its communicative aspects.

Shapiro believes that this trilogy constitutes a kind of general theory of stare decisis that he should have fashioned into a book (letter to author, October 18, 1999). One might speculate on what the book might have looked like as part of his institutional approach to political jurisprudence. On the theoretical side, the central aspect of *Stare Decisis, Policy-Making, and the Courts*—my speculative title for this unwritten book—would have emphasized the indeterminate nature of stare decisis. That is, stare decisis would be of limited use in predicted outcomes of particular cases; Shapiro clearly would express little surprise or distress over the findings of Segal, Spaeth, and Brenner (Brenner and Spaeth 1995; Segal and Spaeth 1996, 1999) that justices of the Supreme Court are unlikely to feel bound by precedents in the mechanical way of legal positivism. At the same time, Shapiro's theory would have emphasized the central role of stare decisis in the decisional process and in the communication of what the law demands of judges deciding the law and of those subject to the law. Just as I regularly tell students that the fact that there is no right answer to a question does not mean that there are no wrong answers, stare decisis points the way for decision makers concerning possible acceptable outcomes. The incrementalism of stare decisis allows for change, but only in small steps. The emphasis in *Stare Decisis, Policy-Making, and the Courts* would be on how similar this process is in key respects to policy-making by other governmental institutions.

These three articles provide Shapiro's most complete analysis of the private law area of torts. The first essay of the trilogy reappeared in his major book on administrative process, *The Supreme Court and Administrative Agencies* (1968b), so it is clear that he had thought about the incrementalist approach to stare decisis vis-à-vis administrative law. Most likely, the explication of the incrementalist approach in the unwritten *Stare Decisis, Policy-Making, and the Courts* would have included a revised version of his analysis of tort law plus case studies from administrative law, statutory interpretation, and constitutional law; he touches on the area of obscenity in the first article in the trilogy, and a significant discussion of this area of jurisprudence would have reflected his long-standing interest in First Amendment issues (his dissertation was on this topic and eventually was published as Shapiro 1966).

CONCLUSION: INSTITUTIONALISM AND THE LEGACY OF MARTIN SHAPIRO

While Shapiro's institutional analyses of courts are regularly cited by persons working in the new institutionalist mode, few authors take the time to consider in depth the ways in which Shapiro anticipated the analytic developments that were to come. His articulation of political jurisprudence as well as his applications of that core concept provide the foundation for the kinds of broad understandings today's institutionalist analysts advance.

The failure to pay detailed attention to some of Shapiro's core insights has had important implications that underlie some of the more heated recent debates among law and politics scholars. A good example is the ongoing dialoguè over whether anything more than attitudes matters in understanding Supreme Court decision making. One can easily imagine what a contribution from Shapiro to this debate would look like. He would acknowledge the importance of the justices' political preferences and would applaud the proponents of the attitudinal model for embedding their argument firmly in the Court's institutional setting. Conversely, he would reject the simplistic portrayal of stare decisis found in much of the work showing that justices act on their own preferences rather than on precedent when the two conflict. He would argue that stare decisis does not bind justices to precedent but rather creates an expectation that the justices will change and develop law incrementally, relying on precedents for information on where the law is and how it has been moving.

Even more important than what Shapiro might say about specific conceptual debates would be his view that the study of courts through the lens of political jurisprudence must involve both the political and the jurisprudential. This means that analysts must be attentive to the political context and the political influences that operate on judges, justices, and courts and to the jurisprudence—the content of what judges and justices say—produced by the courts. This content is central for understanding how judges and justices affect one another as well as how they affect other political actors. Appellate decisions, while often involving elements of rationalization, provide the primary guidance for future action. As shown by the example of the *Oncale* decision discussed earlier in this chapter, what the justices say in their opinions is likely to be more important in the long run than what they do in terms of who wins and who loses the case. Furthermore, as Shapiro so clearly demonstrates in his work, the opinions provide a window onto the justices' struggles in trying to develop logical approaches to the issues presented to them. Because of both the norm of explanation and the need to provide guidance for future actions, the expectations of judicial opinions force justices to explain and defend their courses of action, particularly on collegial courts where dissents are possible.

More generally, even though the term *political jurisprudence* pops up only occasionally in day-to-day discourse among political scientists who study courts, it is clear that this perspective has triumphed. Political scientists have increasingly become concerned about the interaction of courts with other governmental institutions, such as the interaction between the Supreme Court and Congress. In such discussions, the image of the Court is that of one institution of politics interacting with another. The best of such discussions focus on both the political and jurisprudential elements of the Court's role (Epstein and Kobylka 1992; Melnick 1983, 1994; Pickerill 2000).

One might ask why, if political jurisprudence has taken over, do we not find Shapiro's work cited more often? I think that there are probably two reasons for this. First, political jurisprudence has become so dominant that it is effectively taken for granted. To the extent that one can say that there is an analytic paradigm guiding the study of courts by U.S.-trained political scientists, that paradigm is political jurisprudence. Subsumed within political jurisprudence are the other specific theoretical approaches: attitudinal, strategic, interest group theory, small-group theory, systems theory, courts as communities, and so forth. All of these approaches look at courts as political, and the best of the analyses within each approach consider the ways in which jurisprudential issues interact with politics to make courts into courts.

The second reason that Shapiro's influence has been more implicit than explicit is that he focused on a theoretical idea rather than a methodology for analysis. One can argue that the more behavioralist approaches to political jurisprudence came to dominate the institutionalist approaches because the behavioralists applied methods that were relatively easy to teach and apply. Graduate students could be trained to do Guttman scaling, factor analysis, regression, and so on, and the Interuniversity Consortium for Political Research (as it was originally known) provided a vehicle for the distribution of data to be plugged into these methodologies. The statistical methods applied by judicial behavioralists were the same as the methods being applied by other quantitatively oriented political scientists. In contrast, institutionalists have had more of a struggle to identify a method and to communicate that method to the broad community studying U.S. (and comparative) politics; particularly for those studying appellate courts, even the qualitative methods that became standard in the study of institutions such as Congress (e.g., "soaking and poking"; see Fenno 1990), were not available or were extremely difficult to carry out (for exceptions, see Howard 1981; Perry 1991).

One must wonder, however, whether Shapiro's explicit impact on judicial politics would have been greater if he had devoted more effort to working directly with data. Much of his analytic work draws on the opinions of judges and justices; little of his work involves collecting or working with other kinds of data. What if Shapiro had undertaken a study involving extensive interviews with persons who had worked as clerks for Supreme Court justices? What if he had spent significant time talking to mid- to senior-level officials in key administrative agencies, asking about their attentiveness to actual and potential court decisions? Some scholars complain that other people who write about Congress have "never actually met a datum," meaning that these scholars produce work from a distance, drawing largely on roll call voting data or published committee reports. To a significant degree, one might wonder with regard to Shapiro's work how much more interesting and still more influential it might have been if he had directly interacted with the judges and officials about whom he wrote.

Ideas are the core of what we as political scientists argue about, and Shapiro has been a source of many important ideas for scholars of the judiciary. The more deeply I have looked at Shapiro's work, the more I have realized how many of the ideas that have influenced my work on courts and actors within the courts can be traced to Shapiro's insights. Yet most of those influences on my work have been largely indirect. By the time I arrived in graduate school, the more behavioralist element had taken a fairly solid hold of empirical work on the Supreme Court. The core overview text that was assigned in my graduate judicial process class was Murphy and Tanenhaus's *The Study of Public Law* (1972), which has but a single explicit mention of Shapiro and political jurisprudence (in the concluding chapter). Yet a reexamination of that book clearly illustrates that the idea of political jurisprudence was inherent in the text. Still, the institutionalists explicitly working at the lower-court level had the most influence on my work: Kenneth Dolbeare (Dolbeare 1969; Dolbeare and Hammond 1968, 1971), Richard Richardson (Richardson and Vines 1970), and, most importantly, Herbert Jacob (1965; 1967; 1969; 1973). In retrospect, I see much cross-influence between the work of these scholars and Shapiro's political jurisprudence. Shapiro's call for more subtle analysis of the role of courts as political agencies was heeded in the work of scholars writing about the lower courts or the impact of the Supreme Court on other political actors. Institutional analyses of the Supreme Court's decision-making process were largely nonexistent during the 1970s and 1980s.

The rediscovery of the power of institutional analysis was the major development in the study of judicial politics in the 1990s, and central to the interpretivist strand of this work were the ideas underlying political jurisprudence. Less clear is political jurisprudence's influence on the positive theory of institutions strand. In fact, political jurisprudence should be important for any institutional analysis of courts, whether interpretivist or game theoretic: when one speaks of courts' "legislative," "administrative," or "representative" role, political jurisprudence contends that these roles must be understood to function within constraints imposed by jurisprudential expectations. Courts legislate, but that does not make them legislatures; courts administer, but that does not make them administrators. Courts are courts. Courts must respect limits created by attention to jurisprudence. However, courts are political, and the combination of the political and the jurisprudential makes courts what they are. This is the contribution and legacy of Martin Shapiro.

NOTES

1. In electronic correspondence with Howard Gillman (dated June 22, 2000), Shapiro observed that the publication date of *Law and Politics in the Supreme Court* might make it appear to be a product of his graduate training at Harvard; in fact, he describes it as a "reaction to [his] graduate training." The contract for the book came as a result McCloskey's urging the editor at the Free Press to give Shapiro a contract to write a book about the Supreme Court. Only after the contract was signed did Shapiro begin to formulate his ideas about the book's specific content, and only after he had developed the arguments for the *Kentucky Law Journal* piece did the book's argument crystallize.

2. Shapiro defines sociological jurisprudence as the view that "law must be understood not as an independent organism but as an integral part of the social system" (1964b, 294). In fact, in his correspondence with Howard Gillman in connection with the essay in this volume about Robert McCloskey, Shapiro reports that the title of this essay arose because Kentucky was doing a symposium on jurisprudence, had lined up Gilbert Geis to write about sociological jurisprudence (1964), and approached Shapiro to write about jurisprudence from the viewpoint of political science; he agreed and said he would "do political jurisprudence" even though at that point he was not sure what he meant by the term.

3. While this argument is developed most clearly in Shapiro 1964a, the seeds of it can be found in Shapiro 1962. This article became the core of the first chapter of Shapiro 1966, the book based on his dissertation. The basic argument advanced in this work before the political jurisprudence articles is that the Supreme Court is a political institution making political choices through which it creates frameworks for analysis to be used by lower courts and other political actors. Central to this argument is the need to place the Court in its "actual political environment" (1962, 31). More broadly, Shapiro's analysis is an effort to place judicial review within the broader framework of group theory that was dominant during the 1950s and 1960s and was reflected in the work of Bentley, Truman, Latham, and Dahl. One does not find the phrase *political jurisprudence* in Shapiro 1966, but the book can be read as a work of "political jurisprudence."

4. While the newness of empirical studies of judicial decision making may be said to account for the attacks on Shapiro's work, one still sees such attacks today. For example, Judge Harry Edwards described two empirical studies of the D.C. Circuit, on which he serves, as "the heedless observations of academic scholars who misconstrue and misunderstand the work of judges" (1998, 1335).

5. While the Court can discover issues not presented by the parties, this appears to be relatively rare (Epstein, Segal, and Johnson 1996; McGuire and Palmer 1995, 1996; Palmer 1999).

6. This grouping was sometimes referred to as "iron triangles" (Safire 2000; Seidman 1970, 37)

7. Shapiro would also point to *Baker v. Carr* as an example of another Court strength: it can act in situations where other government agencies' direct interests in the issue make it impossible for those other agencies to act (1964a, 241).

8. Although Shapiro 1966 was his second published book, Shapiro 1968b is the second book devoted to political jurisprudence. The phrase *political jurisprudence* does not appear in the index to Shapiro 1966.

9. The success of agencies before the Supreme Court is clear: between 1946 and 1994, federal agencies have won 70 percent of the Supreme Court cases in which they were parties (Epstein et al. 1996, 636). This phenomenon has been widely discussed in the judicial politics literature (Canon and Giles 1972; Crowley 1987; Handberg 1979; Kilwein and Brisbin 1996; Sheehan 1990, 1992; Tanenhaus 1960). Interestingly, it appears that agencies have had somewhat less success before the U.S. Court of Appeals, winning only 58 percent of cases between 1969 and 1988 (Humphries and Songer 1999, 215).

10. This idea has been extensively developed in the literature on procedural justice (see Lind and Tyler 1988; Tyler 1990, 1994).

11. This is not to say that comparative judicial work in political science was unknown before Shapiro's book (see, e.g., Becker 1970; Kommers 1975; Morrison 1974; Schubert and Danelski 1969; Tate 1975; Wenner, Wenner, and Flango 1978); in fact, the earliest work on comparative constitutional law by a political scientist was published more than one hundred years ago (Burgess 1890–91). However, the work was relatively obscure except to the small group of people doing it.

12. This can be overstated. Gavin Drewry, one of the coauthors of a book on the House of Lords (Blom-Cooper and Drewry 1972), was a political scientist. However, other major works advancing political analyses of English courts were largely written by legal academics or sociologists (Abel-Smith and Stevens 1967; Griffith 1977; Paterson 1982; Paterson 1974; Stevens 1978), not by political scientists.

13. Shapiro had previously developed his argument about the political role of appeal in Shapiro 1980.

14. *Judicial review* refers to the general idea of courts reviewing government actions broadly defined, not simply reviewing the constitutionality of legislative enactments, which is the way the term is typically used in discussions of American courts.

15. For the appellate courts, the appointments are by the Crown based on recommendations by the prime minister, but the prime minister relies on the lord chancellor in making these recommendations.

16. This hierarchical promotion system existed well before Shapiro had even thought about writing *Courts* (see Karlen 1963, 120).

17. The article later reappeared as part of chapter 1 of Shapiro 1968b. The article's importance at the time is reflected in its inclusion in the old Bobbs-Merrill Reprint Series in Political Science (no. 554).

18. Writing just before the radical growth in law school enrollments,

Shapiro also points to the dominance of one or two tort teachers within specific jurisdictions. As an example, he points to a teacher at the University of Texas who held his post for many years and instructed a generation of Texas practitioners. That type of dominance is probably less common today, with the increased number of law schools and the growth in the number of students enrolled at each, requiring the employment of multiple teachers for each subject.

REFERENCES

Abe, Masaki. 1995. "The Internal Control of a Bureaucratic Judiciary: The Case of Japan." *International Journal of the Sociology of Law* 23:303–20.

Abel-Smith, Brian, and Robert Stevens. 1967. *Lawyers and the Courts: A Sociological Study of the English Legal System, 1750–1965.* Cambridge: Harvard University Press.

Becker, Theodore L. 1970. "Comparative Judicial Politics: The Political Functionings of Courts." Chicago: Rand McNally.

Bickel, Alexander M. 1962. *The Least Dangerous Branch: The Supreme Court at the Bar of Politics.* Indianapolis: Bobbs-Merrill.

Blom-Cooper, Louis, and Gavin Drewry. 1972. *Final Appeal: A Study of the House of Lords in Its Judicial Capacity.* Oxford: Clarendon.

Braybrooke, David, and Charles E. Lindblom. 1963. *A Strategy of Decision: Policy Evaluation as a Social Process.* New York: Free Press of Glencoe.

Brenner, Saul, and Harold J. Spaeth. 1995. *Stare Indecisis: The Alteration of Precedent on the Supreme Court, 1946–1992.* New York: Cambridge University Press.

Brent, James C. 1999. "An Agent and Two Principals: U.S. Court of Appeals Responses to *Employment Division, Department of Human Resources v. Smith* and the Religious Freedom Restoration Act." *American Politics Quarterly* 27 (2):236–68.

Burgess, John William. 1890–91. *Political Science and Comparative Constitutional Law.* Boston: Ginn.

Canon, Bradley C., and Michael Giles. 1972. "Recurring Litigants: Federal Agencies before the Supreme Court." *Western Political Quarterly* 25:183–91.

Clayton, Cornell W., and Howard Gillman, eds. 1999. *Supreme Court Decision-Making: New Institutionalist Approaches.* Chicago: University of Chicago Press.

Cox, Archibald. 1975. *The Role of the Supreme Court in American Government.* New York: Oxford University Press.

Crowley, Donald W. 1987. "Judicial Review of Administrative Agencies: Does the Type of Agency Matter?" *Western Political Quarterly* 40:265–83.

Cyert, Richard M., and James G. March. 1963. *A Behavioral Theory of the Firm.* Englewood Cliffs, N.J.: Prentice-Hall.

Dahl, Robert. 1957. "Decision Making in a Democracy: The Supreme Court as a National Policy-Maker." *Journal of Public Law* 6:279–95.

Dolbeare, Kenneth M. 1969. "The Federal District Courts and Urban Public Policy: An Exploratory Study, 1960–1967." In *Frontiers of Judicial Research*, ed. J. Grossman and J. Tanenhaus. New York: John Wiley.

Dolbeare, Kenneth M., and Phillip E. Hammond. 1968. "The Political Party Bias of Attitudes toward the Supreme Court." *Public Opinion Quarterly* 32:16–30.

Dolbeare, Kenneth M., and Phillip E. Hammond. 1971. *The School Prayer Decisions: From Court Policy to Local Practice*. Chicago: University of Chicago Press.

Edwards, Harry. 1998. "Collegiality and Decision Making on the D.C. Circuit." *Virginia Law Review* 84:1335–70.

Epp, Charles E. 1998. *The Rights Revolution: Lawyers, Activists, and Supreme Courts in Comparative Perspective*. Chicago: University of Chicago Press.

Epstein, Lee, and Joseph F. Kobylka. 1992. *The Supreme Court and Legal Change: Abortion and the Death Penalty*. Chapel Hill: University of North Carolina Press.

Epstein, Lee, Jeffrey A. Segal, and Timothy Johnson. 1996. "The Claim of Issue Creation on the U.S. Supreme Court." *American Political Science Review* 90:845–52.

Epstein, Lee, Jeffrey A. Segal, Harold J. Spaeth, and Thomas G. Walker. 1996. *The Supreme Court Compendium: Data, Decisions, and Developments*. 2d ed. Washington, D.C.: Congressional Quarterly Press.

Epstein, Lee, and Thomas G. Walker. 1995. "The Role of the Supreme Court in American Society: Playing the Reconstruction Game." In *Contemplating Courts*, ed. L. Epstein. Washington, D.C.: Congressional Quarterly Press.

Eskridge, William N., Jr. 1991a. "Overriding Supreme Court Statutory Interpretation Decisions." *Yale Law Journal* 101:331–456.

Eskridge, William N., Jr. 1991b. "Reneging on History? Playing the Court/Congress/President Civil Rights Game." *California Law Review* 79:613–84.

Farole, Donald J., Jr. 1999. "Reexamining Litigant Success in State Supreme Courts." *Law and Society Review* 33:1043–57.

Fenno, Richard F. 1990. *Watching Politicians: Essays on Participant Observation*. Berkeley: Institute of Governmental Studies, University of California.

Galanter, Marc. 1974. "Why the 'Haves' Come Out Ahead." *Law and Society Review* 9:95.

Geis, Gilbert. 1964. "Sociological Jurisprudence: Admixture of Lore and Law." *Kentucky Law Journal* 52:267–93.

Gillman, Howard, and Cornell W. Clayton, eds. 1999. *The Supreme Court in American Politics: New Institutionalist Interpretations*. Lawrence: University Press of Kansas.

Greenburg, Jan Crawford. 1999. "Sex Suit Fallout Alarms Its Advocates." *Chicago Tribune*, August 2, 1, 7.

Griffith, J. A. G. 1977. *The Politics of the Judiciary*. Manchester: Manchester University Press.

Handberg, Roger. 1979. "The Supreme Court and Administrative Agencies, 1965–1978." *Journal of Contemporary Law* 6:161–76.

Heclo, Hugh. 1978. "Issue Networks and the Executive Establishment." In *The New American Political System*, ed. A. King. Washington, D.C.: American Enterprise Institute.

Holland, Kenneth M., ed. 1991. *Judicial Activism in Comparative Perspective*. New York: St. Martin's Press.

Howard, J. Woodford, Jr. 1981. *Courts of Appeals in the Federal Judicial System: A Study of the Second, Fifth, and District of Columbia Circuits*. Princeton: Princeton University Press.

Humphries, Martha Anne, and Donald R. Songer. 1999. "Law and Politics in Judicial Oversight of Federal Administrative Agencies." *Journal of Politics* 61 (1):207–20.

Jackson, Donald W., and C. Neal Tate, eds. 1993. *Judicial Review and Public Policy*. New York: Greenwood Press.

Jacob, Herbert. 1965. *Justice in America*. Boston: Little, Brown.

Jacob, Herbert. 1967. *Law, Politics, and the Federal Courts*. Boston: Little, Brown.

Jacob, Herbert. 1969. *Debtors in Court: The Consumption of Government Services*. Chicago: Rand McNally.

Jacob, Herbert. 1973. *Urban Justice: Law and Order in American Cities*. Englewood Cliffs, N.J.: Prentice-Hall.

Jacob, Herbert, Erhard Blankenburg, Herbert M. Kritzer, Doris Marie Provine, and Joseph Sanders. 1996. *Courts, Law, and Politics in Comparative Perspective*. New Haven: Yale University Press.

Karlen, Delmar. 1963. *Appellate Courts in the United States and England*. Westport, Conn.: Greenwood Press.

Kenney, Sally J., William M. Reisinger, and John C. Reitz, eds. 1999. *Constitutional Dialogues in Comparative Perspective*. New York: St. Martin's Press.

Kilwein, John C., and Richard A. Brisbin Jr. 1996. "Supreme Court Review of Federal Administrative Agencies." *Judicature* 80:130–37.

Knight, Jack, and Lee Epstein. 1996. "On the Struggle for Judicial Supremacy." *Law and Society Review* 30:87–120.

Kommers, Donald P. 1975. *Judicial Politics in West Germany: A Study of the Federal Constitutional Courts*. Beverly Hills, Calif.: Sage.

Lafon, Jacqueline Lucienne. 1991. "The Judicial Career in France: Theory and Practice under the Fifth Republic." *Judicature* 75:97–106.

Levi, Edward H. 1961. *An Introduction to Legal Reasoning*. Chicago: University of Chicago Press.

Lind, E. Allan, and Tom Tyler. 1988. *The Social Psychology of Procedural Justice*. New York: Plenum.

Lindblom, Charles E. 1959. "The Science of 'Muddling Through.'" *Public Administration Review* 19:79–88.

Llewellyn, Karl N. 1960. *The Common Law Tradition—Deciding Appeals.* Boston: Little, Brown.

Lowi, Theodore J. 1969. *The End of Liberalism: Ideology, Policy, and the Crisis of Public Authority.* New York: W. W. Norton.

Malleson, Kate. 1997. "Judicial Training and Performance Appraisal: The Problem of Judicial Independence." *Modern Law Review* 60:655–67.

Marks, Brian A. 1989. "A Model of Judicial Influence on Congressional Policymaking: *Grove City v. Bell.*" Ph.D. diss., Washington University, St. Louis.

McGuire, Kevin T., and Barbara Palmer. 1995. "Issue Fluidity on the U.S. Supreme Court." *American Political Science Review* 89:691–702.

McGuire, Kevin T., and Barbara Palmer. 1996. "Issues, Agendas, and Decision Making on the Supreme Court." *American Political Science Review* 90:853–65.

Melnick, R. Shep. 1983. *Regulation and the Courts: The Case of the Clean Air Act.* Washington, D.C.: Brookings Institution.

Melnick, R. Shep. 1994. *Between the Lines: Interpreting Welfare Rights.* Washington, D.C.: Brookings Institution.

Melnick, R. Shep. 1995. Review of *Dynamic Statutory Interpretation*, by William N. Eskridge. *Georgetown Law Journal* 84:91–121.

Mezey, Susan Gluck. 1988. *No Longer Disabled: The Federal Courts and the Politics of Social Security Disability.* New York: Greenwood Press.

Mishkin, Paul. 1965. "Foreword." *Harvard Law Review* 79:56–102.

Morrison, Fred. 1974. *Courts and the Political Process in England.* Beverly Hills, Calif.: Sage.

Murphy, Walter F., and Joseph Tanenhaus. 1972. *The Study of Public Law.* New York: Random House.

Palmer, Barbara. 1999. "Issue Fluidity and Agenda Setting on the Warren Court." *Political Research Quarterly* 52 (1): 39–65.

Paterson, Alan. 1974. "Judges: A Political Elite?" *British Journal of Law and Society* 1:118–35.

Paterson, Alan. 1982. *The Law Lords.* London: Macmillan.

Perry, H. W. 1991. *Deciding to Decide: Agenda Setting in the United States Supreme Court.* Cambridge: Harvard University Press.

Pickerill, J. Mitchell. 2000. "Congress and Constitutional Deliberation: The Role of Judicial Review in a Separated System." Ph.D. diss., University of Wisconsin, Madison.

Pritchett, C. Herman. 1948. *The Roosevelt Court: A Study in Judicial Politics and Values, 1937–1947.* New York: Macmillan.

Richardson, Richard J., and Kenneth N. Vines. 1970. *The Politics of Federal Courts.* Boston: Little, Brown.

Rosenberg, Gerald N. 1991. *The Hollow Hope: Can Courts Bring about Social Change?* Chicago: University of Chicago Press.

Safire, William. 2000. "On Language: Iron Triangle." *New York Times Magazine*, March 12, 34.

Schubert, Glendon A., and David J. Danelski, eds. 1969. *Comparative Judicial Behavior: Cross-Cultural Studies of Political Decision-Making in the East and West*. New York: Oxford University Press.

Segal, Jeffrey A. 1997. "Separation-of-Powers Games in the Positive Theory of Congress and Courts." *American Political Science Review* 91:28–44.

Segal, Jeffrey A., and Harold J. Spaeth. 1996. "The Influence of *Stare Decisis* on the Votes of United States Supreme Court Justices." *American Journal of Political Science* 40:971–1003.

Segal, Jeffrey A., and Harold J. Spaeth. 1999. *Majority Rule or Minority Will: Adherence to Precedent in the U.S. Supreme Court*. New York: Cambridge University Press.

Seidman, Harold. 1970. *Politics, Position and Power*. New York: Oxford University Press.

Shapiro, Martin. 1962. "Judicial Modesty, Political Reality and Preferred Position." *Cornell Law Quarterly* 47: 175–204.

Shapiro, Martin. 1964a. *Law and Politics in the Supreme Court: New Approaches to Political Jurisprudence*. New York: Free Press of Glencoe.

Shapiro, Martin. 1964b. "Political Jurisprudence." *Kentucky Law Journal* 52: 294–345.

Shapiro, Martin. 1965. "Stability and Change in Judicial Decision-Making: Incrementalism or Stare Decisis?" *Law in Transition Quarterly* 2: 134–57.

Shapiro, Martin. 1966. *Freedom of Speech: The Supreme Court and Judicial Review*. Englewood Cliffs, N.J.: Prentice-Hall.

Shapiro, Martin. 1968a. "Decentralized Decision-Making in the Law of Torts." In *Political Decision Making*, 44–75, ed. S. Sidney Ulmer. New York: Van Nostrand Reinhold.

Shapiro, Martin. 1968b. *The Supreme Court and Administrative Agencies*. New York: Free Press.

Shapiro, Martin. 1972. "Toward a Theory of Stare Decisis." *Journal of Legal Studies* 1:125–34.

Shapiro, Martin. 1980. "Appeal." *Law and Society Review* 14:629–61.

Shapiro, Martin. 1981. *Courts: A Comparative and Political Analysis*. Chicago: University of Chicago Press.

Sheehan, Reginald S. 1990. "Administrative Agencies and the Court: A Reexamination of the Impact of Agency Type on Decisional Outcomes." *Western Political Quarterly* 43:875–85.

Sheehan, Reginald S. 1992. "Federal Agencies and the Supreme Court: An Analysis of Litigation Outcomes, 1953–1988." *American Politics Quarterly* 20:478–500.

Songer, Donald R., Jeffrey A. Segal, and Charles M. Cameron. 1994. "The Hierarchy of Justice: Testing a Principal-Agent Model of Supreme Court–Circuit Court Interactions." *American Journal of Political Science* 38:673–96.

Songer, Donald R., Reginald S. Sheehan, and Susan Brodie Haire. 1999. "Do the 'Haves' Come out Ahead over Time? Applying Galanter's Framework to the Decisions of the U.S. Courts of Appeals, 1925–1988." *Law and Society Review* 33:811–32.

Spaeth, Harold J., and Jeffrey A. Segal. 1999. *Majority Rule or Minority Will: Adherence to Precedence on the U.S. Supreme Court.* New York: Cambridge University Press.

Stevens, Robert. 1978. *Law and Politics: The House of Lords as a Judicial Body, 1800–1976.* Chapel Hill: University of North Carolina Press.

Stone, Alec. 1992. *The Birth of Judicial Politics in France: The Constitutional Council in Comparative Perspective.* New York: Oxford University Press.

Sunkin, Maurice. 1993. "The Incidence and Effect of Judicial Review Procedures against Central Government in the United Kingdom." In *Judicial Review and Public Policy*, ed. D. W. Jackson and C. N. Tate. New York: Greenwood Press.

Tanenhaus, Joseph. 1960. "Supreme Court Attitudes toward Federal Administrative Agencies." *Journal of Politics* 22:502–24.

Tate, C. Neal. 1975. "Paths to the Bench in Britain: A Quasi-Experimental Study of the Recruitment of a Judicial Elite." *Western Political Quarterly* 28:108–29.

Tate, C. Neal, and Torbjörn Vallinder. 1995. "The Global Expansion of Judicial Power: The Judicialization of Politics." In *The Global Expansion of Judicial Power*, ed. C. N. Tate and T. Vallinder. New York: New York University Press.

Truman, David. 1951. *The Governmental Process: Political Interests and Public Opinion.* New York: Knopf.

Tyler, Thomas R. 1990. *Why People Obey the Law.* New Haven: Yale University Press.

Tyler, Thomas R. 1994. "Governing amid Diversity: The Effect of Fair Decisionmaking Procedures on the Legitimacy of Government." *Law and Society Review* 28:809–32.

Wechsler, Herbert. 1959. "Toward Neutral Principles of Constitutional Law." *Harvard Law Review* 73:1–35.

Wenner, Manfred, Lettie M. Wenner, and Victor E. Flango. 1978. "Austrian and Swiss Judges: A Comparative Study." *Comparative Politics* 10:499–519.

Wildavsky, Aaron. 1964. *Politics of the Budgetary Process.* Boston: Little, Brown.

Afterword

Nancy Maveety

As the essays in this volume demonstrate, the study of judicial behavior has been the occasion for the public law field to define itself as the political science of courts. Like political science itself, it has sought at times to define itself by distancing itself from the interpretive enterprise of its law and history roots. Yet the development of the study of judicial behavior arguably illustrates that "scientific" knowledge is of necessity "interpretive" knowledge. Kuhnian scientific paradigms are, after all, interpretive communities. The three approaches to the study of judicial behavior that this volume traces have been labeled "paradigms," though each approach is less certain of itself and less self-contained than that term implies. What the development of the study of judicial behavior better exemplifies is a conversation *about* paradigms, not really between them. And this conversation is rooted in the fundamental difficulty of scientific theorizing about the interpretive project of judging. While scientifically self-conscious "paradigms" such as attitudinalism or rational choice theory do grip the field (and the discipline), we do well to remember that "the decisions by which scientific paradigms are modified or abandoned are processes of consensus in which the exact moment of decision cannot be isolated and intellectualized, and into which the politics of group behavior may conspicuously enter" (Pocock 1971, 16).[1] The "politics of group behavior" at instance here proceeds from three approaches to the study of judicial behavior that parry with one another on both professional and theoretical levels. A professional victory is not necessarily an intellectual one, and neither guarantees a warm reception from those external to the battle—such as those political actors who are the subjects of those approaches. Yet if there is anything into which political scientists can lay a claim to insight, it is the politics of group behavior—surely including that of their own methodological groups. And to evoke an old adage of groups and politics, we can fight, or we can talk.

Where we are at the end of this volume, then, is where we began: in conversation. Ironically, the field that once called itself public law began as the study of conversation—that of judges, in judicial opinions—and developed as a body of scholarship from the debate over whether these artifacts of the judicial conversation were keys to the judicial decision-making process. The contemporary conversation in the field of law and courts is still about opinions, judicial and scholastic. But it is one in which no majority voice dominates; in fact, stubborn conversational silences and side conversations threaten to proliferate. One response is obviously to redirect the conversation—or even to direct it. One of the pioneers profiled in this volume recently offered this description of the "next giant in the field": a scholar who can "take account of the dramatic expansion of subject matter [in judicial studies] by developing a larger array of concepts and methods and by formulating a broad synthesis through empirical or legal theory" (Cook 1994a, 83). Some would probably argue that a pioneer discussed here—if only properly understood—provides such a synthesis. Some no doubt aspire to be this next giant. And some doubt whether a grand theory of law and courts is possible or even desirable, suggesting that communication, not consensus, is the only sort of unity for which the field can and should hope, at least at present. Perhaps while we await synthetic giants and consensual unity, we can content ourselves with a shared language for refuting the claims of rival views and for consciously constructing our studies to encompass political actions that adherents of conflicting theories recognize as important (see Smith 1996, 143). Hopefully, this volume furnishes a grammar that makes such a communicative conversation possible.

NOTE

1. The references cited in this section are listed in the references to chapter 1.

Contributors

DAVID ADAMANY is president and professor of law and political science at Temple University. He previously served as president and distinguished professor of law and political science at Wayne State University. His research interests include U.S. constitutional law and judicial process, campaign finance, and political parties.

LAWRENCE BAUM received his Ph.D. from the University of Wisconsin-Madison and teaches at Ohio State University. Subjects of his research include the sources of judicial behavior, voting behavior in judicial elections, and the creation and behavior of specialized courts. He is the author of *The Puzzle of Judicial Behavior* (1997), *The Supreme Court* (7th ed., 2001), and *American Courts* (5th ed., 2002).

SARA C. BENESH is assistant professor of political science at the University of Wisconsin-Milwaukee. She received her Ph.D. in 1999 from Michigan State University. Her work has been published in *Jurimetrics*, *Justice System Journal*, and *Law and Courts*. Her major research focus is on the U.S. Courts of Appeals and their relationship to the U.S. Supreme Court, although she also conducts some research on decision making at the Supreme Court level. She is currently working on a revision of the Supreme Court Judicial Databases funded by the National Science Foundation.

ROBERT C. BRADLEY received his B.A. and M.A. degrees from the University of Akron and his Ph.D. from the University of Kentucky, where he studied under the direction of S. Sidney Ulmer. His teaching interests include public law, judicial process and behavior, science and the law, Web-based instruction, and civic education. He has received several teaching awards. His current research interests include comparative judicial behavior and the relationship between civic education and democracy. He has published and presented on various aspects of judicial decision making and different applications of instructional technology.

SAUL BRENNER is professor of political science at the University of North Carolina, Charlotte. He is author or coauthor of three books and more than fifty professional journal articles. Much of his research

concerns fluidity in voting on the U.S. Supreme Court, majority opinion assignment on the Court, and strategies in certiorari voting.

ROBERT A. CARP received his Ph.D. from the University of Iowa in
1969 and is currently professor of political science at the University of
Houston. He is coauthor of *Policy Making and Politics in the Federal
Courts, Politics and Judgment in Federal District Courts, Judicial Process in
America* (5th ed.), *The Federal Courts* (3d ed.), and numerous articles.

CORNELL W. CLAYTON is professor of political science at Washington
State University. He received his D.Phil. from Oxford University in
1990. He is the author or editor of numerous books on American law
and politics, including *The Politics of Justice* (1992), *Government Lawyers:
The Federal Legal Bureaucracy and Presidential Politics* (1995), *Supreme
Court Decision-Making: New Institutionalist Approaches* (with Howard
Gillman, 1999), and *The Supreme Court in American Politics: New Insti-
tutionalist Interpretations* (with Howard Gillman, 1999).

SUE DAVIS is professor of political science at the University of
Delaware. She is the author of *Justice Rehnquist and the Constitution*
(1989) and *American Political Thought: Four Hundred Years of Ideas and
Ideologies* (1996) and is coauthor with Jack Peltason of the fifteenth edi-
tion of Corwin and Peltason's *Understanding the Constitution* (2000).
She is currently working on a study of the political thought of Elizabeth
Cady Stanton.

LEE EPSTEIN is the Edward Mallinckrodt Distinguished University
Professor of political science and professor of law at Washington Uni-
versity. She is the author or coauthor of twelve books, including *The
Supreme Court and Legal Change*, the *Constitutional Law for a Changing
America* series (now in its fourth edition), *The Supreme Court Compendium* (winner of a Special Recognition Honor from the Law and
Courts Section of the American Political Science Association and an
Outstanding Academic Book Award from *Choice*), and *The Choices Justices Make* (winner of the C. Herman Pritchett Award for the best book
on law and courts). Between 1990 and 2000, she received seven grants
from the National Science Foundation to conduct research on various
topics pertaining to law and courts, including interest group participation in litigation and strategic interaction among judges on collegial
courts.

HOWARD GILLMAN is professor of political science at the University of
Southern California. He has written or edited three books on Supreme

Court politics, including *The Constitution Besieged* (1993), which received the C. Herman Pritchett Award for the best book in the field of public law by a political scientist. He has published numerous articles in leading journals of political science and legal studies, and he is currently on the editorial board of *Law and Social Inquiry*. He recently completed a book on judicial politics and the rule of law in the 2000 presidential election dispute, *The Vote that Counted: How the Court Decided the 2000 Presidential Election* (2001).

JACK KNIGHT is the Souers Professor of Government and chair of the department of political science at Washington University in St. Louis. His primary areas of interest are modern social and political theory, law and legal theory, political economy, and philosophy of social science. His publications include *Institutions and Social Conflict* (1992), *Explaining Social Institutions* (with Itai Sened, 1995), and *The Choices Justices Make* (with Lee Epstein, 1997) as well as articles in various journals and edited volumes.

HERBERT M. KRITZER is professor of political science and law at the University of Wisconsin-Madison and serves director of the undergraduate program in legal studies and the criminal justice certificate program. He has conducted extensive empirical research on the U.S. civil justice system as well as research on other common law systems. He is the author of *The Justice Broker* (1990), *Let's Make a Deal* (1991), and *Legal Advocates: Lawyers and Nonlawyers at Work* (1998) and is coauthor of *Courts, Law, and Politics in Comparative Perspective* (1996). He is currently working on a study of U.S. Supreme Court decision making that focuses on ways that law can be systematically incorporated in empirical models of the justices' voting decisions.

JOHN ANTHONY MALTESE is associate professor of political science at the University of Georgia. His book *The Selling of Supreme Court Nominees* (1995) won the 1996 C. Herman Pritchett Award for best book in judicial politics from the Law and Courts Section of the American Political Science Association. He is also the author of *Spin Control: The White House Office of Communications and the Management of Presidential News* (1992). In addition to his many publications in political science, he has written extensively about classical music and won a Grammy Award from the National Academy of Recording Arts and Sciences in 1996 for his liner notes to *The Heifetz Collection* (1994), a sixty-five CD set.

LYNN MATHER is the Nelson A. Rockefeller Professor of Government at Dartmouth College. She received her Ph.D. from the University of

California at Irvine and has published extensively on lawyers, dispute transformation, trial courts, and antitobacco litigation. Books she has written or edited include *Plea Bargaining or Trial? The Process of Criminal Case Disposition* (1979), *Empirical Theories about Courts* (with Keith Boyum, 1983), and *Divorce Lawyers at Work: Varieties of Professionalism in Practice* (with Craig McEwen and Richard Maiman, 2001). She served as president of the Law and Society Association in 2001–2.

NANCY MAVEETY received her Ph.D. from Johns Hopkins University in 1987 and currently serves as associate professor and chair of political science at Tulane University. Her works in the area of judicial studies include *Representation Rights and the Burger Years* (1991) and *Justice Sandra Day O'Connor: Strategist on the Supreme Court* (1996). She is also the author of a satirical novel, *The Stagnant Pool, Scholars below Sea Level* (2000), is a member of the Krewe of Muses, and was a 2001 Fulbright lecturer at Tartu University in Estonia.

STEPHEN MEINHOLD received his Ph.D. from the University of New Orleans and is currently associate professor of political science at the University of North Carolina at Wilmington. His research interests include attitudes toward the legal system, the role of lawyers in politics, the consequences of using attorneys, and why undergraduates pursue a legal education. His work has appeared in *Political Research Quarterly*, *Social Science Quarterly*, and *Justice System Journal*.

JEFFREY A. SEGAL received his Ph.D. from Michigan State University in 1983 and currently serves as professor of political science at SUNY–Stony Brook. He is coauthor (with Harold J. Spaeth) of *The Supreme Court and the Attitudinal Model Revisited* (2002). His articles have appeared in many political science journals, including the *American Political Science Review* and the *American Journal of Political Science*. He is the recipient of the American Political Science Association's 1996 Franklin L. Burdette Pi Sigma Alpha Award for best paper presented at the 1995 APSA meeting.

THOMAS G. WALKER is professor and chair of the political science department of Emory University, where he teaches courses in constitutional law and judicial behavior. He received his B.A. degree from St. Martin's College and his Ph.D. from the University of Kentucky, where he studied under the direction of S. Sidney Ulmer. His book with Deborah Barrow, *A Court Divided: The Fifth Circuit Court of*

Appeals and the Politics of Judicial Reform (1988), received the Southern Political Science Association's V. O. Key Award for the best book on southern politics. In addition, his *Constitutional Law for a Changing America*, coauthored with Lee Epstein, is currently in its fourth edition (2001). Along with Lee Epstein, Jeffrey Segal, and Harold Spaeth, he also wrote *The Supreme Court Compendium* (3d ed., 2001).

Index